The History
of the Crusades
Vol. III

by

J. Fr. Michaud

The History of the Crusades
Vol. III
by J. Fr. Michaud

ISBN: 978-93-62761-96-5

Published by

DOUBLE 9 BOOKS

2/13-B, Ansari Road
Daryaganj, New Delhi – 110002
info@double9books.com
www.double9books.com
Tel. 011-40042856

This book is under public domain

ABOUT THE AUTHOR

J. Fr. Michaud was a French historian and publicist. Michaud was born in either La Biolle or Albens in the Duchy of Savoy. He was schooled in Bourg-en-Bresse and then worked as a writer in Lyon, where the French Revolution instilled in him a deep distaste for revolutionary beliefs that would last his entire life. In 1791, he traveled to Paris and worked as an editor for various royalist periodicals, putting his life in danger. One of these was the Gazette Universelle, which he formed alongside Pascal Boyer and Antoine Marie Cerisier. His Bourbon sympathies landed him in prison briefly in 1800, and when he was released, he temporarily abandoned journalism in favor of writing and editing books. In 1806, he wrote the first work of its sort, Biographie moderne ou dictionnaire des hommes qui se sont fait un nom en Europe since 1789, with his brother Louis Gabriel Michaud and two collaborators. In 1811, he published the first volume of his Histoire des Croisades (History of the Crusades) and the first volume of his Biographie Universelle. In 1813, he was elected Academician, filling the vacancy caused by the death of Jean-François Cailhava de L'Estandoux. In 1814, he resumed editing La Quotidienne.

CONTENTS

BOOK XV
A.D. 1255-1270

EIGHTH CRUSADE

Louis IX., during his sojourn in Palestine, had not only employed himself in fortifying the Christian cities; he had neglected no means of establishing that union and harmony among the Christians themselves, which he felt would create their only security against the attacks of the Mussulmans: unhappily for this people, whom he would have preserved at the peril of his life, his counsels were not long in being forgotten, and the spirit of discord soon displaced the generous sentiments to which his example and discourses had given a momentary life.

It may have been observed in the course of this history, that several maritime nations had stores, counting-houses, and considerable commercial establishments at Ptolemaïs, which had become the capital of Palestine. Among these nations, Genoa and Venice occupied the first rank: each of these colonies inhabited a separate quarter, and had different laws, besides interests, which kept them at constant variance; the only thing they possessed in common, [1] was the Church of St. Sabbas, in which the Venetians and the Genoese assembled together to celebrate the ceremonies of their religion.

This common possession had often been a subject of quarrel between them; a short time after the departure of St. Louis, discord broke out anew, and roused all the passions that the spirit of rivalry and jealousy could give birth to between two nations which had so long contended for the empire of the sea and pre-eminence in commerce. Amidst this struggle, in which the very object of the contest ought to have recalled sentiments of peace and charity to their hearts, the Genoese and Venetians often came to blows in the city of Ptolemaïs, and more than once, the sanctuary, which the two parties had fortified like a place of war, resounded with the din of their sacrilegious battles.

Discord very soon crossed the seas, and carried fresh troubles into the West. Genoa interested the Pisans in her cause, and sought allies and auxiliaries even among the Greeks, at that time impatient to repossess

Constantinople. Venice, in order to avenge her injuries, courted the alliance of Manfroi, who had been excommunicated by the head of the Church. Troops were raised, fleets were armed, and the parties attacked each other both by land and sea; and this war, which the sovereign pontiff was unable to quell, lasted more than twenty years, sometimes to the advantage of the Venetians, as frequently to that of the Genoese; but always fatal to the Christian colonies of the East.

This spirit of discord likewise extended its baneful influence to the rival orders of St. John and the Temple; and the blood of these courageous defenders of the Holy Land flowed in torrents in cities of which they had undertaken the defence; the Hospitallers and Templars pursued and attacked each other with a fury that nothing could appease or turn aside, both orders invoking the aid of the knights that remained in the West. Thus the noblest families of Christendom were dragged into these sanguinary quarrels, and it was no longer asked in Europe whether the Franks had conquered the Saracens, but if victory had been favourable to the knights of the Temple or to those of the Hospital.

The brave Sergines, whom Louis IX. had at his departure left at Ptolemaïs, and the wisest of the other defenders of the Holy Land, had neither authority enough to reëstablish tranquillity, nor troops enough to resist the attacks of the Mussulmans. The only hope of safety which appeared to be left to the Christians of Palestine, arose from the divisions which also troubled the empire of the Saracens; every day new revolutions broke out among the Mamelukes; but, by a singular contrast, feuds, that weakened the power of the Franks, often seemed only to increase that of their enemies. If, from the feeble kingdom of Jerusalem, we pass into Egypt, we there behold the strange spectacle of a government founded by revolt, and strengthening itself amidst political tempests. The Christian colonies, since the taking of Jerusalem, by Saladin, had no longer a common centre or a common tie; the kings of Jerusalem, in losing their capital, lost an authority which served at least as a war-cry, by which to rally ardent spirits around them. Nothing was preserved of royalty but the name, nothing was gained from republicanism but its license. As to the Mamelukes, they were less a nation than an army, in which they at first quarrelled for a leader, and in which they afterwards obeyed him blindly. From the bosom of each of their revolutions sprang a military despotism, armed with all the passions that had given birth to it, and, what must have redoubled the alarm of the Christians, this despotism breathed nothing but war and conquest.

We have said, in the preceding book, that Aibek, after having espoused the sultana Chegger-Eddour, had mounted the throne of Saladin; but it was not long before his reign was disturbed by the rivalries of the emirs. The death of Phares-Eddin Octhaï, one of the leaders opposed to the new sultan, disconcerted the projects of the faction, but the jealousy of a woman did that which neither faction nor license had been able to effect. Chegger-Eddour could not pardon Aibek for having asked the hand of a daughter of the prince of Mossoul, and the faithless husband was assassinated in the bath by slaves. The sultana, after having gratified her woman's vengeance, called in the ambition of the emirs and the crimes of policy to her aid. [2] She sent for the emir Saif-Eddin, to ask his advice, and to offer him her hand and empire. Upon being introduced into the palace, Saif-Eddin found the Sultana seated, with the bleeding body of her husband at her feet: at this spectacle, the emir was seized with horror, and the calmness which the sultana displayed, together with the sight of the bloody throne, upon which she proposed to him to take his seat with her, added to his fright; Chegger-Eddour summoned two other emirs, who could not endure her presence, but fled away, terrified at what they saw and heard. This scene passed during the night. At break of day, the news of it was spread throughout Cairo, and the indignation of the people and the army was general and active: the mother of Aibek amply revenged the death of her son. Chegger-Eddour, in her turn, perished by the hands of slaves, and her body, which was cast into the castle ditch, might teach all the ambitious who were contending for the empire, that revolutions, likewise, sometimes have their justice.

Amidst the tumult, a son of Aibek, fifteen years of age, was raised to the throne; but the approach of a war soon caused a new revolution to break out, and precipitated the youth from his giddy eminence: great events were ripening in Asia, and a storm was brewing in Persia, which was soon to burst over both Syria and Egypt. [3]

The Moguls, under the command of Oulagon, had laid siege to Bagdad, at a moment when the city was divided into several sects, all more earnest in their conflicts with each other than in their preparations to repulse a formidable enemy. The caliph, as well as his people, was sunk deep in voluptuous effeminacy, and the pride created by the vain adulation of the Mussulmans, made him neglect true and available means of defence. The Tartars took the city by storm, and gave it up to all the horrors of war. The last and thirty-seventh of the successors of Abbas, dragged away like the vilest captive, lost his life in the midst of such tumult and disorder, that history [4] is unable to say whether he died of despair, or whether he fell beneath the sword of his enemies.

This violence, committed upon the head of the Mussulman religion, with the march of the Moguls towards Syria, threw the Mamelukes into the greatest consternation. They then deemed it necessary to displace the son of Aibek, and elect a leader able to guide them amidst the perils that threatened them, and their choice fell upon Koutouz, the bravest and most able of the emirs.

Whilst Egypt was earnestly engaged in preparations to resist the Moguls, the Christians appeared to expect their deliverance from this war against the Mussulmans; the khan of Tartary had promised the king of Armenia to carry his conquests as far as the banks of the Nile; and oriental chronicles relate that the Armenian troops were united with those of the Moguls. [5] The latter, after having crossed the Euphrates, took possession of Aleppo, Damascus, and the principal cities of Syria. On all sides, the Mussulmans fled before the Tartars, and the disciples of Christ were protected by the victorious hordes; from that time the Christians only beheld liberators in these redoubtable conquerors. In the churches, and even upon the tomb of Christ, prayers were put up for the triumph of the Moguls, and in the excess of their joy, the Christians of Palestine abandoned their general practice of imploring aid from the powers of Europe.

In the mean time Europe itself entertained a very different idea of this war; the progress of the Moguls created the greatest terror in all the nations of the West; they not only dreaded the Mogul arms on account of the Christian colonies of the East; they trembled for themselves; [6] for whilst the hordes of Oulagon were ravaging Syria, other armies of the same nation were desolating the banks of the Dniester and the Danube. Pope Alexander, addressing the princes, prelates, and all the faithful, exhorted them to unite against the barbarians. Councils were assembled in France, England, Italy, and Germany, to deliberate upon the dangers of Christendom; the head of the Church ordered prayers to be offered up and processions to be made, blasphemies to be punished, and luxury to be suppressed at the table and in dress,—measures which might be conceived proper to mitigate the anger of Heaven, but very insufficient to stop the invasion of the Moguls.

The hordes, however, which ravaged Hungary and Poland were dispersed, and terror again took possession of the Christians of the East, whose hopes had been so sanguine. Oulagon, recalled into Persia by civil wars, left his lieutenant, Ketboga, in Syria, with directions to follow up his conquests. The Christians were still applauding the victories of the Moguls, when a quarrel, provoked by some German Crusaders, all at once changed the state of things, and made enemies of those who had been considered as auxiliaries. Some Mussulman villages which paid tribute to the Tartars, having been pillaged, Ketboga sent to demand a reparation of the Christians, which they refused. In the course of the dispute raised on this subject, the nephew of the Mogul commander was killed. From that time the Tartar leader declared open war against the Christians, ravaged the territory of

Sidon, and menaced that of Ptolemaïs. At the aspect of their desolated plains, all the hopes of the Christians vanished; they had had no bounds to their hopes and their joy, they had now none to their grief or their fears. The alarm created in them by a barbarous people, made them forget that most of their misfortunes came from Egypt, and as they had given over all idea of succours from the West, many of them now placed all their confidence in the arms of the Mamelukes.

A great portion of Palestine had already been invaded by the Moguls, when the sultan of Cairo set out on his march to meet them at the head of his army; he remained three days in the neighbourhood of Ptolemaïs, where he renewed a truce with the Christians. Soon after, a battle was fought in the plain of Tiberias; Ketboga lost his life in the middle of the conflict, and the army of the Tartars, beaten and scattered, abandoned Syria.

To whichever side victory might have inclined, the Christians had nothing to hope from the conqueror; the Mussulmans could not pardon them for having sought the support of the victorious Moguls, and having taken advantage of the desolation of Syria, to insult the disciples of Mahomet. The churches were demolished at Damascus; the Christians were persecuted in all the Mussulman cities, and these persecutions were the presage of a war in which fanaticism exercised all its furies. On all sides complaints and menaces arose against the Franks of Palestine; the cry of *war with the Christians* resounded through all the provinces in the power of the Mamelukes; the animosity was so great, that the sultan of Cairo, who had just triumphed over the Tartars, was the victim to his fidelity in observing the last truce concluded with the Franks. Bibars, who had killed the last sultan of the family of Saladin, took advantage of this effervescence of the public mind to endeavour to raise a party against Koutouz, by affecting great hatred for the Christians, and by reproaching the sultan with a criminal moderation towards the enemies of Islamism.

When the fermentation had been worked up to the highest point, Bibars, having assembled his accomplices, surprised the sultan whilst hunting, struck him several mortal blows, then, all stained as he was with the blood of his master, he hastened to the Mameluke army, at that time collected at Sallhie; he presented himself to the atabek or lieutenant of the prince, announcing the death of Koutouz. Upon being asked who killed the sultan. "It was I," answered he. "In that case," said the atabek, "reign in his place." [7] Strange words, which characterize at a single stroke the spirit of the Mamelukes, as well as of the government they had founded! The army proclaimed Bibars sultan of Egypt, and the ceremonies prepared at Cairo for the reception of the conqueror of the Tartars, served to celebrate the coronation of his murderer.

This revolution gave the Mussulmans the sovereign most to be dreaded by the Christians. Bibars was named *the pillar of the Mussulman religion and the father of victories*; and he was destined to merit these titles by completing the ruin of the Franks. He had scarcely mounted the throne before he gave the signal for war.

The Christians of Palestine being totally without means of resisting the Mameluke forces, sent deputies to the West to solicit prompt and efficient succour. The sovereign pontiff appeared affected by the account of the perils of the Holy Land, and exhorted the faithful to take the cross; but the tone of his exhortations, and the motives that he named in his circulars, only too plainly evinced his desire to see Europe take up arms against other enemies than the Mussulmans. "The Saracens," said he, "know that it will be impossible for any Christian prince to make a long abode in the East, [8] and that the Holy Land will never have any but transient succour from distant countries."

Alexander IV. was much more sincere and far more eloquent in his manifestoes against the house of Swabia; the interest he took in the contest he was carrying on in the kingdom of Naples could not be diverted by the undertaking of a holy war. Clement IV., who succeeded him, made some few demonstrations of zeal to engage the European nations to take arms against the Mussulmans; but the policy of his predecessors had left too many germs of discord and trouble in Italy, to allow him to give much attention to the East. On one side, Germany, still without an emperor, though with three pretenders to the empire, could spare no warriors for the Holy Land. England was a prey to a civil war, in which the barons wore a white cross as their badge of union against the king, and in which priests exhorted them to the fight, pointing to heaven as the reward of their bravery and their rebellion. This strange crusade precluded all thoughts of one beyond the seas. France was the only kingdom from which the prayers of the Christians of Palestine were not repulsed; some French knights took the cross, and chose Eudes, count of Nevers, son of the duke of Burgundy, as their leader; and these were all the succours Europe could afford to send to the East.

At the same time that the afflicting news arrived from the Holy Land, an event was announced which would have plunged the whole West in mourning, if the conquests of the Crusaders had then excited anything like the interest to which they had given birth in former ages. We have frequently had occasion to deplore the rapid decline of the Latin empire of Constantinople; for a length of time, Baldwin had had no means for supporting the imperial dignity, or paying his scanty troop of soldiers, but the alms of Christendom, and some loans obtained from Venice, for which he was obliged to give his own son as a hostage, or, more properly, a pledge. In pressing moments of want, he sold the relics, he tore the lead from the roofs of the churches, and the timber of public edifices was used for heating the fires of the imperial kitchens. Towers half-demolished, ramparts without defences, palaces smoky and deserted, houses and whole streets abandoned, such was the spectacle presented by the queen of eastern cities.

Baldwin had concluded a truce with Michael Palæologus. The facility with which this truce was made ought to have inspired the Latins with some suspicion; but the deplorable state of the Franks did not prevent them from despising their enemies or dreaming of fresh conquests. In hopes of pillage, and forgetful of the perfidious character of the Greeks, a Venetian fleet bore such as remained of the defenders of Byzantium in an expedition against Daphnusia, situated at the embouchure of the Black Sea. The Greeks of Nice, informed by some peasants from the shores of the Bosphorus, did not hesitate to take advantage of the opportunity fortune thus presented. These peasants pointed out to the general of Michael Palæologus, who was about to make war in Epirus, an opening that had been made under the ramparts of Constantinople, close to the Golden Gate, by which more troops might be introduced than would be necessary for the conquest of the city. Baldwin had none with him but children, old men, women, and traders; among the latter of whom were the Genoese newly allied to the Greeks. When the soldiers of Michael had penetrated into the city, they were surprised to find no enemy to contend with; whilst they preserved their ranks, and advanced with precaution, a troop of Comans, whom the Greek emperor had in his pay, traversed the city, sword and fire in hand. The small, terrified crowd of the Latins fled towards the port; whilst the Greek inhabitants hastened to meet the conqueror, shouting, "Long life to Michael Palæologus, emperor of the Romans!" Baldwin, awakened by these cries and the tumult that drew near to his palace, hastened to quit a city that no longer was his. The Venetian fleet, returning from the expedition to Daphnusia, arrived in time to receive the fugitive emperor and all that remained of the empire of the Franks upon the Bosphorus. Thus the Latins were deprived of that city that it had cost them such prodigies of valour to obtain; the Greeks reëntered it without striking a blow, seconded only by the treachery of a few peasants and the darkness of night. Baldwin II., after having reigned in Byzantium during thirty-seven years, resumed the mendicant course he had practised in his youth, and wandered from one court to another, imploring the assistance of Christians. Pope Urban received him with a mixture of compassion and contempt. In a letter addressed to Louis IX., the pontiff deplored the loss of Constantinople, and groaned bitterly over the obscured glory of the Latin Church. Urban expressed a desire that a crusade should be undertaken for the recovery of Byzantium; but he found men's minds but very little disposed to undertake such an enterprise: the clergy of both England and France refused subsidies for an expedition which they pronounced useless. The pope was obliged to content himself with the submission and presents of Michael Palæologus, who, still in dread in the bosom of his new conquest, promised, in order to appease the Holy See, to recognise the Church of Rome, and to succour the holy places.

In the mean time the situation of the Christians of Palestine became every day more alarming, and more worthy of the compassion of the nations and princes of the West. The new sultan of Cairo, after having ravaged the country of the Franks, returned a second time, with a more formidable army than the former. The Franks, alarmed at his progress, sent to him to sue for peace; his only reply was to give up the church of Nazareth to the flames; the Mussulmans ravaged all the country situated between Naïn and Mount Thabor, and then encamped within sight of Ptolemaïs.

The most distinguished of the Christian warriors had attempted an expedition towards Tiberias; but this gallant troop, the last resource of the Franks, had just been defeated and dispersed by the infidels; fifty knights had arrived in Palestine with the duke of Nevers; but what could such a feeble reinforcement do to arrest the progress of a victorious army.

The country was laid waste, and the inhabitants of the cities kept themselves closely shut up behind their ramparts, in the constant apprehension of beholding the enemy under their walls. After threatening Ptolemaïs, Bibars threw himself upon the city of Cæsarea; the Christians, after a spirited resistance, abandoned the place, and retired into the castle, which was surrounded by the waters of the sea. This fortress, which appeared inaccessible, was only able to resist the attacks of the Mussulmans a few days. [9] The city of Arsouf was the next object of the Mussulman leader. The inhabitants defended themselves with almost unexampled bravery; several times the machines of the besiegers and the heaps of wood which they raised to the level of the walls, were consigned to the flames. After having fought at the foot of the ramparts, the besieged and the besiegers dug out the earth beneath the walls of the city, and sought each other, to fight in the mines and subterranean passages; nothing could relax the ardour of the Christians or the impatient activity of Bibars. Religious fanaticism animated the courage of the Mamelukes; the imauns and doctors of the law flocked to the siege of Arsouf, to be present at the triumph of Islamism: at length the sultan planted the standard of the prophet upon the towers of the city, and the Mussulmans were called to prayers in the churches at once converted into mosques. The Mamelukes massacred a great part of the inhabitants; the remainder were condemned to slavery. Bibars distributed the captives among the leaders of his army; he then ordered the destruction of the city, and the Christian prisoners were compelled to demolish their own dwellings. The conquered territory was divided and shared among the principal emirs, according to an order of the sultan, which the Arabian chronicles have preserved as an historical monument. This liberality towards the conquerors of the Christians, appeared to the Mussulmans worthy of the greatest praise, and one of the historians of Bibars exclaims, in his enthusiasm, "That so noble an action was written in the book of God, before being inscribed upon the book of the life of the sultan."

Such encouragements bestowed upon the emirs, announced that Bibars still stood in need of their valour to accomplish other designs. The sultan returned into Egypt, to make fresh preparations and recruit his army. During his sojourn at Cairo, he received ambassadors from several kings of the Franks, from Alphonso, king of Arragon, the king of Armenia, and some other princes of Palestine. All these ambassadors demanded peace for the Christians; but their pressing solicitations only strengthened the sultan in his project of continuing the war; the more earnest their entreaties, the greater reason he had to believe they had nothing else to oppose to him. He answered the envoys of the count of Jaffa: "The time is come in which we will endure no more injuries; when a cottage shall be taken from us, we will take a castle; when you shall seize one of our labourers, we will consign a thousand of your warriors to chains."

Bibars did not delay putting his threats into execution; he returned to Palestine, and made a pilgrimage to Jerusalem, to implore the protection of Mahomet for his arms. His army immediately received the signal for war, and ravaged the territory of Tripoli. If some Oriental chronicles may be believed, the project of Bibars then was to attack Ptolemaïs; and in so great an enterprise, he did not disdain the assistance of treachery. The prince of Tyre, says Ibn-Ferat, united with the Genoese, was to attack Ptolemaïs with a numerous fleet on the sea side, whilst the Mamelukes attacked it by land. Bibars in fact presented himself before Ptolemaïs, but his new auxiliaries no doubt repented of the promises they had made him; and did not second his designs. The sultan retired filled with fury, and threatened to avenge himself upon all the Christians whom war should place in his power.

He first went to discharge his anger upon the fortress of Sefed, which was situated in lower Galilee, fifteen leagues from Ptolemaïs. This fortress had to defend itself against all the forces that the sultan had gathered together for his great enterprise. When the siege had begun, Bibars neglected no means of forcing the garrison to surrender; he was constantly at the head of his troops, and in one conflict, his whole army burst into a loud cry to warn him of a danger that threatened him. To inflame the ardour of the Mamelukes, he caused robes of honour and purses of money to be distributed on the field of battle; the great cadi of Damascus had come to the siege to animate the combatants by his presence; and the promises he addressed, in the name of the prophet, to all the Mussulman soldiers, added greatly to their warlike enthusiasm.

The Christians, however, defended themselves valiantly. This resistance at first astonished their enemies, and soon produced discouragement; in vain the sultan endeavoured to reanimate his soldiers, in vain he ordered that all who fled should be beaten back with clubs, and placed several emirs in chains for deserting their posts; neither the dread of chastisements, nor the hopes of reward, could revive the courage of the Mussulmans. Bibars would have been obliged to raise the siege, if discord had not come to his assistance. He himself took great pains to give birth to it among the Christians; in the frequent messages sent to the garrison, perfidious promises and well-directed threats sowed the seeds of suspicion and mistrust. At length the divisions burst forth; some were anxious that they should surrender, others that they should hold out to death: from that moment the Mussulmans met with a less obstinate resistance, and renewed their own attacks with greater ardour; whilst the Christians accused each other of treacherous proceedings or intentions, the war-machines made the walls totter, and the Mamelukes, after several assaults, were upon the point of opening themselves a road into the place. At length, one Friday (we quote an Arabian chronicle), the cadi of Damascus was praying for the combatants, when the Franks were heard to cry from the top of their half-dismantled towers, "O Mussulmans, spare us, spare us!" The besieged had laid down their arms, and fought no longer—the gates were immediately opened, and the standard of the Mussulmans floated over the walls of Sefed.

A capitulation granted the Christians permission to retire wherever they wished, upon condition that they should take away with them nothing but their clothes. Bibars, when seeing them defile before him, sought for a pretext to detain them in his power. Some were, by his orders, arrested and accused of carrying away treasures and arms; and the command was instantly issued to stop all. They were reproached with having violated the treaty, and were threatened with death if they did not embrace Islamism. They were loaded with chains and crowded together in a mass upon a hill, where they expected nothing but death. A commander of the Temple and two Cordeliers exhorted their companions in misfortune to die like Christian heroes. All those warriors, whom discord had divided, now reunited in one common evil, had only one feeling and one thought; [10] they wept as they embraced each other, they encouraged each other to die becomingly; they passed the night in confessing their sins towards God, and in deploring their errors and their differences. On the morrow, two only of these captives were set at liberty; one was a brother Hospitaller, whom Bibars sent to Ptolemaïs, to announce to the Christians the taking of Sefed; the other was a Templar, who abandoned the faith of Christ, and attached himself to the fortunes of the sultan; all the others, to the number of six hundred, fell beneath the sword of the Mamelukes. This barbarity, committed in the name of the Mussulman religion, appears the more revolting, from the Franks never having given an example for it, and that amidst the furies of war, they were never known to require the conversion of infidels, sword in hand. [11]

It is impossible to describe the despair and consternation of the Christians of Palestine, when they learnt the tragical end of the defenders of Sefed. Their superstitious grief invented or blindly received the most marvellous accounts, which the Western chroniclers have not disdained to repeat; it was said that a celestial light shone every night over the bodies of the Christian warriors that remained unburied. [12] It was added that the sultan, annoyed by this prodigy, which was every day renewed before his eyes, gave orders that the martyrs of the Christian faith should be buried, and that around their place of sepulture high walls should be built, in order that nobody might witness the miracles operated in favour of the victims he had immolated to his vengeance.

After the taking of Sefed, Bibars returned into Egypt, and the Franks hoped for a few days of repose and safety; but the indefatigable sultan never gave his enemies much time to rejoice at his absence. He only remained in Egypt till he had recruited his army with fresh troops, and soon brought back additional desolation to the states of the Christians. In this campaign, Armenia was the point to which his anger and the power of his arms were directed; he reproached the Armenian monarch with forbidding Egyptian merchants to enter his dominions, and could not pardon him for preventing his own subjects from obtaining merchandise from Egypt. These differences were quickly settled on the field of battle; one of the sons of the king of Armenia lost his liberty, and the other his life: the army of Bibars returned loaded with booty, and followed by an innumerable multitude of captives.

As, after each of his victories, the sultan presented himself before Ptolemaïs, the capital of the Christian states, he did not fail on his return from this last expedition, to exhibit before the walls of this city the spoils of the people of Armenia, together with his own machines of war; but the moment was not yet arrived in which such a great undertaking as the capture of Ptolemaïs could be attempted. After terrifying the inhabitants by his appearance, he suddenly departed, for the purpose of surprising Jaffa. This city, the fortifications of which had cost Louis IX. a considerable sum, [13] after a very slight resistance, fell into the hands of Bibars, who caused all the walls to be levelled with the ground. During this excursion, the sultan of Cairo obtained possession of the castle of Carac and several other forts, and then marched towards Tripoli. Bohemond having sent to demand of him what the purpose of his coming was: "I am come," replied he, "to gather in your harvests; in my next campaign I will besiege your capital." Nevertheless, he concluded a truce with Tripoli, in the midst of these hostilities; foreseeing that a treaty of peace would serve as a veil for the project of another war, and that he should soon find an opportunity of violating the truce with advantage.

The author of the life of Bibars, who was sent to Bohemond, count of Tripoli and prince of Antioch, says that the sultan was in the train of the ambassador, in the character of a herald-at-arms. His project was to examine the fortifications and the means of defence of the city of Tripoli. In drawing up the treaty, the Mussulman deputies only gave Bohemond the title of count, whilst he claimed that of prince; the discussion becoming warm, the envoys of Bibars naturally turned their eyes towards their master, who made them a sign to yield. [14] On his return to his army, the sultan laughed heartily with his emirs at this adventure, saying, "The time is come in which God will curse the prince and the count."

By this, Bibars alluded to his project of conquering and ruining the principality of Antioch. The Egyptian army received orders to march towards the banks of the Orontes; and but very few days had passed away before this same army was encamped under the walls of Antioch, badly defended by its patriarch, and abandoned by most of its inhabitants. Historians say very little of this siege, in which the Christians made but a feeble resistance, and appeared more frequently as suppliants than as warriors: their submission, their tears, their prayers, however, made no impression upon a conqueror whose sole policy was the destruction of the Christian cities.

As the Mussulmans entered Antioch without a capitulation, they gave themselves up to all the excesses of license and victory. In a letter which Bibars addressed to the count of Tripoli, the barbarous conqueror takes a pleasure in describing the desolation of the subdued city, and all the evils which his fury had caused the Christians to undergo. [15] "Death," says he, "came among the besieged from all sides and by all roads: we killed all that thou hadst appointed to guard the city or defend its approaches. If thou hadst seen thy knights trampled under the feet of the horses, thy provinces given up to pillage, thy riches distributed by measures-full, the wives of thy subjects put to public sale; if thou hadst seen the pulpits and crosses overturned, the leaves of the Gospel torn and cast to the winds, and the sepulchres of thy patriarchs profaned; if thou hadst seen thy enemies, the Mussulmans, trampling upon the tabernacle, and immolating in the sanctuary, monk, priest, and deacon; in short, if thou hadst seen thy palaces given up to the flames, the dead devoured by the fire of this world, the Church of St. Paul and that of St. Peter completely and entirely destroyed, certes, thou wouldst have cried out: *Would to Heaven that I were become dust!*"

Bibars distributed the booty among his soldiers, the Mamelukes reserving as their portion, the women, girls, and children. At that time, says an Arabian chronicle, "*there was not the slave of a slave that was not the master of a slave.*" A little boy was worth twelve dirhems, a little girl, five dirhems. In a single day the city of Antioch lost all its inhabitants, and a conflagration, lighted by order of Bibars, completed the work of the barbarians. Most historians agree in saying that seventeen thousand Christians were slaughtered, and a hundred thousand dragged away into slavery.

When we recall to our minds the first siege of this city by the Crusaders, and the labours and the exploits of Bohemond, Godfrey, and Tancred, who founded the principality of Antioch, we are afflicted at beholding the end of all that which the glory of conquerors had produced. When, on the other side, we see a numerous population, inclosed within ramparts, making but a feeble defence against an enemy, and allowing themselves to be slaughtered without resistance, we cannot help asking what can have become of the posterity of so many brave warriors as had defended Antioch, during almost two centuries, against all the Mussulman powers.

Complaints were made among the Christians against William, the patriarch, whom they accused of having at least favoured the invasion and conquest of the Mussulmans, by a weak pusillanimity. Without offering an opinion upon the accusation, we content ourselves with saying, that the timid prelate did not long enjoy the fruit of his base conduct; for the Mamelukes, after having permitted him to retire to Cosseïr, with all his treasures, dragged him from his retreat by violence; and the faithless pastor, despoiled of his wealth, and plunged in ignominy, underwent at last a much more cruel death than he might have expected amidst his flock, and upon the ramparts of a Christian city.

After the taking of Antioch, the Christians had nothing left to arrest the progress of the Mussulmans, but the cities of Tripoli and Ptolemaïs. Bibars was impatient to attack these last bulwarks of the Franks; but he did not dare to put trust in his fortune, and aim the last fatal blow at that power before which the Mussulman nations so lately trembled. The sultan of Cairo could not forget that the dangers of the Christians had often roused the whole West, and this thought alone was sufficient to keep him in inaction and dread. Thus the sad remains of the Christian colonies of the East, were still protected by the warlike reputation of the nations of Europe, and by the remembrance of the wonders of the early crusades.

Fame had not failed to carry the news of so many disasters across the seas. The archbishop of Tyre, the grand masters of the Temple and the Hospital, passed over into the West, to repeat the groans of the Christian cities of Syria; but on their arrival, Europe seemed but little disposed to give ear to their complaints. In vain a crusade was preached in Germany, Poland, and the more remote countries of the North; the inhabitants of northern Europe evinced nothing but indifference for events that were passing at such a distance from them. The king of Bohemia, the marquis of Brandenburg, and some other lords that had taken the cross, seemed in no hurry to perform their oath. No army set forward on its march; everything was reduced to preachings and vain preparations.

The misfortunes of the Holy Land were deeply deplored in the kingdom of France; in a *sirvente*, [16] composed on this subject, a contemporary troubadour appears to reproach Providence with the defeats of the Christians of Palestine, and in his poetical delirium, abandons himself to an impious despair:—"Sadness and grief," cried he, "have taken possession of my soul to such a degree, that little is wanting to bring me to instant death; for the cross is disgraced,—that cross which we have taken in honour of him who died upon the cross. Neither cross nor faith protects us longer, or guides us against the cruel Turks,—whom God curse! But it appears, as far as man can judge, that it is God's will to support them for our destruction. And never believe that the enemy will stop in his career after such success; on the contrary, he has sworn and publicly announced that not a single man who believes in Jesus Christ shall be left alive in Syria; that the temple even of the holy Mary will be converted into a mosque. Since the son of Mary, whom this affront ought to afflict, wills it to be so, *since this pleases him, does it follow that it should please us likewise?*

"He is then mad who seeks a quarrel with the Saracens, when Jesus Christ opposes them in nothing, as they have obtained victories, and are gaining them still (which grieves me) over the Franks, the Armenians, and the Persians. Every day we are conquered; for he sleeps,—that God that was accustomed to be so watchful: [17] Mahomet acts with all his power, and the fierce Bibars seconds him."

We cannot believe that these exceedingly remarkable words expressed the feelings of the faithful; but at a time when poets ventured to speak in this manner, we may well suppose that men's minds were not favourable to a crusade. The troubadour we have quoted does not advise the making of any war against the Saracens, and inveighs bitterly against the pope, who sold *God and indulgences* to arm the French against the house of Swabia. In fact, the dissensions raised by the disputed succession of the kingdom of

Naples and Sicily, then occupied the entire attention of the Holy See, and France was not quite free from party spirit on the occasion.

Not satisfied with launching excommunications and ecclesiastical thunders against Frederick and his family, the sovereign pontiffs wished to add the force of arms to the authority conferred upon them by the Church, and the right of conquest to that which they thought they possessed over a kingdom so near to their own capital. As they had no experience in war, and their lieutenants were equally deficient in capacity and courage, their armies were defeated. The court of Rome, thus conquered in the field of battle, was compelled to acknowledge the ascendancy of victory, and in this profane struggle lost some of that spiritual power which alone rendered it formidable.

With the exception of Mainfroy, a natural son of Frederick, and Conradin, his grandson, the family of Swabia was extinct. Mainfroy, who possessed both the abilities and courage of his father, had recently elevated the German cause in Italy, and braved both the arms and the power of the pontiffs. The court of Rome, upon finding it could not retain the kingdom of Sicily for itself, offered it to any one who would undertake the conquest of it. The crown to which Mainfroy pretended was first offered to Richard of Cornwall, and upon his prudent refusal, to Edmund, younger son of the king of England; but the English parliament would not grant the subsidies necessary for so great an undertaking. It was then offered to Louis IX. for his brother, the count of Anjou; and although the scruples of the pious monarch for a moment checked the projects of Pope Urban, Clement IV., on his accession, used fresh persuasions, and Louis at length suffered himself to be overcome by the prayers of Charles; at the same time entertaining a secret hope that the conquest of Sicily would some day prove instrumental to the defence of the Holy Land.

Charles, after being crowned by the pope in the church of St. John of the Lateran, entered the kingdom of Naples at the head of a considerable force, preceded by the fulminations of the court of Rome. The soldiers of Charles wore a cross, and fought in the name of the Church; priests exhorted the combatants, and promised them the protection of Heaven. Mainfroy succumbed in this, miscalled, holy war, and lost both his life and his crown at the battle of Cosenza.

The pope being delivered from the cares of this political crusade, turned his attention to the holy one beyond the seas; his legates solicited various princes, some to take the cross, others to accomplish their vows. Clement did not neglect to press Michael Palæologus to prove the sincerity of his promises. Charles, who was the acknowledged vassal of the pope, and who owed his kingdom to him, received many messages, representing the dangers of the Holy Land, and reminding him of what he owed to Jesus Christ, who was outraged by the victories of the Mussulmans. The new king of Sicily contented himself with sending an embassy to the sultan of Cairo, and with commending the unfortunate inhabitants of Palestine to the mercy of Bibars. The sultan replied to Charles, that he did not reject his intercessions; but the Christians were destroying themselves with their own hands; that no one among them had the power to enforce the observance of treaties, *and that the most contemptible of them were constantly undoing that which the greatest had done*. Bibars, in his turn, sent ambassadors to Charles, less for the purpose of following up any negotiations, than to obtain information upon the state and views of Christendom. [18]

Young Conradin, who was preparing to dispute the crown of Sicily with Charles of Anjou, in order to avail himself of every means of supporting his claim, sent deputies to the sultan of Cairo, in the character of king of Jerusalem, conjuring him to protect his rights against his rival. Bibars, in his reply, pretended to endeavour to console Conradin, but, doubtless, received with joy these proofs of the divisions that existed among the princes of Europe.

In the state in which Europe then was, one monarch alone took serious interest in the fate of the Christian colonies of Asia. The remembrance of a land in which he had so long dwelt, and the hope of avenging the honour of the French arms in Egypt, [19] once more directed the thoughts of Louis IX. to a new crusade. He however concealed his purpose, and this great project, says one of his historians, [20] was formed, so to say, between God and himself. Louis consulted the pope, who hesitated to answer him, reflecting upon the dangers that his absence might bring upon France, and even upon Europe. The first letter of Clement [21] aimed at diverting the French monarch from so perilous an enterprise; but, upon being consulted again, the sovereign pontiff showed none of the same scruples, and declared it to be his duty to encourage Louis in his design, as he was persuaded, he said, that this design came from God.

The purpose, however, of this negotiation remained still buried in profound mystery. Louis, no doubt, was fearful of prematurely announcing his designs, lest reflection might weaken the enthusiasm of which he must stand in so much need, or that a powerful opposition to the undertaking of a crusade might be formed in both his court and his kingdom; he thought that, by announcing his project unexpectedly, at the moment of its being ripe for execution, he should affect men's minds more forcibly, and induce them more easily to follow his example. An assembly of the barons, nobles, and prelates of the kingdom was solemnly convoked at Paris towards the middle of Lent. The faithful Joinville was not forgotten in this convocation; the seneschal foresaw, he says in his Memoirs, that Louis was about to take the cross, and the cause of his having this presentiment was, that in a dream he had seen the king of France clothed in a chasuble of a bright red colour, made of Rheims serge, which signified the cross. His almoner, when explaining this dream to him, added, that the chasuble being of Rheims serge, denoted that the crusade would be but a trifling or small exploit.

On the twenty-third day of March, the great parliament of the kingdom being assembled in a hall of the Louvre, the king entered, bearing in his hand the crown of thorns of Christ. At sight of this, the whole assembly became aware of the monarch's intentions. Louis, in a speech delivered with great animation, described the misfortunes of the Holy Land, and proclaimed that he was resolved to go and succour it; he then exhorted all who heard him to take the cross. When he ceased to speak, a sad but a profound silence expressed at once the surprise and grief of the barons and prelates, with the respect that all entertained for the will of the holy monarch.

Cardinal de St. Cecilia, the pope's legate, spoke after him, and in a pathetic exhortation, called upon the French warriors to take arms. Louis received the cross from the hands of the cardinal, and his example was followed by three of his sons. Among these princes, the assembly was affected at beholding John, count of Nevers, who was born at Damietta amidst the calamities of the preceding crusade. At the same time the legate received the oath of John, count of Brittany, of Alphonso de Brienne, count of Eu, of Marguerite, the ancient countess of Flanders, and of a great number of prelates, nobles, and knights.

The determination of St. Louis, of which a sad presentiment had been entertained, spread deep regret throughout his kingdom; his people could not behold without sorrow the departure of a prince whose presence alone preserved peace, and maintained order and justice everywhere. The health of the king was very much weakened, and there was great reason to fear that he would not be able to support the dangers and fatigues of a crusade; he took his sons with him; which circumstance added greatly to the public grief. The disasters of the first crusade were still fresh in the memory of his subjects, and whilst they thought of the captivity of the whole of the royal family, they dreaded greater misfortunes in the future. Joinville does not fear to say, "that they who had advised the king to undertake this voyage beyond the seas, had sinned mortally."

Notwithstanding the general regret, there were neither complaints nor murmurs against the king; the spirit of resignation, which was one of the virtues of the monarch, appeared to have passed into the minds of all his subjects, and, to employ the very expressions of the pope's bull, "the French people saw in the devotion of their king nothing but a noble and painful sacrifice to the cause of the Christians, to that cause for which God had not spared his only Son."

The greater that was the affection for the king, the greater was the general grief; but the zeal to partake his perils more than kept pace with these. [22] Louis alone thought of delivering the tomb of Christ and the Christian colonies; the warlike nobility of the kingdom only thought of following their king in an expedition which was already looked upon as unfortunate.

Among those who took the cross after the assembly of the Louvre, history names Thibault, king of Navarre; Henry, count of Champagne, and his brother, the count d'Artois, son of Robert, killed at Mansourah; the counts of Flanders, de la Marche, St. Pol, and Soissons; the seigneurs de Montmorency, de Nemours, de Pienne, &c. The sieur de Joinville was warmly pressed to take the cross, but he resisted all the persuasions that could be made to him, alleging the vast injuries sustained by his vassals during the last expedition. The good seneschal also was not forgetful of the predictions of his almoner; he earnestly wished to accompany the king, whom he loved sincerely; but he was not yet recovered from the terrors he had experienced in Egypt, and no earthly motive could induce him to revisit the land of the Saracens.

The determination of the king of France created a lively sensation throughout Europe, and revived in men's minds the little that remained of the old enthusiasm for the crusades. As he was the chief of the enterprise, most of the warriors were ambitious of fighting under his immediate banners; the confidence entertained for his wisdom and virtues, in some sort fortified minds that dreaded distant expeditions, and restored hopes to the Christian nations, that they appeared to have forgotten. The remembrance, even, of the misfortunes of the first voyage added to the security of the future, and created a belief in many that the triumph of the Christian armies would at length be the reward of past labours and calamities, and the fruit of a salutary experience.

Clement IV. wrote to the king of Armenia to console him for the evils he had suffered by the invasion of the Mamelukes, and to announce to him that the Christians of the East were about to receive powerful succours. Abaga, khan of the Tartars, who was then prosecuting a war against the Turks of Asia Minor, sent ambassadors to the court of Rome, and to several princes of the West, proposing to attack the Mamelukes in concert with the Franks, and drive them from Syria and Egypt. The pope received the

Mogul ambassadors with great solemnity; he told them that an army, led by a powerful monarch, was about to embark for the East, that the hour fatal to the Mussulmans was come, and that God would bless his nation, and all the allies of his nation.

Louis, constantly occupied by his expedition, fixed the period of his departure for 1270; so that three long years must pass away before the assistance promised by the sovereign pontiff could arrive in the East. Vessels to transport the Crusaders were demanded of the republics of Genoa and Venice: the Venetians at first refused; but upon learning that applications were being made to the Genoese, they sent ambassadors to offer a fleet. After protracted negotiations, in which Venice evinced more jealousy of the Genoese than zeal for the crusade, she again refused to concur in the embarkation of the Christian army, being in less dread of the anger of Louis IX. than of that of the sultan of Cairo, who had it in his power to ruin her mercantile establishments in the East. At length the Genoese engaged to furnish vessels for the expedition.

But the greatest difficulty was to find the money necessary for the preparations of the war. Up to this period, the tenths levied upon the clergy had supplied the expenses of the crusades; [23] and an opinion generally prevailed, that a holy war ought to be paid for by men attached to the Church and devoted to the altars of Jesus Christ. Urban IV., the predecessor of Clement, had already ordered throughout the West, that a levy of a hundredth should be made upon the revenues of the clergy; and, what might be considered a traffic in holy things, the court of Rome permitted the distributing of indulgences, which faculty was granted in proportion with what was given beyond the tribute required. The French clergy had addressed several petitions to the pope upon this subject; but these petitions always remained unnoticed.

When the late determination of Louis IX. became known, the Holy See had recourse to the customary means, and, without the least attention to complaints, which were not without foundation, the order was issued to levy again a tenth during three years. Upon this the clergy redoubled their opposition, and were much more earnest in the defence of their own revenues than in the defence of the Holy Land. They complained to the king, and they sent deputies to Rome, to show the depth of the misery into which the Church of France was plunged by the burdens imposed upon it; [24] these deputies represented to the sovereign pontiff that the exactions of latter times became every day more intolerable, and that the property of the clergy was no longer sufficient to support the altars and feed the poor of Jesus Christ. They added, that injustice and violence had formerly separated the Greek Church from that of Rome; giving his holiness to understand, that new rigours would not fail to produce new schisms. They further said, that if most crusades, particularly the expedition of Louis IX. into Egypt, had been unfortunate, it no doubt arose from the sanctuary having been plundered, and the churches ruined for the sake of them; as a last reason, they prognosticated much greater calamities for the future than any that had been experienced.

Such an address necessarily inflamed the anger of the sovereign pontiff. Clement, in his reply, warmly reproached the deputies, and they who had sent them, with their indifference for the cause of all Christians, and for their avarice, which made them deny their superfluous wealth for the prosecution of a war in which so many princes and illustrious warriors perilled their lives. He pointed to the excommunication ready to fall upon their heads, and, what must have much more terrified them, he threatened to deprive them of their property and their benefices. Such was then the power of Rome, that nothing could be possessed without its pleasure: the clergy were obliged to submit, and pay the tenth during four years. The pope further empowered the king to dispose of all the sums bequeathed by will for the assistance of the Holy Land; he equally abandoned to him the money that might be drawn from those who, having taken the cross, were desirous of redeeming their vows; which latter means must have produced a considerable sum, as the clergy gave the cross to everybody, and refused dispensation to nobody.

Louis IX. neglected none of the resources that his position as king of France placed in his hands; at this period no regular impost was known, and, to support the splendour of their thrones, kings had nothing to depend upon but the revenues of their domains. [25] In order to provide for all the expenses he was obliged to incur on this occasion, the king had recourse to the impost called the capitation-tax, which suzerain lords, according to feudal customs, required of each of their vassals in any extraordinary circumstances. Usage authorized him to levy this contribution on account of the crusade, but he had also the right, on the occasion of a ceremony, at that time very important, in which his eldest son Philip was to be received as a knight. Thus, the impost was demanded in the name of chivalry and in the name of religion; it was paid without a murmur, because Louis confided the gathering of it to men of acknowledged integrity.

When Philip received the sword of knighthood, the French, and particularly the Parisians, expressed their love for Louis IX. and his family by public rejoicings; all the nobility hastened from the provinces to be present at the festivities and spectacles that were celebrated in the capital on this occasion. Amidst the tournaments, the exercises of the tilt-yard, and the sports in which the skill and courage of the *preux* and the *paladins* were displayed, the crusade was not forgotten. The pope's legate pronounced a discourse, in the isle of St. Louis, upon the misfortunes of the Holy Land; all the people appeared to be deeply moved by the exhortations of the prelate; a crowd of knights, and warriors of all classes, took the cross; thus Louis IX. found in this circumstance an opportunity of raising money for the support of his army, and of procuring recruits for the holy war.

Whilst all France was engaged in preparing for the expedition beyond the seas, the crusade was preached in the other countries of Europe. A council was held at Northampton, in England, in which Ottobon, the pope's legate, exhorted the faithful to arm themselves to save the little that remained of the kingdom of Jerusalem; and Prince Edward took the cross, to discharge the vow that his father Henry III. had made when the news reached Europe of the captivity of Louis IX. in Egypt. After the example of Edward, his brother Prince Edmund, with the earls of Pembroke and Warwick, and many knights and barons, agreed to take arms against the infidels. The same zeal for the deliverance of the holy places was manifested in Scotland, where John Baliol and several nobles enrolled themselves under the banners of the cross.

Catalonia and Castile furnished a great number of Crusaders: the king of Portugal, and James, king of Arragon, took the cross. Dona Sancha, one of the daughters of the Arragonese prince, had made a pilgrimage to Jerusalem, and had died in the hospital of St. John, after devoting many years to the service of pilgrims and the sick. James had several times conquered the Moors; but neither his exploits against the infidels, nor the remembrance of a daughter who had fallen a martyr to Christian charity, could sustain his piety against the attacks of his earthly passions, and his shameful connection with Berengaria scandalized Christendom.

The pope, to whom he communicated his design of going to the Holy Land, replied that Jesus Christ could not accept the services of a prince *who crucified him every day by his sins*. The king of Arragon, by a strange combination of opposite sentiments, would neither renounce Berengaria nor give up his project of going to fight against the infidels in the East. He renewed his oath in a great assembly at Toledo, at which the ambassadors of the khan of Tartary and of the king of Armenia were present. We read in a Spanish dissertation [26] upon the crusades, that Alphonso the Wise, who was not able to go to the East himself, furnished the king of Arragon with a hundred men and a hundred thousand marvedis in gold; the order of St. James, and other orders of knighthood, who had often accompanied the conqueror of the Moors in his battles, supplied him also with men and money. The city of Barcelona offered him eighty thousand Barcellonese sols, and Majorca fifty thousand silver sols, with two equipped vessels. The fleet, composed of thirty large ships and a great number of smaller craft, in which were embarked eight hundred men-at-arms and two thousand foot-soldiers, set out from Barcelona on the 4th of September, 1268. When they arrived off Majorca, the fleet was dispersed by a tempest; one part of the vessels gained the coasts of Asia, another took shelter in the ports of Sardinia; the vessel the king of Arragon was on board of was cast upon the coast of Languedoc.

The arrival at Ptolemaïs of the Arragonese Crusaders, commanded by a natural son of James, restored some hopes to the Franks of Palestine. An envoy from the king of Arragon, according to the Oriental chronicles, repaired to the khan of the Tartars, to announce to him that the Spanish monarch would soon arrive with his army. But whether he was detained by the charms of Berengaria, or whether the tempest that dispersed his fleet made him believe that Heaven was averse to his pilgrimage, James did not arrive. His departure, in which he appeared to despise the counsels of the Holy See, had been severely censured; and his return, which was attributed to his disgraceful passion, met with an equal share of blame. Murmurs likewise arose against the king of Portugal, who had levied the tenths, but did not leave his kingdom.

All those who in Europe took an interest in the crusade had, at this time, their eyes directed towards the kingdom of Naples, where Charles of Anjou was making great preparations to accompany his brother into the East; but this kingdom, recently conquered, was doomed again to be the theatre of a war kindled by vengeance and ambition. There fell out in the states of Naples and Sicily, which had so often changed masters, that which almost always takes place after a revolution: deceived hopes were changed into hatreds: the excesses inseparable from a conquest, the presence of an army proud of its victories, with the too violent government of Charles, animated the people against their new king. Clement IV. thought it his duty to give a timely and salutary warning: "Your kingdom," he wrote to him, "at first exhausted by the agents of your authority, is now torn by your enemies; thus the caterpillar destroys what has escaped the grasshopper. The kingdom of Sicily and Naples has not been wanting in men to desolate it; where now are they that will defend it?" This letter of the pope announced storms ready to break forth. Many of those who had called Charles to the throne, regretted the house of Swabia, and directed their new hopes towards Conradin, heir of Frederick and of Conrad. This young prince quitted Germany with an army, and advanced towards Italy, strengthening himself in his march with the party of the Ghibellines, and with all those whom the domination of Charles had irritated. All Italy was in flames, and the pope, Charles's protector, retired to Viterbo, had no defence to afford him, except the thunders of the Church.

Charles of Anjou, however, assembled his troops, and marched out to meet his rival. The two armies met in the plain of St. Valentine, near Aquila; the army of Conradin was cut to pieces, and the young prince fell into the power of the conqueror. Posterity cannot pardon Charles for having abused his victory even so far as to condemn and decapitate his disarmed and vanquished enemy. [27] After this execution, Sicily and the country of Naples were given up to all the furies of a jealous, suspicious tyranny; for violence produces violence, and great political crimes never come alone. It was thus that Charles got ready for the crusade; but, on the other hand, Providence was preparing terrible catastrophes for him: "So true it is," says an historian, "that God as often gives kingdoms to punish those he elevates, as to chastise those whom he brings low."

Whilst these bloody scenes were passing in Italy, Louis IX. was following up the establishment of public peace and his darling object, the crusade, at the same time. The holy monarch did not forget that the surest manner of softening the evils of war, as well as of his absence, was to make good laws; he therefore issued several ordinances, and each of these ordinances was a monument of his justice. The most celebrated of all is the Pragmatic Sanction, which Bossuet called the firmest support of Gallican liberties. He also employed himself in elevating that monument of legislation which illustrated his reign, and which became a light for following ages.

The count of Poictiers, who was to accompany his brother, was in the mean time engaged in pacifying his provinces, and established many regulations for maintaining public order. He, above everything, endeavoured to abolish slavery; having for a maxim, "That men are born free, and it is always wise to bring back things to their origin." This good prince drew upon himself the benedictions of his people; and the love of his vassals assured the duration of the laws he made.

We have said that Prince Edward, son of Henry III., had taken the oath to combat the infidels. He had recently displayed a brilliant valour in the civil war that had so long desolated England; and the deliverance of his father and the pacification of the kingdom had been the reward of his exploits. It was his esteem for the character of Louis IX., more than the spirit of devotion, that induced him to set out for the East. The king of France, who himself exhorted him to take the cross, lent him seventy thousand livres tournois for the preparations for his voyage. Edward was to follow Louis as his vassal, and to conduct under his banners the English Crusaders, united with those of Guienne. Gaston de Béarn, to whom the French monarch advanced the sum of twenty-five thousand livres, prepared to follow Prince Edward to the Holy Land.

The period fixed upon for the departure of the expedition was drawing near. By order of the legate, the curés in every parish had taken the names of the Crusaders, in order to oblige them to wear the cross publicly, and all had notice to hold themselves in readiness to embark in the month of May, 1270. Louis confided the administration of his kingdom, during his absence, to Matthew, abbot of St. Denis, and to Simon, sieur de Nesle; he wrote to all the nobles who were to follow him into the Holy Land, to recommend them to assemble their knights and men-at-arms. As religious enthusiasm was not sufficiently strong to make men forget their worldly interests, many nobles who had taken the cross entertained great fears of being ruined by the holy war, and most of them hesitated to set out. Louis undertook to pay all the expenses of their voyage, and to maintain them at his own cost during the war,—a thing that had not been done in the crusades of Louis VII. or Philip Augustus, in which the ardour of the Crusaders did not allow them to give a thought to their fortunes, or to exercise so much foresight. We have still a valuable monument of this epoch in a charter, by which the king of France stipulates how much he is to pay to a great number of barons and knights during the time the war beyond the seas should last.

Early in the month of March, Louis repaired to the church of St. Denis, where he received the symbols of pilgrimage, and placed his kingdom under the protection of the apostles of France. [28] Upon the day following this solemn ceremony, a mass for the crusade was celebrated in the church of Notre Dame, at Paris. The monarch appeared there, accompanied by his children and the principal nobles of his court; he walked from the palace barefooted, carrying his scrip and staff. The same day he went to sleep at Vincennes, and beheld, for the last time, the spot on which he had enjoyed so much happiness in administering justice to his people. And it was here too that he took leave of Queen Marguerite, whom he had never before quitted,—a separation rendered so much the more painful by the sorrowful reflection it recalled of past events, and by melancholy presentiments for the future.

Both the people and the court were affected by the deepest regret, and that which added to the public anxiety was the circumstance that every one was ignorant of the point to which the expedition was to be directed: the coast of Africa was only vaguely conjectured. The king of Sicily had taken the cross without having the least inclination to embark for Asia; and when the question was discussed in council, he gave it as his opinion that Tunis should be the object of the first attack. The kingdom of Tunis covered the seas with pirates, who infested all the routes to Palestine; it was, besides, the ally of Egypt, and might, if subdued, be made the readiest road to that country. These were the ostensible reasons put forth; the true ones were, that it was of importance to the king of Sicily that the coasts of Africa should be brought under European subjection, and that he did not wish to go too far from Italy. The true reason with St. Louis, and that which, no doubt, determined him, was, that he believed it possible to convert the king of Tunis, and thus bring a vast kingdom under the Christian banners. The Mussulman prince, whose ambassadors had been several times in France, had himself given birth to this idea, by saying, that he asked nothing better than to embrace the religion of Jesus Christ: [29] thus, that which he had said to turn aside an invasion, was precisely the cause of the war being directed against his territories. Louis IX. often repeated that he would consent to pass the whole of his life in a dungeon, without seeing the sun, if, by such a sacrifice, the conversion of the king of Tunis and his nation could be brought about; an expression of ardent proselytism that has been blamed with much bitterness, but which only showed an extreme desire to see Africa delivered from barbarism, and marching with Europe in the progress of intelligence and civilization, which are the great blessings of Christianity.

As Louis traversed his kingdom on his way to Aigues-Mortes, where the army of the Crusaders was to embark, he was everywhere hailed by the benedictions of his people, and gratified by hearing their ardent prayers for the success of his arms; the clergy and the faithful, assembled in the churches, prayed for the king and his children, and all that should follow him. They prayed also for foreign princes and nobles who had taken the cross, and promised to go into the East; as if they would, by that means, press them to hasten their departure.

Very few, however, responded to this religious appeal. The king of Castile, who had taken the cross, had pretensions to the imperial crown, nor could he forget the death of his brother Frederick, immolated by Charles of Anjou. It was not only that the affairs of the empire detained the German princes and nobles; the death of young Conradin had so shocked and disgusted men's minds in Germany, that no one from that country would have consented to fight under the same banners as the king of Sicily. So black a crime, committed amidst the preparations for a holy war, appeared to presage great calamities. In the height of their grief or indignation, people might fear that Heaven would be angry with the Christians, and that its curse would fall upon the arms of the Crusaders.

When Louis arrived at Aigues-Mortes, he found neither the Genoese fleet nor the principal nobles who were to embark with him; the ambassadors of Palæologus were the only persons who did not cause themselves to be waited for; for a great dread of the crusade was entertained at Constantinople, and this fear was more active than the enthusiasm of the Crusaders. Louis might have asked the Greek emperor why, after having promised to send soldiers, he had only sent ambassadors; but Louis, who attached great importance to the conversion of the Greeks, contented himself with removing the apprehensions of the envoys, and, as Clement IV. died at that period, he sent them to the conclave of the cardinals, to terminate the reunion of the two churches.

At length the unwilling Crusaders, stimulated by repeated exhortations, and by the example of Louis, set forward on their march from all the provinces, and directed their course towards the ports of Aigues-Mortes and Marseilles. Louis soon welcomed the arrival of the count of Poictiers, with a great number of his vassals; the principal nobles brought with them the most distinguished of their knights and their most brave and hardy soldiers; many cities likewise contributed their supply of warriors. Each troop had its banner, and formed a separate corps, bearing the name of a city or a province; the battalions of Beaucaire, Carcassonne, Châlons, Perigord, &c., attracted observation in the Christian army. These names, it is true, excited great emulation, but they also gave rise to quarrels, which the wisdom and firmness of Louis had great difficulty in appeasing. Crusaders arrived from Catalonia, Castile, and several other provinces of Spain; five hundred warriors from Friesland likewise ranged themselves with full confidence under the standard of such a leader as Louis, saying, that their nation had always been proud to obey the kings of France.

Before he embarked, the king wrote once more to the regents of the kingdom, to recommend them to watch carefully over public morals, to deliver France from corrupt judges, and to render to everybody, particularly to the poor, prompt and perfect justice, so that He who judges the judgments of men might have nothing to reproach him with.

Such were the last farewells that Louis took of France. The fleet set sail on the fourth of July, 1270, and in a few days arrived in the road of Cagliari. Here the council of the counts and barons was assembled in the king's vessel, to deliberate upon the plan of the crusade. Those who advocated the conquest of Tunis, said that by that means the passages of the Mediterranean would be opened, and the power of the Mamelukes would be weakened; and that after that conquest the army would go triumphantly into either Egypt or Palestine. Many of the barons were not of this opinion; they said, if the Holy Land stood in need of prompt assistance, they ought to afford it without delay; whilst they were engaged on the coast of Africa, in a country with which they were unacquainted, the Christian cities of Syria might all fall into the hands of the Saracens; the most redoubtable enemy of the Christians was Bibars, the terrible sultan of Cairo; it was him they ought first to attack; it was into his states, into the bosom of his capital, that the war should be carried, and not to a place two hundred leagues from Egypt. They added to this, remembrances of the defeats of the French army on the banks of the Nile,—defeats that ought to be avenged upon the very theatre of so many disasters.

Contemporary history does not say to what extent Louis was struck with the wisdom of these last opinions; but the expedition to Tunis flattered his most cherished hopes. It had been proposed by the king of Sicily, whose concurrence was necessary to the success of the crusade. It was, therefore, decided that the Genoese fleet should direct its course towards Africa; and two days after, on the twentieth of July, it arrived in sight of Tunis and Carthage.

On the western coast of Africa, opposite Sicily, is a peninsula, described by Strabo, whose circumference is three hundred and forty stadii, or forty-two miles. This peninsula advances into the sea between two gulfs, one of which, on the west, offers a commodious port; the other, on the south-east, communicates, by means of a canal, with a lake which extends three leagues into the land, and which modern geographers term the Gullet. It was upon this spot was built the great rival of Rome, whose site extended over the two shores of the sea. Neither the conquests of the Romans, nor the ravages of the Vandals, had been able to entirely destroy this once flourishing city; but in the seventh century, after being invaded and laid waste by the Saracens, it became nothing but a mass of ruins; a moderate-sized village upon the port, called Marsa, a tower on the point of the cape, a pretty strong castle on the hill of Byrsa,—these were all the remains of that city whose power so long dominated over the Mediterranean and the coasts of Africa and Asia.

At five leagues' distance, towards the south-east, a little beyond the gulf and the lake of the Gullet, arose a city, called in ancient times Tynis or Tunissa, [30] of which Scipio made himself master before he attacked Carthage. Tunis had thriven by the fall of other cities, and in the thirteenth century she vied in wealth and population with the most flourishing cities of Africa. It contained ten thousand houses, and had three extensive suburbs; the spoils of nations and the produce of an immense commerce had enriched it; and all that the art of fortification could invent had been employed to defend the access to it.

The coast on which Tunis stood was the theatre of many revolutions, of which ancient history has transmitted accounts to us; but modern history has not, in the same manner, consecrated the revolutions of the Saracens. We can scarcely follow the march of the barbarians who planted the standard of Islamism upon so many ruins. All that we positively know is, that Tunis, for a long time united to the kingdom of Morocco, was separated from it under a warlike prince, whose third successor was reigning in the time of St. Louis.

At the sight of the Christian fleet, the inhabitants of the coast of Africa were seized with terror, and all who were upon the Carthage shore took flight towards the mountains or towards Tunis. Some vessels that were in the port were abandoned by their crews; the king ordered Florent de Varennes, who performed the functions of admiral, to get into a boat and reconnoitre the coast. Varennes found nobody in the port or upon the shore; he sent word to the king that there was no time to be lost, he must take immediate advantage of the consternation of the enemy. But it was remembered that in the preceding expedition the descent upon the coast of Egypt had been too precipitate; in this it was determined to risk nothing. Inexperienced youth had presided over the former war; now it was directed by old age and ripe manhood: it was resolved to wait till the morrow.

The next day, at dawn, the coast appeared covered with Saracens, among whom were many men on horseback. The Crusaders, not the less, commenced their preparations for landing. At the approach of the Christians, the multitude of infidels disappeared; which, according to the account of an eye witness, was a blessing from Heaven, for the disorder was so great, that a hundred men would have been sufficient to stop the disembarkation of the whole army.

When the Christian army had landed, it was drawn up in order of battle upon the shore, and, in accordance with the laws of war, Pierre de Condé, almoner to the king, read, with a loud voice, a proclamation, by which the conquerors took possession of the territory. This proclamation, which Louis had drawn up himself, began by these words: "I proclaim, in the name of our Lord Jesus Christ, and of Louis, king of France, his sergeant," &c. [31]

The baggage, provisions, and munitions of war were landed; a vast space was marked out, and the Christian soldiers pitched their tents. Whilst they were digging ditches and raising intrenchments to protect the army from a surprise, they took possession of the tower built on the point of the cape; and on the following day, five hundred sailors planted the standard of the lilies upon the castle of Carthage. The village of Marsa, which was close to the castle, fell likewise into the hands of the Crusaders; the women and the sick were placed here, whilst the army remained beneath their tents.

Louis still hoped for the conversion of the king of Tunis, but this pious illusion was very quickly dissolved. The Mussulman prince sent messengers to the king, to inform, him that he would come and meet him at the head of a hundred thousand men, and would require baptism of him on the field of battle; the Moorish king added, that he had caused all the Christians in his dominions to be seized, and that every one of them should be massacred if the Christian army presumed to insult his capital.

The menaces and vain bravadoes of the prince of Tunis effected no change in the plans of the crusade; the Moors, besides, inspired no fear, and they themselves could not conceal the terror which the sight only of the Christians created in them. Not daring to face their enemy, their scattered bands sometimes hovered around the Christian army, seeking to surprise any stragglers from the camp; and at others, uniting together, they poured down towards the advanced posts, launched a few arrows, showed their naked swords, and then depended upon the swiftness of their horses to secure them from the pursuit of the Christians. They not unfrequently had recourse to treachery: three hundred of them came into the camp of the Crusaders, and said they wished to embrace the Christian faith, and a hundred more followed them, announcing the same intention. [32] After being received with open arms, they waited for what they deemed a favourable opportunity, and fell upon a body of the Christians, sword in hand; but being overwhelmed by numbers, most of them were killed, and the rest were allowed to escape. Three of the principals fell on their knees, and implored the compassion of the leaders. The contempt the Franks had for such enemies obtained their pardon, and they were driven out of the camp.

At length the Mussulman army, emboldened by the inaction of the Christians, presented itself several times on the plain. Nothing would have been more easy than to attack and conquer it; but Louis had resolved to act upon the defensive, and to await the arrival of the king of Sicily for beginning the war,—a fatal resolution, which ruined everything: the Sicilian monarch, who had advised this ill-starred expedition, was destined to complete, by his delays, the evil he had begun by his counsels.

The Mussulmans flocked from all parts of Africa to defend the cause of Islamism against the Christians. Preparations were carried on in Egypt to meet the invasion of the Franks, and in the month of August, Bibars announced by messengers, that he was about to march to the assistance of Tunis. The troops which the sultan of Cairo maintained in the province of Barka received orders to set forward. Thus, the Moorish army was about to become formidable; but it was not this host of Saracens that the Crusaders had most to dread. Other dangers, other misfortunes threatened them: the Christian army wanted water; they had none but salted provisions; the soldiers could not endure the climate of Africa; winds constantly prevailed, which, coming from the torrid zone, appeared to the Europeans to be the breath of a devouring fire. The Saracens upon the neighbouring mountains raised the sand with certain instruments made for the purpose, and the dust was carried by the wind in burning clouds down upon the plain upon which the Christians were encamped. At last, dysentery, that fatal malady of warm climates, began to commit frightful ravages among the troops; and the plague, which appears to be born of itself upon this burning, arid sand, spread its dire contagion through the Christian army.

They were obliged to be under arms night and day; not to defend themselves from an enemy that always fled away from them, but to guard against surprise. A vast number of the Crusaders sunk under fatigue, famine, and disease. The French had soon to regret the loss of Bouchard, count de Vendome, the count de la Marche, Gauthier de Nemours, the lords de Montmorency, de Pienne, de Bressac, Guy d'Aspremont, and Raoul, brother of the count de Soissons. It became impossible to bury the dead; the ditches of the camp were filled with carcases, thrown in heaps, which added to the corruption of the air and to the spectacle of the general desolation.

At length Olivier de Termes, a Languedocian gentleman, coming from Sicily, announced that King Charles was quite ready to embark with his army. This news was received with joy, but had no power to alleviate the evils the Crusaders were then exposed to. The heats became excessive; the want of water, bad food, disease, which continued its ravages, and the grief at being shut up in a camp without the power to fight, completed the despondency that had taken possession of the minds of leaders and soldiers. Louis endeavoured to cheer them both by his words and his example; but he himself fell ill with dysentery. Prince Philip, the duke de Nevers, the king of Navarre, and the legate also felt the effects of the contagion. The duke de Nevers, surnamed Tristan, was born at Damietta during the captivity of the king, and was particularly the object of his father's love. The young prince remained in the royal tent; but as he appeared to be sinking under the effects of the disease, it was judged best to convey him on board one of the vessels. The monarch incessantly demanded news of his son; but all who surrounded him preserved a melancholy silence. At length they were obliged to inform him that the duke de Nevers was dead; the feelings of the father prevailed over the resignation of the Christian, and he wept bitterly. A short time afterwards, the pope's legate died, deeply regretted by the clergy and the soldiers of the cross, who regarded him as their spiritual father.

In spite of his sufferings, in spite of his griefs, Louis IX. was constantly engaged in endeavours to alleviate the situation of his army. He gave orders as long as he had any strength left, dividing his time between the duties of a Christian and those of a monarch. The fever, however, increased; no longer able to attend either to his cares for the army or to exercises of piety, he ordered the cross to be placed before him, and stretching out his hands, he in silence implored Him who had suffered for all men.

The whole army was in a state of mourning; the soldiers walked about in tears, demanding of Heaven the preservation of so good a prince. Amidst the general grief, Louis turned his thoughts towards the accomplishment of the divine laws and the destinies of France. Philip, who was his successor to the throne, was in his tent; he desired him to approach his bed, and in a faltering voice gave him counsels in what manner he should govern the kingdom of his fathers. The instructions he gave him comprise the most noble maxims of religion and loyalty; and that which will render them for ever worthy of the respect of posterity is, that they had the authority of his example, and only recalled the virtues of his own life. After having recommended Philip to respect, and cause to be respected, religion and its ministers, and at all times, and above all things, to fear to offend God: [33] "My dear son," added he, "be charitable and merciful towards the poor and all who suffer. If thou attainest the throne, show thyself worthy, by thy conduct, of receiving the holy unction with which the kings of France are consecrated. When thou shalt be king, show thyself just in all things, and let nothing turn thee aside from the path of truth and rectitude. If the widow and orphan contend before thee with the powerful man, declare thyself of the party of the feeble against the strong, until the truth shall be known to thee. In affairs in which thou thyself shalt be interested, support at first the cause of the other; for if thou dost not act in that sort, thy counsellors will hesitate to speak against thee, which thou oughtest not to desire. My dear son, above all things I recommend thee to avoid war with every Christian nation; if thou art reduced by necessity to make it, at least take care that the poor people, who are not in the wrong, be kept safe from all harm. Give all thy efforts to appease the divisions that may arise in thy kingdom, for nothing is so pleasing to God as the spectacle of concord and peace. Neglect nothing to provide good lieutenants (baillis) and provosts in thy provinces. Give power freely to men who know how to use it, and punish all who abuse it; for if it is thy duty to hate evil in another, much greater reason hast thou to hate it in them who hold their authority of thee. Be just in the levying of thy public taxes, and be wise and moderate in the expenditure of them; beware of foolish expenses, which lead to unjust imposts; correct with prudence all that is defective in the laws of thy kingdom. Maintain with loyalty the rights and franchises that thy predecessors have left, for the happier that thy subjects shall be, the greater thou wilt be; the more irreproachable thy government shall be, the more thy enemies will fear to attack it."

Louis gave Philip several more counsels upon the love he owed to God, his people, and his family; then pouring out his full heart, he uttered nothing but the language of a parent who is about to be separated from a son he loves tenderly. "I bestow upon thee," said he, "all the benedictions that a father can bestow upon a dear son. Aid me by masses and prayers, and let me have a part in all the good actions thou shalt perform. I beseech our Lord Jesus Christ, by his great mercy, to guard thee from all evils, and to keep thee from doing anything contrary to his will; and that after this mortal life we may see Him, love Him, and praise Him together in a life everlasting."

When we reflect that these words were pronounced on the coast of Africa by a dying king of France, we experience a mixture of surprise and emotion, which even the coldest and most indifferent hearts can scarcely fail to partake of. Judge, then, of the effect they must have produced upon the feelings of a desolate son! Philip listened to them with respectful sorrow, and commanded them to be faithfully transcribed, in order that he might have them before his eyes all the days of his life. [34]

Louis then turned to his daughter, the queen of Navarre, who sat, drowned in tears, at the foot of his bed: in a precept which he had prepared for her, he laid before her all the duties of a queen and a wife. Above all, he recommended her to take the greatest care of her husband, who was then sick; and, never forgetful of even the smallest circumstances, he advised the king of Navarre, on his return to Champagne, to pay all his debts before he began to rebuild the convent of the Cordeliers of Provins.

These instructions were the last words that Louis addressed to his children; from that time they never saw him again. The ambassadors of Michael Palæologus arriving in the camp, the king consented to receive them. In the state in which Louis then was, it was impossible for him to see through the false promises of the Greeks, or the alarms and deceitful policy of their emperor; he no longer gave attention to the things of this world. He confined himself to the expression of his earnest wishes that the reunion of the two churches might at length be effected, and promised the ambassadors that his son Philip would do everything in his power to bring it about. These envoys were Meliteniote, archdeacon of the imperial chapel, and the celebrated Vechus, chancellor of the church of Constantinople. They were both so much affected by the words and the virtues of St. Louis, that they afterwards gave their most zealous endeavours to promote the reunion, and both ended by becoming victims to the policy of the Greeks.

After this interview Louis thought of nothing but his God, and remained alone with his confessor. His almoners recited before him the prayers of the Church, to which he responded. He then received the Viaticum and extreme unction. "From Sunday, at the hour of nones," says an ocular witness, "till Monday, at the hour of tierce, his mouth never ceased, either day or night, to praise our Lord, and to pray for the people he had brought to that place." He was heard to pronounce these words of the prophet-king: "Grant, Lord, that we may despise the prosperities of this world, and know how to brave its adversities." He likewise repeated, as loudly as his feeble state would permit, this verse of another psalm: "Oh, God! deign to sanctify thy people, and to watch over them." Sometimes he invoked St. Denis, whom he was accustomed to invoke in battle, and implored him to grant his heavenly support to this army he was about to leave without a leader. In the night between Sunday and Monday he was heard to pronounce the word *Jerusalem* twice, and then he added: "We will go to Jerusalem." His mind was constantly occupied with the idea of the holy war. Perhaps, likewise, he saw nothing then but the heavenly Jerusalem, the last country of the just man.

At nine o'clock in the morning of Monday, the twenty-fifth of August, he lost his speech; but he still looked upon all who were round him kindly (*débonnairement*). His countenance was calm, and it was evident that his mind was, at the same time, divided between the purest of earthly affections and the thoughts of eternity. Feeling that death was approaching fast, he made signs to his attendants to place him, covered by hair-cloth, upon a bed of ashes. Between the hours of tierce and mid-day he appeared to sleep, and lay with his eyes closed for more than half an hour at a time. He then seemed to revive, opened his eyes, and looking towards heaven, exclaimed: "O Lord! I shall enter into thy house, and shall worship thee in thy holy tabernacle!" Hi died at three o'clock in the afternoon.

We have spoken of the profound grief which prevailed among the Crusaders when Louis fell sick. There was not a leader or a soldier that did not forget his own ills in his anxiety for the king. At every hour of the day and night these faithful warriors crowded round the monarch's tent, and when they beheld the sad and apprehensive air of all who came out of it, they turned away, with their eyes cast to the earth, and their souls filled with the most gloomy thoughts. In the camp, the soldiers scarcely durst ask each other a question, for they heard none but sorrowful tidings. At length, when the event that all had dreaded was announced to the army, the French warriors abandoned themselves to despair; they saw in the death of Louis a signal for all sorts of calamities, and anxiously inquired of each other what leader was to conduct them back to their homes. With the general groans and tears were mingled many bitter reproaches against those who had advised this fatal expedition, particularly the king of Sicily, whom all accused of being the cause of the disasters of the war.

On the very day of the king's death Charles of Anjou and his army landed near Carthage; trumpets and other warlike music resounded along the shore, but a profound and melancholy silence was preserved in the camp of the Crusaders, and not a man went forth to meet the Sicilians, whom they had looked for with so much impatience. Sad forebodings rushed into the mind of Charles; he galloped forward, and flying to the tent of the king, found his royal brother dead, and stretched upon his bed of ashes. The features of Louis were scarcely altered, his death had been so calm. Charles prostrated himself at his feet, watering them with his tears, and calling him sometimes his brother, sometimes his lord. He remained a long time in this attitude, without seeing any of those who surrounded him, continuing to address Louis as if he had been still living, and reproaching himself, in accents of despair, with not having heard, with not having received, the last words of the most affectionate of brothers and best of kings.

The mortal remains of Louis were deposited in two funereal urns. The entrails of the holy monarch were granted to Charles of Anjou, who sent them to the abbey of Montréal, where these precious relics, for a length of time, attracted the devotion and respect of the faithful. The bones and the heart of Louis remained in the hands of Philip. This young prince was desirous of sending them to France, but the leaders and soldiers would not consent to be separated from all that was left to them of their beloved monarch. The presence of this sacred deposit amongst the Crusaders appeared to them a safeguard against new misfortunes, and the most sure means of drawing down the protection of Heaven upon the Christian army.

Philip was still sick, and his malady created great anxiety. The army considered him the worthy successor of Louis, and the affection that had been felt for the father descended to the son; he received, amidst the public grief, the homage and oaths of the leaders, barons, and nobles. His first care was to confirm the regency, and all that his father had established in France before his departure. Geoffrey de Beaulieu, William de Chartres, and John de Mons, confessors and almoners to the king, were directed to carry these orders of Philip's into the West. Among the letters which these ecclesiastics took with them into France, history has preserved that which was addressed to the clergy *and to all people of worth* in the kingdom. [35] After having described their labours, the perils and the death of Louis IX., the young prince implored God to grant that he might follow the steps of so good a father, might accomplish his sacred commands, and put in practice all his counsels. Philip concluded his letter, which was read aloud in all churches, by supplicating the ecclesiastics and the faithful "to put up to the King of Kings their prayers and their offerings for that prince, with whose zeal for religion, and tender solicitude for the kingdom of France, which he loved as the apple of his eye, they were so well acquainted."

The death of Louis had greatly raised the confidence of the Saracens. The mourning and grief which they observed in the Christian army were, by them, mistaken for discouragement, and they flattered themselves they should obtain a triumph over their enemies; but these hopes were speedily dispelled. The king of Sicily took the command of the Christian army during the sickness of Philip, and resumed the war. The troops he had brought with him were eager for fight, and all the French seemed anxious to seek a distraction from their grief in the field of battle. The disease which had desolated their army appeared to have suspended its ravages, and the soldiers, a long time imprisoned in their camp, felt their strength revive at the sight of the perils of war. Several conflicts took place around the lake of the Gullet, of which the Christians wished to get possession, to facilitate their approach to Tunis. The Moors, who, but a few days before, threatened to exterminate or make slaves of all the Crusaders, were not able to sustain the shock of their enemies; the cross-bowmen alone were frequently sufficient to disperse their numberless multitude. Horrible howlings, with the noise of kettle-drums and other instruments, announced their approach; clouds of dust descending from the neighbouring heights announced their retreat, and screened their flight. In two encounters they were overtaken, and left a great many of their host stretched upon the plain. Another time their camp was carried, and given up to pillage. The sovereign of Tunis could not reckon upon his army for the defence of his states, and he himself set them no example of bravery, for he remained constantly shut up in his subterranean grottoes, to avoid at the same time the burning rays of the sun and the perils of fight. Pressed by his fears, he at length could see no hopes of safety but in peace, and he resolved to purchase it, even at the cost of all his treasures. His ambassadors came repeatedly to the Christian army with directions to make proposals, and, above all, to endeavour to seduce the king of Sicily by brilliant promises. [36]

When the report of these negotiations was spread through the camp of the Crusaders, it gave birth to very different opinions. The soldiers, to whom the plunder of Tunis had been promised, wished to continue the war; some of the leaders, to whom other hopes had been given, did not evince the same ardour as the soldiers. By the death of Louis IX. and the apostolic legate, the crusade had lost both its principal motive and that moral force which had animated everything. The spirit of the Crusaders, which nobody directed, worked upon by a thousand various passions, floated in uncertainty, and this uncertainty was likely, in the end, to keep the army in a state of inaction, and bring about the abandonment of the war. Philip was desirous of returning to France, whither the affairs of his kingdom peremptorily called him. Most of the barons and French nobles began to sigh for their country. At length it was agreed that the pacific proposals of the king of Tunis should be deliberated upon.

In the council, those to whom no promise had been held out, and who were not so impatient as the others to quit the coast of Africa, were of opinion that they ought to prosecute the war. "It was for the conquest of Tunis that Louis IX. had embarked at Carthage, and that the Christian army had undergone so many evils. How could they pay higher honour to the memory of Louis and so many Frenchmen, like him, martyrs to their zeal and their faith, than by carrying on and completing their work? All Christendom knew that the Crusaders threatened Tunis, that the Moors fled at the sight of them, and that the city was ready to open its gates. What would Christendom say on learning that the Crusaders had fled before the vanquished, and robbed themselves of their own victory?"

Those who were of opinion that the peace should be concluded, answered, that the question was not only to enter Tunis, but to conquer the country, which could only be done by exterminating the population. "Besides, a prolonged siege would very much weaken the Christian army. Winter was approaching, in which they could procure no provisions, and in which continual rains would, perhaps, cause more diseases than excessive heat had done. The taking of Tunis was not the principal object of the crusade; it was necessary to make peace upon advantageous conditions, to obtain means to carry the war afterwards where circumstances might require." The leaders who spoke thus were themselves the same that had promoted the expedition against Tunis: the king of Sicily was at their head; they no longer urged the necessity for clearing the Mediterranean of pirates who infested the route of pilgrims; they said no more about depriving the sultan of Egypt of his most powerful ally. The reasons they gave for putting an end to the war were precisely the same as they had given for commencing it. Their opinion, however, prevailed; not because others were convinced by what they heard, but, as it often happens in the most important deliberations, the majority decide rather from motives they do not avow, than from those they appear to support. [37]

On the thirty-first of October a truce of ten years was concluded between the king of Tunis and the leaders of the Christian army. All the prisoners were to be given up on both sides, and Christians who had been previously captives were to be set at liberty. The sovereign of Tunis engaged not to require of the Franks any of the dues imposed in his kingdom upon foreign commerce. The treaty granted all Christians liberty to reside in the states of Tunis, to build churches there, and even to preach their faith there. The Mussulman prince was bound to pay to the king of Sicily an annual tribute of forty thousand crowns, and two hundred and ten thousand ounces of gold to the leader of the Christian army for the expenses of the war.

It was, doubtless, the last condition that decided the question: the two hundred and ten thousand ounces of gold exceeded the sum that Louis IX. had paid in Egypt for the ransom of his army; but a part of it only was received at first. Who could assure the payment of the rest when the Christian army had quitted the coast of Africa? The king of Sicily alone could derive any advantage from this treaty, so disgraceful to the French arms; he had not only found means of making a Mussulman prince pay the tribute of forty thousand gold crowns, which he owed the Pope as vassal of the Holy See; but the peace which they had concluded, in some sort, placed at his disposal an army capable of undertaking much greater conquests than that of Tunis. Thus, complaints immediately arose reproaching the king of Sicily with having, at his pleasure, changed the aim of the crusade, in order to make the Christian army subservient to his ambition.

A few days after the signing of the truce, Prince Edward arrived off the coast of Carthage, with the English and Scotch Crusaders. Having sailed from Aigues-Mortes, he directed his course towards Palestine, and came to take orders from the king of France. The French and Sicilians were prodigal in their expressions of sincere friendship for the English. Edward was received with great honours, but when he learned they had made peace, he retired into his tent, and refused to be present at any of the councils of the Christian army.

The Crusaders became impatient to quit an arid and murderous land, which recalled to them nothing but misfortunes, without the least mixture of glory. The Christian army embarked on the eighteenth of November for Sicily; and, as if Heaven had decreed that this expedition should be nothing but a series of misfortunes, a frightful tempest assailed the fleet just as it was about to enter the port of Trapani. Eighteen large ships and four thousand Crusaders were submerged, and perished in the waves. Most of the leaders and soldiers lost their arms, equipments, and horses. If one historian is to be believed, the money received from the king of Tunis was lost in this shipwreck.

After so great a misfortune, the king of Sicily neglected no means of succouring the Crusaders. We may believe in the generous sentiments which he expressed upon the occasion; but there is little doubt that, with his feelings a hope was mixed of deriving something favourable to his projects from this deplorable circumstance. When all the leaders were arrived, several councils were held to ascertain what remained to be done. As every one deplored his own losses, Charles proposed a sure means of repairing them, which was the conquest of Greece. This was the plan he had arranged; in the first place, all the Crusaders should pass the winter in Sicily; in the spring, the count of Poictiers should set out for Palestine with a part of the army, the rest was to follow Charles to Epirus, and from thence to Byzantium. This project had something adventurous and chivalric in it, very likely to seduce the French barons and nobles; but letters to the young king arrived from France, in which the regents represented in strong colours the grief and alarms of his people. Philip declared that he could not stay in Sicily, but should immediately return to his own dominions. This determination destroyed all Charles's hopes; the French lords would not abandon their young monarch, and the princes and all the leaders of the Christian army laid aside the cross. An Italian chronicle reports that Charles, in his vexation, confiscated to his own profit all the vessels and all the effects which, after the late shipwreck, were thrown upon the coasts of Sicily. He had profited by the misfortunes of the army before Tunis, and he now enriched himself with the spoils of his companions in arms. This act of injustice and violence completed the dislike that most of the Crusaders had conceived for him; this was particularly the case with the Genoese, to whom the fleet belonged in which the Christian army had embarked.

It was, however, decided that they should resume the crusade four years later. The two kings, the princes, and the most influential leaders, engaged themselves by oath to embark for Syria with their troops in the month of July of the fourth year;—a vain promise, that not one of them was destined to keep, and which they only made then to excuse in their own eyes the inconsistency of their conduct in this war. Edward, who had announced his resolution of passing the winter in Sicily, and setting out for Palestine in the spring, was the only one that did not break his promises.

The French warriors abandoned all thoughts of the crusade; but they were yet far from seeing the closing of that abyss of miseries which it had opened beneath their feet. The king of Navarre died shortly after landing at Trapani, and his wife Isabella was so deeply affected by his death, that she immediately followed him to the tomb. Philip set out on his return to France in the month of January, and the young queen, who had accompanied him, became another victim of the crusade. In crossing Calabria, whilst fording a river near Cosenza, her horse fell, and she being pregnant, this fall caused her death. Thus Philip pursued his journey, bearing with him the bodies of his father, his brother, and his wife. He learnt on his march that the count and countess of Poictiers, returning to Languedoc, had both died in Tuscany from the effects of the contagious malady of the coast of Africa. Passing by Viterbo, Philip witnessed the tragical end of one of the most illustrious of his companions in arms; Henry d'Allemagne was attacked by the sons of the earl of Leicester, pursued into a church, and massacred at the foot of the altar. Thus, great crimes were joined with great calamities, to add to the cruel remembrances that this crusade was destined to leave behind it.

Philip, after crossing Mount Cenis, returned to Paris through Burgundy and Champagne. What days of mourning for France! At the departure of Louis IX. for the East, the whole nation had been impressed by the most melancholy presentiments; and, alas! all these presentiments were but too fully realized!

It was not the flag of victory, but a funeral pall that preceded the French warriors in their march. Funereal urns, the wreck of an army but lately so flourishing, a young sick prince, who had only escaped by a miracle the death that had swept away his family—this was all that came back from the crusade! The people came from all parts to meet the melancholy train; they surrounded the young king, they strove to approach the remains of St. Louis, and it was made evident, by their pious propriety and their religious sadness, that the sentiments which led them there were not such as generally precipitate the multitude upon the steps of the masters of the earth.

On the arrival of Philip in his capital, the bones and the heart of St. Louis were conveyed to the church of Notre Dame, where ecclesiastics sang the hymns of the service of the dead during the whole night. On the following day the funeral of the royal martyr was celebrated in the church of St. Denis. In the midst of an immense assemblage of all classes of the people, deeply affected by what they saw, the young monarch advanced, bearing on his shoulders the mortal remains of his father. He stopped several times on his way, and crosses, which were placed at every station, recalled, up to the last century, this beautiful picture of filial piety.

Louis IX. was deposited near his grandfather Philip Augustus, and his father Louis VIII. Although he had forbidden his tomb to be ornamented, it was covered with plates of silver, which were afterwards carried away by the English. At a later period a more terrible revolution broke into his tomb and scattered his ashes; but this revolution has not been able to destroy his memory.

No, posterity will never cease to praise that passion for justice which filled the whole life of Louis IX., that ardour in search of truth, so rare even among the greatest kings; that love of peace, to which he sacrificed even the glory he had acquired in arms; that solicitude for the good of all; that tender consideration for poverty; that profound respect for the rights of misfortune and for the lives of men:—virtues which astonished the middle ages, and which our own times still perceive in the descendants of so good a prince.
[38]

The ascendancy which his virtue and piety gave him he only employed in defending his people against everything that was unjust. This ascendancy, which he preserved over his age, gave to his laws an empire, which laws, whatever they may be, rarely obtain but with time. A few years after his reign, provinces demanded to be united to the crown, under the sole hope and the sole condition of enjoying the *wise ordinances of the king, who loved justice*. Such were the conquests of St. Louis. It is well known, that after his victories over the English he restored Guienne to them, in spite of the advice of his barons, who considered this act of generosity to be contrary to the interests of the kingdom. Perhaps it only belongs to elevated minds like his to know how much wisdom there is in the counsels of moderation! An illustrious writer of the last age has said, when speaking of Louis IX., *that great moderate men are rare*, and it is doubtless on that account that the world does not understand them.

In the position in which France at that time was placed, a vulgar genius would have fomented divisions; whereas Louis only sought to appease them; and it was this spirit of conciliation which rendered him the arbitrator of kings and nations, and gave him more strength and power than could have been procured by the combinations of the wisest policy. Among the contemporaries of St. Louis persons were not wanting who blamed his moderation, and many who pride themselves upon being skilful politicians blame him even now. Strange skill, which tends to create a belief that morality is foreign to the happiness of nations, and which cannot afford to the leaders of empires the same virtues that God has bestowed upon man for the preservation of society!

The more we admire the reign of Louis IX. the greater is our astonishment at his having twice interrupted the course of its blessings, and quitted a people he rendered happy by his presence. But, whilst beholding the passions which agitate the present generation, who will dare to raise his voice for the purpose of accusing past ages! If at the moment in which I write this history all Europe is moved by the rumour of a general rising against the Mussulmans, now masters of Byzantium;—if the most ardent disciples of the modern school of philosophy are putting up vows for the triumph of the Gospel over the Koran, for the deliverance of the Greeks, and the resurrection of Athens and Lacedæmon, how can we believe that in the middle ages princes and Christian nations would not be affected by the horrible state of slavery of Jerusalem, and all those holy regions from which the light first broke upon Christendom? Consistently with the character which Louis IX. displayed in all the circumstances of his life, how could he remain indifferent to the calamities of the Christian colonies, which were principally peopled by Frenchmen, and which were considered as another France,—the France of the east? We must not forget, likewise, that the great aim of his policy was to unite the nations of the east and west by the ties of Christianity; and that this aim, if he had succeeded in it, would have been greatly to the advantage of humanity. Ambition itself has been sometimes pardoned for projects much more chimerical, and wars much more unfortunate. [39]

However it may be, we can venture to say that the captivity and death of St. Louis in distant regions did not at all lessen the respect in which his name and his virtues were held in Europe. Perhaps even such extraordinary misfortunes, suffered in the name of religion and of all that was then reverenced, added something to the splendour of the monarchy; for the times we have seen were then far distant in which the misfortunes of kings have only served to despoil royalty of that which makes it respected among men. The death of Louis IX. was a great subject of grief for the French; but with the regret which his loss created, there was mingled, for the whole people, the thoughts of the happy future which Louis had prepared, and for pious minds the hope of having a guardian and a support in heaven. Very shortly the death of a king of France was celebrated as a fresh triumph for religion,—as a fresh glory for his country; and the anniversary of the day on which he expired became thereafter one of the solemn festivals of the Christian Church and of the French monarchy.

A beautiful spectacle was that canonical inquiry in which the common father of the faithful interrogated the contemporaries of Louis IX. upon the virtues of his life and the benefits of his reign! Frenchmen of all classes came forward to attest, upon the Gospel, that the monarch whose death they lamented was worthy of all the rewards of heaven. Among them were many of his old companions in arms, who had shared his chains in Egypt, and beheld him dying on his bed of ashes before Tunis. The whole of Europe confirmed their religious testimony, and repeated these words of the head of the Church:—"*House of France, rejoice at having given to the world so great a prince; rejoice, people of France, at having had so good a king!*" [40]

The death of Louis IX., as we have already said, had suddenly suspended all enterprises beyond the seas. Edward only, accompanied by the count of Brittany, his brother Edmund, and three hundred knights, had gone into Syria at the head of a small army of five hundred Crusaders from Friesland. All these Crusaders together only formed a body of a thousand or twelve hundred combatants; and this was all that reached Asia of those numberless armies that had been raised in the West for the deliverance of the Holy Land. So feeble a reinforcement was not calculated to inspire confidence or restore security to the Christians of Palestine, not yet recovered from their consternation at hearing of the retreat of the Crusaders from before Tunis, and their return into Europe.

Most of the princes and Christian states of Syria, in the fear of being invaded, had concluded treaties with the sultan of Cairo; many must have hesitated at engaging in a war from which the slender succours from Europe could allow them no hopes of great advantages, and in which likewise they had to dread being abandoned by the Crusaders, ever eager to return to the West. Nevertheless, the Templars and the Hospitallers, who never missed an opportunity of fighting with the Saracens, united themselves with Prince Edward, whose fame had preceded him into the East. Bibars, who was then ravaging the territories of Ptolemaïs, drew his forces off from a city which he had filled with alarm, and appeared for a moment to have abandoned the execution of his projects.

The little army of the Christians, composed of from six to seven thousand men, advanced upon the Mussulman territories, directing its course towards Phœnicia, in order to re-establish the communication that had been interrupted between the Christian cities. In this expedition the Crusaders had much to suffer from excessive heat; many died from indulging in fruits and honey, which the country produced in abundance. They marched afterwards towards the city of Nazareth, upon the walls of which they planted the standard of Christ. The soldiers of the cross could not remember without indignation that Bibars had completely destroyed the church of this city, consecrated to the Virgin. Nazareth was given up to pillage, and all the Mussulmans found in the city expiated by being put to the sword, the burning and destruction of one of the most beautiful monuments raised by the Christians in Syria.

After this victory, for which we cannot praise the Crusaders, the Christian army had to combat the Mussulman troops, who were impatient to avenge the excesses committed at Nazareth. Whether he had learnt to respect the superiority of his enemies, or whether he had cause to complain of the warriors of Palestine, Edward returned within the walls of Ptolemaïs, and sought for no more contests. The frequent excursions of the Saracens could not provoke him to take up arms; but whilst he remained thus safe from the perils of war, he was on the point of perishing by the hand of a Mussulman whom he had taken into his service. Some of the chronicles of the time tell us that the emir of Jaffa armed the hand of the assassin; others say that the blow was directed by the sect of the Ismaëlians, who still subsisted, notwithstanding the war declared against them by both the Tartars and the Mamelukes.

After having thus run the danger of losing his life, Edward, cured of his wounds, only thought of concluding a truce with Bibars; and being recalled into England by the prayers of Henry III., whose successor he was, he quitted the East without having done anything important for the cause he had sworn to defend. Thus all the results of this crusade, which had so much alarmed the Mussulmans, were reduced, on one side, to the massacre of the unarmed population of Nazareth, and on the other, to the vain conquest of the ruins of Carthage. Another result of this war, and the only one it had for Europe, was to entirely discourage the Christian warriors, and make them forget the East. After Edward, no prince from the West ever crossed the seas to combat with the infidels in Asia, and the crusade in which he took a part so little glorious, was the last of those which had for object the deliverance or recovery of the Holy Land.

Among the circumstances that produced the failure of this crusade, history must not forget the protracted vacancy of the papal throne, during which no voice was raised to animate the Crusaders, in which there was no authority powerful enough, particularly after the death of St. Louis, to direct their enterprise. After a lapse of two years, however, the conclave chose a successor of St. Peter; and, fortunately for the eastern Christians, the suffrages fell upon Thibault, archdeacon of Liege, who had followed the Frisons into Asia, and whom the intelligence of his elevation found still in Palestine. The Christians of Syria had reason to hope that the new pontiff, for so long a time a witness of their perils and their miseries, would not fail to employ all his power to succour them. Thibault gave them an assurance of it before he quitted Ptolemaïs, and in a discourse which he addressed to the assembled people, he took for his text this verse of the hundred and thirty-seventh Psalm: "If I forget thee, O Jerusalem, may I myself be forgotten among men!"

The patriarch of Jerusalem, and the grand masters of the Temple and the Hospital accompanied Gregory X. into the West. On his return, the pontiff applied himself at once to the re-establishment of peace in Italy and Germany. He engaged the princes, particularly the king of France, to unite their efforts in assisting the Holy Land. Philip contented himself with sending a few troops into the East, and with advancing thirty-six thousand silver marks to the Pope, for which sum he held as security all the possessions of the Templars in his kingdom. Pisa, Genoa, and Marseilles furnished several galleys, and five hundred warriors were embarked for Ptolemaïs, at the expense of the sovereign pontiff.

This assistance was far from answering the hopes or the wants of the Christian colonies. Gregory resolved to interest all Christendom in his project, and for that purpose convoked a council at Lyons, in 1274. This council was much more numerous and more solemn than that which Innocent IV. had assembled thirty years before in the same city. At this were present the patriarchs of Jerusalem and Constantinople, more than a thousand bishops and archbishops, the envoys of the emperors of the East and of the West, those of the kings of France and Cyprus, and of all the princes of Europe and beyond the seas. In this numerous assembly, no persons attracted so much attention as the Tartar princes and ambassadors, sent by the powerful head of the Moguls, to form an alliance with the Christians against the Mussulmans; several of these Tartar princes received baptism from the hands of the Pope, and Christians who were witnesses of this ceremony saw in it an assured pledge of the Divine promises.

All admired the power of God who had chosen the instruments of his designs from remote and little known regions; the crowd of the faithful looked upon the supreme head of the hordes of Tartary as another Cyrus, whom Providence had charged with the destruction of Babylon and the deliverance of Jerusalem. At the last sitting, the Council of Lyons decreed that a new crusade should be undertaken, and that during ten years a tenth should be levied upon all ecclesiastical property. Palæologus, who at length submitted to the Latin church, promised to send troops for the deliverance of the heritage of Christ; the Pope recognized Rodolph of Hapsbourg as emperor of the West, upon condition that he would go into Palestine at the head of an army.

But notwithstanding the grand spectacle of such a council, the decisions and the exhortations of the Pope and the prelates could not arouse the enthusiasm of the faithful, which was no longer anything, to borrow an expression from Scripture, "but the smoking remains of a burnt cloth." Gregory X. had succeeded in re-establishing peace among the Italian republics, and in terminating all the discords of Germany relative to the succession to the empire: no war interfered with the crusade; but the minds of both princes and nations had taken a fresh direction. We still possess a written document of this period, which, doubtless, obtained the approbation if not the encouragement of the pope, and which appears to us well calculated to throw a light upon the spirit of the age, and show us what was then the general opinion of expeditions to the East. In this document, which will be considered whimsical, at least in its form, the author, Humbert de Romanis, endeavours to revive the zeal of Christians for the holy war, and, while deploring the indifference of his contemporaries, he points out eight obstacles to the effects of his preaching: 1st. *A sinful habit*; 2nd. *The dread of fatigue*; 3rd. *Repugnance to quit their native country*; 4th. *An excessive love of family*; 5th. *The evil discourses of men*; 6th. *A weakness of mind that creates a belief that every thing is impossible;* 7th. *Bad examples;* 8th. *A faith without warmth.* To all these motives for indifference the author might have added other reasons drawn from the policy and the new interests of Europe; but without allowing himself to be stopped by so many obstacles, the intrepid defender of the crusades, proceeding always by enumerations and categories, hastens to denote seven powerful passions, which, according to him, ought to cause the partisans of the holy to triumph; these reasons were: 1st. *Zeal for the glory of God;* 2nd. *Zeal for the Christian faith;* 3rd. *Brotherly charity;* 4th. *Devotional respect for the Holy Land;* 5th. *The war commenced by the Mussulmans;* 6th. *The example of the first Crusaders;* 7th. *The blessings of the Church.* After these enumerations, Humbert de Romanis repeats the objections that were made in his time against undertaking crusades. Some said that wars, of whatever kind they might be, only served to promote the shedding of blood, and that there were quite enough of those that could not be avoided, and of those that people were obliged to make in self-defence; others said that it was tempting God to quit a land in which his will had caused us to be born, and in which his goodness heaped blessings upon us, to go into a country which God had given to other nations, and in which we were constantly abandoned by him to all the miseries of exile. It was further said, that it was not permissible to invade the territories of the Saracens, that there was no more reason for pursuing the Mussulmans than the Jews, that the wars made against them would never effect their conversion, and in short, that this war did not appear to be agreeable to God, since he permitted so many misfortunes to overwhelm the Crusaders.

Humbert de Romanis, in his book, answers all these and many other objections; but these objections themselves were founded upon the spirit of the age, which could not be changed by reasoning. He in vain repeated that the Holy Land originally belonged to the Christians, and that they had the right to endeavour to reconquer it; that the vine of the Lord ought to be defended by the sword against those who wished to root it up; that if they extirpated the brambles from a barren soil, they were much more strongly bound to drive from a holy land a rude and barbarous nation. He in vain repeated what had been so often said before, that the misfortunes of the crusades did not happen because those crusades were displeasing to God, but because it was God's will to punish the Crusaders, and try their constancy and faith. All this display of ecclesiastical erudition and argumentation persuaded nobody; not because people were more enlightened than they had been some years before, but because they entertained other thoughts: similar discourses would have succeeded admirably in the preceding century, when addressed to dominant passions; but they produced no effect when addressed to indifference.

This European indifference was fatal to the Christian colonies of the East; it gave them up without defence to the mercy of an enemy who every day became more powerful, and whose fanaticism was inflamed by victory. On the other hand, fresh symptoms of decay, and new signs of approaching ruin, were observable in the confederation of the Franks of Syria. All those petty principalities, all those cities scattered along the Syrian coasts were shared among them; and all the passions which the spirit of rivalry gives birth to became the auxiliaries of the Saracens. Every one of these petty states, in a constant state of fear, eagerly purchased a few days of peace, or a few months of existence, by treaties with Bibars, treaties in which the common honour and interests of the Christians were almost always sacrificed. The sultan of Cairo did not disdain to conclude a treaty of alliance with a single city, or even with a town; and nothing is more curious than to see figuring in these acts of policy, on the one side the sovereign of Egypt, Syria, Mesopotamia, and twenty other provinces; and on the other a little city like Sidon [41] or Tortosa, with its fields, its orchards, and its mills: a deplorable contrast, which must have made the Christians feel the extent of their humiliation, and proved to them all they had to fear. In all these treaties it was the Mussulman policy to promote division among the Franks, and to hold them in a state of dependence, [42] never considering them as allies, but as vassals, farmers or tributaries.

Such was the peace enjoyed by the Christian states in Syria; and a further matter to be deplored was, that there were then three pretenders to the kingdom of Jerusalem:—the king of Cyprus, the king of Sicily, and Mary of Antioch, who was descended from the fourth daughter of Isabella, the wife of Amaury. Parties disputed, and even fought for a kingdom half destroyed; or rather they contended for the disgrace of ruining it entirely, and giving it up, rent by discord, to the domination of the Saracens.

Bibars, in the meanwhile, steadily pursued the course of his conquests; every day fame spread abroad an account of some fresh triumph; at one time he re-entered Cairo, dragging in his train a king of Nubia, whom he had just conquered; at another, he returned from Armenia, whence he brought thirty thousand horses and ten thousand children of both sexes. These accounts spread terror among the Christian cities, a terror that was very little mitigated by their treaties with the sultan of Egypt; no one could tell what might be the next conquest Bibars contemplated, and every city was trembling lest it should be the next object of his ambition or his fury, when the death of this fierce conqueror afforded the Christians a few moments of security and joy.

The end of Bibars is related after various manners; we will follow the account of the historian Ibn-Ferat, with whose expressions even we shall sometimes make free. Bibars was about to set out for Damascus, to fight the Tartars in the neighbourhood of the Euphrates; but before his departure he demanded an extraordinary impost. The imaun Mohyeddin Almoury addressed remonstrances to him on the subject; but the sultan replied: "Oh! my master, I will abolish this tax when I shall have conquered our enemies." When Bibars had triumphed over the Tartars, he wrote in the following terms to the chief of the divan at Damascus: "We will not dismount from our horse until thou hast levied an impost of two hundred thousand dirhems upon Damascus, one of three hundred thousand upon its territories, one of three hundred thousand upon its towns, and one of ten hundred thousand dirhems upon the southern provinces." Thus the joy created by the victory of Bibars was changed into sadness, and the people prayed for the death of the sultan. Complaints were carried to the cheick Mohyeddin, a pious and respected man; [43] and scarcely was the levy of the tribute begun when Bibars was razed from the roll of the living—he died poisoned.

The Arabian historians place Bibars among the great princes of the dynasty of the Baharite Mamelukes. He was originally sold as a slave, and although he only lived among soldiers, a penetrating sagacity of mind supplied the place of education. When afterwards, he had become familiar with war, and had been cast among the factions of the army, he had acquired all the knowledge that was necessary to enable him to reign over the Mamelukes. The quality which was of most service to him in the career of his ambition was his incredible activity; during the seventeen years of his reign, he did not allow himself one day of repose; he was present, almost at the same time, in Syria, in Egypt, and upon the banks of the Euphrates: the chronicles relate that he was frequently perambulating the streets of Damascus, whilst his courtiers were awaiting the moment of his waking at the gates of the palace of Cairo. As two sultans of Egypt had perished beneath his hands, and as he had arrived at empire by means of violent revolutions, that which he most dreaded was the influence of his own example; all those whose ambition he feared, or whose fidelity he doubted, were immediately sacrificed. The most simple communications between man and man were sufficient to alarm his fierce and suspicious temper; if oriental historians may be credited, during the reign of Bibars, friends shunned each other in the streets, and no man durst enter into the house of another. When it was important to him to conceal his designs, to cast a veil over his proceedings, or himself to avoid the public eye, woe to him who should divine his thought, pronounce his name, or salute him on his way. Severe with his soldiers, a flatterer with his emirs, entertaining no repugnance for artifice, preferring violence, sporting with treaties and oaths, practising a dissimulation that nobody could penetrate, possessed by an avarice that made him pitiless in the levying of tributes; having never retreated before an enemy, before an obstacle, or before a crime, his genius and character seemed made for the government, which he had in some sort founded, a monstrous government, which sustained itself by vices and excesses, and which could not possibly have subsisted in conjunction with moderation and virtue.

His enemies and his subjects trembled equally before him; they trembled still around that litter which transported his remains from Damascus to Cairo. But so many excesses, so many violences, so many triumphs, which only ministered to his personal ambition, were not able to fix the crown in his family; his two sons only ascended the throne to descend from it again. Kelaoun, the bravest of the emirs, soon usurped the sovereign power; a uniform line of succession to the throne was not at all likely to be preserved in an army constantly exposed to sedition. Every Mameluke believed himself born for empire, and in this republic of slaves it appeared permissible for every one to dream of tyranny. A thing almost incredible,— that which appeared most calculated to ruin this band of turbulent soldiery, was precisely that which saved it; weakness or incapacity could never support itself long upon the throne, and amidst the tumult of factions, it almost always happened that the most brave and the most able was chosen to direct the government, and lead in war.

Bibars had commenced the ruin of the Christians; Kelaoun was destined to complete it. In the West, Gregory in vain prosecuted the preparations, or rather the preachings of the crusade; he several times renewed his intreaties to Rodolph of Hapsburg, but Rodolph had an empire to preserve; it was useless for the pope to threaten to deprive him of his crown; the new emperor saw much less danger for him in the anger of the sovereign pontiff than in an expedition which would lead him so far from his states. At length Gregory died, without having been able to fulfil the promises he had made to the Christians of the East. Palestine received, from time to time, some succours from Europe; but these succours, scarcely ever arriving seasonably, appeared less likely to increase than to compromise its safety. The king of Sicily, who had caused himself to be proclaimed king of Jerusalem, sent some soldiers and a governor to Ptolemaïs; he was preparing to make a formidable expedition into Syria, [44] and his ambition, perhaps, might, in this circumstance, have been serviceable to the cause of the Christians, if a revolution had not suddenly put an end to his projects.

The discontent of the people in his states, particularly in Sicily, continually increased. The people had been burdened with a heavy tax for the last crusade, and the publication of a new one was received with many murmurs; the enemies of Charles saw nothing in the assumption of the cross but a signal for violence and brigandage; it is under this sacred banner, they said, that he is accustomed to shed innocent blood: they further remembered that the conquest of Naples had been made under the standard of the cross. At length the signal of revolt being given, eight thousand Frenchmen were immolated to the manes of Conradin, and the Sicilian vespers completed the destruction of all Charles's Eastern projects.

Kelaoun from that time had it in his power to attack the Christians; but busied in establishing his authority among the Mamelukes, and in repulsing the Tartars, who had advanced towards the Euphrates, he consented to conclude a truce with the Franks of Ptolemaïs. It may plainly be perceived by this treaty, which the Arabian authors have preserved, what were the designs of the sultans of Cairo, and the extent of the ascendancy they assumed over their feeble enemies. [45] The Christians engaged, in the event of any prince of the Franks making an expedition into Asia, to warn the infidels of the coming of Christian armies from the West. This was at the same time signing a dishonourable condition, and renouncing all hopes of a crusade.

The armies of the West, besides, were fighting for other interests than those of the Holy Land, and there was no reason to believe they would be seen in Asia for a length of time. Most of the princes of Europe at that time never bestowed a thought upon the Mussulmans or their victories; such princes or states as had any interests to guard in the East, [46] not only allied themselves without scruple with the sultan of Egypt, but promised by treaties, and swore upon the Gospel, to declare themselves the enemies of all the Christian powers that should attack the states of their Mussulman ally.

Thus all these treaties, dictated sometimes by ambition and avarice, and sometimes by fear, raised every day a new barrier between the Christians of the East and those of the West. Besides, these treaties were no checks upon the sultan of Cairo, who always found some pretext for breaking them, when war presented more advantages than peace. It was thus with the fortress of Margat, situated upon the river Eleuctera, in the neighbourhood of Tripoli. The Hospitallers who guarded this castle were accused of making incursions upon the lands of the Mussulmans; and this accusation, which was not perhaps without foundation, was soon followed by the siege of the place. The towers and ramparts for a long time resisted the shock of the machines of war; the garrison repulsed every attack; but whilst they were fighting upon the walls, and at the foot of the walls, miners were digging away the earth from beneath them. At length the fortress, undermined on all sides, was ready to fall to pieces at the first signal. The Hospitallers made an honourable capitulation, and Margat opened its gates to the Mussulman army.

Upon the seacoast, between Margat and Tortosa, stood another castle, to which a Frank nobleman had retired, whom some of the Arabian chroniclers call the sieur de Telima, and others, the sieur Barthélemi. This Frank lord never ceased ravaging the lands of his neighbourhood, and every day returned home to his fortress loaded with the spoils of the Saracens. Kelaoun was desirous of attacking the castle of the sieur Barthélemi, but thinking it impregnable, he wrote to the count of Tripoli,—"It is thou who hast built, or hast allowed to be built, this castle; evil be to thee, evil be to thy capital, evil be to thy people, if it be not promptly demolished." [47] The count of Tripoli was the more alarmed at these menaces, from the Mussulman troops being, at the moment he received the letter, in his territories: he offered the seigneur Barthélemi considerable lands in exchange for his castle; he made him the most brilliant promises and offers, but all in vain. At length the son of Barthélemi interfered in the negotiation, and set out to implore the compassion of the sultan of Cairo. The enraged old man flew after his son, overtook him in the city of Ptolemaïs, and poniarded him before the assembled people. This parricide disgusted all the Christians; and Barthélemi was at last abandoned by his own soldiers, who held his crime in great horror. The castle, which was left unprotected, was shortly after demolished. From that time the sieur Barthélemi became the most inveterate enemy of the Christians; and, retired among the infidels, was constantly employed in associating them with his vengeance, and in urging the destruction of the Christian cities.

His pitiless hatred had but too many opportunities of being satisfied. The sultan of Cairo pursued the war against the Christians, and everything seemed to favour his enterprizes. He had for a long time entertained the project of gaining possession of Laodicea, whose port rivalled that of Alexandria; but the citadel of that city, surrounded by the waters of the sea, was inaccessible; an earthquake, which shook the towers of the fortress, facilitated his conquest of it. The castle of Carac and some other forts, built on the coast of Phœnicia, fell into the hands of the Mussulmans. After having thus laid open all the avenues to Tripoli, the sultan turned the whole of his attention to the siege of that city. Neither the faith of treaties, nor the recent submissions of Bohemond, were able to retard for a moment the fall of a flourishing city: no Christian city, no prince of Palestine offered the least assistance to Tripoli. Such indeed was the spirit of division that always reigned among the Franks, that the Templars, in conjunction with the seigneur de Giblet, had entertained the project of introducing some Christian soldiers into Bohemond's city, and taking it by surprise. They were not able, it is true, to execute their design; but what evils must not these odious jealousies, these black treacheries, have brought upon the feeble remains of the Christian colonies!

A formidable army appeared before the walls of Tripoli, and a great number of machines were erected against the ramparts: after a siege of thirty-five days, the Mussulmans penetrated into the city, fire and sword in hand. Seven thousand Christians fell under the arms of the conqueror; the women and children were dragged away into slavery, and the terrified crowd vainly sought an asylum from the blood-thirsty Mamelukes in the island of St. Nicholas. Aboulfeda relates, that having occasion to go to that island, a few days after the taking of Tripoli, he found it covered with dead bodies. Some of the inhabitants having succeeded in getting on board ships, fled away from their desolate country; but the sea drove them back again upon the shore, where they were massacred by the Mussulmans. Not only the population of Tripoli was almost exterminated, but the sultan gave orders that the city should be burnt and demolished. The port of Tripoli attracted a great part of the commerce of the Mediterranean; the city contained more than four thousand silk-looms; its palaces were admired, its towers and its fortifications appeared impregnable. So many sources of prosperity, all that could cause peace to nourish or serve for defence in war, all perished under the flame, the axe, and the hammer! The principal aim of the Mussulman policy in this war, was to destroy all that the Christians had done; to leave no traces of their power upon the coasts of Syria; nothing which could afterwards attract thither the princes and warriors of the West, nothing that could yield them the means of maintaining themselves there if ever they should be tempted again to unfurl their standards in the East.

Ptolemaïs, which remained neuter in this cruel war, learnt the fall and destruction of a Christian city from some fugitives, who, having escaped the sword of the Mussulmans, came to intreat an asylum within its walls. From this sad intelligence, it might easily predict the misfortunes that awaited it. Ptolemaïs was then the capital of the Christian colonies, and the most considerable city of Syria. Most of the Franks, upon being driven from the other cities of Palestine, had taken refuge there, bringing with them all their portable wealth. In its port anchored all the warlike fleets that came from the West, with the richest trading vessels from most countries of the world. The city had not less increased in extent than population; it was constructed of square-cut stones; all the walls of the houses rose to an equal height, and a platform or terrace surmounted most of the buildings. [48] The interior of the principal houses was ornamented with paintings, and they received light by the means of glass windows, which was at that time an extraordinary luxury. In the public places, coverings of silk or transparent stuffs screened the inhabitants from the ardours of the sun. Between the two ramparts which bounded the city on the east, were built castles and palaces, the residences of the great; the artizans and traders occupied the interior of the city. Among the princes and nobles who had mansions in Ptolemaïs, were the king of Jerusalem, his brothers and his family, the princes of Galilee and Antioch, the lieutenants of France and Sicily, the duke of Cæsarea, the counts of Tripoli and Jaffa, the lords of Barouth, Tyre, Tiberias, Ibelin, Arsaph, &c. We read in an old chronicle that all these magnates were accustomed to walk in the public places, wearing crowns of gold like kings, whilst the vestments of their numerous trains glittered with gold and precious stones. Every day was passed in festivity, spectacles or tournaments; whilst the port was a mart of exchange for the treasures of the East and the West, exhibiting at all times an animated picture of commerce and industry.

Contemporary history deplores with severity the corruption of morals that prevailed in Ptolemaïs, the crowds of strangers bringing with them the vices of all countries. Effeminacy and luxury pervaded every class, the clergy themselves being unable to escape the general contagion: the inhabitants of Ptolemaïs were esteemed the most voluptuous and dissolute of all the nations of Syria. Ptolemaïs was not only the richest city of Syria, it was further supposed to be the best fortified. St. Louis, during his abode in Palestine, had neglected nothing to repair and increase its fortifications. On the land side, a double wall surrounded the city, commanded at distances by lofty battlemented towers; and a wide and deep ditch prevented access to the ramparts. Towards the sea, the city was defended by a fortress built at the entrance of the port, by the castle of the temple on the south, and by the tower called the King's Tower, on the east.

Ptolemaïs appears then to have possessed much better means of defence than at the period at which it stood out for three years against all the forces of Europe. No power could have subdued it if it had been inhabited by true citizens, and not by foreigners, pilgrims, and traders, at all times ready to transport themselves and their wealth from one place to another. The persons who represented the king of Naples, the lieutenants of the king of Cyprus, the French, the English, the pope's legate, the patriarch of Jerusalem, the prince of Antioch, the three military orders, the Venetians, the Genoese, the Pisans, the Armenians, the Tartars, had all and each their separate quarter, their jurisdiction, their tribunals, their magistrates—all independent of each other, and all enjoying the right of sovereignty. All these quarters were as so many different cities, opposed to each other by customs, by language, by manners, and above all, by rivalries and jealousies. It was impossible to preserve order in a city in which so many sovereigns made laws, which had no uniform government, and in which the crime pursued in one part, was protected in another. Thus all the passions were without a check, and often gave birth to sanguinary and disgraceful scenes: in addition to the quarrels that took their rise in the country, there was not a feud in Europe, particularly in Italy, that was not felt in Ptolemaïs. The discords of the Guelphs and the Ghibelines were here carried on with warmth, and the rivalries of Venice and Genoa had caused torrents of blood to flow. Each nation had fortifications in the quarter it inhabited, against the others; and the churches even were fortified. At the entrance to each division was a fortress, with gates and iron chains; it was plainly to be perceived that all these means of defence had been employed less for the purpose of stopping the progress of an enemy, than as a barrier against neighbours and rivals.

The leaders of all the quarters and the principal inhabitants of the city sometimes assembled; but they seldom, agreed, and were at all times mistrustful of each other: these assemblies never laid down any settled plan of conduct, never established any wholesome fixed rule, and, above all, never showed the least foresight.

The city at the same time demanded succours from the West, and solicited a truce with the Saracens. When a treaty was concluded, no one had sufficient power to secure its observance; on the contrary, every one had it in his power to violate it, and thus bring upon the city all the ills that this violation would produce.

After the taking of Tripoli, the sultan of Cairo menaced the city of Ptolemaïs; nevertheless, whether he dreaded the despair of the inhabitants, or thought that the favourable moment was not yet arrived, he yielded to their solicitations, and renewed a truce with them for two years, two months, two weeks, two days, and two hours. According to a chronicle, the pope's legate disapproved of the treaty, and caused some Mussulman traders, who came to Ptolemaïs, to be insulted: the Templars and the other military orders were desirous of making reparation to the sultan of Egypt; but the legate opposed them, and threatened to excommunicate all who should have the least intercourse with the infidels. [49]

An Arabian author assigns another motive for the violences committed against the Mussulmans. He relates that the wife of a rich inhabitant of Ptolemaïs, being deeply enamoured of a young Mussulman, had appointed a meeting with him in one of the gardens that surround the city; the husband, warned of this outrage against conjugal fidelity, gathers together some friends, goes out from Ptolemaïs with them, [50] surprises his wife and her seducer, and immolates them both to his injured honour. Some Mussulmans are drawn to the spot; the Christians come up in still greater numbers; the quarrel becomes angry and general; and every Mussulman is massacred.

These violences, which fame did not fail to exaggerate whilst narrating them, might give the sultan of Egypt a pretext for renewing the war; and the Christians, who plainly perceived their new perils, implored the assistance of the sovereign pontiff. The pope engaged Venice to furnish twenty-five galleys, and this fleet transported to Ptolemaïs a troop of sixteen hundred men, levied in haste in Italy. This reinforcement, which was sent to the inhabitants of Palestine for their defence, provoked their ruin; the soldiers of the Holy See, levied among adventurers and vagabonds, gave themselves up to all sorts of excesses. Having no regular pay, they plundered Christians and Mussulmans indiscriminately; at last, this undisciplined troop marched out of the city in arms, and made an incursion upon the lands of the Saracens. Everything was laid waste on their passage; towns and villages were pillaged, the inhabitants insulted, and many of them massacred. The sultan of Cairo sent ambassadors to the Christians to complain of these outrages, committed in a time of peace. On the arrival of the Mussulman envoys several councils were held in Ptolemaïs. Opinions were at first divided; some were willing to take the part of those who had broken the truce; others thought it more just and prudent to give satisfaction to the sultan, and solicit the continuation of the treaty. In the end, it was determined to send a deputation to Cairo, commissioned to make excuses and offer presents. Upon being admitted to an audience of Kelaoun, the deputation alleged that the offences had been committed by some soldiers who had come from the West, and in no case by the inhabitants of Ptolemaïs. The deputies, in the name of their city, offered to punish the authors of the disorders; but their submission and prayers produced no effect upon the sultan, who reproached them severely with making a jest of the faith of treaties, and with giving an asylum to disturbers of peace and foes to the laws of nations. He was the more inflexible, from thinking the opportunity a favourable one for carrying out his projects; he was aware that no crusade was in preparation in Europe, and he knew that all the succour from the West was reduced to this band of adventurers who had just broken the truce. Kelaoun sent back the ambassadors, threatening the city of Ptolemaïs with the whole weight of his anger: his orders were already given for preparations for war throughout all his provinces.

Immediately after the return of the ambassadors [51] a grand council was called, at which were present the patriarch of Jerusalem, John de Gresli, who commanded for the king of France, Messire Oste de Granson for the king of England, the grand masters of the Temple and the Hospital, the principal persons of the city, and a great number of citizens and pilgrims. When the deputies had rendered an account of their mission, and repeated the threats of the sultan, the patriarch addressed the assembly; his virtues, his gray hairs, his zeal for the cause of the Christians, all inspired confidence and respect. This venerable prelate exhorted all who heard him to arm themselves for the defence of the city, to remember that they were Christians, and that it was their duty to die for the cause of Christ; he conjured them to forget their discords, to have no other enemies but the Mussulmans, and to show themselves worthy of the holy cause for which they were about to fight. His eloquence awakened the generous feelings of his audience, and all swore to obey the exhortations of the patriarch: happy would it have been for the city of Ptolemaïs if its inhabitants and its defenders had preserved the same dispositions and the same enthusiasm amidst the perils and mischances of war!

They asked for succour in all quarters; a few pilgrims arrived from the West, and a few warriors from the isles of the Mediterranean: the king of Cyprus landed with five hundred men. These new auxiliaries and all who were able to bear arms in the city, amounted to nine hundred horsemen and ten thousand foot soldiers. They were divided into four bodies, charged with the defence of the towers and the ramparts. The first of these divisions was under the command of Oste de Granson and John de Gresli, the one with the English and the Picards, the other with the French; the second division was commanded by the king of Cyprus, in conjunction with the grand master of the Teutonic order; the third by the grand master of St. John, and the grand master of the knights of Canterbury; the fourth by the grand masters of the Temple and of St. Lazarus: a council of eight leaders was to govern the city during the siege.

The Mussulmans were preparing for the war in all quarters; everything was in motion from the banks of the Nile to those of the Euphrates. The sultan Kelaoun having fallen sick on leaving Cairo, sent before him seven principal emirs, each having four thousand horse and twenty thousand foot under his command. On their arrival upon the territories of Ptolemaïs, gardens, country-houses, the vines which covered the hills—everything was destroyed. The sight of the conflagration which arose on all sides, the distracted crowd of the inhabitants of the neighbourhood, who fled from their homes, with their goods, their flocks, and their families, warned Ptolemaïs of the execution of the threats and the sinister projects of the Saracens: there were several battles fought on the plain, but nothing remarkable or decisive; the Mussulmans waited the arrival of the sultan to commence the labours of the siege.

In the meanwhile, Kelaoun was still detained in Egypt by sickness, and feeling his end approach, the sultan sent for his son and his principal emirs; he recommended to the latter, to serve his son as they had served himself; and to the former, to follow up the war against the Christians without any intermission, conjuring him not to grant his remains the honour of sepulture before he had conquered the city of Ptolemaïs. Chalil swore to accomplish the last wishes of his father; and when Kelaoun had closed his eyes, the ulemas and the imauns assembled in the chapel in which his remains were deposited, and read during the whole night verses from the Koran, never ceasing to invoke their prophet against the disciples of Christ. Chalil did not delay setting forward on his march with his army. The Franks hoped that the death of Kelaoun would give birth to some disorders among the Mamelukes; but hatred for the Christians was a sufficient bond of union for the Mussulman soldiers; the siege even of Ptolemaïs, the hope of annihilating a Christian city, stifled all the germs of discord, and consolidated the power of Chalil, whom they proclaimed beforehand the conqueror of the Franks, and the *pacificator of the Mussulman religion*.

The sultan arrived before Ptolemaïs; his army covering a space of several leagues, from the sea to the mountains. More than three hundred machines of war were ready to batter the ramparts of the city. Aboulfeda, who was present at this siege, speaks of one of these machines which a hundred chariots were scarcely sufficient to transport.

This formidable preparation spread consternation among the inhabitants of Ptolemaïs. The grand master of the templars, despairing of the defence or of the salvation of the city, assembled the leaders to consult if there were any means of renewing the truce, and thus escaping inevitable ruin. [52] Repairing to the tent of the sultan, he demanded peace of him; and seeking to produce an effect upon his mind, he exaggerated the strength of Ptolemaïs; the sultan, dreading doubtless the difficulties of the siege, and hoping to find another opportunity of making himself master of the city, consented to a truce upon condition that every inhabitant should pay him a Venetian denier. The grand master on his return convoked an assembly of the people in the church of the Holy Cross, and laid before them the conditions the sultan placed upon the conclusion of a fresh truce. His advice was, that they should comply with these conditions, provided there were no other means of saving Ptolemaïs. Scarcely had he expressed his opinion, when the multitude rushed in in fury, uttering loud cries of *treachery*! and very nearly did the grand master expiate on the spot his foresight and zeal for the salvation of the city. From that time the only thought of this generous warrior was to die arms in hand for an ungrateful and frivolous people, incapable of repelling war by war, and not enduring to be saved by peace.

The presence of the sultan had redoubled the ardour of the Mussulman troops. From the day of his arrival the siege was prosecuted with incredible vigour. The army of the besiegers amounted to sixty thousand horse and a hundred and forty thousand foot, who constantly relieved each other, and left the besieged not a moment of repose. The machines hurled stones and enormous pieces of wood, the fall of which shook the palaces and houses of the city to their foundation. A shower of arrows, darts, fire-pots, and leaden balls was poured night and day upon the ramparts and towers. In the first assaults, the Christians killed a great number of the infidels who approached the walls with arrows and stones; they made many sorties, in one of which they penetrated to the tents of the Saracens. Being at length repulsed, some of them fell into the hands of the Mussulmans, and the Syrian horsemen, who had fastened the heads of the vanquished to the necks of their horses, went to display before the sultan of Cairo the barbarous trophies of a dearly-bought victory.

Danger at first united all the inhabitants of Ptolemaïs, and animated them with the same sentiments. In the early combats nothing could equal their ardour; they were sustained by the expectation of receiving succours from the West, and they hoped, also, that some advantages gained over the Saracens would force the besiegers to retreat; but in proportion as these hopes vanished, their zeal diminished; most of them were incapable of supporting lengthened fatigue; the sight of a peril which unceasingly returned exhausted their courage; the defenders of the ramparts perceived that their numbers were lessened daily; the port was covered with Christians departing from the city, and bearing their treasures with them. The example of those who thus fled completed the discouragement of those who remained; and in a city which numbered a hundred thousand inhabitants, and which, at the commencement of the siege, had furnished nearly twenty thousand warriors, only twelve thousand could at length be mustered under arms.

To desertion, another evil was soon added, which was dissension among the leaders; several of them disapproved of the measures that were adopted for the defence of the city, and because their opinions did not prevail in the council, they remained inactive, forgetful of the perils and evils which threatened both the city and themselves.

On the fourth day of May, after the siege had lasted nearly a month, the sultan of Cairo gave the signal for an assault. From daybreak, all the drums of the army, placed upon three hundred camels, spread a fearful and stunning noise. The most formidable of the machines of war were employed in battering the ramparts towards the gate and tower of St. Antony, on the east side of the city. This post was guarded by the soldiers of the king of Cyprus; the Mussulmans planted their ladders at the foot of the walls; the defence was not less spirited than the attack; the conflict lasted during the whole day, and night alone forced the Saracens to retreat. After this severe struggle, the king of Cyprus became more anxious for safety than glory, and determined to abandon a city which he had now no hopes of saving.

He retired with his troop in the evening, under the pretence of taking some necessary repose, and, confiding the post of peril to the Teutonic knights, promised to return with daylight; but when the sun arose, the king of Cyprus had embarked with all his knights and three thousand soldiers. What were the surprise and indignation of the Christian warriors at the news of this dastardly desertion! "Would to heaven," says the author of an account that lies before us, [53] —"would to heaven that a whirlwind had arisen, had submerged these base fugitives, and that they had sunk like lead to the bottom of the sea!"

On the morrow, the Mussulmans gave a fresh assault; covered by their long bucklers, they advanced in good order towards their machines, carrying a vast number of ladders. The Christians defended the approach to the walls for some time; but when the besiegers perceived that the towers, occupied on the preceding day by the Cypriots, were abandoned, their audacity increased, and they made incredible efforts to fill up the ditch, by casting into it stones, earth, and the carcases of their dead horses. Contemporary historians relate a circumstance of this part of the siege to which it is very difficult to give credit: a troop of sectaries, who were called Chages, followed the army of the Mamelukes; the devotion of these sectaries consisted in suffering all sorts of privations, and even in immolating themselves for the sake of Islamism: the sultan ordered them to fill up the ditch; they filled it up with their living bodies, and the Mussulman cavalry marched over them, to gain the foot of the walls! [54]

The besiegers fought with fury; some planted their ladders and mounted in crowds to the ramparts; whilst others continued to batter the walls with the rams, and brought every available instrument into play to demolish them. At length a large breach opened a passage into the city, and this breach soon became the scene of a bloody and obstinate contest. Stones and arrows were abandoned, they now fought man to man, with lance, sword, and mace. The multitude of Saracens increased every instant, whilst no fresh succours were received by the Christians. After a long and brave resistance, the defenders of the rampart, worn out with fatigue and overwhelmed by numbers, were obliged to retreat into the city; the Saracens rushed forward in pursuit of them, and, what is scarcely to be believed, most of the inhabitants remained idle spectators, not because their courage was subdued by the sight of danger, but because the spirit of rivalry and jealousy was not stifled even by the feelings of a public and general calamity. "When the news of the entrance of the Saracens [we borrow the expressions of a contemporary historian] was spread through the city, many of the citizens, from malice towards each other, entertained not near so much pity for the common calamity as they ought to have done, and took no account of what might happen to them, thinking in their hearts that the sultan would do them no harm, because they had not consented to the violation of the truce." In their infatuation they preferred owing their safety to the clemency of the conqueror, rather than to the bravery of the Christian warriors; [55] far from lending assistance to their neighbours, every one rejoiced in secret at their losses; the principal leaders of each quarter, or of each nation, were sparing of their soldiers, not in order to preserve their means of contending with the Saracens, but for the sake of having more empire in the city, and of husbanding their strength, so as to be on a future day the most powerful and formidable in the public dissensions.

True bravery, however, did not allow itself to be misled by such base passions; the troops of the Temple and the Hospital were found wherever danger called them. William de Clermont, marshal of the Hospitallers, hastened with his knights to the spot where peril was most imminent and the carnage the greatest. He met a crowd of Christians flying before their enemies; this brave warrior checked their flight and reanimated their courage, rushing among the Saracens, and cutting down all that came in his way; the Mussulmans, says an old chronicle, "fled away at his approach, like sheep before a wolf." Then most of those who had turned their backs on the enemy returned to the fight; the shock was terrible, the slaughter frightful: towards evening the trumpets of the Saracens sounded a retreat, and all who had escaped from the swords of the Christians retired in disorder through the breach they had made. This unexpected advantage had a wonderful effect upon the spirits of the besieged. Such as had taken no part in the contest, but remained quietly in their dwellings, began to fear that they should be accused of betraying the Christian cause. They set forward, with banners displayed, and directed their course towards the gate of St. Antony. The sight of the field of battle, still covered with traces of carnage, must have awakened in them some generous feelings, and if they had not exhibited their bravery, their brother warriors, stretched upon the earth, who implored them to help them and dress their wounds, at least offered them an opportunity of exercising their humanity. The wounded were attended to, the dead were buried, and they then set about repairing the walls and placing the machines: the whole of the night was employed in preparing means of defence for the day which was to follow.

Before sunrise the next morning, a general assembly was convoked in the house of the Hospitallers. Sadness was depicted on every countenance; they had lost two thousand Christian warriors in the battle of the preceding day; there now were only seven thousand combatants left in the city; these were not enough to defend the towers and the ramparts; they were no longer sustained by the hope of conquering their enemies; the future presented nothing but one terrible prospect of perils and calamities. When all were met, the patriarch of Jerusalem addressed the melancholy assembly. The venerable prelate directed no reproaches against them who had not assisted in the fight of the preceding day; the past must be forgotten; he did not praise them who had signalized their bravery, for fear of awakening jealousy; in his discourse he did not venture to speak of country, for Ptolemaïs was not the country of most of those who listened to him. The picture of the misfortunes which threatened the city and every one of its inhabitants, was presented in the darkest colours; there was no hope, no asylum for the vanquished; nothing was to be expected from the clemency of the Saracens, who always accomplished their threats, and never fulfilled their promises. It was but too certain that Europe would send them no succour; they had not vessels enough to enable them to think of flying by sea:—thus the patriarch took less pains to dissipate the alarms of his auditors than to animate them by despair. He terminated his speech by exhorting them to place all their confidence in God and their swords, to prepare for fight by penitence, to love each other, to help each other, and to endeavour to render their lives or their death glorious for themselves and serviceable to Christianity.

The speech of the patriarch made the deepest impression upon the assembly; nothing was heard but sobs and sighs; every person present was in tears; the religious sentiments which are generally awakened by the aspect of a great peril, filled all their hearts with an ardour and an enthusiasm they had never before experienced; most of them embraced each other, and exchanged reciprocal exhortations to brave every danger; they mutually confessed their sins, and even expressed a hope for the crown of martyrdom; those who had meditated desertion the day before, swore that they would never abandon the city, but would die on the ramparts with their brethren and companions.

The leaders and soldiers then went to the posts entrusted to their bravery. Such as were not employed in the defence of the ramparts and towers, made themselves ready to contend with their enemies, if they should gain access to the city; barriers were erected in all the streets, and heaps of stones were collected on the roofs, and at the doors of houses, to crush the Mussulmans, or impede them on their march.

Scarcely were these preparations finished, than the air resounded with the notes of trumpets and the beating of drums; a horrible noise, proceeding from the plain, announced the approach of the Saracens. After having discharged a multitude of arrows, they advanced confidently towards the wall they had broken through the day before. But they met with a resistance they did not expect; many were slain at the foot of the ramparts; but as their number momentarily increased, their constantly renewed attacks necessarily exhausted the strength of the Christians, at first in small numbers, and receiving no reinforcements. Towards the end of the day, the Christians had scarcely the power to hurl a javelin or handle a lance. The wall began again to give way beneath the strokes of the rams; then the patriarch, ever present at the point of danger, exclaimed in a supplicating tone,—"Oh, God! surround us with a rampart that men cannot destroy, and cover us with the ægis of Thy power!" At hearing this, the soldiers appeared to rally and make a last effort; they precipitated themselves upon the enemy, calling upon the *blessed Jesus, with a loud voice.* The Saracens, adds our chronicler, *called upon the name of their Mahomet,* and uttered the most fearful threats against the defenders of the Christian faith.

Whilst this conflict was going on upon the ramparts, the city awaited in great dread the issue of the battle; the agitation of men's minds gave birth to a thousand rumours, which were in turn adopted and rejected. It was reported in the most remote quarters, that the Christians were victorious, and the Mussulmans had fled; it was likewise added, that a fleet with an army on board had arrived from the West. To these news, which created a momentary joy, succeeded the most disheartening intelligence; and in all these reports there was nothing true but that which announced something inauspicious.

It was soon known that the Mussulmans had entered the city. The Christian warriors who defended the gate of St. Antony, had not been able to resist the shock of the enemy, and fled into the streets, imploring the assistance of the inhabitants. These latter then remembered the exhortations of the patriarch; reinforcements hasten from all quarters; the knights of the Hospital, with the valiant William at their head, reappear. A storm of stones falls from the tops of the houses; iron chains are stretched across the passage of the Mussulman cavalry; such as have been exhausted by fight recover their strength, and rush again into the *mêlée*; they who have come to their assistance follow their steps, break through the Mussulman battalions, disperse them and pursue them beyond the ramparts. In every one of these combats was exhibited all that valour can accomplish when united with despair. On contemplating, on one side the inevitable ruin of a great city, and on the other the efforts of a small number of defenders who put off, day after day, scenes of destruction and death, we cannot help feeling both compassion and surprise. The assaults were renewed without ceasing, and always with the same fury. At the end of every day's conflict, the unfortunate inhabitants of Ptolemaïs congratulated themselves upon having triumphed over their enemies; but on the morrow, when the sun appeared above the horizon, what were their thoughts when they beheld from the top of their ramparts the Mussulman army still the same, covering the plain from the sea to the foot of Karenba and Carmel!

The Saracens, on their part, became astonished at the resistance which all their attacks met with; so many combats, in which their innumerable multitude had not been able to obtain a decided advantage, began to give them discouragement. In the infidel army it was impossible to explain the invincible bravery of the Christian soldiers without assigning miraculous causes for it. A thousand extraordinary tales flew from mouth to mouth, and struck the imagination of the gross crowd of the Mussulmans. They believed they saw two men in every one of those with whom they fought; [56] in the excess of their astonishment, they persuaded themselves that every warrior who fell beneath their stroke was reborn of himself, and returned stronger and more terrible than ever to the field of battle. The sultan of Cairo appeared to have lost all hope of taking the city by assault. It is asserted that the renegadoes, whose apostasy made them desirous of the ruin of the Christian name, sought every means to revive his courage; the sieur Barthélemi, who had sworn an eternal hatred to the Franks, followed the Mussulman army; [57] this implacable deserter neglected nothing to encourage the leaders, to reanimate them for battle, and awaken in their hearts the furious passions that constantly devoured his own. In addition to these, the imauns and sheiks, who were numerous in the Mameluke camps, pervaded the ranks of the army to inflame the fanaticism of the soldiers: the sultan threatened all who flew before the enemy with punishment, and offered immense rewards for those who should plant the standard of the Prophet, not upon the walls of Ptolemaïs, but in the centre of the city.

On the 4th of May, a day fatal to the Christians, the signal for a fresh assault was given. At dawn the Mussulman army was under arms, the sultan animating the soldiers by his presence. Both the attack and the defence were much more animated and obstinate than they had been for some days before. Among those who fell on the field of battle, there were seven Mussulmans for one Christian; but the Mussulmans could repair their losses; those of the Christians were irreparable. The Saracens still directed all their efforts against the tower and the gate of St. Antony.

They were already upon the breach, when the knights of the Temple formed the rash resolution of making a sortie, and attacking the camp of the Mussulmans. They found the enemy's army drawn up in order of battle; after a bloody conflict, the Saracens repulsed the Christians, and pursued them to the foot of the ramparts. The grand master of the Temple was struck by an arrow and fell in the midst of his knights. The grand-master of the Hospital, at the same time received a wound which disabled him. The rout then became general, and all hope of saving the city was lost. There were scarcely a thousand Christian warriors left to defend the gate of St. Antony against the whole Mussulman army.

The Christians were obliged to yield to the multitude of their enemies; they directed their course towards the house of the Templars, situated on the seacoast. It was then that a death-pall seemed stretched over the whole city of Ptolemaïs: the Saracens advanced full of fury; there was not a street that did not become the theatre of carnage; a battle was fought for every tower, for every palace, and at the entrance of every public building; and in all these combats, so many men were killed, that, according to the report of an historian, *they walked upon the dead as upon a bridge.*

As if angry heaven gave the signal for destruction, a violent storm, accompanied by hail and rain, burst over the city; the horizon was all at once covered with such impenetrable darkness, that the combatants could scarcely distinguish the colours they fought under, or see what standard floated over the towers; all the scourges contributed to the desolation of Ptolemaïs; the flames appeared in several quarters, without any one making an effort to extinguish them; the conquerors only thought of destroying the city, the only object of the conquered was to escape. A multitude of people fled away at hazard, without knowing where they could hope to find an asylum. Whole families took refuge in the churches, where they were stifled by the flames, or cut to pieces at the foot of the altars; nuns and timid virgins mixed with the multitude which wandered through the city, or disfigured with wounds their faces and their bosoms, [58] to escape the brutality of the conquerors: what was most deplorable in the spectacle then presented in Ptolemaïs, was the desertion of the leaders, who abandoned a people in the height of its despair. John de Gresly and Oste de Granson, who had scarcely shown themselves upon the ramparts during the siege, fled away at the very commencement of the battle. Many others, who had taken the oath to die, at the aspect of this general destruction, only thought of saving their lives, and threw away their arms to facilitate their flight. History however is able to contrast some acts of true heroism with these base desertions. Our readers cannot have forgotten the brilliant actions of William de Clement. Amidst the ruins of Ptolemaïs, amidst the universal destruction, he still defied the enemy; attempting to rally some Christian warriors, he rode to the gate of St. Antony, which the Templars had just abandoned; though alone, he wished to renew the fight; he pierced through the ranks of the Saracens several times, and returned, still fighting; when he came back to the middle of the city, his war-horse (we copy a relation of the time) was much fatigued, as was he himself also; the war-horse no longer answered to the spur, and stopped in the street, as unable to do any more. The Saracens shot Brother William to the earth with arrows; and thus this loyal champion of Jesus Christ rendered up his soul to his creator. [59]

We cannot refuse our highest praise to the patriarch of Jerusalem, who, during the whole siege, shared all the dangers of the combatants; when he was dragged away towards the port by his friends, to evade the pursuit of the Mussulmans, the generous old man complained bitterly at being separated from his flock in the hour of peril. He was induced at last to embark, but as he insisted upon receiving on board his vessel all that presented themselves, the boat was sunk, and the faithful pastor died the victim of his charity.

The sea was tempestuous, the vessels could not approach close to land; the shore presented a heart-rending spectacle: here a mother called upon her son, there a son implored the assistance of his father; many precipitated themselves into the waves, in despair; the mass of people endeavoured to gain the vessels by swimming; some were drowned in the attempt, others were beaten off with oars. Several women of the noblest families flew in terror to the port, bringing with them their diamonds and their most valuable effects; they promised the mariners to become their wives, to give themselves and all their wealth up to them, if they would bear them away from this horrid scene; most of them were conveyed to the Isle of Cyprus: no pity was shown but to such as had treasures to bestow in return; thus, when tears had no effect upon hearts, avarice assumed the place of humanity, and saved some few victims. At length the Mussulman horsemen came down upon the port, and furiously pursued the Christians even into the waves: from that moment no one was able to escape the carnage.

Still, amidst the city given over to pillage, and a prey to the flames and the barbarity of the conquerors, several fortresses remained standing, and were defended by some Christian soldiers; these unfortunate warriors died sword in hand, without any other witnesses of their glorious end but their implacable enemies.

The castle of the Templars, in which all the knights who had escaped the steel of the Saracens had taken refuge, was soon the only place in the city that held out. The sultan having granted them a capitulation, sent three hundred Mussulmans to execute the treaty. Scarcely had these entered one of the principal towers, the tower of the grand-master, than they began to outrage the women who had taken refuge there. This violation of the rights of war irritated the Christian warriors to such a degree, that all the Saracens who had entered the tower were instantly immolated to their too just vengeance. The angry sultan ordered the siege to be prosecuted against the Christians in their last asylum, and that all should be put to the sword. The knights of the Temple and their companions defended themselves for several days: at length the tower of the grand-master was undermined, and fell at the very moment the Mussulmans were mounting to an assault: they who attacked it and they who defended it were equally crushed by its fall;

women, children, Christian warriors, all who had come to seek refuge in the house of the Templars, perished, buried beneath the ruins. Every church of Ptolemaïs was plundered, profaned, and then given up to the flames. The sultan ordered all the principal edifices, with the towers and ramparts, to be demolished.

The Mussulman soldiers expressed their joy by ferocious clamours; which joy formed a horrible contrast with the desolation of the conquered. Amidst the tumultuous scenes of victory were mingled the screams of women, upon whom the barbarians were committing violence in their camp, and the cries of little children, borne away into slavery. A distracted multitude of fugitives, driven from ruin to ruin, and finding no place of refuge, directed their course to the tent of the sultan, to implore his mercy; Chalil distributed these Christian supplicants among his emirs, who caused them all to be massacred. Macrisi makes the number of these unhappy victims amount to ten thousand.

After the taking and the destruction of Ptolemaïs, the sultan sent one of his emirs with a body of troops to take possession of the city of Tyre; this city, seized with terror, opened its gates without resistance. The conquerors likewise possessed themselves of Berytus, Sidon, and all the Christian cities along the coast. These cities, which had not afforded the least succour to Ptolemaïs, in the last great struggle, and which believed themselves protected by a truce, beheld their population massacred, dispersed, and led into slavery; the fury of the Mussulmans extended even to the stones, they seemed to wish to destroy the very earth which the Christians had trod upon; their houses, their temples, the monuments of their piety, their valour and their industry, everything was condemned to perish with them by the sword or by fire.

Most of the contemporary chronicles attribute such great disasters to the sins of the inhabitants of Palestine, and in the scenes of destruction only behold the effect of that divine anger which fell upon Nineveh and Babylon. History must not reject these easy explanations; but it is, doubtless, permitted to penetrate deeper into human affairs, and whilst recognising the intervention of Heaven in the political destinies of nations, it is bound at least to endeavour to discover the means which Providence has employed to raise, to maintain for a time, and at length, to destroy empires.

We have shown, in the course of our recital, to what point the ambition of the leaders, the want of discipline among the soldiers, the turbulent passions of the multitude, the corruption of morals, the spirit of discord and dissension, with egotism and selfishness, had urged on the kingdom of Jerusalem towards its decline and its destruction. We shall here offer but one general observation which belongs to our subject, and which ought not to be omitted in a history of the crusades.

This power of the Franks had been cast upon Asia, as by a tempest, and could not support itself there by its own strength. The true support of the kingdom of Jerusalem remained in the West, and the principle of its preservation, the source of its power was foreign to itself; its safety depended upon a crowd of circumstances which its leaders could not possibly foresee, upon a crowd of events which passed far from it; it depended above all upon feelings and opinions which prevailed among distant nations. Whilst the enthusiasm which had founded the Christian colonies was kept up in Europe, these colonies might hope to prolong their existence; the greatest of their calamities [60] was the indifference of the nations which dwelt beyond the seas; the kingdom of Jerusalem began with the crusades, it was destined to terminate with them.

A Mussulman chronicler, after having described the desolation of the coasts of Syria, and the expulsion of the citizens, terminates his account by this singular reflection: "Things, if it please God, will remain thus till the last judgment." The wishes of the Arabian historian, have hitherto been but too completely fulfilled; the Mussulmans, for more than five centuries, have reigned over the countries occupied by the Christians, and with them has reigned the genius of destruction which presided over the wars we have described. The philosopher who contemplates these desolated regions, these fields uncultivated and deserted, these towns in ruins, these cities without industry, without laws, and almost without inhabitants, and who compares them with what they were in the times of the crusades, cannot avoid being deeply impressed by regret and compassion. Without dwelling upon the motives which governed the actions of the Crusaders, without approving all that a frequently blind enthusiasm inspired, he must at least acknowledge that these distant expeditions did some good, and that if they sometimes carried desolation to the coasts of Syria, they also carried thither the germs of prosperity and civilization.

BOOK XVI
A.D. 1291-1396

ATTEMPTED CRUSADES

CRUSADES AGAINST THE TURKS

We are now arrived at the end of the brilliant epoch of the crusades, but our task is not yet completed; for, as the curiosity of readers attaches a high value to the knowledge of the causes of events, in the same degree must it be desirous of knowing the influence that these events have had upon the laws, manners, and destinies of nations. After having witnessed the kindling of so many passions, which inflamed Europe and Asia during two centuries, who but must be curious to see in what manner these passions were progressively extinguished; what were the political combinations that weakened this universal enthusiasm; and what were the interests, the opinions, and the institutions which took place of the spirit of the holy wars. Here the philosophy of history comes at our wish to enlighten us with its lamp, and make clear to us the eternal course of human things. The end of a great revolution may be compared, in some sort, to the decline of the life of man, it is then that the fruits of long experience may be gathered, it is then that the past, with its remembrances and its lessons, is reflected as in a faithful mirror.

We will pursue, then, with confidence the work we have begun; if, in the career we have still to go through, we may have little to say that will awaken the curiosity of common minds, enlightened spirits will, doubtless, find some interest, in following with us all these long reverberations of a revolution which deeply agitated the world, and whose consequences will be felt by remotest posterity.

When the news of the taking of Ptolemaïs arrived in the West, Pope Nicholas IV. gave his whole attention to the preaching of a crusade. A bull addressed to all the faithful, deplored in pathetic terms the late disasters of the Christians; and the greater that these misfortunes were, the more fully did the pope offer the treasures of divine mercy and pontifical indulgences to new Crusaders. An indulgence of a hundred days was granted to those who would attend the sermons of the preachers of the crusade, or would come to the churches to listen to the groans of the city of God. The holy orators had permission to preach the war of the East in forbidden places; and, that great sinners might be induced to become soldiers of the cross, the preachers received the faculty of granting certain absolutions that had till that time been reserved for the supreme authority of the Holy See.

In many provinces, the clergy assembled in consequence of the directions of the pope, to deliberate upon the means of recovering Palestine. The prelates employed themselves in this pious mission with much zeal, and in order to secure the success of the enterprise, all united in conjuring the sovereign pontiff to labour without intermission in bringing about the reëstablishment of peace among Christian princes.

Several monarchs had already taken the cross; and Nicholas sent legates to press them to accomplish the vow they appeared to have forgotten. Edward, king of England, although he had levied the tenths upon the clergy for the expenses of the crusade, showed very little inclination to quit his states for the purpose of returning into Asia. The emperor Rodolph, who, in the conference of Lausanne, had promised the pope to make the voyage beyond the seas, died at this period, much more deeply engaged in the affairs of Germany, than in those of the Christians of the East. Nicholas IV. gave Philip to understand that the whole West had its eyes fixed upon him, and that his example might influence all Christendom; the sovereign pontiff at the same time exhorted the prelates of the Church of France to join with him in persuading the king, the nobles, and the people, to take arms against the infidels.

The father of the Christian world did not confine his endeavours to awakening the zeal of the princes and nations of the West; he sent apostolic messages to the Greek emperor, Andronicus Palæologus, the emperor of Trebizond, and the kings of Armenia, Georgia, and Cyprus, in which he announced to them the approaching deliverance of the holy places. As the Christians in their distress had sometimes turned their looks towards the Tartars, two missionaries were sent to the coast of Argun, with directions to offer the Mogul emperor the benedictions of the sovereign pontiff, and to solicit his powerful aid against the Mussulmans.

The exertions and exhortations of the pope did not succeed in arming Europe against the Saracens; contemporary chronicles say that Nicholas was not able to endure this indifference of the Christians, and that he died in despair. After his death, the conclave could not agree in the nomination of a head of the Church, and the Holy See remained vacant during twenty-seven months. In this long interval, the pulpits which had resounded with the complaints of the faithful of the East, remained mute, and Europe forgot the last calamities of the Holy Land.

In the East, the affairs of the Christians took a not more favourable turn. The discord that had arisen between the princes of the family of Hayton desolated Armenia, and gave it up to the invasion of the barbarians. The kingdom of Cyprus, the last asylum of the Franks established in Asia, only owed a transitory security to the sanguinary divisions of the Mamelukes of Egypt, and appeared to be fully engaged by its own dangers.

But whilst Christendom gave up all thoughts of the deliverance of Jerusalem, the Tartars of Persia, to whom the pope had sent missionaries, all at once revived the hopes of the Christians, by forming a project for wresting Syria and Palestine from the hands of the Mussulmans; an enterprize which only wanted to be a crusade, to have been proclaimed by the head of the Church.

The Tartars, for a long time, threatened the Mussulman powers, whom the Christians regarded as their most cruel enemies. Argun, when he died, was busied in preparations for a formidable war. These preparations had spread such serious alarm among his enemies, that the disciples of Mahomet considered his death as one of the number of miracles operated in favour of Islamism.

Among the successors of Argun, who were by turns the enemies and the friends of the Mussulmans, there was one able leader, who was warlike, and more animated by the thirst for conquests than the others. The Greek historian Pachymerus, and the Armenian Hayton, lavish the highest praises upon the bravery, the virtue, and even the piety of Cazan. This Mogul prince considered the Christians as his most faithful allies; and in his armies, in which the Georgians served, the standard of the cross floated by the side of the imperial standard. The conquest of the banks of the Nile and the Jordan engaged all his thoughts. When new cities were built in his states, he took a delight in bestowing upon them the names of Aleppo, Damascus, Alexandria, and of several other places in Egypt and Syria.

Cazan quitted Persia at the head of an army; and the king of Cyprus with the orders of St. John and the Temple, being made aware of his projects, joined his standards. A great battle was fought near Emessa, which was decided against the sultan of Egypt, who lost the greater part of his army, and was pursued by the Armenian cavalry to the verge of the desert. Aleppo and Damascus opened their gates to the conquerors; and if we may believe the historian Hayton, Christians once more entered Jerusalem, and the emperor of the Tartars visited in their company the tomb of Christ.

It was from that place Cazan sent ambassadors to the pope and the sovereigns of Europe, to solicit their alliance, and to offer them possession of the Holy Land. Among the singularities of this period, our readers will no doubt be astonished to find a Mogul emperor endeavouring to revive the spirit of the crusades among the princes of Christendom; and to see barbarians from the banks of the Irtis and the Jaxartes waiting upon Calvary and Mount Sion for the warriors of France, Germany, and Italy, in order to combat the enemies of Christ. The sovereign pontiff received the ambassadors of Cazan with distinction; but could only answer their demands and propositions by promises doomed to remain unexecuted. The haughtiness with which Boniface VIII., the successor of Nicholas, spoke to the Christian princes, together with his exhortations, which resembled commands more than entreaties, disgusted the sovereigns, particularly the king of France. Genoa, which then lay under an interdict, was the only city of Europe in which a crusade was seriously spoken of; and by a whimsical circumstance, it was the ladies who gave the signal and set the example.

We are still in possession of a brief of the pope's, in which the holy father felicitates the ladies who had taken the cross, upon their following the steps of Cazan, the emperor of the Tartars, *who, although a pagan, had conceived the generous resolution of delivering the Holy Land.* History has preserved two other letters of the pope, one addressed to Porchetto, archbishop of Genoa, and the other to four Genoese nobles, who had undertaken to direct the expedition. "Oh, prodigy! oh, miracle!" says he to Porchetto; "a weak and timid sex takes the advance of warriors in this great enterprise, in this war against the enemies of Christ, in this fight against the workers of iniquity. The kings and princes of the earth, regardless of all the solicitations that have been made to them, refuse to send succours to the Christians banished from the Holy Land, and here are women who come forward without being called! Whence can this magnanimous resolution come, if not from God, the source of all strength and all virtue!!!" The pope terminated his letter by directing the archbishop to call together the clergy and the people, and proclaim the devotion of the noble Genoese ladies, in order that their example may cast seeds of good works into the hearts of the people.

This crusade, notwithstanding, never took place; it was doubtless only preached to rouse the emulation of the knights, and the pope only directed his attention to it to give a lesson to the princes of Christendom, by which they did not at all profit. The letters written upon this occasion by Boniface VIII. were preserved in the archives of the republic of Genoa for a long time. Even in the last century, the helmets and cuirasses which were to have been worn by the Genoese ladies in this expedition were exhibited in the arsenal of that city.

The Tartars, in spite of their victories, were not able to triumph over the constancy and discipline of the Mamelukes, who, like themselves, had issued from the deserts of Scythia. That which had so often happened to the Franks in the height of the crusades, now happened to the Moguls; they at first obtained great advantages, but events foreign to the Holy War recalled them into their own country, and forced them to abandon their conquests. Cazan was obliged to quit Syria and return into Persia; he attempted a second expedition, which he again abandoned; and he died in the third, amidst his triumphs, bearing with him to the tomb the last hopes of the Christians.

The Armenian and Cyprian warriors left the holy city, the ramparts of which they had begun to re-erect, and which was doomed never again to see the standard of the cross unfurled within its walls. This last reverse of the Christians of the East was scarcely known in Europe, where the name of Jerusalem was still pronounced in the congregations of the faithful, but had no longer the power to awaken the enthusiasm of knights and warriors. At the Council of Vienna, Pope Clement V. proclaimed a crusade; but in this assembly, in which the abolition of the Templars was determined upon, Christians were exhorted very feebly to take up arms against the infidels.

The sovereign pontiff was then much more busy in levying tenths than in preparations for a holy war. One thing worthy of remark is, that Clement found himself obliged on this occasion to recommend moderation to the collectors of the tenths, and forbade them *to seize the chalices, the books, or the ornaments of the churches.* This prohibition of the pope's proves to us that violence had often been committed in collecting the tributes destined to the expenses of the holy wars; this violence must have assisted in relaxing the zeal and ardour of nations for distant enterprises, as the results of which, Christian cities were ruined, and the altars of Christ plundered.

Europe at that time awaited with great impatience the issue of an expedition undertaken by the knights of St. John of Jerusalem. A great number of warriors, excited by the relation of the adventures of chivalry, and by a passion for military glory, followed the Hospitallers in their enterprise; women even were desirous of taking a part in this expedition, and sold their diamonds and jewels to provide for the expenses of the war.

This army of new crusaders embarked at the port of Brendisi, and it soon became known in the West that the knights of the Hospital had taken possession of the isle of Rhodes.

Renown published everywhere the exploits of the Hospitallers and their companions in arms; and these exploits, and the admiration they inspired throughout Christendom, naturally turned the attention and remembrances of the faithful to the Templars, who were reproached with the disgraceful repose in which they forgot both the Holy Land and the tomb of Christ.

The knights of the Temple, after having been received in the Isle of Cyprus, had returned to Sicily, where they were employed by the king in an expedition against Greece. United with the Catalans and some warriors from Italy, this warlike body took possession of Thessalonica, made themselves masters of Athens, advanced towards the Hellespont, and ravaged a part of Thrace. After this expedition the Templars disdained the possession of the cities which had fallen into their power, and leaving the conquered provinces to their companions in arms, they kept for themselves the riches of the people they had subdued. It was then that, loaded with the spoils of Greece, they came to establish themselves in the West, particularly in France, where their opulence, their luxury, and their idleness, scandalized the piety of the faithful, awakened envy, and provoked the hatred of both the people and the great.

It does not enter into the plan of this work to dilate upon the process instituted against the Templars; but if we have followed these noble knights in all their wars against the Mussulmans,—if we have been so long witnesses of their exploits, and, as it were, companions of their labours, we shall perhaps have acquired the right of expressing our opinion upon the accusations directed against them. We must at once declare that we have found nothing up to the period of the process, either in the chronicles of the East, or those of the West, which can give birth to or establish an idea, or even a suspicion, of the crimes imputed to them. How can it, in fact, be believed, that a warlike and religious order, which twenty years before had seen three hundred of its knights sacrifice themselves upon the ruins of Saphet, rather than embrace the Mussulman faith, that this order which had almost entirely buried itself under the ruins of Ptolemaïs could possibly have contracted an alliance with infidels, outraged the Christian religion with horrible blasphemies, and given up to the Saracens that Holy Land filled with its military glory.

And at what period were all these odious reproaches addressed to the Templars? at a time when Christendom seemed to have forgotten Jerusalem, and in which the name of Christ was not sufficient to awaken the bravery of a Christian warrior. No doubt the order of the Templars had degenerated from the austerity of early times, and that it was no longer animated by that spirit of humility and religion of which St. Bernard so much boasted; no doubt some of the knights had brought with them that corruption which was then the reproach of all the Christians of the East, and of which Europe itself could offer them numerous examples; no doubt, in short, some among them might have wounded morality by their conduct, and offended the religion of Christ by their irregularities; but we do not hesitate to say that it was not the province of men to judge them, and that upon this occasion the merciful God of the Christians had not deputed his vengeance to human laws.

The real error of the Templars was having quitted the East, and renounced the spirit of their institution, which was to receive and protect pilgrims, and to combat with the enemies of the Christian faith. This order, richer than the most powerful monarchs, and whose knights were as a regular army, always ready for fight, became, naturally, dreaded by the princes who granted them an asylum. The Templars had not been free from all reproach during their abode in Cyprus; accustomed to rule in Palestine, they must have contracted a habit of obedience with difficulty. The example of the Teutonic knights, who, after quitting the East, founded a power in the north of Europe which was dreaded by the neighbouring states, was not likely to reassure princes who mistrusted the warlike spirit, and the active and enterprising genius, of the knights of the Temple.

Such, probably, were the motives which armed the policy rather than the justice of sovereigns against them; nothing so clearly proves the fear they inspired as the rancour with which they were pursued, and the care that was taken to render them odious. As soon as their persecution began, they were only considered as enemies whom it was necessary to treat as criminals. As rigours without example preceded their abolition, it was necessary to justify that measure by fresh rigours. Vengeance and hatred finished that which the policy of princes had begun; a policy which had, perhaps, reasons for being suspicious, but which had none for proving itself barbarous. It is thus we must explain the tragical issue of this process, in which all the forms of justice were so violated, that even if the accusations be considered proved, we must still regard the Templars as victims and their judges as executioners. [61]

Philip-le-Bel had promised the council of Vienna to go into the East to combat the infidels, without doubt to procure pardon for having pursued the knights of the Temple with so much inveteracy. Amidst the festivals that welcomed the arrival of Edward in Paris, the French monarch and the princes of his family took the cross. Most of the nobles of his court followed his example, and the ladies promised to accompany the knights to the holy war; but no one took any measures for setting out. Promises were then made to cross the seas by persons who had not any serious intention of leaving their homes. The vow to combat the Saracens appeared to be a vain ceremony, which engaged the swearer to nothing. It was taken with perfect indifference, and violated in the same manner; *considered as not more sacred than the vows the knights made to the ladies.*

Philip-le-Bel died without ever having thought of accomplishing his vow. Philip-le-Long, who succeeded him, entertained for a moment the project of going into the East. Edward, who had already several times sworn to fight the Saracens, at the same time renewed his promise. But the sovereign pontiff, whether that he doubted their sincerity, or whether that he stood in need of the concurrence of these two monarchs to reëstablish tranquillity in Europe, and to resist the emperor of Germany, against whom he had armed himself with the thunders of the Church, or whether, in short, he thought the moment an unfavourable one, did not approve of their expedition into Syria. "Before thinking of the voyage beyond the seas," wrote he to the king of England, "we would wish you to establish peace, first in your own conscience, then in your kingdom." The father of the faithful represented to the king of France that the peace, so necessary to be firm before a crusade should be undertaken, was almost banished from Christendom. England and Scotland were at war; the states of Germany were divided against each other; the king of Sicily and the king of Naples were only bound by a truce of short duration; reciprocal mistrust prevented the kings of Cyprus and Armenia from uniting their forces against the common enemy; the kings of Spain were quite sufficiently employed in defending their states against the Moors; the republics of Lombardy were all in arms against each other; all the cities of Italy were torn by factions, the provinces a prey to tyrants, the sea impracticable, the route by land thickly strewed with dangers. After having given this picture of the deplorable state of Christendom, the pope pressed Philip to inquire seriously how he could provide for the expenses of the war without ruining his people, *or without attempting*, he added, *to do that which is impossible, as has been done before.*

The paternal advice of the sovereign pontiff, and some troubles which arose in the bosom of his kingdom, determined Philip to postpone the execution of his project. A multitude of herdsmen and shepherds, of adventurers and vagabonds, setting up, as in the time of the captivity of St. Louis, the pilgrims' cross, assembled in many places, persecuted the Jews, and committed most culpable excesses. Force of arms and the full severity of the laws were obliged to be resorted to, in order to quell these disorders, of which the crusade was only a pretext. At the same time several provinces of France suffered greatly from an epidemic disease; the Jews were accused of having poisoned the wells, with the design of suspending the preparations for the holy war. They were accused of all sorts of plots against the Christians; and the general fermentation was the greater from the suspicions being vague, and from the impossibility of proving or contradicting the crimes alleged. Policy could discover no other means of dissipating the troubles than that of entering into the passions of the multitude, and driving all the

Jews out of the kingdom. Amidst these unhappy circumstances, Philip fell ill, and died regretting his not having accomplished the vow he had made of warring against the Saracens.

In the state of abandonment to which the crusades had fallen, we are surprised at seeing the minds of the French still occasionally directed towards the delivery of the holy places. This last flickering of enthusiasm, which our ancestors kept alight amidst the general indifference, was not confined to religious sentiments, but extended to a feeling of patriotism and national glory. It was France which had given the first impulsion to the holy wars, as we have several times observed. The name of Palestine, the names of St. Jean d'Acre or Ptolemaïs, and that of Jerusalem appealed no less to patriotism than to piety. Although the two expeditions of Louis IX. had been unsuccessful, the example of the holy monarch was a great authority for the princes of his family, and often carried their thoughts to the places where he had suffered the glory of martyrdom. The memory of his exploits and even of his misfortunes, the memory of the heroes who had died on the banks of the Nile and the Jordan, interested all the families of the kingdom; and the city in which reposed the ashes of Godfrey and Baldwin of Bouillon, those distant regions in which so many glorious battles had been fought, could not be forgotten by French warriors.

After the death of Philip-le-Long, ambassadors arrived in Europe from the king of Armenia; this prince, abandoned by the Tartars, and threatened by the Mamelukes of Egypt, requested the assistance of the West. The pope wrote to Charles-le-Bel, the successor of Philip-le-Long, and conjured him to take up arms against the infidels. Charles received with respect the counsels and the exhortations of the sovereign pontiff, and was engaged in preparations for a crusade when the succession of the county of Flanders caused a war to break out in the Low Countries. From that time France became attentive only to the events that were passing before her eyes, and in which her own independence and safety were deeply interested. At the approach of death, and at a time when the kingdom had no longer anything to fear, Charles-le-Bel remembered his oath, and his last thoughts were directed towards the deliverance of Jerusalem. "I bequeath," says he in his will, "to the Holy Land fifty thousand livres, to be paid and delivered when the general passage shall be made; and it is my intention, if the passage be made in my lifetime, to go thither in person." [62] It was thus that at this period the spirit of the crusades still occasionally showed itself; most of the testaments [63] then made by princes and *rich men* (these words designated the nobility) contained some dispositions in favour of the Holy

Land; but we must add, also, that the facility of purchasing the merit of pilgrimage for money must necessarily have greatly diminished the number of pilgrims and Crusaders.

Whilst dying people were thus prodigal of their treasure for the holy war, nobody took up arms. There still, however, remained some men endowed with a vivid imagination and an ardent temperament, who made incredible efforts to rekindle an enthusiasm on the point of being extinguished. The greater the indifference of nations, the greater were the ardour and zeal displayed by these men in their preachings. Among these latter apostles of the crusades, history cites the name of Raymond Lulli, one of the luminaries of the schools of the middle ages. [64]

Lulli was possessed during his life but by one thought, and that was, to combat and convert the infidels. [65] It was upon the proposition of this zealous missionary that the council of Vienna decided that chairs should be established in the universities of Rome, Bologna, Paris, and Salamanca, for instruction in the languages of the East. He presented to the pope several memorials upon the means of annihilating the worship of Mahomet and the domination of his disciples. Lulli, constantly occupied with his project, made a pilgrimage into Palestine, travelled through Syria, Armenia, and Egypt, and came back to Europe to describe the misfortunes, the captivity, and the disgraces of the Christians beyond the seas. On his return, he visited all the courts of the West, seeking to communicate to sovereigns the sentiments by which he was animated. Finding his efforts were vain, his zeal carried him to the coast of Africa, where he endeavoured to convert by his eloquence those same Saracens against whom he had invoked the arms of Christian warriors. He returned to Europe, passed through Italy, France, and Spain, preaching everywhere the necessity for another crusade. He embarked again for Jerusalem, and brought back, as the fruit of his pilgrimage, some useful notions upon the best manner of attacking the countries of the infidels. All his labours, all his researches, all his prayers, produced no effect upon the indifference of kings and nations. Lulli, at length despairing of seeing his projects realised, and deploring the blindness of his contemporaries, retired to the island of Majorca, which was his native country. From the depth of his retreat he still issued memorials upon an expedition to the East; but solitude soon wearied his ardent and restless spirit, and he quitted Majorca, no more to waste his words upon the princes of Europe, who would not listen to him, but to return to the Mussulmans, whom he still hoped to lead to the Gospel by his eloquence. He repaired a second time to Africa, and at length suffered, as the reward of his preachings, the torments and the death of martyrs.

Whilst Lulli was striving to direct the efforts of the faithful to the deliverance of the holy places, a noble Venetian likewise consecrated his life and his talents to the revival of the spirit of the crusades. Sanuti thus describes the first audience he obtained of the sovereign pontiff: "I am not sent hither," said he, "by any king, any prince, or any republic; it is from the impulse of my own mind that I come to throw myself at the feet of your holiness, and to propose to you an easy means of crushing the enemies of the true faith, of extirpating the sect of Mahomet, and of recovering the Holy Land. [66] My voyages in Cyprus, Armenia, and Egypt, together with a long sojourn in Romania, have furnished me with knowledge and information that may be turned to the profit of Christianity." On finishing these words, Sanuti presented two books to the pope, one covered with red and the other with yellow, and four geographical charts, the first of the Mediterranean Sea, the second of the earth and of the sea, the third of the Holy Land, the fourth, of Egypt. The two books of the noble Venetian contained the history of the Christian establishments in the East, and wise counsels respecting the undertaking of another crusade. His zeal, enlightened by experience, did not allow him to neglect the least detail upon the route that was to be followed, upon the point that it would be best to attack, upon the number of troops, and upon the fitting out and provisioning of the vessels. He advised that operations should commence by landing in Egypt, and weakening the power of the sultans of Cairo. The most certain means of effecting this latter purpose was to obtain directly from Bagdad the Indian merchandises which European commerce was accustomed to get by the cities of Alexandria and Damietta. Sanuti, at the same time, advised the sovereign pontiff to redouble the severity of his censures against those who carried into Egypt arms, metals, timber for building, or anything that could assist in equipping fleets or arming the Mameluke soldiery.

The pope bestowed great praises upon Sanuti, and furnished him with introductions to several sovereigns of Europe. The Christian princes, particularly the king of France, received him with kindness, lauded his piety, and admired his talents—but took care not to follow his advice. Sanuti addressed himself likewise to the emperor of Constantinople, to engage him in an expedition against the infidels; he sought everywhere, and by every means, to raise up enemies against the Mussulmans, and passed his life in preaching a crusade, without obtaining any more success than Raymond Lulli had done.

The zeal of the two men of whom we have just spoken can only be compared to that of Peter the Hermit; they were both much more enlightened than the cenobite Peter, but they could get no one to listen to them, and the fruitlessness of their efforts proves how much the times were changed. Peter preached in cities and in public places, and the multitude, inflamed by his discourses, led away and awakened the feelings of the great. In the times of Lulli and Sanuti, sovereigns alone could be addressed, and sovereigns, occupied by their own affairs, showed very little interest for projects which only concerned Christendom in general. In the early times of the crusades, the deliverance of the holy places was a matter of importance; simply to pronounce the name of Jerusalem was sufficient to appease differences among princes; later, the least interest of jealousy, ambition, or self-love had the power to arrest the progress of, or completely put an end to, a holy enterprise. Frequently, in the twelfth century, popes and simple preachers, arming themselves with the authority of Christ, commanded princes to take up the cross and set out for the East; in the thirteenth, but more particularly in the fourteenth century, it was necessary to pray and solicit; and, generally, the most humble prayers produced no effect. [67]

Thus, the groans of Sion no longer melted hearts, and Christian eloquence was powerless against infidels. In order to awaken attention, it was necessary to mingle something of profane grandeur with the pathetic exhortations of religion; thus, Europe, which scarcely listened to the missionaries of the cross, appeared, all at once, to be aroused by the arrival of the king of Cyprus, soliciting, in person, the assistance of Christian princes. The pope, who was then at Avignon, eagerly announced to the faithful that an Eastern king was come to his court, and conjured the warriors of the West to take up arms against the Saracens. The king of Cyprus and Jerusalem described the invasions of the Mamelukes, the progress of the Turks, the dangers which surrounded his kingdom, that of Armenia, and the isle of Rhodes, and omitted no instance of the numerous persecutions endured by the Christians who remained in Syria and Egypt. These sad recitals, coming from a royal mouth, awakened some generous sentiments in men's minds; a league was formed between the sovereign pontiff, the king of France, and the republic of Venice; and the pope published a bull by which he ordered the bishops to cause a crusade to be preached.

Philip of Valois convoked an assembly at Paris, in the Holy Chapel, at which were present John, king of Bohemia, the king of Navarre, the dukes of Burgundy, Brittany, Lorraine, Brabant, and Bourbon, with most of the prelates and barons of the kingdom. Peter de la Palue, named patriarch of Jerusalem, and who had recently passed through Egypt and Palestine, harangued the auditory upon the necessity for attacking the infidels, and stopping the progress of their domination in the East. Philip, who had already taken the cross, renewed the vow he had made, and as he was preparing to quit his kingdom, the barons took the oath of obedience to his son Prince John, by raising their hands towards the crown of thorns of

Christ. John of Bohemia, the king of Navarre, and a great number of princes and nobles, received the cross from the hands of the archbishop of Rouen. The crusade was preached throughout the kingdom, "and gave to all noble lords," says Froissart, "great delight, particularly to those who wished to pass their time in arms, and knew no means then of employing it otherwise more reasonably." [68]

The king of France sent to the pope the archbishop of Rouen, who afterwards ascended the chair of St. Peter under the name of Clement VI. The archbishop, in full consistory, pronounced a discourse upon the crusade, and declared, in the presence of divine majesty, to the holy father, to the church of Rome and all Christendom, that Philip of Valois would set out for the East in the month of August, in the year 1336. The pope felicitated the French monarch upon his resolution, and granted him the tenths during six years. These circumstances are related by Philip Villani, who was at Avignon at the time, and who, after having spoken in his history of the promise made in the Dame of the king of France, exclaims:—"And I, the historian, I heard the oath pronounced which I have just related."

Philip gave orders that a fleet, assembled in the port of Marseilles, should be made ready to receive forty thousand Crusaders. Edward III., to whom the crusade offered an easy means of imposing taxes, promised to accompany the king of France with an army in the pilgrimage beyond the seas. Most of the republics of Italy, with the kings of Arragon, Majorca, and Hungary, engaged to supply money, troops, and vessels for the expedition. In the midst of their preparations, the Crusaders lost him who directed and was the soul of the enterprise. Everything was interrupted by the death of Pope John XXI., and in this place it becomes necessary to point out one of the causes which rendered abortive, in the thirteenth and fourteenth centuries, so many attempts to carry the war into the East. As the successors of St. Peter scarcely ever succeeded to the pontifical chair before they were of an advanced age, they were wanting in the energy and activity necessary for exciting the Christian world, directing distant wars, and kindling an enthusiasm, formerly so difficult to be restrained, now so difficult to be revived. Each crusade requiring long preparations, the life of one sovereign pontiff scarcely sufficed for the completion of such great enterprises. It most frequently happened, that he who had preached a holy war could not behold the departure of the Crusaders; and that he who saw the Christian armies set out, never lived long enough to follow them through their expeditions, conduct them in their triumphs, or succour them in their reverses. Thus we never find in the projects which circumstances had formed, that spirit of sequence and wholeness necessary to secure execution and success. Add to this, that since the popes had been established at Avignon, and their apostolic seat was no longer in the centre of Christendom, they did not exercise the same ascendancy over the distant provinces, and their authority every day lost something of that influence attached to the name only of Rome, considered, during so many centuries, the capital of the world.

The news of a fresh crusade having reached the East, the Christians who dwelt in Syria or Egypt, with pilgrims and European merchants, were exposed to all sorts of persecutions. The sultan of Cairo and several Mussulman princes assembled armies for the purpose of resisting the Crusaders, or to go and attack the Christians in the West. A descendant of the Abassides, who resided in Egypt, and assumed the title of caliph, sent letters and messages in every direction to engage all true believers to take up arms; promising the martyrs of the Mussulman faith that they should be present at delicious banquets, and that each of them should have seven virgins for wives.

The aim of this crusade, preached in the name of the prophet of Mecca, was to penetrate into Europe by the way of Gibraltar; the Mussulman warriors swore to annihilate Christianity, and to convert all the Christian temples into stables. In proportion as the Saracens were thus becoming inflamed for an expedition, which they also called a holy war, Europe beheld the zeal of the princes and warriors who had sworn to combat the enemies of Christ, grow fainter and fainter, and at length die away. When Benedict XI. succeeded John XXI., he found the minds of all changed; hatreds, mistrusts and jealousies had taken place of a transitory and insincere enthusiasm; it was in vain that Christians from the East described the persecutions they had undergone and the preparations of the infidels against the nations of the West; it was in vain that the pope continued his exhortations and his prayers; the greater that the reason was for undertaking a crusade, the more indifferent people became, and the more all ranks seemed to shun the idea of contending with the Saracens. It was at this period that Brother Andrew of Antioch came to Avignon with the design of imploring the aid of the pope and the princes of Christendom. Philip of Valois had come to the court of the sovereign pontiff, to inform him that he should defer his voyage into the East, and had mounted his horse to return to Paris, when Brother Andrew presented himself before him, and said: "Art thou Philip king of France, who promised God and his Church to deliver the Holy Land?" The king answered, "Yes." Then the monk resumed: "If thy intention is to perform that which thou hast promised, I implore Jesus Christ to direct thy steps, and grant thee the victory; but if the enterprise thou hast commenced is only to turn to the shame and misfortunes of Christians, if thou art not, with the help of God, determined to finish it, if thou hast deceived the holy Catholic Church, divine justice will fall heavily on thy family and on thy kingdom, and the blood which the news of thy expedition has caused to flow will rise up against thee." The king surprised at this strange appeal, answered: "Brother Andrew, come with us:" and Brother Andrew replied without being moved, and in an inspired tone: "If thou wast going into the East, I would go before thee, but as thou art going to the West, go on; I will return to perform penance for my sins in the land thou hast abandoned."

Such was even then the authority of the orators who spoke in the name of Jerusalem, that the last words of Brother Andrew left trouble and uneasiness in the mind of a powerful monarch; but fresh political storms had recently broken out. Edward III. had laid claim to the throne of the Capets, and his ambition was the signal for a war which lasted more than a century, and brought the greatest calamities upon France. Philip, attacked by a formidable enemy, was obliged to renounce his expedition beyond the seas, and employ, for the defence of his own kingdom, the troops and fleets that he had collected for the deliverance of the heritage of Christ.

The pope did not, however, abandon the project of the holy war. The poet Petrarch, who was then at Avignon, proved one of the most ardent apostles of the crusade. This illustrious poet, whom we are now accustomed to consider only as the ingenious singer of the praises of the fair Laura, and who was then deemed the most worthy interpreter of the wisdom of the ancients, and one of the great spirits of his age, addressed an eloquent letter to the Doge of Venice, to induce him to enter into a war against the Mussulmans. Some of the states of Italy united their forces to make an expedition into the East. A chronicle of the counts of Ason relates that a great number of Crusaders, clothed in white, with a red cross, marched out of Milan; and that a fleet, equipped by the sovereign pontiff, passed through the Archipelago, and surprised the city of Smyrna, in which the Crusaders were themselves quickly besieged by the Turks. The pope's legate and several knights perished in a sortie, which circumstance determined the sovereign pontiff to employ new efforts to revive a zeal for the crusade. It was at this period that the dauphin of Viennois, Humbert II., resolved to take the cross, and came to Avignon, to supplicate the pope to allow him to be the captain of the holy voyage against the Turks, and against the faithless vassals of the church of Rome. Humbert easily obtained all he asked, and returned to his states to make preparations for his expedition. He alienated his domains, he sold privileges to the nobility, and immunities to his cities; he levied considerable sums upon the Jews, and upon the Italian merchants established in the Viennois; he exacted a tribute from all his subjects who would not accompany him to the crusade, and having embarked, with a hundred men-at-arms, he went to seek in Asia either the fortune of a conqueror or the glory of a martyr. He found neither the one nor the other, and returned to Europe without renown and burdened with debts. History represents Humbert as a weak, inconstant and irresolute prince. He ruined himself, in the first place, by his dissipation, then by the expenses of the crusade; weary of the world and its affairs, he finished by abandoning to the crown of France his principality, which he had pledged to Philip of Valois, and retired to a monastery of Dominican Friars. In order to console him for not having conquered Egypt or any other country, the pope bestowed upon him the title of patriarch of Alexandria; and the king of France, to make him forget Dauphiny, named him archbishop of Rheims.

Such were the events and the consequences of the crusade occasioned in Europe by the arrival of Hugh of Lusignan, king of Cyprus. Some years having glided away, this prince came again to solicit the aid of the sovereign pontiff; at this period most of the sovereigns were in a state of war, and the pope not being able to do anything for the king of Cyprus, conceived the singular idea of naming him tribune of Rome. Hugh of Lusignan accepted this function, and died in Italy, without having been able to send any succour to the East.

War was not then the only scourge that ravaged the world; the horrors of the plague were added to the destruction of arms; this contagion which was called the black plague, and which took its rise upon the great level plain of Tartary, extended its devastations over all the countries of the East and West, and in a few years carried off more than thirteen millions of men. Historians have remarked that this scourge in its funeral march followed the footsteps of the merchants who brought into Europe the productions of India, and of the pilgrims who returned from Palestine.

As soon as pestilence had ceased its ravages, war resumed all its fury. The deplorable state in which discord had plunged Europe at that time, and particularly France, must have made people regret the periods when the preaching of a crusade imposed silence upon all passions and suspended all hostilities. The pope had several times undertaken to reëstablish peace: he at first addressed supplications to the English monarch; he afterwards threatened him with the thunders of the Church, but the voice of the father of the faithful was lost in the din of arms.

Philip of Valois died amidst the terrible struggle he had to maintain against England. The loss of the battle of Poictiers and the captivity of King John became the signal for the greatest troubles that afflicted the kingdom of France in the middle ages. The plots of the king of Navarre, the intrigues of the great, the disorders of the people, the fury of factions, the sanguinary scenes of the Jacquerie, spread terror and desolation in the capital and through the provinces. When France had completed the exhaustion of her treasures by paying the ransom of King John, the presence of her monarch was not able to restore to her the repose she required to repair her misfortunes. The soldiers of both nations, who were disbanded without pay, and who found themselves without an asylum, formed themselves into armed bands, and under the name of white companies, pervaded the kingdom, braving the orders of the king and the excommunications of the pope, and carrying wherever they went license, murder and devastation. All that had escaped the sword of the English, and the avidity of the collectors of the imposts, became the prey of these brigands, whose numbers increased in proportion with their impunity and their excesses. The fields remained uncultivated; all commercial pursuits were interrupted; and terror and misery reigned in the cities. Thus the suspension of hostilities had brought no relief to the evils of nations, and the disorders which broke out during the peace were more insupportable than those which had been endured during the war.

It was in these unfortunate circumstances that Peter, the son of Hugh of Lusignan, came, after the example of his father, to solicit the assistance of the Christian princes against the infidels, and caused Urban V. to adopt the project of a new crusade. Perhaps he hoped that the state of confusion in which France was plunged offered him a means of raising troops, and that he might turn against his enemies of the East, all the furies of war which desolated the kingdom.

Peter of Lusignan proposed to attack the power of the sultans of Cairo, whose dominions extended to Jerusalem. Christendom had at that time more redoubtable enemies among the Mussulman nations than the Mamelukes of Egypt. The Turks, who had become masters of Asia Minor, had recently passed the Hellespont, pushed their conquests as far as Mount Hemus, and placed the seat of their empire at Adrianople. That was the enemy that doubtless ought to have been attacked, but the Turks did not as yet inspire serious alarm, except in the countries they had invaded or menaced. At the court of Avignon, at which were assembled the king of Cyprus, the king of France, and the king of Denmark, there was no mention made of the invasion of Romania, or of the dangers of Constantinople, but of the loss of the Christian colonies in Syria, and of the captivity in which the city of Christ was still held.

Peter of Lusignan spoke with enthusiasm of the war against the infidels, and of the deliverance of the holy places; King John did not listen to him without emotion, and finished by forgetting his own misfortunes, to interest himself about those of the Christians beyond the seas. Waldemar III., king of Denmark, was equally affected by the discourse and the accounts of the king of Cyprus. The pope preached the crusade before the three monarchs: it was holy week; the remembrance of the sufferings of Christ appeared to add authority to the words of the pontiff, and when he deplored the misfortunes of Jerusalem, the princes who listened to him could not refrain from shedding tears, and swore to go and fight the Saracens.

We may, doubtless, believe that the king of France was led to take the cross by a sentiment of piety, and by the eloquence of the pope; but we must likewise suppose that the counsels of policy were not entirely foreign to this determination. The spirit of the holy war, if once really awakened, would necessarily go far to appease, if not extinguish, the discords and passions kindled by revolution and civil war. King John might entertain the hope of uniting under the standard of the crusade, and seducing to follow him beyond the seas, the *white companies*, over whom he could exercise no authority; and the sovereign pontiff was no less anxious to get rid of these bands of brigands, who braved his spiritual power, and threatened to make him a prisoner in Avignon.

Several great nobles, John of Artois, the count of Eu, the count Dammartin, the count de Tancarville, and Marshal Boucicault, followed the example of King John. The Cardinal Talleyrand de Périgord was named legate of the pope in the crusade. The king of Denmark promised to unite his forces with those of the French. To encourage his zeal, the sovereign pontiff gave him a fragment of the true cross, and several other relics, the sight of which would constantly remind him of the holy cause he had sworn to defend. Waldemar III. had come to the court of Avignon to place his kingdom under the protection of the Holy See; he took all the oaths required of him; but the bulls he obtained from Urban, as the price of his submission, had no efficacy in restoring peace to his dominions, and the troubles which followed his return soon made him forget his promises regarding the holy war.

The king of Cyprus, with most pressing recommendations from the pope, visited all the courts of Europe; the zeal and the chivalric eloquence of the hero of the cross were universally admired; but he derived nothing but vague promises from his enterprise, and received nothing but vain felicitations for a devotion which found no imitators.

The king of France was the only one of all the Christian princes who appeared to engage himself earnestly in the crusade. Urban V., however, showed but little confidence in the firmness of his resolution, as he felt it necessary to threaten with excommunication all who should seek to divert him from the holy enterprise. But all these precautions of the pope, with the example of the king and the indulgences of the crusade, were powerless in inducing the nation to take arms, or in persuading the *white companies* to *leave the chamber*, as they called the kingdom they desolated with their brigandages. The time fixed for the expedition was very near at hand, and nothing was ready; there was neither an army nor a fleet. It was at this period King John died in London, whither he had returned to offer himself as an hostage for the duke of Anjou, who had escaped from prison; and perhaps also to get rid of the cares of an enterprise which he had no means of executing or directing with success.

The pope trembled in Avignon, and was compelled to use his utmost efforts to free himself from these formidable bands, whose leaders styled themselves *the friends of God and the enemies of all the world*. History says that he employed in his contests with them the small quantity of money which had been raised for the crusade, and that this excited violent murmurs. In this state of things, Charles IV., emperor of Germany, in concert with the king of Hungary, proposed to take the companies into their pay, and send them against the Turks. If this project had been executed, we should have been able to join the name of Bertrand Duguesclin to the glorious names that adorn the pages of this history; the Breton hero was to have been the leader of the troops destined to contend with the Mussulmans on the banks of the Danube. The sovereign pontiff himself wrote several letters to him to induce him to take part in this crusade; but the project of Charles IV. was in the end abandoned, and Duguesclin led the white companies into Spain.

The king of Cyprus, however, had succeeded in enrolling under his banners a great number of adventurers of all sorts and conditions, men who were accustomed to live amidst perils, and who were attracted by the hope of pillaging the richest countries of the east. The republic of Venice did not disdain to take part in an expedition from which her commerce was likely to derive great advantages. Peter of Lusignan likewise received succours from the brave knights of Rhodes, and, on his return to the isle of Cyprus, he embarked at the head of ten thousand men to realize his projects of conquests over the infidels. The Crusaders, to whom the pope sent a legate, went to attack Alexandria, which they found almost without defence. When the place had fallen into their power, the king of Cyprus wished that they should fortify themselves in it, and there await the armies of Cairo; but his soldiers and allies could not resist their inclination to plunder a flourishing city, and fearing to be surprised by the Mamelukes, they set fire to Alexandria, and abandoned it on the fourth day after the conquest. Without subduing the Mussulmans, they irritated them. After the precipitate departure of the Crusaders, the Egyptian people, listening to nothing but hatred and vengeance, indulged in all sorts of violence against the unfortunate Christians who dwelt in Egypt. By the orders of the sultan of Cairo, everything was seized that belonged to the Venetians; and the Mamelukes, having prepared a fleet, threatened, in their turn, to make descents upon the isles of Rhodes and Cyprus. Again the nations of the West were applied to; the pope intreated all Christian princes to take arms against the infidels; but not one of them would assume the cross, and the king of Cyprus was left alone, to fight out the war he had provoked.

To the ardour for crusades, in the minds of European warriors, had succeeded a passion for distinguishing and enriching themselves by chivalric enterprizes and adventurous expeditions, in which, however, some remembrances of the holy wars were always mingled. The Genoese having formed the project of making war upon the coasts of Barbary, whose piratical inhabitants infested the Mediterranean, demanded a leader and troops of the king of France. On the report alone of such an enterprize, a crowd of warriors, eager to signalize their bravery, issued from all the provinces; the count d'Auvergne, the sieur de Coucy, Guy de la Trimouille, and Messire Jean de Vienne, admiral of France, solicited the honour of combating the infidels in Africa; fourteen hundred knights and nobles, under the orders of the duke of Bourbon, repaired to Genoa, and embarked on board the fleet of that republic; the French and the Genoese, the first led by a desire for booty and the love of glory, the latter by the more positive interests of their commerce, went to this war beyond the sea as to a banquet. "Beautiful and pleasant," says Froissart, "was it to behold the order of their departure, and how those banners, pennons, and streamers, fairly and richly wrought with the arms of the noble knights, floated to the wind and glistened in the sun; and to hear those trumpets and clarions sound and resound, and other musicians performing their parts, with pipes, flutes, and macaires, as well as the sound and the voice which issued from them, reverberate over all the sea." After a few days' sailing, the Christian army arrived on the coast of Barbary, and laid siege to the city of *Africa*. The inhabitants offered some resistance, and not being able to conceive why they were thus attacked by an enemy they did not know, and of whom they had never heard, they sent deputies to the camp of the Christians to demand of them what motive had brought them beneath their walls. The Genoese, doubtless, reminded the deputies of the piracies carried on in the Mediterranean and upon the coasts of Italy; but the knights could not allege any grievance, and must have felt considerably embarrassed how to answer the questions of the besieged. Froissart, who gives an account of this expedition, informs us that the duke of Bourbon called a council of the principal leaders, and after they had deliberated upon the question proposed by the Saracens, he addressed this reply to them, which we shall report in the old language as near that of the times as we are able: "They who demand why war is made against them, must know that their lineage and race put to death and crucified the son of God named Jesus Christ, and that we wish to avenge upon them this fact and evil deed. Further, they do not believe in the holy baptism, nor in the Virgin Mary, the mother of Jesus Christ; and all these things being considered is why we hold the Saracens and all their sect as enemies." The besieged were not likely to be convinced by this explanation, "so," adds the good Froissart, "they only laughed at it, and said it was neither reasonable nor proved, for it was the Jews who put Christ to death, and not they."

The French knights had more bravery than knowledge, and were much more expert in fighting than in reasoning. They prosecuted the siege and made several assaults, but in all their attacks met with a determined resistance. They were, however, persuaded that Heaven declared in their favour, and performed miracles to assure them the victory. It was said in the camp, that a battalion of ladies in white had appeared amidst the combatants, and created great terror among the Saracens. They likewise told of a miraculous dog which God had sent to the Christian soldiers as a vigilant sentinel, and which had several times prevented their being surprised by the Mussulmans. We repeat these marvellous stories, in order to exhibit the spirit of the knights, who saw nothing but ladies under circumstances in which the early Crusaders would have seen saints and angels. The story of the miraculous dog serves to prove that the French warriors kept but a bad watch around their camp, and that they carried on the siege with more bravery than prudence. Several battles were fought, in which the most rash lost their lives. The heat of the climate and the season gave birth to contagious diseases. In proportion as obstacles multiplied around them, the ardour of the besiegers inclined daily towards depression. Discord, likewise, broke out in the Christian army, in which the French and the Genoese mutually reproached each other with their miseries: winter was drawing near, and they despaired of reducing the place; the duke of Bourbon resolved to raise the siege, and to return to Europe with his knights and soldiers.

During several months no news of this expedition had arrived in France; processions were made and public prayers were put up in all the provinces to ask of Heaven the safe return of the Crusaders. Old chronicles inform us, — "that the lady of Coucy, the lady of Sully, the dauphiness of Auvergne, and all the ladies of France whose lords and husbands were engaged in this voyage, were in great dismay for them whilst the voyage lasted; and when the news came to them that they had already passed the sea, they were all much rejoiced."

This expedition, which the Genoese had promoted with the intention of defending their commerce against the brigandages of pirates, only served to increase the evil they wished to remedy; vengeance, indignation, and fear armed the infidels against the Christians in every direction. Vessels issued from all the coasts of Africa, covered the Mediterranean, and intercepted the communications with Europe; the merchandizes which had been accustomed to flow from Damascus, Cairo, and Alexandria, no longer appeared; and the historians of the times deplore, as a calamity, the impossibility of procuring spices in either France or Germany.

The war which had begun between Egypt and the kingdom of Cyprus was prosecuted with equal animosity on both sides. Whilst the sultan of Cairo threatened the poor remains of the Christian colonies of the East, the king of Cyprus and the knights of Rhodes spread terror along all the coasts of Syria; in one incursion they took possession of Tripoli, and gave the city up to the flames. Tortosa, Laodicea, and Belinas met with the same fate: this manner of making war in a country that they professed to wish to conquer for the sake of delivering it, excited everywhere the fury of the Mussulmans, without raising the hopes or the courage of the Christians who dwelt there. Pilgrimage to the Holy Land became impracticable, and, during several years, no European Christians were able to visit Jerusalem.

The sultan of Egypt, however, after many fruitless efforts to avenge the expedition against Alexandria, made peace with the king of Cyprus and the knights of Rhodes. It was agreed that the prisoners should be liberated on both sides, and that the king of Cyprus should receive half of the dues levied upon the merchandize which entered at Tyre, Berouth, Sidon, Alexandria, Jerusalem, and Damascus. The treaty regulated the tribute which pilgrims should pay in those places of the Holy Land to which their devotion called them. The sultan of Egypt restored to the knights of St. John the house they had formerly possessed in Jerusalem, and the knights had permission to cause the churches of the holy sepulchres of Bethlehem, of Nazareth, &c. to be repaired.

Europe at this period turned its eyes from countries which had so long excited its veneration and enthusiasm to direct them towards regions invaded or threatened by the Turks. We have seen, towards the end of the eleventh century, hordes from this nation spread themselves as conquerors over the whole of Asia. It may be remembered that it was their invasion of Palestine, and their violent domination over the holy city, which roused Christendom, and provoked the first crusade. Their power, which then extended as far as Nice, and which, even at that time, alarmed the Greeks, was checked by the victorious armies of the West. The Turks of whom we are now speaking, and of whom Christendom, towards the end of the fourteenth century, began to be very much in dread, like those who had preceded them, drew their origin from the Tartars. Their warlike tribes, formerly established in Carismia, had been driven thence by the successors of Gengiskhan; and the remains of this conquering nation, after ravaging

Syria and Mesopotamia, came, a few years before the first crusade of St. Louis, to seek an asylum in Asia Minor.

The weakness of the Greeks and the division of the Mussulman princes enabled them to conquer several provinces, and to found a new state among the ruins of several empires. The terror inspired by their fierce and brutal valour facilitated their progress, and opened for them the road to Greece. Countries which had been the cradle of civilization, of the arts, and of knowledge, soon succumbed beneath the laws of Ottoman despotism.

There can be no doubt that despotism, such as it was known then in Asia, and as it is seen in our days, is the most fragile of human institutions. The violent measures which it took to preserve itself, showed plainly that it itself felt a consciousness of its own fragility. When we see it immolate all the laws of nature to its own laws, hold the sword constantly suspended over all that approach it, and itself experience more fear than it inspires, we are tempted to believe that it has no veritable support. Whilst reading the oriental history of the middle ages, we are astonished to see all those empires which the genius of despotism raised in Asia, fall almost without resistance, and disappear from the scene of the world. But we must admit, when this monstrous government supports itself upon religious ideas, and upon the prejudices and passions of a great nation, it has also its popular ascendancy; it is also, to employ a mode of speaking very common at present, the expression of all its wills, and nothing can resist its action, or arrest the development of its power.

Thus arose the Ottoman empire, which had for its springs of action a hatred of the Christians, and the conquest of the Greek empire, and which sustained itself by the double fanaticism of religion and victory. The Turks had but two ideas, or rather two ever-acting passions, which with them supplied the place of patriotism,—to extend their dominions and propagate the Mussulman faith. The ambition which led the sovereign to conquer Christian provinces, was found to be that of the whole nation, accustomed to enrich themselves by all the violences of war, and who believed they obeyed the most sacred precept of the Koran, by exterminating the race of infidels. If the prince was unceasingly obliged to animate the religious enthusiasm and the warlike ardour of his subjects, the subjects, in their turn, kept the prince as constantly in exercise. The absolute leader of the Ottomans might commit all sorts of crimes with impunity; but he could not live long in a state of peace with his neighbours, without risking his authority and his life. The Turks could not endure either a pacific prince, or a prince unfortunate in war; so thoroughly were they persuaded that they ought to be always fighting, and that they ought always to conquer. The Ottoman people, to whom nothing was good or right but conquest, would obey none but a conqueror; and if they consented to be slaves, and tremble beneath the frown of a master, it was upon the sole condition that this all-powerful master should carry abroad the terror of his arms, and should give chains to other nations.

The Ottoman dynasty which began with the Turkish nation and gave its name to it, that dynasty, always the object of veneration, and respected by revolt itself, has presented by its stability a new spectacle in the East. It has exhibited to the world a succession of great princes, who have in history almost all the same physiognomy, and resemble each other in their pride, their ambition and their military genius: which proves that all these barbarian heroes were formed by their national manners, and that among the Turks, there is but one single road to greatness. We may judge what advantages this harmony between subjects and sovereign must have given to the Ottoman nation, in its wars against the Christians, or even against other Mussulman people.

Whilst the only defence of Europe consisted in feudal troops which were assembled at certain periods, and could not be held beneath their banners for any length of time together, the Ottomans were the only people who had a regular army always under arms. Their warriors, always animated by one same spirit, had moreover the advantage of discipline over the insubordinate chivalry of the Franks, who were constantly agitated by discord, and were put in action by a thousand different passions.

As the population of the Turks was not always sufficient for their armies, they forced each family of the countries they conquered to give up a fifth part of its male children for the military service. They thus levied a tribute upon the population of the Christians, and the sons of the effeminate Greeks became those invincible janissaries who were one day to besiege Byzantium, and destroy even the ruins of the empire of the Cæsars. Such were the new people who were about to place themselves between the East and the West, and engross all the attention of Christian Europe, until that time occupied with the deliverance of the holy places.

When we are acquainted with the power and the character of the Ottomans, we are astonished at seeing what remained of the Greek empire subsist a long time in their vicinity. We must here resume from a past period, the history of the feeble successors of Constantine, sometimes forming alliances with the Turks ready to plunder them, at others, imploring the assistance of the Latins, whom they hated, and seeking to awaken the spirit of the crusades whose consequences they dreaded.

At the period of the first invasions of Greece by the Turks, the emperor Andronicus sent an embassy to the Pope, to promise him to obey the Romish

Church, and to request of him apostolic legates, with an army capable of driving away the infidels and opening the route to the Holy Sepulchre. Cantacuzenes, who followed the example of Andronicus, said to the envoys from the sovereign pontiff: "I shall consider it my glory to serve Christendom; my states shall afford the Crusaders a free and safe passage; my troops, my vessels, my treasures shall be devoted to the common defence, and my fate will be worthy of envy if I obtain the crown of martyrdom." Clement VI., to whom Cantacuzenes addressed himself, died without having been able to interest the Christian warriors in the fate of Constantinople. A short time afterwards, the emperor buried himself in a cloister; and the brother *Josaphat Christodulus*, confounded among the monks of Mount Athos, troubled himself no longer with a crusade among the Latins.

Under the reign of John Palæologus, the progress of the Turks became more alarming. The emperor himself went to solicit the aid of the sovereign pontiff. After having, in a public ceremony, kissed the hands and feet of the pope, he acknowledged the double *procession* [69] of the Holy Ghost, and the supremacy of the Church of Rome. Touched by this humble submission, the pope protested he would come to the succour of the Greeks; but when he applied to the sovereigns of Europe, he could obtain nothing from them but vain promises. At the moment at which Palæologus was about to embark on his return to the East, he was arrested by his creditors, and remained thus during several months, without the pope or the princes he had come to solicit, and who had promised to assist him in the deliverance of his empire, making the least attempt to deliver him himself. Palæologus returned to Constantinople, to his divided family; and his subjects, who despised him, waited in vain for the performance of the promises of the pope and the European monarchs. In his despair, he at length formed the resolution of imploring the clemency of the sultan Amurath, and of purchasing by a tribute, permission to continue to reign over the wreck of his empire. He complained of this hard necessity to the pontiff of Rome, who caused a new crusade to be preached; but the Christian monarch beheld with indifference, a prince who had returned to the bosom of the Catholic Church, condemned to declare himself the vassal of infidels. The emperor of Byzantium and the head of the Church, by promising, the one, to arm the West in the cause of Greece, and the other, to subject the Greeks to the Roman Church, had formed engagements that they every day found it more difficult to fulfil. Whilst they were reciprocally upbraiding each other with not having kept their word, Amurath, who accomplished his threats better than the pope and the Christian princes did their promises, added new rigours to the fate of Palæologus, and interdicted even the repairing of the ramparts of his capital. Again the supplications to the sovereign were renewed, and again these supplications were passed on to the monarchs of Christendom; but they made no reply, or at most contented themselves with expressing pity for the emperor and people of Byzantium.

There is no doubt that the Greek emperors stood in great need of succour from the Latins, but this pusillanimous policy, which unceasingly invoked the assistance of other nations, only proclaimed the weakness of the empire, and necessarily deprived the Greeks, in the hour of peril, of all confidence in their own strength. On the other side, these cries of alarm, which constantly resounded throughout Europe, met with nothing but incredulous minds and indifferent hearts. It was in vain that the warriors of the West heard it for ever repeated that Constantinople was the barrier of Christendom; they could not consider a city which was unable to provide for its own defence, and was always in want of succour, as a barrier capable of arresting the course of a powerful enemy. When Gregory XI. solicited the emperor of Germany to assist Constantinople, that prince replied sharply that the Greeks had opened the gates of Europe to the Turks, and *let the wolf into the sheep-fold.*

At this time the miserable remains of the empire of the Cæsars was comprised within the extent of less than twenty leagues, and in this narrow space there was an empire of Byzantium, and an empire of Rodesto or Selivrea; the princes, whom ties of blood ought to have united, quarrelled with inveterate fury for the rags of the imperial purple. Brother was armed against brother, and father and son declared open war; all the crimes that had formerly been inspired by the ambition of obtaining the sceptre of the Roman world, were still committed for the advantage of reigning over a few miserable cities. Such was the empire of the East, upon which the Ottoman dominions continued on all sides to encroach.

At the period of which we are speaking, all the princes of the family of Palæologus having been commanded to repair to the court of Bajazet, obeyed his supreme order tremblingly; and if they came out safe and sound from the palace of the sultan, which was for them the den of the lion, it was because pity disarmed the executioner, and because the contempt they inspired among the Mussulmans was their safeguard. The Ottoman emperor contented himself with commanding Manuel, the son and successor of John Palæologus, not to deliver Constantinople up to him, but to remain shut up in it as in a prison, under the penalty of losing both his crown and his life.

Whilst the Greeks were thus trembling in the presence of the Turks, the janissaries passed through the straits of Thermopylæ without obstruction, and advanced into the Peloponnesus. On the other side, Bajazet, for whom the rapidity of his conquests procured the surname of *Iberim*, or *Lightning,* invaded the country of the Servians, afterwards that of the Bulgarians, and was preparing to carry the war into Hungary.

A deplorable schism then divided Christendom. Two popes shared the empire of the Church, and the European republic had no longer a head that could warn it of its dangers, an organ that could express its wishes and its fears, or a tie that could bind together its forces; religious opinions had no longer sufficient influence to bring about a crusade, and Christendom had nothing left to defend it but the spirit of chivalry, and the warlike character of some of the nations of Europe.

The ambassadors whom Manuel sent into the West, repeating the eternal lamentations of the Greeks over the barbarities of the Turks, solicited in vain the piety of the faithful. The envoys of Sigismund, king of Hungary, were more fortunate in their appeal to the bravery of the knights and barons of France. Charles VI. had not renounced, if the historians of the time may be believed, the idea of undertaking some great enterprise against the enemies of the true faith: "in order," says Froissart, "to free the souls of his predecessors, King Philip, of excellent memory, and King John, his grandfather." The Hungarian envoys took care to insinuate in their speeches, that the sultan of the Turks held Christian chivalry in contempt; nothing more was wanting to inflame the ardour of the French warriors; and when their monarch declared his intention of entering into the league against the infidels, every gallant knight in the kingdom flew to arms. This brave band was commanded by the duke de Nevers, son of the duke of Burgundy, a young prince whose rash courage afterwards procured for him the surname of Jean-sans-Peur (John the Fearless). Among other leaders were the count de la Marche, Henry and Philip de Bar, relations of the king of France, Philip of Artois, constable of the kingdom; John of Vienne, admiral; the sieur de Coucy, Guy de la Tremouille, and the marshal de Boucicault, whose name is mixed with the history of every war of his time.

All ideas of glory, all sentiments of religion and chivalry were bound up with this expedition. The leaders ruined themselves to make preparations for their voyage, and to astonish the East by their magnificence; the people implored the protection of Heaven for the success of their arms. The enterprise of the new Crusaders was already compared to that of Godfrey of Bouillon, and the poets of the times celebrated the near deliverance of the Holy Land.

The French army, in which were fourteen hundred knights and as many squires, traversed Germany, and was increased on its way by a crowd of warriors from Austria and Bavaria. When they arrived on the banks of the Danube, they found the entire nobility of Hungary and Bohemia under arms. Whilst reviewing the numerous soldiers thus assembled to oppose the Turks, Sigismund exclaimed with delight: "If heaven were to fall, the lances of the Christian army would stop it in its descent."

Never was a war begun under more happy auspices; not only had the spirit of chivalry drawn together a great number of warriors beneath the banners of the cross, but several maritime nations of Italy had taken up arms for the defence of their eastern commerce. A Venetian fleet, commanded by the noble Mocenigo, joined the vessels of the Greek emperor and of the knights of Rhodes near the mouth of the Danube, to procure the triumph of the standard of the Franks in the Hellespont, whilst the Christian army should march against Constantinople.

As soon as the signal for war was given, nothing could resist the impetuous valour of the Crusaders; they beat the Turks everywhere; they took several towns of Bulgaria and Servia, and laid siege to Nicopolis: happy had it been if these first advantages had not given them a blind confidence in victory!

The French knights, who were always found at the head of the Christian army, could not believe that Bajazet would dare to attack them; and when it was announced to them that the sultan, with his army, was drawing near, they chastised the bold scout who gave them the first intelligence of it. The Mussulman army, however, had crossed Mount Hemus, and was advancing towards Nicopolis. When the two armies were in presence of each other, Sigismund conjured his allies to moderate their warlike ardour, and to wait for a favourable opportunity of attacking an enemy with whom they were totally unacquainted. The duke de Nevers and the young nobles who accompanied him, listened with impatience to the advice of the Hungarians, and believed that they were desirous of disputing with them the honour of beginning the fight. Scarcely had the standard of the crescent [70] met their eyes, than they rushed out of the camp and fell upon the enemy; the Turks retreated, and appeared to fly; the French pursued them in a disorderly manner, and soon became separated from the Hungarian army. All at once, clouds of spahis and janissaries poured down from the neighbouring forests, in which they had been placed in ambush. All about the country, pikes had been planted to impede the march of cavalry. The French warriors being unable either to advance or retreat, and surrounded by an innumerable army, no longer fought to conquer, but to die with glory, and sell their lives dearly. After having, during several hours, carried slaughter into the enemy's ranks, all the French engaged in the conflict either perished by the swords of the Mussulmans, or were made prisoners.

Bajazet, after this first victory, directed all his forces against the Hungarian army, which terror had already seized, and which was dispersed at the first shock. Sigismund, who, on the morning of that day, had counted a hundred thousand men beneath his banners, threw himself into a fishing-boat, and coasting along the shores of the Euxine, found refuge in Constantinople, where his mere presence announced his defeat, and spread consternation.

Such were the fruits of the presumption and want of discipline of the French warriors. History has lamented their reverses more than it has blamed their conduct; it has satisfied itself with saying, that in order to conquer the Turks, the Hungarians should have shown the valour of the French, or the French should have imitated the prudence of the Hungarians.

Bajazet, who was wounded in the battle, proved barbarous after victory. Some historians have said that the sultan had to avenge the death of many Mussulman captives, who had been massacred by the Christian army. He commanded all the prisoners, many of whom were wounded and plundered of their clothes, to be brought before him, and then gave order to his janissaries to slaughter them before his eyes. Three thousand French warriors were immolated to his vengeance; but he spared the duke de Nevers, the count de la Marche, the sieur de Coucy, Philip of Artois, the count de Bar, Marshal Boucicault, and some other leaders, on account of the ransom he hoped to procure for them.

When fame carried the news of so great a disaster into France, the first who spoke of it were threatened with being thrown into the Seine: many were imprisoned in the châtelet of Paris by the king's orders. At length the most sinister reports were confirmed by the account of messire de Hély, whom Bajazet sent into France to announce the defeat of the Christians and the captivity of their leaders. This intelligence spread desolation through both the court of Charles VI. and the kingdom of France. Froissart adds, in his natural style, "that the high dames of France were much enraged, and had good cause, for this affected their hearts too closely."

In order to mitigate the wrath of the Turkish emperor, Charles VI. sent him magnificent presents. Messengers passing through Hungary and the territory of Constantinople, bore to the sultan white falcons from Norway, fine scarlet cloths, white and red linens from Rheims, *draps de hautes-lices*, or tapestries, worked at Arras, in Picardy, representing the history of Alexander, "which thing," add contemporary chronicles, "was very agreeable to all persons of worth and honour to look upon." At the court of France means could not be devised for sending into Turkey the money required for the liberation of the princes and nobles detained in the prisons of Bajazet. A banker of Paris performed that which no sovereign of Europe could then have done; in concert with some merchants of Genoa, he negotiated for the ransom of the prisoners, and undertook to pay for this ransom the sum agreed upon, of two hundred thousand ducats.

The noble captives, whom the sultan had dragged in his train as far as Brusa, at length were allowed to return to Europe. Of the number, all regained their native country, with the exception of two: Guy of Tremouille died in the isle of Rhodes. The lady de Coucy, who was incapable of consolation, sent a faithful knight among the Turks, to learn the fate of her husband, and the knight returned with the fatal intelligence that the sieur de Coucy had died in his prison.

When the duke de Nevers, with his companions in misfortune, quitted the camp of Bajazet, the sultan addressed the following words to him, as reported by Froissart:—"Count de Nevers, I know right well and am informed that thou art in thine own country a great lord, and the son of a great lord. Thou art young; thou mayest, perchance, take as an injury that requires vengeance that which has befallen thee in thy first chivalry, and wouldst willingly, to recover thy honour, assemble forces to come and give me battle; if I suspected this, and if it were my will, I would make thee swear upon thy faith and upon the law that thou shouldst never arm thyself against me, nor any of those that are in thy company; but no, I will neither require thee nor them to take this oath; but I wish to tell thee that if, when thou shalt have returned, it may please thee to assemble a power to come against me, thou wilt find me always ready and prepared for both thee and thy people."

This speech, which exhibited all the Ottoman pride, must, without doubt, have been a lesson for young warriors, whose mad presumption had brought on all the evils of the war. They despised Bajazet before their defeat; and his haughty disdain after victory could not appear in their eyes a vain bravado. "So," says Froissart, "they remembered it well as long as they lived."

On their return to France, the noble knights were received with the interest that unfortunate bravery inspires. The court of Charles VI. and that of Burgundy were never tired of hearing them recount their exploits, their tragical adventures, and the miseries of their captivity; they told wonders of the magnificence of Bajazet; and when they repeated the speeches of the sultan, who was accustomed to *say that he would be lord over all the world, that he would yet come to Rome, and make his horse eat his oats on the altar of St. Peter;* when they spoke of the armies which the emperor raised daily to accomplish his menaces, what fear must, doubtless, have been mixed in the minds of his auditors with feelings of curiosity and surprise.

The accounts of the duke de Nevers and his companions awakened, however, the emulation of the warriors, and their misfortunes in Asia inspired less compassion than a desire to avenge their defeat. A new expedition against the Turks was soon announced in France, and a crowd of young nobles and knights eagerly took up arms. The duke of Orleans, the brother of the king, was inconsolable at not being able to obtain permission to place himself at their head, and go with them to combat the infidels. It was the Marshal Boucicault, scarcely returned from captivity, who led these new Crusaders into the East. Their arrival on the shores of the Bosphorus delivered Byzantium, which was then besieged by Bajazet. Their exploits raised the courage of the Greeks, and redeemed the honour of the soldiers of the West among the Turks. When, after a year of labours and glorious combats, they returned to their own country, the Greek emperor Manuel believed he saw fresh evils ready to overwhelm him, and he resolved to follow Marshal Boucicault and solicit more assistance from Charles VI.; thus placing all the hopes of his empire in the French warriors. He was received with great honours on his passage through Italy; when he had crossed the Alps, brilliant festivities awaited him in all the great cities. At two leagues from Paris he found Charles VI., who, with all his nobles, had come out to meet him. He made his public entry into the capital, clothed in a robe of white silk, and mounted on a white horse, marks of supreme rank among the Franks. It was gratifying to see a successor of the Cæsars imploring the arms of chivalry; and the confidence which he placed in the bravery of the French, flattered the pride of the nation; but in the condition of France at that period, it was much more easy to offer Manuel the spectacle of tournaments, and the brilliant ceremonies of courts, than to furnish him with the treasures and armies of which he stood in need. Charles VI. began to feel the approach of that fatal malady which left the field open to factions, and threw the kingdom into the greatest misfortunes. England, whose assistance the emperor of Constantinople likewise solicited, was disturbed by the usurpation of Henry of Lancaster; and if the English monarch then took the cross, it was less with the intention of succouring the Greeks than to divert attention from his own injustice, and to have a pretext for levying imposts upon his people. At the same time, the deposition of Winceslaus set the whole German empire in motion; and the nascent heresy of John Huss already gave the signal for the disorders that were destined to trouble Bohemia during the fifteenth century. Amidst all these agitations in Christendom, the only power that could have reëstablished harmony was itself divided, and the Catholic Church, still a prey to the rival pretensions of two pontiffs, could neither give its attention to promote peace among the Christians, nor war against the Turks.

This state of France and Europe completely destroyed all the hopes of the Greek emperor. After passing two years in Paris, without obtaining anything, he determined to leave the West, and having embarked at Venice, he stopped in the Peloponnesus, where he waited patiently till Fortune should herself take charge of the entire ruin or the deliverance of his empire.

This deliverance, which could no longer be expected from the Christian powers, arrived all at once by means of a people still more barbarous than the Turks, whose conquests made the entire East tremble. Tamerlane, or Timour, from the bosom of civil wars, had been elevated to the throne of the Moguls, and revived in the north of Asia the formidable empire of Gengishan. History is scarcely able to follow this new conqueror in his gigantic expeditions. The imagination is terrified at the rapidity with which, to make use of an expression of Timour himself, he carried "the destroying wind of desolation" from Zagathaï to the Indus, and from the Indus to the icy deserts of Siberia. Such was the scourge that Heaven sent to destroy the menacing pride of Bajazet. The historians of the times are not agreed as to the motives which armed the leader of the Moguls against the Ottoman emperor; some attribute Tamerlane's determination to the complaints of the Mussulman princes of Asia Minor, whom the sultan of the Turks had driven from their states; others, faithful to the spirit of their age, and seeking the causes of great events in celestial phenomena, explain the invasion of the Tartars by the appearance of a comet, which was visible during two months to affrighted Asia. Disdaining marvellous explanations, we will confine ourselves to saying that peace could not last between two men urged on by the same ambition, and who were not likely to pardon each other for having at the same time entertained the thought of conquering the world. Their character, as well as their policy, is plainly enough indicated in the violent threats they reciprocally addressed to each other before hostilities, and which became the signal for the most sanguinary catastrophes.

Tamerlane, having set out from Samarcand, first reduced Seborto, and as if he wished to give Bajazet, before he attacked him, the spectacle of the ravages which accompanied his arms everywhere, he all at once directed the course of his Tartar hordes towards Syria and the provinces governed by the Mamelukes of Egypt. The valour of his soldiers, the discords of his enemies, the treachery and perfidy which he never disdained to call in to the assistance of his power, opened for him the gates of Aleppo, Damascus, and Tripoli. Torrents of blood and pyramids of human heads marked the passage of the Mogul conqueror. His approach spread terror everywhere, as well among the Christians as among the Mussulmans; and although he boasted in his discourses of avenging the cause of the oppressed, Jerusalem might, on this occasion, be grateful that he did not think of delivering her.

At length the Tartars advanced towards Asia Minor. Timour traversed Anatolia with an army of eight hundred thousand men. Bajazet, who raised the siege of Constantinople to come to meet his redoubtable adversary, encountered him in the plains of Ancyra. At the end of a battle which lasted three days, the Ottoman emperor lost at once his empire and his liberty. The Greeks, to whom fame soon brought the news of this victory, tremblingly returned thanks to their fierce liberator; but the indifference with which he received their embassy, proved that he had had no intention of meriting their gratitude. Arrived on the shores of the Bosphorus, the conqueror of Bajazet directed his looks and his projects towards the West; but the master of the vast kingdoms of Asia had not a single barque in which to transport himself to the other side of the canal. Thus Constantinople, after having escaped the yoke of the Ottomans, had the good fortune to escape also the presence of the Tartars, and Europe saw this violent tempest dissipate itself at a distance from her.

The conqueror vented his anger upon the city of Smyrna, which was defended by the Knights of Rhodes. This city was carried by assault, delivered up to pillage, and reduced to ashes; the Mogul emperor returned to Samarcand in triumph, dragging the sultan Bajazet in his train, and meditating by turns the conquest of Africa, the invasion of the West, and a war against China.

After the battle of Ancyra, several princes of the family of Bajazet disputed the ravaged provinces of the Ottoman empire. If the Franks had then appeared in the Strait of Galliopoli and in Thrace, they might have profited by the defeat and discords of the Turks, and have driven them back beyond the Taurus; but the indifference of the Christian states, with the perfidy and cupidity of some of the maritime nations of Europe, allowed the Ottoman dynasty time and means to renovate its depressed power.

The Greeks derived no more advantage from the victory of Tamerlane than the Latins. Twenty years after the battle of Ancyra, the Ottomans had retaken all their provinces; their armies again environed Constantinople, and it is at this point we may apply to the power of the Turks the oriental comparison of that serpent of the desert which an elephant had crushed in its passage, which joins its dispersed rings together again, raises its head by degrees, reseizes the prey it had abandoned, and clasps it within its monstrous folds.

As long as the Greek emperors were in no fear for the safety of their capital, they kept up very little intercourse with the Christian princes of Europe; but upon the appearance of danger, the court of Byzantium renewed its supplications and its promises of obedience to the Church of

Rome. A conversation of Manuel, reported by Phrantza, throws a light upon the situation of the Greeks, and upon the policy of the timid successors of Constantine. "The only resource we have left against the Turks," said this prince to his son, "is their fear of our union with the Latins, and the terror with which the warlike nations of the West inspire them. Whenever you are pressed by the infidels, send to the court of Rome, and prolong the negotiations, without ever taking a decisive part." Manuel added, that the vanity of the Latins and the obstinacy of the Greeks would always prevent any real or durable harmony; and that a union of any kind with the pope, by arousing the passions of both parties, would only give Byzantium up to the mercy of the barbarians.

Such counsels, which announce but little frankness in the policy of the Greeks, could not be long followed up with success. The dangers became more pressing, the circumstances more imperative; as Christendom only replied to vain negotiations by vain promises, the successor of Manuel found himself obliged to give pledges of his faith and sincerity. The idea of a council was at length adopted, in which the two churches should come to an understanding, and should approximate. The emperor John Palæologus and the doctors of the Greek Church repaired to Ferrara, and afterwards to Florence. After long debates, the union was sworn to on both sides, and solemnly proclaimed. In the West this event was celebrated as a victory; at Constantinople it raised cries of blasphemy, apostasy, and impiety. Thus was the prediction of Manuel accomplished; all the efforts employed to unite opinions, only served to raise a new barrier between the Greeks and the Latins.

At the councils of Ferrara and Florence, the deputies of the Armenians, the Maronites, the Jacobites of Syria and Egypt, the Nestorians, and the Ethiopians submitted, as well as the Greeks, to the pontifical authority, and without doubt also, in the same hope of being succoured by the Latins, and delivered from the tyranny of the Mussulmans. This solemn proceeding was less a submission to the Holy See than a homage rendered to the bravery of the Franks, in whom all the Christians of Asia and Africa beheld liberators.

Pope Eugenius, however, on receiving the submission of the Greeks, had promised to send succours to Constantinople and to the Christians of the East. The pontiff hoped that the union of the two churches and the preaching of a crusade would fix upon him the eyes of the Christian world, and restore to the pontifical authority the confidence and power of which the schisms of the West and the seditious decrees of the council of Bâle had deprived it. He wrote to all the princes of Christendom, exhorting them to unite to put a stop to the invasions of the Mussulmans. Eugenius, in his letter, described all the evils which the faithful suffered in the countries under the domination of the barbarians. "The Turks tied troops of men and women together, and dragged them along in their train. All the Christians whom they condemned to slavery, were confounded with the vilest booty, and sold like beasts of burden. In their barbarity, they separated the son from the father, the brother from the sister, and the husband from the wife. Those whom age or infirmities prevented from walking were killed upon the high roads or in the middle of cities. Even infancy could not excite their pity; they put to death innocent victims that had scarcely begun to exist, and who, being yet ignorant of fear, smiled upon their executioners whilst receiving the mortal blow. Every Christian family was compelled to give up its own sons to the Ottoman empire, in the same manner as the people of Athens had been formerly forced to send as a tribute the flower of their youth to the monster of Crete. Wherever the Turks had penetrated, the fields were cursed with barrenness, and the cities were without laws or industry; the Christian religion had no longer either priests or altars; humanity no longer either support or asylum." In fact, the father of the faithful forgot none of the cruelties committed by the enemies of Christ; he could not restrain the sadness which so many painful images caused him, and conjured princes and nations to send assistance to the kingdom of Cyprus, the isle of Rhodes, and particularly to Constantinople, as these were the last bulwarks of the West.

The exhortations of the sovereign pontiff were addressed to none but indifferent hearts in the nations of England, France, and Spain. Neither the sentiment of humanity, nor that of patriotism, had power to revive the enthusiasm to which the spirit of religion and chivalry had in past times given birth. Distant crusades, whatever was their object, began to be considered as only the work of a jealous policy, the springs of which were set in motion, to banish the princes and nobles whose power and wealth were coveted. In the state in which Europe then was, such as loved war, had but too many opportunities for exercising their bravery, without quitting their homes. The Germans, who had set on foot forty thousand men to combat the heretics of Bohemia, remained motionless, when the Turks were represented to them as ready to carry the standard of Islamism to the extremities of the West.

The pope, however, was not satisfied with exhorting the faithful to take up arms, he was desirous of setting them the example; the pontiff levied soldiers and equipped vessels to make war against the Turks. The maritime cities of Flanders, and the republics of Genoa and Venice, which had great interests in the East, made some preparations; their fleets united under the standard of St. Peter, and directed their course towards the Hellespont. The fear of an approaching invasion awakened the zeal of the nations inhabiting the shores of the Dneister and the Danube. The crusade was preached in the diets of Poland and Hungary. Upon the frontiers threatened by the barbarians, the people, the clergy, and the nobility obeyed the voice of religion and patriotism.

The sovereign pontiff named, as legate with the Crusaders, Cardinal Julian, a prelate of an intrepid character of an ardent genius, arming himself by turns with the sword of fight and with that of speech; as redoubtable in the field of battle as in the learned contests of the schools. After having obtained the confidence of the council of Bâle, Cardinal Julian distinguished himself in the council of Florence, by defending the dogmas of the Latin church. His eloquence had roused up all Germany against the Hussites; now he burned to rouse up all Christendom against the Turks. The army collected under the banners of the cross had for leaders Hunniades and Ladislaus; the first, the waywode of Transylvania, was celebrated among Christian warriors, and the epithet of the *brigand*, which the Turks attached to his name, denoted the hatred and terror he inspired among the infidels. Upon the head of Ladislaus were united the two crowns of Poland and Hungary, and he merited, by the brilliant qualities of his youth, the love of both Poles and Hungarians. The Crusaders assembled on the Danube, and quickly received the signal for war. The fleets of the sovereign pontiff, of Venice, and Genoa cruised in the Hellespont. The inhabitants of Moldavia, Servia, and Greece promised to join the Christian army; the sultan of Caramania, the implacable enemy of the Ottomans, was to attack them in Asia. The Greek emperor, John Palæologus, announced great preparations, and got ready to march at the head of an army to meet his liberators.

Hunniades and Ladislaus advanced as far as Sophia, the capital of the Bulgarians. Two battles opened for them the passages of Mount Hemus and the road to Byzantium. The rigours of winter alone arrested the victorious march of the Christian warriors; and the army of the Crusaders returned into Hungary, to await the favourable season for renewing the war. They returned to Buda in triumph, amidst the acclamations of an immense population. The clergy celebrated, by hymns and thanksgivings, the first victories of the Christians, and Ladislaus repaired, barefooted, to the church of Notre Dame, in which he hung up the standards taken from the infidels.

Before the beginning of the war, the Mussulmans had been persuaded that the destruction of the Christians was written in the book of destiny. "When all the enemies of the prophet," said they among themselves, "shall be destroyed, each of us will have nothing to do but to guide his plough, and look at his war-horse in his stable." This opinion, the offspring of pride and victory, had proved sufficient to relax the zeal of the Ottoman warriors; and most of them remained in their homes, whilst the Christians marched towards Adrianopolis.

When fame informed them of the victories of the Franks upon the Danube, this blind security all at once gave place to fear. The sultan Amurath immediately sent ambassadors to sue for peace. History is silent as to the means of seduction employed by the Ottoman envoys to win the victorious Crusaders; but it is well known that they succeeded in obtaining a favourable hearing for their proposals. Peace was determined upon in the council of the leaders of the Christian army. The parties swore, the one upon the Koran, and the other upon the Gospel, to a truce of ten years. This unexpected resolution irritated the pride and zeal of Cardinal Julian, whose mission was to stimulate the Christians to war. When he saw the leaders of the crusade unite in a desire for peace, he preserved a haughty silence, and refused to sign a treaty he disapproved of. The inflexible legate waited for an opportunity in which he might give vent to his discontent, and force the Crusaders to resume their arms. This opportunity was not long in presenting itself.

Amurath, satisfied with having restored peace to his states, and fatigued with earthly grandeur, renounced the cares of empire, and buried himself in a retreat at Magnesia. The sultan of Caramania informed the Christians that their most redoubtable enemy *had lost his senses*, and had just exchanged the imperial crown for the cap of a cenobite. He added that Amurath had left the supreme authority in the hands of a child, and in his message compared this child *to a young plant which the slightest wind might tear up by the roots*.

The same sultan was so thoroughly persuaded that the Ottoman empire was in its decline, that he entered Anatolia at the head of an army. About the same time reports were spread that the emperor of Constantinople was advancing towards Thrace; that the Greeks of the Peloponnesus had taken up arms, and that the confederate fleets still awaited a fresh signal for war in the Hellespont. Another circumstance, not less important, seemed calculated to awaken the warlike ardour of the Crusaders; the victory gained near Sophia had given them a powerful ally in Greece. In this battle, the son of John Castuct, who commanded the van of the Ottoman army, suddenly abandoned the banners and the religion of the Turks, to defend the worship and the heritage of his ancestors in Albania. The messengers of Scanderberg announced to the leaders of the Christian army, that he was ready to join them at the head of twenty thousand Albanians, assembled under the standard of the cross.

All these news, arriving at once, had an immediate effect in changing men's minds as well as the face of affairs. A fresh council was called; Cardinal Julian arose among the leaders, and reproached them with having betrayed both their fortune and their glory; he reproached them in severe terms, with having signed a disgraceful peace, which was sacrilegious, fatal to Europe, and fatal to the Church. "You had sworn," said he, "to combat the eternal enemies of Christendom, and now you have sworn upon the Gospel, to lay down your arms. To which of these two oaths will you be faithful? You have just thought proper to conclude a treaty with the Mussulmans; but have you not also treaties with your allies? Will you abandon these generous allies at the moment that they are flying from all parts to your assistance, and are coming to share the perils of a war in which God has so visibly protected your first labours?

"But, what do I say? You not only abandon your allies, you leave, without support and without hope, that crowd of Christians whom you have promised to deliver from an insupportable yoke, and who must now remain a prey to all the outrages of the Mussulmans whom your victories have irritated. The groans of so many victims will pursue you into your retreat, and will accuse you before God and before men.

"You close for ever the gates of Asia against the Christian phalanxes, and you restore to the Mussulmans the hopes they had lost of invading the countries of Christendom. To what interests, answer me, have you sacrificed your own glory and the safety of the Christian world? Had not war already given you all that the sultan Amurath promises? Would he not have already given you still more; and do not the pledges obtained by victory inspire more confidence than the promises of infidels?

"What shall I say to the sovereign pontiff who has sent me to you, not to treat with Mussulmans, but to drive them beyond the seas? What shall I say to all the pastors of the Christian Churches, and to all the faithful of the West, who are now offering up prayers to Heaven for the success of your arms?

"There is no doubt that the barbarians, whom we have twice conquered, would never have consented to a peace, if they had had the means of carrying on the war. Do you believe they will observe the truce, when fortune shall become more favourable to them? No; Christian warriors cannot remain bound by an impious compact which gives up the Church and Europe to the disciples of Mahomet. Learn that there is no peace between God and his enemies, between truth and falsehood, between Heaven and Hell. There is no necessity for me to absolve you from an oath evidently contrary to religion and morality, to all that which constitutes, among men, the sanctity and faith of promises. I exhort you then, in the name of God, in the name of the Gospel, to resume your arms and follow me in the road of salvation and glory."

The safety of Christendom may, no doubt, be pleaded in extenuation of the violence of this discourse; but impartial history, whatever may be the reasons alleged, cannot approve of this open violation of the faith of oaths. The leaders of the crusade might merit the reproaches of the apostolic legate, who accused them of having made a peace disgraceful in itself and dangerous to Christian Europe; but they certainly also deserve the contempt of posterity for violating treaties they had so recently concluded. When Cardinal Julian began to speak, the minds of his auditors were already wavering; when he had finished his discourse, the warlike ardour which animated him seized upon the whole assembly, and manifested itself by the loud acclamations of a general approbation. With one unanimous voice they all swore to recommence the war, on the same spot where they had just sworn to maintain peace.

The enthusiasm of most of the leaders was at its height it scarcely allowed them to observe that they had lost half their army. A great number of the Crusaders had quitted their colours, some impatient to return to their homes, but by far the greater part dissatisfied with a treaty, which rendered their bravery and their exploits useless. The prince of Servia, a near neighbour of the Turks, and in dread of their vengeance, did not dare to run the risk of a new war, and sent no troops to the army of Hunniades and Ladislaus. They waited in vain for the reinforcements promised by Skanderberg, who was obliged to defend Albania. There remained not more than twenty thousand men under the banners of the cross. A chief of the Wallachians, on joining the Crusaders with his cavalry, could not refrain from expressing his surprise to the king of Hungary, at the smallness of his numbers; and told him that the sultan they were going to contend with, was frequently followed to the chase by more slaves than the Christian warriors amounted to.

The principal leaders were advised to defer the commencement of the war till the arrival of fresh Crusaders, or the return of those that had left them; but Ladislaus, Hunniades, and particularly Julian, were persuaded that God protected the defenders of the cross, and that nothing could resist them. They set forward on their march, and crossing the deserts of Bulgaria, encamped at Warna, on the shores of the Black Sea.

It was there the Crusaders, instead of finding the fleet which was to second them, learned that Amurath had left his retreat at Magnesia, and was hastening to meet them at the head of sixty thousand combatants. At this intelligence all the extravagant confidence infused by the Cardinal Julian faded away, and in their despair they accused the Greeks of having betrayed or abandoned them; and the Genoese, with the nephew of the Pope, who commanded the Christian fleet, of having yielded the passage of Galliopoli to the Turks. This accusation is repeated in all the chronicles of the West; but the Turkish historians make no mention of it; they, on the contrary, say that Amurath crossed the Hellespont at a considerable distance from the places occupied by the Christian fleet; and that the grand vizier, who was upon the European shore, protected the passage of the Ottoman army by a battery of cannon. "As soon as the troops of Amurath," adds the Turkish historian Coggia Effendi, "gained the shore, they offered up prayers and thanks to the God of Mahomet, *and the zephyr of victory breathed upon the Mussulman banners.*" The sultan pursued his march, swearing by the prophets of Islamism, to punish its enemies for the violation of treaties. If some authors may be believed, the emperor of the Turks supplicated Jesus Christ himself to avenge the outrage committed upon his name by the perjured warriors. At the approach of the Ottomans, Hunniades and the legate advised retreat; but retreat became impossible, and Ladislaus determined to conquer or die. The battle began: and it was then, says the Ottoman historian, "that an infinite number of valiant men were borne to the valley of shadows by torrents of blood." At the commencement of the battle both the right and left wings of the Mussulman army were broken. Some authors say that Amurath thought of flying, and that he was stopped by a janissary, who retained him by the bridle of his horse; others celebrate the firm courage of the sultan, and compare him to a rock which resists all the blasts of the tempest. Coggia Effendi, whom we have already quoted, adds that the Ottoman emperor addressed, upon the field of battle, a prayer to the God of Mahomet, and conjured him with tears to remove from the Mussulmans the bitter cup of contempt and affliction.

Fortune appeared to favour the arms of the Crusaders. A great part of the Ottoman army fled before twenty-four thousand Christian soldiers, and nothing could resist the impetuous courage of the king of Hungary. A crowd of prelates and bishops, armed with cuirasses and swords, accompanied Ladislaus, and intreated him to direct his attacks towards the point at which Amurath still fought, defended by the bravest of his janissaries. He listened but too willingly to their imprudent advice, and having rushed among the enemy's battalions, he was instantly pierced by a thousand lances, and fell with all who had been able to follow him. His head, fixed upon the point of a lance, and shown to the Hungarians, spread consternation through their ranks. It was in vain Hunniades and the bishops endeavoured to revive the courage of the Crusaders, by telling them they were not fighting for an earthly king, but for Jesus Christ; the whole Christian army disbanded, and fled in the greatest disorder. Hunniades himself was carried away with the rest: ten thousand soldiers of the cross lost their lives, and the Turks made a great number of prisoners. Cardinal Julian perished either in the battle or the flight.

After his victory, Amurath traversed the field of battle; and as he observed he did not see among the Christian bodies one with a gray beard, his vizier replied that men arrived at the age of reason would never have attempted such a rash enterprize. These words were nothing more than a piece of flattery addressed to the sultan; but they might, nevertheless, serve to characterize a war in which the leaders of the Christian armies obeyed rather the impulses of the imprudent passions of youth, than the cooler dictates of experience and matured age.

The expeditions of the Christians against the Turks began almost all, like this, by brilliant successes, and finished by great disasters. Most frequently a crusade was terminated at the first or the second battle, because the Crusaders had only valour, and were totally deficient in qualities which could improve a victory or repair reverses. When conquerors, they quarrelled for the glory of the fight or the spoils of the enemy; when conquered, they were at once depressed and discouraged, and returned to their homes, accusing each other reciprocally of their defeats.

The battle of Warna secured to the Turks the European provinces they had invaded, and permitted them to make fresh conquests. Amurath, after having triumphed over his enemies, again renounced the imperial crown, and the solitude of Magnesia once more beheld the conqueror of the Hungarians clothed in the humble mantle of a hermit; but the janissaries, whom he had so often led to victory, would not permit him to renounce the world or enjoy the repose he was so anxious for. Forced to resume the command of armies and the reins of empire, he directed his views against Albania; and he afterwards returned to fight with Hunniades on the shores of the Danube. He passed the remainder of his days in making war against the Christians, and with his last breath recommended his successor to direct his arms against Constantinople.

Mahomet II., to whom Amurath bequeathed the conquest of Byzantium, did not succeed his father till six years after the battle of Warna. It was then that began the days of mourning and calamity for the Greeks; and it is at this period that history offers us, as a spectacle, a last and terrible conflict; on the one side, an old empire whose glory had filled the universe, and which had no defence or limits left but the ramparts of its capital; and on the other, a new empire, the name of which was scarcely known, and which already threatened the whole world with invasion.

Constantine and Mahomet, elevated almost at the same time,—the one to the throne of Otman, the other to that of the Cæsars, presented no less difference in their characters than in their destinies. The moderation and piety of Constantine were admired, and historians have celebrated his calm and prudent valour in the field of battle, with his heroic patience in reverses. Mahomet brought to the throne an active and enterprising spirit, an ardent and passionate policy, and an indomitable pride. It is asserted that he loved letters and the arts; but these peaceful pursuits were not able to soften his savage ferocity. In war, he neither spared the lives of his enemies nor of his soldiers; and the violences of his character often ensanguined even peace. Whilst in Constantine a monarch could be recognized brought up in the school of Christianity, in Mahomet was as easily known a prince formed by the warlike and intolerant maxims of the Koran. The last of the Cæsars had all the virtues that can honour and teach the endurance of a great misfortune. The son of Amurath exhibited the dark qualities of a conqueror, with all the passions which, in the day of victory, must leave nothing but despair to the vanquished.

When Mahomet succeeded to the empire, his first thought was the conquest of Byzantium. In the negotiations which preceded the rupture of the peace, Constantine did not conceal the weakness of the Greek empire, and displayed all the resignation of a Christian. "My confidence is in God," said he to the Ottoman prince; "if it should please him to soften your heart, I shall rejoice at that happy change; if it should please him to deliver up Constantinople to you, I shall submit to his will without a murmur."

The siege of Byzantium was fixed to begin in the spring of the year 1453; and the Greeks and the Turks passed the winter in preparation for the defence and the attack. Mahomet entered with ardour upon an enterprise to which, for a length of time, all the wishes of the Turkish nation and all the Ottoman policy has been directed. In the middle of a night, having sent for his vizier: "Thou seest," said Mahomet, "the disorder of my couch. I have carried to it the trouble which agitates and devours me; henceforth there will be neither repose nor sleep for me but in the capital of the Greeks."

Whilst Mahomet was getting together all his forces to commence the war, Constantine Palæologus implored assistance from the nations of Europe. Cries of alarm had so often been heard from Constantinople, that some regarded the dangers of the Greek empire as imaginary, and others, its ruin as inevitable. In vain Constantine promised, as all his predecessors had done, to unite the Greek Church with the Roman Church; the remembrance of so many promises, made in the hour of peril and forgotten in times of safety, added to the antipathy of the Latins for the people of Greece. The Pope exhorted feebly the warriors of the West to take arms, and satisfied himself with sending to the Greek emperor a legate and some ecclesiastics versed in the art of argumentation and in the study of theology. Although the Cardinal Isidore brought with him a considerable treasure, and had in his suite some Italian soldiers, his arrival at Constantinople must have spread discouragement among the Greeks, who expected other succours, and appeared to have attached a very high value to their submission to the Church of Rome.

The princes of the Morea and the Archipelago, with those of Hungary and Bulgaria, some, in dread of being themselves attacked, the others, restrained by indifference or the spirit of jealousy, refused to take any part in a war in which victory would decide their own fate. As Genoa and Venice had counting-houses and commercial establishments at Constantinople, two thousand Genoese soldiers and five or six hundred Venetians presented themselves to assist in defending the city. A troop of Catalans also arrived, an intrepid soldiery, by turns the scourge and hope of Greece, whom a love of war and peril brought to the imperial city. And this was all that was to represent warlike Europe at the siege of Byzantium.

At this period, several Christian powers were at war with each other: the continuator of Baronius remarks on this subject, that the soldiers who then perished in battles fought in the bosom of Christendom, would have been sufficient to disperse the Turks, and drive them back to the outward verge of Asia. But if history, on this occasion, accuses the nations of the West of indifference, what ought it to say of that of the Greeks for their own defence? The efforts of Constantine to unite the two Churches had weakened the confidence and zeal of his subjects, who prided themselves upon being orthodox. Among the Greeks, some, in order to owe nothing to the Latins, declared that God himself had undertaken to save his people, and upon the faith of some prophecies they had made, they awaited in inaction a miraculous deliverance. Others, more dark in their scholastic reveries, were not willing that Constantinople should be saved, because they had predicted that the empire must perish to expiate the crime of the union. Every hope of victory had in their eyes something impious and contrary to the will of Heaven. When the emperor spoke of the means of safety that still remained, and of the necessity for taking arms, these atrabilarious doctors drew back with a kind of horror, and the multitude they had misled ran after the monk Genadius, who, from the depth of his cell, cried out constantly to the people, that there was nothing to be done, and that all was lost.

When we study the whimsicalities of the human mind, that which most affects the enlightened observer is, to see there are men whose passion is words, whom self-love attaches to vain subtleties, and for whom the ruin of the world would be a less painful spectacle than the triumph of an opinion they have opposed. On the eve of the greatest perils, Constantinople was filled with people whom hatred for the Latins made forgetful of even the approach and menaces of the Turks. The grand duke Notares went so far as to say that he would like better to see in Byzantium the turban of Mahomet than the tiara of the pontiff of Rome.

It is not useless to remind our readers here, that in all these debates there was no question that affected the truths of Christianity,—nothing but some points of ecclesiastical discipline: celebrating the mass in the Latin tongue, consecrating unleavened bread, mixing some cold water in the chalice, communicating with Azymites—these were things that were to be hated, things that were to be feared much more than Islamism. Such were the motives for which the Greeks repulsed the Franks, their natural allies, loaded them with anathemas, and invoked the maledictions of Heaven upon their own city.

Amidst these deplorable disputes the voice of patriotism was never listened to, and indifference, selfishness, and cowardice were able to conceal themselves under the respectable appearance of religion and orthodoxy. A great part of the population of Constantinople had abandoned the city; among those that remained, the richest had buried their treasures, which they might have employed in the general defence, and which they soon lost, with their liberty and their lives. The imperial city only contained within its bosom four thousand nine hundred and seventy defenders, and the emperor was obliged to plunder the churches to support them. Thus, from eight to nine thousand combatants formed the entire garrison of Byzantium, and the last hope of the empire of the East.

Mahomet had completed his immense preparations. As the conquest of Byzantium and the pillage of Constantinople were the richest recompense that could be offered to the valour of the Ottomans, all the soldiers were, in some sort, associated with the ambition of their leader. The warlike ardour and fanaticism which had distinguished the companions of Omar and the first champions of Islamism were now revived. From all the regions which extend from the chain of Taurus to the banks of the Ebro and the Danube came crowds of warriors, attracted to the army by the hopes of booty or the desire of distinguishing themselves in a religious and national war. In order at once to give a clear idea of the decay and weakness of the Greeks, and of the strength and power of the Ottomans, it will suffice to say, that Constantinople and all that remained of the territory of the empire contained a smaller number of inhabitants of all kinds than Mahomet mustered soldiers beneath his banners.

The Ottoman army set out from Adrianople at the beginning of March; and on the sixth of April Mahomet pitched his tent before the gate of St. Romanus. The signal for battle was speedily given on both sides. In the early days of the siege, the Greeks and the Turks displayed all that the art of war had invented or perfected among the ancients and moderns. Among his formidable preparations, Mahomet had not neglected artillery, the use of which was then spread through the West. One of his cannons, founded under his own eyes at Adrianople, was of such gigantic proportions, that three hundred oxen dragged it along with difficulty, and it launched a ball of seven hundred quintals (seven hundred pounds weight) to a distance of more than six hundred toises (six hundred fathoms). Almost all the historians of the time speak of this terrible instrument of war, but say very little of the effect it produced in the field of battle. On examining with care the accounts of contemporaries, and particularly the descriptions they have left us of these enormous machines of bronze, which they had so much trouble to move, we feel persuaded that at the siege of Byzantium the Ottoman artillery inspired more fright and surprise than it did execution. The Turks showed very little skill or zeal in seconding the Frank engineers and artillerymen whom Mahomet had taken into his service; and it was a great blessing for Christendom that so powerful a discovery was not perfected at once in the hands of barbarians, whom Europe could not have resisted if they had joined this new force to the advantages they already possessed in war.

The Turks employed other arms and other means of attack with much more success; such as mines dug under the ramparts, rolling towers, which were brought close up to the walls, rams which battered the walls, balistæ, which launched beams and stones, arrows, javelins, and even the Greek fire, which still rivalled gunpowder, although the latter was destined soon to make it neglected and forgotten. All these means of destruction were employed at the same time, and assaults were renewed unceasingly. The besieged could not avail themselves of all their machines, from the want of hands to work them; and when we reflect on the smallness of the number of the defenders of Constantinople, we are astonished that they were able to resist, for more than fifty days, the innumerable host of the Ottomans. This generous soldiery occupied a line of more than a league in length, repelling, night and day, the assaults of the enemy, repairing the breaches in the walls, and making sorties; they appeared to be everywhere at the same time, and to be equal to everything, animated by the presence of their leaders, and particularly by the example of Constantine. Several times fortune favoured the efforts of this heroic troop, and tingled a few gleams of hope with the sentiment of sadness and terror which prevailed in Constantinople. The besieged preserved one advantage, the city was inaccessible towards the Propontis and on the side of the port. Mahomet had assembled a numerous fleet in the canal of the Black Sea; but it only served for the transmission of provisions and warlike stores. The Ottoman marine could not contend with the marine of the Greeks, particularly with that of the Franks; and the Turks themselves acknowledged that they must yield the empire of the seas to the Christian nations.

About the middle of the siege, five vessels from the coasts of Italy and Greece arrived in the canal. The whole Ottoman fleet was immediately in motion, and advanced to meet them; from their numbers they surrounded them, and attacked them several times, with the view of getting possession of them, or of turning them from their course. Mahomet encouraged the combatants with voice and gesture from the shore. When the Ottomans appeared to be failing in their attempt, he could not restrain his anger; urging his horse into the sea, he seemed to threaten the elements, and, like a barbarian king of antiquity, to accuse the waves of being obstacles to his conquests. On the other side, the Greeks, collected on the ramparts of the city, awaited the issue of the combat in great anxiety. At length, after an obstinate and bloody conflict, all the Turkish ships were dispersed or cast upon the shore; and the Christian fleet, laden with provisions and soldiers, sailed in triumph into the port of Constantinople.

The sultan burned to avenge this disgrace to his arms, and resolved to make a last effort to render himself master of the port of Constantinople. As the entrance of it was guarded by several large vessels, and closed by a chain of iron that could neither be broken nor passed, the Ottoman monarch employed an extraordinary method, which the besieged had not foreseen, and the success of which displayed the force of his will and the extent of his power. In a single night, between seventy and eighty vessels, which were at anchor in the canal of the Black Sea, were transported by land to the gulf of Ceras. The road was covered with planks, plastered with grease, along which a multitude of soldiers and workmen made the vessels slide. The Turkish fleet, commanded by pilots, with sails unfurled, as if upon a maritime expedition, advanced over a hilly country, and traversed a space of two miles by the light of torches and flambeaux, to the sound of clarions and trumpets, without the Genoese, who inhabited Galata, daring to offer any opposition to its passage. The Greeks, fully occupied in guarding their ramparts, had no suspicion of the designs of the enemy. They could not comprehend what could be the cause or the object of all the tumult that was heard during the whole night from the seashore, until the dawn of day showed them the Mussulman standards floating in their port.

We naturally here inquire what resistance was made by the vessels which guarded the iron chain, and by those which had entered the port, after having dispersed the Ottoman fleet. We may suppose that every warrior who had fought in the Christian ships was then employed in defending the ramparts of the city; or, it is probable, that the part of the gulf in which the Turkish ships descended, was not deep enough to be accessible to large vessels. However this may have been, the Mussulmans lost no time in taking advantage of their success. Scarcely were the Turkish boats launched, when a multitude of workmen were busily engaged in constructing floating batteries on the same spot where the Venetians made their last assault in the fifth crusade.

This bold enterprise, carried out with such audacity and success, spread trouble and consternation among the besieged. They made several attempts to burn the fleet and destroy the works the enemy had begun; but they in vain had recourse to the Greek fire, which had so often saved Constantinople from the attacks of the barbarians. Forty of their most intrepid warriors, betrayed by their imprudent valour, and perhaps also by the Genoese, fell into the hands of the Turks, and a death amidst tortures was the reward of their generous devotion.

Constantine used reprisals, and exposed the heads of seventy of his captives upon the ramparts. This mode of making war announced that the combatants no longer listened to anything but the inspirations of despair or the furies of vengeance. The Mussulmans, who daily received supplies of all kinds, prosecuted the siege without intermission. The certainty of victory redoubled their ardour; Constantinople was assaulted on several sides at once, and the garrison, already weakened by the conflicts and labours of a long siege, were obliged to divide their forces to defend all the points attacked.

The repairs of the fortifications on the side of the port had been neglected. Towards the west, several of the towers, particularly that of St. Romanus, were falling into ruins. In this almost desperate situation, what was, if possible, still more deplorable, the garrison of Byzantium was possessed by the spirit of discord. Violent debates arose between the grand duke Notares and Justiniani, who commanded the Genoese troops. The Venetians and the Genoese were several times on the point of coming to blows; and yet history can scarcely point out the subjects of these unfortunate quarrels. Such was the blindness produced by the spirit of jealousy, or rather by despair, that in this chosen band of warriors, who were every day sacrificing their lives in the noble cause they had embraced, it was not uncommon to hear mutual accusations of cowardice and treachery.

Constantine endeavoured to appease them; and himself, always calm in the midst of discord, appeared to be actuated by no other feeling than a love of country and a thirst for glory. The character he exhibited when surrounded by dangers, ought to have procured him the confidence and the affection of the people; but the turbulent and seditious spirit of the Greeks, and the vanity of their disputes would not permit them to appreciate true greatness. They reproached Palæologus with misfortunes which were not his work, and which his virtue alone could have repaired. They accused him of completing the ruin of an empire which all the world abandoned, and which he alone was willing to defend. They not only no longer respected the authority or the intentions of the prince; but every one who was exalted either by rank or character, became an object of reprobation or mistrust. By a consequence of that restless spirit which, in public disorders, urges the multitude to seek obscure supports, certain predictions, fully credited by the people, announced that the city of the Cæsars could only be saved by a miserable mendicant, in whose hand God would place the sword of his wrath.

As the day of their great calamities approached, the congregations of the churches proportionately increased. The image of the holy Virgin, the patroness of Constantinople, was solemnly exhibited, and carried in procession through the streets. These pious ceremonies, doubtless, presented something edifying, but they did not inspire the bravery necessary for the defence of a country and a religion in extreme danger; and Heaven, amidst the perils of war, did not listen to the prayers of an unarmed trembling people.

During the siege, capitulation had been several times spoken of. Mahomet required that the capital of an empire, of which he already possessed all the provinces, should be given up to him, and he would permit the Greeks to retire with their treasures. Palæologus was willing to consent to pay a tribute, but he would not give up Constantinople. At length, in a last message, the sultan threatened to immolate the Greek emperor with his family, and scatter his captive people throughout the earth, if he persisted in defending the city. Mahomet offered his enemy a principality in the Peloponnesus; Constantine rejected this proposition, and preferred a glorious death. From that moment peace was no more mentioned, and Byzantium was left to the chances of an implacable war.

The sultan announced to the army an approaching general assault: the wealth of Constantinople, the captives, the Greek women, were to be the rewards of the valour of the soldiers; he for himself, only reserved the city and the edifices. To add religious enthusiasm to that of war, dervises pervaded the ranks of the Ottoman army, exhorting the soldiers to purify their bodies by ablutions, and their souls by prayer; and promising the delights of paradise to the defenders of the Mussulman faith. At the end of the day, great fires, lighted by the orders of the sultan, spread a lurid splendour over all the shores of the sea, from the point of Galata to the Golden Gate. The Ottoman emperor then appeared in the midst of his army, promising again the plunder of Byzantium to his soldiers; and, to render his promise more solemn, he swore to it *by the soul of Amurath, by four thousand prophets, by his children, and lastly by his cimeter.* The whole army burst forth in exclamations of joy, and repeated several times: *God is God, and Mahomet is the messenger of God.* When this warlike ceremony was finished, the sultan ordered, under pain of death, that profound silence should be observed throughout the camp; and from that moment nothing was to be heard around Constantinople but the confused tumult of an army in which everything was in motion, preparing for a terrible and decisive combat.

In the city, the garrison kept watch upon the ramparts, and observed with anxiety the movements of the Ottoman army. They had heard with affright the noisy exclamations of the Turks; but the sudden silence which followed them redoubled their alarm. The light from the enemy's fires was reflected from the summits of the towers and from the domes of the churches, and rendered the darkness which covered the city more awful. Constantinople, in which the labours of industry and all the ordinary cares of life were suspended, was plunged in a profound calm, which, however, afforded neither sleep nor repose to any one; it was the dismal aspect of a city which some great scourge has rendered desolate. Only around the temples some few plaintive sounds were heard, imploring with the voice of prayer the mercy of heaven. Already might the words of the Persian poet be applied to that unfortunate city, which the conqueror repeated on the morrow in the pride of his triumph: *The spider silently spins his web beneath the roofs of the palaces, and the bird of darkness utters his mournful cries upon the towers of Efrasiab.*

Constantine called together the principal leaders of the garrison to deliberate upon the dangers which threatened the empire. In a pathetic discourse, he endeavoured to revive the courage and the hopes of his companions in arms; speaking to the Greeks of patriotism, and to the Latin auxiliaries of religion and humanity, he exhorted them all to have patience, but above all to preserve concord. The warriors who were present at this last council, listened to the emperor in melancholy silence; they did not dare to interrogate each other upon the means of defence, which all knew to be useless. They embraced each other with tears, and returned to the ramparts, filled with the most sinister forebodings.

The emperor entered the church of St. Sophia, where he received the sacrament of the communion; the sadness which was observable on his countenance, the pious humility with which he solicited forgetfulness of injuries, pardon for his faults, the touching words which he addressed to the people, which resembled eternal adieus, redoubled the general consternation. The sun of the last day of the Roman empire arose: it was the 29th of May; the signal for assault was given to the Turkish army before dawn: the multitude of Mussulman soldiers rushed towards the walls of the city. The attack was made at the same time on the side of the port, and near the gate of St. Romanus. In the first charge, the assailants everywhere met with a firm resistance; the Catalans and the Genoese did all that the courage of Franks could effect. Palæologus fought at the head of the Greeks, and the sight alone of the imperial banner filled the Ottoman soldiers with terror. Three hundred archers from the isle of Crete, sustained gloriously the ancient renown of the Cretans for their skill with the bow. Among this brave band it is but just to point out Cardinal Isidorus, who had caused the fortifications he was charged to protect to be repaired at his own expense, and who fought till the end of the siege, at the head of the soldiers he had brought from Italy. History likewise owes great praise to the monks of St. Basil, who had no doubt adopted the party of the union, and whose valour and glorious death expiated the blind and fatal obstinacy of the Byzantine clergy.

The historian Phrantza compares the close ranks of the Mussulmans to an extended tightened cord, which might have been placed round the city. The towers which defended the gate St. Romanus crumbled away beneath the blows of the rams and the discharges of the Ottoman artillery. The exterior walls were carried; the dead and the founded, confounded with the ruins, filled up the ditches. And yet upon this horrible field of battle the defenders of Byzantium fought still; nothing could weary their constancy nothing could shake their courage.

After two hours of frightful conflict, Mahomet advanced with his chosen troops and ten thousand janissaries. He appeared in the midst of them, with his mace in his hand, like the angel of destruction; his threatening looks animated the ardour of his soldiers, and he pointed out to them by his gestures the points that were to be attacked. Behind the battalions he led, a troop of those men whom despotism charges with the execution of its vengeance, punished or constrained all who wished to fly, and forced them forward to the carnage. The dust which arose from the steps of the combatants, with the smoke of the artillery, covered both the army and the city. The clang of the trumpets, the crash of the ruins, the explosion of the cannons, and the shock of arms completely drowned the voices of the leaders. The janissaries fought in disorder; and Constantine, who had remarked it, was exhorting his soldiers to make one last effort, when the aspect of the fight became all at once changed. Justinian having been struck by an arrow, the pain of the wound was so intense as to force him to quit the field of battle. The Genoese and most of the Latin auxiliaries followed his example. The Greeks, left alone, are soon overwhelmed by numbers; the Turks pass the ramparts, get possession of the towers, and break open the gates. Constantine fought still; but soon, covered with wounds, he fell among the heap of dead, and Constantinople was without a head and without defenders.

What a spectacle is that of an empire which has but one moment of existence left, and which is about to finish amidst the furies of war, and beneath the sword of barbarians! All at once every tie of society is broken; religion, patriotism, nature have no longer laws that can be invoked; even wisdom and experience can yield none but useless counsels. All the ascendancy and splendour of virtue, genius, or even valour, have no longer power to distinguish or protect the citizens. Those magnificent palaces which constituted the pride of princes, nobody possesses them now. Among all the numerous edifices of a great capital, no one can find an asylum or an abode. The city has no longer warriors or magistrates, nobles or plebeians, poor or rich; the whole population is but a troop of slaves, who await with terror the presence of an irritated master. Such was Constantinople at the moment the conquerors were preparing to enter it.

When some of those who had defended the ramparts retreated into the city, announcing the coming of the Turks, they could not obtain belief; when the Turkish battalions came pouring in, the people, says the Greek historian Ducas, "were half dead with fear, and could scarcely breathe." The multitude rushed about the streets, without knowing whither to go, and uttering piercing cries. Women, children, and old people flocked to the churches, as if the altars of Christ could prove an asylum against the savage disciples of Mahomet!

It is not our task to describe the disasters which followed the taking of Constantinople. The massacre of the unarmed inhabitants, the city given up to pillage, holy places profaned, virgins and matrons overwhelmed with outrages, an entire population loaded with chains; such are the horrible pictures that are to be found in the annals of the Turks, the Greeks, and the Latins. Such was the fate of that city which frequent revolutions had covered with ruins, and which became at length the ridicule and the prey of a nation it had long despised. If there be anything consolatory amidst so many distressing scenes, it is the virtue of Constantine, [71] who would not survive his country, and whose death was the last glory of the empire of the East. [72]

When we consider the weakness of the Greek empire and the power of its enemies, we are astonished it was able to resist so long. The Ottomans were governed by all the passions which favour conquests; the Greeks had not one of the qualities which are useful in defence: to be convinced of this, we have but to see how the two nations acted. When Mahomet proclaimed his enterprise, the Ottomans flocked to his army from all parts of his empire; whilst at the first report of the siege, a great part of the population of Constantinople deserted the city. We have seen that the dervises encouraged the Mussulman soldiers, and held up to them the war against the Greeks as a holy war. The Greek priests, on the contrary, discouraged the defenders of Byzantium, and were not far from considering the resistance of Constantine as a sacrilegious action. During the assaults made upon the imperial city, the Turkish soldiers, to fill up the ditches, cast into them their tents and their baggage, preferring victory to all they possessed. It is well known that at the same time the richest Greeks were employed in burying their wealth, preferring treasures to patriotism. We could add other remarkable features, but these quite sufficiently show on which side the strength was. What most strongly foretold the ruin of Byzantium, was the small degree of confidence the Greeks had in the duration of their empire. Never did the ancient Romans more clearly show the power and ascendancy of their patriotism, than when they designated Rome, the *eternal city*. Constantinople saw the number of its defenders diminish, and their courage became weaker, in proportion with the facility with which the sinister predictions of its approaching ruin found credit among the people.

When Byzantium, at the beginning of the thirteenth century, fell into the hands of the Latins, the empire still possessed great means of defence, and yet twenty thousand Crusaders achieved the conquest of it; which places the valour of the Franks much above that of the Turks. This would perhaps be the best place to examine what was the influence of the crusades over the destiny of the empire of the East. In the first expedition of the Latins, Asia Minor was delivered from the Turks, who were already masters of Nice, and threatened Constantinople; but the Crusaders sold the services they had rendered at too high a price: on the one part, violence, on the other, perfidy, disturbed the harmony that ought to have subsisted between the Greeks and the Latins. At length the taking of Constantinople by the Franks was a mortal blow to the empire of Byzantium. Amidst the war, schism became enlarged by hatred; and schism, in its turn, doubled the reciprocal hatred. This division favoured the progress of the Turks, and opened the gates of Constantinople to them.

What is most unfortunate in the conquest of the Ottomans is, that they preserved nothing, not even the name of Byzantium. The barbarians who overthrew the empire of the West, adopted the religion and manners of the conquered nations; which, by degrees, caused the traces of invasion and conquest to disappear. The Turks, on the contrary, were resolved to make the Koran triumph wherever they carried their arms. As soon as they were masters of Constantinople, the altars of Christ were overturned, and everything changed with religion. The city of Constantine became more widely than ever separated from Christendom; and as it was for the infidels the gate of the West, Christian Europe, which during nearly three centuries had sent its fleets and its armies into Asia, had reason at last to tremble for itself. From that period crusades took a new character, and were nothing but defensive wars.

BOOK XVII
A.D. 1453-1481

CRUSADES AGAINST THE TURKS

The West had heard of the dangers which threatened the Greek empire with indifference; but on learning the last triumph of the arms of Mahomet, all the Christian nations were seized with terror; and it was believed that the janissaries were already overturning the altars of the Gospel in the richest provinces of Germany. People trembled at the idea of one day hearing the Koran preached in the churches of Rome, changed into mosques. Murmurs arose on all sides against the Pope, Nicholas V., who was reproached with not having preached a crusade, to prevent the misfortune which all Christendom deplored. Assistance sent before the siege might, in fact, have saved Constantinople; but the city once in the power of the barbarians, the evil became irreparable. A union of all the Christian powers alone could wrest their conquests from the hands of the Turks, and against this union fresh obstacles arose daily.

In vain, to excite the West once more, the eloquence of Christian orators was addressed sometimes to the grief, and at others to the piety, of the faithful; in vain, by turns, the ascendancy of religious ideas and that of chivalry were employed: everybody deplored the progress of the Turks, but a blind resignation, or rather a cruel indifference, soon took place of the general consternation.

A short time after the taking of Constantinople, Philip the Good, duke of Burgundy, assembled at Lille, in Flanders, all the nobility of his states; and in a festival of which history has preserved a faithful account, he endeavoured to awaken the zeal and valour of the knights, by the spectacle of everything that could at that period affect their chivalric imagination. In the first place, a great number of pictures and curious scenes were exhibited to the spectators, among which were the labours of Hercules, the adventures of Jason and Medea, and the enchantments of Melusina. [73] After these, an elephant was led into the banquetting-hall by a Saracen giant; on the back of the elephant was a tower, from which issued a lady clothed in mourning, representing the Christian Church. The elephant having arrived in front of the table of the duke of Burgundy, the lady recited a long complaint, in verse, upon the evils with which she was afflicted; and addressing herself to the princes, dukes, and knights, she complained of their tardiness and their indifference in assisting her. Then appeared a herald-at-arms, who carried in his hand a pheasant, a bird which chivalry had adopted as the symbol and the prize of bravery. Two noble demoiselles, and several knights of the order of the Golden Fleece, approached the duke, and presented to him the bird of the brave, praying him to *hold them in remembrance*. Philip the Good, who knew, says Oliver de la Marche, with what intention he held this banquet, cast a look of compassion upon the Lady Holy Church, [74] and drew from his bosom a writing, which the herald-at-arms read with a loud voice. In this writing, the duke vowed *in the first place by God his Creator, and by the holy Virgin, and next by the ladies and the pheasant,* "that if it pleased the king of France to expose his body for the defence of the Christian faith, to resist the damnable enterprize of the Grand Turk, he would serve him with his person and his power in the said voyage, in the best manner that God would give him grace; if the said king committed this expedition to any prince of his blood, or other great lord, he swore to obey him; and if, on account of his great affairs, he was nut disposed to go or to send, and other potent princes would take the cross, he offered to accompany them as soon as he possibly could. If, during the holy voyage, he could by any means or manner learn or know that the said Grand Turk would be willing to meet him body to body, he, Philip, for the sake of the said Christian faith, would willingly fight with him, with the help of the all-powerful God, and of his very sweet Virgin Mother, whom he always called upon to aid him."

The Lady Holy Church thanked the duke for the zeal he showed for her defence. All the lords and knights who were present, invoked, in their turns, the names of God and the Virgin, without forgetting the ladies and the pheasant, and swore to consecrate their wealth and their lives to the service of Jesus Christ, *and of their very redoubtable lord the duke of Burgundy.* All expressed the most ardent enthusiasm. Some distinguished themselves by the whimsicality and the singularity of their promises. The count d'Etampes, nephew to Philip the Good, engaged himself to offer a *challenge to any of the great princes and lords of the Grand Turk's company,* and promised to fight them *body to body, two to two, three to three, four to four, five to five, &c.* The bastard of Burgundy swore to fight with a Turk in any manner he might please, and engaged to have his challenge sent to *the hostel of the Turk.* The lord of Pons swore never to sojourn in any city till he had met with a Saracen with whom he might fight body to body, by the help of our Lady, for the love of whom *he would never sleep in a bed on a Saturday,* before the entire accomplishment of his vow.

Another knight undertook, from the day of his departure, never to eat anything on a Friday that had been killed, until he had exchanged blows with one or many enemies of the faith; if the banner of his lord and that of the Saracens were unfurled as the signal for fight, he made a vow to go straight to the banner of the Grand Turk, and *to strike it to the earth, or die in attempting to do so.* [75] The seigneur de Toulongeon, on his arrival in the country of the infidels, vowed to challenge one of the men-at-arms of the Grand Turk, and fight him in the presence of his lord, the duke of Burgundy; or if the Saracen were not willing to come, he proposed to go and fight him in the presence of the Grand Turk, *provided he might have good assurance of safety.*

All these promises, which were never accomplished, serve at least to show us the spirit and the manners of chivalry. The simple confidence which the knights had in their arms, proves how little they were acquainted with the enemies against whom they declared war in this fashion. [76]

When each one had pronounced his vows, a lady clothed in white, bearing upon her back this inscription in letters of gold, — *Grace-Dieu*, came and saluted the assembly, and presented twelve ladies with twelve knights. These ladies personated twelve virtues or qualities, the name of which each wore upon her shoulder:—Faith, Charity, Justice, Reason, Prudence, Temperance, Strength, Truth, Bounty (largesse), Diligence, Hope, Valour,— such were the chivalric virtues that were to preside over the crusade.

After this ceremony, says the chronicler we have quoted, the ladies *began to dance like mummers, and to give themselves up to gaiety, in order to carry on the festival more joyously.*

The details of this chivalric feast make us perceive a great change in the spirit and the manners of Europe. When we call to our minds the Council of Clermont, the preachings of Peter the Hermit and of St. Bernard, with the grave enthusiasm and the austere devotion which presided at the taking of the oaths of the early Crusaders; and when we afterwards behold the brilliant solemnities of chivalry, the half-profane and half-religious promises of the knights, in short, all the worldly spectacles amidst which a holy war was proclaimed, we can fancy ourselves transported not only into another age, but amongst new nations. The religion which had precipitated the West upon Asia had no longer an empire, unless the ladies were its interpreters. It was less piety, or the desire of obtaining heavenly crowns, than the sentiment of gallantry with which they were animated in tournaments, that brought knights beneath the standard of the cross.

We likewise know that this kind of preaching produced only a transient effect upon the minds of the warriors; and that they had not any influence whatever upon the multitude. This observation must convince us of one truth, which is, that the most active and powerful motive among men will always be the spirit of religion, and that no other motive, emanating from human passions, could have excited the world like that which produced and kept up the crusades.

Some pious men, however, made incredible efforts to revive the spirit of the early times of the holy wars. John Capistran, a monk of St. Francis, and Æneas Sylvius, bishop of Sienna, neglected no means that they thought would inflame the minds of the people, and reanimate religious enthusiasm. The first, who passed for a saint, travelled through the cities of Germany and Hungary, describing to the assemblies of the people, the perils of the faith, and the threats of the wicked. The second, one of the most enlightened bishops of his age, versed in Greek and Latin literature, an orator and a poet, exhorted princes to take up arms to keep off invasion from their own states, and save the Christian republic from approaching destruction.

Æneas Sylvius wrote to the sovereign pontiff, and endeavoured to rouse his zeal by telling him, that the loss of Constantinople would weaken his credit and tarnish his name, if he did not use every effort to destroy the power of the Turks. The pious orator repaired to Rome, and preached the crusade in a consistory; and to show the necessity for a holy war, he quoted by turns, before the pope and cardinals, the authority of Greek philosophers, and that of fathers of the Church. He deplored the captivity of Jerusalem, the cradle of Christianity; and the slavery of Greece, the mother of the sciences and the arts. Æneas celebrated the heroic courage of the Germans, the noble devotion of the French, the generous pride of the Spaniards, and the love of glory which animated the nations of Italy. The king of Hungary, whose kingdom was threatened by Mahomet, was present at this assembly. The orator of the crusade, pointing out this monarch to the sovereign pontiff and the prelates, conjured them to have pity on his tears.

Frederick III., emperor of Germany, at the same time wrote to Pope Nicholas V., to implore him to save Christendom. "The words that issue from the mouth of man cannot give an idea of the calamity the Catholic Church has just experienced, or make known the ferocity of the people who are now desolating Greece, and who menace the West." The emperor pressed the pope to unite all the Christian powers against this formidable enemy; announcing that he himself was about to convoke the princes and states of Germany. The pope applauded the intentions of the emperor, and legates were sent to the diets of Ratisbon and Frankfort. Æneas Sylvius again preached the crusade against the Turks in these two assemblies. The duke of Burgundy, who was present at both, renewed, in the presence of the princes and states of the German empire, the vow he had made *to God, to the*

Blessed Virgin, to the ladies, and to the pheasant. Hungarian deputies came to announce that the banks of the Danube and the frontiers of Germany were about to be invaded by the Turks, if Christians did not hasten, in all parts, to take up arms to repel them.

The diet decreed that ten thousand horse and thirty thousand foot should be sent against the Turks; but as nothing was decided as to the manner of levying this army, or as to how it should be maintained, the enthusiasm for the crusade soon declined, and nobody put himself forward to oppose the progress of the Ottomans. Æneas Sylvius explains to us, in one of his letters, the causes of this indifference and inaction of Christendom. "The Christian republic was nothing but a body without a head; they who ought to have been the leaders had nothing great about them but the name; Europe was divided into a crowd of inimical or rival states; discords that could not be appeased, diversity of interests, languages, and customs, left no hope of raising a common army, or of carrying on an active and regular war against the Turks."

Æneas Sylvius thus demonstrated the impossibility of a crusade, and yet, carried away by his zeal, he passed his whole life in preaching one. Whilst he was uselessly haranguing the princes of Germany, the pope was endeavouring to establish concord among the states of Italy. The ascendancy of the pontifical authority was not sufficient to calm angry spirits, and peace was the work of a poor hermit, whose words exercised a supreme authority over the hearts of the faithful. Brother Simon issued all at once from his retreat, perambulated the cities, and addressing both princes and people, exhorted them to unite against the enemies of Jesus Christ: at the voice of the holy orator, Venice, Florence, and the duke of Milan, laid down their arms, and a league was formed, into which most of the republics and principalities of Italy entered.

Advantage might have been taken of this union to declare war against the Turks. But the confederation had no leader capable of directing it. Two men were able to set both Germany and Italy in motion,—the Emperor Frederick and Pope Nicholas. They alone could have insured success to a crusade which they themselves had preached: but the one was restrained by the avarice and indolence of his character; the other, passionate in the pursuit of learned antiquity, always surrounded by scholars, employed himself much more earnestly in collecting the literary treasures of Greece and Rome, than in promoting attempts for the deliverance of the city of Constantine. When the Turks took Byzantium, he was causing translation to be made, at great expense, of the most celebrated Greek authors; and it would not be harsh to believe that the tenths levied for the crusade, were sometimes employed in the acquisition of the masterpieces of Plato, Herodotus, or Thucydides.

Nicholas confined himself to a few exhortations addressed to the faithful, and died without having removed any of the difficulties which opposed themselves to the undertaking of a holy war. Calixtus III., who succeeded him, showed more zeal, and at the very commencement of his pontificate, he sent legates and preachers throughout Europe, to proclaim a crusade and levy tenths. An embassy from the pontiff went to solicit the kings of Persia and Armenia, and the khan of the Tartars, to unite with the Christians of the West, to make war against the Turks. Sixteen galleys, constructed with the produce of the tenths, put to sea under the command of the patriarch of Aquileia, and displayed the banner of St. Peter in the Archipelago, and on the coasts of Asia Minor; Æneas Sylvius harangued the pope in the name of the emperor of Germany, and promised him the concurrence of all the powers of Christendom, if his holiness opened the treasures of the Church, and, by his evangelical exhortations, called *all the workmen to the harvest*. Calixtus III. thanked the head of the empire for his advice, and pressed him to set the example. But the indolent Frederick contented himself with renewing his promises; and whilst the emperor was thus exhorting the pope to maintain a crusade, and that the pope, on his side, was urging the emperor to take arms, the Ottomans penetrated into Hungary, and advanced against Belgrade.

This city, one of the bulwarks of the West, received no succour from Christendom. There remained no hope for it but in the valour of Hunniades, and in the apostolic zeal of John of Capistran. The one commanded the troops of the Hungarians, and excited them by his example; the other, who, by his preachings had got together a great number of German Crusaders, animated the Christian soldiers, and inspired them with an invincible ardour.

Contemporary chronicles inform us, that at this period a hairy comet appeared blazing in the east. The Christian nations believed they saw in this phenomenon a prophetic signal of the greatest evils; and as the evil then most to be dreaded was the invasion of the Turks, Calixtus was desirous of profiting by this feeling of the people, to revive the idea of a crusade. He exhorted the Christians to penitence; and pointed out the holy war as a means by which they might expiate their sins and appease the anger of Heaven.

In no country, notwithstanding, did the people arm, except in those that were immediately menaced by the Turks. It was at this time that the pope ordered that every day at noon, the bells should be rung in all parishes, to call upon the faithful to pray for the Hungarians, and for those who were contending with the Turks. Calixtus granted indulgences to all Christians who, at this signal, would repeat the Dominical prayer and the angelic salutation three times. Such was the origin of the *Angelus*, which the customs of the Church have consecrated, and continued to modern times.

Heaven was doubtless touched by these fervent prayers, which arose at the same time and together, from all parts of Christian Europe. On the 6th of August, 1456, the Turks were defeated under the walls of Belgrade, which they had besieged forty days, and which they had threatened to treat in the same manner as they had treated the Greek capital. The presence of Hunniades and the ardent zeal of John Capistran had so excited the valour of the Hungarians, that they destroyed the Ottoman fleet, which covered the Danube and the Save, and the army commanded by Mahomet himself. More than twenty thousand Mussulmans lost their lives in the battle; the sultan was wounded amidst his janissaries, and escaped the pursuit of the victors with much difficulty. All Europe returned Heaven thanks for a victory, for the obtaining of which it had only concurred by its prayers, and which it must have considered a miracle. The tent and the arms of Mahomet were sent to the pope, as a trophy of the holy war, and as a homage rendered to the father of the faithful. Religion celebrated by its ceremonies, a day in which its most cruel enemies had been vanquished. The festival of the Transfiguration, instituted by a bull of the pope, and marked to take place on the 6th of August, reminded the universal Church, every year, of the defeat of the Turks before Belgrade.

Hunniades and Capistran did not long survive their triumphs; but both died whilst Christendom was still mixing their names with hymns of gratitude. The passion of jealousy empoisoned their last moments; and the scarcely evangelical warmth with which each of them claimed the honour of having saved Belgrade, left a stain upon their renown. Æneas Sylvius, when commending their memory to the esteem of posterity, celebrates the virtues of Capistran, and expresses astonishment that an humble cenobite, who had trampled under-foot all the riches of this world, should not have had sufficient strength to resist the charms of glory.

Whilst the Hungarians were beating the Turks before Belgrade, the pope's fleet gained some advantages in the Archipelago. Calixtus took care not to neglect to remind the faithful of the exploits and triumphs of the patriarch of Aquileia; persuaded that the news of victories gained over the Mussulmans would restore hope and courage to all those whom the reverses of the Christians had discouraged and terrified. A fresh crusade was preached in France, England, Germany, and even in the kingdoms of Castile, Arragon, and Portugal. The people everywhere listened with pious seriousness to the preachers of the crusade; but murmurs generally arose against the levying of the tenths. The clergy of Rouen, with the university and parliament of Paris, opposed the impost openly. In Germany complaints were more violent than elsewhere. In proportion as the spirit of the holy wars cooled, the means employed by the popes to renew these distant expeditions were judged with greater severity. It must likewise be admitted, that there were great abuses in the collection and the employment of the tenths. An open traffic of the indulgences of the court of Rome for the crusade was carried on, and the tribunal of penitence, on certain occasions, seemed to be nothing but a means of levying taxes upon the faithful. It was only by money that the favours of the Church and the mercies of Heaven could be obtained; the sins of Christians might be said, in some sort, to have a tariff; and we find in the history of Arragon, that disobedience to the decrees of the pope even had become the source of a new tribute. It may be remembered that the sovereign pontiffs had frequently forbidden Christians to convey munitions or arms to the infidels. The trade of the maritime cities often braved the menaces of the Holy See, and avarice led the merchants to transgress the severest orders on this point. A sum of money was then required, in the name of the pope, of all who were accused of this offence. They were condemned to pay the fourth or the fifth of the profits arising from their illicit commerce. Commissaries were appointed to levy this impost, and decrees regulated the collection of it, as in that of all other public revenues.

But that which most completely exposes the spirit of this age, and particularly that of the court of Rome, is, that in the preachings of the crusades, the faithful were much less earnestly exhorted to take arms than to pay a tribute in money. The levies raised in the name of the Holy See, were termed *succours for the Hungarians*; and as the Hungarians always stood in need of being succoured, the levying of the tenths became a permanent state of things, which the people and the clergy endured every day with less patience and resignation.

We ought likewise to add, that the Holy See did not always receive the produce of the tribute it imposed upon the Christians. Princes, under pretence of making war against the Turks, sometimes took possession of it; and the tenths destined for the holy war were too often employed in carrying out the quarrels of ambition.

At length the complaints of the Germans against the commissaries and agents of the court of Rome became so serious and so numerous, that the pope found himself obliged to reply to them. In his apology, drawn up by Æneas Sylvius, he declared that Scanderberg and the king of Hungary had received numerous succours; that fleets had been armed against the infidels, and that vessels and munitions of war had been sent to Rhodes, Cyprus, and Mytilene; that, in a word, the money levied for the defence of the faith and of Christendom upon the faithful, had never been otherwise employed. The apologist of the pope, after having thus justified him, felicitated him with having saved Europe.

This apology, which explains nothing, and which finishes with an eulogy, too strongly resembles that of the ancient Roman, who, upon being accused of having embezzled the public money, as his only reply, proposed that they should go to the Capitol, and give thanks to the gods for the victories he had gained over the enemies of the republic. It must, however, be admitted, that that which Æneas Sylvius said was not totally void of truth; and history can but applaud the zeal which the sovereign pontiff displayed, in order to arrest the progress of Mahomet, and save a crowd of victims from the tyranny of the Ottomans.

Calixtus never ceased soliciting the Christian princes to unite with him, and was particularly anxious to kindle the warlike enthusiasm of the French against the Turks. "If I were but seconded by the French," said he, "we would destroy the race of the infidels." He spared neither prayers nor promises to induce Charles VII. to succour Hungary, and defend the barriers of Europe. He sent him that golden rose which the popes were accustomed to bless on the fourth Sunday of Lent, and of which they made a present to Christian princes, as a particular mark of esteem and affection. These caresses and these civilities of the pontiff were a great change from the times in which the heads of the Church only spoke to monarchs in the name of irritated Heaven; and only exhorted them to take the cross whilst reproaching them with their sins, and recommending them to expiate them by the holy war. The popes, when preaching the crusades, were no longer the interpreters of dominant opinions; their wishes were no longer laws, and princes made ample use of the faculty they possessed of not obeying. Charles VII., who was in constant dread of the enterprises of the English, resisted the reiterated entreaties of Calixtus. It was in vain that the dauphin, who afterwards reigned under the title of Louis XI., and was then living at the court of Burgundy, openly declared himself favourable to the crusade, and wished to create a party for himself in the kingdom, by taking the cross; France remained uninterested in the war preached against the infidels, and Charles contented himself with permitting the levy of the tenths in his states, upon the express condition that he should superintend the employment of them.

Whilst the pope was imploring the assistance of Christendom for the Hungarians, Hungary was a prey to troubles created by the succession of Ladislaus, who was killed at the battle of Warna. The family of Hunniades was proscribed, and the ambition of the princes disputed the possession of the provinces threatened by the Turks. Calixtus employed the paternal authority of the Holy See to appease the furies of discord, and to reconcile the pretensions of the emperor of Germany with the rights of justice and with the rights of nations; and these generous efforts at length succeeded in reëstablishing peace. His conduct appeared less praiseworthy, and particularly less disinterested, when the succession of Alphonso, king of Naples, brought fresh wars upon Italy. History relates that the sovereign pontiff, on this occasion, forgot the perils of Christianity, and employed the treasures collected for the holy war in the defence of a cause which certainly was not that of religion.

But the indefatigable orator of the crusades, Æneas Sylvius, succeeded Calixtus III. in the chair of St. Peter. The tiara appeared to be the reward of his zeal for the war against the Turks, and everything gave reason for hope that he would neglect nothing to execute himself the projects he had conceived; and awaken among the nations of Christendom, that warlike enthusiasm, that religious patriotism, which breathed in his discourses.

Mahomet II. continued to follow up the course of his victories, and his power every day became more redoubtable. He was then employed in despoiling all the Greek princes who had escaped his first invasions, and whose weakness was concealed under the pompous titles of emperor of Trebizond, king of Iberia, and despot of the Morea. All these princes, to whom acts of submission cost nothing, provided they enabled them to reign a few days longer, had been eager, a short time after the taking of Constantinople, to send ambassadors to the victorious sultan, to congratulate him upon his triumphs; and the fierce conqueror saw nothing in them but a prey which it would be easy for him to devour,—enemies that he could subdue at leisure. Most of them dishonoured the last moments of their reign or their existence, by all that ambition, jealousy, and the spirit of discord could inspire that was perfidious, cruel, or treacherous. When the Mussulmans penetrated into the Greek provinces, stained with all the crimes of civil war, it might have been believed that they were sent to accomplish the menaces of heavenly anger.

Mahomet did not deign to put forth all his strength against the pusillanimous tyrants of Greece. Other enemies were worthy of employing his arms; he had but to speak a word, to pull the throne from under the prince of Synope or the emperor of Trebizond; and if all that remained of the family of the Comnenas were massacred by his orders, he, in this circumstance, was less obedient to the fears of a dark policy than to his natural ferocity. Seven years after the taking of Byzantium, he led his janissaries into the Peloponnesus: at his approach, all the princes of Achaia either took to flight, or became his slaves. Meeting with scarcely any resistance, he gathered with disdain the fruits of an easy conquest. He meditated projects more vast than such conquests; and when he unfurled the banner of the cross amidst the ruins of Sparta and Athens, he fixed his eyes earnestly upon the Sea of Sicily, and wished to find a route that might conduct him to the shores of Italy.

The first care of Pius II. was to proclaim the fresh dangers of Europe. He wrote to all the powers of Christendom, and convoked a general assembly at Mantua, to deliberate upon the means of arresting the progress of the Ottomans. The bull of the pontiff reminded the faithful, that the Church of Christ had often been beaten by the tempest, but that He who commands the winds was ever watchful over its safety. "My predecessors," added he, "have declared war against the Turks, both by land and by sea; it is for us now to carry it on; we will spare neither labour nor expense for a war so useful, so just, and so holy."

All the states of Christendom promised to send ambassadors to Mantua. Pius II. went thither himself; and in his opening discourse, he expatiated with strength against the indifference of princes and sovereigns. He pointed to the Turks then ravaging Bosnia and Greece, and ready to extend, like a rapid conflagration, their devastations over Italy, Germany, and all the countries of Europe. The pontiff declared he would not quit Mantua before the Christian princes and states had given him pledges of their devotion to the cause of Christendom; and at length protested, that if he were abandoned by the Christian powers, he would alone maintain this glorious struggle, and would die in defending the independence of Europe and of the Church.

The language of Pius II. was full of religion, and his religion was full of patriotism. When Demosthenes and the Greek orators mounted the tribune to press their fellow-citizens to defend the liberties of Greece against the enterprises of Philip, or the invasions of the great king, they spoke, without doubt, with more eloquence; but never were they inspired by greater interests or nobler motives.

Cardinal Bissarion, to whom Greece had given birth, and whom the Church of Rome had adopted, spoke after Pius II., and declared that the whole college of cardinals was animated by the same zeal as the father of the faithful. The deputies of Rhodes, Cyprus, Epirus; those of Illyria, Peloponnesus, and of several of the countries the Turks had invaded, made, before the council, a lamentable recital of all the evils the Christians were suffering under the domination of the Mussulmans; but the ambassadors of the great powers of Europe were not yet arrived; and this delay announced but too plainly the indifference of the Christian monarchs for the crusades. The debates which afterwards arose relative to the pretensions of the families of Anjou and Arragon to the kingdom of Naples; and then the disputes upon etiquette and precedence, which occupied the council during several days, completely proved that the minds of the assembly were not sufficiently impressed by the dangers of Christian Europe, and that no generous resolution would be there taken to prevent them.

The pope proposed to levy for the crusade a tenth upon the revenues of the clergy, a twentieth upon the Jews, and a thirtieth upon princes and seculars. He proposed at the same time, to raise an army of a hundred thousand men in the different states of Europe, and to intrust the command of this army to the emperor of Germany. These propositions, in order to be executed, required the approbation of the sovereigns, and most of the ambassadors made only vague promises. A great number of conferences were held; the council lasted many months, and the pope quitted Mantua without having done anything decisive for the enterprise he meditated. He returned to Rome, whence he wrote again to the Christian princes, conjuring them to send ambassadors, to deliberate afresh upon the war against the Turks.

Constantly pursued by the thought of delivering the Christian world, and losing hope daily of being able to affect the West, he conceived the strange idea of addressing Mahomet II. himself, and of employing all the powers of reasoning and eloquence to convert the Mussulman prince to Christianity. His letter, which we still possess, presents a complete treatise of the philosophy and the theology of the time. The pontiff opposes to the apostles of Islamism, the authority of the prophets and the fathers of the Church, and the profane authority of Lycurgus and Solon. Aiming particularly at interesting the ambition of the Ottoman emperor, he proposes to him the example of the great Constantine, who obtained the empire of the world on receiving baptism, and investing himself with that sign by which it was given to him to conquer. The sultan had only to acknowledge the God from whom all authority comes, to have the Abyssinians, the Arabs, the Mamelukes, the Persians, with all the nations of Asia, submit to his domination; and if the intercession of the court of Rome were necessary for him to reign over the East, the head of the Church promised him the assistance of his prayers, and the support of the pontifical sovereignty.

In this singular negotiation with Mahomet II., the pope was not more fortunate than with the Christian princes. The latter, when he urged them to defend their own states, answered by vain protestations. Mahomet, to whom he offered the conquest of the world, contented himself with replying, that "he was innocent of the death of Jesus Christ, and that he thought with horror of those who had fastened him to the cross."

The Ottoman emperor had just obtained possession of Bosnia, and had caused the king of that unfortunate country, who had submitted to his arms, to perish in the midst of tortures. Ottoman troops ravaged the frontiers of Illyria, and threatened the city of Ragusa. The dangers of Italy became every day more pressing. The pope assembled his consistory, and represented to the members, that the time was come to stop the progress of the Turks, and to commence the holy war he had preached. "The duke of Burgundy and the Venetian republic were ready to second his enterprise. Whilst the Hungarians and the Poles were preparing to fight the Ottomans on the Dniester and the Danube, the Epeirots and the Albanians were about to raise the standard of liberty among the Greeks: in Asia, the sultan of Caramania and the king of Persia would attack the Turks, and second the united efforts of the Christians. The pontiff declared that he was resolved to march himself against the infidels. When the Christian princes should behold the vicar of Jesus Christ setting out for the holy war, would they not be ashamed to remain inactive? Loaded with years and infirmities, he had but a few moments to live; it would be hastening to an almost certain death; but of what consequence was the hour or the place of his decease, provided he died for the cause of Christ, and for the safety of Christendom."

The cardinals gave a unanimous assent to the resolution of Pius II. From that time the pope employed himself in preparations for his departure, and addressed an exhortation to the faithful to engage them to second his designs. After having, in this apostolic exhortation, retraced, with lively eloquence, the misfortunes and the perils of the Christian Church, the pontiff expressed himself thus:—

"Our fathers lost Jerusalem and all Asia; we have lost Greece and a great part of Europe. Christendom is now nothing but a corner of the world. In this extreme peril, the common father of the faithful is himself going to meet the enemy. Doubtless, war is ill suited to the weakness of old age, or to the character of pontiff; but when religion is ready to succumb, who could restrain us? We will take our place during fight, either upon the poop of a vessel, or upon a lofty hill, pouring our benedictions upon the soldiers of Christ, and invoking for them the God of armies. Thus the patriarch Moses prayed upon the mountain, and raised his hands towards heaven, whilst Israel combated with the nations whom God had reproved. We shall be followed by our cardinals, and by a great number of bishops; we will march with the standard of the cross displayed, with the relics of saints, with Jesus Christ himself in his eucharist. What Christian will refuse to follow the vicar of God, going with his holy senate, and all the revered train of the Church, to the defence of religion and humanity?

"What war was ever more just or more necessary? The Turks attack all that we hold most dear, all that Christian society considers most holy. If you are men, can you be wanting in compassion for your fellow-men? If you are Christians, religion commands you to carry succour to your brethren. If the misfortunes of others touch you not, think of your own safety—have pity on yourselves. You imagine yourselves to be in safety, because you are as yet at a distance from peril: to-morrow the sword will be suspended over your heads. If you convey not assistance to those who are before you, those who are behind you will, in like manner, abandon you in the hour of danger.

"Do you feel yourselves strong enough to support the opprobrium and the humiliation of a barbarous domination? Remain in your dwellings, await your enemies there; await there those vile Asiatics, who are not even men, and yet have the insolent pretension to govern all the nations of Europe. But if you possess a noble heart, an elevated mind, a generous character, a Christian soul, you will follow the banners of the Church; you will send us succours; you will aid the army of the Lord.

"Such as will aid us, God will bless them; but such as remain indifferent shall have no part in the treasures of divine mercy. May the wicked and the impious, who shall trouble the public peace, be accursed of God! May Heaven pour upon them the scourges of its wrath! Let them live in unceasing fear, and may their life be as if suspended by a thread! Neither power nor riches shall defend them; the arrows of remorse shall reach them everywhere; the flames of the abyss shall consume their hearts."

The pontiff addressed this exhortation to the princes, the nobility, and the people of all nations. He fixed upon the city and port of Ancona as the place of meeting for the Crusaders. He promised the remission of their sins to all who would serve, during six months, at their own expense, or who would maintain one or two soldiers of the cross during the same space of time. He had nothing to bestow in this world upon the faithful who should take part in the crusade; but he conjured Heaven to direct all their steps, to multiply their days, to preserve and increase their kingdoms, their principalities, and their possessions. On terminating his apostolical discourse, he addressed the Omnipotent God: "Oh thou, who searchest reins and hearts, thou knowest if we have any other thought than that of combating for thy glory, and for the safety of the flock thou hast committed to our charge. Avenge the Christian blood which flows beneath the sword of the Turks, and which on all sides rises up towards thee. Turn a favourable eye upon thy people; guide us in the war undertaken for the triumph of thy faith. Do so, that Greece may be restored to thy worship, and that all Europe may bless thy name!"

This bull of the pope was sent throughout all the West, and read publicly in the churches. The assembled faithful shed tears at the recital of the misfortunes of Christendom. The cross and arms were taken in countries apparently most secure from the invasions of the Turks, even in the remotest north of Europe. Some repaired to Ancona; others directed their course towards Hungary, to join the army of Matthias Corvinus, ready to set out on its march against the Turks.

The pope wrote to the doge of Venice, to entreat him to assist in person in the war about to be made against the infidels. He told him that the presence of princes in armies inspired confidence in the soldiers and terror in their enemies. As the doge was advanced in years, Paul reminded him that his own hair was blanched by time, [77] and that the duke of Burgundy, who promised to accompany the Crusaders to the East, had attained the days of old age. "We shall be," added the holy father, "three old men at the head of an army of Christians. God takes delight in the number three, and the Trinity which is in heaven, will not fail to protect this trinity upon earth."

These singular expressions of the pope belonged to the bad taste of the age. But in presenting old age as the only mover and the last hope of the crusade, they painted sufficiently clearly the spirit of the times with regard to holy wars, and might be believed to presage the little success of an enterprise, which, in order to succeed, stood in need of the ardour and activity that are only to be found in youth. The doge of Venice hesitated to embark; but as the republic was at war with Mahomet II., and as it was of importance to mix its interests with those of the crusade, it threatened to employ force, in order to compel the doge to follow the pontiff of Rome. The duke of Burgundy, who had been the first of all the Christian princes to swear to go and combat with the infidels, showed no inclination to join the Crusaders. The pope, in his letters, reminded him of his solemn promises, and reproached him with having deceived men,—with having deceived God himself. He added, that his breach of faith would throw the whole of Christendom into mourning, and might bring about the entire failure of the enterprise. Philip, in spite of the severe remonstrances of Pius II., could not make up his mind to leave his states, but contented himself with sending two thousand men-at-arms to the Christian army. He was at that time in dread of the crooked policy of Louis XI., who, when he was dauphin, was eager to fight the Turks; but having ascended the throne of France, had no other enemies but his neighbours.

Pius II., after having implored the protection of God, in the basilic of the holy Apostles, left Rome in the month of June, 1464. Being attacked by a slow fever, and fearing that the sight of his infirmities might discourage the soldiers of the cross, he concealed his sufferings, and desired his physician to be silent on the subject of his malady. All along his route the people put up prayers for the success of his enterprise. The city of Ancona received him in triumph, and saluted him as the liberator of the Christian world.

A great number of Crusaders had arrived in this city; but most of them were without arms or stores, and were almost naked. The earnest exhortations of the pope had had no effect upon the knights and barons of Christendom. The poor, and men of the lowest class of the people, appeared to have been more struck with the dangers of Europe than the rich and the great of the earth. [78] The crowd of Crusaders collected at Ancona resembled a troop of vagabonds and mendicants much more than an army. Every day, want and disease made martyrs of them. Pius II. was touched with their misery; but as he could not provide for their maintenance, he retained such as were in a condition to go to the war at their own expense, and dismissed the others with the indulgences of the crusade.

The Christian army was to direct its course to the coasts of Greece, and join Scanderberg, who had recently beaten the Ottomans in the plains of Ocrida. Deputies were sent to the Hungarians, the king of Cyprus, and to all the enemies of the Turks in Asia, without forgetting the king of Persia, to warn them to hold themselves in readiness to commence the war against the followers of Mahomet.

The little city of Ancona attracted the attention of all Europe. In fact, what spectacle could be more interesting than that of the father of the faithful braving the perils of war and of the seas, to go into distant countries, for the purposes of avenging outraged humanity, breaking the chains of Christian captives, and visiting his children in their affliction? Unfortunately, the physical strength of Pius II. was not equal to his zeal, and would not permit him to perfect his sacrifice. The fleet was ready to set sail, when the fever which he had had on leaving Rome, aggravated by the fatigues of the voyage and his subsequent anxiety, became a mortal malady. Feeling his end approach, he called the cardinals around him, and made them swear to prosecute the war against the infidels. He died whilst commending the Christians of the East to their care; and the last looks he cast upon earth were directed towards Greece, then labouring under the oppression of the enemies of Christ.

Paul II., who was elected pope, promised, amidst the conclave, to follow the example of his predecessor. But the Crusaders assembled by Pius II. were already returned to their homes. The Venetians, left alone, carried the war into the Peloponnesus, without being able to obtain any great advantages over the Turks. They devastated the country they went to deliver; and the most remarkable of their trophies was the pillage of Athens.

The Greeks of the canton of Lacedæmon and some other cities, who, in the hope of being succoured, had raised the standard of liberty, could not stand against the janissaries, and fell victims to their devotion to the cause of religion and patriotism. Scanderberg, whose capital the Turks besieged, came himself to solicit the assistance of the pope. Being received by Paul II. in presence of the cardinals, he declared before the sacred college, that there was no longer in the East any place but Epirus, and in Epirus only his little army, that still fought for the cause of the Christians. He added, that if he succumbed, nobody would be left to defend the routes to Italy. The pope bestowed the greatest praises upon Scanderberg, and made him a present of a sword which he had blessed. He at the same time wrote to the princes of Christendom, to persuade them to assist Albania. In a letter addressed to the duke of Burgundy, Paul II. lamented the fate of the nations of Greece, driven from their country by the barbarians; he deplored the exile and the misery of the Greek families coming to seek refuge in Italy, dying with hunger and in nakedness, crowded together upon the seashore, holding their hands up to Heaven, and supplicating their brothers the Christians to succour them or to avenge them. The head of the Church reminded them of all that his predecessors had done, and of all he himself had done, to avert such great misfortunes. He blamed the indifference of both monarchs and nations; and menaced Europe with the same calamities, if they did not speedily take up arms against the Turks. The exhortations of the pope remained without effect; Scanderberg, carrying nothing back with him but some sums of money which he had obtained from the Holy See, returned to his kingdom, then ravaged by the Ottomans, and a short time afterwards died at Lissa, covered with glory, but despairing of the noble cause for which he had fought all his life.

Such was the ascendancy of one great man, that under his banners the Greeks, for such a length of time degenerate, recalled the remembrance of the brightest days of the military glory of their country; the little province of Albania resisted during twenty years the whole power of the Ottoman empire. The death of Scanderberg threw his companions in arms into despair. "Hasten, brave Albanians," cried they in the public places, "redouble your courage; for the ramparts of the empire and of Macedon are now crumbled into dust." These words were at once the funeral oration of a hero and that of his people. Two years had scarcely passed away before most of the cities of Epirus fell into the power of the Turks; and, as Scanderberg himself had foretold to the pontiff of Rome, not a soldier of Christ remained east of the Adriatic Sea.

All enterprises against the infidels were from that time confined to a few maritime expeditions of the Venetians and the Knights of Rhodes.

These expeditions were not sufficient to arrest the progress of the Ottomans. Mahomet II. never ceased to meditate an invasion of Germany and Italy. Resolved to aim one last blow at his enemies, he determined, after the example of the Roman pontiffs, to employ the ascendancy of religion, to excite the bravery and the enthusiasm of the Mussulmans. In the midst of a solemn ceremony, and in the presence of the divan and the mufti, he swore "to renounce all pleasures, and never to turn his countenance from the West to the East, until he had overthrown and trampled under the feet of his horses the gods of the nations,—those gods of wood, brass, silver, gold, and painting, that the disciples of Christ made with their hands." He swore "to exterminate the iniquity of the Christians from the face of the earth, and to proclaim, from the rising to the setting, the glory of the God of Sabaoth and of Mahomet." After this threatening declaration, the Turkish emperor pressed all the circumcised nations that followed his laws to join him, in order to obey the command of God and his prophet.

The oath of Mahomet II. was read in all the mosques of the empire, at the hour of prayer. The Ottoman warriors flocked to Constantinople from all parts. An army of the sultan's was already ravaging Croatia and Carniola; and soon a formidable fleet issued from the canal, and attacked the island of Eubœa or Negropont, separated by the Euripus from the city of Athens, which the Turkish historians call the city or the country of the philosophers. At the first news of the danger, the pope ordered public prayers in the city of Rome. He himself walked barefooted in procession before the image of the Virgin; but Heaven, says one of the annalists of the Church, did not deign to listen to the prayers of the Christians; Negropont fell into the hands of the Turks, and the entire population of the island was either exterminated or dragged into slavery. A great number of those who had defended their country with courage expired in tortures. Fame soon carried to Europe an account of the excesses of Ottoman barbarity, and all Christian nations were filled with horror and fright.

After the last victories of the Turks, Germany had reason to dread a prompt invasion, and the coasts of Italy were at the same time threatened. Cardinal Bessarion addressed an eloquent exhortation to the Italians, and conjured them to unite against the common enemy. The pope did everything in his power to appease discord, and at length succeeded in forming a league among the Italian states, similar to that which was entered into after the taking of Constantinople. His legates solicited the assistance of the kings of France and England. Upon his pressing request, Frederick convoked a diet at Ratisbon, and afterwards at Nuremberg, in which appeared the deputies of Venice, Sienna, Naples, Hungary, and Carniola, who described the ravages of the Turks, and painted in the most striking colours the misfortunes which menaced Europe. In these two assemblies, several resolutions were formed for war against the Mussulmans; but not one of them was executed. Such was the general blindness, that neither the exhortations of the pope, nor the frightful progress of the Turks, were able to awaken the zeal of princes or people. The chronicles of the times speak of several miracles by which God manifested his power in these unfortunate days; but there can be no doubt that the greatest miracle of Providence was, that Italy and Germany did not fall into the hands of the Ottomans, when not a human hand was raised to defend them.

After the death of Paul II., who had not time to achieve his work, and did not witness the effect of his preachings, his successor, Sextus IV., neglected nothing for the defence of Christendom. When scarcely seated on the pontifical throne, he deputed cardinals to several states of Europe, to preach peace among Christians and war against the Turks. The legates were specially intrusted to press the levying of the tenths for the crusade. They were authorized to launch the thunders of excommunication against those who should oppose this impost, or who misapplied the produce of it. This severity, which occasioned troubles in England, and still more in Germany, succeeded in other countries, and furnished the sovereign pontiff with means for preparing for war. But none of the princes of the West took up arms, and Christendom was still exposed to the greatest perils, when fortune sent succour it had no reason to look for from the depths of Asia.

Of all the powers that had promised to combat the Ottomans, the only one that did not fail, was the king of Persia, to whom Calixtus III. had sent a missionary, and who declared himself the faithful ally of the Christians. In his reply, the king of Persia bestowed the greatest praises on the pope, encouraged him in his resolution of attacking Mahomet, and announced to him that he himself would commence hostilities. At the time his letter was received at Rome, his troops were already crossing Armenia, and several Ottoman cities had fallen into the hands of the Persians. Mahomet was obliged to abandon or to suspend his projects of conquest on the side of Europe, to march against these new enemies, with the greater part of the strength of his empire.

Great advantage might have been taken of this powerful diversion of the Persians. But the Venetians, the king of Naples, and the pope, alone put themselves forward to make war against the Ottomans. The sovereign pontiff had caused twenty-four galleys to be built with the produce of the tenths levied for the crusade. This fleet, commanded by Cardinal Caraffa, and collected in the Tiber, after having been blessed by Sextus IV., went to join that of Venice and Naples, and cruised along the coasts of Ionia and Pamphylia, to the great terror of all the maritime Ottoman cities. The

Venetians did not fail to direct the operations of the Christian fleet against the cities whose wealth and commerce gave them any cause for jealousy. Satalia and Smyrna were given up to the horrors of war; the first of these, situated on the coast of Pamphylia, was the *entrepôt* for the productions and the merchandise of India and Arabia. The second, situated in the Ionian Sea, possessed rich manufactures and a flourishing trade. The Christian soldiers committed in these two cities all the kinds of excess with which the Turks were then reproached. After this piratical expedition, the fleet regained the ports of Italy, and Cardinal Caraffa returned triumphant to Rome, followed by twenty-five captives mounted upon superb horses, and by twelve camels, loaded with the spoils of the enemy. The ensigns taken from the Mussulmans, and the chain of the port of Satalia, were solemnly suspended over the gate and in the vaulted roof of the Vatican.

Whilst these poor advantages over the Mussulmans were being celebrated at Rome, Mahomet was inflicting terrible blows upon his enemies; and when he returned to Constantinople, he had destroyed the armies of the king of Persia. That which gave the Turkish emperor an immense advantage over the powers which took up arms against him, was that they never acted in concert, either for defence or attack. Discord was not long in being revived among the Christian princes, and particularly among the states of Italy. The pope himself forgot the spirit of peace and union he had preached; he forgot the holy war; and Venice, left alone in the struggle against the Ottomans, was obliged to sue to Mahomet for peace.

The Ottomans took as much advantage of peace as of war to increase their power. There now remained nothing of the sad wreck of the Greek empire. Venice had lost all its possessions in the Archipelago and Greece; Genoa at length lost the rich colony of Caffa, in the Crimea. Of all the conquests of the Crusaders, the Christians had only preserved the kingdom of Cyprus and the isle of Rhodes.

During more than a century, the kings of Cyprus had implored the assistance of the West, and contended with some successes against the Saracens, particularly the Mamelukes of Egypt. The maritime cities of Italy protected a kingdom from which trade and navigation derived great advantage. Every day fresh warriors from Europe afforded it the support of their arms. A few years after the taking of Constantinople, history remarks Jacques Cœur, who had obtained the restitution of his wealth, establishing himself in the isle of Cyprus, and consecrating his fortune and his life to the defence of the Christians of the East. After his death, there was to be seen, in a church at Bourges which he had founded, this inscription:—"The Seigneur Jacques Cœur, Captain-general of the Church against the infidels." [79]

The kingdom of Cyprus, after having resisted the Mussulmans for a long time, became at last the theatre and the prey of revolutions. Abandoned, in some sort, by the Christian powers, and obliged to defend itself against the Turks, it placed itself under the protection of the Mamelukes of Egypt. In time of trouble, the malcontents retired to Cairo, and procured the protection of a power which had a great interest in keeping up discord. The family of Lusignan being nearly extinct, a daughter, the only scion of many kings, at first married a Portuguese prince, and afterwards Louis, count of Savoy. But the sultan of Cairo and Mahomet II. would not permit a Latin prince to wear the crown of Cyprus, and caused a natural son of the last king to be elected. James, whose illegitimate birth kept him from the throne, and who had disturbed the kingdom by his ambitious pretensions, was crowned king of Cyprus in the city of Cairo, under the auspices and in the presence of the Mamelukes. That which must have greatly added to the scandal of this coronation was, that the new king promised to be faithful to the sultan of Egypt, and to pay five thousand gold crowns for the support of the great mosques of Mecca and Jerusalem. It was upon the Gospel that he swore to keep this promise, and to omit nothing that the Mamelukes required. "If I break my word," added he, "I shall be an apostate and a forger; I shall deny the existence of Jesus Christ, and the virginity of his mother; I shall slay a camel upon the font of baptism, and I shall curse the priesthood." Such were the words which a desire of reigning placed in the mouth of a prince who was about to govern a kingdom founded by the soldiers of Jesus Christ. He died a short time after having taken possession of the supreme authority. His people thought the days of his life and his reign were shortened by divine justice.

The republic of Venice, which adopted Catherine Cornaro, the widow of James, then took possession of Cyprus, which it defended against the Mamelukes and against the Turks, and held it till the middle of the following century.

The eyes of the whole Christian world were fixed upon the isle of Rhodes. This isle, defended by the Knights of St. John, recalled to the faithful the remembrance of the Holy Land, and prevented the extinction of the hope of one day seeing the standard of Christ again floating over the walls of Jerusalem. The martial youth of all the countries of the West unceasingly flocked thither, and, in some sort, revived the ardour, the zeal, and the exploits of the first crusades. The order of the Hospitallers, faithful to its first institution, always protected pilgrims repairing to Palestine, and defended Christian vessels against the attacks of Turks, Mamelukes, and pirates. At the commencement of his reign, Mahomet II. summoned the grand-master to pay him a tribute, as to his sovereign. The latter contented himself with answering: "We only owe the sovereignty of Rhodes to God and our swords. It is our duty to be the enemies, and not the tributaries, of the Ottomans!" This reply wounded the pride of the sultan; but he dissembled his anger, persuaded that victory would soon give that which was refused, and at the same time avenge him for the noble disdain of the Knights of St. John.

The Ottoman emperor, after having triumphed over the Persians, returned to Constantinople with fresh projects for conquests in Europe, and with increased animosity against the Christians; and the whole of his empire prepared to minister to his ambition and his anger. If the Turks had not till that period carried their invasions into the West, it was because the difference of religion and manners kept them from all communication with the Christian nations; and because they were entirely ignorant of the state and dispositions of Christendom, of the forces that might be opposed to them, and even of the best routes for them to pursue. They became gradually acquainted with the frontiers of Europe, and with the sea-coasts; and, like the lion of Holy Writ, which prowls constantly about in search of its prey, were ever on the watch for favourable opportunities. They secured advanced posts, and marched with precaution towards the country they wished to conquer, as an army draws round a place it is about to besiege. By frequently-repeated incursions, they spread terror among the nations they intended to attack; and by the ravages they exercised, they weakened the means of resistance of their enemies. Mahomet at first made himself master of Scutari and Negropont, in order to dominate, in a manner, over the coasts of the Adriatic and the Sea of Naples; on the other side, several of his armies directed their course towards the Danube, to lay open the routes to Germany; and Ottoman troops had penetrated, with fire and sword, as far as Friuli, to terrify the republic of Venice, and reconnoitre the avenues that lead to Italy.

When everything was ready for the execution of his terrible designs, the leader of the Ottoman empire resolved to attack Christendom at several points at once. A numerous army set out on its march to invade Hungary, and all the countries in the vicinity of the Danube. Two numerous fleets, with a vast number of troops on board, were despatched, one against the Knights of Rhodes, whose bravery Mahomet dreaded; and the other against the coast of Naples, the conquest of which would open the way towards Rome and southern Italy. In such a pressing danger, the hopes of the Germans, and even of a portion of the Italian states, reposed entirely upon the Hungarians. The king of Hungary was then considered as the guardian of the frontiers of Europe; and to be always in a condition to meet the Turks, he received every year succours in money from the republic of Venice and the emperor of Germany. The pope added to these succours a part of the tenths levied for the crusade, and his legates and missionaries were always present to excite the valour of the Hungarian soldiers.

At the approach of the Ottoman army, all Hungary, governed by Matthias Corvinus, son of Hunniades, flew to arms. The Hungarian army met the Turks in the plains of Transylvania, and gave them battle. Victory was obtained by the Christians, who, in a single battle, destroyed the enemy's army. Contemporary chronicles take less pains to describe this terrible conflict, than to exhibit the joy of the conquerors after their triumph. The entire victorious army assisted at a banquet prepared upon the field of battle, still covered with dead, and all smoking with carnage. The leaders and the soldiers mingled their songs of joy with the cries of the wounded and the dying, and in the intoxication of victory and festivity performed barbarous dances upon the bloody carcasses of their enemies.

The war between the Christians and the Turks became every day more cruel, and presented nothing but scenes of barbarity and destruction. The menaces of Mahomet; the constant violation by the Turks, in peace as well as in war, of the rights of nations and the faith of oaths; many thousands of Christians condemned to die in tortures for having defended their country and their religion, with twenty years of combats and misfortunes, had altogether excited the hatred of the soldiers of the cross; the thirst of vengeance rendered them sometimes as ferocious as their enemies; and in their triumphs they too frequently forgot that they were fighting in the cause of the Gospel.

Whilst the Turkish army experienced a sanguinary defeat upon the Danube, the fleet of Mahomet, which was directed against the isle of Rhodes, was destined to find, in the Knights of St. John, enemies not less intrepid or less to be dreaded than the Hungarians. The pacha who commanded this expedition, belonged to the imperial family of Palæologus, whose humble prayers had so frequently solicited the aid of Christian Europe. After the taking of Constantinople, he embraced the Mussulman religion, and from that time only sought to second Mahomet in his project of exterminating the race of the Christians in the East.

Several historians have related at great length the events of the siege of Rhodes; and this is, perhaps, a fitting opportunity to repair a great injustice committed upon one of the writers who have preceded us. An expression, escaped from the Abbé de Vertot, and with which criticism has armed itself, has proved sufficient to deprive him of the noblest reward of the labours of an historian,—the reputation for veracity. [80] After having examined with much care the historical monuments we possess, and according to which the author of the *History of the Knights of Malta* has described the siege of Rhodes, we feel great pleasure in rendering homage to the fidelity of his account, and we do not hesitate to refer our readers to it. In this elegant historian will be found the heroic constancy of Aubusson, grand-master of the order of St. John, and the indefatigable intrepidity of his knights, defending themselves amidst ruins, against a hundred thousand Mussulmans, armed with all that the art of sieges and the genius of war had invented. At the approach of the Turks, the grand-master of Rhodes implored the arms and aid of the Christian princes; but all the succours that were sent them consisted of two Neapolitan vessels, which did not arrive till after the siege was raised, and some sums of money which were the produce of a jubilee ordered by the pope at the request of Louis XI.

The third expedition of Mahomet, and the most important for his projects of conquest, was that which was to have been directed against the kingdom of Naples. The Ottoman fleet stopped before Otranto. After a siege of a few days, this city was taken by assault, given up to pillage, and its population massacred or dragged away into slavery. This invasion of the Turks, which was quite unexpected, spread terror throughout Italy. Boufinius informs us that the pope entertained for a moment the thought of quitting the city of the Apostles, and of going beyond the Alps, to seek an asylum in the kingdom of France.

It is probable that if Mahomet II. had united all his forces in an invasion of the kingdom of Naples, he might have pushed his conquests as far as Rome. But the loss of his army in Hungary, and the check experienced by his best troops before the city of Rhodes, must have suspended or stopped the execution of his projects. Sextus IV., when recovered from his first terrors, implored the assistance of Christendom. The sovereign pontiff addressed all the ecclesiastical and secular powers, as well as the Christians of all conditions; he conjured them, by the mercy and sufferings of Christ; by the last judgment, in which every one would be placed according to his works; by the promises of baptism; by the obedience due to the Church, — he supplicated them, to preserve among themselves, at least during three years, charity, peace, and concord. He sent legates in all directions, charged to appease the troubles and wars which divided the Christian world. These legates were instructed to act with moderation and prudence; to lead nations and kings, by means of persuasion, to the true spirit of the Gospel, and to resemble, in their pious courses, the dove which came back to the ark, bearing the pacific olive-branch. In order to encourage princes by his example, the pontiff ordered the galleys he had destined to succour Rhodes, to set sail for the coast of Naples. At the same time he commanded public prayers to be put up; and, to draw down the blessings of Heaven upon the arms of the Christians, and excite the piety of the faithful, he directed that the octave of All Saints should be celebrated in the universal Church, to begin with the year 1480, which he called in his bull the "Octave of the age."

Previously to the taking of Otranto, Italy had been more divided than ever. The heat of factions and the animosities which were created by jealousy had so perverted men's minds, that several states and many citizens only contemplated in an invasion of the Turks the ruin of a neighbouring state or of a rival faction. Venice was accused of having drawn the Ottoman troops into the kingdom of Naples. We must, however, in justice, say that the presence of danger, and particularly the account of the cruelties practised by the fierce conquerors of Otranto, awakened generous sentiments in all hearts; and when the sovereign pontiff, addressing the Italians, said that the moment was come to rise in arms, if they wished to defend their lands, their families, their faith, their liberty, all Italy listened to his exhortations, and united as one man against the common enemy.

The discourses and the prayers of the head of the Church did not produce the same effect in England, Germany, or France. The legates were everywhere received with respect, but they could not put an end to the war between England and Scotland, or stifle the germs of a quarrel always ready to break out between Louis XI. and the emperor Maximilian. In a Germanic diet which was convoked, as usual, pathetic speeches were made upon the calamities which threatened Christian Europe; but no one took up arms.

The Ottomans, shut up in Otranto, had not, it is true, strength enough to advance into Italy; but they might every day expect reinforcements. After having raised three armies, the Turkish emperor levied a fourth in Bithynia, to be employed, according to circumstances, against the Mamelukes of Egypt, or against the Christians of the West. But even these preparations, or the fresh invasions which they had reason to fear, were not able to remove the general indifference. The nations and the princes who did not believe themselves threatened with approximate danger, returned to their divisions and their quarrels. They had abandoned the safety of Christendom to the care of Providence, when they learnt the death of Mahomet II.; this news appeared to be spread everywhere at once, and was received like the announcement of a great victory, particularly in the countries which were in dread of the Ottoman invasions. At Rome, where the dread had been most lively, the pope ordered prayers, festivals, and processions, which lasted three days; and during those three days, the pacific artillery of the castle of St. Angelo never ceased to thunder forth the intelligence of the deliverance of Italy.

This joy of the Christians paints better than the long recitals of history the ambition, the genius, the fortune, and the policy of the barbarous hero of Islamism. During the course of this reign, [81] five pontiffs had succeeded to the chair of St. Peter; all had employed the ascendancy of their spiritual and temporal power in endeavouring to check the progress of his arms, and all died with the grief of seeing the growth and extension of that empire, before which all the East trembled, and of whose invasions the West was in constant dread.

A.D. 1481-1571

The Turks abandoned Otranto, and the divisions which arose in the family of Mahomet suspended for a time the projects of Ottoman policy. Jem-Jem, whom the Latin chronicles call Zizim, disputed the empire with Bajazet, and being conquered, came into the West to await a favourable opportunity for recommencing the war. The Knights of Rhodes received him with great honours. He was afterwards sent into France, and, by one of the whimsical sports of fortune, an obscure commandery in the province of Auvergne became for a moment the asylum of a prince who pretended to the vast empire of the Crescent. His presence among the Christian powers gave serious uneasiness to Bajazet. The king of Hungary and the king of Naples had already promised to give the fugitive prince the support of their armies. The Ottoman emperor sent ambassadors to Charles VIII.; he informed the French monarch that his design was to conquer Egypt, and that he would voluntarily cede Jerusalem to him if he would place Zizim in his hands. At the same time, the sultan of Cairo sent one of the Latin fathers of the Holy Sepulchre to the pope, and requested also that the brother of Bajazet should be delivered up to him, as he wished to show him at the head of his army in a war against the Turks. He offered the sovereign pontiff, in exchange for such a great service, a hundred thousand gold ducats, the possession of the holy city, and even of the city of Constantinople, if they succeeded in driving the Turks from it. Charles VIII. had not arrived at the age for reigning, and the queen regent, engaged in reëstablishing peace in the kingdom, did not listen to the proposition of Bajazet. Neither did the pope accept the splendid offers of the sultan of Egypt; but the importance that appeared to be attached to the person of Zizim gave him the idea that he could himself derive some advantage from him. He demanded and obtained that the brother of Bajazet should be given up to him, and then he exhorted the Christian princes to unite with him, and promised to go in person to the conquest of Greece and Syria. The enterprise of Innocent VIII. reminds us of that of Pius II., and was destined to be equally unfortunate. The pontiff was employed in his scheme, with more zeal than success, when he died. Alexander VI., who succeeded him, had created for himself a name which repelled the confidence of the faithful, and left no hope that the preparations for a holy war would ever be able to divert him from the cares of his personal ambition, or tear him away from his profane affections.

The kingdom of Naples, however, which had occasioned so many wars, begun and carried on under the banners of the cross, gave rise, under these circumstances, to the idea of an enterprise which resembled a crusade. The duke of Milan, and several other small states, constantly occupied in disturbing Italy, and in calling thither foreign arms, for the purpose of increasing or preserving their own power, persuaded Charles VIII., then seated on the throne, to endeavour to establish the rights of the house of Anjou. Their solicitations and their brilliant promises awakened the ambition of the young king, who resolved to conquer the kingdom of Naples, and proclaimed the design of extending his views to the territories of the infidels.

The passion for arms, the spirit of chivalry, and the little that remained in men's hearts of the ancient ardour for crusades and distant expeditions, seconded the enterprise of the French monarch. Public prayers were offered up, and processions were formed throughout the kingdom, for the success of an expedition against the Turks. The preachings, or rather the poetical inspirations of some writers of the time, announced to all Europe the deliverance of the East.

When Charles VIII. had passed the Alps with his army, all the nations of Italy received him with the most lively demonstrations of joy; the love of liberty, the spirit of devotion, the sentiment of gallantry, all the passions which then prevailed, appeared to attach some hope to the issue of this expedition. The nations looked to the king of France and his knights for their independence. Amidst the brilliant festivities of chivalry, the French warriors were received as the *champions of the honour of ladies*. They gave Charles VIII. the titles of *envoy of God*, of *liberator of the Romish Church*, and of *defender of the faith*. All the acts of the king gave reason to believe that his expedition had for its object the glory and safety of Christendom. He wrote to the bishops of France to demand of them the tenths of a crusade. "Our intention," said he to them in his letters, "is not only to recover our kingdom of Naples, but to secure the welfare of Italy, and to effect the deliverance of the Holy Land."

Whilst the nations on both sides of the Alps gave themselves up to hope and joy, terror reigned in the kingdom of Naples. Alphonso addressed himself to all his allies; he, in particular, implored the succour of the Holy See, and, by a singular contrast, whilst he placed his greatest hopes in the court of Rome, he sent ambassadors to Constantinople, to warn Bajazet of the projects of Charles VIII. respecting Greece, and to conjure the Mussulman emperor to assist him in defending his kingdom against the invasion of the French. Alexander VI., who had embraced the cause of the princes of Arragon, beheld with the most lively inquietude the triumphant march of the king of France, who was advancing towards Rome without encountering any obstacles. In vain he called to his aid both the states of Italy and the Mussulman masters of Greece; in vain he employed the ascendancy of his spiritual power; he soon found himself obliged to submit, and to open the gates of his capital to a prince whom he regarded as his enemy, and whom he had by turns threatened with the anger of Heaven and with that of Bajazet.

Thus the war which the king of France had sworn to make against the infidels began by a victory obtained over the pope. According to one of the conditions imposed upon the sovereign pontiff, the brother of Bajazet was placed in the hands of Charles VIII. The unfortunate *Jem-Jem*, who knew nothing of the policy of which he was soon to become the victim, thanked the pope for having restored him to liberty. He congratulated himself upon being *protected by the great king of the West*, and entertained no doubt that the victorious arms of the Christians would replace him on the Ottoman throne. Charles VIII., however, appeared but very little disposed to restore to him the empire of Constantinople, which he had just purchased for himself. In the course of the last century, an act was found in the chancery of Rome, by which Andrew Palæologus, the despot of Achaia, and nephew of Constantine, sold to the king of France all his claims to the empire of the East, for the sum of four thousand three hundred gold ducats! This act, by which an empire was sold in the presence of a notary, and which could only be ratified by victory, appears to us a very curious historical monument; and serves to enlighten us upon the spirit and policy of these remote times. We must admit, however, that the French monarch seemed even then to attach very little value to this kind of treaty, and fulfilled none of the conditions of it. His attention was principally directed towards the kingdom of Naples, which fortune was about to place in his hands, without requiring him to fight a single battle.

Whilst Charles prolonged his sojourn at Rome, Alphonso II., abandoned to his own resources, a prey to terror and remorse, and pursued by the complaints of the Neapolitans, descended from his throne, and went to bury himself in a monastery of Sicily. His son Ferdinand, who succeeded him, although he had driven the Turks out of the city of Otranto, and had been proclaimed liberator of Italy, could neither revive the courage of his army nor the fidelity of his subjects. From the moment the arrival of the French was announced, the yoke of the house of Arragon appeared to become every day more insupportable. When Charles quitted the Roman states, instead of encountering the armies of an enemy, he only met on his road with deputations which came to offer him the crown of Naples. The capital soon received him in triumph, and the whole kingdom placed itself under his subjection.

Fame was not long in carrying into Greece the news of the marvellous conquests of Charles VIII. The Turks of Epirus, struck with terror, dreaded every instant to see the French arrive. Nicolas Vignier adds, that Bajazet was possessed by such fear, that he caused all his navy to come to the Straits of St. George, to enable him to escape into Asia.

The presence of Zizim in the Christian army particularly excited the alarms of the Mussulmans; but fortune had exhausted all her prodigies in favour of the French. *Jem-Jem*, whom the king of France hoped to exhibit to the enemies of the faith, died almost suddenly on arriving in the kingdom of Naples. Alexander VI. was accused of bringing about this death; Bajazet having promised him three hundred thousand gold ducats, *if he would aid his brother in escaping from the miseries of this life.* Turkish historians relate this event after a different manner: they say that a barber of Constantinople, named Mustapha, was sent to poison Zizim; and, what paints with a single stroke the spirit and the character of the Ottoman despotism, when the barber returned to announce that the brother of the sultan was dead, Bajazet raised him to the post of vizier; so important did the service appear, and so worthy of reward was the crime.

The conquests of Charles VIII., which gave the Turks so much alarm, began to create lively inquietudes in several Christian states. A league was formed against the French, into which entered the pope, the emperor Maximilian, the king of Spain, and the principal states of Italy. After the example of Charles VIII., this league assumed as a pretext a war against the Turks; but its real design did not remain long concealed; for it solicited the approbation and the assistance of Bajazet. Policy, on this occasion, did not hesitate to sacrifice Christian victims, to cement an alliance with the disciples of the Koran. As the Greeks of Epirus and the Peloponnesus were eager to profit by the enterprise of the king of France to shake off the yoke of the Ottomans, they sent deputies into Italy. The senate of Venice caused these deputies to be arrested, and gave up their papers to the envoys of the sultan. Fifty thousand of the inhabitants of Greece perished victims to this base act of treachery.

On another side, the inconstancy of the people, who had at first been favourable to the arms of the king of France, and the discontent which is always inspired by the presence of a victorious army, all at once changed the state of things in the kingdom of Naples. The French, who had been received with so much enthusiasm, became odious, and the hopes of all were directed towards the family of Arragon, so recently abandoned. Charles, instead of directing his looks towards Greece, turned them towards France. Whilst he was in the act of causing himself to be crowned emperor of Byzantium and king of Sicily, his thoughts were fixed upon the abandonment of his conquests. It was a singular contrast which the spectacle presented, of preparations for a retreat, and a triumphal ceremony, going on at the same time. Whilst the nobility, the clergy, and all the public bodies of the state, came to congratulate the victorious prince, the people were invoking the protection of Heaven against him, and the French awaited in silence the order and signal for its departure. On the day following his coronation, and as if he had only come to Naples for the sake of this vain ceremony, Charles VIII. set out, accompanied by the most distinguished of his knights, and resumed sorrowfully the road to his own kingdom. On his arrival in Italy, he had heard nothing in his march but benedictions and songs of triumph. On his return, he heard only the maledictions of the people and the threats of his enemies. In the first place he had crossed Italy without opposition; in order to leave it, he was forced to give battle; and considered as a victory the liberty which was left to him to drag back the wreck of his army over the Alps.

Thus terminated this enterprise of Charles VIII., which at first was pretended to be a holy war, which was directed by a short-sighted policy, and the consequences of which became so fatal to France and Italy. Whilst the preparations for this war were going on, there appeared, as we have said above, several writings in prose and verse, in which great victories were predicted. The aim of these predictions was not only to excite the enthusiasm of the people, but to strengthen a weak and irresolute prince in his undertaking. When we read the prophetic songs and hymns of the poets, we may fancy we see the French setting out for the conquest of the holy places. But the scene changes when we turn our eyes to the pages of history. Everything leads us to conclude, that on this occasion religious opinions and sentiments of chivalry were but the auxiliaries of unfortunate ambition. It is particularly to this expedition that we may apply what J. J. Rousseau somewhere says of the crusades: "The intrigues of cabinets embroiled affairs, and religion was the pretext."

The policy of Venice did not preserve her from the anger of Bajazet, who declared war against her. Alexander VI. published a jubilee, and demanded tenths of the clergy of Europe for the preparations for a crusade against the Turks. The emperor Maximilian, Louis XII., and the kings of Castile,

Portugal, and Hungary, appeared to listen for a moment to the propositions of the pope. But reciprocal mistrust speedily dissolved this Christian league: in vain the preachers of the crusade repeated in their discourses the menaces of Bajazet; they could not overcome the indifference of the people; and the sovereign pontiff found everywhere equal obstacles to the levying of the tenths and the distribution of indulgences. The French clergy on this occasion braved ecclesiastical censures; and what shows the decline of the pontifical power, at least as far as regards the crusades, a simple decision of the Faculty of Theology of Paris was at that time sufficient to stand against all the terrible array of the menaces and thunders of Rome.

We have shown how and by what causes the spirit of the crusades had become enfeebled. Towards the end of the fifteenth century and the commencement of the sixteenth, two great events completed the diversion of attention from the East. America had recently been revealed to the ancient world, and the Portuguese had doubled the Cape of Good Hope. There is no doubt that the progress of navigation during the holy wars had contributed to the discoveries of Vasco de Gama and Christopher Columbus. But these discoveries, when they once became known in Europe, entirely occupied that active, enterprising, and adventurous spirit which had so long kept up the ardour for expeditions against the infidels. The direction of men's minds, views of policy, speculations of commerce, all were changed; and the great revolution of the crusades on its decline, was seen, in some sort, to clash with the new revolution which was born of the discovery and conquest of a new world.

The Venetians, masters of the ancient routes and commerce of India, were the first to be aware of the changes that were in operation, the consequences of which must prove so injurious to them. They secretly sent deputies to the sultan of Cairo, as much interested as themselves in opposing the interests of the Portuguese. The deputation from Venice advised the sultan of Egypt to ally himself with the king of Calcutta and other Indian powers, to attack the fleets and troops of Portugal. The republic undertook to send into Egypt and to the coasts of Arabia artisans to found cannon, and carpenters to construct vessels of war. The Egyptian monarch, whose interests were the same as those of Venice, readily entered into the plan proposed to him; and in order to arrest the progress of the Portuguese in India, he endeavoured to inspire a fear with regard to the holy places, which had so long been, and still were, objects of veneration for the faithful of the West. He threatened to raze to the ground the church of the Holy Sepulchre, to cast the ashes and monuments of the martyrs to the winds, and to force all the Christians of his states to abjure the faith of Christ. A Cordelier of Jerusalem came to Rome to express the alarms of the Christians of Palestine, and of the guardians of the holy tomb. The pope was seized with terror, and hastened to send the Cordelier to the king of Portugal, whom he conjured to make the sacrifice of his new conquests to God and Christendom. [82] The Portuguese monarch received the envoy of the pope and the Oriental Christians with kindness, gave him considerable sums for the support of the holy places, and replied to the sovereign pontiff, that he did not at all fear seeing the threats of the sultan carried out, but, on the contrary, he hoped to burn both Mecca and Medina, and bring vast regions under the law of the Gospel, if the princes of Christendom were willing to coöperate with him.

The sultan of Egypt, who received tribute from all pilgrims, did not destroy the churches of Jerusalem, but he attempted an expedition against the Portuguese, in concert with the king of Cambay and Calcutta. They equipped at Suez a fleet composed of six galleys, a galleon, and four store-ships, in which were embarked eight hundred Mamelukes. The Egyptian fleet descended along the shores of the Red Sea, coasted Arabia, doubled the Gulf of Persia, and cast anchor at the island and in the port of Diu, one of the most important points for the commerce of India. It is of this expedition the author of the Lusiad speaks in his ninth book: "With the help of the fleets from the port of Arsinoë, the Calicutians hoped to reduce those of Emanuel to ashes; but the arbiter of heaven and earth always finds means to execute the decrees of his profound wisdom."

The expedition of the Mamelukes, notwithstanding the success it at first obtained, produced not the results that the sultan of Cairo and the republic of Venice expected. The Portuguese, in their despair, endeavoured to persuade the king of Ethiopia to divert the course of the Nile. A project for shutting up the new routes of commerce and the passage of the Cape of Good Hope was scarcely more reasonable. Instead of having recourse to arms, the sultans of the Mamelukes would have much better served the interests of Venice, and those of their own power, if they had multiplied canals in their provinces, and opened a commodious, quick, and safe passage for the commerce of India: by that means they would have preserved for the navigation of the Mediterranean the advantage it had enjoyed for ages over the navigation of the ocean; and the maritime cities of Egypt and Italy would not have seen the sources of their prosperity suddenly dried up.

Whilst the republic of Venice contemplated with terror the causes of her future decline, she still inspired considerable jealousy by the splendour of her wealth and magnificence. Many complaints arose against the Venetians, who were universally accused of sacrificing everything to the interests of their commerce, and of betraying or serving the cause of the Christians, as fidelity or treachery became most profitable to them. In a diet which Maximilian convoked at Augsburg, Hélian, the ambassador of Louis XII., pronounced a vehement discourse against the Venetian nation. He reproached them, in the first place, with having thwarted, by their hostility and their intrigues, a league formed by the pope, the emperor of Germany, the king of France, and the king of Arragon, against the Turks. The orator then reproached the Venetians with having refused to succour Constantinople when besieged by Mahomet II. "Their fleet was in the Hellespont during the siege; they could hear the groans of a Christian people, sinking under the sword of the barbarians. Nothing could excite their pity. They remained unaffected and motionless, and when the city was taken, they purchased the spoils of the vanquished, and sold to the Mussulmans the unfortunate inhabitants of Greece, who had taken refuge beneath their banners. At a later period, when the Ottomans were besieging Otranto, not only cities and princes, but the mendicant orders, sent assistance to the besieged. The Venetians, whose fleet was then at anchor before Corfu, beheld with indifference, perhaps with joy, the dangers and the misfortunes of a Christian city. No, God cannot pardon a nation, which, by its avarice, its jealousy, and its ambition, has betrayed the cause of Christendom, and appears to maintain an understanding with the Turks, in order to reign with them over the East and over the West." Hélian, on terminating his discourse, pressed the states and the princes to combine their efforts, to execute the decrees of divine justice, and complete the ruin of the republic of Venice.

This discourse, in which the name of Christianity was invoked, but which breathed nothing but vengeance and hatred, made a lively impression upon the assembly. The passions which inflamed the diet of Augsburg, and which left no room for a thought of a war against the Turks, but too plainly showed the state of agitation and discord in which Christendom was then plunged. It is not consistent with our purpose to speak of the league formed, in the first place, against Venice, or of the league afterwards formed against Louis XII., or of the events which brought trouble into Italy, and even into the bosom of the Church, then threatened with a schism.

At the council of the Lateran, convoked by Julius II., the disorders of Christendom were deplored, without the least remedy being proposed for them. They touched upon the war with the Turks, without bestowing any attention upon the means for carrying it on. The exhortations of the pope, which were supposed to be animated by an ambitious policy, inspired no confidence. The pontiff, whom Voltaire represents as a bad priest but a good prince, entered in an active manner into the wars between Christian powers. Since war was carried on in his name, he could not fill the honourable part of a conciliator, and enjoyed no longer the consideration attached to the title of Father of the Faithful. He was not able to reëstablish the peace he had himself broken, and found it impossible to direct an enterprise against the infidels.

The preaching for a crusade, so often repeated, no longer made any impression on men's minds; misfortunes which never arrived had been so often announced to nations, that they ceased to awaken any alarm. After the death of Mahomet, the Turks seemed to have renounced all idea of conquering Europe. Bajazet at first attacked the Mamelukes of Egypt without success; he afterwards sunk into voluptuousness and the pleasures of the seraglio, which gave the Christians a few years of repose and safety. But as an indolent and effeminate prince did not fulfil the first condition of Ottoman despotism, which was war, he irritated the army, and his pacific tastes brought about his fall from the throne. Selim, who succeeded him, more ambitious and more cruel than Mahomet, accused of poisoning his father, and covered with the blood of his family, had scarcely attained empire before he promised to the janissaries the conquest of the world, and threatened, at the same time, Italy, Germany, Persia, and Egypt.

In the twelfth and last sitting of the fifth council of the Lateran, Leo X. took upon him to preach a crusade against the redoubtable emperor of the Ottomans. He ordered to be read before the fathers of the council a letter from the emperor Maximilian, who expressed great grief at seeing Christendom always exposed to the invasions of a barbarous nation.

At the same time the emperor of Germany, writing to his counsellor at the diet of Nuremberg, expressed the desire he had always felt of reëstablishing the empire of Constantine, and delivering Greece from the domination of the Turks. "We would willingly," said he, "have employed our power and even our person in this enterprise, if the other leaders of Christendom had assisted." When reading these letters of Maximilian, we might be led to believe that this prince was touched more than others by the misfortunes of the Greeks and the perils of Christendom. But the inconstancy and levity of his character would not allow him to carry on with ardour an enterprise to which he appeared to attach so much importance. He passed his life in forming projects against the Turks, and in making war against Christian powers; and in his old age consoled himself by thinking that the glory of saving Europe might perhaps one day belong to a prince of his family.

Whilst the Christian princes were thus reciprocally exhorting each other to take arms, without any one of them renouncing the interests of his own ambition, or offering an example of a generous devotion, Selim, after having conquered the king of Persia, attacked the army of the Mamelukes, dethroned the sultan of Cairo, and united to his vast dominions all the countries that the Franks had inhabited or possessed in Asia. Jerusalem then beheld the standard of the crescent floating over its walls, and the son of Bajazet, after the example of Omar, profaned by his presence the church of the Holy Sepulchre. [83] Palestine only fell under a fresh domination, and no change took place in the fate of the Christians. But as Europe dreaded the Turks more than the Mamelukes, against whom war had ceased to be carried on, the news of the conquests of Selim spread consternation and grief everywhere. It appeared to Christendom as if the holy city passed for the first time under the yoke of the infidels; and the sentiments of grief and mourning that the Christians then experienced, necessarily revived the idea of delivering the tomb of Christ.

We must add that the late victories of Selim completed the overthrow of all the powers in the East that had rivalled the Turks, and that whilst increasing in a fearful manner the strength of the Ottoman empire, they left it no other enemies to contend with but the nations of the West.

Leo X. contemplated seriously the dangers which threatened Christendom, and resolved to arm the principal powers of Europe against the Turks. The sovereign pontiff announced his project to the college of cardinals. The prelates most distinguished for their learning and their skill in negotiations, were sent into England, Spain, and Germany, with the mission of appeasing all quarrels that divided princes, and forming a powerful league against the enemies of the Christian republic. Leo X., who declared himself beforehand the head of this holy league, proclaimed a truce of five years among all the states of Europe, and threatened those who disturbed the peace with excommunication.

Whilst the pope was thus giving all his attention to preparations for a crusade, the poets and orators, whose labours he encouraged, represented him as already the liberator of the Christian world. The celebrated Vida, in a Sapphic ode addressed to Leo X., sang the future labours and conquests of the pontiff. Carried away by his poetical enthusiasm, he swore to go, clad in shining steel, to the extremities of the world, and to drink from a brazen helmet the waters of the Xanthus and the Indus. He boasts of cutting down with his sword the barbarous heroes of Asia, and fancies that he already sees posterity placing his name among those of warriors who had never known fear. Vida, in his ode, speaks of neither Christ nor the cross, but of Bellona and Apollo. His verses appear to be much less an inspiration of the Gospel than an imitation of Horace; and the praises he addresses to the head of the Christian Church resemble, both in tone and form, those which the bard of the Tiber addressed to Augustus. Whilst Vida, in profane verses, thus felicitated Leo X. upon the laurels he was about to gather amidst the labours and perils of a holy war, another writer not less celebrated, in a prose epistle printed at the head of the Orations of Cicero, addressed the sovereign pontiff with the same congratulations and the same eulogies. Novagero took delight in celebrating beforehand those days of glory in which the pope would return in triumph to the eternal city, after having extended the limits of the Christian world,—those happy days in which all Italy, in which all nations, should revere him as a divinity descended from heaven for their deliverance.

Italy was then filled with fugitive Greeks, amongst whom were some illustrious scholars, who exercised a great influence over men's minds, and never ceased to represent the Turks as a barbarous and ferocious people. The Greek tongue was taught with success in the most celebrated schools, and the new direction of studies, with the admiration which the masterpieces of Greece inspired, added greatly to the hatred of the people for the fierce dominators of Byzantium, Athens, and Jerusalem. Thus all the disciples of Homer and Plato associated themselves, in some sort, by their wishes and their discourses, with the enterprise of the sovereign pontiff. It may have been remarked, that the manner of preaching the crusades, and the motives alleged to excite the ardour of the Christians, differed according to circumstances, and were almost always analogous to the prevailing ideas of each period. In the times of which we now speak, everything naturally bears the character and stamp of the great age of Leo X.; and if the crusade had been able to contribute to the restoration of letters, it was just that letters in their turn should do something in a war undertaken against the enemies of civilization and intelligence.

The envoys of the court of Rome were received with distinction in all the states of Europe, and neglected neither evangelical exhortations, nor seductions, nor promises, nor any of the resources of profane policy, to induce Christian princes to join the crusade proclaimed by the pope. The sacred college rejoiced at the success of their mission, and the pope, to prove his gratitude to Heaven, and to draw down divine blessings upon his enterprise, ordered that processions should be made and prayers put up, during three days, in the capital of the Christian world. He himself celebrated the divine office, distributed alms, and walked barefooted and with his head uncovered to the church of the Holy Apostles.

Sadoletus, secretary to the Holy See, one of the most distinguished favourites of the Muses, and who, in the judgment of Erasmus, possessed in his writings the copiousness and the manner of Cicero, pronounced, in the presence of the clergy and the Roman people, a discourse, in which he celebrated the zeal and the activity of the sovereign pontiff, the eagerness of the Christian princes to make peace with each other, and the desire they evinced to unite their powers against the Turks: the orator reminded his auditory of the emperor of Germany and the king of France, glorious pillars of Christendom; of the army of Charles, king of Castile, whose youth exhibited all the virtues of ripened age; of the king of England, the invincible defender of the faith; of Emanuel, king of Portugal, always ready to sacrifice his own interests to those of the Church; of Louis II., king of Hungary; and Sigismund, king of Poland; the first, a young prince, the hope of Christians; the second, worthy to be their leader; of the king of Denmark, with whose devotion to religion Europe was well acquainted; and of James, king of Scotland, the examples of whose family must keep him in the road of virtue and glory. Among the Christian states, upon which humanity and religion must build their hopes, Sadoletus did not forget the Helvetians, a powerful and warlike nation, which burned with such zeal for the war against the Turks, that its numerous bands of soldiers were already prepared to march, and only waited for the signal of the head of the Church. The holy orator finished by a vehement apostrophe against the race of the Ottomans, whom he threatened with the united forces of Europe, and by an invocation to God, whom he conjured to bless the arms of so many princes, of so many Christian nations, in order that the empire of the world might be wrested from Mahomet, and that the praises of Jesus Christ might at length resound from the south to the north, and from the west to the east.

Leo X. was constantly engaged with the crusade he had preached. He consulted with able captains, and acquired information concerning the strength of the Turks, and upon the means of attacking them with advantage: the most certain means was to raise numerous armies. In his letters to the princes and the faithful, he exhorted Christians not to neglect prayers and the austerities of penitence; but he recommended them above all things to prepare their arms, and to oppose their redoubtable enemies with strength and valour. In concert with the principal states of Christendom, he laid down the plan of the holy war. The emperor of Germany was to furnish an army to which the Hungarian and Polish cavalry should be united. The king of France, with all his forces, all those of the Venetians, and several states of Italy, and sixteen thousand Swiss, was to embark at Brindisi, and make a descent upon the coast of Greece; whilst the fleets of Spain, Portugal, and England, should set sail from Carthagena and the neighbouring ports, to transport Spanish troops to the shores of the Hellespont. The pope proposed to embark himself at the port of Ancona, to repair to Constantinople, under the walls of which city all the forces of the Christian powers were to meet.

This plan was gigantic, and never would the Ottoman empire have been in greater danger, if such vast designs could have been carried into execution. But the Christian monarchs were only able to observe the truce proclaimed by the pope, and which they had accepted for a very few months; each of them had engaged to furnish for the crusade troops which every day became more necessary to them in their own states, and which they wished to aggrandize or defend. The old age of Maximilian, and the approaching vacancy of the imperial throne, at that time held all the ambitious in a state of expectation: very shortly the rivalry of Charles V. and Francis I. rekindled war in Europe, and Christendom, disturbed by the quarrels of princes, no longer thought it probable they should be invaded by the Turks.

But these political dissensions were not the only obstacles to the execution of the projects of Leo X. Another difficulty arose from the levy of the tenths. The clergy everywhere appeared to have the same indifference for the wars which ruined them. The people dreaded to see their alms employed in enterprises which had not for object the triumph of religion. The legate of the pope in Spain addressed himself first to the Arragonese, who replied by a formal refusal, expressed in a national synod. Cardinal Ximenes declared, in the name of the king of Castile, that the Spaniards did not believe in the threats of the Turks, and that they would not give their money until the pope had positively announced how he would employ it. If the dispositions and the will of the court of Rome found less resistance and occasioned no troubles in England or France, it was because Cardinal Wolsey, minister of Henry VIII., was associated in the mission of the apostolic legate, and that Leo X. abandoned the tenths of his kingdom to Francis I.

We have before us several historical documents which have never been printed, and which throw a great light upon the circumstances of which we are speaking. The first is a letter from Francis I., dated from Amboise, the 16th of December, 1516, by which *Master Josse de Lagarde, doctor in theology, vicar-general of the cathedral church of Thoulouse*, is named commissary, *touching the fact of the crusade in the diocese*. The king of France exposes in another letter the aim of the jubilate that is about to be opened: *it was to implore means to make war against the infidels, and conquer the Holy Land and the empire of Greece, detained and usurped by the said infidels*. To these letters patent are joined instructions given by the king, in concert with the legate of the pope, for the execution of the bull which orders the preaching of the crusade in the kingdom of France during the two years 1517 and 1518. These instructions, in the first place, recommend the choice of good preachers, charged *to make good and devout sermons to the people, and to explain the faculties and dispensations which are contained in the bull*, as well as why *the just and holy causes for which it is ordered, that during two years all other indulgences, all other general and particular pardons, are suspended and revoked*.

After having spoken of the choice of preachers, and of the manner in which they ought to preach, the letters patent of the king give some instructions upon the choice of confessors. The commissary-general of the crusade could appoint as many as seemed necessary to him for every church in which were *troncs et questes* (poor-boxes and gatherings) for the jubilee. He was commanded to name six for the cathedral of the diocese, *gens de bonne conscience, hors de suspicion* (worthy people, above suspicion). The ecclesiastics thus chosen by the commissary had the mission to confess all such as were desirous of indulgences; and to avoid the disorders that might arise from the spirit of rivalry, they had, to the exclusion of all others, the power to make compositions and restitutions, and give absolution, &c. &c.

In short, the royal ordinance omitted none of the circumstances which accompanied the preaching of a crusade, or of the forms which ought to be adopted in the distribution of indulgences. It goes so far as to regulate the shape of the *troncs* placed in the churches to receive the offerings of the faithful, and the religious ceremonies that were to be observed during the jubilee. [84] Among other orders, one commanded that a great number of confessionals, or bills of absolution and indulgence, should be made; that these bills, signed by a notary, should be sent to the commissary-general, who would seal them WITH THE SEAL sent by the king, and that there should be left upon them a blank space for the name of him or her who wished to procure them. The royal instruction added, that the commissary should cause his *tronc* to be properly and handsomely set up, and that there should be in the centre of it a large handsome cross, upon which should be written, in great, fair letters, IN HOC SIGNO VINCES. In order that nothing might be wanting to excite the people to devotion, it was besides ordered, that solemn processions should be made, and that in them a handsome banner should be carried, upon which should be, on one side, the portraits of the pope and the king of France, and on the other, *paintings full of Turks and other infidels*.

In this ordinance, of which it gives us great pleasure to recall the spirit and the expressions, that which history particularly observes, is the numerous precautions against infidelity and fraud. The distributors of the indulgences were obliged to consult an assessment for their government in all expenses and reinstatements. The *troncs*, in which the money of the faithful was deposited, had three locks and three keys, and were only to be opened in the presence of witnesses; among the documents we have quoted, is one which is the legal order for the opening of the *troncs*, [85] with an account rendered of the receipts and expenditure, in which the most minute details are not neglected, and which shows to what a degree exactitude and watchfulness were carried. These rigorous precautions were the more necessary, from the people being led to be suspicious by the examples of past times; it was pretty well known that many of the collectors of the money for the crusades were not *people of worth, and above suspicion*. The more sacred the motive for levying this tribute was said to be, the more promptly was suspicion awakened; and the more anxious did charity itself appear as to the manner in which its offerings might be expended. Upon this point, as upon others, authority had so much the more necessity for keeping a severe watch, from there always being among the orators of the crusades some who showed more zeal than wisdom, and whose preachings were really a subject of scandal. As most of them received a salary proportionate with the amount of money dropped into the *troncs* of the churches, many did not hesitate to exaggerate the promises of the sovereign pontiff and the privileges attached to gifts of charity. History gives us the example of a preacher who put forth from the evangelical pulpit the following culpable maxim: *When a piece of money shall be placed in the tronc of the crusade for the deliverance of a soul from purgatory, immediately that soul will be delivered, and will fly away towards heaven.* The Faculty of Theology of Paris censured this proposition as contrary to the dogmas of the Church. The prudence of the heads of the Gallican Church, and the wise measures adopted by the king of France, thus prevented great disorders. It was not so in Germany, where the greatest excitement and dissatisfaction prevailed, and where seeds of heresy and trouble began to spring up even in the bosom of the clergy.

It may have been observed, how much more easy the court of Rome had hitherto daily made the opening of the treasury of pontifical indulgences. In the early expeditions to the East, these indulgences were only granted to the pilgrims of the Holy Land. They were afterwards granted to all who contributed to the support of the Crusaders. Still later, they were granted to the faithful who listened to the sermons of the preachers of the crusades; sometimes even to those who were present at the mass of the pope's legates. As the distribution or sale of indulgences was an inexhaustible source of wealth, Leo X. took upon him to grant them not only to those who, by their alms, were willing to aid in defraying the expenses of the war against the Turks, but to all the faithful whose pious liberality should contribute to the amount necessary for the completion of the building of the church of St. Peter, which had been begun by his predecessor Julius II. Although this destination might have something noble and truly useful in it; although it might be worthy, in some sort, of an age in which the arts burst forth with great splendour, many Christians, particularly in Germany, saw nothing in it but an actual profanation, and a new means by which the court of Rome sought to enrich itself at the expense of the faithful.

Albert, archbishop of Mayence, charged with appointing the preachers of the jubilee and the distributors of papal indulgences, named for Saxony, Dominicans, to the exclusion of Cordeliers or Augustines, who had sometimes filled these kinds of missions. The latter showed themselves jealous of this preference; and as no precaution had been taken either to avert the effects of this species of rivalry, or put a stop to the abuses which might be committed, it happened that the Augustines censured severely the conduct, manners, and opinions of the Dominicans, and that the latter but too well justified the complaints of their adversaries.

Luther, an Augustine monk, put himself forward in these violent quarrels, and distinguished himself by his fervid eloquence; [86] he spoke strongly against the preachers that had been selected to receive the contributions of the faithful; and among the propositions he put forth from the pulpit, history has preserved the following, which was censured by Leo X.: "It is a sin to resist the Turks, seeing that Providence makes use of this faithless nation, to visit the iniquities of his people." This strange maxim obtained faith amongst the partisans of Luther; and when the pope's legate demanded, at the diet of Ratisbon, the levy of the tenths destined for the crusade, he met with a warm opposition. Murmurs and complaints arose in all parts of Germany. The court of Rome was reproached with putting holy things up to sale: it was compared to the unfaithful shepherd, who shears the sheep confided to his care; it was accused of despoiling credulous people; of ruining nations and kings; and of accumulating upon Christians more miseries than the domination of the Turks could cause them.

For more than a century, these kinds of accusations resounded throughout Germany, every time that money was raised for crusades; or that any tribute whatever was imposed upon the Christians by the sovereign pontiff. The reformers took advantage of this disposition of men's minds to circulate new ideas, and to attempt a revolution in the Church. Among a nation led by its genius and character to speculative ideas, philosophic and religious novelties were sure to find more warm partisans and ardent apostles than elsewhere. It must likewise be added, that Germany was one of the countries of Christendom that Rome had, in its omnipotence, spared the least; and that the spirit of opposition had *there* taken rise, amidst long quarrels between the priesthood and the empire. When once the tie that united the minds of people was broken, and the yoke of an authority consecrated by time was shaken off, opposition knew no bounds; there was no longer a limit to opinions: the Church was attacked on all sides at once, and by a thousand different sects, all opposed to the court of Rome, and most of them opposed to each other. From that period burst forth that revolution which was destined to separate for ever many nations of Christendom from the Romish communion.

It is not our task to describe the events which accompanied the schism of Luther; but it is curious to observe, that the origin of the Reformation should be connected, not directly with the crusades, but with the abuse of the indulgences promulgated for the crusades.

Like all who begin revolutions, Luther was not at all aware of the extent to which his opposition to the court of Rome might be carried: he at first began by attacking some abuses of the pontifical authority, and soon finished by attacking the authority itself. The opinions he had kindled by his eloquence, the passions he had given birth to among his disciples, led him himself much further than he could possibly have foreseen: those who had the greatest reason to combat the doctrines of the reformers saw, no more than he did, what those doctrines were to bring with them. Germany, divided into a thousand different states, and given up to all kinds of disorders, had no authority sufficiently strong and sufficiently prescient to anticipate the effects of a schism. At the court of Rome nobody could have believed that a simple monk could ever shake the pillars of the Church. Amidst the pomp and the splendour of the arts which he patronized, and diverted by the cares of an ambitious policy, Leo X. perhaps was too neglectful of the progress of Luther. Above all, he was wrong in entirely abandoning the expedition against the Turks, which he had announced to the Christian world, and which might, at least at the first, have offered a useful distraction to minds agitated by ideas of reformation. The undertaking of a holy war which he had followed up with so much warmth at the beginning of his pontificate and for which the poets promised him eternal glory,—this enterprise, at his death, no longer engaged his thoughts, or those of his contemporaries.

In the mean time Soliman, the successor of Selim, had recently taken possession of Belgrade, and threatened the isle of Rhodes. This isle was then the last colony of the Christians in Asia. As long as the Knights of St. John remained masters of it, the sultan of the Turks had reason to fear that some great expedition might be formed in the West for the recovery of Palestine and Syria, or even for the conquest of Egypt, which had lately been united to the Ottoman empire.

The grand-master of the Hospitallers sent to solicit the assistance of Christian Europe. Charles V. had just united, in his own person, the imperial crown with that of the Spains. Entirely occupied with opposing the power of France, and anxious to draw Pope Adrian VI. into a war against the most Christian king, the emperor was very little affected by the danger which threatened the Knights of Rhodes. The sovereign pontiff did not dare to succour them, or solicit for them the support of Christendom. Francis I. exhibited more generous sentiments; but in the situation in which his kingdom was then placed, he was unable to send them the assistance he had promised.

The Knights of Rhodes were left to their own resources. History has celebrated the labours and the prodigies of heroism by which the order of the Hospitallers illustrated its defence. After many months of combats, Rhodes fell into the hands of Soliman. It was a sad spectacle to behold the grand-master L'Isle-Adam, the father of his knights and of his subjects, dragging with him the sad remains of the order, and all the people of Rhodes, who had determined to follow him. He landed at first upon the coast of Naples, not far from the spot where Virgil makes the pious Æneas land, with the glorious wreck of Troy. If the spirit of the crusades could have revived, what heart could have remained unmoved, at seeing this venerable old man, followed by his faithful companions in misfortune, seeking an asylum, imploring compassion, and soliciting, as a reward of their past services, a little corner of earth upon which he and his warriors might still unfurl the standard of religion, and combat the infidels.

When the grand-master set forward on his march towards Rome, Adrian VI. had declared war against the king of France; a league was formed by the sovereign pontiff, the emperor, the king of England, and the duke of Milan. In this state of affairs, the Christians of the East could not hope for any succour. After the death of Adrian, Pope Clement VII. showed himself more favourable to the order of the Hospitallers. He received the grand-master with all the demonstrations of a paternal tenderness. When the chancellor of the order related, in the consistory, the exploits and the reverses of the knights, the sovereign pontiff and the Romish prelates shed tears, and promised to interest all the powers of the Christian world for such noble sufferers. Unfortunately for the order of St. John, the powers of Europe were more than ever divided among themselves. Francis I. was made prisoner at the battle of Pavia. The pope, who had wished to resume the old papal title of the conciliator, only drew down upon himself the hatred and the anger of Charles V. Amidst these divisions, the Knights of Rhodes were forgotten; and it was not till ten years after the conquest of Soliman, that these noble warriors were able to obtain from the emperor, the rock of Malta, where they became again the terror of the Mussulmans.

Whilst Europe was thus troubled, the conqueror of Rhodes and Belgrade reappeared in a threatening attitude upon the banks of the Danube. Louis II. endeavoured to reanimate the patriotism of the Hungarians, and caused the old custom of exposing in public a bloody sabre to be revived, as a signal of war and of danger for the country. But neither the exhortations of the monarch, nor those of the clergy, nor even the approach of the enemy, were able to appease the discords, born of feudal anarchy and the lengthened misfortunes of Hungary. The Hungarian monarch was only able to get together an army of twenty-two thousand men, to oppose to that of Soliman. Louis, a young prince without experience, who allowed himself to be led, even in war, by ecclesiastics, named, as general of his army, Paul Temory, lately issued from a convent of Cordeliers, to become archbishop of

Colotza. We are unable to ascertain whether, in this circumstance, the king of Hungary was obliged to put himself in the hands of the clergy, because he was abandoned by the nobility; or, if the nobility abandoned him, because he had put himself in the hands of the clergy. As the pope constantly excited the Hungarians to defend their own country, the ecclesiastics of Hungary, who were his interpreters to the faithful, and even to the king, must naturally have exercised a great influence in all that concerned the crusade.

In this war twenty-two thousand Christians had to contend with an army of a hundred thousand Ottomans; and this was the Hungarian army which, according to the advice of the bishops, offered battle to the infidels. What is very remarkable in holy wars is, that the clergy may almost always be recognised by the rashness of the enterprises. The persuasion of the ecclesiastics, that they were fighting for the cause of God, with their ignorance of the art of war, prevented them from seeing perils, did not allow them to doubt of victory, and made them often neglect the means of human prudence. It was then, in the confidence of a miraculous success, that the archbishop of Colotza did not hesitate to venture upon a decisive battle. The clergy who accompanied him animated the combatants by their discourses, and set an example of bravery; but religious and warlike enthusiasm cannot triumph over numbers, and most of the prelates received the palm of martyrdom in the *mêlée*. Eighteen thousand Christians were left upon the field of battle; and what added greatly to the misfortune, Louis II. disappeared, and perished in the general rout, leaving his kingdom torn by factions and ravaged by the Turks.

The defeat of the Hungarians brought despair to the mind of Clement VII. The pontiff wrote to all the sovereigns of Europe; he even formed the project of visiting them in person, and to engage them by his prayers and his tears to defend Christendom. Neither the touching exhortations of the pope, nor his suppliant attitude, were able to move the princes; and it is here that we can plainly perceive the rapid decline of the pontifical power, which we have so lately seen armed with all the terrors of the Church, and whose decisions were considered as the decrees of Heaven. War was about to be rekindled in Italy, and the pope was not long in becoming himself the victim of the disorders he would willingly have prevented. The imperial troops entered Rome as into an enemy's city. The emperor, who assumed the title of temporal head of the Church, did not fear to offer to Europe the scandal of the captivity of a pontiff.

Although the authority of the head of the Church no longer inspired the same veneration, or exercised the same ascendancy over men's minds, nevertheless the violences of Charles V. excited general indignation. England and France flew to arms. All Europe was troubled: some wished to avenge the pope, others to take advantage of the disorder; but none thought of defending Christendom against the invasion of the Turks.

Clement VII., however, from the depths of the prison in which the emperor detained him, still watched over the defence of Christian Europe: his legates went to exhort the Hungarians to fight for their God and their country. As the pontiff had been ruined by the calamities of war, he implored the charity of the faithful; he ordered that the plate should be sold in all the churches of Italy; he solicited the assistance of several Italian states; and he ordered that indulgences might be distributed and the tenths collected to support the expenses of the holy war.

The active solicitude of the pope went so far as to seek enemies against the Turks even in the East and among the infidels. Acomath, who had in Egypt shaken off the yoke of the Porte, received encouragement from the court of Rome. A legate of the pope went to promise him the support of the Christians of the West. The sovereign pontiff kept up continual relations on all the frontiers and in all the provinces of the Turkish empire, in order to be made aware of the designs and preparations of the sultans of Constantinople. It is not out of place to say here, that most of the predecessors of Clement had taken, as he did, the greatest care in watching the projects of the infidels. Thus the heads of the Church did not confine themselves to exciting the Christians to defend themselves upon their own territories; but, like vigilant sentinels, they constantly kept their eyes fixed upon the enemies of Christendom, to warn Europe of the perils which threatened it.

When the emperor broke the chains of Clement VII., the holy pontiff forgot the outrages he had received, to give all his cares to the danger of the German empire, which was about to be attacked by the Turks. The capital of Austria was soon besieged, and only owed its safety to the bravery of its garrison. In the diets of Augsburg and Spire, the pope's legate endeavoured, in the name of religion, to rouse the ardour of the people of Germany for their own defence. A physician, named Riccius, spoke in the name of the emperor, and added his exhortations to those of the apostolic legate; he made an appeal to the ancient virtue of the Germans, and reminded his auditors of the example of their ancestors, who had never endured a foreign domination. He pressed princes, magistrates, and people, to fight for their own independence and safety. Ferdinand, king of Bohemia and Hungary, urged the princes and states of the empire to adopt prompt and effective measures against the Turks. These exhortations and counsels met with but little success, but had to encounter a strong opposition from the still too active spirit of the new doctrines. All the cities, all the provinces, were occupied by questions agitated by the Reformation. We may at this time compare the nations of Germany, menaced by the Turks, to the Greeks of the lower empire, whom history represents as given up to vain disputes, when the barbarians were at their gates. As among the Greeks, there was a crowd of men among the Germans, who entertained less dread of seeing in their cities the turban of Mahomet than the tiara of the pontiff of Rome; some, governed by a spirit of fatalism scarcely to be equalled in the Koran, asserted that God had judged Hungary, and that the safety of that kingdom was not in the power of men; others (the Millenarians) announced with a fanatical joy the approach of the last judgment; and whilst the preachers of the crusades were exhorting the Germans to defend their country, the jealous pride of an impious sect called for the days of universal desolation.

The paternal proceedings and counsels of the pope were neither able to calm men's minds, nor to rekindle an enthusiasm for the holy war, in Germany, or even among the Hungarians. Ferdinand, brother of Charles V., whom the imperial power had caused to be declared king of Hungary; and the vaiwode of Transylvania, who, with permission of the Turks, reigned over the ruins of his country, were contending for this unfortunate kingdom, oppressed at the same time by its enemies and its allies. When Soliman returned, for the third time, to the banks of the Danube, called thither by a party of the Hungarian nobility, he found no army to oppose his march. The Ottomans advanced towards the capital of Austria, and prepared to invade the richest provinces of Germany. So pressing a danger determined the head and the princes of the empire to unite their forces against the common enemy. But when the Turks retired in disorder, no one thought of either fighting with them, or pursuing them in their precipitate retreat. The king of Hungary, abandoned all at once by the Germans, and fearing fresh attacks, had no resource but to sue to his enemies for peace. It is a circumstance worthy of remark, that the pope was comprised in the treaty: Soliman gave the title of father to the Roman pontiff, and that of brother to the king of Hungary. Clement VII., after so many useless attempts to interest the princes of Christendom, appeared to entertain no hope but in Providence; and exclaimed with bitterness, when approving the issue of the pacific negotiations, "We have nothing left but to supplicate Heaven to watch itself over the Christian world."

It might be believed that the holy wars were drawing towards an end, when the head of the Church had laid down his arms, and made peace with the infidels. But this treaty of peace, like others that had preceded it, could only be considered as a truce, and war would most likely break out again when either the Christians or the Mussulmans saw any hopes of carrying it on with advantage. Such was the policy of the times; particularly that which governed the Christian and Mussulman powers in their mutual relations. Soliman had abandoned his projects upon Germany and Hungary, less out of respect for treaties, than because he was employing his forces against the Persians, or that he required his army to quell some revolts which had broken out in Asia against his authority. On the other side, Christendom left the Ottomans in peace, because it was a prey to discord; and because most Christian princes, occupied by their own interests, listened to nothing but the counsels of their ambition.

Europe had at that time three great monarchs, whose united strength would have been quite sufficient to crush the power of the Turks; but these three princes were as much opposed to each other by their policy as by their character and their genius. Henry VIII. of England, who had refuted Luther, and leagued himself with the king of France, to deliver the captive pope, had just separated himself from the Romish Church. Sometimes allied with France, sometimes allied with the emperor, occupied in bringing about the triumph of the schism of which he was the apostle and the head, he had no time to bestow upon war with the infidels. Francis I. had, in the first place, made pretensions to the imperial crown, and afterwards to the duchy of Milan and the kingdom of Naples. These pretensions, which were a source of misfortunes to himself and France, disturbed the whole of his reign, and never allowed him an opportunity for seriously undertaking a crusade against the Turks, a crusade which he himself had preached in his states. The feeling of vengeance and jealousy which animated him against a fortunate and powerful rival, inspired him twice with the idea of seeking an alliance with Soliman. To the great scandal of Christendom, an Ottoman fleet was received in the port of Marseilles, and the standard of the lilies was mingled with the crescent under the walls of Nice. Charles V., master of all the Spains, head of the German empire, sovereign of the Low Countries, and possessor of several empires in the new world, was much more anxious to humble the French monarchy, and establish his domination in Europe, than to defend Christendom against the invasion of the Turks. During the greater part of his reign, this monarch conciliated the Protestants of Germany, on account of the Ottomans; and avoided collision with the Ottomans, on account of his enemies in the Christian republic. He satisfied himself with protecting, by his arms, the capital of Austria, when threatened by the Turks; but when the pope conjured him to employ his forces for the deliverance of Hungary, he preferred attempting an expedition to the coast of Africa. A war against the Moors of Africa was more popular in Spain than an expedition upon the Danube; and Charles was more desirous of acquiring popularity among the Spaniards, than of meriting the gratitude of Christendom. The Barbary powers were recently formed, under the protection of the Ottoman Porte, and began to render themselves formidable in the Mediterranean. Charles carried his arms twice to the coast of Africa: in the first expedition, he got possession of Tunis, planted his standards upon the ruins of Carthage, and delivered twenty thousand captives, who went to publish his victories in every part of the Christian world; in the second expedition, he would have annihilated the Barbary powers, so destructive to the navigation of the Franks; but a hurricane, which destroyed his fleet and his army, dispersed the hopes of commerce and navigators.

At the time Charles experienced so great a disaster whilst combating the Mussulmans of Africa, the Ottomans, invited by Francis I., were ravaging the coasts of Italy, and had recently entered Hungary, from whence they threatened Germany.

Then fresh cries of alarm resounded all over Europe, and among those who exhorted the nations to oppose the Turks, the voice of Martin Luther was heard. In a book entitled *Prayer against the Turk*, the reformer condemned the indifference of people and kings, and advised the Christians to resist the Mussulmans, if they did not wish to be led into captivity, as the children of Israel had formerly been. In a formula of prayer which he had composed, he expressed himself thus: "Arise, Lord, great God, and sanctify thy name, which thy enemies outrage; strengthen thy reign, which they wish to destroy, and suffer us not to be trampled under-foot by those who are not willing that thou shouldst be our God."

Murmurs had several times arisen against Luther, who was accused of having, by his doctrines, weakened the courage of the Germans. Some time before the period of which we are speaking, he published an apology, in which, without disavowing the famous proposition censured by the pope, he gave to his words a different sense from that which the court of Rome gave them, and which he himself, no doubt, had given them in the first instance. All his explanations, which it is not very easy to analyze, were reduced to this idea: — "That it was allowable to fight with the Turks, but that it was not allowable to fight with them under the banners of Christianity." Although the leader of the Reformation required all the qualities of a perfect Christian in the warriors called upon to fight the Mussulmans, and although he drew all the principles of his preaching from the religion of Christ; the standard of the cross in a Christian army, caused him, he said, more horror than the sight of the demon. The true motive for his repugnance for a crusade may be easily guessed; a crusade appeared necessarily to require the concurrence of the pope; and the concurrence of the pope, in a war which interested Christendom, was the thing in the world most dreaded by Luther. He had so strong an aversion to the court of Rome, that in his writings he asks himself if war ought not to be made against the Pope as well as the Turk; and in the excess of his hatred, does not hesitate to answer, *against the one as against the other.*

We will not repeat here the declamations and the sophisms of Luther. Through the puerile subtleties and the contrary reasonings which he employs for his justification, we must, however, remark the distinction he has made between civil authority and ecclesiastical authority: it is to the first, says the reformer, that it belongs to combat the Turks; the duty of the second is to wait, to submit, to pray, and to groan. He adds, that war was not the business of bishops, but of magistrates; that the emperor, in this circumstance, ought to be considered as the head of the German confederation, and not as the protector of the Church, nor as the support of the Christian faith; a title which can only properly be given to Jesus Christ. All these arguments, doubtless, had something reasonable in them; and the opinion of Luther upon the civil authority, although he might have adopted it only out of opposition to the papal power, would have obtained the approbation of enlightened minds, if he had not employed, in supporting it, all the passion of irritated pride; and if his apology, in particular, had not been stained by abuse which decency will not allow history to repeat.

Not content with this apology, which had for title, *Of the War against the Turks*, Luther, two years after the siege of Vienna, published another work, entitled, *A Military Discourse*, in which he also urges the Germans to take arms. This second discourse begins, as the first had done, by theological distinctions and subtleties; by declamations against the pope and the bishops; by predictions upon the approaching end of the world; and upon the power of the Turks; which the author finds clearly announced in Daniel. Although he endeavours to prove, as in his first writing, that the war against the Mussulmans is not at all a religious war, but an enterprise entirely political; he promises, not the less, the palms of martyrdom to those who shall die with arms in their hands. He represents this war as agreeable to the Divinity, and as the duty of a true disciple of the Gospel. "Thy arm and thy lance," says he to every Christian soldier who shall take arms against the infidels, "shall be the arm and the lance of God. In immolating Turks, thou wilt not shed innocent blood, and the world will consider thee as the executioner of the decrees of divine justice; for thou wilt but kill those whom God has himself condemned. The Turk," adds he, "ravishes terrestrial life from Christians, and procures them eternal life; he at the same time kills himself, and precipitates himself into hell." Luther appears to be so penetrated with this idea, that he is on the point of deploring the fate of the Mussulmans; and to chastise indifferent Christians, and pusillanimous Germans, he has no punishment to wish them, unless it be that they should become Turks, and thus be the property of the devil.

A short extract is not sufficient to show what whimsical and singular ideas are contained in Luther's discourse; it may, however, be easily perceived how much this kind of preaching differs from that of the orators who preached the crusade in preceding ages. In the second part of his discourse, the leader of the Reformation addressed himself to the various classes of society; to the nobility, who are immersed in luxury and pleasures, but for whom the hour of fight is at length come; to the citizens and merchants, for too long a time addicted to usury and cupidity; to the labourers and peasants, whom he accuses of deceiving and robbing their neighbours. The tone of the preacher is full of an excessive severity; he speaks like a man who feels no sorrow at the misfortunes which are about to happen, because he has foretold them, and his warnings and prophecies have been despised. He says, with a sort of satisfaction, that after days of joy and debauchery, after seasons of festivity and pleasures, comes the time of tears, miseries, and alarms. He finishes by a vehement apostrophe, addressed to all who shall remain deaf to his voice, and whom the enemy shall find without defence: "Listen now, then, to the devil in the Turk, you who are not willing to listen to God in Jesus Christ; the Turk will burn your dwellings; he will bear away your cattle and your harvests; he will outrage and slaughter your wives and your daughters before your eyes; he will impale your little children upon the very stakes of the hedge which serves as an inclosure to your heritage; he will immolate you yourselves, or will carry you away into Turkey, to expose you in the market, like unclean animals; it is he who will teach you what you will have lost, and what you ought to have done. It is to the Turk belongs the task to humble the haughty nobility, to render citizens docile, and to chastise and tame the gross multitude."

Luther then gives his advice upon the manner of making war against the Turks; he is desirous that all should defend themselves even to death, and that all the countries through which the enemy was about to pass should be laid waste; he terminates his discourse by addressing consolations to them who shall fall into the hands of the Turks, and traces out for them a plan of conduct for the time of their captivity among the infidels.

This language, of which we are far from exaggerating the singularity, was not at all calculated to warm and rally men's minds for a struggle against the enemies of Germany and Christendom. At this period, the princes and the states of the empire frequently met to deliberate on their own dangers. It was more easy to convoke diets than to get together armies. The Protestants were not willing to take arms against the Turks, for fear of strengthening their adversaries; and the Catholics were restrained by their fear of the Protestants: amidst the violent debates that agitated Germany, the Church, and even the civil authority which Luther had proclaimed, lost all that unity of action, without which it is impossible to combat a formidable enemy with advantage. Among the Germans, the spirit of sect weakened by degrees the spirit of patriotism; among Christians, the hatred they conceived for one another caused them to lose that pious ardour which had animated them against the Mussulmans. In proportion as the Reformation proceeded, Germany became divided into two parties, which were like two enemies face to face. Both parties soon had recourse to arms, and, in the fury of civil wars, the invasions of the Turks were forgotten. It was thus that the Reformation, which took its birth at the end of the crusades, completely extinguished the enthusiasm for holy wars, and no longer permitted the nations of Christendom to unite against the infidels.

The name of the Turks was still pronounced in the diets of Germany, and even in the council of Trent; but no measures were adopted for making war against them. From that time there passed nothing in either Hungary or the East which was able to fix the attention of the Christian world. The only event upon which Europe seemed interested was the defence of Malta against all the forces of Soliman. This defence increased the reputation of the military order of St. John. The port of Malta became the only place of shelter for Christian vessels on the route to Egypt, Syria, or Greece. The corsairs of Tunis and Algiers, and all the pirates who infested the Mediterranean, trembled at the sight of the rock, and of the galleys over which floated the standard of the cross. This military colony, always armed against the infidels, and constantly recruited from the warlike nobility of Europe, offered, up to the end of the eighteenth century, a living image of ancient chivalry, and of the heroic epoch of the crusades. We have described the origin of this illustrious order,—we have followed it in its days of triumph, and in its reverses, still more glorious than its victories. We will not say by what revolution it is fallen, nor how it has lost that isle which was given to it as the reward of its bravery, and which it defended, during more than two hundred years, against the Ottoman forces and the barbarians of Africa.

Whilst the Turks miscarried in their expedition against Malta, Soliman was pursuing the war in Hungary, and still threatening Germany. He died on the banks of the Danube, in the midst of victories obtained over the Christians. Christendom must have rejoiced at his death, as it had rejoiced at the death of Mahomet II. Under the reign of Soliman, who was the greatest prince of the Ottoman dynasty, the Turks not only invaded a part of the German empire, but their marine, seconded by the genius of Barberossa and Dragut, made a progress that must have alarmed all the maritime powers of Europe. Selim II., who succeeded him, had neither his qualities nor the genius of most of his predecessors; but he followed not the less their projects of aggrandizement, or the views of their ambitious policy. The Ottomans, masters of the coasts of Greece, Syria, and Africa, were desirous of adding to their conquests the kingdom of Cyprus, which was then possessed by the Venetians.

After a siege of several months, the Ottoman army obtained possession of the cities of Famagousta and Nicosia. The Turks stained their victory by cruelties without example. The bravest of the defenders of Cyprus expiated in tortures the glory of an obstinate resistance; and it may be said, it was the executioners that finished the war. The barbarity of the Turks disgusted the Christian nations afresh; and the maritime countries of the West beheld with terror an invasion which threatened to exclude Europeans from every road to the East.

At the approach of the danger, Pope Pius V. exhorted the Christian powers to take up arms against the Ottomans. A confederation was formed, consisting of the republic of Venice, Philip II., king of Spain, and the pope himself, always ready to add the authority of his example to his preaching. A numerous fleet, equipped for the defence of the isle of Cyprus, arrived too late in the eastern seas, and was only able to repair the disgrace of the Christian arms. This fleet, commanded by Don John of Austria, met that of the Ottomans in the Gulf of Lepanto. It was in this sea Antony and Augustus disputed the mastership of the Roman world. The battle which took place between the Christians and the Turks reminds us in some degree of the spirit and enthusiasm of the crusades. Before the commencement of the conflict, Don John hoisted on board his ship the standard of St. Peter, which he had received from the pope, and the army saluted with cries of joy this religious signal of victory. The leaders of the Christians passed along the line of barques, exhorting the soldiers to fight for the cause of Christ. All the warriors, falling upon their knees, implored divine protection, and arose full of confidence in their own bravery and the miracles of heaven.

No naval battle of antiquity can be compared to this of Lepanto, in which the Turks fought for the empire of the world, and the Christians for the defence of Europe. The courage and skill of Don John and the other leaders, the intrepidity and ardour of the soldiers, and the superiority of the Franks in manœuvring their vessels, and in their artillery, procured for the Christian fleet a decisive victory. Two hundred of the enemy's ships were taken, burnt, or sunk. The wreck of the Turkish fleet, whilst announcing the victory of the Christians, carried consternation to the coasts of Greece and to the capital of the Ottoman empire.

Terrified by the results of this battle, Selim caused the famous castle of the Dardanelles to be built, which to the present day defends the entrance to the canal of Constantinople. At the time of the battle, the roof of the temple of Mecca fell in, and the Turks believed they saw in this accident a sign of the anger of Heaven. The roof was of wood; and that it might become, says Cantemir, a more solid emblem of the empire, the son of Soliman ordered it to be reconstructed of brick.

Whilst the Turks deplored the first reverse their arms had met with, the whole of Christendom learnt the news of the victory of Lepanto with the greatest joy. The Venetians, who had awaited in terror the issue of the battle, celebrated the triumph of the Christian fleet by extraordinary festivities. In order that no feeling of sadness should be mingled with the universal joy, the senate set all prisoners at liberty, and forbade the subjects of the republic to wear mourning for their relations or friends who had been killed fighting against the Turks. The battle of Lepanto was inscribed upon coins, and as the infidels were defeated on the day of St. Justin, the seigneury ordered that this happy day should be every year a festival for the whole population of Venice.

At Toledo, and in all the churches of Spain, the people and the clergy offered up hymns of gratitude to Heaven for the victory it had granted to the valour of the Christian soldiers. No nation, no prince of Europe, was indifferent to the defeat of the Turks; and, if one historian may be believed, the king of England, James I., celebrated in a poem the glorious day of Lepanto.

As the pope had effectively contributed to the success of the Christian arms, it was at Rome that the strongest symptoms of delight were exhibited. Mark Antony Colonna, who had commanded the vessels of the sovereign pontiff, was received in triumph, and conducted to the Capitol, preceded by a great number of prisoners of war. The ensigns taken from the enemy were suspended in the church of Ara-Cœli. After a solemn mass, Mark Antony Mureti pronounced the panegyric of the triumphant general. Thus the ceremonies of ancient Rome were mingled with those of the modern, to celebrate the valour and exploits of the defenders of Christendom. The Church itself was desirous of consecrating a victory gained over its enemies among its festivals; Pius V. instituted one in honour of the Virgin, by whose intercession it was believed the Mussulmans had been conquered. This festival was celebrated on the 7th October, the day of the battle of Lepanto, under the denomination of "Our Lady of Victories."

Thus a unanimous concert of prayers and thanksgivings arose towards heaven, and all Christians at the same time showed their gratitude to the God of armies for having delivered Europe from the invasion of the Mussulmans. But it was not long before this happy harmony was disturbed: ambition, reciprocal mistrusts, diversity of interests, all that had till that time favoured the progress of the Turks, prevented the Christians from deriving the proper advantages from their victory. The Venetians were anxious to pursue the war, in order to recover the isle of Cyprus; but Philip II., dreading any increase in the power of Venice, withdrew from the confederation. The Venetian republic, abandoned by its allies, hastened to make peace. It obtained it by sacrificing all the possessions it had lost during the war,—a strange result of victory; by which the vanquished dictated laws to the conqueror, and which plainly shows us to what extent the pretensions of the Turks would have been carried if fortune had favoured their arms.

The war which was terminated by the battle of Lepanto, was the last in which the standard of the cross animated or rallied Christian warriors.

The spirit of the holy wars at first arose from popular opinions. When these opinions became weakened and great powers were formed, all that relates to war or peace became concentrated in the councils of monarchs. No more projects for distant expeditions were formed in public councils; no more warlike enterprises were recommended from the pulpits of the churches, or before assemblies of the faithful. States and princes, placed at the head of human affairs, even when they made war against the Mussulmans, obeyed much less the influence of religious ideas than interests purely political. From that period the enthusiasm of the multitude, and all the passions that had given birth to the crusades, were reckoned as nothing.

The alliance of Francis I. with Soliman was at first a great scandal for all Christendom. The king of France justified himself by accusing the ambition and the perfidy of Charles V. His example was quickly followed by Charles himself, and by other Christian states. Policy, disengaging itself more and more from that which was religious in it, came at last to consider the Ottoman Porte, no longer an enemy against whom it was a duty always to be fighting, but as a great power, whom it was sometimes necessary to conciliate, and whose support might be sought without outraging the Deity, or affecting the interests of the Church.

As the voice of the sovereign pontiff was always the instrument to summon Christians to take arms against the infidels, the spirit of the crusades necessarily grew weaker as the authority of the popes declined. It may be added, that the political system of Europe was making its development, and the ties and springs which were to found the equilibrium of the Christian republic had an increasing tendency to their establishment. Each state had its plan of defence and aggrandisement, which it followed with a constant activity; all were employed in endeavouring to attain the degree of power, force, and influence to which their position and the fortune of their arms entitled them. Hence those restless ambitions, those mutual mistrusts, that ever active spirit of rivalry, which scarcely ever permitted sovereigns to turn their attention towards distant wars.

Whilst ambition and the desire of increasing and defending their power detained princes in their own states, the people became attached to their homes by the blessings and the enjoyments of a rapidly-rising civilization.

In the eleventh century, the Franks, the Normans, and other barbarians from the north, had not quite lost the character and habits of nomadic races, which favoured the rise and the progress of that warlike enthusiasm which had precipitated the Crusaders upon the East. In the sixteenth century, institutions consecrated by time, the precepts of Christianity better understood, respect for ancestry, love of settled property, the constantly increasing wealth of cities, with the progress of industry and of agriculture, had changed the character of the Franks, destroyed their partiality for a wandering life, and had become so many ties to attach them to their country.

In the preceding century the genius of navigation had discovered America and the passage of the Cape of Good Hope. The results of this discovery effected a great revolution in commerce, attracted the attention of all nations, and gave a new direction to the human mind. All the speculations of industry, for so long a time founded upon the crusades, were directed towards America or the East Indies. Great empires, rich climates, offered themselves all at once to the ambition or the cupidity of all who sought for glory, fortune, or adventures—the wonders of a new world made men forgetful of those of the East.

At this so memorable epoch, a general emulation arose in Europe for the cultivation of arts and of letters. The age of Leo X. produced masterpieces of all kinds. [87] France, Spain, and still more Italy, turned the newly-discovered art of printing greatly to the advantage of knowledge. The splendid geniuses of Greece and Rome were everywhere revived. In proportion as men's minds became enlightened, the new career opened before them expanded. Another enthusiasm succeeded to that of religious enterprises; and the exploits of the heroic times of our history excited much more admiration in our romances and poets, than they created desire in people of the world to imitate them. Then the Epic Muse, whose voice only celebrates distant events, sang the heroes of the holy wars; and the crusades, for the same reason that Tasso became at liberty to adorn the recital of them with all the wealth of his imagination,—the crusades, we say, were no longer anything for Europe but a poetical remembrance.

One fortunate circumstance for Christendom is, that at the period when the crusades, which had for their object the defence of Europe, drew near to their end, the Turks began to lose some part of that military power which they had displayed in their contests with the Christian nations. The Ottomans had at first been, as we have already said, the only nation that kept on foot a regular standing army, which gave it a vast superiority over powers that it was desirous of subduing. In the sixteenth century, most of the great states of Europe had likewise armies which they could at any time bring against their enemies. Discipline and military tactics had made great progress in Christendom; artillery and marine became more perfect in the West every day, whilst the Turks, in all that concerns the art of war, or that of navigation, gathered no advantage from either the lessons of experience, or from the knowledge to which time and circumstances had given birth among their neighbours. We ought to add, that the spirit of superstition and intolerance which the Turks associated with their wars, was very injurious to the preservation and extent of their conquests. When they took possession of a province, they insisted upon making their laws, their customs, and their worship paramount. They must change everything, they must destroy everything, in the country in which they wished to establish themselves; they must either exterminate the population, or reduce it to the impossibility of disturbing a foreign domination. Thus it may be remarked, that, although several times masters of Hungary, they retired from it after every campaign, and were never able, amidst all their victories, to found a colony or make any durable establishment there. The Ottoman population which had sufficed for occupying and enslaving the Greek empire, could not people and preserve more distant countries. It was this, above everything, which saved Germany and Italy from the invasion of the Turks. The Ottomans might, perhaps, have conquered the world if they had been able to impose their manners upon it, or furnish it with inhabitants.

After the battle of Lepanto, although they had preserved the isle of Cyprus, and dictated laws to the republic of Venice, the Turks not the less lost the idea of their being invincible, or that all the world must submit to their arms. It was observed that from that time most of the leaders of Turkish armies or fleets became more timid, and felt less assured of victory, when in the presence of an enemy. Astrologers, who had till then beheld in the phenomena of the heavens the increase and the glory of the Ottoman empire, saw nothing during the reign of Soliman and following reigns but sinister auguries in the aspects of the celestial bodies. We mention astrologers, because their predictions have considerable influence upon the policy of the Turks. It is not improbable that these pretended conjurers did not confine their observations to the celestial bodies, but that they watched the manners and the opinions of the people, and the march of events and affairs. It is for this reason that their prophecies were found true, and that they belong, in some sort, to history.

The spirit of conquest, however, which had so long animated the nation, still subsisted, and sometimes fortune favoured the Ottoman banner with victory.

Towards the end of the sixteenth century, the Turks carried war to both the banks of the Danube and to the frontiers of Persia. Among the Christian warriors who flew to the aid of Germany, the duke of Mercœur, brother of the duke of Mayenne, must not be forgotten; he was followed by a crowd of French soldiers, who had fought against Henry IV., and who went to expiate the crimes of civil war by fighting the infidels. The duke of Mercœur, to whom the emperor Rodolph II. gave the command of the imperial army, gained several advantages over the Ottomans.

Whilst the war was being carried on in Hungary, the king of Persia sent an embassy to the emperor of Germany and the princes of the West, to persuade them to form an alliance with him against the Turks. The Persian ambassadors repaired to the court of the sovereign pontiff, and to those of several Christian powers, conjuring them to declare war against the Ottomans. This embassy of the king of Persia, and the exploits of the French on the Danube, created great uneasiness in the Divan, and an ambassador was sent to the king of France, as the most to be feared of the Christian princes. The letters of credit of the Turkish envoy bore this title: "To the most glorious, magnanimous, and greatest lord of the faith of Jesus, pacificator of the differences which arise among Christian princes, lord of greatness, majesty, and riches, and glorious guide of the greatest, Henry IV., emperor of France." The sultan of the Turks conjured the French monarch, in his letter, to bring about a truce between the Porte and the emperor of Germany, and to recall from Hungary the duke of Mercœur, whose valour and skill brought victory to the banners of the Germans. Henry IV. interrogated the Ottoman ambassador, and asked him why the Turks dreaded the duke of Mercœur so much. The ambassador replied, that a prophecy, credited by the Turks, declared that the sword of the French would drive them from Europe, and overthrow their empire. Henry IV. did not recall the duke of Mercœur: this able captain continued to beat the Ottomans, and having covered himself with glory in the war against the infidels, he was seized, whilst on his return to France, by a purple fever, "which," says Mezerai, "sent him to triumph in heaven."

In their wars against the Christians, the Turks often found themselves on the defensive, which was for them a sign of decline. History remarks that at no period did their reverses cause them more alarm, or their victories more surprise and joy. Their defeats were almost always a signal for sedition and revolt, which the decline of power rendered bold.

And yet the Ottoman empire still carried on war, and advanced like a storm ready to burst. In the middle of the seventeenth century, the isle of Chio, which had belonged to the Genoese, was added to its maritime possessions, and the Turks directed their victorious arms towards Candia, an important colony of the Venetians. At the same time an Ottoman army entered Transylvania, and greatly alarmed Austria.

Pope Alexander VII., pressed by the emperor Leopold I. and by the Venetian senate, endeavoured to form a league among the princes and states of Christendom, and addressed the king of Poland, the king of Spain, and more particularly the king of France, to implore their succour against the Turks.

Louis XIV. yielded to the prayers of the sovereign pontiff, and sent to Rome an ambassador charged to announce to his holiness, that he entered into the confederation of the Christian princes. On the other side, the states of the Germanic empire, which were the allies of France, assembled at Frankfort, and engaged to raise money and troops, promising to unite their efforts with those of the French monarch, for the defence of Christendom.

This generous forwardness on the part of the king of France and his allies merited, no doubt, the gratitude of Leopold; but, what is difficult to be believed, the zeal they showed for the common cause, and which exceeded what was first hoped for, only awakened the jealous uneasiness of the emperor. We have even reason to think that this uneasiness extended to the sovereign pontiff; for his holiness welcomed the propositions of Louis XIV. very coldly; and when the resolutions of the Germanic body reached Rome, Alexander received with indifference news for which any other pope, say the memoirs of the time, would not have failed to go and return solemn thanks in the church of St. Peter or of St. John of the Lateran. The king of France could not dissemble his surprise; and in a letter, which he caused to be written to his ambassador, are these remarkable words: "For the rest, it is more an affair of his holiness than ours; it will suffice for his majesty, for his own satisfaction and his duty towards God, to have made all the advances with respect to this league, that a king, the eldest son of the Church, and the principal defender of religion, could do in a danger imminent for Christendom."

It was soon known that the Turks were making progress, and had penetrated into Moravia. The emperor Leopold, at their approach, quitted his capital. The pope then consented to resume the suspended negotiations. But they were resumed with a sentiment of jealousy and reciprocal mistrust, that left no hope of a happy result. Louis XIV., nevertheless, omitted nothing to prove the frankness of his intentions, or to forward the formation of a league. It was then believed that an enterprise against the Turks was the business of all Christendom, and that, in this case, one Christian power alone, ought not to decide for peace or war.

We enter into some details here, because these details have not been hitherto generally known, and that present circumstances may give them additional interest. We know, likewise, in the days in which we live, we must search for examples in old remembrances, and often for our true titles to glory likewise.

The emperor could not be reassured by the demonstrations of the French monarch; and the rancour which he retained on account of the treaty of Westphalia, made him forgetful of his own dangers and of those of the Germanic body. Louis XIV. engaged to set on foot an army of twenty thousand men, and the confederates of Germany offered as many. Leopold feared this army on his own account. In the end, Louis satisfied himself with furnishing six thousand soldiers, under the command of the count de Coligny and the marquis de la Feuillade. The pope, not to remain neuter in a war against the Mussulmans, granted the emperor a subsidy of 70,000 florins, and the faculty of levying tenths upon all the ecclesiastical property in the Austrian states. All the united succours of Germany, the king of France, and the other confederate states, formed an army of thirty thousand men. This army marched to Hungary. When united to the troops of the emperor, they gained many advantages over the Turks, and defeated them completely at the battle of St. Gothard. The Ottomans solicited a suspension of arms, and the jealous passions which had at first prevented the war being carried on with vigour, allowed the Divan to conclude an advantageous peace.

The Ottomans, thus delivered from a formidable war, were able to direct all their strength against Candia, which Venice, now left alone, was not strong enough to defend. A great number of French warriors then flew to the succour of a Christian city besieged by the infidels: among the knights whom the love of glory led to this perilous and distant war, history takes pleasure in naming the marquis de Fénelon, whose care had brought up the archbishop of Cambrai, and whom his age considered as the model of gallant gentlemen. His young son, whom he took with him, was wounded in an affair against the Turks, and died of his wounds. France, in the same expedition, had to lament another hero, the young duke of Beaufort; Mascaron, who pronounced the funeral oration of this new Maccabeus, thus describes his death: "After the flight of all the others, yielding rather to number than to strength, he fell upon his own trophies, and died the most glorious death that a Christian hero could wish, sword in hand against the enemies of his God and his king, in the sight of Europe, Asia, and Africa; and more than all that, in the sight of God and his angels." Louis XIV., always considering it consistent with his glory to protect the Christian states, sent fresh succours to Candia: four French vessels appeared before the isle; but they arrived too late; the city of Candia, after a siege of two years and four months, had just capitulated.

This conquest revived the courage of the Turks, and their power, sustained by the genius of Kiouprouli, whom the Mussulmans called *the great destroyer of the bells of impiety*, might have still rendered themselves formidable to the Christian nations, if their policy had not been governed by a foolish pride. Intoxicated with some trifling successes, the Turks resumed their project of invading Germany. Towards the end of the seventeenth century, they made a last attempt, and the capital of Austria beheld beneath its walls an army of two hundred thousand infidels.

Germany was exhausted by the thirty years' war. The king of Poland, urged by the pope to come to the succour of the Germanic empire, hastened with his Polish cavalry to the scene of action, and revived the courage of the Germans and the garrison of Vienna. The Turks, upon being attacked with impetuosity, abandoned their camp, their artillery, and their baggage. The wreck of the Ottoman army did not rally till they reached the banks of the Raab, where they encamped around the tent of the grand vizier, the only one that had not fallen into the hands of the conquerors. John Sobieski entered in triumph into the city he had saved by his courage. This happy event was celebrated throughout Germany by public rejoicings; and, as had been done after the victory gained by Don John of Austria, amidst the ceremonies of the Church, these words from Scripture were repeated: "There was a man sent from God, named John."

The defeat of Vienna was for the Turks a signal for the greatest reverses. The vengeance of the people and the army pursued the grand vizier, who had conducted the war; and the sultan, Mahomet IV., fell from the throne at the report of these sanguinary disasters, the effects of which were felt to the very heart of the empire. The famous treaty of Carlowitz testifies the losses that the Ottoman nation had undergone, and the incontestable superiority of its enemies. The decline of Turkey, as a maritime power, had commenced at the battle of Lepanto; its decline as a military or conquering power, dates from the defeat of Vienna. History has two things to remark in the negotiations of Carlowitz. Hungary, which had for so long a time resisted the Turks, weakened at length by civil discords and foreign wars, and given up at the same time to the emperors of Germany and the sultans of Constantinople, then lost its national independence, and became united to the possessions of the house of Austria. Among the states and princes who signed the treaty, the czars of Muscovy, who were destined, at a later period, to inflict such terrible blows upon the Ottoman empire, appeared for the first time as a power interested in the Christian struggle against the infidels.

We have described the origin and progress of the Turks; it only remains for us now to speak of the causes of their decline.

The Turks were only constituted to contend with a barbarous people, like themselves, or with a degenerate people, like the Greeks. When they met with nations that were not corrupted, and were not deficient in bravery or patriotism, their career was checked. It is a circumstance worthy of remark, that they were never able to make an impression upon any of the nations of the Latin Church; the only nation that was separated from Christendom by the conquests of the Turks was one that had separated itself from it. When the Ottomans were no longer able to prosecute their scheme of general invasion, all the passions which had stimulated them to conquest only served to disturb their own empire; which is the ordinary destiny of mere conquering nations.

The wars they prosecuted at the same time against Christian Europe and Persia, were the principal causes of the decay of the military power of the Turks. The efforts they made against the Persians, diverted their forces from their expeditions against the Christians; and their expeditions against the Christians crippled their means for the wars in Asia. In these two kinds of war they had a very different manner of fighting. After having for any length of time contended with the warriors of the Oxus or Caucasus, they were incapacitated for making war in Europe. They were never able to triumph completely over either Persia or the Christian nations; and remained at last pressed between two enemies, equally interested in their ruin, and equally animated by religious passions.

The Turks, like all the hordes from the north of Asia, brought with them the feudal government. The first thing to be done by all nomadic nations, who established themselves in conquered countries, was the division of the lands, with certain conditions of protection and obedience. From this division naturally emanated feudalism. The difference, however, which existed between the Turks and the other barbarians who conquered the West, was, that the jealous despotism of the sultans never allowed fiefs to become hereditary, or that an aristocracy should grow up round it, as in the monarchies of Christendom. Thus in the Turkish empire nothing was to be seen on one side, but the authority of an absolute master; and on the other, nothing but a military democracy. The Ottoman monarchy was thus built upon that which is weakest in political societies—the will of a single man, or that of the multitude.

The Turks have been compared to the Romans. Both nations began in the same manner; for both were nothing but bands of brigands. What distinguishes them in history is, that the Turks have remained the same as they were in their origin; whilst the Romans, in their conquests, never rejected the knowledge, the customs, or even the gods of the people they conquered. The Turks, on the contrary, took nothing from other nations, and made it their pride to continue barbarians.

We have said above, that hereditary aristocracy has never been established by the side of despotism; and this is, perhaps, the reason why the Ottoman nation has remained in a state of barbarism. They who have studied the march of human societies know that it is by the aristocracy that the manners and morals of a people are formed, and that it is in the middle classes that knowledge has its birth, and civilization begins. [88] The absence of an aristocracy in oriental governments, not only explains to us the fragility of those governments, but it assists us also in explaining why progress has not been made in a country where nothing distinguished the men from each other, where no one had sufficient influence to guide the crowd, or was sufficiently elevated to serve as an example or model.

In consequence of the indifference of the Turks for the arts and sciences, the labours of industry, agriculture, and navigation, were confided to their slaves, who were their enemies. As they held in horror everything new, or that they had not brought from Asia with them, they were obliged to have recourse to foreigners for everything that was invented or perfected in Europe. Thus the sources of prosperity and power, the strength of their armies and their fleets, were not at all in their own hands. Every one knows what the Turks have lost by neglecting to learn or to follow the progress of the military tactics of the Europeans. At the battle of Lepanto, disorder was introduced into their fleet entirely from their having promised liberty to their sailors, who were all Christians.

Some modern writers, seeking everywhere for similitudes, have compared the janissaries to the pretorian cohorts. This comparison has nothing exact in it: among the Romans, the empire was elective, and the pretorians got possession of it for the purpose of putting it up to sale. Among the Turks, the idea of choosing their prince never suggested itself to the minds of either the people or the soldiery. The janissaries contented themselves with disturbing the government, and keeping it in such a state of disorder, that they could never be dismissed, and might always remain masters. All their opposition consisted in preventing any amelioration whatever in discipline or military usages. The abuses and prejudices the most difficult to be destroyed in a nation, are those which adhere to a body or a class in which power happens to be placed. All-powerful despotism was never able to overcome the opposition of the janissaries and spahis; and those redoubtable corps, which had so effectively contributed to ancient conquests, became the greatest obstacle to the making of new ones.

The Turks established in Greece had more respect for old usages and old prejudices, than they had of love for the country they inhabited. Masters of Stamboul, they had their eyes constantly fixed upon the places of their origin, and appeared to be but travellers, or passing conquerors of Europe. They preserved the manners of Asia, the laws of Asia, the remembrances of Asia; and the West was, in their estimation, less a country than a theatre for their exploits.

Amidst their decline, nothing was more fatal to the Turks than the memory of their past glory; nothing was more injurious to them than that national pride which was no longer in harmony with their fortune, or in proportion with their strength. The illusions of a power that no longer existed prevented them from foreseeing the obstacles they were likely to meet with in their enterprises, or the dangers with which they were threatened. When the Ottomans made an unsuccessful war, or an unfavourable treaty, they never failed to lay the blame on their leaders, whom popular vengeance devoted to death or exile; and whilst they thus immolated victims to their vanity, their reverses became the more irreparable, from their persisting in mistaking the true causes of them.

Tacitus somewhere expresses the joy he felt in seeing barbarians making war upon one another; and we experience something of this joy when we see despotism threatened by its own institutions, and tormented by the very instruments of its power. Another spectacle, no less consoling to all who love humanity and justice, is to behold this family of fierce despots, before whom the entire East trembled, devouring itself. It is well known what victims each sultan, on ascending the throne, was compelled to offer to the suspicious genius of despotism. But Heaven does not permit the most sacred laws of nature to be constantly violated with impunity; and the Ottoman dynasty, in expiation of so many crimes against family ties, sunk at last into a species of degradation. The Ottoman princes, brought up in subjection and fear, lost the energy and the faculties necessary for conducting the government of a great empire. Soliman II. only increased the evil by decreeing a constitutional law, that no son of the sultan's should command armies or govern provinces. From that time none but effeminate princes, timid and senseless men, occupied the Ottoman throne.

If the will of the prince became corrupt, it was quite sufficient to render the corruption general. In proportion as the character of the sultans degenerated, everything degenerated around them. A universal apathy displaced the noisy activity of war and victory. To the passion for conquests succeeded cupidity, ambition, selfishness, and all the vices that signalize and complete the decline of empires. When states rise and march on towards prosperity, there is an emulation to increase their powers; when they decline, there is also an emulation to urge on their destruction, and take advantage of their ruin.

The empire had always a numerous army; but that army, in which discipline every day degenerated, was only formidable in time of peace. A crowd of *Thimariots*, or possessors of fiefs for life, having nothing to leave to their families, passed over the lands that were given to them like locusts, which, in the plains where the winds have wafted them, destroy even to the germs of the harvests. The pachas governed the provinces as conquerors. The wealth of the people was for them like the booty which conquerors distributed among themselves on the day of victory. Such as could amass treasures were able to purchase impunity. Such as had armies proclaimed their independence. Subalterns everywhere followed the example of the leaders. In the government, as well as in the army, everything was put up to sale, everything was subject to pillage. Thus this empire, which had displayed such energy, fell like a prey into the hands of all those whom fortune or the favour of the prince called to authority; and if we may be permitted to employ a not very elevated comparison to express the degree of abasement of a nation, the Ottoman power no longer presented any aspect but that of those lifeless bodies in which we can perceive no motion but in the insects that are devouring them.

The sultans of Constantinople, while slumbering in their seraglios, were often awakened by the thunder of popular revolts. Violences of the army or the people were the only justice able to reach despotism. But this justice itself was one calamity the more, and only assisted in precipitating the general decline.

Although the successors of Othman, after the reign of Selim, were the pontiffs of the national faith, this important dignity added nothing to their power. The Mussulman faith, which commanded with severity the observance of many minute practices, did not at all repress the passions of the multitude. A religious belief which permitted a prince to commit fratricide could be no safeguard for either the authority or the life of the prince. A religion always ready to consecrate the triumph of force, could find no motives in its moral code for the condemnation of revolt, particularly when the revolt happened to be crowned with success. [89]

But what is remarkably singular, the Turks, when they rose against a prince of the Ottoman dynasty, preserved a profound veneration for that dynasty. They immolated the tyrant to their vengeance, and were ready to immolate themselves for the tyranny. Thus license, in its greatest excesses, always respected despotism; and what carried disorder to its highest pitch was, that despotism in its turn respected license.

The Turks lived in this state of decline as in their natural condition. Nothing is more remarkable in history than the carelessness of a nation in the midst of a revolution that is dragging it down to its ruin; and this revolution with the Turks was not brought about by new ideas, but by old ideas, not by love of liberty, but by habits of slavery. They respected the causes of their ruin, because these causes were connected with the history of barbarous times; and religion, by constantly repeating to them that "he who is in the fire ought to be resigned," prevented them from seeking a remedy for the ills they suffered.

Among nations which incline towards destruction, in the very bosom of corruption a certain politeness, a certain polish or elegance of manners, may be observed. The Turks, on the contrary, had a brutal and savage corruption, and their empire grew old without the nation's losing anything of that fierceness of character, of that proud roughness, which belong to the infancy of society.

We shall be asked why Christendom did not take advantage of this decline of the Turks to drive them back again into Asia. We have seen in this history, that the nations of Christian Europe were never able to combine and agree for the defence of Constantinople, when it was attacked by the Turks; and they showed no more inclination to combine to deliver it after it was taken. We may add that the less redoubtable the Turks became, the fewer were the efforts made to conquer them. They inspired, besides, no jealousy in the commercial nations of Christendom. It was in vain that fortune placed them between the East and the West; that she rendered them masters of the Archipelago, of the coasts of Africa, of the ports of the Black Sea and the Red Sea: their finest provinces were deserts, their cities were abandoned. Everything perished in the hands of an indolent and unpolished people. The Turks were spared, because they made no use of their advantages; and because they were, to employ an expression of Montesquieu's, the men the most fit to hold great empires carelessly.

Before we terminate this rapid sketch of the Turkish empire in the seventeenth century, we beg to be allowed to add some reflections which circumstances may cause to be appreciated. Nothing was more monstrous than the presence, upon the same territory, of two nations and two religions that hated and cursed each other reciprocally. Spain had presented a similar spectacle; but the energy and the magnanimous constancy of the Spaniards triumphed over an adverse people and an adverse religion; and at the very time at which the Turks established themselves in Greece, the Moors, carrying with them their foreign worship, abandoned their conquests and returned to Africa, from whence they came. The Greeks, after the invasion of the Ottomans, neither showed the same energy nor the same courage;

although their patriotism ought to have been constantly animated by the soil they trod on, and by their very name, of which the conqueror had not been able to deprive them.

Nevertheless, amidst their abasement and their misery, they were still able to place their hope in the ascendancy of religious ideas, and in the wish for civilization, which acted as a tie between all Christian societies. Whilst the manners and the worship of Islamism rendered the Turks foreign and even odious to Christendom, the religion of Christ and the remembrances of history placed the Greeks in relation with the other nations of Europe.

In proportion as the knowledge derived from antiquity made progress among the Franks, Greece became for them a sacred country. The language of Plato and Demosthenes, in which the charms of liberty had been celebrated with so much eloquence, became more dear to them than their own maternal tongue. The poetical sites of Greece, which the love of letters rendered so familiar to the studious class, were for us like places in which we had passed our infancy. Europe had not a scholar in whom the city of Aristotle, that of Lycurgus, or that of Epaminondas, did not inspire something resembling the sentiments we feel for our own country. If the Greeks were degenerated; if they viewed with indifference the ruins of their country, ancient Greece still lived for every enlightened man, and was ever present, wherever a taste for the arts or a love of learning existed.

The warmer that the interest for the Greeks became, the more barbarous the Turks appeared. The Ottoman nation came and established itself in the richest countries of Europe, and remained in sight of all European people, without becoming acquainted with their languages, their laws, or their policy; like those troops of wild animals which sometimes stop in the neighbourhood of the dwellings of man, ignorant of that which is going on in these places, and having no means to seize their prey or defend themselves, but their activity, their natural strength, and the means which a gross instinct gives them. This state of things was opposed both to the laws of society and the laws of nature, which do not permit men or nations to live together and in the same place, except when they possess similar qualities, and are able to employ their faculties in common. The Turks may have been protected, at first by the fortune of their own arms, and afterwards by the policy of certain cabinets; but what real support could they have in the West, when they were repulsed by the manners, feelings, and opinions of the European nations, to whom they became every day more foreign?

On one side, the antipathy entertained for a barbarous people; on the other, the relations which united nations civilized by Christianity, were likely, sooner or later, to revive that spirit of fraternity which produced the crusades; and God has willed that this spirit, from which the holy wars were born, should manifest itself in the same century which had for a long time refused to acknowledge the effects or to admire the prodigies of them.

At the moment in which we are finishing this history, the Greeks have thrown forth a cry of alarm, and this cry has resounded throughout the Christian world. Is the moment of their deliverance arrived? When we examine the present state of Europe, we find a much greater force than would be necessary to conquer Byzantium; but on the other side, the diversity of interests and opinions will not permit the Christian republic to unite for this great enterprise. We have seen that the Turks really possess nothing but the soil of their vast empire; the riches that are there produced belong to the nations of Christendom, and these nations are for the Turkish provinces, which they cultivate to their profit, that which an active and industrious farmer is for the fields he ploughs and reaps. Add to this, that most of the Christian powers appear to fear that the displacing of a great empire may break the ties of the European confederation; they do not, as formerly, dread the strength of the Ottomans, but the difficulties and divisions that the conquest would produce. That which may add to their fears is that impatience for change, that ardent passion for novelty, which is spread all at once among the nations like a contagious fever; whilst the Greeks are imploring Europe for their liberty, restless and dissatisfied spirits look to the East for I do not know what signal for a revolution in Europe. Thus Christendom, divided by its various interests, tormented by a thousand different passions, and fearing for its own repose, awaits with anxiety the events that are preparing, and appears to recoil from victories which the superiority of her intelligence and her armies hold out to her.

What will be the issue of all the warlike demonstrations and all the pacific negotiations of which fame informs us every day? There is no doubt the cross will again arise in the East, and the fate of Christians residing there will receive some amelioration; but are we arrived at the moment which is to render Europe entirely Christian? Will the Ottoman empire, whose weakness now appears so great, yield to the power of its enemies, or will it hasten its own ruin? Will Greece, so long enslaved, resume that rank among nations from which she formerly descended so ingloriously, or will she fall into the hands of her liberators? A thousand other questions present themselves to the mind; but we will not forestall events; above all, we will avoid multiplying conjectures and hypotheses, or producing here the brilliant reveries of philosophers and poets, which the severity of history rejects. When we set a high value upon truth, and have sought it for a length of time in all that the remembrances of the past contain that is most positive, we learn to speak of the future with much circumspection and reserve.

It may be thought that we have dwelt too long upon the Ottoman empire; but the origin of that empire, its progress and its decline, are connected with all the events we have had to describe. The sketch we have traced of it may have been sometimes serviceable in making our readers acquainted with the spirit and the character of the wars against the infidels; and is this view our labour has not been useless.

At the period we have now gained, the passions which had given birth to the prodigies of the crusades had become speculative opinions, which occupied the attention of writers rather than that of kings or nations. Thus the holy wars, with their causes and effects, became the objects of the discussions of doctors and philosophers. We may remember the opinion of Luther; and although he had partly disavowed or retracted his first opinion upon the war against the Turks, most of his partisans continued to evince a great aversion for the crusades.

The minister Jurieu goes much further than Luther. That ardent apostle of the Reformation, far from thinking that war ought to be made against the Mussulmans, did not hesitate to consider the Turks as auxiliaries of the Protestants, and said that the fierce sectaries of Mahomet were sent to "labour with the Reformers in the great work of God," which was the ruin of the papal empire. After the raising of the last siege of Vienna, in 1683, and the revocation of the edict of Nantes, the same Jurieu was afflicted at the disgrace of the Reformers and the defeat of the Turks; adding, at the same time, "that God had only abased them, in order to raise them together again, and make them the instruments of his vengeance against the popes." Such is the excess of blindness to which the spirit of party or sect has power to carry us, when misled by hatred, and irritated by persecution.

Other writers, however, celebrated for their genius, and who also were connected with the Reformation, maintained that wars against the infidels ought to be carried on: they deplored the indifference of Christendom, and the wars that were breaking out daily among Christian nations, whilst they left in peace a people, a foe to all other peoples. Chancellor Bacon, in his dialogue *de bello sacro*, employs all his logic to prove that the Turks are excluded from the law of nations. He invokes, by turns, natural right, the rights of nations, and divine right, against the barbarians, to whom he refuses the name of a people, and maintains that war should be carried on against them as against pirates, anthropophagi, or wild animals. The illustrious chancellor quotes, in support of his opinion, maxims from Aristotle, maxims from the Bible, with examples from history, and even from fable. His manner of reasoning savours a little of the policy and philosophy of the sixteenth century, and we do not feel ourselves called upon to repeat arguments, of which many would not be of a nature to convince minds of the present century.

We prefer developing some of the ideas of Leibnitz, who, in order to revive the spirit of distant expeditions, addressed himself to the ambition of princes, and whose political views have received a memorable application in modern times. At the moment in which Louis XIV. was preparing to carry his arms into the Low Countries, the German philosopher sent him a long memorial, to persuade him to renew the expedition of St. Louis into Egypt. The conquest of that rich country, which Leibnitz calls the Holland of the East, would favour the triumph and the propagation of the faith; it would procure for the Most Christian king the renown of Alexander, and for the French monarchy vast means of power and prosperity. After the occupation of Alexandria and Cairo, fortune would offer the conquerors some happy opportunity for restoring the empire of the East; the Ottoman power, attacked by the Poles and the Germans, and troubled by internal divisions, was ready to sink into ruin; Muscovy and Persia were already preparing to take advantage of its fall; if France put forth her strength, nothing would be more easy than to gather together again the immense heritage of Constantine, to dominate over the Mediterranean, to extend her empire over the Red Sea, over the Sea of Ethiopia, over the Persian Gulf, and obtain possession of the commerce of India; everything the most brilliant in the glory and grandeur of empires then presented itself to the imagination of Leibnitz; and this exalted genius, dazzled by his own idea, and allying his policy with the prejudices of his age, could see nothing greater than the conquest of Egypt, *but the discovery of the philosopher's stone*: he beheld already, in a shortly distant futurity, the Christian religion flourishing again in Asia, the empire and the commerce of the East and the West divided between the king of France and the house of Austria and Spain, the world rendered peaceful, and governed by these two conquering powers!

After having developed the advantages of the vast enterprise he proposed, Leibnitz neglected none of the means that would be likely to secure the success or facilitate the execution of it. It was in this part of his memorial that he showed all the superiority of his genius; and when we read the account of the last war of the French in Egypt, we cannot but feel persuaded that Buonaparte was well acquainted with the plan of campaign addressed by Leibnitz to Louis XIV. But certainly this gigantic enterprise, whose result was likely to be more brilliant than either solid or durable, was less suited to a monarch guided in his policy by the sentiments of real greatness, than to the modern hero, always enamoured of an adventurous and romantic glory. Nevertheless, the ideas of Leibnitz, although not favourably received by the cabinet of Versailles, did not fail to produce a lively impression upon the statesmen of the seventeenth century. It is known likewise, that the king of France had already thought seriously of a war against the Turks; and we have reason to believe that Boileau alluded to all these projects of distant conquests, when he said in his epistle to the king:

Je t'attends dans six mois aux bords de l'Hellespont. [90]

The eloquence, or even the flattery of authors, could not induce princes to take up arms against the infidels; and the Crusaders finished, as they began, with pilgrimages. Among the celebrated pilgrims who repaired to the East after the holy wars, one of the most remarkable was Ignatius Loyola. He visited the holy places twice, and, like St. Jerome, would have ended his days in Palestine, if the Latin priests had not advised him to return into Europe, where he established the order of the Jesuits. As was the case before the crusades, princes mixed with the crowd of Christians who went to the Holy Land. Frederick III., before he ascended the imperial throne, went on a pilgrimage to the holy city. We still possess an account of the voyages which were made successively into Palestine by a prince of Radziwil, a duke of Bavaria, a duke of Austria, and three electors of Saxony, among whom was he who was the protector of Luther.

Pilgrims from the West were no longer received at Jerusalem, as in the early times, by the Knights of St. John, but by the Latin fathers of the order of St. Francis of Assisi, who devoted themselves to the guardianship of the holy sepulchre. Preserving the hospitable manners of ancient times, the guardian father himself washed the feet of travellers, and furnished them with the necessary assistance for their pilgrimage. Pilgrims embarked at Venice, where vessels were always ready to transport them to the coast of Syria. People could obtain all the benefits attached to the pilgrimage of the Holy Land, without quitting their homes; either by commissioning pious men who were sent beyond the seas, or cenobites who resided on the spot.

The greater part of the sovereigns of Christendom, after the example of Charlemagne, thought it consistent with their glory, not only to deliver, but to protect the city of Jesus Christ from the outrages of the Mussulmans. The capitulations of Francis I., renewed by most of his successors, contain [91] several conditions which contribute to secure peace to the Christians, with the free exercise of their religion in the East. In the reign of Henry IV., Deshayes, the ambassador from France to Constantinople, went to visit the faithful at Jerusalem, and conveyed to them the consolations of a charity worthy of royalty. The count of Nointel, who represented Louis XIV. at the court of the sultan of Turkey, also went into the Holy Land; and Jerusalem received in triumph the envoy of the powerful monarch, whose credit and renown were employed to protect the Christians beyond the seas.

Most of the princes of Christendom every year sent their tributes to the holy city; and in solemn ceremonies, the church of the Resurrection displayed the treasures offered by the kings of the West. The guardians of the holy places, who entertained and took charge of pilgrims, possessed nothing on earth; but the gifts of the faithful were for them like the manna of the desert, sent every day from heaven. By a species of miracle constantly renewed, the holy monuments of the Christian religion, for a long time defended by the armies of the West, having no longer any defence but religious remembrances, preserved themselves amidst the barbarous sectaries of Islamism: the security enjoyed by the city of Jerusalem made its deliverance less thought of. That which produced the spirit of the crusades in the eleventh century was, above all other causes, the persecution directed against pilgrims, and the state of misery in which the Christians of the East existed. When they ceased to be persecuted, and had fewer miseries to endure, lamentable accounts no longer awakened the pity and indignation of the western nations; and Christendom satisfied itself with addressing prayers to God for the preservation of peace in the places he had sanctified by his miracles. There was then a spirit of resignation [92] which took place of the enthusiasm of the crusades; the city of David and of Godfrey became confounded in the minds of Christians with the heavenly Jerusalem, and as sacred orators said, "it was necessary to pass through Heaven to arrive at the Holy Land," it was of no use appealing to the bravery of warriors, but to the devotion and charity of the faithful.

BOOK XVIII
A.D. 1571-1685

REFLECTIONS UPON THE STATE OF EUROPE, UPON THE VARIOUS CLASSES OF SOCIETY, AND UPON THE PROGRESS Of NAVIGATION, INDUSTRY, ARTS, AND GENERAL KNOWLEDGE, DURING AND AFTER THE CRUSADES.

We have made known the origin, the spirit, and the character of the crusades; it is now our task to show their influence on the state of society. Before giving our opinion upon the results of the holy wars, it has appeared to us desirable to lay before our readers, in a few words, the judgments that others have passed upon them. In the seventeenth century, so abounding in men of genius, the heroic bravery of the Crusaders was admired, their reverses were deplored, and, without a question as to the good or evil which these distant expeditions had brought about, the pious motives which had made the warriors of the West take arms were respected. The eighteenth century, which had adopted all the opinions of the Reformation, and exaggerated them,—the eighteenth century did not spare the crusades, and did not fail to accuse the ignorance, barbarity, and fanaticism of our ancestors as the causes of them. [93] Voltaire published a history of the crusades, in 1753; the subject he had chosen was at that time so low in public opinion, and he himself cast so much ridicule upon the events he described, that his book created no curiosity, and found no readers. Nothing can equal the violence with which the authors of the *Encyclopédie*, a short time afterwards, surpassed even the acerbity of Voltaire. This manner of judging the crusades became so general, that the panegyrists of St. Louis allowed themselves to be drawn into it, and several among them, in their discourses, were scarcely inclined to pardon the pious monarch for his exploits and his misfortunes in Egypt and before Tunis.

A philosophy, however, enlightened by the spirit of research and analysis, traced events to their causes, studied their effects, and, from holding truth as the only object worthy of inquiry, neglected declamation and despised satire. The judicious Robertson, in his introduction to the History of Charles V., gave it as his opinion, that the crusades had favoured the progress of liberty and the development of the human mind. Whether this perception flattered some of the opinions of the time, or whether it exercised over the public the natural ascendancy of truth, it met with a sufficient number of partisans; and from that time the expeditions of the Crusaders into the East have been judged with less severity.

A few years ago the Institute of France proposed a question, by which they invited the learned to point out all the advantages society had derived from the crusades; and if we may judge by the memorials which obtained the prize in this learned contest, [94] the holy wars brought more benefits for posterity in their train, than they produced calamities for the generations contemporary with them. Thus, opinions upon the crusades had changed several times in less than two centuries; a great lesson for those who pronounce with so much assurance upon the revolutions which we have seen begin, but which we shall not see end; when there is so much difficulty in judging of revolutions long ago accomplished, and whose results are all before our eyes!

Perhaps we are arrived at the favourable moment for appreciating with some truth the influence of the crusades, and the opinions of those who have reflected upon them before us: we may say, that the revolutions of the present age are for us a torch which enlightens the history of past times; none of the lessons which are afforded by great political concussions have been wanting for the present generation, and on that account, no doubt, our age will some day merit the title of the age of enlightenment.

We may safely say, that that which the crusades were deficient in, in order to have found more indulgent judges, was success; let us suppose for a moment that the crusades had succeeded, as they who undertook them hoped they would, and let us see, in that case, what would have been their results. Egypt, Syria, and Greece would have become Christian colonies; the nations of the East and the West would have pursued together the great march of civilization; the languages of the Franks would have penetrated to the extremes of Asia; the Barbary coast, now inhabited by pirates, would have received the morals and the laws of Europe; and the interior of Africa would not have been for a long time a land impenetrable to the relations of commerce and the researches of learned men and travellers. In order to judge what nations under the same laws and the same religion would have gained by this union, we have but to remember the state of the Roman world under the successors of Augustus, forming, as it were, one people, living under the same law, speaking the same language. All the seas were free, and the most distant provinces communicated with each other by easy and commodious routes; cities exchanged the objects of their arts and their industry, climates their various productions, nations their knowledge. If the crusades had subdued the East to Christianity, it is fair to believe that this grand spectacle, which the human race had only once beheld, would have been repeated in modern times, and opinions would not now be divided as to the advantages of the holy wars. Unfortunately, the Crusaders were unable to extend or preserve their conquests. The results of the crusades are thus more difficult to seize, and the good attributed to them does not strike all minds with equal force.

Among the results of the crusades, impartial history cannot pass over the evils they caused humanity to undergo; but these evils were felt in the time itself of the holy wars; and the faithful picture of that period has been quite sufficient to make us acquainted with them. As to the good the crusades produced, it has been like the germ, which remains a long time concealed in the earth, and develops itself slowly. After the account of each crusade, our readers will remember that, in a short summary, we have pointed out the immediate results of it. Now we will embrace all the epochs of the Eastern expeditions in a general review. When the ages to which the events of which we have spoken belonged become better known, the spirit of these events and their consequences will be better understood and better judged of: we are about to exhibit societies such as they were in the middle ages, and the progress they have made towards civilization; leaving to enlightened readers the care of appreciating that which belongs to the crusades.

We will in the first place examine the state of the different powers of Europe, and will begin with France.

When we remember the state of weakness and decay in which the commencement of the twelfth century found the French monarchy, we are astonished at the degree of prosperity and splendour it attained in subsequent ages. Skilful negotiations, successful wars, useful alliances, the decay of the feudal system, and the progressive enfranchisement of the commons, favoured the dynasty of the Capets, in the aggrandizement of their states, and in the increase of their authority. Several centuries were employed in consummating this great work of fortune and policy; and the more slowly that this revolution was operated, the more durable proved its effects. One plan of conduct, followed up by all the princes of one same family, and the success it obtained in the prosperity and aggrandizement of the kingdom, and the glory and independence of the nation, at the present day, merit all the attention of history. Frenchmen cannot help feeling both gratitude and admiration when they reflect that the union of so many rich provinces—that this French monarchy, which has grown from age to age, and which finished by extending from the Rhine to the Pyrenees; that this beautiful France, in a word, such as we see it, is the work of the august family which governs it at the present day. [95]

The policy of our kings was no doubt seconded by the great events of the crusades; it was natural that the nation which took the greatest share in these events should profit more than others by it, in the increase of its power and the amelioration of its social condition. The glory which the French arms acquired beyond the seas gave a new lustre to the monarchy; royal authority profited equally by the exploits and the reverses of the numerous warriors whom the holy wars attracted into Asia; the absence, the death, or the ruin of the great vassals permitted royalty to rise from the bosom of feudal anarchy, and establish order in the kingdom.

More than a century before the first crusade, the barons and prelates had ceased to meet in general assembly to regulate the forms of justice, and lend to the acts of royal authority the support of their political influence. At the second crusade, there were several assemblies of the great men of the kingdom, in which preparations for the expedition, and measures for the maintenance of public order and the execution of the laws during the absence of Louis VII., were deliberated upon. In these meetings, which were very numerous, the French might trace at least a faint image of those assemblies, so celebrated under the first races, in which the kings and their subjects deliberated together upon the means of securing the independence of the nation and the safety of the throne.

Thus the crusades aided the kings of France in resuming their legislative power, and the most enlightened part of the nation, in recovering those ancient prerogatives which they had exercised under the children of Clovis and Charlemagne.

It may be remembered, that after the accession of Hugh Capet, the great vassals not only did no longer assemble around their prince, but had entirely separated their cause from that of the crown; several even scarcely acknowledged a king of France, and covering their opposition with a pious pretext, they, in their public acts, designated the year of the reign of Jesus Christ, instead of that of the king. This opposition, which lasted more than a century, at last gave way to other feelings, when they saw the French monarchs at the head of those expeditions which attracted the attention of all Christendom, and in which the cause of Jesus Christ himself, as well as of all Christian nations, seemed interested. In order to perceive clearly what the kings of France owed to the holy wars, and what in particular they gained by taking part in them, it would suffice to compare Philip I., shut up in his palace, in a melancholy manner, during the Council of Clermont, excommunicated by Urban, condemned by the bishops, and abandoned by his nobles, with Philip Augustus, in the first place conqueror of Saladin in Syria, and afterwards triumphant at Beauvines, over the enemies of his kingdom; or with Louis IX., surrounded in his reverses by a faithful nobility, ever respected by the clergy and the people, revered as the firmest support of the Church, and proclaimed by his own age the arbiter of Europe.

We will speak hereafter of the changes which were then effected in the different classes of society; we will confine ourselves here to saying that the crusades were the signal for a new order of things in France, and that this new order of things cast solid foundations during the holy wars.

If royalty in France was weak at the period of the first crusade, in England it was strong and powerful; royalty and feudalism oppressed England with all the weight of the conquests of William; but an authority founded upon victory, and sustained by violence, created at an early period in men's minds a feeling of opposition, which time and circumstances were destined to develop. Military despotism had been able to impose silence upon opinions; but it had not entirely changed the manners of the English, or destroyed their attachment to old customs. Passions suppressed by the sword broke out with greater violence in the end.

An all-powerful monarchy exhibited a tendency to decline, and in England was seen the contrary of that which had been seen in France. Liberty made advances at the expense of royal authority. It does not enter into our plan to explain in detail the causes of this revolution. Several English monarchs allowed themselves to be led away by an imprudent and passionate policy, which threw them into fatal extravagances; their excesses, their violences, and particularly the crimes of John Lack-land, alienated the minds of their subjects, and united the whole nation in one feeling of resistance to absolute power. Another cause of decline not less remarkable, and to which history has not sufficiently drawn attention, was the ambition of the English princes, which inspired them with the senseless project of conquering the kingdom of France. The ruinous wars which they maintained against an enemy they could not subdue, placed them at the discretion of the barons and the English people, who furnished them with subsidies and fought under their banners.

The crusades had, perhaps, less influence upon the civilization of England than upon that of several other states of Europe. They might, however, concur with many circumstances of that period in effecting the changes which the English monarchy underwent.

Richard Cœur de Lion was more anxious to acquire the renown of a great captain than the reputation of a great king; the glory of arms made him forget the cares of his kingdom. It may be remembered that before his departure he sold the charges, the prerogatives, and the domains of the crown; he would have sold, as he himself said, the city of London, if he could have found a purchaser; his reverses and his captivity ruined his people, and his long absence kept up the spirit of faction among his nobles, and more especially in his own family.

The English barons were several times desirous of going into the East, against the will of the king; and the idea of opposing a monarch they did not love, often added to their impatience to embark for Palestine. Kings likewise took advantage of the opinions of their times, and engaged themselves to set out for the crusades, with the sole view of obtaining subsidies, which they employed in other enterprises. These means, too often employed, drew contempt upon the policy of princes, and only served to increase the public mistrust.

But that which completed the overthrow of the foundations of an absolute monarchy in England, was the violent enterprises of the popes against the English kings; enterprises which the spirit of religious wars favoured. In the league of the barons against Henry III., the rebels wore a cross, as in the wars beyond the seas; and the priests promised the palms of martyrdom to those who should die in the cause of liberty. One very curious circumstance is, that the head of the league formed for the independence of the English nation, was a French gentleman, the son of that count de Montfort so renowned [96] in the crusade against the Albigeois.

But the long efforts of England to obtain liberty deserve so much the more to fix the attention of history, from their having, in the end, attained a positive and durable result. So many other nations, after having contended for a long time, sometimes against license, sometimes against tyranny, have only met with misery, shame, and slavery. If the English revolution produced in the end salutary effects, it was because all classes of society concurred together in it; because it was made in the interests of all, according to the character and the manners of the nation, and according to the spirit of Christianity, which then presided over all which ought to last among men. Unanimity of opinions and sentiments, the accordance of manners and laws, of policy and religion, founded from that time that public spirit of which England still offers us the model; and this public spirit became in the end the most firm support and the most sure safeguard of liberty.

Whilst England was wresting liberty from its kings, and France was requiring hers back again of royalty, Germany presented another spectacle; the German empire, which had thrown out great splendour up to the eleventh century, declined rapidly during the crusades.

The emperors, in order to resist the great vassals, granted several advantages to the clergy, and bestowed privileges upon the cities. The clergy employed these advantages in favour of the popes, who attacked the imperial power; the cities profited by the concessions which were made to found their independence. All the efforts of the emperors had proved unable to prevent the crown continuing elective, whilst the great fiefs became hereditary. Thus the heads of the empire depended for their election upon the princes and nobles whom they themselves had freed from all dependence. In the competition of the pretenders to the throne, in a competition which was almost always decided by fortune, intrigue, or victory, it may easily be supposed that ambition was often more successful than moderation and virtue. Among the princes who ascended the imperial throne, many were men of great character; but their active and restless genius led them into adventurous and gigantic enterprises, which exhausted their strength and hastened the decline of the empire.

The memories of ancient Rome and of the power of the Cæsars were always present to their imagination. One of the greatest errors of their policy was turning their views towards Italy; they encountered on their way thither the popes, who declared a war of extermination against them; two families of emperors succumbed beneath the thunders of Rome; they were never able to reign over Italy, and whilst they exhausted themselves in vain efforts to establish their domination there, they completed the loss of their influence in Germany.

It is a consoling remark for humanity, that most of the conquerors of the middle ages weakened themselves by their undertakings, victory itself only serving to bring about the ruin of their power. The kings of France of this period evinced, perhaps, less talent and genius than the emperors of Germany; but their policy was wiser and more fortunate; they confined themselves to conquering their own kingdom; their conquests only tended to unite the scattered members of a large family; and their authority became more popular in proportion with their being considered as a natural tie between the French of all the provinces.

The glory which the emperors of Germany acquired by their conquests was but a personal glory, and did not at all interest the German people. This manifestation of their power had nothing in common with the nations of which they were the head. As soon as this power was no longer a bond or a support for the people, they separated themselves from it, and every one sought his safety or his aggrandizement in his own strength.

A state of things arose from this which was, perhaps, more fatal to Germany than the absolute authority of the emperors; upon the ruins of the imperial grandeur arose a crowd of states, opposed to each other by diversity of laws and the spirit of rivalry. All those ecclesiastical and secular principalities in which the spirit of monarchy prevailed; those cities in which the spirit of liberty fermented; that nobility animated by the pretensions of aristocracy, could not possibly have the same interests or the same policy to direct their efforts towards one common and salutary aim.

The popes, after having weakened the power of the emperors, wished to dispose of the broken sceptre of Charlemagne, and offered it to all who appeared likely to promote their scheme of vengeance. A crowd of princes then started up as pretenders to the empire thus held out by the popes, and the greater the number of these, the more rapidly the empire declined. Amidst civil discords, Germany completed the loss of its political unity, and at last its religious unity.

In order to judge to what a degree it was difficult to put in motion that enormous mass called the German confederation, it is only necessary to contemplate, in the history of the fourteenth and fifteenth centuries, those numerous diets which assembled to deliberate upon the war against the Turks, in which the presence of imminent peril even was never able to produce one energetic decision for the safety of Germany.

The popes sometimes made use of the pretext of the crusades to drive the emperors to a distance, and to precipitate them into disastrous expeditions; thus the enthusiasm for the holy wars, which had a tendency to establish union among Christian nations, had no power to bring together the members of the German nation, and only served to keep up trouble and disorder in the bosom of the empire. We must, however, repeat here what has been read in this history; it was under the auspices and by the influence of the court of Rome, when occupied seriously by a crusade, that the family of Rodolph of Hapsburg arose, a family whose power restored the empire to something of its ancient splendour, and saved Europe from the invasion of the Turks.

We have likewise to add that, at the period of the crusades, Germany augmented its territories and its population. The expeditions against the infidels of the East gave birth to the idea of attacking the pagans and idolaters, whose hordes inhabited the banks of the Vistula and the coasts of the Baltic. These races, when subdued by the Crusaders, entered into the Christian republic, and formed part of the German confederation. At the aspect of the cross, such cities as Dantzic, Thorn, Elbing, Kœnigsberg, &c., sprang up from the bosom of forests and deserts. Finland, Lithuania, Pomerania, and Silesia became flourishing provinces; new nations arose, new states were formed, and, to complete these prodigies, the arms of the Crusaders marked the spot in which a monarchy was to appear that did not exist in the middle ages, but which the present age has seen all at once take its place in the rank of the great powers of Europe. At the end of the thirteenth century, the provinces from which the Prussian monarchy derives both its name and its origin, were separated from Christendom by idolatry and savage manners; the conquest and the civilization of these provinces were the work of the holy wars.

If from Germany we pass into Italy, we there meet with other forms of government, and other revolutions.

When the last columns of the Roman empire crumbled away, Italy was covered with ruins. The Huns, the Franks, the Vandals, the Goths, the Germans, and the Lombards, held over this beautiful country, in turns, the scourge of their domination, and all left behind them traces of their manners, their legislation, and their character.

In the tenth century, the emperors of Constantinople being unable any longer to retain Italy, other powers arose, some from conquests, others by good fortune, and others from circumstances which history has much difficulty in indicating. The influence of the popes sometimes defended the independence of Italy against the invasions and the yoke of the German emperors; but the struggle was so long, and the war between the two powers exhibited so many vicissitudes, that it only served to perpetuate trouble and discord; during several centuries, the Guelphs and the Ghibellines desolated Italy without defending it.

In every nation of Europe there was then a power, or rather a preponderating authority, which was as a rallying-point, or centre, around which society formed and united its forces to defend its political existence.

Italy had not, like France and other countries, this precious means of conservation. Nothing proves better the dissolution in which this rich country was plunged, than the manner by which it endeavoured to establish its independence in the middle ages. That division into many states, that parcelling out of territory, that numerous population split into a thousand fractions, all announced the absence of any tie, of any common centre. Italy comprised many nations; twenty republics had each their own laws, their own interests, and their own history. Those perpetual wars between the citizens of the same cities; those animosities between republic and republic; that necessity of the inhabitants for calling in strangers in their internal quarrels; those mistrusts which bore harder upon the citizens than upon the stipendiary adventurers, tended to efface the true sentiment of patriotism, and at length caused even the name of the Italian nation to be forgotten.

The feudal system was abolished earlier in Italy than elsewhere; but with feudalism departed the ancient honour of brave knights, and the virtues of chivalry. In republics defended by mercenaries, bravery, and all the generous sentiments that accompany it, ceased to be esteemed. Violent passions had no longer any check, either in the laws or in the opinions of men; it was at this unhappy period that those hatreds and vengeances displayed themselves which appear so improbable to us in our tragedies; no spectacle can be more afflicting than that of Italy in the fourteenth century; and we may safely say that Dante had but to look around him to find the model for his Hell.

Society, always ready to split to pieces, appeared to have no other motive but the fury of parties, no other principle of life but discord and civil war; there was no other guarantee against license but tyranny; or against tyranny, but the despair of factions, and the poniard of conspirators. As the strength of most of the little states which covered Italy was seldom equal to their ambition; and as princes and citizens, by the same reason that they were weak, wanted both moderation and courage; they sought their elevation or their safety in all the means that treachery and perfidy could suggest. Plots, political stratagems, odious crimes, everything appeared right to them; everything seemed properly available that could sustain their quarrels, and satisfy their ambition or their jealousy. At length, all morality disappeared; and it was then that school of policy was formed, which is to be found in the lessons, or rather in the satire, of Machiavel's book.

It is said that the Italians were the first to form the idea of what publicists call the balance of power. We do not think that Italy merits such a glory; that which is understood by the balance of power is not an invention: it is nothing but the natural resource of the weakness which seeks a support. If we follow the progress of events, we shall find that this system, so long boasted, became fatal to Italy, by calling thither conquerors, who made it, even up to our own days, the theatre of most sanguinary wars.

At the period of the crusades, the cities of Lombardy, and the republics of Genoa, Pisa, and Venice, had attained great prosperity; and that which gave them this prosperity was the commerce of the East, which Italy carried on before the crusades, and persevered in, with all the advantages accruing from the expeditions beyond the seas.

But these republics, which contended for the empire of the sea, and only occupied a little corner of land upon the Mediterranean,—which had their eyes constantly fixed upon Syria, Egypt, and Greece,—which left to strangers the care of defending their territories, and only armed their citizens for the defence of their commerce,—these mercantile republics were much better calculated to enrich Italy than to keep up the sentiment of a true independence among the Italian nations.

We cannot, however, refrain from admiring that republic of Venice, whose power everywhere preceded the arms of the Crusaders, and which the nations of the middle ages looked upon as the queen of the East. The decline of this great republic did not begin before the period at which the progress of navigation, that it had so much contributed to, at length opened the route to India, and led to the discovery of a new world. Most of the other republics of Italy neither displayed the same splendour nor enjoyed the same duration; many among them—particularly those in which democracy prevailed—had disappeared at the end of the crusades, in the chaos and tumult of discords and civil wars. In their place arose dukes and princes, who substituted the intrigues of policy for popular passions, and sometimes made it their ambition to favour the revival of arts and letters, the true glory of Italy.

The kingdom of Naples and Sicily, situated at the extremity of Italy, was for the Crusaders the road to Greece and the East. The riches of this country, which appeared never to have any guardians,—a territory which its inhabitants were never able to defend, must have often tempted the cupidity and the ambition of the princes and even of the knights who went to seek their fortunes in Asia. The history of this fine country is mixed up during two centuries with that of the holy wars, the crusades often furnishing a pretext or an opportunity for the conquest of it. The wars undertaken for the kingdom of Naples,—those wars which produced more monstrous crimes than glorious exploits, more revolts than battles, completed the corruption of the Neapolitan character, in which has always been remarked, on the one part, an inclination to shake off the yoke of present domination, and, on the other, an extreme resignation in submitting to the yoke of victory.

Whilst glancing thus at the principal states of Europe, we are particularly struck with the great diversity that exists in the manners, the institutions, and the destinies of nations. How is it possible to follow the march of civilization amidst so many republics and monarchies, some bursting with splendour from the bosom of barbarism, others sinking into ruins? And how is it possible to point out the influence of the crusades through so many revolutions, which have often the same causes, but whose effects are so different, and sometimes so opposite? Spain, to which we are now about to turn our attention, will present us with other pictures, and must furnish fresh subjects for meditation.

During the course of the crusades, we see Spain occupied in its own boundaries with defending itself against those same Saracens whom the other nations of Europe went to contend with in the East; in the north of the Peninsula, some Christian sovereignties had maintained themselves, which began to be formidable under Sancho the Great, king of Castile and Arragon. The valour of the Castilians, sustained by the example of the Cid, and by the influence of chivalric manners, and seconded by warriors from all the provinces of France, took Toledo, before the end of the eleventh century. But the conquests of the Spaniards did not afterwards correspond with the splendour of their early triumphs; as fast as they retook provinces from the Moors, they made separate kingdoms of them; and the Spanish power, thus divided, became, in some sort, weakened by its own victories.

The invasion of the Moors in Spain bore some resemblance to that of the Franks in Asia. It was the religion of Mahomet that animated the Saracen warriors to the fight, as the Christian religion inflamed the zeal and ardour of the soldiers of the cross. Africa and Asia often answered to the appeal of the Mussulman colonies in Spain, as Europe did to the cries of alarm of the Christian colonies in Syria. Enthusiasm gave birth on both sides to prodigies of heroism, and held fortune for a long time suspended between the two inimical nations and the two inimical religions.

A spirit of independence naturally grew up among the Spaniards, during a war in which the state had need of all its citizens, and in which every citizen, by that means, acquired a great degree of importance. It has been remarked, with reason, that a people that has done great things, that an entire people called to the defence of its country, experiences an exaggerated sentiment of its rights, shows itself more exacting, sometimes more unjust towards those who govern, and often feels tempted to employ against its sovereigns the strength it had employed against its enemies. Thus we may see in the Spanish annals, that the nobility and the people were more turbulent than in other countries, and that monarchy was there at first more limited than among the other nations of Europe.

The institution of the Cortes, the enfranchisement of the commons, and a crowd of privileges granted to cities, signalized very early, among the Spaniards, the decay of the feudal system and of the absolute authority of the monarchs. If we may judge by public acts of legislation, we might believe that the Spanish people enjoyed liberty before all the other nations of Europe. But, in times of trouble, we must be guarded in judging of the liberty of a nation by that which is said in political rostrums, or in charters and institutions, by turns obtained by violence and destroyed by power, always placed between two rocks,—anarchy and despotism. The history of Spain, at this period, is full of crimes and monstrous deeds, that stain the cause of princes as well as that of the people: which proves at least that morals did not keep pace with laws, and that institutions, created among public discords, did not soften the national character.

Amidst the revolutions which agitated Spain, political passions sometimes caused even the domination of the Moors to be forgotten. When at the end of the thirteenth century, the Mussulmans, conquered by James of Arragon, abandoned the Balearic isles and the kingdom of Valencia and Murcia, the Spaniards all at once suspended the progress of their arms. Whilst in the East, the victorious Mamelukes redoubled their efforts to completely drive the Franks from the coast of Syria; in the West, the Moors remained, during two centuries, in possession of a part of Spain, without the Spaniards ever seriously attempting to complete the conquest of their own country. The standard of Mahomet floated over the cities of Granada, up to the reign of Ferdinand and Isabella. It was only at this period that the Spanish monarchy issued all-powerful from the chaos of revolutions, and revived in the people the warlike and religious enthusiasm which completed the expulsion of the Moors. Then terminated the struggle which had lasted during eight centuries, and in which, according to Spanish authors, three thousand seven hundred battles were fought. So many combats, which were nothing but one long crusade, must have been a school of bravery and heroism; thus the Spaniards, in the sixteenth and seventeenth centuries, were considered the most brave and warlike nation of Europe. Philosophers have sought to explain by the influence of climate that spirit of haughtiness and pride, that grave and austere character which to this day distinguish the Spanish nation. It appears to us that a much more natural explanation of this national character is to be found in a war at once patriotic and religious, in which twenty successive generations were engaged, the perils of which must have inspired serious thoughts as well as noble sentiments.

The aversion for the yoke and the religion of the Moors, redoubled the attachment of the people for their religion and their ancient customs. The remembrance of that glorious struggle has not failed to animate the ardour and courage of the Spaniards at a recent period;—fortunate had it been for Spain if, at the moment at which I am speaking, she had not forgotten her own examples!

Towards the end of the war against the Moors, Spain adopted the Inquisition with more warmth than the other Christian nations. I will not attempt to repel the reproaches which modern philosophers have addressed to her; but it appears to me that sufficient account has not been taken of the motives which would render more excusable in Spain than elsewhere, those suspicions and those dark jealousies for all which was not the national religion. How could they forget that the standard of a foreign worship had so long floated over the Peninsula, and that during many ages, Christian warriors had fought, not only for the faith of their fathers, but for the very soil of their country against the infidels? According to my opinion, may it not be believed, that among the Spaniards, religious intolerance, or rather a hatred for all foreign religion, had something in itself which was less a jealous devotion than an ardent, restless patriotism?

Spain took no part in the crusades, till the spirit of these wars began to die away in the rest of Europe. We must, however, remark, that this kingdom derived some advantages from the Eastern expeditions. In almost all the enterprises of Christendom against the Mussulmans of Asia, a great number of the Crusaders stopped on the coast of Spain to combat the Moors. Many crusades were published in the West against the infidels who were masters of the Peninsula. The celebrated victory of Tolosa over the Moors was the fruit of a crusade preached in Europe, and particularly in France, by order of the sovereign pontiff. Expeditions beyond the sea were likewise favourable to the Spaniards, by retaining in their own country the Saracens of Egypt and Syria, who might have joined those on the coast of Africa. It has been shown in this history that the kingdom of Portugal was conquered and founded by Crusaders. The crusades gave the idea of those orders of chivalry, which, in imitation of those of Palestine, were formed in Spain, and without the succour of which the Spanish nation would not perhaps have triumphed over the Moors.

We may add, that Spain is the country in which the memory of the crusades was preserved the longest. In the last century, the bull called *Crusada* was there published every year in all the provinces. This solemn publication reminded the Spaniards of the triumphs they had formerly obtained over the Mussulmans.

We have shown the state of the principal powers of Europe during the crusades; it now remains for us to speak of a power which dominated over all the others, and which was as a tie or centre to all the powers;—we mean the authority of the heads of the Church.

The popes, as a temporal power and as a spiritual power, presented a singular contrast in the middle ages. As sovereigns of Rome, they had almost no authority, and were often banished from their own states: as heads of Christendom, they exercised an absolute empire to the extremities of the world, and their name was revered wherever the Gospel was preached.

It has been said that the popes made the crusades; they who maintain this opinion are far from being acquainted with the general movement which then affected the Christian world; no power on earth could have been able to produce such a great revolution; it only belonged to Him whose will gives birth to and disperses tempests, to throw all at once into human hearts that enthusiasm which silenced all other passions, and drew on the multitude as if by an invisible power. In the first book of this volume we have shown how the enthusiasm for the holy wars developed itself by degrees, and how it broke forth towards the end of the eleventh century, without any other influence but that of the dominant ideas: it led away the whole of society, and the popes were led away as nations of people were; one proof that the sovereign pontiffs did not produce this extraordinary revolution is, that they were never able to revive the spirit of the crusades, when that spirit became extinct among Christian nations.

It has likewise been said that the crusades very much increased the authority of the popes; we shall soon see what truth there is in that assertion. Among the causes which contributed to the growth of the pontifical authority, we may name the invasion of the barbarians of the North, who overthrew the empire of the West, and the progress of the Saracens, who would not allow the emperors of the East leisure to turn their attention towards Italy, or even to preserve any domination over that country. The popes thus found themselves freed from two powers upon which they depended; and remained in possession of the city of Rome, which appeared to have no other master. Other circumstances added from that time to the authority of the successors of St. Peter. However it may be, everybody knows that this authority had already made immense progress before the crusades; the head of the most powerful monarchs had already bowed before the thunders of the Vatican; and Christendom seemed to have already adopted the maxim of Gregory VII., that "the pope, in quality of Vicar of Jesus Christ, ought to be superior to every human power."

It cannot be doubted that a religious war was calculated to favour the development of the pontifical authority. But this war itself produced events, and gave rise to circumstances which were less a means of aggrandizement for the power of the popes, than a rock against which that power was dashed and injured. But it is positive, that the end of the crusades left the sovereign pontiffs less powerful than they had been at the commencement of the holy wars.

Let us, in the first place, say a few words of the advantages which the heads of the Church derived from the expeditions against the infidels. Recourse was always had to the sovereign pontiffs when the question of a crusade was agitated; the holy war was preached in their name, and carried on under their auspices. Warriors enrolled under the banners of the cross, received from the pope privileges which freed them from all other dependence but that of the Church; the popes were the protectors of the Crusaders, the support of their families, the guardians of their properties; it was to the popes the Crusaders submitted all their differences, and confided all their interests.

The sovereign pontiffs were not at first aware of the advantages they might derive from the crusades. In the first crusade, Urban, who had enemies to contend with, did not think of asking the assistance of the warriors he had persuaded to take the cross; it was not till the second crusade that the popes perceived the ascendancy the holy wars must give them. At this period a king of France and an emperor of Germany were, in a manner, lieutenants of the Holy See; in the third crusade, the pope compelled Henry II. to take the cross, to expiate the murder of Thomas à Becket. After the death of Henry, his son Richard set out for the East, at the signal of the sovereign pontiff. In consequence of this crusade, great disorders, as we have related, disturbed the kingdom of England; the popes took advantage of them to give laws to the English people, and a few years after the death of Richard, his brother and successor acknowledged himself the vassal of the court of Rome.

The crusades were for the popes a pretext to usurp, in all the states of Europe, the principal attributes of sovereignty; they became possessed, in the name of the holy war, of the right of levying everywhere both armies and imposts; the legates they employed in all the countries of Christendom exercised supreme authority in their name; the presence of these legates inspired respect and fear; their wills were laws. Armed with the cross, they commanded all the clergy as masters; and as the clergy, among all Christian nations, had the greatest ascendancy, the empire of the popes had no longer any opposition or limits.

It may be perceived that we have forgotten none of the advantages the heads of the Church found in the crusades: here are the obstacles and the rocks they met with in the exercise of their power.

It must be allowed that the empire of the popes received but very little increase in Asia during the holy wars; the quarrels and disputes which constantly disturbed the Christian colonies in the East, and in which they were obliged to interfere, multiplied their embarrassments, without adding to their power.

Their voice was not always listened to by the multitude of the Crusaders; sometimes even the soldiers of the cross resisted the will and despised the counsels of the pontiffs. The legates of the Holy See were frequently in opposition to the leaders of the army, and their character was not always respected in camps. As the popes were supposed to direct the crusades, they were, in some sort, responsible for the misfortunes and disorders they had no power to prevent: this moral responsibility exposed them sometimes to be judged with rigour, and was injurious to their reputation for wisdom and ability.

By an abuse of the spirit of the crusades, the popes were dragged into wars in which their ambition was often more interested than religion; they then thought of their temporal power, and that was their weakest point; they were never strong but when they depended upon a higher support;

the crusades became for them as a lever, which they employed to elevate themselves; but it must be allowed that they depended upon it too much, and when this lever failed them, their authority trembled. Seeking to regain what they had lost, the popes made, in the fourteenth and fifteenth centuries, incredible efforts to revive the spirit of the crusades; the question then being no longer to go and fight the Saracens in Asia, but to defend Europe against the invasion of the Turks. Amidst the perils of Christendom, the conduct of the popes merited the greatest praise, and the zeal they displayed has not been sufficiently appreciated by historians. But the time of the fervour for crusades was past. The success obtained by the sovereign pontiffs was never proportionate with their efforts, and the uselessness of their attempts necessarily weakened the idea entertained of their ascendancy and their power.

The crusade against the Albigeois procured them very little advantage; the intolerance which gave birth to that war proceeded from the crusades; the Inquisition, which arose from it, awakened more passions than it suppressed. By the Inquisition, the Church assumed in this world a jurisdiction which partook too strongly of humanity; her decrees were much more respected when they were referred to heaven or to a future life.

Nothing can equal the enormity of the tributes that were imposed upon the clergy for carrying on the holy wars. The tenths were not only levied for the crusades, but for every attempt at a crusade; not only for expeditions to the East, but for every enterprise against the enemies of the court of Rome. They were at length levied under the most vain pretexts; all Europe addressed warm remonstrances to the popes; at first the rigour with which the agents collected the tributes was complained of; and afterwards their infidelity in the application of the treasures extorted from the faithful became equally a subject of scandal. Nothing could be more injurious to the pontifical authority than these complaints, which arose from all quarters, and which, in the end, furnished weapons for the formidable heresy of Luther.

The history of the popes in the middle ages completes the proof of that which we have said. Their domination went on constantly increasing during a century up to Innocent III.; it after that period declined during another century, down to Boniface VIII., at which time crusades beyond the seas ended.

In latter days, publicists have said a great deal about the power of the heads of the Church; but they have judged rather according to systems than according to facts,—more after the spirit of our own age than that of the middle ages. The genius of the sovereign pontiffs has been much lauded, particularly for the purpose of placing their ambition in a stronger light. But if the popes really had the genius and the ambition attributed to them, we must believe they would have been principally employed in aggrandizing their states, and increasing their authority as sovereigns. Nevertheless, they did not succeed in this, or else they never attempted it. In fact, what could men do, who were mostly arrived at the age of decrepitude?—what could princes do, who merely passed over the throne, to strengthen their authority, and master the passions belonging to the infancy and the youth of societies? Among the crowd of popes who succeeded each other, many were endowed with a superior genius, whilst others only possessed a moderate capacity; men of all characters and all turns of mind occupied, in succession, the chair of St. Peter; nevertheless, these men, so different by their tastes, their passions, and their talents, all aimed at and all did the same thing; they had, therefore, an impulsion which was not in themselves, the motive of which must be sought elsewhere than in the vulgar policy of princes.

That would be a curious history which would trace, in the same picture, the spiritual empire and the temporal empire of the popes. Who would not be surprised at seeing in it, on one side, a force which nothing could resist, which moves the very world,—a will always the same, which is transmitted from pontiff to pontiff, like a deposit, or like a sacred heritage; on the other, a policy weak and changeable, like man,—a power which can scarcely defend itself against the lowest of its enemies, and which at every moment the breath of revolutions has power to shake? In this parallel, the imagination would be dazzled when such an empire should be presented to it as has never been seen upon earth, and which would lead to the belief that the popes did not belong to this fragile and transitory world,—a power which hell cannot pull down,—which the world cannot corrupt,—which, without the help of any army, and by the simple ascendancy of a few words, subdues things sooner, and proves itself more formidable, than ancient Rome, with all her victories. What more magnificent spectacle can the history of empires present to us? But, in the other part of the picture, who would not be moved to pity at beholding a government without vigour, an administration without foresight,—that people, descended from *the king people*, led by an indolent, timid old man, the eternal city falling into ruins, and as hidden beneath the grass? When we see—so near to a power almost supernatural—weakness, uncertainty, the fragility common to things below, and humanity with all its miseries, why may we not be permitted to compare the double power of the popes to Jesus Christ himself, of whom they were the vicars and images upon earth,—to Jesus Christ, whose double nature presents us, on one side, a God beaming with splendour, and on the other a simple mortal, loaded with the cross, and crowned with thorns?

If the principal features of this picture are not wanting in truthfulness, how can we believe in the policy of the popes as it is represented to us?—is it not more natural to think that the sovereign pontiffs, in all they did that was great, followed the spirit of Christianity? In the middle ages, which was the period of their power, they were much more directed by this spirit than they directed it themselves; later, and when popes entertained projects like those that are attributed to their genius and ambition, their power declined. We have but to compare Gregory VII., giving himself up to the spirit of his age, and supporting himself by the ascendancy of the Church, with Julius II., whom Voltaire calls a great prince, and who only employed the known combinations of policy.

The pontifical authority was the only one that had its bases and roots in opinions and beliefs. This power gave the world, or, rather, the world asked of it, laws, knowledge, and a support. The popes were right in the famous comparison of the two great luminaries. The authority of the heads of the Church was much more in advance towards civilization than the authority of princes. In order that the world might be civilized, it was important for the popes to have great power; and the need that was felt for their power favoured the progress of it.

As long as the world was governed by opinions and beliefs, rather than by civil laws and political authorities, the popes exercised the greatest influence; when the interests and rights of princes and nations became better regulated; when the world passed from the empire of opinions to that of laws; when, in a word, temporal power was well established in Europe, and prevailed over the spiritual of society, the pontiffs necessarily lost their ascendancy. Such is the history of the origin, of the progress, and of the decay of the pontifical power in the ages which have preceded us.

That which we have said of the popes clearly shows what influence the Church exercised over the society of Europe in the middle ages; but gross minds were not yet prepared to receive all the benefits of Christianity. The alliance of barbarism with superstition retarded the progress of true knowledge. The passions and customs of barbarians were still mingled with some salutary institutions.

The Franks, the Germans, and Goths, when obtaining possession of the richest countries of Europe, had employed all the rights of conquest, and these rights had become the laws of European society. We may form an idea of the government of the middle ages by representing to ourselves a victorious army, which disperses itself throughout the conquered country, shares the territory and those who inhabit it, and is always ready to march at the signal of its officers and its supreme general, to combat the common enemy, and defend its possessions.

As long as discipline and subordination subsisted in this military colony, public order was not entirely disturbed; and this kind of government might supply the place of wiser institutions. But as soon as the relations of assistance and fidelity, obedience and protection, became weakened, society—or rather the feudal government—no longer presented anything but the aspect of an army given up to license,—of an army whose officers and soldiers no longer acknowledged a head, were no longer subject to direction, and fought at hazard under a thousand different standards.

The vassals depended, in the first place, on the prince, because they held their lands and their offices of him. These lands and these offices becoming hereditary, their holders soon desired to render themselves independent, and to arrogate to themselves privileges which only belonged to the sovereign; such as coining money, holding a jurisdiction, and making war in their own name. From that time there remained scarcely any trace of subordination.

This decline of society, or, rather, this corruption of the feudal system, is referrible to the end of the second race. Charlemagne, in his endeavours to reëstablish the empire of the Cæsars, committed violence upon the social compact, and his extraordinary efforts exhausted the powers of royalty. The bow which he had too strongly bent, broke in the hands of his successors, and his empire crumbled away, when no longer sustained by the ascendancy of a great character. Charlemagne wished to emancipate himself from the laws of feudalism; under his feeble successors, feudalism, in its turn, was desirous of emancipating itself from the crown. The greatest evil of the feudal system was that it destroyed all protective power, all tutelary legislation, which could watch over the order and safety of society.

The monarch, despoiled of all authority, could neither be the support of innocence nor the avenger of crime; nor the mediator in war, nor the arbitrator in disputes that disturbed peace. Sovereignty, exercised by every man who wore a sword, was spread everywhere, without any one acknowledging its power anywhere; such was the disorder and confusion among those who disputed, sword in hand, for the wreck of sovereign power.

Nothing is more afflicting than this picture; the excesses which accompanied feudal anarchy no one is ignorant of. It does not form part of our plan to speak of it to any extent; the task we have to perform is a less painful one: if we turn our looks towards old times, it is only in order to discover the origin of our institutions; and among the revolutions of a barbarous age, we have only to make known what they produced that is salutary and durable. Before we proceed further, and in order to mix a few consolatory ideas with sad and painful images, we will show, by the side of the abuses of feudalism, the advantages contemporary society received from the feudal system, and the happy germs of civilization which grew from it for the benefit of following ages.

If the feudal government contained sources of disorder, it prevented disorder being carried to its height, and the evil from remaining without remedy. If it favoured anarchy and civil wars, it preserved Europe from the fury of conquerors, and from that of despotism. Vassals did not willingly consent to leave their lands; they were only bound to follow their sovereign to war for a stipulated time. This condition of the feudal compact, which was general in Europe, was found favourable for the defence of territory, and placed obstacles in the way of every project of invasion. Forces, spread about in all parts, served to protect every country against a foreign enemy, and could not be collected anywhere to assist the designs of an ambitious leader.

At a time in which passions did everything and laws were nothing, in which no political interest bound people together, what could have prevented a prince from assembling armies and ravaging Europe? What could have prevented a conqueror from subduing several kingdoms, and subjecting the people to all the excesses of tyranny, supported by the force of arms alone? It was then to the spirit of resistance of the feudal nobility that European society owed, in the midst of barbarism, the advantage of not becoming a prey to Eastern despotism, and security from wars of invasion.

Feudalism had rights and privileges to defend; the defence of these rights and privileges naturally led to ideas of independence, and these ideas of independence spread in the end through all classes of society. It must not be forgotten that the English barons established liberty in their country, whilst defending the privileges and rights of the feudal compact.

The reciprocity of obedience and protection, of services and duties, kept alive some generous sentiments. From feudal relations was born that spirit of devotion and respect for the sovereign which is neither the blind submission of the slave, nor the reasonable submission of the republican. This sentiment, which was considered, up to modern times, as the conservative principle of society in monarchies, became particularly the distinctive character of the French nobility.

The history of the crusades presents us with several examples of this devotion of the barons and knights to their monarch. When the kings of France who took the cross, were in any dangers in the East, what proofs of respect and love did they not receive from the gallant knights who accompanied them? What spectacle can be more touching than that of the imprisoned army in Egypt, forgetting its own captivity to deplore that of Louis IX.! Who is not affected at seeing, upon the coast of Africa, the French warriors overwhelmed with evils, but finding no tears in their miseries but to weep for the death of a king of France?

These ties of fidelity, which arose from feudal relations, were so powerful over men's minds, that the preachers of the crusades sometimes invoked them in their exhortations. They preached the duties of feudalism concurrently with the precepts of the Gospel, and in order to excite Christian warriors to take the cross, they called them "the vassals of Jesus Christ."

It is to the times of the feudal government we must go back, to find in all its purity, that susceptibility upon the point of honour, that inviolable fidelity to the word, which then supplied the absence of laws, and which in polished societies often render men better than laws themselves. All our ideas of military glory, that boundless esteem which we accord to bravery, that profound contempt which, amongst us, is attached to falsehood or felony, are to be traced to this remote period. Feudalism was so completely mixed up with the spirit and character of nations, that modern societies have no institutions that have not some relation with it; and we have everywhere traces of it in our habits, our manners, and even in our speech.

Let me be allowed to add here one single observation. It is in vain we protest against our origin by our words; we are incessantly reminded of it by our tastes, by our sentiments, and sometimes by our pleasures. In fact, if, on one side, our reason, formed in the school of new ideas, finds nothing that is not revolting in the middle ages, why, on the other, does our imagination, moved by the spectacle of generous passions, delight in representing to itself olden times, and mingling with gallant knights and paladins? Whilst a severe philosophy heaps measureless blame upon the barbarous customs of feudalism, and the gothic manners of our ancestors, how is it that the remembrances which these manners and these customs have left us inspire still our poets with pictures which appear to us so full of charms? Why are these remembrances revived every day with the same success, in our poems, in our romances, and upon our stage? Would it be true to say that there is more patriotism in our imagination than in our reason, since the one would make us forget the history of our country, and the other unceasingly reminds us of it?

The crusades assisted in destroying the abuses of the feudal system; they served to preserve all that the system inspired of generous sentiments, and concurred at the same time in developing that which it contained that was favourable to civilization. We will finish our sketch of the manners of feudalism and the salutary effects of the crusades, by describing the revolution which operated at this time upon the different classes of society. The nobility will fix our attention in the first place.

Nobles are found in every nation where the memory of ancestors is reckoned for anything. There can be no doubt that nobility was common among the Franks and other barbarous people who invaded Europe. But in what point of view was this nobility looked upon before the eleventh and twelfth centuries? How was it at first constituted? How was the illustration of races transmitted? We are in possession of very few monuments to assist in deciding these questions; and when we have thoroughly studied the history of the middle ages, we have nothing better to do than to imitate the genealogists, who, when embarrassed in explaining the origin of the most ancient families, content themselves with assigning it to the night-time of the past.

When we reflect upon the rapidity with which generations pass away, and how difficult it is, even in civilized times, for most families to make out their own history during a single century, can we be astonished that, in times of ignorance and barbarism, there have been so few means of preserving the memory of the most illustrious families? In addition to the almost entire absence of written documents, the idea of true grandeur, the idea of that which constitutes heroic illustration, did not yet strike men's minds sufficiently forcibly to make them preserve a long remembrance of it. [97] In these barbarous times, men, and even princes, were most frequently only distinguished by their physical qualities or their bodily defects. To be convinced of this truth we have but to glance at the list of kings of the middle ages, in which we find the names of Pepin-le-Bref (Pepin the Short), Charles-le-Chauve (Charles the Bald), William-le-Roux (William Rufus, or the Red), Louis-le-Gros (Louis the Fat), Frederick-Barbereusse (Frederick Barbarossa, or Red Beard), and many others, whom their age only designated by that which struck their eyes and was obvious to the grossest perception. There are few things more curious for an observer, than to see how old chronicles make us acquainted with the personages whose actions they give an account of. They never omit in their pictures, either the colour of the hair, or the stature, or the countenance of the princes and heroes; and their historical portraits (may I be allowed the comparison?) bear much less resemblance to a passage of history, than to those descriptions which are now-a-days written upon the passports of travellers.

If, as a writer has said, entire man was not yet understood, it cannot be said that virtue was not known, as at any other period; but the idea of virtue was then lost in that of duty, and with the single sentiment of duty, which was but the voice of conscience or the modest instinct of habit, they dreamt not of living in the memory of men. [98] The desire for illustrating a name belongs to a nascent civilization. When civilization threw forth its first rays, moral ideas of greatness were attached to the name of ancient families; and it may be safely said that nobility was not truly instituted before the value of glory began to be felt. But what is very certain is, that in the crusades nobility acquired an eminence that it had never before enjoyed. The exploits of nobles in the cause of Christianity, were very different affairs from those wars of castle against castle, with which they employed themselves in Europe. Nobility from that time found its archives in history, and the opinion the world entertained of its valour became its loftiest title.

If we consult the most authentic facts and the most probable opinions, we have reason to believe that the distinctions of nobility were at first founded upon great offices, but principally upon property. It was for the land or estate that, in the feudal system, the oath of fealty or homage was taken, and the protection of the sovereign claimed. For the man who was not a proprietor there was no contract, no privilege; he had nothing to give, nothing to receive; in the times of Joinville, nobles were called *rich men*. In France, a great proprietor was, by right, noble; if he was ruined or despoiled, his descendants sank into the crowd again: thus had the customs of a barbarous age established it. A strange thing it is, that there are times in which extreme civilization can make a nation revert to the same estate as extreme barbarism. When political illusions shall be dispersed, and there shall remain nothing but the mere substance of society, it is still property, it is the estate which will establish pre-eminence and denote ranks. Lands will no longer furnish soldiers, but they will pay taxes for the support of them; they will no longer be held by the tenure of complying with the duty of feudal aid; but they will still owe the sovereign the support of their influence, in exchange for the protection they shall receive from the sovereign authority.

If, in the middle ages, aristocracy was founded upon land, society derived a great advantage from the circumstance; for territorial property, which does not change, which is always the same, preserves the institutions and manners of a people better than industrial property, which most frequently belongs no more to one country than another, and which, on that account, bears within itself the germs of corruption. If it was for this reason that formerly nobility was degraded by giving itself up to the speculations of commerce and industry, it must be agreed that the usage thus established, had at least a respectable aim, and arose from a salutary principle. [99]

Territorial property had then such an influence over the social state, that it is quite enough to be acquainted with the changes it experienced, to judge of the changes to which society was subjected. "As soon as the state of the property of a certain period is discovered," says Robertson, "we may determine with precision what was at the same time the degree of power then enjoyed by the king or the nobility." During the crusades, ecclesiastical and civil laws permitted nobles to alienate their domains. A great number of them availed themselves of this fatal privilege, and did not hesitate to sell their lands; which displaced property, and consequently power. The nobility thus lost its power, and the crown gained that which the aristocracy lost.

The crusades, however, were not unproductive of good fruit for the nobility; gentlemen acquired principalities in the East; most of the cities of Greece and Syria became so many lordships, which recognised as masters counts and barons enrolled under the banners of the holy wars; some, still more fortunate, ascended the throne of David, or that of Constantine, and took place among the greatest monarchs of Christendom.

The military orders likewise presented the nobility with amends for the losses they experienced in ruinous wars. These orders had immense possessions in both the West and the East; they were for the European nobility, an asylum in peace, and a school of heroism in war.

It was at this period that the use of surnames was introduced, and coats of arms were assumed. Every gentleman added to his own name the name of his estate, or the title of the lordship he possessed; he placed in his coat of arms a sign which distinguished his family and marked his nobility; genealogy became a science, and consecrated, by its researches, the illustration of races. Whatever value may be now-a-days attached to this science, it must be admitted that it often threw a great light upon the history of illustrious families, and sometimes upon the general history of a country to which these families belonged.

Everything leads us to believe that the origin of surnames, [100] but more particularly of coats of arms, is due to the Crusaders. The lord stood in no need of a mark of distinction when he did not go off his own manor; but he became aware of the necessity for distinguishing himself from others when he found himself at a distance from home, and confounded in the crowd of the Crusaders: a great number of families ruined themselves, or became extinct, in the holy wars. Such as were ruined attached themselves more strongly to the remembrance of their nobility, the only wealth that was left them; after the extinction of families, the necessity for replacing them was felt; it was under Philip-le-Hardi that the practice of creating nobles was introduced. [101] As soon as there were new nobles, it became of more consequence to be considered ancient ones. Property did not appear sufficient to preserve and transmit a name which itself became a property, consecrated by history and acknowledged by society. It was then that nobility attached more value to marks of distinction.

At the end of the feudal government, the nobility, it is true, still constituted, in a great degree, the strength of the army; but it served the state in a new character; it conformed more with the spirit of chivalry than with that of feudalism. A gentleman no longer paid homage to his sovereign for his estate, but he swore upon his sword to be faithful to him.

As soon as feudal services ceased to be required, the nobility increased in zeal for personal service. Kings eagerly welcomed them when they were no longer formidable; thus they recovered in the favour of courts a great portion of the advantages they had lost. As they still held the first rank in society, and preserved a great ascendancy over the other classes, they continued, by their example, to polish the spirit and the manners of the nation; and it is by their means particularly, that those elegant manners were formed which have so long distinguished the French among all the nations of Europe.

It is difficult, however, to say with precision what the nobility gained and what they lost by the changes that were effected. Their existence, doubtless, had something more brilliant in it, but also something less solid. The honorary prerogatives which they retained, without giving them any real strength, armed more jealous passions against them than territorial power had done; for it may be remarked, that man's self-love endures riches and power in others, with a better grace than it endures distinctions.

We must add, likewise, that as society progressed, new means of illustration, new kinds of notability arose; the moral power of opinion, which had been attached exclusively to nobility, communicated itself by degrees to those who contributed to the prosperity of society by their talents, their knowledge, or their industry.

We have seen the brilliant side of feudalism; we have now to speak of the state in which the inhabitants of the cities and the country groaned. Most of the villages and cities depended upon some baron, whose protection they purchased, and who exercised an arbitrary jurisdiction over them. Man, reduced to servitude, or rather slavery, had no law which guarded him against oppression; the produce of labour, the wages of his sweat, did not belong to him; he was himself a property which could be claimed anywhere, if he fled away from his home. Chained to the glebe, he must often have envied the animal who helped him to trace the furrow, or the palfrey, the noble companion of his master. The serf had no other hope but that which religion afforded him, and left nothing to his children but the example of his patience in suffering. He could neither make a contract during his lifetime, nor a testament at the hour of death. His last will was not recognised by law; it died with him. To excuse the barbarity of this gross age, we must remember the still more frightful fate of slaves among the Greeks and Romans. We have no need to point out the obstacles this state of things must have opposed to the development of the industry and the social faculties of man. Thus the country was covered with forests, and most of the cities presented nothing but an aspect of poverty and misery.

The cities of Lombardy, and a great part of Italy, were the first places that shook off the yoke of feudalism. The emperors of Germany, as we have seen, were almost always at variance with the popes. The cities took advantage of these quarrels, to arrogate rights which no one disputed. Others purchased them of the emperors, who believed they made a good bargain when they sold that which they had not the power to refuse. Towards the middle of the eleventh century, the clergy and nobility had already no more influence in the cities of Italy. According to the evidence of Otho of Freisengen, a contemporary author, Italy was full of free cities, all of which had obliged their bishops to reside within their walls; there was scarcely a noble who was not subject to the laws and government of a city. In Germany the cities obtained their freedom at a later period. These Germans, who, according to Tacitus, considered dwelling in cities as a mark of servitude, not only in the end built cities, but sought liberty in them. The cities of the Rhine appear to have been made free by the emperors in the eleventh century. But most of these cities were poor, they contained but few inhabitants, and were not able to defend themselves against the German oligarchy. At the commencement of the fourteenth century, several free cities, enriched by the commerce of the East, and by the communications opened by the crusades, formed a confederation, and by that means made their independence respected.

In England, the spirit of liberty did not take its spring before the holy wars; the cities, with the exception of that of London, which had obtained several privileges, scarcely dreamt of independence; the Britons, as in the times of Virgil, appeared still separated from the rest of the world. It may be said that liberty in the English nation was not an affair of locality, but a general affair, which was to be decided at a later period.

In Spain, the war against the Moors, as we have already said, favoured the independence of the commons. We are in possession of historical documents of the eleventh century, which prove that several Spanish cities enjoyed certain immunities at this period. But the first of these cities which were summoned to the Cortes, urged by a spirit of jealousy, refused to admit the others, which was very injurious to the development and progress of liberty in Spain.

In the south of France, the archives of the communes present us with some traces of liberty, a long time before the period of the crusades. The influence of a fine climate, the vivacity which animated the inhabitants, with some traditions of the Roman law, preserved, in the provinces which border on Spain and Italy, habits of independence which might serve as models or examples. When the kings of France thought of enfranchising some communes, it was from the south of the kingdom they must have taken the idea.

These enfranchisements of the southern cities, however, were rather consecrated by custom than by positive laws. According to the best opinions, the formal and legal enfranchisement of communes in France dates from Louis-le-Gros, who granted privileges to some cities situated within the domains of the crown. The example of Louis-le-Gros was followed by Louis VII. and Philip Augustus. A great number of cities saw all sorts of slavery excluded from their walls, chose their own magistrates, levied their own taxes, kept up a military force, and had a jurisdiction entirely their own. Such was the first blow given in France to the feudal government.

Before this period it was customary to implore the aid of the barons against violence and robbery. This support was abandoned as soon as another tutelary power arose. The serfs, and even the freemen, who had at first sought safety in castles, soon sought it in cities, against their former protectors, the castellans; the first engagements of the inhabitants of cities were mutual defence and reciprocal protection.

The liberty of cities began by the corporations; men could only be strong when united. This necessity for union in moments of crisis or peril is so natural, that when society is disturbed, factions and parties are formed which are like corporations. The spirit of a public body, or the spirit of party, in whatever way it may be considered, holds essentially with the social character. Liberty was much more considered in relation with the community than in relation with individual man; it was considered a benefit that could only be enjoyed in common. Thus society did not find itself subordinate to the individual, but the individual to society. Isolated man could do nothing; strength lay with the association, which effectually protected the rights of all, and watched over the conservation of individual liberty and public liberty.

When cities situated within the royal domains had obtained their franchises, the spirit of independence soon possessed the other cities of the kingdom. The communes which succeeded in gaining their enfranchisement, did not all obtain the same advantages; they were, more or less, favoured by circumstances. Here, liberty was purchased of the lord; there, the yoke was shaken off by force; in other places, treaties were effected, in which the spirit of liberty and feudal power made mutual concessions.

During the crusades, the long absence of the barons must have multiplied, for the communes, opportunities of enfranchising themselves. Most of the lords who ruined themselves for the holy wars, exchanged, for the money of which they stood in need, all their rights over the cities which depended upon them—rights which they yielded the more willingly from hoping to win principalities in Asia.

This enfranchisement of communes produced a very different effect for the great vassals and the crown. It weakened the authority of the lords, because the spirit of liberty was against them; it increased the royal authority, because the cities which were free, or had a desire to be so, looked to the king. Cities, when their independence was threatened, implored the king's protection. We find in old chronicles, that Philip Augustus granted letters of protection to cities dependent upon barons. Thus kings became the hope of all the communes of the kingdom, and liberty supported itself by royalty. This is why the cities of France, to defend their franchises, formed no league, as they did in other countries; for they found a natural defence in royal power.

The revolution which was destined to destroy feudalism, appeared to act as of itself. There is, in the possession of a newly-acquired good, a restlessness, an anxiety, a fear of losing it, which kept the communes always on the alert; there is, on the contrary, in the possession of an anciently-acquired good, an indolent security, which did not permit the barons to see the true state of things. The lords only opposed new ideas by a short-sighted disdain, and believed they had lost nothing as long as they retained their swords by their sides.

If, however, we may judge by the complaints of Guibert, abbot of Nogent, a contemporary historian, the enfranchisement of the communes met with some opposition. There was no want of sour spirits, who considered it a dangerous and destructive innovation. But we may believe that these complaints were only inspired by that natural repugnance which the greater part of men entertain for seeing anything change which is consecrated by time, and by that vague mistrust which novelty produces, under whatever form it may appear. The truth is, that nobody knew, or could possibly judge, of the extent of the changes that were then in operation. Revolutions, whatever may be their object or their character, are never thoroughly understood before they have finished their course, and never reveal their secret at their commencement.

A century after Louis-le-Gros, Louis VIII. pretended to have the right of immediate sovereignty over all the communes. This was a signal for all the cities to complete their emancipation from the barons; this was the mortal blow to the feudal aristocracy. This great revolution of the social state went on so rapidly, that history can with difficulty follow its progress, and cannot assign the part which the crusades bore in it.

Happy had it been for society if that spirit of liberty which then set it in motion, and which advanced without ceasing, sowing blessings and evils on its route, had produced none but wise institutions; if, always confined within just bounds, it had not frequently kindled bloody discords, and had not at last mingled itself with the blind passions of the multitude! What a picture were that which should exhibit the consequences of this revolution up to modern times, which should represent monarchy rising from the ruins of feudalism and then itself succumbing in a new revolution! What a subject for serious thoughts in the historian, when, embracing with a rapid glance ancient and modern times, he sees the two most active forces of society, at the revival of civilization,—royalty and liberty, marching constantly one towards the other, demanding of each other reciprocal support, overthrowing all the barriers that separated them, destroying all they found in their passage; at last, after several ages of endeavours, meeting face to face upon the ruins accumulated round them, taking each other at first sight for enemies, declaring war against each other, and falling together on the same field of battle! [102]

God forbid that I should here be thought to present discouraging images! I have only wished to show the fragility of human affairs, and the want of foresight in those who direct societies. The revolution we have beheld is, perhaps, less the work of liberty than of the equality which is seen to figure, for the first time, in the political world.

This equality, such as the moderns have constituted it, was scarcely known in the ancient republics, of which the language had no word to express it. The first book that spoke of equality was the Gospel. Christianity constantly represents all men as equal before God. The object of the Gospel was to lower the pride of the great; which was salutary. I know not what false philosophy made use of equality to raise the pride of the low;—and then society was shaken to its very foundations.

The great revolution which has been effected in the manners and laws of Europe, and which began at the times of the crusades, may be divided into two principal epochs. At first it was desirable to wrest from the feudal lords a power which they abused: that was the first epoch,—that was the revolution of liberty. When the feudal lords had nothing left but distinctions, these distinctions irritated pride and jealousy, which, in the end, persuaded themselves that every political superiority was a tyranny, which must be brought low. This was the second epoch,—the revolution of equality; much more terrible than the first, because it had for motive, passions much more difficult to satisfy than the love of liberty.

But the peasants and serfs of the country, whilst the cities were in the enjoyment of liberty, still groaned in slavery. Up to the fourteenth century, this numerous class found no abatement in the rigours of their servitude. The greatest advantage the crusades could have bestowed upon the peasants, was the momentary cessation of brigandage, and the peace which reigned in the country, all the time the wars against the Saracens were being carried on.

It is probable that serfs in Europe were not better treated, according to the legislation and customs of the West, than they were in the Holy Land, according to the *Assizes of Jerusalem*. There is no doubt that peasants taken from the glebe for the crusade became free men; but most of them perished by misery or by the swords of the Mussulmans. What became of the few who revisited their homes cannot be ascertained.

A population dispersed and scattered about a country did not present, as in cities, a formidable mass, capable of resistance. Peasants rarely communicated with each other, and could not support any demand, or establish any common right. Man requires some intelligence to make him sensible of the advantages of liberty, and the peasant class was then brutified by ignorance. We must likewise add, that the love of independence came with riches; and this is why it arose earlier in cities than in the country, and earlier in flourishing cities than in poorer ones. The serfs of the country were poor; they would not have known what use to make of liberty. Liberty is of little value to him who is in want of the first necessaries of life. Among warlike and barbarous hordes, who entertained a repugnance for labour, it was natural that they should be despised who gave themselves up to the painful toil of cultivating the earth. This repugnance was necessarily more strong among nomad nations, like those that conquered Europe. The contempt felt in the middle ages for the peasantry was injurious to their liberty; and this contempt even survived their servitude. People felt, in some sort, forced to treat as slaves men who performed a task which was considered necessary, but which every free man disdained.

The inhabitant of the country, abandoned to his own resources, did not aspire to independence; the only good he could pretend to was the choice of slavery. As the Church inspired more confidence than the nobles, a crowd of unfortunate beings took refuge, in a manner, at the foot of the altars, and devoted their liberty and that of their children to this church or that monastery, to which they looked for protection. Nothing is more curious than the formulæ by which the clergy received this sacrifice of individual liberty. They congratulated the new serfs with having preferred "the domination of Jesus Christ to the liberty of the age;" they added, that "to serve God was to reign," and that "a holy servitude was true independence." These words must have been in harmony with the manners and ideas of the times, since a multitude of men and women were seen every day flocking to the monasteries, and conjuring the Church to admit them among "the serfs of Jesus Christ." That they should believe themselves, on that account, much more free than other men, we may at the present day be astonished; but was there not a sort of liberty in wearing chains they had chosen, and with which they had fettered themselves?

Some free cities of Germany contributed to the enfranchisement of the peasants of their territory. The same thing happened in Italy and in Spain, where the territory of cities was considerable; in England, the peasantry waited a long time for any amelioration of their fate. But nothing is more difficult than to ascertain with certainty the destiny which, during many ages, this multitude of men who covered the plains of Europe underwent; in the darkness of the middle ages, numberless generations of serfs passed over the earth, without leaving any traces in history. We can with difficulty catch, in old chronicles and acts of administration, here and there a few scattered gleams to throw a light upon our researches.

In France, it is not till the commencement of the fourteenth century that any ordinances of the kings upon the enfranchisement of the serfs are to be found. In an ordinance of 1315, Louis X. made use of these remarkable words: "Many persons among our common people are enchained in the bonds of servitude, which displeases us greatly.... Our kingdom," he added, "is called and named the kingdom of the Franks; we are desirous that the thing should in truth be in accordance with its name," &c. In this ordinance, made only for the royal domains, the king of France pressed the nobles to follow his example. "We are in possession of a letter-patent of the same king, by which commissaries were commanded to transport themselves to the bailiwick of Senlis, and "to give freedom to all who required it," on condition, nevertheless, of paying a sum for the rights of servitude, which reverted to the crown.

All the historical documents of this period prove, more and more, that the kings had placed themselves at the head of the general movement of society. In all they then did, their motive, doubtless, was to reëstablish order in the kingdom, and to found their authority upon the protection granted to those who suffered from the violences and excesses of feudal anarchy. If, however, we may judge by the ordinance just quoted, and by many other similar ones, their policy was not always disinterested, and, like most of the barons, they sometimes sold rather than granted the freedom of the serfs and the communes.

Many peasants showed themselves but little disposed to receive a liberty which was to be sold to them. Some from poverty, others from mistrust, a great number from unwillingness to change their condition, refused the benefit that was offered to them. Such is the spirit of man, that they resolved to remain serfs, because they were condemned to be such no longer. In several provinces, even disorders were created by their resistance. This was slaves fighting, with their chains, against Liberty herself. At a later period, the *jaquerie* proved that it was more easy to kindle the passions of a gross people, than to make them free; and that it was far, as regarded the serfs, from impatience under the yoke and hatred for their masters, to the true love of liberty.

When we are desirous of breaking the chains of the multitude, it is never to the multitude that we must address ourselves; in order that the fate of the lower classes should be ameliorated, the amelioration must come from the superior classes, by whom knowledge is spread and institutions are established. This is what happened at the period of which we are speaking. The servitude of the country was much softened by the maxims of the clergy, but more particularly by the influence of that French magistracy which had arisen contemporaneously with civilization.

In the middle of the fifteenth century, some serfs of Catalonia, who had taken refuge in France, being claimed by their lords, the parliament of Thoulouse declared that every man who entered into the kingdom crying *France!* became free. Mezerai, [103] who relates this fact, adds: "Such is the kingdom of France, that its air communicates liberty to those who breathe it, and our kings are so august that they only reign over free men."

At the beginning of the sixteenth century, scarcely a trace of servitude could be found in the cities or the country. History could but applaud this revolution, if the fall even of feudalism, whilst destroying ancient abuses, had not placed governments in antagonism with difficulties which had not been foreseen, and whose consequences were destined to be deplorable. When the feudal government, which cost the people nothing, [104] was quite overthrown, it became necessary to provide for the expenses of a new administration; when the state had lost the defenders which the feudal laws provided for it, others were to be sought, and their services to be remunerated. Thence came the necessity for stipendiary armies and regular and permanent taxes. To provide the money wanted, the coinage was debased, the Jews were persecuted, violence was had recourse to, and justice was sold, — all of which tended to corrupt both the government and the nation. The embarrassment of the finances, and the disorders it produced, have only increased up to the present day. To remedy this, the moral strength and life of society have often been neglected, and means of raising money have constituted the whole policy of states. To have credit, or not to have it, that is, now-a-days, life or death for governments. *Credit, deficit, bankruptcy,* are three words, of which the ancients and the middle ages were quite ignorant; but which are now constantly present to the restless, uneasy minds of kings and ministers. These three words will perhaps one day be sufficient to explain the decline and fall of empires.

Whatever was the weight of the public impositions, it must be allowed that the taxes gave rise to more frequent relations between governments and the people, which proved advantageous to liberty. People gave more attention to the administration which they paid for with the fruit of their industry and labour. Sovereigns had more consideration for the different classes of citizens of whom they demanded tribute; and were constrained to consult them in certain circumstances, in order that the people, says Pasquier, might not have occasion to be dissatisfied or murmur. The origin of representative government, as it exists in many European nations in our days, has been sought for in remote times; but everything leads us to believe that it owed its birth to the relations which the wants of states and the necessity for taxes naturally established between peoples and governments.

That which most increased the embarrassments of the majority of European monarchies, after the fall of feudalism, was the excessive enlargement of their military establishments. At the moment I am writing, there is no necessity to point out this fearful rock of modern societies It is not a century since Montesquieu predicted that Europe would perish by its armies. [105] God grant that this prophecy be not about to be accomplished! The military force of Europe has given us reason to dread all the evils it was intended to prevent. It was to defend every kingdom from foreign invasions; and yet there is not a kingdom in Europe that has not been invaded, or threatened with invasion. It was deemed necessary to restrain the multitude by means of armies; and armies have been raised to such numbers of men, that they have become the multitude itself under arms. Can it be true, as has been said, that there is no remedy for this evil? Deplorable state of things, without which society cannot last, with which it cannot exist!

The crusades have been reproached with having given birth to the idea of imposts; this idea is too simple not to have arisen without the help of the crusades. [106] It is probable that the manner in which the tenths were collected for the holy war, might serve as a model for those who afterwards established regular contributions. As to regular armies, the expeditions to the East might furnish the first idea of them. It is certain that these distant expeditions changed the conditions of the feudal service, and accustomed people to see permanent armies maintained and commanded by princes.

Among the institutions which contended with the barbarism of the middle ages, we will, in the first place, consider chivalry, the exploits of which are much better known than its origin. At a time when everything was decided by force, and everything was determined by the sword;—in which, as Montesquieu says, to judge was to fight—women, children, and orphans were not able to defend their rights, and were abandoned a prey to iniquity. Generous warriors came forward to defend them; their devotion was applauded,—their example was followed. Shortly the order of Paladins was formed, who perambulated the world, seeking for wrongs to redress, and felons to combat with. Such was, doubtless, the origin of chivalry, which is so uselessly sought for in the forests of Germany. This institution sprang from the extreme disorder of society, and arose like a bulwark, which human generosity opposed to the irruptions of license, and the passions of a barbarous age.

Chivalry was known in the West before the crusades. These wars, which appeared to have the same aim as chivalry,—that of defending the oppressed, serving the cause of God, and combating with infidels,—gave this institution more splendour and consistency,—a direction more extended and salutary.

Religion, which mingled itself with all the institutions and all the passions of the middle ages, purified the sentiments of the knights, and elevated them to the enthusiasm of virtue. Christianity lent chivalry its ceremonies and its emblems, and tempered, by the mildness of its maxims, the asperities of warlike manners.

Piety, bravery, and modesty were the distinctive qualities of chivalry: "Serve God, and he will help you; be mild and courteous to every gentleman, by divesting yourself of all pride; be neither a flatterer nor a slanderer, for such people seldom come to great excellence. Be loyal in words and deeds; keep your word; be helpful to the poor and to orphans, and God will reward you." [107] Thus said the mother of Bayard to her son; and these instructions of a virtuous mother comprised the whole code of chivalry.

The most admirable part of this institution was the entire abnegation of self,—that loyalty which made it the duty of every knight to forget his own glory, and only publish the lofty deeds of his companions in arms. The deeds of valour of a knight were his fortune, his means of living; *and he who was silent upon them was a robber of the property of others.* Nothing appeared more reprehensible than for a knight to praise himself. "If the squire," says le Code des Preux, "be vain-glorious of what he has done, he is not worthy to become a knight." An historian of the crusades offers us a singular example of this virtue, which is not entirely humility, and might be called the false modesty of glory, when he describes Tancred checking his career in the field of battle, to make his squire swear to be for ever silent upon his exploits.

The most cruel insult that could be offered to a knight, was to accuse him of falsehood. Want of truth, and perjury, were considered the most shameful of all crimes. If oppressed innocence implored the succour of a knight, woe to him who did not respond to the appeal! Shame followed every offence towards the weak, and every aggression towards an unarmed man.

The spirit of chivalry kept up and strengthened among warriors the generous sentiments which the military spirit of feudalism had given birth to: devotion to his sovereign was the first virtue, or rather the first duty, of a knight. Thus in every state of Europe grew up a young military power, always ready for fight, and always ready to sacrifice itself for prince or for country, as for the cause of justice and innocence.

One of the most remarkable characteristics of chivalry, and that which at the present day most strongly excites our surprise and curiosity, was the alliance of religious sentiments with gallantry. *Devotion and love,*—such was the principle of action of a knight: *God and the ladies,*—such was his device.

To form an idea of the manners of chivalry, we have but to glance at the tournaments, which owed their origin to it, and which were as schools of courtesy and festivals of bravery. At this period, the nobility were dispersed, and lived isolated in their castles. Tournaments furnished them with opportunities for assembling; and it was at these brilliant meetings that the memory of ancient gallant knights was revived,—that youth took them for models, and imbibed chivalric virtues by receiving rewards from the hands of beauty.

As the ladies were the judges of the actions and the bravery of the knights, they exercised an absolute empire over the minds of the warriors; and I have no occasion to say that this ascendancy of the softer sex threw a charm over the heroism of the *preux* and the *paladins.* Europe began to escape from barbarism from the moment the most weak commanded the most strong,—from the moment when the love of glory, when the noblest feelings of the heart, the tenderest affections of the soul, everything that constitutes the moral force of society, was able to triumph over every other force.

Louis IX., a prisoner in Egypt, replies to the Saracens, that he will do nothing without Queen Marguerite, "who is his lady." The orientals could not comprehend such deference; and it is because they did not comprehend this deference, that they have remained so far in the rear of the nations of Europe, in nobleness of sentiment, purity of morals, and elegance of manners.

Heroes of antiquity wandered over the world to deliver it from scourges and monsters; but these heroes were not actuated by religion, which elevates the soul, nor by that courtesy which softens the manners. They were acquainted with friendship, as in the cases of Theseus and Pirithous, and Hercules and Lycas; but they knew nothing of the delicacy of love. The ancient poets take delight in representing the misfortunes of certain heroines abandoned by their lovers; but, in their touching pictures, there never escapes from their plaintive muse the least expression of blame against the hero, who thus caused the tears of beauty to flow. In the middle ages, or according to the manners of chivalry, a warrior who should have imitated the conduct of Theseus to Ariadne, or that of the son of Anchises towards Dido, would not have failed to incur the reproach of treachery.

Another difference between the spirit of antiquity and the sentiments of the moderns is, that among the ancients love was supposed to enervate the courage of heroes; and that in the days of chivalry, the women, who were the judges of valour, constantly kept alive the love of glory and an enthusiasm for virtue, in the hearts of the warriors. We find in Alain Chartier, a conversation of several ladies, who express their opinions upon the conduct of their knights, who had been present at the battle of Agincourt. One of these knights had sought safety in flight, and the lady of his thoughts exclaims: "According to the law of love, I should have loved him better dead than alive." In the first crusade, Adela, countess of Blois, wrote to her husband, who was gone to the East with Godfrey of Bouillon: "Beware of meriting the reproaches of the brave." As the count of Blois returned to Europe before the taking of Jerusalem, his wife made him blush at his desertion, and forced him to return to Palestine, where he fought bravely, and found a glorious death. Thus the spirit and the sentiments of chivalry gave birth to prodigies equally with the most ardent patriotism of ancient Lacedæmon; and these prodigies appeared so simple, so natural, that the chroniclers only repeat them in passing, and without testifying the least surprise at them.

This institution, so ingeniously called "Fountain of courtesy, which comes from God," is still much more admirable when considered under the all-powerful influence of religious ideas. Christian charity claimed all the affections of the knight, and demanded of him a perpetual devotion for the defence of pilgrims and the care of the sick. It was thus that were established the orders of St. John, of the Temple, of the Teutonic Knights, and several others, all instituted to combat the Saracens and solace human miseries. The infidels admired their virtues, as much as they dreaded their bravery. Nothing is more touching than the spectacle of these noble warriors, who were seen by turns in the field of battle and in the asylum of pain; sometimes the terror of the enemy, and as frequently the consolers of all who suffered. That which the paladins of the West did for beauty, the knights of Palestine did for poverty and misfortune. The former devoted their lives to the ladies of their thoughts; the latter devoted theirs to the poor and the infirm. The grand-master of the military order of St. John took the title of "Guardian of the poor of Jesus Christ," and the knights called the sick and the poor "Our lords." It appears almost an incredible thing, but the grand-master of the order of St. Lazarus, instituted for the cure and the relief of leprosy, was obliged to be chosen from among the lepers. [108] Thus the charity of the knights, in order to be the better acquainted with human miseries, in a manner ennobled that which is most disgusting in the diseases of man. Did not this grand-master of St. Lazarus, who was obliged himself to be afflicted with the infirmities he was called upon to alleviate in others, imitate, as much as is possible on earth, the example of the Son of God, who assumed a human form in order to deliver humanity?

It may be thought that there was ostentation in so great a charity; but Christianity, as we have said, had subdued the pride of the warriors, and that was, without doubt, one of the noblest miracles of the religion of the middle ages. All who then visited the Holy Land could but admire in the knights of St. John, the Temple, and St. Lazarus, their resignation in suffering all the pains of life, their submission to all the rigours of discipline, and their docility to the least wish of their leader. During the sojourn of St. Louis in Palestine, the Hospitallers having had a quarrel with some Crusaders who were hunting on Mount Carmel, the latter brought their complaint before the grand-master. The head of the Hospital ordered before him the brothers who had outraged the Crusaders, and to punish them, condemned there to eat their food on the ground upon their mantles. "It happened," says the sieur de Joinville, "that I was present with the knights who had complained, and we requested the master to allow the brothers to arise from their mantles, which he refused." Thus the rigour of the cloisters and the austere humility of cenobites had nothing repulsive for these warriors. Such were the heroes that religion and the spirit of the crusades had formed. I know that this submission and humility in men accustomed to arms may be turned into ridicule; but an enlightened philosophy takes pleasure in recognising the happy influence of religious ideas upon the manners of a society given up to barbarous passions. In an age when all power was derived from the sword, in which passion and anger might have carried warriors to all kinds of excesses, what more agreeable spectacle for humanity could there be than that of valour humbling itself, and strength forgetting itself?

We are aware that the spirit of chivalry was sometimes abused, and that its noble maxims did not govern the conduct of all knights. We have described in the history of the crusades, the lengthened discords which jealousy created between the two orders of St. John and the Temple. We have spoken of the vices with which the Templars were reproached towards the end of the holy wars. We could speak still more of the absurdities of knight-errantry; but our task is here to write the history of institutions, and not that of human passions. Whatever may be thought of the corruption of men, it will always be true that chivalry, allied with the spirit of courtesy and the spirit of Christianity, awakened in human hearts virtues and sentiments of which the ancients were ignorant.

That which proves that everything was not barbarous in the middle ages is, that the institution of chivalry obtained, from its birth, the esteem and admiration of all Christendom. There was no gentleman who was not desirous of being a knight. Princes and kings took honour to themselves for belonging to chivalry. In it warriors came to take lessons of politeness, bravery, and humanity. Admirable school, in which victory laid aside its pride, and grandeur its haughty disdain; to which those who had riches and power came to learn only to make use of them with moderation and generosity.

As the education of the people was formed upon the example of the higher classes of society, the generous sentiments of chivalry spread themselves by degrees through all ranks, and mingled with the character of the European nations; gradually, there arose against those who were wanting in their duties of knighthood, a general opinion, more severe than the laws themselves, which was as the code of honour, as the cry of the public conscience. What might not be hoped from a state of society, in which all the discourses held in camps, in tournaments, in meetings of warriors, was reduced to these words: "Evil be to him who forgets the promises he has made to religion, to patriotism, to virtuous love; evil be to him who betrays his God, his king, or his lady?"

When the institution of chivalry fell by the abuse that was made of it, or rather in consequence of the changes in the military system of Europe; there remained still in European society some of the sentiments it had inspired, in the same manner as there remains with those who have forgotten the religion in which they were born, something of its precepts, and particularly of the profound impressions which they received from it in their infancy. In the times of chivalry, the reward of good actions was glory and honour. This coin, which is so useful to nations, and which costs them nothing, did not fail to have some currency in following ages. Such is the effect of a glorious remembrance, that the marks and distinctions of chivalry serve still in our days to recompense merit and bravery.

Since it can with truth be said that the crusades added some lustre and gave some ascendancy to chivalry, it must be agreed that they rendered essential service to humanity.

If the institution of chivalry was a barrier against license and barbarism, the institution of the clergy, founded upon more fixed and durable principles, ought to have rendered still greater services to civilization.

The ascendancy and wealth of the clergy placed them on an equality with the nobility, in the feudal system; but it must be allowed that the rank assigned them in this order of things was repugnant to their character and to the state of society. We do not hesitate to say that the feudal system had a tendency to corrupt the institution of the clergy, as the clergy corrupted the feudal system. The clergy, instructed in principles of peace, were not fit to carry out the conditions of the military régime; on the other side, the military régime was sure to change the pacific manners of the clergy. It was not at all uncommon to see prelates clad in cuirass and helmet. Sometimes country priests led to battle the flock which a religion of peace had confided to them. This military spirit in ecclesiastics was much increased by the crusades, in which their arms were sanctified by the object of the war. The clergy, however, never became sufficiently warlike to fulfil all the feudal engagements; and we may add likewise, that they were not always sufficiently pacific to fulfil all their religious duties.

It may be concluded, from what we have just said, that the ecclesiastical order and the feudal government would, in the long run, repel each other. If we consult the history of the middle ages, we shall see that the barons and nobles often showed themselves jealous of the power of the clergy, and that the clergy, in the end, contributed to the ruin of the foundations of feudalism.

The existence of the clergy underwent many modifications, according to times, places, and circumstances. In Italy, they enjoyed but very little credit, and took part in most popular factions. In Germany, the high clergy shared with the nobility the wrecks of imperial power. In Spain, they contributed greatly to the expulsion of the Moors, and the spoils of the vanquished added to their wealth. In England, the clergy associated themselves with the barons, and contended with the crown. In France, they attached themselves to royalty, and favoured the constantly increasing power of the monarchs.

If we may judge by the councils which were held during the crusades, most of which were occupied with reforming ecclesiastical discipline, we have reason to believe that the morals of the clergy had then a strong tendency to corruption. Old chronicles are particularly severe against the Crusaders and the clergy of the East, whom they unceasingly accuse of outraging morality and religion by their excesses. Some of the chroniclers even, like James of Vitry, draw such hideous pictures, that they are suspected of injustice, or at least of exaggeration. It is not useless, for the sake of historical truth, to remark here, that most of the historians of whom we now speak, belonged to the class of preachers charged with the task of censuring their age, and who were often obliged to darken their colours in order to move the multitude. In all times, sacred orators have been seen exaggerating the vices it was their object to combat; and if we were not aware of the charity which animates them, we might sometimes mistake their discourses for violent satires. This is an observation of which we ought not to lose sight whilst reading the chronicles of the middle ages, which are almost all drawn up by ecclesiastics, accustomed by their profession to judge their contemporaries with severity. Another observation proved by history is, that corruption is spoken of with more bitterness in times in which it is scarcely known, than in times in which it has become general. In ages in which some ideas of virtue still prevail, people accuse themselves; and in ages quite corrupted, they praise themselves.

A chronicle of the time of the first crusades tells us, that the iniquities of men had then reached their height; and, what at once characterizes the spirit of the chronicler and that of his age, he adds that these iniquities would have shortened the duration of the world, "if it had not been that some new monastic congregations were formed." In fact, during the twelfth and thirteenth centuries, more monasteries were founded than in all the other centuries of the middle ages. The enthusiasm for the holy wars, by exalting the imaginations of nations, had produced a mental revolution; prodigies were everywhere seen that had never been observed till that time; devotion itself believed that it could no longer attain salvation by ordinary ways: whilst a crowd of warriors precipitated themselves upon the East, many pious souls, to perform penance, sought for private mortifications, and devoted themselves to the rigours of a voluntary exile, or buried themselves in deserts.

At the head of the monastic congregations which were formed at this period, we must place that of the Brothers of Mercy, which had its birth in the third crusade, and was instituted for the purpose of delivering captives. These venerable cenobites, after the example of the heroes of chivalry, sought for victims to console, and for the miserable to succour. Like knights, they exposed themselves to a thousand dangers, and braved death in the exercise of beneficence and charity. It was during the sixth crusade that the two orders of St. Dominic and St. Francis arose, orders which, according to the expression of the abbot of Usberg, renewed the youth of the Church. From the thirteenth century these two orders sent missions into the East, and into the north of Asia. Whilst the Tartar hordes were overturning empires, ravaging Europe, and threatening all Christendom, poor priests traversed the solitudes of Tartary, penetrated even into China; and, peaceful conquerors, armed with the Gospel, extended the empire of Christianity, and planted the standard of the cross at the extremities of the known world. The religious colonies which they then founded in Asia lasted much longer than the colonies founded by the Crusaders.

We will not attempt to enumerate all the services which religious communities rendered society. They had regulations which might serve for models in the infancy of political legislation. They were in all respects like the corporations of cities. Whilst anarchy disturbed cities, the woods had their legislation; and the germs of civilization developed themselves in silence and in solitude.

It was in monasteries that were found the only schools in which letters were taught, and that the Latin language, and the wonders it produced, were preserved. It was in them that studious men kept a faithful register of events, and employed themselves in transmitting to us those historical documents without which the glory and the manners of our ancestors would be unknown to us.

Besides that the clergy contributed greatly to the fertilizing of uncultivated lands, they protected the labourers with the whole power of the Church. The Truce of God, which was the work of the clergy, placed under the safeguard of Heaven, the inhabitants of the fields, the oxen, the companions of their labours, and even the instruments of their tillage. The Church went still further; it multiplied the festivals of the calendar, for the sake of the people. By augmenting the number of religious solemnities, the Church had two motives: the first, to bring more frequently to the foot of the altar an ignorant and gross multitude, who there found the instruction necessary for the amelioration of their morals and the consolation of their evils; the second, to procure some days of repose for that crowd of serfs, condemned by the avarice of their masters to labours which had no end, and of which they did not gather the fruit. [109]

Amidst wars which revived without ceasing, the peasantry often found an asylum near a monastery inhabited by peaceful men, and protected by the opinions of the times. Nothing can prove better the ascendancy of the Church, than seeing, on one side, the nobility shut up in their strong castles, and on the other, cenobites dwelling in cloisters scarcely closed, and defended only by faith and confidence. As might be expected, the peace which reigned in the neighbourhood of monasteries attracted a numerous population around them. Many towns, and even cities, owed their origin to the vicinity of a monastery, whose name they still preserve.

The maxims of the clergy, more perhaps than their example, contributed to the enfranchisement of serfs. Gregory the Great, when giving liberty to some slaves, said that the Redeemer came upon earth to release men from slavery, and to substitute the rights of the people for the code of servitude. In the middle ages, many charters of liberty were granted for "the love of God,—for the salvation of the soul,—for the remission of sins." It was at the hour of death, and by testamentary dispositions, that most enfranchisements were granted; from which we may conclude that it was the work of the priests who assisted the dying. The clergy represented the enfranchisement of slaves as a thing agreeable to God; the ceremony of manumission was performed in the church as a solemn religious act. It was at the foot of the altars that the holy words were pronounced which broke the bonds of slavery. Thus everything announced that the spirit of the Gospel was everywhere mingled with the progress of civilization, and that the liberty of modern nations was to be one of the blessings of Christianity.

There was another mode of gaining liberty, which was by entering into holy orders, or to take vows in a monastery. So great a number of slaves escaped by that means from the yoke of their masters, that this custom was obliged to be restrained, and at last entirely abolished, in almost all the states of Europe. The crusades often bestowed upon the serfs the same privileges that the clergy did. Beneath the banners of the cross, serfs found the enfranchisement they had before found in monasteries. This facility which peasants possessed, of breaking their chains by going to the Holy Land, would have depopulated the plains, if new regulations had not placed restrictions and limits to it.

It has been said that the clergy became enriched by the crusades. This assertion, which has been so often repeated by the writers of the last century, requires to be examined by the impartiality of history. The clergy were rich at the period of the first crusade. Their enemies accused them for a long time of having usurped immense properties. In France, under the two first races, their wealth had given umbrage to the barons, who had several times despoiled them, under the pretext that they did not defend the state, and that the property they held belonged to them whose bravery watched over the safety of the kingdom.

If the crusades enriched the clergy, it might be supposed that the clergy would be most rich in countries which took the greatest part in the crusades. Now, the clergy of Germany, and several other states of Europe, surpassed in wealth the clergy of the kingdom of France, where the crusades excited so much enthusiasm, and caused so many warriors to take arms. The clergy, it is true, found new possessions in the East; but, after the crusades, nothing of them was left but vain titles.

The first crusade must have been, as we have said, very profitable to the clergy; they were not obliged to pay the expenses of it; the zeal of the faithful furnished them. Nevertheless they did take part in this crusade; and the priests who set out, with the other Crusaders, certainly did not enrich themselves in their pilgrimage. Many, no doubt, shared the fate of Robert, abbot of St. Remi, the historian of the first crusade, who, on his return from Jerusalem, was expelled by his monks for having ruined his convent.

At the second crusade, contributions were levied upon the churches, without any regard to the warm remonstrances of the ecclesiastics. From that time an opinion, which became very injurious to the clergy, was established throughout the Christian world, which was, that wars undertaken for the glory of Jesus Christ and the deliverance of the holy places, ought to be paid for by the Church. Tributes were at once levied upon the clergy, without consulting any other authority, or following any other regulations than those of necessity and circumstances. To reckon from the third crusade, after the publication of the *Saladin tenth*, more regular imposts were established, which were fixed by the popes or councils, and which were collected with such rigour, that churches were despoiled of their ornaments, and sometimes the sacred vases were put up to sale. It is true that the clergy sometimes received offerings and bequests from those who went to the Holy Land, or had made a vow to go; but what did such tributes of piety amount to when compared to the tributes they themselves were compelled to pay? We do not hesitate to affirm that, in the space of two hundred years, the clergy paid towards the holy wars more money than would have been required to purchase all their property; and thus the zeal of ecclesiastics for the deliverance of the holy places was observed perceptibly to cool; and it may be said that the indifference which followed among Christian nations the ardour for the crusades, began by the clergy. In Germany, and many other countries, their discontent was carried so far, that at last the popes did not dare to trust the preaching of crusades to the bishops, and only gave this mission to the mendicant orders, who possessed nothing, and had nothing to pay for the expeditions against the infidels. [110]

It has been said that the clergy took advantage of the crusades to buy at low prices the property of the nobility, as, in our days, we have seen many people take advantage of a revolution, to purchase at a moderate price the property of the clergy themselves. We find, in fact, examples of such acquisitions in the first crusades; but these examples must have been more rare in the holy wars, of which the clergy were obliged to pay the expenses. [111] The great advantage that the clergy had over the nobility was, that the nobles were able to pawn or alienate their possessions, and that ecclesiastics were never allowed to pledge or alienate their property. Another advantage the clergy possessed was, that they formed a body always animated by the same spirit, and always governed by the same laws. Whilst everything changed around them, they never changed. It was thus they resisted the revolution which was effected in property.

We have seen, that in the twelfth and thirteenth centuries a great number of monasteries were established. By that means wild, uncultivated places became fertile lands; and these conquests made over the desert added to the domains of the clergy. We must likewise add, that the jurisdiction of the clergy, which every day made fresh progress, was for them a source of wealth. It was in the nature of things, as we have already remarked, that the most enlightened class should become the richest. The clergy had therefore no need of profiting by the ruin of the Crusaders in order to become rich; their knowledge, their spirit of order and economy, *with the ascendancy they possessed over the people*, offered them ample means for increasing or preserving their possessions.

Everybody, besides, had reason to rejoice at seeing the clergy acquire wealth; for this wealth belonged to everybody. In fact, every man could enter into the clergy, and the clergy belonged to all families. This order, so powerful in the middle ages, was as a natural link, as an intermediate point, which drew together and united all the classes of society. In the quarrels which jealousy sometimes raised between the clergy and the nobility, the great vassals reproached the ecclesiastics with being *the children of serfs*. It was not uncommon to see men who had issued from the lowest class of the people, in the highest functions of the Church; a certain proof that the clergy offered every one a way by which he might elevate himself, and that they thus assisted in reëstablishing the harmony destroyed by feudal inequality.

The clergy—such as our fathers saw it—only now exists in the memory of men. [112] In proportion as this institution, with all the advantages we have spoken of, shall be further removed from us, we shall perhaps become the more aware of its value. There are things of which we judge more favourably when memory recalls them to us, than when they are present.

After a revolution which has ruined so many families, in which so many hopes have been deceived,—at a time in which a numerous youth is crowded in the confined circle of public employments,—in which the divers professions, among the enlightened class, by no means suffice for the vast number of the candidates,—let me ask whether the Church, with its riches and its consolatory morality, would not be as a port in the storm,—as a refuge always open for those to whom the world has nothing to give? At a time in which everything is uncertain, moving, and transitory,—in which no man is sure of his destiny, who but must envy those men whose fate never changed,—who lived always in the same manner,—who saw the present without complaining,—to whom the future gave no uneasiness, and who might justly be compared to the young ones of the birds, of which Scripture speaks? If I durst utter all my thought—and I speak less in the name of religion than in the names of philosophy and humanity—I should even regret those austere retreats, open to piety, and consecrated by peace and prayer. There, at least, a shelter was found from the passions which disturb society, as they trouble the heart of man. Why, in fact, should there not be hospitals for the miseries of the soul, as there are for other human infirmities? Why are not they who have suffered from the storms of life, and whose heart is torn by deep wounds, to find a refuge against their ills, as well as those whom indigence overtakes, or as well as the war-mutilated soldier? Who does not know that great revolutions, like great griefs, inspire a desire for concealing existence, and seeking repose in solitude? "When the storm growls," says Pythagoras, "worship echo." Let us look back to the times which preceded the middle ages,—to those times in which the world was ready to fall to pieces with the Roman empire: it was at this deplorable epoch that the deserts of the Thebais were peopled with pious cenobites, who were no longer able to support the spectacle of human passions. It was not only simple and vulgar men who flocked to the solitudes of Cetteus and Memphis, but learned men, warriors,—men who had been seen in the courts of emperors. Whilst society was shaken to its foundations,—whilst disorder and corruption spread their baneful influence everywhere, elevated minds, whom this state of things drove to despair, went to bury themselves in retirement, embracing the altars of that Christian religion which was the only support left to unfortunate virtue, and was the last hope of civilization.

The swords of knights and the maxims of the clergy, as we have seen, contended with advantage against the excesses of barbarism; but no institution had yet attained sufficient consistence to guarantee the security of European societies. In spite of all efforts for the reëstablishment of order, anarchy still subsisted. In order to know what, either in an age or a people, is the spirit of civilization, it is sufficient to be acquainted with the progress that has been made in that same age, or among that same people, in the administration of justice. Of all the monuments the human mind can raise, a civil and criminal code is that which requires the most extensive knowledge, and the profoundest acquaintance with the passions of man.

In the middle ages, society, immersed in darkness, had lost the lessons and examples of antiquity in all which concerned judicial order; and found itself, in a manner, reduced to the experience of the barbarians.

When the barons usurped from the crown the right of administering justice, there were as many jurisdictions in France as there were lordships.

Judicial administration then lost that spirit of *wholeness*, that uniformity, which gives weight and rectitude to its decisions. Judgment was no longer given but according to local customs, or uncertain traditions. [113] When, in the seventeenth century, the judicial customs and traditions which had been found in preceding ages were collected, there were found two hundred and eighty-five of them; a certain proof that in the times of which we speak, there could be no fixed rule, and that anarchy had invaded the sanctuary of justice.

Royalty could not watch over seignorial jurisdictions, and the ordinances of the kings were powerless out of the domains of the crown. The great vassals had no mutual understanding that might modify or regulate legislation. It is a remarkable thing that France, after the decline of the empire of Charlemagne, remained more than two centuries without recognising any authority to which it could carry its griefs and its complaints,—without having, either in the person of the monarch or the assemblies of the great, a power which could establish regulations, repair injustices, correct abuses, and consecrate the maxims of experience. If the kingdom was able to subsist for so long a time in this state, have we not reason to believe that there is in every society an unknown force, which defends that society against its own excesses, and saves the people in spite of their passions,—in spite of all which seems calculated to bring on their ruin?

To decide in civil and criminal causes, there was no other guide, no other intelligence, but the instincts and the conscience of the judges. These feeble means were not competent, in complicated cases, to assign to actions their true intention, or to appreciate the language of innocence or the denegations of crime. All matters were then treated according to verbal conventions, and judged according to unwritten testimonies. Words, often ill-interpreted, sometimes partially effaced from the memory, frequently contradicted or falsified, could not enlighten justice. Good faith was implored; the consciences of witnesses and parties were appealed to; but it was too frequently perjury that answered, and which commanded the decisions of the judges. At length, it was believed that an infallible means was discovered for detecting falsehood and fraud; an appeal was made from the consciences of men to the justice of Heaven. He who was accused, he whose evidence was contradicted, submitted to the ordeals of fire, boiling water, or red-hot iron. It was believed that Heaven would not permit injustice, and that it would rather suspend the laws of nature than the laws of society.

These proofs, however, were abandoned to the vulgar; judicial combat was the ordeal of nobles or of freemen. This species of justice, in which every warrior had only his own valour as the arbiter of his destiny, conformed exceedingly well with the military spirit of the age.

So barbarous a custom was generally adopted: not satisfied with having recourse to judicial combat in criminal cases, civil questions were subject to its decisions. A gentleman had not only a right to defy his adversary, he might also challenge the witnesses themselves, and force sometimes even the judges to descend with him into the arena. Justice was then only seen in victory, or rather victory became the sole justice. Thus the Franks, in the crusades, often expressed their astonishment that God should sometimes allow the Mussulmans to conquer the Christians.

The sword decided everything; the places where justice pronounced her decrees resounded with the cries of fury and hatred. They were stained, by turns, with the blood of the innocent or with the blood of the guilty, as skill, strength, or fortune favoured the arms of the combatants. In the face of such combats, how was it possible to preserve the idea of justice or injustice? Must not ferocity of manners have increased, and education become unnatural?

We ought, however, to remember the circumstances which brought about this custom, and which may render it excusable in the eyes of enlightened philosophy. In the impossibility in which the judges often found themselves of ascertaining the truth or pronouncing with certainty, fraud, perjury, and falsehood triumphed over the laws, and threatened to invade the whole of society. No better means could be discovered to prevent this misfortune than to terrify imposture and perfidy, by the preparations, "pomp, and circumstance," of a judicial combat. Justice, being unable to reveal herself amidst the darkness of barbarism, surrounded herself with terrible images, and would only allow her sanctuary to be approached with mistrust and fear. The terror which the idea even of a judicial combat inspired, the uncertainty of such a judgment, must have prevented many contests, and that was a great advantage. No other more certain means, besides, were to be found to appease quarrels, which could not be prolonged without perilling the whole of society. In an age in which the passions were mixed with everything, it was doubtless important for society that justice should terminate debates in an equitable manner; but it was likewise important that these debates should terminate promptly.

At the first aspect, we only see in this custom a privilege and a monstrous employment of physical force. But without this employment of physical force, the world was perhaps likely to become the prey of perjured, faithless men. We ought then to sigh less over this revolting abuse than over the state of society in which it appeared necessary, in order to prevent abuses still more revolting. It required much trouble afterwards to reform the judicial combat. The prejudices most difficult to be destroyed are those in which bravery and the point of honour believe themselves interested. Neither the power of kings, nor religion, nor philosophy, have been able to abolish duels among modern nations; and duels, in some respects, are nothing but the justice which was rendered by the sword in the middle ages.

We have not yet made known all the obstacles which the triumph of justice met with in the manners and customs of these remote times. The absence of laws caused great disorders; but the yoke of the laws was more insupportable to the barons than anarchy itself. The confidence which the barons felt in their arms, rendered them at least indifferent to all kinds of legislation. In any society whatever, the men who have power or force in their hands are seldom the first to appeal to laws; because nobody can be unjust towards them with impunity, and they have always the means of doing themselves justice. [114]

Judicial order, as we understand it now-a-days, could be nothing, in the twelfth century, but an abstraction which did not enter into men's minds. The warlike nobility of Europe would have had nothing to do with any kind of justice which did not present an image of war. The barons could not form an idea that legislation might be a safeguard for themselves as well as society. They only felt an injustice as they felt a wound in the field of battle; and personal resentment was the only motive which animated them to the pursuit of the guilty. Equity then scarcely passed for a virtue, but revenge was a duty. There were no laws against those who were unjust, but there were laws against those who did not avenge themselves.

With these manners and this character, the barons were not able to renounce the practice of private wars, which the Franks and other barbarians had brought with them into Europe. Every noble who fancied himself attacked in either his honour or his property, took arms to defend his rights or avenge his quarrel. All the relations and vassals of the belligerent parties were obliged to take part in the quarrel. Fields were ravaged, towns and villages were burnt, and it was thus they demanded or rendered justice. During many centuries Europe was desolated by these intestine wars. Sanguinary discords, which were transmitted from generation to generation, became an habitual state, for which customs and regulations were invoked; and whilst society was without laws, civil war had its jurisprudence.

It was not easy to remedy such vast disorders. How could force be disarmed, and despoiled of a prerogative it seemed to prefer to all other privileges? Society, such as it then was, had but one single power capable of counterbalancing that of the warlike passions which desolated Europe; this was the force of religious ideas and the ascendancy of Christianity.

The authority of councils was invoked against private wars; the saints were made to speak; superstition itself was called in; visions, revelations, and prodigies were had recourse to. The Church put forth all its threats and launched all its thunders. These means sometimes suspended the progress of the evil, but the principle of discord always subsisted. It was not possible to put an end to private wars, but they were at length suppressed during certain days of the week; and all the good that such a powerful religion could do was to bring about the adoption of the Truce of God. It was here the crusades wonderfully seconded the zeal of the clergy. Whenever war was declared against the Saracens, discords were all at once appeased, as if by miracle, and Europe remained in profound silence before the standard of the cross.

The efforts of the clergy, however, in conjunction with some other favourable circumstances, were destined in the end to bring about the triumph of justice and humanity. Before civil justice was established, the Church possessed a holy jurisdiction which judged the faithful. This justice stood in no need of pursuing the guilty; the guilty came to give themselves up to its judgments: it was not blind, like human justice; the most secret folds of the conscience developed themselves before it: it met with no resistance, it excited no murmurs; those whom it condemned, condemned themselves. To cause its laws to be executed, and to sanction its decisions, it had the power of remorse, the fear of an avenging God, the promises of heaven, the menaces of hell. Such was the tribunal of penitence, which, in the absence of civil laws, held the place sometimes of other tribunals, and watched over public order, as a triumph of religion. A tribunal so formidable necessarily increased the influence of the clergy, and contributed, no doubt, to extend their jurisdiction even to affairs in which evangelical morality was not at all interested. People, persuaded that all justice comes from God, were likely to be led to believe that God pronounced his least judgments by the organs of his ministers upon earth. When the popes were reproached with interfering in the policy of princes, they answered that the acts of that policy might be sins, and thence these acts came under the pontifical jurisdiction. The clergy usurped judicial authority in civil affairs, as the sovereign pontiffs had usurped temporal authority. [115] In the middle ages the clergy declared themselves arbiters of the just and the unjust; and as their jurisdiction was much more favourable to humanity, more conformable to reason than that of the barons, it made rapid progress. Among the privileges which the popes granted to the Crusaders, that of being judged by the ecclesiastical laws was placed in the first rank. The clergy took advantage of the absence, the death, or the ruin of the nobles who were gone to the crusades, to extend their jurisdiction, as the commons availed themselves of this circumstance to obtain their liberty, and kings to increase their power. At last this jurisdiction became so powerful that it awakened the jealousy of the feudal nobility. Towards the middle of the thirteenth century, the nobles formed a league against the clergy, and in a manifesto, which we still possess, they demanded that "they should render to Cæsar that which belonged to Cæsar." They forbade their vassals to appeal to the ecclesiastical tribunals, except in cases of heresy, marriage, and usury, and threatened delinquents with the loss of their property and the mutilation of a member. "The clerks," added they, "enriched at our expense, shall be brought back to the state of the primitive church and to a contemplative life, leaving to us the action which becomes us, and presenting to us the miracles which we have not seen for a long time."

As the influence of the clergy arose from Christianity, the nobles, in their manifesto, wished to claim the advantage of having alone converted the Gauls by their arms. All that they said in support of this assertion gave reason to predict that they would not triumph in a contest in which Victory would range herself on the side of knowledge and intelligence.

This was not an ordinary war, but a veritable war of opinions; and as the lords had, to sustain it, nothing but their swords, they were at last obliged to renounce their pretensions.

The society of Europe, however, arrived at that period so fatal to nations, at that crisis, almost always a sanguinary one, in which new opinions and old opinions declare an obstinate war against each other; in which all that is new ferments, and is agitated violently; in which all that is ancient resists, and falls to pieces with a crash. For a length of time old laws were powerless; and the laws which were endeavoured to be established, had, in their execution, neither the force that is acquired by habit, nor that which is conferred by experience. A universal crisis was experienced throughout Europe; and the West, troubled by revolutions and civil wars, was, for a moment, upon the point of falling back into the darkness and chaos of the tenth century.

It was at this period that was established in Germany the imperial chamber, instituted for the purpose of appeasing discords and repressing brigandage. In Arragon the tutelary authority of the *justiza* was created, who was armed against license with all the power of a dictator. In all countries brotherhoods and associations were formed against the excesses of anarchy. It was in France, above all, that the necessity was felt to call in justice to the support of shaken social order, and to place it under the safeguard of royalty. Royal power was born, in some sort, amongst the perils and fears of society. There is an instinct which, in moments of crisis, guides people towards the authority which is to protect them; and this authority becomes all-powerful, from the reason that its assistance is implored, and that it is the object of all hopes.

Ecclesiastical jurisdiction had already dealt a mortal blow to feudal justice. The study of the Roman law caused something of the experience of the ancients to revive among nations scarcely escaped from barbarism. A new judicial order sprang up in Europe, particularly in France. [116] This judicial order was at first very complicated, in consequence of that natural disposition of men of the pen and of the robe to multiply forms in all affairs. To follow the clue through the labyrinth of the new laws, the barons were deficient in knowledge, and more particularly in patience. If it be true that lawyers complicated legislation in order to remain the sole interpreters of it, their hopes were not deceived; for they in the end took the places of the feudal nobles in judicial functions.

It is true that seignorial justices were not abolished; but an appeal was permitted from their decisions to the judgment of the crown. There were, besides, cases in which the justice of the barons was found incompetent, and as this incompetence was almost always judged of by the jurisdiction of the king, the latter finished by attracting to itself most of the causes of any weight or importance. As it is otherwise important that justice should be protected by a force that can make it respected, as the power of the barons declined, and as that of the king increased daily, the royal jurisdiction prevailed, and custom sanctioned the maxim that all justice emanates from the king. When once this maxim was recognised and proclaimed in all the provinces, Beaumanier was right in saying, "that the king was sovereign over everything, and that he had by right the general guardianship of the kingdom."

It was at this period arose that French magistracy which afterwards became so eminent. The parliaments exhibited the frankness and loyalty of old times, united with the intelligence of modern times. They sometimes defended the rights of the people against the crown, and were often a buckler for the crown against factions. Perhaps their roots did not strike deeply enough into the society whose rights they defended. The fundamental laws of the kingdom had neither regulated their rights, nor fixed with precision the limits of their power. Their authority was due less to written constitutions than to that want of justice which is felt among civilized people, than to that supreme ascendancy which they almost always obtain whose function it is to be exponents of the law. We have seen parliaments perish amidst public disorders, for which they themselves gave the imprudent signal. They saw the faults of administration, but they were deficient in positive knowledge to point out the proper remedy: they appealed to the people, and factions answered; they invoked liberty, and the revolution burst forth. Now, when this magistracy no longer exists among us, and that it can have no place in the order of things which events have given birth to, it appears to us the moment is come for everybody to be just towards it, and to praise that noble disinterestedness, that enlightened firmness, that inflexible probity, which formed its principal character. "It is for the observer of the present period," says an English writer, "and not for the historian of past times, to decide if those virtues which distinguished the ancient French magistracy are sufficiently common now-a-days, not to be remembered with great praise, and exhibited to our contemporaries as useful examples."

In the revolution which was effected, we are astonished that the barons showed so little foresight; they opposed the privileges of an order of things which no longer existed, when, without their intervention and without their concurrence, a new order of things was established; the greater that was their need of union to defend themselves, the more obstinacy they showed for maintaining the too fatal privilege of making war upon each other. The habit of warlike and feudal manners made them prefer to all other functions the occupation of arms, which they considered, with reason, as the most glorious career; but which ruined them, kept them in their ignorance, and drove them from affairs, whilst others enriched themselves in peaceful employments, exercised their faculties usefully, and employed themselves exclusively with power. In the end, the nobility, after the most generous sacrifices, became nothing but an aristocracy without action in the government, whilst those who lent a hand to the administration became really the masters.

The revolutions we have just described have made us for a moment forget the crusades; the holy wars, however, may be reckoned among the causes which ameliorated legislation. The departure of the Crusaders gave occasion for a number of actions; precautions against fraud were multiplied; public notaries were called in; the use of charters,—called *chartres chirographaires,* or *chartres parties,*—was adopted, or rather revived. We have already said that many regulations were made to limit the numbers of the Crusaders, and these regulations were so many laws added to those which existed. The Crusaders, whilst passing through distant countries, might remark many wise customs, which they brought back into their own country. Villehardouin informs us with what astonishment the French nobles, on their arrival at Venice, beheld the senate, the doge, and the people deliberating in their presence. This spectacle could not fail to enlighten them. When the Latins were masters of Constantinople, they there became acquainted with the legislation of Greece; in Palestine, the Assizes of Jerusalem gave them an idea of a legislation less imperfect than their own; the code which for a long time governed the Christian colonies led Louis IX. to think of making a collection of laws, which he did not, it is true, put in practice, but which no doubt spread much useful information. The example of St. Louis, and the encouragement that jurisconsults received on his return from Egypt, contributed to create among the people the love of justice; and this love of justice, which began to be felt among all classes, was the best guarantee of a nascent civilization.

Skilful writers have gone over before us this epoch, so abundant in great events and in lessons of policy. They have shown how royalty rose from the bosom of disorder; how legislation progressively prevailed over anarchy; and how several states of Europe—particularly France—attained that degree of strength and splendour in which we have seen them during the eighteenth century. There would remain but very little for us to say, after the great publicists who have preceded us, if recent revolutions had not broken forth to enlighten us. The experience of the present times has thrown a new light over past ages; and we are better acquainted with the nature and origin of old institutions, since we have seen them sink into ruins. The tree of our ancient monarchy has not been able to resist the concussions which have shaken society; its branches have strewed the earth, and its roots have been laid bare. It then became easy for us to see by what secret conduits strength and life had been circulated; how had grown, and how had fallen,—

"That tree whose head approached to heaven,
And whose feet touched the empire of the dead." [117]

After having gone through the different classes of society, and shown the origins of our institutions during the crusades, we are about to see what was, at the same period, the progress of navigation, commerce, industry, the sciences, letters, the arts, and general knowledge.

Before the twelfth century, the seas of Europe and Asia, with the exception of the Mediterranean, were scarcely frequented even by the nations who dwelt upon their shores. At the period of the first crusades, that which formed the kingdom of France had but two or three ports upon the coast of Normandy, and had not a single one upon the ocean, or the Mediterranean, when, in the seventh crusade, Louis IX. caused that of Aigues-Mortes to be dug. [118] England was scarcely more advanced; that kingdom abandoned the navigation of the seas which surrounded it to pirates. It appeared that the world was not yet large enough for the ambition and genius of the English nation, which at the present day dominates over all the known seas. Some cities on the shores of the Baltic, of Holland, Flanders, and Spain, made maritime expeditions, but which scarcely deserve to be described in the history of the crusades. When the crusades began, the spirit of devotion, united with that of commerce, gave a new and more extended direction to the voyages and labours of navigators. The inhabitants of Denmark appeared in the seas of Syria; and Norwegians, who came by sea, assisted at the taking of Sidon. Citizens of Lubeck and Bremen were present at the siege of Ptolemaïs. From all the coasts of the West, vessels and fleets transported pilgrims, provisions, and arms into the kingdom of Jerusalem and the other Christian principalities established in Asia by the victories of the Crusaders.

Thus navigators from all countries met in the seas of the East. It was, in some sort, under the auspices of the cross, that advantageous relations began to be established among the maritime nations of Europe. At the commencement of the twelfth century, a fleet of Pisans, joined with some other Italians, came to assist the Arragonese in conquering the Balearic Isles. The navigators of Italy were so little acquainted with the seas of Spain, that they took the coasts of Arragon for the country of the Moors. This first alliance between distant nations was the work of a crusade preached by Pope Pascal III., and seconded by a great number of knights of Provence and Languedoc.

The navigators of Lubeck, Bremen, and Denmark, after having tried their strength in long voyages, took advantage of the experience they had gained, to visit the unknown seas of the Baltic. These new enterprises presented to their pious zeal and their ambition a nearer sea, and savage peoples which they might bring under their faith, and make subservient to their commercial views. Maritime expeditions were mixed with the crusades preached against nations still living in a state of paganism. At the aspect of the cross and the flag of navigators, rich cities sprang up, and barbarous regions began to be acquainted with the blessings of civilization.

It was at this period that navigation opened for itself a new career, and saw the theatre of its useful labours expand. Nothing could have favoured its progress like the communication that was then established between the Baltic, the Mediterranean, the Spanish Ocean, and the seas of the north. By uniting nations in pursuit of the same advantages, it multiplied their relations, their ties, and their interests, and redoubled their emulation. In this career thus opened to all the nations of Europe, practical knowledge became rectified, was much increased, and spread everywhere; the configuration of coasts, the position of capes, ports, bays, isles, &c. &c., were all ascertained; the depth of the ocean was fathomed; the direction of winds, currents, and tides was observed; much information was gained upon all the points of hydrography, and very soon that ignorance of the eleventh and twelfth centuries was dispersed, which had occasioned so many shipwrecks, that the chroniclers of the times of the first crusades, as they tremblingly recount them, can only ascribe them to the anger of Heaven.

We would here speak of the mariner's compass, if the period of its invention could be ascertained clearly. A passage of James of Vitry, which we have elsewhere given, does not permit us to doubt that the properties of the loadstone were known in the time of the crusades, and that navigators derived great assistance from it in their long voyages; but, on the other hand, there is nothing to prove that the use of the mariner's compass was then general. We may believe that so valuable a discovery was still a secret for the vulgar, and that those who were in possession of this secret, only sought to profit by it for their own interest, without thinking of the advantages that might be drawn from it for the progress of navigation. We will add that that which has happened to the mariner's compass, has happened also to most of the inventions of industry, of which history can rarely assign the epochs, because their authors, from a spirit of cupidity or jealousy, have not only not promulgated them, but have concealed them carefully from the knowledge of their contemporaries.

Naval architecture was much improved during the crusades. The vessels were greatly enlarged, to enable them to contain the multitudes of pilgrims to be transported. The dangers incidental to long voyages, caused the ships destined for the East to be constructed in a more solid manner. The art of setting up several masts in the same vessel, the art of multiplying the sails, and of disposing them so as to enable the ship to sail against the wind, were the happy fruit of the emulation which then animated navigators.

Thus the activity and the genius of man triumphed over all obstacles, commanded the elements, and took possession of the empire of the sea. But this empire, like that of the land, was, in the middle ages, a prey to brigandage and violence; tempests, contrary winds, shipwrecks, were not the only evils to be apprehended in long voyages. On every sea no right was known but the right of the strongest, and the absence of a maritime code added greatly to the perils of distant navigation.

The necessity for a legislation that might assure the interests and the freedom of navigators was strongly felt. It was Spain that furnished the first model of one. At the commencement of the twelfth century a code of maritime rights was drawn up by the ancient *prudhommes* [119] of the Sea of Barcelona. The Venetians adopted it in an assembly held at St. Sophia, in 1255. This code was afterwards adopted by the Pisans and Genoese, and, under the name of the Consulat of the Sea, became the common law or right of the eastern seas. Another code, published at first by Eleanor of Guienne, and afterwards by Richard Cœur-de-Lion, under the title of "Rolls of Oleron," obtained the assent of several maritime nations, and was at last accepted in all the seas of the West.

Protected by this code, navigators were enabled to gather the fruit of their long labours, and soon disputed advantageously the empire of the Mediterranean with the infidels. If Italy and several other countries of the West escaped the yoke of the Saracens, they owed their safety more to the superiority of their fleets than to that of their armies.

I have spoken in the preceding book of the discovery of America, and of the passage to India by the Cape of Good Hope. It is probable that, without the crusades, the genius of navigators would, although later, have surmounted the immense space and numberless dangers that separated the Baltic and the Mediterranean from the Indian Ocean, and the Old World from the New. We may at least say that the distant expeditions and the perilous enterprises undertaken beneath the banners of the cross, prepared the way for the last prodigies of navigation, by opening everywhere new routes for industry, and, above all, by favouring the progress of commerce, the natural and necessary link between the divers nations and the different countries of the globe.

Each climate has its productions; and this diversity of riches creates for men an obligation for exchanges. This obligation for exchanges produces communication among all nations, so that in time the most widely-separated regions cannot remain unknown to each other. It may truly be said, that Providence has thus placed various productions in different climates, that it has denied to some countries what it has granted to others, to create for men dispersed over the face of the earth, the necessity for reciprocally seeking each other, for trading to supply their mutual wants, for communicating their knowledge, and for marching together towards civilization.

In the middle ages, the indolent and effeminate Greeks neglected to bring into the West the merchandises of Asia. The Saracens only anchored on the coasts of Europe, to bring thither the scourges of war. The commerce of the West went to seek that which was not brought to it; and frequent voyages to the East were all for the profit of the West.

A long time before the crusades, the merchandises of India and Asia had arrived in Europe, sometimes by land, crossing the Greek empire, Hungary, and the country of the Bulgarians; but more frequently by the Mediterranean, in which were all the ports of Italy. These routes were both made more familiar by the holy wars, and from that time nothing could stop the rapid progress of commerce, protected in its march by the standard of the cross.

Most of the maritime cities of the West not only got rich by furnishing Europe with the productions of the East, but they found further a considerable advantage in the transport of pilgrims and Christian armies.

Fleets followed along the coasts of the countries in which the Crusaders were fighting, and sold them the munitions of war and the provisions of which they always stood in need. Thus commerce brought back into Europe a part of the treasures which the princes and barons, who ruined themselves to go and fight the infidels, carried into Asia.

All the wealth of the maritime cities of Syria, and even of Greece, belonged to merchants of the West. They were the masters of a great part of the Christian cities of Asia; we know what was the share of the Venetians after the taking of Constantinople. They possessed all the isles of the Archipelago, and half of Byzantium. The Greek empire was as another Venice, with its laws, its fleets, and its armies.

The Latins soon lost Constantinople, Jerusalem, and most of the countries which submitted to their arms. Commerce, more fortunate, preserved its conquests after the crusades. The city of Tana, built at the mouth of the Tanais, became for Venice a colony, which opened for her useful relations with Persia and Tartary, and which dominated in the markets of Tauris, Trebizond, Bagdad, and Bassora. Some Genoese, assembled in a little city of the Crimea,—Caffa, at the time even when the Turks were threatening Europe, employed themselves in working the mines of the Caucasus, and receiving the treasures of India by way of Astracan. European commerce established stores even among nations that made cruel war against the Christians. The terror which the Mamelukes inspired did not prevent colonies of merchants establishing themselves in Egypt. Africa, particularly the coast of the Mediterranean, was all subservient to their mercantile ambition, and the places which St. Louis had not been able to conquer, became tributaries to their industry.

Whilst the commerce of all parts of the world was thus placed in the hands of a few maritime cities, many of the great kingdoms of Europe were still strangers to it. England, which had no other wealth but its wools, gladly received in its capital the merchandises of Asia, brought thither by Italian and Spanish merchants. The cities of France took but little part in the commerce of the East. The crusades were the work of the French; others gathered the fruits of them. Marseilles was, in the middle ages, the only French city which kept up any relation with distant nations. This city founded by the Phocians, for the sake of the commerce with the Gauls, had never ceased to turn its eyes towards the places of its origin, and have commercial relations with Syria and Greece. Spain, whose industry developed itself early, took more advantage from the crusades, and, towards the end of the holy wars, the Spaniards had warehouses upon all the coasts of Asia.

No country, however, derived more advantage from the trade of the East than Italy. This country, which dominated over the Mediterranean, and which lay open to all parts of the known world, was placed in the most favourable position. This position, which had formerly facilitated the conquests of the Romans, assisted the nations of Italy in their new enterprises, and subdued the world to their speculations, as it had subdued it to their arms. Whilst their fleets set out for the East, they sent into Europe, not legions and proconsuls, as Rome had done, but caravans of merchants, who subdued the provinces they passed through to the calculations and the wants of commerce. These merchants disposed of, by their industrious traffic, all the money which then circulated in the West. In all countries they had numerous colonies and considerable establishments. Europe has no great cities in which the name of the Lombards, given to a street, to a quarter, does not, even at the present day, attest the long sojourn of the Italian merchants.

We cannot help admiring this power of commerce; but it had likewise its principle of destruction. What rivalries, what jealous passions, did it not give birth to daily! Pacific conquests were contended for without ceasing, swords in hand. In this struggle many cities succumbed; Pisa was destroyed by Genoa; Genoa, in her turn, could not maintain its rivalry against Venice. Another rock for these commercial powers, was the mobility of the commerce which had elevated them, and which carried unceasingly its favours and its gifts from one place to another. If commerce changed its route or its direction, that was quite enough to make a city prosper, or to precipitate its fall. In the middle ages, a crowd of cities disappeared, without discord or war having at all contributed to their ruin. It appeared as if fortune took a pleasure in destroying her own work, and as if she disdained on that account to associate herself with human passions.

It is not possible to separate the progress of industry and even of agriculture from that of commerce. To ascertain what industry and agriculture could gain by relations with the East, it would perhaps be sufficient to ascertain in what state these two sources of prosperity then were among the Orientals. Among so many travellers, there were, doubtless, some who had an interest in observing the usages and practices of the distant countries they visited. We know that in the expeditions of the Crusaders, such as were masters of a trade, or were skilful in a mechanical art, were enrolled in preference to others. These industrious pilgrims did not always make a voyage barren of advantages for their country; and in those holy wars, in which the knights of the cross only sought victory and renown, industry, if I may venture to say so, had also its crusade, whose peaceful trophies consisted in precious discoveries, stolen from the Greeks or the Saracens, and in the happy imitation of that which they had admired in the arts of the East.

The Saracens had manufactures of stuffs before the crusades. At Damascus, and in the cities of Egypt, metals were worked with greater perfection than in the West. Old chronicles inform us that the Christians of Palestine went sometimes to Damascus to purchase arms. Joinville relates that, being on a pilgrimage to our lady of Tortosa, he bought at Tripoli some camlets, fabricated in that city. He sent some pieces of them to Queen Marguerite, who, he tells us, at first took them for relics, and fell on her knees to receive them; but upon discovering her mistake arose, saying, "Mischief upon the seneschal! who has made me kneel to his camlets." [120] Joinville was directed by Louis IX. to purchase a quantity of this stuff, which proves that the manufactory in which it was fabricated had some reputation.

There were at this period, in the same city of Tripoli, and in several cities of Greece, a great number of silk-looms, the produce of which must have excited great attention in the merchants and pilgrims who visited the East. About the middle of the twelfth century, Roger II., king of Sicily, caused several of these looms to be transported to Palermo; this was the fruit of an expedition to the coasts of Greece. The mulberry-tree flourished and multiplied under the beautiful sky of Italy, as well as under that of the Morea, and this useful conquest gave the Sicilians the means of soon surpassing the industry of the Greeks. The principal workshop was placed in the palace of the kings, as if to display the richness and magnificence of this new art.

Many useful inventions came to us at this period from the countries of the East. Some writers affirm that windmills were known in Europe before the crusades; but we should remember that they might have been due to the early pilgrimages into Asia, which it is so difficult to separate, upon such matters, from the holy wars. [121]

Tyre was at this time famous for its glass. The sand found in its vicinity gave to the fabrication of glass a perfection unknown in other countries. The use of glass was much more common in Palestine than in the West. The Venetians obtained from Tyre the idea of their beautiful works in glass, so celebrated in the middle ages.

The Crusaders, as has been seen in this history, always evinced great surprise at witnessing the explosion of the Greek fire. But what appears very strange, they never seemed to envy the Saracens this great advantage. The Frank warriors, in the field of battle, preferred the sword and lance to a means of fighting which, in their minds, took away something from personal bravery. It is not at all improbable, however, that the Greek fire, in the end, furnished the idea of gunpowder; an invention fatal to humanity, but which placed a formidable weapon in the hands of European society, when threatened by the Turks and Tartars.

We have already spoken of the maize, or Turkish wheat, sent into Italy by Boniface of Montferrat, in the fourth crusade. The Damascus plum was brought at the same time into Europe by a duke of Anjou, who visited Jerusalem. Our gardens owe to the holy wars the ranunculus, so prized by Orientals, and shalots, which take their name from Ascalon; the knowledge, or rather the use of saffron, alum, and indigo, in Europe, may be traced to the times of the crusades.

We may remember with what delight the Crusaders saw for the first time the sugar-canes of the territory of Tripoli. The plant was transported to Sicily, about the middle of the twelfth century. It is not correct, however, to say that it passed from thence into the new world. If the Spaniards afterwards transported the sugar-cane to the island of Madeira, we may believe they found it in the kingdom of Granada, whither the Moors had brought it from Africa. But it is also probable that notice was only taken of this plant because the taste for sugar was widely spread, and that the substance, which was brought from Egypt, became an important branch of commerce. It is thus we may render honour to the crusades.

Natural history, which is connected with the progress of industry and agriculture, was enriched likewise by some useful notions. Distant climates not only exchanged their vegetable productions, but the crusades procured for Europe an acquaintance with several animals of Africa and Asia. We have mentioned that the Mamelukes of Egypt sent Louis IX. an elephant, of which the French monarch made a present to the king of England. A short time after the first expedition of Louis IX., Bibars sent to Mainfrey, son of Frederick II., several Mogul prisoners, with their horses, which were of Tartar breed. Among the Oriental productions which the Egyptian ambassadors were directed to present to the king of Sicily, was a giraffe, an animal that had never till that time been seen in the West.

The curious circumstances which we could further produce, would add nothing to the opinion that must be already entertained of the happy influence of the crusades upon the progress of agriculture and industry. The riches of Asia, when brought into Europe, soon gave birth to a desire for the cultivation of the arts which embellish life, and of the sciences which double the faculties of man.

In the tenth century, architecture consisted in the construction of towers, ramparts, and fortresses. In the habitations of the great, everything was sacrificed to the necessity of providing defences against an enemy; nothing could be afforded to comfort or magnificence. The dwellings of the people, even in cities, scarcely protected them from the injuries of weather or the intemperance of seasons. The only architectural monuments were those which devotion raised to ancestors. Before magnificent palaces for princes, or convenient houses for the rich were thought of, edifices consecrated to religion were constructed. It is scarcely possible to enumerate the churches and monasteries built in the eleventh and twelfth centuries. According to the opinion of the time, the most certain mode of expiating sins, was to build a church or a monastery. Thus architectural monuments arose at the voice of repentance, and religious inspirations revived, in some sort, the prodigies which fabulous antiquity attributed to the lyre of Amphion.

In every city, in every town, the inhabitants made it their pride to ornament their cathedral, and the altars at which they invoked the saint whom the parish had chosen for its patron. It may be said that there was something like patriotism in this pious zeal; for the basilic, or paternal church, was then the most noble and the most sensible image of the country.

At the commencement of the crusades, there existed a religious confraternity composed of men practised in the labours of building; they travelled about the world, offering their services to the faithful to build or repair churches. Another confraternity was formed with the useful design of constructing bridges for pilgrims and travellers. A chapel or an oratory reminded passengers that the bridge they were crossing was the work of charity.

The clergy, who were rich, and could only display their opulence in buildings, made it their glory to erect churches. To complete their work, they called in the aid of painting and sculpture, which, like architecture, owed their first encouragement to piety, and whose earliest masterpieces were consecrated to the ornamenting of the altars of the Christian religion.

Nothing was more common than to see noble Crusaders, on their departure for Palestine, or on their return to the West, found a monastery or a church. Several pilgrims are named, who, on coming back from Jerusalem, employed their treasures in constructing churches, the form of which might offer them an image of the holy sepulchre they had visited. The treasures conquered from the infidels were often appropriated to such buildings. Before the first crusade, some cities of Italy undertook an expedition into Africa, and the spoils were reserved for the ornamenting of churches. We read in an Italian chronicle, that the Pisans ceded to the Greek emperor Calo-John several cities which belonged to them in Asia Minor, upon the condition that this emperor would defray the expenses necessary for the building of the archbishop's palace at Pisa, and ornamenting the cathedral of Palermo.

During the crusades, the sight of the monuments of architecture which were admired in the East, must have awakened the emulation of the western pilgrims. Nothing could exceed the surprise of the Crusaders at beholding the city of Constantine. Foucher de Chartres exclaimed in his enthusiasm: "Oh, what a vast and beautiful city is Constantinople!" The German historian Gunther likewise expresses his admiration, and says that such magnificence could not be believed if it were not seen. The marshal of Champagne relates that the French knights, on seeing the beautiful towers and the superb palaces of Byzantium, could not persuade themselves *that there could be such a rich city in all the world!*

Italy, which derived such advantages from its relations with the East, profited greatly by the masterpieces of Greece. The inhabitants of Rome, and of several other cities founded and embellished by the Romans, had before them remains of antiquity that might serve them as models. The riches which their commerce brought them furnished them with the means of encouraging industry and the arts, which assist in the embellishment of cities. The cities of Italy, — Venice in particular, — had palaces and sumptuous edifices before the crusades. In the thirteenth and fourteenth centuries, the taste for beautiful architecture changed the face of Italy, and spread by degrees throughout the rest of Europe.

We must add, however, that the fine arts, with the exception of architecture, owed very little to the frequent communications with the East. Painting was despised among the Mussulmans, to whom the Koran forbade the reproduction of the images of man or of animated beings. The Latins likewise, as our readers may remember, after the taking of Constantinople, destroyed most of the monuments raised by the genius of sculpture, and converted the masterpieces of Phidias and Praxiteles into pieces of coin.

The indolent and silent character of the orientals was not calculated to carry music to perfection, as this art bespeaks a lively and warm imagination in a people; and the Greeks had for a long time lost the secret of those melodious songs which, in the times of Linus and Orpheus, charmed the heights of Rhodope and the woods of Mænalus. The history of music, then, has very little to do with that of the holy wars. When Italy saw the fine arts revive, they sprang up as a natural production of the soil, as plants indigenous to the climate; they owed their splendour to the prosperous state of society, and followed, as a consequence of the opulence and luxury which commerce and industry had produced. [122]

The revival of the fine arts announced that of letters. But if it be true that letters owed a part of their progress to the influence of the crusades, it must be confessed that the Crusaders did not always show themselves disposed to profit by them for themselves: nothing can exceed the ignorance of the Crusaders who then set out for the East. History informs us that after the taking of Jerusalem, they burnt at Tripoli a library which contained the most precious monuments of oriental literature: at the taking of Constantinople, a conflagration devoured the literary treasures of ancient Greece. The Crusaders beheld this misfortune with so much indifference, that not one of their chronicles makes mention of it, and posterity would have been ignorant of it but for the eloquent complaints of Nicetas.

The science which gained most by these distant expeditions was doubtless geography. Before the crusades, this science was quite unknown. Countries, the least distant from each other, had no intercommunication. Burgundy was scarcely known at Paris; in Burgundy Paris was considered as a very remote place. The Crusaders who followed Peter the Hermit were not acquainted with the names of the cities of Germany and Hungary which they passed through. They experienced a defeat at Mersbourg, and the contemporary chronicles that speak of it content themselves with calling the Hungarian city *Malleville*, or the city of misfortune.

If the Franks scarcely knew their own country, what must have been their ignorance of the countries of the East? We may judge by the necessity they felt for taking their guides from among the Greeks, whom they mistrusted, and by their extreme embarrassment whenever these guides abandoned them. Several armies perished from want of knowing the places to which victory conducted them. Most of the chroniclers knew no more about the matter than the Crusaders; and this it is that renders it so difficult to follow them in Asia Minor and Syria.

One most remarkable circumstance is, that out of more than two hundred chronicles that speak of Egypt, we have not been able to find more than one that makes mention of the Pyramids. James of Vitry, who sojourned for a long time in Syria, and who appears to have possessed as much knowledge as was then common to the learned, repeats, in his descriptions of the East, the fables of Herodotus; such as the history of the Amazons and that of the phœnix. We can scarcely forbear laughing at the simple credulity of Joinville, who tells us gravely, in his memoirs, that the trees of the terrestrial paradise produce cinnamon, ginger, and cloves, and that these spices are fished out of the waters of the Nile, whither they have been carried by the winds.

The Crusaders, constantly engaged in fighting, never entertained the idea of making themselves acquainted with the countries subdued by their arms. Nevertheless, in consequence of them, religion and commerce,— the one led by the desire of spreading the Gospel, the other by the hopes of gaining wealth, opened some new routes, and gained useful notions concerning the East during the crusades. The missionaries sent by the court of Rome and by St. Louis travelled over the vast regions of Asia, and commerce either followed or went before them in these distant journeys. The accounts of Rubruquis, Asselin, John Plan Carpin, and Marco Paolo, contain observations of which the truth and correctness are recognised at the present day.

We may add that the Crusaders, who went from all the countries of Europe, became acquainted with each other beneath the standard of the cross. Nations were no longer foreign to each other; which dissipated the ignorance in which they had been regarding the names of the cities and provinces of the West.

The geographical charts of this period neither give the configuration of the globe, nor the extent of countries, nor the position or limits of emperors; they merely trace, by vague designations, that which struck travellers most forcibly,—such as the curiosities of each country, the animals, the buildings, and the various dresses of men. We have seen a map of the world, which is attached to the chronicle of St. Denis, and which appears to have been made in the thirteenth century: we do not find, as in modern maps, the names of the four cardinal points set down, but on the four sides are written the names of the principal winds, to the number of twelve. Jerusalem, according to the opinion of the time, is placed in the centre of the three parts of the known world; a large edifice surmounted by a cross represents the holy city. Around this queen of cities, the author of the map has figured, by other edifices, the cities of Palestine, Syria, Egypt, &c.: the distances are marked without any attention to exactness; all appears thrown at random on the paper: this confused mass of edifices or houses, seems to be less a representation of the universe than the shapeless picture of a great city, built without plan or regularity.

We may judge by this how completely geography was then in its infancy; but, at the same time, it renders it evident that it was not quite neglected, as till that time it had been. Thus, we have a right to believe they would not stand still there, and that geographical knowledge would soon advance. In the fourteenth century, the countries of the East were already much better known, if we may judge by the chart which Sanuti presented to the pope, and which may be seen in the collection of the historians of the crusades by Bengars.

The sciences most useful to man, such as medicine, might have made some progress during the crusades, if the Crusaders had profited by the knowledge of the Orientals. In medicine particularly, the Arabians had more positive knowledge than the Latins. At the siege of Ptolemaïs, we have seen that Saladin sent his physicians to Richard; but we do not learn that the king of England sent his to Saladin, when he fell ill. In the first crusade of St. Louis, the physicians who accompanied the army of the Crusaders understood nothing of the scurvy and other epidemic diseases, which exercised such ravages in the camp of the Christians. Their ignorance was not less fatal than the contagion: when Louis IX. and his warriors became the prisoners of the Mussulmans, the diseases which desolated them ceased all at once, because they were no longer attended by their own physicians, but were placed under the care of the Arabians.

The East then furnished Europe with several processes and remedies from which modern medicine, for a length of time, derived great advantage. Cassia and senna came from Asia, and became known in the West at the period of the crusades. Theriaca, which played so great a part in the medicine of the middle ages, was brought from Antioch to Venice. Robert of Normandy, on his return from the Holy Land, after the taking of Jerusalem, obtained from the school of Salerno a collection of Hygeian precepts, which became proverbs among all the nations of Europe.

And yet these discoveries, and this knowledge of the Orientals, did not much enlighten the West in the art of curing. Properly to receive lessons of experience of this kind, preliminary studies were necessary, and the physicians of Europe were then too ignorant to profit by the learning of the Arabians. At this period, religious charity raised a great number of open asylums for suffering humanity. But this charity, however admirable, when its object was to attend the sick, and comfort them in their sufferings, knew but very little of the symptoms or the character of the numberless diseases which attack the life of man. It may be safely said, that during the crusades, we received from the East many more serious diseases than true instruction in medicine. We know that there were numerous lazar-houses established in Europe in the time of the crusades; but we know nothing of the remedies employed for the cure of leprosy. Isolation appears to have been the only curative or preservative means known for this malady, which many learned physicians now look upon as mere prejudice. The spirit of devotion richly endowed lepers, without doing anything for their cure. Leprosy, in the end, disappeared without the assistance of medicine, and the property bestowed upon lazar-houses was transferred to the hospitals; which was advantageous to humanity, and may be set down as one of the benefits of the crusades. [123]

We will say nothing of the other sciences, which owed still less than geography and medicine to the holy wars.

The Saracens of Syria were very little enlightened in the middle ages. In the East, the state of knowledge, like everything else, depended upon the reign of a great prince; whilst this prince reigned, knowledge flourished by his influence; at his death, everything returned to darkness, as the natural state of countries governed by Islamism. [124]

The Franks gained more by their commerce with the Greeks than by that with the Saracens. The Crusaders established continual relations between the cities of Italy and the empire of Byzantium. Some sparks of the genius of the Greeks were glimmering in Italy before the taking of Constantinople by the Turks.

A college for young Greeks was established at Paris in the reign of Philip Augustus. In the thirteenth century universities flourished at Bologna, Paris, and Salamanca, in which the Greek language was taught; and later, the Oriental languages were added, by a decree of the council of Vienna.

We find in a chronicle of St. Denis these remarkable words:—"This year, 1257, William, a physician, brought some Greek books from Constantinople." Thus, the arrival of some volumes from Greece was an event worthy of being recorded, and the importance attached to it, already announced the disposition of men's minds.

When the Turks became masters of Constantinople, the learned, exiled from their country, came to establish themselves in Italy, where the Greek muses formed an alliance with the Latin muses. The venerable interpreters of antiquity were hailed everywhere with eagerness, and the communication of their knowledge was repaid by generous hospitality. Among the distinguished men to whom the muses of ancient Greece owed an honourable protection, we must not forget Nicholas V., who, as the head of the Christians of the West, excommunicated the Greek Church, and, as a scholar, seemed to have vowed a worship to the genius of Homer and Plato. [125] Printing, which had then recently been invented, was employed to preserve the literary treasures brought from the East, and made them for ever safe from the scythe of Time, the furies of war, or the hands of barbarians. The Iliad and the Odyssey found readers in places which had inspired the Æneid; the orations of Demosthenes were again read amid the wrecks of the forum, where the learned might believe they still listened to the voice of Cicero. The genius of the Italians, kindled by the masterpieces of ancient Rome and of old Athens, produced fresh masterpieces; and Italy presented a phenomenon which the world will, perhaps, never see again,— that of a nation which, in the space of a few centuries, obtained twice the palm of literature in two different languages.

It was from Constantinople we received the philosophy of Aristotle. We can scarcely say to what extent the true friends of intelligence ought to congratulate themselves on this head. Aristotle had disciples, partisans, and martyrs; the philosopher of Stagyra was very near being preferred to the Bible; the contemners of Aristotle were called *Biblici*. At that period a mania for subtleties was introduced into the schools, which dishonoured the teaching of philosophy. Reason was no longer studied in the mind of man, but in a book; nature was no longer studied in the universe, but in Aristotle. The schools became like fencing-matches. In an age in which everything was decided by violence, the human mind wished to have its species of warfare; so that victory in most affairs was considered justice; and became, in the schools, the only reason. We may believe that this philosophy did not much assist the march of true wisdom; but we must admit, that if it did, for a moment, lead the human mind astray, it did not quite arrest its progress. It exercised the faculties of man, and by that means assisted in their development. At the commencement of societies, it is less the errors of the mind than its inaction that retains nations in the darkness of barbarism.

Universities had never been so attended as at this period. The number of students in the schools of Paris, Bologna, and Oxford were said to amount to ten thousand. The great privileges granted to universities, prove the esteem in which learning was then held. The doctors disputed for precedency with knighthood itself. If Bartholo is to be believed, ten years' teaching of the Roman law conferred the title of *knight*. This dignity was called *the knighthood of learning*, and they who attained it were called *knights-clerks*.

Among all the productions of mind, those which ought to be ranked first, were such as had for object the preservation of the memory of events. At all periods of the middle ages, chronicles appeared, to which were consigned the important facts of history. In many monasteries were kept registers or journals, in which was inserted everything remarkable that happened in the various parts of the world. Monks, in the general assemblies, sometimes communicated these registers to each other, and this communication assisted them in rendering their chronicles more complete. In ages less remote from us, other cenobites have collected, with laborious care, these same chronicles, concealed in the solitude of cloisters, and have transmitted them to posterity as the most precious monuments of old times.

The ancient chroniclers were simple and pious men; they considered the least falsehood as a mortal sin; they were scrupulous in telling the truth, when they were acquainted with it. Most of them would have thought themselves deficient in the duties of an historian, if they had not gone back to the creation of the world, or at least to the deluge. Among the events which they relate, they never forgot such as would strike the vulgar, and which struck themselves; as the revolutions of nature, famines, prodigies, &c. According to the spirit of their age, the foundation of a monastery holds a more conspicuous place in their recitals than that of a kingdom or of a republic. Politics are quite unknown to them; and everything which astonishes them, everything they do not easily comprehend, they rarely fail to account for by a miracle.

Such is the character of our old chroniclers; and even when they do not inform us of that which we desire to know, their simplicity touches us, and their ingenuousness interests us. When they tell us of wonderful things which were believed in their times, and of which they appear fully persuaded, they do nothing but paint themselves and their age.

But we must beware of fancying the Oriental chronicles of the same period more perfect than our own. We find in them the same spirit of superstition and credulity, united to that spirit of fatalism which characterizes the Mussulman faith.

It is quite in vain for us to seek in Arabian historians any of those thoughts that instruct us in the knowledge of human passions or political revolutions. They almost always neglect the most important circumstances of events, in order to describe whimsical particularities, or to enter into insignificant details; thus, obeying the spirit of oriental despotism, which wills that man should be always occupied with little things. When they relate the fall of an empire, if asked why it has fallen, they reply: "God knows, God has willed it so." In all their chronicles which we have consulted, whenever the Mussulmans triumph over the Christians, we never find any other reflection but this: "God is God, and Mahomet is his prophet." When the Christians gain a victory, the Mussulman chronicles preserve a perfect silence, contenting themselves with saying: "May God curse them!"

Oriental historical productions are very far from redeeming this absence of remark by another merit, such as order, clearness, or elegance; most of their accounts are nothing but a nomenclature of facts confusedly arranged. Quotations from the Koran, verses made upon the occurrence of an event, some comparisons which belong rather to poetry than history,—such are the only ornaments of their narrations.

We see by this that our chronicles of the middle ages have nothing to envy in those of the East. Most of them, it is true, are of an extreme dryness, and have neither precision nor method. But still some few of them do not appear unworthy of attracting the attention of scholars and men of taste. As their authors wrote in Latin, we have reason to believe that the great works of antiquity were not unknown to them, and in many of their recitals, we may easily perceive they have had models.

History must have made some progress during the crusades. These long wars between the Christians and the Mussulmans were like a great spectacle at which Europe and Asia were present. The importance of the events, and the lively interest which Christendom took in them, inspired several writers with the desire of retracing the history of them. A crowd of chroniclers arose in the West, among whom some were not unworthy of the name of historians. Everybody is acquainted with William of Tyre, who may be called the Livy of the crusades, Albert d'Aix, Baudry, archbishop of Dol, Odo of Deuil, and particularly James of Vitry, in whom we meet with vivid and animated descriptions, a rapid and flowing style, and a narration almost always elegant:—and, though last, not least, Villehardouin and Joinville, who wrote in the French language, and whose memoirs are the earliest monuments of French literature.

But all these events which presented to historians such rich pictures, the wonders of nascent institutions, the prodigies of the social world issuing from the chaos of barbarism, must not only have awakened the curiosity, they must have struck vividly the minds of new generations. This grand spectacle, without doubt, contributed to the development of the faculties connected with the imagination. After having seen the simple and faithful relations of events, the genius of poets was called upon to add something to the truthful pictures of the chroniclers. The troubadours who flourished during the crusades were not likely to neglect the exploits of so many gallant knights. We hear their voices constantly mingling with those of the preachers of the holy wars, and find their poetical fictions everywhere confounded with the narrations of history.

Among the warriors who went into the East to combat the infidels, a great number of troubadours and trouvères distinguished themselves. We have seen the romance of Raoul de Couci, and the verses of Thibault, count of Champagne. We may add to these names known in the *fasti* of the French muses, those of the count of Poictiers, the count of Anjou, the duke of Brittany, Frederick II., and Richard Cœur-de-Lion. Often would these princely and lordly Crusaders charm the tediousness of a long pilgrimage by poetical relaxations and remembrances. The count of Soissons, when a prisoner with St. Louis, sang the praises of the dames of France, in the presence and beneath the very swords of the Saracens. One chronicle relates that at the end of the third crusade, the duke of Burgundy made a satire against Richard, and that Richard replied by a poem. The example of these princes was enough to arouse the emulation of the poets; and as they composed their verses in the French language, this language, which was then spoken at Jerusalem, Constantinople, and many other places in the East, must have prevailed over all contemporary idioms.

The muse of the troubadours celebrated chivalry, love, and beauty; that of the trouvères, who dwelt on the banks of the Loire, and in the provinces situated beyond that river, delighted in songs of a more serious kind. The trouvères had rivals in England and Germany. These poets had created for themselves an heroic and new world, which inspired them with noble actions. They celebrated the lofty deeds of Arthur and Rinaldo, the knights of the Round Table, Charlemagne, Roland, and the twelve peers of France. They added to these names those of Godfrey, Tancred, Richard, and Saladin, the remembrance of whom vividly interested all the Christian nations of the middle ages.

The marvellous, among a people, belongs to their habits, to the effects of climate, and to the great revolutions of society. In consequence of the mixture and confusion of divers nations in the middle ages, the wonderful traditions of the North became confounded with those of the South, and produced a semi-barbarous mythology, which differed widely from the laughing mythology of the Greeks. But the labours, the perils, the exploits of a religious war, of a distant war, like those of the crusades, must have given a more noble direction to the imagination of poets, and preserved it from that which was common and whimsical in the romantic conceptions of a gross age. That which was then passing upon the real theatre of events, was more extraordinary than the inventions of poetry; and the marvellous of that period was the more easy to be seized, from being all to be found in actual history.

A new literature then was born, conforming with the genius of a new state of society. If this literature, which, to employ the expression of the learned Heren, bore a character of national and contemporary originality, had produced great works like the Iliad and the Odyssey, the muses would have opened for themselves a career unknown to the ancients; language would have been, from that time enriched, perfected, fixed by the masterpieces themselves; and history would have spoken of the age of the crusades, as it speaks to us of the age of Augustus or Pericles.

Unfortunately, our literature of the middle ages only produced indifferent poems, which were not able to make us forget the great works of antiquity. There were none but romantic productions, in which the interest of the subject was not at all raised by talent, and poems whose authors, though witty and ingenious, had none of that authority of genius which carries away the opinions of an age, and even of posterity.

We have more than one reason for regretting that the human mind did not open for itself a new career at the period of the crusades. There is no doubt that the ancients offer us the more perfect models of taste; but in proportion as people, in the end, became impassioned for the Greeks and the Latins, modern nations disdained their own antiquities for those of Athens and Rome. With the study of masterpieces which had nothing to do with our own glory, the remembrance of our own ancestors was not at all mixed; and the knowledge they have given us has added nothing to our patriotism. What an interest and what a value would the remembrances of our country have had for us, if they had been traced by a literature, formed according to the manners of the nation, and which would, in some sort, have commenced with the nation itself!

Most of the romancers, and even the poets of these times, who had no models and wanted taste, found no other means of interesting their readers, than by exaggerating the sentiments of chivalry. Imitation, pushed to the extreme, was taken for reality, and there were found knights who wished to do that which they saw in romances and poems. Thence came knight-errantry. Thus, in all times, the state of society has acted upon literature, and literature, in its turn, has reacted upon the state of society.

The romances which were consecrated to chivalry and the crusades, underwent the modifications that manners and customs received; and this species of composition has come down to our days, expressing, by turns, the tastes, sentiments, and opinions of each age. This was quite unknown to antiquity. It was born with the Romance language, whose name it took; and they who now derive pleasure from it ought to be thankful for it to the age of the crusades.

These kinds of productions, which attracted the curiosity and attention of the vulgar, contributed to form the national language, which then appeared to be scorned by the learned. The Latin language still remained the language of the sciences and of learning. But it lost its correctness and its purity. The Latin of the fifteenth century was more corrupt than that of the twelfth. The Romance language and the Latin language had a tendency to corrupt each other, by their mixture and their reciprocal borrowings.

Knowledge, however, continued to increase and spread, and assisted greatly in polishing the manners of the nations of Europe. One proof that the crusades were not unconnected with these first steps of civilization is, that knowledge and letters first flourished among the peoples enriched by the commerce which the holy wars favoured, as in Italy; and with the peoples who had most communication with the Orientals, as the Spaniards. Two inventions were destined to complete this happy revolution, and mark the commencement and the end of the period of the crusades. The first was the invention of paper, which became known in Europe just before the first expedition into the East; the second, the invention of printing, which took place towards the end of the holy wars.

There remains but little for us to say upon the results of the crusades. Several distinguished writers have spoken of them before us, and the information they have given upon this important subject, whilst it facilitates our labour, only leaves us the advantage of expressing an opinion which their authority has consecrated, and which has no longer any need of being defended.

The better to explain and make clear all the good that the holy wars brought with them, we have elsewhere examined what would have happened if they had had all the success they might have had. Let us now attempt another hypothesis, and let our minds dwell for a moment upon the state in which Europe would have been, without the expeditions which the West so many times repeated against the nations of Asia and Africa. In the eleventh century, several European countries were invaded, and others were threatened by the Saracens. What means of defence had the Christian republic then, when most of the states were given up to license, troubled by discords, and plunged in barbarism? If Christendom, as M. De Bonald remarks, had not then gone out by all its gates, and at repeated times, to attack a formidable enemy, have we not a right to believe that this enemy would have profited by the inaction of the Christian nations, and that he would have surprised them amidst their divisions, and subdued them one after another? [126] Which of us does not tremble with horror at thinking that France, Germany, England, and Italy might have experienced the fate of Greece and Palestine?

We have said, when commencing our history, that the crusades offered the spectacle of a sanguinary and terrible struggle between two religions which contended for the empire of the world; the victory to belong to that one of these two religions which would inspire its disciples and defenders with the most generous sentiments, and which, favouring among them the progress of civilization, would give them the greater force and power to defend their territories and assure their conquests.

In this formidable struggle, the true means of defence consisted in superiority of knowledge and of social qualities. As long as the ignorance of barbarism reigned over the nations of the West as well as over those of Asia, victory continued uncertain; perhaps even the greater strength was then on the side of the more barbarous people, for they were already possessed of all the conditions of their political existence. But when the dawn of civilization rose over Europe, she became aware of her own security, and her enemies began to be sensible of fear.

The Mussulman religion, by its doctrine of fatalism, appeared to interdict all foresight to its disciples, and in days of mischance contained nothing to revive the courage of its warriors. The Christians, on the contrary, lost none of their faculties in reverses: reverses often even redoubled their energy and activity. What is most astonishing in the history of the crusades, is to observe that the defeats of the Christians in Asia, excited, among the warlike populations of Europe, much more enthusiasm than their victories. The preachers of the holy wars, to persuade Christian warriors to take up arms against the infidels, said nothing of the glory and the power of Jerusalem; but endeavoured, in their pathetic lamentations, to exaggerate the perils, the misfortunes, and the decline of the Christian colonies.

We see by this what advantage Christianity had over the worship of Mahomet, in the war between the East and the West.

Another vice of the Koran is, that it has a tendency to isolate men; which is injurious to the development of their social qualities. Under the empire of Islamism, there is nothing strong but despotism; but the strength of despotism is, almost always, nothing but the weakness of the nation it rules over. The Christian religion has another aim, when it says to its disciples, *Love one another as brothers*. One of its most admirable characteristics is the spirit of sociability with which it inspires men. By all its maxims, it orders them to unite, to help one another, to enlighten one another. It thus doubles their strength, by placing them constantly in community of labours and dangers, fears and hopes, opinions and feelings. It was this spirit of sociability which gave birth to the crusades, and sustained them during two centuries. If this spirit was unable to assure success, it at least prepared the Christian republic, at a later period, to defend itself with advantage. It made the nations of Europe like fasces that cannot be broken. It created, in the midst of disorders even, a moral force which nothing could conquer; and Christianity, defended by this moral force, was at length able to say to the barbarians, masters of Constantinople, that which God said to the waves of the sea: *You shall go no further*.

Thus Christianity, and the heroic virtues with which it inspired its disciples, were, in the middle ages, an invincible buckler for Christian Europe. When the enthusiasm for crusades beyond the seas began to die away, the heads of the Church still invoked the spirit of the Gospel, to animate the nations against the Mussulmans, on the point of invading Germany and Italy; and, still holding up to Christian warriors the cross of Christ, sometimes succeeded in awakening in hearts sentiments of a religious and patriotic heroism. It cannot then be denied that the crusades contributed to save European societies from the invasion of the barbarians; and this was, without doubt, the first and greatest of the advantages which humanity derived from them.

Here I am, then, arrived at the termination of my labour. To resume my opinions and render a last homage to truth, I must say, that, among the results of the crusades, there are some which appear incontestable, others which cannot be determined with precision. I ought to add, that many circumstances concurred with the civil wars in assisting the progress of knowledge and civilization. Nothing can be more complicated than the springs which set modern societies in motion; and he who would desire to explain the march of things by one single cause, must fall into great error. The same events do not produce always or everywhere similar effects; as may be seen by the picture we have traced of Europe in the middle ages. The holy wars assisted, in France, in abasing the great vassals, whilst feudal power received scarcely any injury from it in Germany and other countries. During this period some states were enlarged, others marched rapidly towards their fall. Among some nations, liberty took deep root, and presided over young institutions; among others, the power of princes was elevated, at times freeing itself from all restraints, at others, being limited by wise laws. Here flourished commerce, the arts and sciences; elsewhere industry made no progress, and the human mind remained immersed in darkness. The germs of civilization, in the times of the crusades, were like those seeds which the storm carries with it, and scatters, some in barren places, where they remain unknown and unproductive; others, upon propitious land, where, the action of the sun, a happy temperature, and the fecundity of the soil, favour their development, and cause them to bear good fruits.

Every age has its dominant opinions; and when these opinions are connected with great events, they leave their impress upon the institutions of societies. Other events, other opinions come, in their turn, to give a new direction to human affairs, and to modify, ameliorate, or corrupt the morals and the laws of nations. Thus, the political world is unceasingly renewed; by turns, disturbed by violent shocks, and ruled by generally-spread truths or errors. If, in the future, societies assume still another new face, there is no doubt their institutions will, one day, be explained by the influence of the revolutions we have seen, as we now explain the institutions of times past, by the influence of the crusades. May posterity gather and preserve the fruit of our misfortunes, better than we ourselves have gathered and preserved the fruit of the experience and of the misfortunes of our fathers! [127]

See Supplementary Chapter.

APPENDIX

No. 1.—Page 2, Vol. I.

In the third and fourth century of the Christian era, pilgrimages to the Holy Land became so frequent, that they led to many abuses. St. Augustine, Serm. 3, de Martyr. Verb., expresses himself thus: "Dominus non dixit, Vade in Orientem et quære justitiam: naviga usque ad Occidentem, ut accipias indulgentiam." The same saint says elsewhere, Serm. 1, de Verb. Apost. Petri ad Christum: "Noli longa itinera meditari; ubi credis, ubi venis; ad eum enim, qui ubique est, amando venitur, non navigando." St. Gregory of Nyssus, in a letter which bears for title, "De Euntibus Hierosolymam," speaks with still greater vehemence against pilgrimages: he thinks that women, in particular, would meet on their route with frequent opportunities for sinning; that Jesus Christ and the Holy Ghost were not in one place more than another; he censures bitterly the morals of the inhabitants of Jerusalem, who committed the greatest crimes, although they had constantly before their eyes Calvary and all the places visited by pilgrims. St. Jerome endeavoured to divert St. Paulinus from the pilgrimage to Jerusalem, by a letter which is still preserved: "De Hierosolymis," said he, "et de Britannia equaliter patet aula cœlestis." He added, that an innumerable crowd of saints and doctors enjoyed eternal life without ever having seen Jerusalem; that from the reign of Hadrian to that of Constantine, an image of Jupiter received the adorations of the pagans upon the rock of Calvary, and that fervent worship was paid to Venus and Adonis within the walls of Bethlehem.

We add an extract from the pilgrimage of St. Eusebius of Cremona, and his friend St. Jerome, taken from a notice, written by Francis Ferrarius, vol. i. of the Bollandists, of the month of April, p. 276.

"(A.D. 390-423.) According to St. Jerome, St. Eusebius was born at Cremona, of distinguished parents, who spared neither pains nor expense for his education. They were rewarded by the rapid progress of their son in knowledge, but particularly by the rare virtues which he showed from his earliest childhood. Solely occupied with religious ideas, Eusebius, when still young, abandoned his parents, his country, and all the advantages which his birth and wealth promised him, to go to Rome, and visit the sacred monuments contained in that city. Very soon becoming united in a strict friendship with St. Jerome, who dwelt in Rome, Eusebius determined to accompany him in a voyage which the latter intended to make to Jerusalem.

"Having embarked, they visited the isle of Cyprus in their passage, passed through Antioch, where they were received by St. Paulinus, who was bishop of that city, [128] and arrived safely at Jerusalem. After having performed their devotions in the spots sanctified with the presence of Christ, they visited Bethlehem, Calvary, Mount of Olives, and Mount Tabor, the valley of Jehoshaphat, the castle of Emmaüs, and extended their pilgrimage as far as Egypt, to witness the fasts and austerities to which the pious solitaries of the Thebaïs abandoned themselves. Returning into Judæa, the city of Bethlehem particularly fixed their attention, and they resolved to found a monastery there, which was soon filled with religious men disposed to follow the rules established by St. Jerome himself. But the crowd of pilgrims becoming daily more considerable, and not knowing how to feed and lodge them, the two friends were obliged to return to Italy, to sell the property they had there, which they destined for these pious purposes. St. Jerome, compelled by his affairs to go to Rome, there met with St. Paulina, descended from the ancient family of the Gracchi. This lady, learning the project that had brought him into Italy, determined to follow his example: she abandoned her fortune, her country, and her children, and accompanied him to Bethlehem, where she founded a monastery for maidens, which she governed herself to the time of her death. St. Jerome, after having employed the large sums he brought back in the construction of an hospital for pilgrims, terminated his pious career at Bethlehem, at an advanced age. Eusebius, who was named abbot after the death of his friend, only survived him two years. Deeply regretted by his monks, of whom he had constantly been the benefactor and the father, he was interred, according to his desire, with St. Jerome, close to the stable in which the Saviour was born. Thus were united in the tomb, as they had been in life, and as they are, without doubt, in heaven, where their virtues have placed them, two men who renounced all they held most dear to strengthen the faith of the faithful, and to become in a distant country the consolers of the unfortunate."

No. 2.—Page 3, Vol. I.

The Itinerary from Bordeaux to Jerusalem.

Although we do not think it necessary, at this time of day, to give, as Mr. Michaud has done, in his "Pièces Justificatives," the whole of this celebrated Itinerary, [129] with remarks upon the places passed through or by; we think we shall gratify the praiseworthy curiosity of many of our readers by so far presenting the details, as to show the route by which early pilgrims travelled to the Holy Land.

This Itinerary is deemed by learned men the most exact and correct that has come down to modern times; it was printed for the first time, in 1588, by the care of the celebrated Pierre Pithon, from a manuscript upon vellum in his own library; and which, when M. Michaud wrote this history, was in the Imperial Library at Paris. This Itinerary was composed about the year 333 of the Christian era. In fact, the author of it informs us that he went from Constantinople to Chalcedon, and that he returned to Constantinople under the consulship of Dalmatius and Xenophilus, who, we learn from Cassiodorus and other authorities, were consuls together in the year 333. The author was a Christian of Bordeaux, whose aim, in this work, was to facilitate for his compatriots the voyage to the Holy Land, which he himself had performed.

The example of the empress Helena, and the magnificence with which she had ornamented the humble spot which gave our Saviour birth, singularly excited, at this period, the zeal and curiosity of Christians for such voyages. A passage from the Psalms, badly interpreted in the Greek, was considered as a prophecy, and a commandment to all the faithful to visit the holy places. In the Psalms was read: "Let us adore the Lord, in the spot where his feet were placed," and the bishops of that time unceasingly repeated: "The psalmist has prophesied, and has said; Let us adore the Lord on the spot where his feet were placed." This is in the 132nd Psalm, and Jerome, Eusebius, and others did not understand it otherwise; the Vulgate translates it: *Adorabimus in loco ubi steterunt pedes ejus*; but the Hebrew only says, *We will prostrate ourselves before thy footstool*, that is to say, before the holy ark; and this is the version in the English.

On leaving this famous city, our pilgrim directed his course towards Thoulouse, passing by Auch—from Thoulouse to Narbonne, passing by Carcassonne—and from Narbonne to Arles, passing by Beziers and Nîmes. Arles was then a city of great note, being called the Little Rome of the Gauls. He continues his route towards Italy, and after having passed through the cities of Avignon, Orange, Valence, Die, Gap, and Embrun, he arrives at the foot of the Cottian Alps (Alpes Cottiæ); at Briançon he begins to climb Mount Genevre, and soon finds himself at Susa in Italy. He afterwards enters Turin, follows the Po, traverses the beautiful plains of Piedmont, which are north of that river, till he gains Pavia; he re-ascends towards the north, and arrives at Milan, then the city of Italy second only to Rome. Continuing his route towards the East, the pilgrim passes through Bergamo, Brescia, Verona, Vicenza, and arrives at Aquileia, then a great city, but afterwards destroyed by Attila. He then ascends the Julian Alps, which separate Friuli from Carniola. He arrives at Æmona (Layback), and at twenty-three miles beyond that place, marks the limits of Italy and Norica; which limits were at that time the boundaries of the Western and the Eastern empires.

Our pilgrim, after quitting the vicariat of Italy, or the ancient Cisalpine Gaul, enters the diocese of Illyria, goes on to Cilley, and reaches the city of Petau, in modern Styria. Crossing the river Drave, he enters Lower, or Second Pannonia; but continues to follow the northern banks of the Drave, or the southern frontiers of modern Hungary, and traversing Pannonia Superior, he directs his course to the south, and gains the banks of the Save at *Cibalis*, which was placed where now the modern village of Svilaï stands, to the east of Brod. Proceeding towards the East, he enters *Sirmium*, then one of the most considerable cities of the Eastern empire, but of which there are now scarcely any vestiges. At a short distance from Sirmium our pilgrim comes to the confluence of the Save and the Danube, at *Singidunum*, where Belgrade is at present, which city, he informs us, terminates Pannonia Superior. Crossing the Save, he finds himself in Mœsia, now Servia, and follows the course of the Danube. At *Viminacium*, now in ruins, near Vi-Palanka and Ram, our pilgrim does not neglect to remark that it was at this place Diocletian killed Carinus, which agrees with the account of Eutropius of this event. After leaving the banks of the Danube at Viminacium, he directs his course towards the south-east, following the Roman way, which deviates little from the banks of the Morava, and at about fifty miles before he comes to Nissa, he points to a station called *Mansio Oromago*, as the limits of Mœsia and Dacia; but which we must observe is the Dacia of Aurelian, and not that of Trajan, of which he speaks. After having traversed Nissa into Servia, he arrives at the city of *Sardica*, whose ruins are now to be seen near Sophia, or Triaditza. Continuing to follow the same route, which is that of the present day, from Belgrade to Constantinople, he sets down the limits between Dacia and Thrace, just beyond the *Mutatio Sencio*. From Philippopolis, or Felibra, our pilgrim journeys to *Heraclia*, now Erekil, on the coast of the Sea of Marmora, and, at length to Constantinople. From Constantinople, says our traveller, you cross the Bosphorus, you arrive at Chalcedon, and go through Bithynia. At Libyssa, near Gebyzeh, on the coast of the Propontis, our pilgrim remarks, is the tomb of Hannibal; which is confirmed by Pliny, Plutarch, Eusebius, &c. Tournefort and Belo, among the moderns, say they have seen the tomb in this place. After arriving in *Nicomedia* (Isnikmid), our pilgrim continues his route, and passing through Nice (Isnik) marks near Ceratæ the limits of Bithynia and Galatia. Then on to *Ancyra*, near Angora—then to Andrapa, where he places the limits of Galatia and Cappadocia. Proceeding still towards the south-east, into the Karismania of the moderns, he gains Tyana, which he tells us is the country of the magician Apollonius. Next is a place called Pilas, and soon after Tarsus, which he does not fail to tell us is the country of the apostle Paul. He then enters Cilicia Secunda, which formed one of the divisions of the empire of the East. At nine miles beyond Alexandria (or Scanderoun) he marks the limits of Cilicia and Syria, and arrives at length at the city of Antioch (Antakia). Our traveller then continues his route along the Roman way which ran along the coast of Syria, and at *Balnea* (Belnia), indicates the limits of Syria and Phœnicia. On passing by a small place called *Antaradus* (Centre-Aradus), which is the Tortosa of the time of the crusades, he takes care to observe that the city of Aradus itself is only two miles from the coast. This powerful city was built in the little island called Ruad by the moderns. Our traveler crosses *Tripolis* (Taraboles), then Berytus (Berouth), and arrives at *Sidona* (Saide). Next to Tyre (now the little village of Sour); thence to Ptolemaïs (St. Jean d'Acre), and at Sycamenes be finds himself at the foot of Mount Carmel. At eight miles from that place he indicates the confines of Syria and Palestine, and arrives at Cæsarea (Qaïsarich). On leaving Cæsarea, our pilgrim quits the direct road that leads to Jerusalem. In order the better to fulfil the object of his voyage, and visit Palestine, he directs his course to the East, towards the revered waters of the Jordan. After interrupting his Itinerary to make several Biblical remarks, he proceeds to the banks of the Jordan, at a place called *Scythopolis* or *Bethsan*, named by the moderns Bisan; then going afterwards to the south of the side of Jerusalem, he passes *Aser*, "in which was the house of Job," and at fifteen miles thence enters *Neapolis* or *Sichem*, the Naboles of the moderns. Here he ceases to follow any direct route, but visits every place that the Old or New Testament has rendered memorable; and gives an account of them in his journey from Neapolis to Jerusalem. After seeing everything that could attract the attention of a pious and well-informed Christian, he returns to Jerusalem, and resumes his Itinerary with as much exactness as at first. As his homeward journey begins by the same route he arrived, we will join company with him at Erekil, on the coast of Marmora, where he begins to deviate. He proceeds to the south of Mount Rhodope, the Despeto-dag of the moderns; he passes through the city of Apris, which, after Theodosius, took the name of Theodosiopolis. At a short distance from Apris, our pilgrim indicates the limits of the province of Europa, and that of Rhodope. To understand this, we must remember that at the period at which the Aquitain pilgrim wrote, the diocese of Thrace was divided into six provinces, amongst which were those of Europa and Rhodope; the cities of Constantinople, Heraclea, and Apris were in the province of Europa. Our pilgrim reaches Trajanopolis, which the Turks call Orichovo, and keeping to the west, through Macedonia, or the Romania of the moderns, and along the northern shores of the Sea of Marmora, and of the Archipelago, he points out, near a place called Pardis, the boundary of the provinces of Rhodope and Macedon—he crosses Neapolis, now Cavale, and Philippi, which is in ruins. Shortly afterwards he visits the celebrated Amphipolis on the Strymon, the ruins of which are now near a little village called Jeni-Keni. Twenty miles farther our pilgrim contemplates the tomb of the poet Euripides, at a station named Arethusa, situated in a valley of the same name. He passes by Thessalonica (Saloniki), which is still one of the most considerable cities of these countries. He arrives at Pella, the celebrated capital of Macedon, which presents nothing at the present day but ruins, known by the name of Palatiæ, or the Palaces. Our pilgrim does not omit to show his erudition by remarking that Alexander the Great was of this city—*civitas Pelli, unde fuit Alexander Magnus Macedo.* Here the pilgrim, directing his course towards the north-west, follows the famous Egnatian way, constructed by the Romans through Macedon. This way passes to Edessa, to Heraclea in Macedon, and there, discontinuing its northward direction, it goes straight to the west to Dyrrachium; but one branch of this way, before arriving at Dyrrachium, now Durazzo, re-descends towards Apollonia, now in ruins under the name of Polina; and it was this last that the pilgrim took. At thirty-three miles from Heraclea, near a station called Brucida, he points out the limits of Macedon and Epirus, two provinces which were then only subdivisions of the great diocese of Macedon. At twenty-four miles from Apollonia, the Aquitain traveller gains the coast at Aulona (Valena), at a place where Epirus, or the coast of Albania of the moderns, comes nearest to Italy. He then crosses the strait between Aulona and Hydruntum, near Otranto. Upon his arrival in Italy, our pilgrim goes to Brindisi, and afterwards takes the Appian way, of all the ways the best and the most frequented. It led him first to Capua. From Capua he continues, by the same way, to Rome, crossing the Pontine marshes. He quits Rome, and follows the Flaminian way, which crosses the Apennines, and which leads out at Ariminum (Rimini), by Spoleto, Fano, and Pesaro.

From Rimini our pilgrim takes the Emilian way, which traced and still does trace a straight line; and traversing Bologna, Modena, Parma, and Placentia, he arrives at last at Mediolanum (Milan); from whence he returns to Bordeaux by the same route he took at starting.

No. 3.—Page 25, Vol. I.

There is so much sameness, accompanied by such incredible marvels, in the numerous pilgrimages described by M. Michaud, that we are certain our readers will willingly dispense with them. The incident which he promises to give of Foulque, count of Anjou, is this:—"Then the count approached to kiss the Holy Sepulchre, and then the divine clemency showed that the good zeal of the count was acceptable, for the stone, which is hard and solid, at the kiss of the count became soft and flexible as wax warmed at the fire. The count bit it, and took away a large piece in his mouth, without the infidels perceiving it; and he then, quite at his ease, visited the other holy places."

There is, indeed, another incident to which we fear M. Michaud alludes; but as the amusement or instruction it could afford would not compensate for its indecency, we do not give it.

No. 4.—Page 53, Vol. I.

Among the chroniclers who give an account of this very memorable event, one of the most esteemed is William of Malmesbury, a monk of the order of St. Bennet. From his learning he was called the Librarian, and his particular study was history. He lived in the early part of the twelfth century. Our author having transferred the spirit of all the chronicles to his text, we deem it quite unnecessary to offer the whole that he has quoted from them in his *Pièces Justificatives*; but there is a curious passage of William of Malmesbury, which shows the character of the writer and his times, that we shall not hesitate to give.

Having said that, after the council, every one retired to his home, he continues thus:—"Immediately the fame of this great event being spread through the universe, penetrated the minds of Christians with its mild breath, and wherever it blew, there was no nation, however distant or obscure it might be, that did not send some of its people. This zeal not only animated the provinces bordering on the Mediterranean, but all who had ever even heard of the name of a Christian in the most remote isles, and among barbarous nations. Then the Welshman abandoned his forests and neglected his hunting; the Scotchman deserted the fleas with which he is so familiar; the Dane ceased to swallow his intoxicating draughts; and the Norican turned his back upon his raw fish. [130] The fields were left by the cultivators, and the houses by their inhabitants; all the cities were deserted. People were restrained neither by the ties of blood nor the love of country; they saw nothing but God. All that was in the granaries or destined for food, was left under the guardianship of the greedy agriculturist. The voyage to Jerusalem was the only thing hoped for or thought of. Joy animated the hearts of all who set out; grief dwelt in the hearts of all who remained. Why do I say, of those who remained? You might have seen the husband setting forth with his wife, with all his family; you would have laughed to see all the penates put in motion and loaded upon cars. The road was too narrow for the passengers, more room was wanted for the travellers, so great and numerous was the crowd."

— — — —

Robert of Normandy.

Robert had, before the crusades, long and serious quarrels with his father, William II. of Normandy and I. of England. In 1080, he quitted his country and sought the protection of his uncles, Robert, count of Flanders, Udo, archbishop of Trèves, and several other princes of the houses of Lorraine, Germany, Aquitain, and Gascony. He made his complaints to them, mingling falsehood with truth, and received great assistance from them. But he squandered their gifts among actors, parasites, and courtezans. He was so prodigal that he soon became straitened again, and was obliged to have recourse to usurers. "Every one," says the chronicler Orderic Vital, "knew Duke Robert for an indolent, weak prince. So the ill-intentioned, despising him, took advantage of his character to excite trouble and factions. The duke was bold, valiant, worthy of praise in many respects, and naturally eloquent; but he was inconsiderate, prodigal in his bounty, free of promises, light and imprudent in his falsehoods, allowing himself to be easily prevailed upon by prayers; mild in character and slow to punish crime; changeable in his decisions, too familiar in his conversation, and by that means drawing upon himself the contempt of the ill-disposed. He was stout, and short of stature, whence his father named him Courte-Heuse. He was anxious to please everybody, and gave, or promised, or granted, all that was asked of him. Prodigal of his patrimony, he diminished it daily by giving imprudently to every one what he desired. Thus he became poor, and furnished others with means to act against him." When the first crusade took place, Normandy, ill-governed by such a prince, was in the most deplorable condition. Duke Robert, in fear of the greatest evils, saw no better means of avoiding them, than by pledging his duchy with his brother William Rufus, for five years, for the sum of ten thousand marks, and setting out for Jerusalem. With his exploits in the Holy Land our readers are acquainted. In the year 1100, Robert, on his return from Palestine, landed in Apulia, where he fell in love with Sibylla, daughter of Geoffrey of Conversana, nephew of Duke Guiscard. He married her, and took her into Normandy, obtaining from his father-in-law the means of redeeming his duchy. He lived there eight years much in the same fashion as before his pilgrimage. At the end of that period, and in consequence of events foreign to our object, he was made prisoner at Tinchebray in Normandy, by his brother Henry, who carried him to London, where he remained confined twenty-seven years, but always living amidst the enjoyments of life.

— — — —

Charlemagne.

Whilst searching the Chronicles for passages illustrative of our work, we met with a portrait of Charlemagne so exceedingly interesting, that although he had nothing to do with the crusades, we cannot refrain from presenting it to our readers, begging them to remember that Charlemagne was considered, even in Asia, as the most powerful prince of Europe.

"Charlemagne, who attained the highest degree of celebrity and glory, of a scrupulous and profound piety, was well informed in letters and philosophy, was the avenger and ardent propagator of the Christian religion, and the defender and supporter of justice and truth. Charlemagne's face was very white (at the time he was crowned by the pope, Leo), his countenance was cheerful, and whether standing or sitting, his carriage was equally majestic. Although his neck was thick and rather short, and his belly too protuberant, all his limbs were well proportioned. On days of festivity he wore a mantle of gold tissue, and a chaussure ornamented with precious stones. His *sagum*, or cloak, was fastened with a golden clasp, and his diadem was enriched with gold and jewels. Towards the end of his career, he was seized, on his return from Spain, with a fever, which lasted four years, and rendered him lame. He followed rather his own inclinations than the advice of his physicians, for whom he had a kind of aversion, because they wished him to abstain from roast meat, of which he was very fond, and to accustom himself to live on boiled meats. Charles was called great on account of his great good fortune, in which he was not inferior to his father, but was, on the contrary, more frequently a conqueror and more illustrious. In his youth his hair was brown, and his complexion ruddy; he was handsome, and had much dignity in his carriage; he was very generous, very equitable in his judgments, eloquent, and very well informed. He enjoyed every day the sports of the chase and the exercise of riding on horseback; he was exceedingly fond of tepid baths, to which he invited not only his children but the lords of his court, his friends, and his guards, so that there were often more than a hundred persons in the bath with him. He was moderate in his eating, and still more so in his drinking; nevertheless he often complained that fasts were injurious to him. He rarely gave great banquets, except upon solemn occasions. There were, ordinarily, not more than four dishes on his table, besides the roast meat which he so greatly preferred. Whilst he ate, a person read to him histories and accounts of the actions of the ancients, or else the book of the *City of God*, by Saint Augustine, for which he had a great predilection. During the repast he never drank more than three times. In summer, he took fruit after dinner, and slept two or three hours, undressed as if at night. His dress was that of the Franks, and he constantly wore a sword; the sword-belt and baldric being of gold or silver. Sometimes he wore two swords. He spoke several languages. He had around him doctors of the seven liberal arts, who instructed him daily; that is to say, a deacon of Pisa, in grammar; a Saxon, in rhetoric, dialectics, and astronomy; and Albin, surnamed Alouin, in the other arts. He himself made some reforms in the art of reading and in that of singing, although he never read in public aloud, and never sang but with the choir. He caused all the laws of his kingdom to be written, that were not so before. He himself wrote the actions and the wars of the ancients, and began a grammar of the language of his country. He had every night a hundred and twenty guards around his bed. Ten were placed at his head, ten at his feet, and ten on each side of him, and each of these forty held a naked sword in one hand and a lighted torch in the other."

— — — —

No. 7.—Page 227, Vol. I.

The Chronicle of Tours.

We think it our duty to give here the passage from Albert d'Aix in its entirety, which contains the motives for the sentence of death pronounced by the leaders of the Christian army against the Mussulmans found in Jerusalem. At the end is the description of the massacres which followed the taking of the city. For all who wish to appreciate the spirit of the times, this document is important.

"Jerusalem civitas Dei excelsi, ut universi nôstis, magnâ difficultate, et non sine damno nostrorum, recuperata, propriis filiis hodie restituta est, et liberata de manu regis Babyloniæ jugoque Turcorum. Sed modo cavendum est, ne avaritiâ, aut pigritiâ vel misericordiâ erga inimicos habitâ, hanc amittamus, captivis et adhuc residuis in urbe gentilibus, parcentes. Nam si forte à rege Babyloniæ in multitudine gravi occupati fuimus. subito ab intus et extra impugnabimur, sicque in perpetuum exilium transportabimur. Unde primum et fidele nobis videtur consilium, quatenus universi Saraceni et Gentiles, qui captivi tenentur, pecunia redimendi, aut redempti, sine dilatione in gladio corruant, ne fraude aut ingenio illorum nobis aliqua occurrant adversa. Consilio hoc accepto, tertio die post victoriam egressa est sententia à majoribus; et ecce universi arma rapiunt, et miserabili cædi in omne vulgus gentilium, quod adhuc erat residuum, exagunt, alios producentes à vinculis, et decollantes; alios per vicos et plateas civitatis inventos trucidantes, quibus antea pecuniæ causâ, aut humanâ pietate pepercerant. Puellis tenellis detruncabant, aut lapidibus obruebant, in nullis aliquam considerantes ætatem. E contra puellæ, mulieres, matronæ, metu momentaneæ mortis angustatæ et horrere gravissimæ necis concussæ, Christianos, in jugulum utriusque sexus debacchantes ac sævientes, medios pro liberandâ vitâ amplexabantur, quædam pedibus eorum advolvebantur, de vitâ et salute suâ illos mirum miserando fletu et ejulatu sollicitantes. Pueri vero quinquennes aut triennes matrum patrumque crudelem casum intuentes, unà miserum clamorem et fletum multiplicabant; sed frustra hæc pietatis et misericordiæ signa fiebant. Nam Christiani sic neci totum laxaverunt animum, ut non sugens masculus aut fœmina, nedum infans unius anni vivens manum percussoris evaderet. Unde plateæ totius civitatis Jerusalem, corporibus extinctis virorum, mulierum, lacerisque membris infantium adeo stratæ et opertæ fuisse referuntur, ut non solùm in vicis, soliis, et palatiis, sed etiam in locis desertæ solitudinis, copia occisorum reperiebatur innumerabilis." — *Alb. Aq.* lib. 6, cap. 30, *ap. Bong.* pp. 282, 283.

————

No. 8.

Letter from Bohemond, Godfrey, Raymond, and Hugh the Great, upon the Peace concluded with the Emperor, and the Victory gained over the Infidels (anno 1097, ex Manuscript. St. Albani).

Bohemond, son of Guiscard; Raymond, count of St. Gilles; Duke Godfrey, and Hugh the Great; to all of the sect of the Catholic faith: may they attain the eternal felicity which we wish them.

In order that the peace concluded between us and the emperor, as well as the events that have happened to us since we have been in the lands of the Saracens, be known to all the world, we despatch to you, very dear brethren, an envoy, who will inform you of all it can interest you to know. We have to tell you, that in the month of May, the emperor promised us that from that time, pilgrims who came from the West to visit the Holy Sepulchre, should be protected from all insults on the lands of his dominions; pronouncing pain of death against whoever should transgress against his orders, and giving us at the same time, as hostages, his son-in-law and his nephew, as guarantees of his word. But let us return to events more capable of interesting you. At the end of the same month of May, we gave battle to the Turks, and, by the grace of God, we conquered them. Thirty thousand were left upon the field of battle. Our loss amounted to three thousand men, who, by that glorious death, have acquired felicity without end. It is impossible to value correctly the immense quantity of gold and silver, as well as precious vestments and arms, that fell into our hands; Nice, a city of importance, with the forts and castles which surround it, immediately surrendered. We likewise fought a bloody battle in Antioch; sixty-nine thousand infidels were killed in the place, whilst only ten thousand of us had the good fortune to obtain eternal life upon this occasion. Never was a joy equal to that which animates us, beheld; for, whether we live, or whether we die, we belong to the Lord. On this subject learn that the king of Persia has sent us a message, by which he warns us of his intention of giving us battle towards the festival of All-Saints. If he should prove the conqueror, his design is, he says, with the help of the king of Babylon and many other infidel princes, to make incessant war upon the Christians; but if he should be conquered, he will be baptized with all those he can persuade to follow his example. We beg you, then, very dear brethren, to redouble your fasts and your alms, particularly the third day before the festival, which will be on a Friday, the day of triumph of Jesus Christ, in which we shall fight with much more hope of success, by preparing ourselves by prayers and other acts of devotion.

P.S.—I, bishop of Grenoble, [131] send these letters, which have been brought to me, to you archbishops and canons of the church of Tours, in order that they may be known by all those who will repair to the festival, and by those of the different parts of the earth into which they shall return; and that some may favour this holy enterprise by alms and prayers, whilst others, taking up arms, will hasten to take a part in it.

———

No. 9.

Letter from Daimbert, Archbishop of Pisa, Godfrey of Bouillon, and Raymond, Count of St. Gilles. They announce the Victories gained by the Christian Armies in the Holy Land (anno 1100, ex Manuscript. Signiensis Monasterii).

I, archbishop of Pisa, and the other bishops; Godfrey, by the grace of God now defender of the Holy Sepulchre, and all the army of the Lord, at present in the land of Israel, to our holy father the pope, to the Romish Church, to all bishops, and to all Christians, health and benediction in our Lord Jesus Christ.

God has manifested his mercy by accomplishing by means of us, that which he promised in ancient times. After the taking of Nice, our army, three hundred thousand men strong, covered the whole of Romania. The Saracen princes and kings having risen up against us, with the help of God were easily conquered and annihilated; but as some of us became vain-glorious upon these advantages, the Lord, to prove us, opposed Antioch to us, a city against which human efforts could do nothing, which stopped us nine months, and the resistance of which so humbled our pride, that it compelled us to have recourse to penitence. God, touched by our repentance, allowed a ray of his divine mercy to shine upon us, introduced us into the city, and gave the Turks with all their possessions up to us.

In our ingratitude, having a second time imputed this success to our own courage, and not to the Omnipotent who had caused us to obtain it, he permitted, for our chastisement, that an innumerable multitude of Saracens should come and besiege us, so that nobody durst go out of the city; we were soon given up to so cruel a famine, that some of us, in their despair, did not appear averse to nourishing themselves upon human flesh. It would be too long to make the recital of all we suffered in this respect. At length the anger of the Lord became appeased, and he so inflamed the courage of our warriors, that even they who were weakened by disease and famine took up arms and fought valiantly. The enemy was conquered; and as our army was fruitlessly consuming itself within the walls of Antioch, we entered Syria, and took from the Saracens the cities of Barra and Marra, as well as several castles and strong places. A horrible famine which assailed our army here, placed us under the cruel necessity of feeding upon the dead bodies of the Saracens, already in a state of putrefaction. Happily, the hand of the Lord aided us again, and opened to us the gates of the cities and fortresses of the countries we passed through. At our approach, they hastened to send us messengers loaded with provisions and presents; they offered to surrender and accept the laws we might please to dictate; but as we were few in number, and as the general desire of the army was to march to Jerusalem, we continued our route, after having required hostages of the cities, the smallest of which contained more inhabitants than we had soldiers.

The news of these advantages induced a great number of our people who had remained at Antioch and Laodicea, to join us at Tyre, so that, under the all-powerful *ægis* of the Lord, we arrived at Jerusalem. Our troops suffered much in the siege of this place from the want of water. The council of war being assembled, the bishops and principal leaders ordered that the army should make a procession barefooted around the city, in order that He who formerly humiliated himself for us, touched by our humility, might open the gates to us, and give up his enemies to our anger. The Lord, appeased by our action, gave up Jerusalem to us eight days afterwards, precisely at the period at which the Apostles composing the primitive Church separated to spread themselves over the different parts of the earth, an epoch which is celebrated as a festival by a great number of the faithful. If you desire to know what we did to the enemies we found in the city, learn that in the portico of Solomon, and in the temple, our horses walked up to their knees in the impure blood of the Saracens. We already marked out those who were to guard the place, and we had already granted to those whom a love of country or a desire to see their families again recalled into Europe, permission to return thither, when we were informed that the king of Babylon was at Ascalon, with an innumerable army, announcing haughtily his project of leading away into captivity the Franks who guarded Jerusalem, and then rendering himself master of Antioch. It was thus he spoke; but the God of heaven had ordained otherwise. This news being confirmed to us, we marched to meet the Babylonians, after leaving in the city our wounded and our baggage, with a sufficient garrison. The two armies being in presence of each other, we bent our knees, and invoked in our favour the God of armies, that it might please Him, in His justice, to annihilate by our hands the power of the Saracens and that of the demon, and by that means extend his Church and the knowledge of the Gospel from one sea to the other. God granted our prayers, and gave us such courage that those who could have seen us rush upon the enemy, would have taken us for a herd of deer going to quench the thirst that devours them in a clear fountain which they perceive. Our army consisted of little more than five thousand horsemen and fifteen thousand foot; the enemy, on the contrary, had more than a hundred thousand horse and forty thousand foot soldiers. But God manifested his power in favour of his servants. Our first charge alone put to flight, even without fighting, this immense multitude. It might be said they feared to offer the least resistance, and that they had not arms upon which they could depend to defend themselves with. All the treasures of the king of Babylon fell into our hands. More than a hundred thousand Saracens fell beneath our swords; a great number were drowned in the sea, and fear was so strong upon them, that two thousand were stifled in the gates of Ascalon, by pressing to get in.

If our soldiers had not been occupied in pillaging the camp of the enemies, scarcely, of such a number, enough would have escaped to announce their defeat. We cannot pass by in silence a very extraordinary event. On the day before that of the battle, we took possession of several thousands of camels, oxen, and sheep. The leaders commanded the soldiers to leave them, in order to march towards the enemy. A wonderful thing to relate, these animals accompanied us still, stopping when we stopped, advancing when we advanced; the clouds even sheltered us from the ardour of the sun, and the zephyrs blew to refresh us. We offered up thanks to the Lord for the victory he had enabled us to gain, and we returned to Jerusalem. The count of St. Gilles, Robert duke of Normandy, and Robert count of Flanders, left Duke Godfrey there, and came back to Laodicea. A perfect concord having been reëstablished between Bohemond and our leaders by the archbishop of Pisa, the Count Raymond prepared to return to Jerusalem for the service of God and his brethren. In consequence we wish for you, heads of the Catholic Church of Jesus Christ, and first of the Latin people; and you all, bishops, clerks, monks, and laymen, that in favour of the courage and admirable piety of your brethren, it may please the Lord to pour his blessings upon you, to grant you the entire remission of your sins, and to make you sit at the right hand of God, who lives and reigns with the Father in the unity of the Holy Ghost, from all eternity. So be it.

We pray you and supplicate you by our Lord Jesus Christ, who was always with us, and who has preserved us through all our tribulations, to show gratitude towards our brethren who return to you, to do them kindness, and pay them that which you owe them, in order by that means to render yourselves agreeable to the Lord, and to obtain a part in the favours they have merited from divine goodness.

————

No. 10.

Letter of the principal Crusaders to Pope Urban. (See Foulcher de Chartres, pages 394, 395, of the Collection of Bongars.)

We are all desirous that you should know how great the mercy of God has been towards us, and by what all-powerful help we have taken Antioch; how the Turks, who had loaded with outrages our Lord Jesus Christ, have been conquered and put to death, and how we have avenged the injuries done to our God; how we have at last been besieged by the Turks from Corasan, Jerusalem, Damascus, and many other countries; and how at length, by the protection of Heaven, we have been delivered from a great danger.

When we had taken Nice, we routed, as you have learnt, a great multitude of Turks who came out against us. We beat the great Soliman (Kilidge-Arslan), we made a considerable booty, and being masters of all Romania, we laid siege to Antioch. We suffered much in this siege, both on the part of the Turks shut up in the city, and on the part of those who came to succour the besieged. At length, the Turks being conquered in all the battles, the cause of the Christian religion triumphed in the following manner. I, Bohemond (*ego Bohemundus*), after having made an agreement with a certain Saracen, who agreed to give up the city to me, I applied ladders to the walls towards the end of the night, and we thus made ourselves masters of the place which had so long resisted Jesus Christ. We killed Accien, the governor of Antioch, with a great number of his people, and we had in our power their wives, their children, their families, and all that they possessed. We could not, however, get possession of the citadel; and when we were about to attack it, we saw an infinite number of Turks arrive, whose approach had been announced to us for some time; we saw them spread over the country, covering all the plains. They besieged us on the third day; more than a hundred of them penetrated to the citadel, and threatened to invade the city from within.

As we were placed upon a hill opposite to that on which the fort stood, we guarded the road which led into the city, and forced the infidels, after several combats, to reënter the citadel. As they saw they could not execute their project, they surrounded the place in such a manner that all communication was cut off; at which we were greatly afflicted and desolated. Pressed by hunger and all sorts of miseries, many among us killed their horses and their asses which they brought with them, and ate them; but at last the mercy of God came to our assistance; the apostle Andrew revealed to a servant of God the place in which the lance was with which Longinus pierced the side of the Saviour. We found this holy lance in the church of the apostle Peter. This discovery, and several other divine revelations, restored our strength and courage to such a degree, that those who were full of despair and fright became full of ardour and audacity, and exhorted each other to the fight. After having been besieged during three weeks and four days, on the day of the festival of St. Peter and St. Paul, full of confidence in God, having confessed all our sins, we marched out of the city in order of battle. We were in such small numbers, in comparison with the army of the Saracens, that the latter might well believe we meant to fly, instead of to provoke them to fight. Having made our dispositions, we attacked the enemy wherever they appeared in force. Aided by the divine lance, we put them at once to flight. The Saracens, according to their custom, began to disperse on all sides, occupying the hills and roads, with the design of surrounding us and destroying the whole Christian army; but we had learnt their tactics. By the grace and mercy of God, we succeeded in making them unite at one point, and when they were united, the right hand of God fought with us; we forced them to fly and abandon their camp, with all that was in it. After having conquered them and pursued them the whole day, we returned full of joy into Antioch. The citadel surrendered; the commander and most of his people being converted to the Christian faith. Thus our Lord Jesus Christ beheld all the city of Antioch restored to his law and his religion; but as something sorrowful is always mixed with the joys of this world, the bishop of Puy, whom you gave us for your apostolic vicar, died after the conquest of the city, and after a war in which he had gained much glory. Now your children, deprived of the father you gave them, address themselves to you who are their spiritual father. We pray you, you who have opened to us the way we are following, you, who by your discourses have made us quit our homes and all we held dearest in our own countries, who have made us take the cross to follow Jesus Christ and glorify his name, we conjure you to complete your work by coming into the midst of us, and by bringing with you all you can bring. It was in the city of Antioch that the name of Christian took its origin; for when St. Peter was installed in that church which we see every day, those who had called themselves Galileans named themselves

Christians. What can be more just or more suitable than to see him who is the head of the Church come to this city, which may be regarded as the capital of Christendom? Come, then, and help us to finish a war which is yours. We have conquered the Turks and the Pagans; we cannot in the same way combat heretics, Greeks, Armenians, Syrians, and Jacobites; we conjure you to do so; we conjure you, holy Father, with earnestness. You, who are the father of the faithful, come amongst your children; you, who are the vicar of St. Peter, come and take your seat in his church; come and mould our hearts to submission and obedience; come and destroy by your supreme and sole authority all kinds of heresies; come and lead us in the road you have marked out for us, and open to us the gates of the one and the other Jerusalem; come, and with us deliver the tomb of Jesus Christ, and make the name of Christian prevail over all other names. If you yield to our wishes, if you come amongst us, every one will obey you. May He who reigns in all ages bring you amongst us, and make you sensible to our prayers. Amen.

————

No. 11.

Council of Naplouse, held by the Authority of Garamond, Patriarch of Jerusalem, to reform the Morals of the Christians of Palestine, in the Presence of Baldwin, King of Jerusalem, in the year of our Lord 1120, in the Pontificate of Calixtus II.

This is the manner in which William of Tyre, book xii. of the *Holy War*, chap. xiii. relates summarily the cause and the acts of the council.

The same year, that is to say the year 1120 of the incarnation of the Word, the kingdom of Jerusalem being tormented, on account of its sins, with many troubles, and in addition to the calamities inflicted by their enemies, a multitude of locusts and gnawing rats destroying the harvests to such a degree that it was feared bread would be wanting; the seigneur Garamond, patriarch of Jerusalem, a man religious and fearing God; the king Baldwin, the prelates of the churches, and the great men of the kingdom, repaired to Naplouse, a small city of Samaria, and held a public assembly and a general court. In a sermon addressed to the people, it was said, that as it appeared plain that it was the sins of the people which had provoked the Lord, it was necessary to deliberate in common upon the means of correcting and repressing excesses, in order that, returning to a better life, and worthily satisfying for their remitted sins, the people might render themselves acceptable to Him who desireth not the death of a sinner, but rather that he should turn from his wickedness and live. Terrified, then, by the menacing signs of Heaven, by frequent earthquakes, by successive defeats, by the pangs of famine, by perfidious and daily attacks of their enemies; seeking to win back the Lord by works of piety, they have, to restore and preserve discipline in morals, decreed twenty-five acts, which shall have the force of laws. If any one be desirous of reading them, they will be easily found in the archives of many churches.

Present at this council, Garamond, patriarch of Jerusalem; the logician Baldwin, second king of the Latins; Ekmar, archbishop of Cæsarea; Bernard, bishop of Nazareth; the bishop of Liddes; Gildon, abbot elect of St. Mary of the Valley of Jehoshaphat; Peter, abbot of Mount Tabor; Achard, prior of Mount Sion; Payen, chancellor of the king; Eustace Granier; William de Buret; Batisan, constable of Jaffa; and many others of the two orders, of whom we forget the number and the names.

"The synod," says Baronius, "towards the end of 1120 succeeded in effecting such a reformation in morals, that by the mercy of Heaven, in the following year, 1121, the leader of the Turks, coming against Antioch with considerable strength, was struck with apoplexy and died."

Chap. 1.—As it is necessary that things which commence by God should finish in him and by him, with the intention of beginning this holy council and terminating it by the Lord, I, Baldwin, second king of the Latins at Jerusalem, opening this holy assembly by God, I render and I grant, as I have ordered, to the holy Church of Jerusalem, and to the patriarch here present, Garamond, as well as to his successors, the tenths of all my revenues, as far as concerns the extent of this diocese; that is to say, the tenths of my revenues of Jerusalem, Naplouse, and Ptolemaïs, which is further called Accon. They are the benefits of my royal munificence, in order that the patriarch, charged with the duty of praying the Lord for the welfare of the state, may have wherewithal to subsist on. And if, one day, in consequence of the progress of the Christian religion, he, or one of his successors, should ordain a bishop in one of these cities, he may dispose of the tenths as well for the king as for the Church.

Chap. 2.—I, Bohemond, in the presence of the members of this council, with the consent of the personages of the assembly and of my barons, who will do the same by their tenths, according to the extent of their ecclesiastical powers, I make restitution of the tenths, as I have said; and agreeing with them as to the injustice with which they and I have retained them, I ask pardon.

Chap. 3.—I, Patriarch Garamond, on the part of the all-powerful God, by my power and that of all the bishops and brethren here present, I absolve you upon the said restitution of the tenths, and I accept charitably with them the tenths you acknowledge to owe to God, to me, and to your other bishops, according to the extent of the benefices of the brethren present or absent.

Chap. 4.—If any one fears being ill-treated by his wife, let him go and find him whom he suspects, and let him forbid him, before legal witnesses, entrance to his house and all colloquy with his wife. If, after this prohibition, he or any one of his friends should find them in colloquy in his house or elsewhere, let the man, without any cutting off of his members, be submitted to the justice of the Church; and if he purges himself by ardent fire, let him be dismissed unpunished. But when he shall have undergone some disgrace for being surprised in colloquy, let him be dismissed unpunished and without vengeance for having violated the prohibition.

M. Michaud inserts the whole of these laws; but we omit the next twelve, as more likely to create disgust than to afford instruction or amusement.

Chap. 16.—The male or female Saracen who shall assume the dress of the Franks shall belong to the state.

Chap. 17.—If any man, already married, has married another woman, he has, to the first Sunday of Lent of our year, to confess himself to the priest and perform penance; afterwards he has but to live according to the precepts of the Church. But if he conceals his crime longer, his goods will be confiscated; he will be cut off from society and banished from this land.

Chap. 18.—If any man, without knowing it, marries the wife of another, or if a woman marries, without knowing it, a man already married, then let the one that is innocent turn out the guilty one, and be in possession of the right of marrying again.

Chap. 19.—If any man, wishing to get rid of his wife, says he has another, or that he has taken her during the lifetime of the first, let him submit to the ordeal of red-hot iron, or let him bring before the magistrates of the Church, legal witnesses, who will affirm by oath that it is so. What is here said of men is applicable to women.

Chap. 20.—If a clerk take up arms in his own defence, there is no harm in it; but if, from a love of war, or to sacrifice to worldly interests, he renounces his condition, let him return to the Church within the time granted, let him confess and conform afterwards with the instructions of the patriarch.

Chap. 21.—If a monk or regular canon apostatize, let him return to his order or go back to his country.

Chap. 22.—Whoever shall accuse another without being able to prove the fact, shall undergo the punishment due to the crime he has accused him of.

Chap. 23.—If any one be convicted of robbery above the value of six sous, let him be threatened with the loss of his hand, his foot, or his eyes.

If the theft be below six sous, let him be marked with a hot iron on the forehead, and be whipped through the city. If the thing stolen be found, let it be restored to him to whom it belongs. If the thief has nothing, let his body be given up to him he has injured. If he repeats the offence, let him be deprived of all his members, and of his life.

Chap. 24.—If any one under age commits a theft, let him be kept until the King's court shall decide what shall be done with him.

Chap. 25.—If any baron surprises a man of his own class in the act of theft, the latter is not to be subject to the loss of his members, but let him be sent to be judged in the King's court.

————

No. 12.

Bull of Pope Eugenius III. for the Second Crusade.

We here give a translation of the bull of Eugenius III., published in 1145, for the second crusade. It is taken from "Bullarum Romanum Novissimum," the first volume.

"The servant of the servants of God, to his dear son Louis, illustrious and glorious king of the French, to his dear sons the princes, and to all the faithful of the kingdom of France, health and apostolic benediction.

"We know by the history of times past, and by the traditions of our fathers, how many efforts our predecessors made for the deliverance of the Church of the East. Our predecessor, Urban, of happy memory, sounded the evangelic trumpet, and employed himself with unexampled zeal, in summoning the Christian nations from all parts of the world to the defence of the Holy Land. At his voice, the brave and intrepid warriors of the kingdom of the Franks, and the Italians, inflamed with a holy ardour, took arms, and delivered, at the cost of their blood, the city in which our Saviour deigned to suffer for us, and which contains the tomb, the monument of His passion. By the grace of God, and by the zeal of our fathers, who defended Jerusalem, and endeavoured to spread the Christian name in those distant countries, the conquered cities of Asia have been preserved up to our days, and many cities of the infidels have been attacked and their inhabitants have become Christians. Now, for our sins, and those of the Christian people (which we cannot repeat without grief and lamentation), the city of Edessa,—which in our own language is called Rohas, and which, if we can believe the history of it, when the East was subjected to the Pagan nations, alone remained faithful to Christianity,—the city of Edessa is fallen into the hands of the enemies of the cross.

"Several other Christian cities have shared the same fate: the archbishop of that city with his clergy, and many other Christians have been killed; relics of saints have been given up to the insults of the infidels, and dispersed. The greatest danger threatens the Church of God and all Christendom. We are persuaded that your prudence and your zeal will be conspicuous on this occasion; you will show the nobleness of your sentiments and the purity of your faith. If the conquests made by the valour of the fathers are preserved by the valour of the sons, I hope you will not allow it to be believed that the heroism of the French has degenerated. We warn you, we pray you, we command you, to take up the cross and arms. I warn you for the remission of your sins,—you who are men of God,—to clothe yourselves with power and courage, and stop the invasions of the infidels, who are rejoicing at the victory gained over you; to defend the Church of the East, delivered by our ancestors; to wrest from the hands of the Mussulmans many thousands of Christian prisoners who are now in chains. By that means the holiness of the Christian name will increase in the present generation, and your valour, the reputation of which is spread throughout the universe, will not only preserve itself without stain, but will acquire a new splendour. Take as your example that virtuous Mattathias, who, to preserve the laws of his ancestors, did not hesitate to expose himself to death with his sons and his family; did not hesitate to abandon all he held dear in the world, and who, with the help of Heaven, after a thousand labours, triumphed over his enemies. We, who watch over the Church and over you, with a parental solicitude, we grant to those who will devote themselves to this glorious enterprise the privileges which our predecessor Urban granted to the soldiers of the cross. We have likewise ordered that their wives and their children, their worldly goods, and their possessions, should be placed under the safeguard of the Church, of the archbishops, the bishops, and the other prelates. We order, by our apostolic authority, that those who shall have taken the cross shall be exempt from all kinds of pursuit on account of their property, until their return, or until certain news be received of their death. We order, besides, that the soldiers of Jesus Christ should abstain from wearing rich habits, from having great care in adorning their persons, and from taking with them dogs for the chase, falcons, or anything that may corrupt the manners of the warriors. We warn them, in the name of the Most High, that they should only concern themselves with their war-horses, their arms, and everything that may assist them in contending with the infidels. The holy war calls for all their efforts, and for all the faculties they have in them; they who undertake the holy voyage with a right and pure heart and who shall have contracted debts, shall pay no interest. If they themselves, or others for them, are under obligations to pay usurious interest, we release them from them by our apostolic authority. If the lords of whom they hold, will not, or cannot lend them the money necessary, they shall be allowed to engage their lands or possessions to ecclesiastics, or any other persons. As our predecessor has done, by the authority of the all-powerful God, and by that of the blessed St. Peter, prince of the apostles, we grant absolution and remission of sins, we promise life eternal to all those who shall undertake and terminate the said pilgrimage, or who shall die in the service of Jesus Christ, after having confessed their sins with a contrite and humble heart."

Given at Viterbo, in the month of December, 1145.

———

No. 13.

A Letter from Saladin, drawn up by the Cdi Alfadhel, to the Imaum Nassir Del-din-illah Aboul Abbas Ahmed, containing the account of the Conquest of Jerusalem, and of the Battle of Tiberias.

After devout wishes for the caliph, he enters thus on his subject:—

"The *servant* (that is Saladin) has written this letter, which contains the account of the auspicious events of which he is the author. The inscription of this letter is the description of divine goodness, which is a sea for pens, a sea in which they may swim for ages. It is a blessing for which the gratitude should be measureless. Let thanks then be rendered to God for this blessing of to-day; it is a blessing which will last for ever; let no one say: *The like has been seen.* The affairs of Islamism are in the happiest condition; the faith of those who believe in it is strengthened. The Mussulmans have destroyed the error which infidels had spread over these places. God has faithfully fulfilled, with regard to his religion, the compact he entered into. Religion was exiled and a stranger; she now inhabits her natural dwelling: the reward is received, that reward purchased at the price of life. The commandment of the truth of God, which was powerless, is now in vigour; his house is re-peopled, though it was abandoned after it had been destroyed. The order of God is arrived, and the noses of the polytheists are abased. Swords advanced by night, and the sick were asleep. (That is to say, I believe, that Saladin surprised the Crusaders, and that the Christians did not expect what happened to them on his part.) God has performed the promise he made to raise his religion above all religions. Its light is more brilliant than that of the morning; the Mussulmans are restored to their heritage, which had been wrested from them. They have been awakened, they have conquered that which they could not have hoped to conquer, even in their dreams; their feet are firmly fixed upon the hill; their standards have floated over the mosque; they have prayed upon *the black stone*. In acting thus, the *servant* proposed to himself nothing short of these great results; he only confronted *this evil* (the evils of this war) in the hope of this great blessing;

he only made war on those who opposed him, that the word of God might be spread; for the word of God is exalted; he has only fought that he might by that means merit eternal life, and not the wealth of this world. Perhaps, tongues may have accused him of having a contemptible object, and men's thoughts have calumniated him; but he has extinguished these thoughts by means of time and patience. He who sought a precious thing placed himself in danger. He who exerted himself to render his life illustrious, exposed himself. Otherwise, the *servant* has only acted after having consulted with the wisest of his doctors. The *servant* has written this letter, and already God has caused him to triumph over his enemies. The towers of the infidel are cast down; he drew his sword, and it became a wand; his attacks became weak; he turned his bridle; and, as a chastisement from God, he has not found hands to act with. His swords have slept in their scabbards, his lances have lost their noses (points), and for a long time they were raised to inflict death. The land of Jerusalem is become pure; it was as a woman who has her rules. God is become one God, and he was *trinary* (or three). The houses of the infidel are destroyed, the dwellings of polytheism are cast down. The Mussulmans have taken possession of the fortified castles. Our enemies will not return to them again, for they are branded with the seal of weakness and degradation. God has placed beauty where deformity was.

The first time the servant attacked them, [132] God came to his succour, and assisted him with his angels; he broke them with a rupture past remedy; he precipitated them with a fall which would not allow the infidels to rise up again. He made a great number of prisoners, and killed many of their people. The field of battle was covered with dead, arms, and horses. How many swords became like saws, with striking! How many horsemen rushed towards the destiny which destroyed them! The king himself (of Jerusalem) advanced and cleared all before him. That day was a day of testimony (of the favour of God and the valour of the Mussulmans). The angels were witnesses. Error was at bay; Islamism took birth. The ribs of the infidels were materials for the fire of hell. The king was taken, and he held in his hand the most firm of his ties, the most strong of the *bonds* of his religion and of his belief. That was the *cross*, the leader, the guide of the partisans of pride and tyranny. They (the Christians) never advanced towards a peril without having this in the midst of them; they flew round it as moths fly round a light. Their hearts gathered together under its shade; they fought under this light with the greatest courage. They considered it as the strongest tie that could bind them together; they believed it to be a wall which would defend them on this day. On that day the greater part of the infidels were taken. Not one of them turned his back, except the Count. [133] May God curse him! He was eager for carnage in the day of victory, and full of base tricks in the day of degradation; he saved himself! but how? he stole away for fear of being struck by the lance or the sword; God afterwards took him in his own hands, caused him to die according to his promise, and sent him from the kingdom of death to hell. After the defeat, the servant passed through the province (Palestine), and gathered together the Abassides subjects that were scattered about it;—those subjects who carried terror to the hearts of their enemies; and he conquered by their aid such and such places.

This province (Palestine) is full of wells, lakes, islands, mosques, minarets, population, armies. The servant will change the tares of error for the good seed of the true faith; he will cast down the crosses of the churches, and will cause the *izan* (the summons of the Mussulmans to prayers) to be heard. He will change into *pulpits* the places on which the infidels immolated (altars), and of churches he will make mosques.

"There remained nothing but Jerusalem; every banished man, every fugitive had here taken refuge; those from afar as well as those near had here shut themselves up; they considered themselves as there protected by the favour of God; they believed that their Church would intercede for them. Then the servant arrived before the city; he beheld a city well peopled; he beheld troops who had agreed to die; for whom death would be sweet if their city was doomed to fall. He came to one side of the city, but he found that the valleys (or the gardens) were deep; that bad passages were numerous; that the walls, like a necklace, surrounded it, and that towers, like large beads, [134] were placed along the middle of the walls. Then he directed his course to another side, where there was such an ascent as he desired, a place and an asylum for the cavalry; he surrounded this side and made his approaches to it; he caused his tent to be pitched in a spot exposed to the attempts of the enemy; he attacked the walls vigorously, and at length got possession of them. The besieged sent to him, offering to pay him a tribute for a certain time; they wished to obtain a cessation of their distress, and wait for reinforcements. The servant deferred his answer, and drew his machines nearer; the machines that are the sticks and cords that punish castles for their resistance. Their strokes prepared the victory. Possession was taken of the towers; the walls were void of combatants; stone crumbled away into dust again, as it had been at first. The gates fell into the hands of the army of the servant. Then the infidels despaired; the leader of the impiety came out then: this was *Ben* or *Bezbar-ran*; he requested that the city should be taken by capitulation and not by storm; the abjection of ruin and distress was imprinted upon his countenance, which before shone with the glory of royalty; he prostrated himself in the dust, he before whom nobody had dared to raise their eyes, and said: There (pointing to the city) are thousands of captive Mussulmans;—this is the determination of the Franks:

if you take the city by force, if you place the burden of war heavily on their backs, they will immediately kill their captives; they will afterwards kill their wives and children; then they will have nothing to wish for but death; but not one of them will die without having sacrificed many of your people.' The officers were of opinion that the city should be taken by capitulation; for, said they, if it is taken by storm, there is no doubt but that the besieged will rush headlong into danger, and will sacrifice their lives for a thing they have so well defended. In the sorties they had precedingly made, they had displayed incredible courage, and their attacks had been terrible.

But God has driven them out of this territory, and has cast them down; he has favoured the partisans of the truth, and has shown his anger against the infidels. These had protected this city by the sword; they had raised buildings at the point of the sword and with columns of soldiers. These (the infidels) have placed churches there, and houses of the Diweieh, Deuïourjeh, &c., and of the Hospitallers. In these houses are precious things in marble.

"The servant has restored the mosque *Alasca* to its ancient destination. He has placed imauns in it, who will there celebrate the true worship. The *khothbeh* (or sermon) was made there on Friday, the 14th of Chaaban. Little was wanting to make the heavens open with joy, and the stars dance. The word of God has been exalted; the tombs of the prophets, which the infidels had stained, have been purified, &c. &c."

Towards the end of his letter, Saladin says that his troops are spread all over the province; he boasts of the fertility and richness of it, and says he is going to complete the conquest of it. He adds that the fleet has put to sea; and that he is about to restore the walls of Jerusalem.

––––

No. 14.

Khothbeh, or Sermon made at Jerusalem, the first Friday after Saladin had taken Possession of that City, by Mohammed Ben Zeky.

Mohammed Ben Zeky ascended the mimber, or pulpit, and commenced the khothbeh, or sermon, by reciting the surate *Falchah* (the first of the Koran) from the beginning to the end. Then he said: "May the crew of the unjust perish! Praises be to God, the master of worlds!" Then he read, 1st, the commencement of the surate *Alin'am*: "Praise to God who has created the Heavens;" 2nd, a verse of the surate *Soubhana*: "Praise to God who has no son;" 3rd, three verses of the surate *Alkehef*: "Praises to God who has sent the book to his servant." Then he read, 1st, the verse: "Praise to God, and salvation to his servants;" 2nd, a verse of the surate *Seba*: "Praises to God to whom belongs all that is in heaven or earth;" 3rd, several verses of the surate *Falhr*: "Praises to God the creator of the Heavens." His intention was to bring together all the *Temeh-houdah* (praises which are contained in the Koran). After this, he commenced the khothbeh in these terms:—

"Praise to God, who has raised Islamism into glory by his aid; who has abased polytheism by his power; who rules worldly things by his will; who prolongs his blessings according to the measure of our gratitude; who defeats infidels by his stratagems; who gives power to dynasties, according to his justice; who has reserved future life for those who fear him, by an effort of his goodness; who extends his shadow over his servants; who has caused his religion to triumph over all others; who gains the victory over his servants without any one being able to oppose him; who triumphs in his caliph, without any one being able to resist him; who orders what he wills, without any being able to make objections to it; who judges according to his will, without any one being able to avert the execution of his decrees. I praise this God for having by his assistance rendered his elect victorious; for the glory he has given them; for the aid he has granted to his defenders; I praise him for having purified the house filled with pollution, from the impieties of polytheism. I praise him inwardly and outwardly. I give testimony that there is no other God but this God; that he is the only one, and has no associate; the only one, the eternal one, who begets not, neither is he begotten, and has no equal. I give testimony that Mahomet is his servant and his messenger, this prophet who has removed doubts, confounded polytheism, extinguished falsehood; who travelled by night from Medina to Jerusalem; who ascended into the heavens, and reached even the cedar Almontéhy. May the eternal felicity of God be with him, with his successor Abou Bekr Alsadic, &c.

"O men! publish the extraordinary blessing by which God has made easy to you the recapture and deliverance of this city which we had lost, and has made it again the centre of Islamism, after having been during nearly a hundred years in the hands of the infidels.

This house was built and its foundations laid for the glory of God and in the fear of Heaven. For this house is the dwelling of Abraham; the ladder of your prophet (peace be with him!); the kiblah towards which you prayed at the commencement of Islamism, the abode of prophets, the aim of saints, the place of revelation, the habitation of order and defence; it is situated in the land of the gathering, the arena of the meeting; it is of this blessed land of which God speaks in his sacred book. It was in this mosque that Mahomet prayed with the angels who approach God. It was this city to which God sent his servant, his messenger, the word which he sent to Mary. The prophet he honoured with a mission did not stray from the rank of his servant. For God said, *the Messiah will not deny that he is the servant of God; God has no son, and has no other God with him.* Certes, they have been in impiety, they who have said that the Messiah, the son of Mary, was God.

"This house is the first of the two kiblah, the second of the mosques, the third of the hérameïn; it is not towards it that the people come in crowds after the two mesdjed; it is towards it that the fingers are pointed after the two places. [I suppose Mecca and Medina.] If you were not of the number of the servants whom God has chosen, certes he would not have favoured you particularly by this advantage which has been granted to no other brave men, the honour of which no one can dispute with you; how fortunate you are in being the soldiers of an army which has made manifest the miracles of the prophet, which has made the expeditions of Abou Bekr, the conquests of Omar, &c. God has rewarded you by the best of rewards in that which you have done for his prophet. He has been grateful for the courage you have shown in punishing rebels; the blood which you have shed for him has been acceptable to him; it has introduced you into the Paradise which is the abode of the blessed; acknowledge, then, the value of this blessing, offer up to him necessary thanksgivings; for God has shown for you a marked beneficence in granting you this blessing, in selecting you for this expedition. For the gates of Heaven have been opened for this conquest; its splendour has cast a light which has penetrated even to the deepest darkness; the angels who approach the Divine Majesty have rejoiced at it; the eye of the prophets and the messengers has beheld it with joy. Since, by the favour of God, you are the army which will conquer Jerusalem at the end of time, the troop which will raise the standards of the faith after the destruction of the prophecy.

This house, is it not that of which God spoke in his book? for he says, Be he praised who made his servant travel by night,' &c.; is this not the house which the nations have revered; towards which the prophets came, in which the four books sent from God have been read? Is this not the house for which God stopped the sun, under Joshua, and retarded the march of day, in order that his conquest should be easy, and should be accelerated? Is this not the house which God committed to Moses, and which he commanded his people to save; but, with the exception of two men, these people would not; God was angry against these people, and cast them into the desert, to punish them for their rebellion.

"I praise the God who has conducted you to the place from which he banished the children of Israel; and yet these were distinguished above other nations. God has seconded you in an enterprise in which he had abandoned other nations that had preceded you; which has caused there to be but one opinion amongst you, whilst formerly opinions differed; rejoice that God has named you among those who are near him, and has made of you his own army, after you became his soldiers by your own free will. The angels (who were sent towards this house) have thanked you for having brought hither the doctrine of the unity.

Now the powers of the heavens pray for you, and pour benedictions upon you. Preserve this gift in you, by the fear of God. Whoever possesses it is saved. Beware of the passions, of disobedience, of falling back, of flying from an enemy. Are you eager to take advantage of the opportunity to destroy what anguish remains? Fight for God as you ought; sacrifice yourselves to please him, you his servants, since you are of the number of the elect. Beware that the devil do not come down among you again, and that irreligion introduce not itself into your hearts. Did you figure to yourselves that your swords of steel, your chosen horses, your untiring perseverance, have gained you this victory? No, it was God; it was from him alone that your success came. Beware, servants of God after having obtained this victory, of becoming disobedient and rebellious; for then you will be like her who cut to pieces that which she had spun, or like him to whom we have sent our verses, and who has rejected them; the devil has laid hold of him, and he has wandered from the faith. The holy war! the holy war! that is the best of your worships, the most noble of your customs; help God, and he will help you; hold to God, and he will hold to you; remember him, and he will remember you; do good towards him, and he will do good towards you; endeavour to cut off every diseased member, to destroy even to the last enemy; purify the rest of the earth of those nations with whom God and his messenger are angry. Lop off the branches of impiety, and fear, for already the days have grown. Vengeance of Mussulman attacks, of the Mahometan nation. God is great: he gives conquests, he degrades impiety; learn that this is a great opportunity—seize it; it is a prey, cast yourselves upon it; it is a booty, get possession of it. It is an important business, apply your whole means to it, give yourselves up to it entirely; put the battalions of your tribes on the march for it. For this business draws towards its end, and the treasuries are filled with wealth. God has already given you the victory over these vile enemies. These enemies were equal to you, or perhaps more numerous than you; but however that might be, he has manifested that one of you is worth twenty other men. God will aid you as you cause his orders to be obeyed, and abstain from that which he has prohibited. He will strengthen all us Mussulmans by a victory; if God helps you, you have no other conqueror to fear; but if he withdraw his help from you, who will be he that shall help you after him?"

Then the preacher prayed for the Imaun Alnassir, the caliph, and said: "O God! eternalize the sultan, thy servant, who humbles himself before thy majesty, who is grateful for thy blessings, who cherishes the remembrance of thy favour. Preserve thy keen sword, thy brilliant star, who protects and defends thy religion, who defends the harem! the seid, the triumphant prince, the *reuniter* of the word, of the faith (that is to say, who has so acted that the Mussulman princes, with one accord, with one unanimous feeling, marched against the infidels); the exterminator of the cross, the good of the state and of religion (salah eddounia wa eddyn). The sultan of the Mussulmans, the purifier of the sacred house, Aboul Modhaffer Yous-ben-Ayoub, the verifier of the power of the emir of the believers; O God! grant that thy angels may surround his throne; make good the reward due to that which he has done for the religion of Abraham; reward his actions for the sake of the Mussulman religion. O God! prolong for Islamism," &c.

–– –– ––

No. 15.

Bull of Gregory VIII., A.D. 1187.

Gregory, bishop, servant of the servants of God; to all those of the worshippers of Our Lord Jesus Christ to whom these letters shall come, health and the apostolic benediction.

Having learnt the terrible severity of the judgments which the divine hand has exercised over Jerusalem and the Holy Land, we have been, we and our brethren, penetrated with such horror, afflicted with such lively grief, that, in the painful uncertainty of what it would be best for us to do on this occasion, we have only been able to partake the sorrows of the psalmist, and to exclaim with him, "Lord, the nations have invaded thy heritage, they have profaned thy holy temple; Jerusalem is no more than a desert, and the bodies of the saints have served as pasture to the beasts of the earth, and to the birds of the heavens." For in consequence of the intestine dissensions which the wickedness of men, by the suggestion of the demon, had given birth to in the Holy Land, behold Saladin, without any warning, at the head of a formidable army, comes pouring down upon the city. The king and the bishops, the Templars and the Hospitallers, the barons and the people, hasten to the rescue, bearing with them the cross of the Lord, that cross which, in memory of the passion of Christ, who was nailed to it, and which thus purchased the redemption of the human race, was regarded as the most secure rampart to be opposed to the attacks of the infidels. The conflict begins; our brethren are conquered, the holy cross falls into the hands of the enemies; the king is made prisoner, the bishops are massacred, and such of the Christians as escape death, cannot avoid slavery. Flight saves a few, and very few; and these tell us that they saw the whole of the Templars and Hospitallers perish before their eyes. We think it useless, beloved brethren, to inform you how, after the destruction of the army, the enemies spread themselves over the whole kingdom, and rendered themselves masters of most of the cities, with the exception of a small number, which still resist. It is here we are compelled to say with the prophet, "Who will change my eyes into a fountain of tears, that I may weep night and day the massacre of my people!" Nevertheless, far from allowing ourselves to be cast down, or to be divided, we ought to be persuaded that these reverses are only to be attributed to the anger of God, against the multitude of our sins; that the most efficacious manner of obtaining the remission of them is by tears and groans, and that at last, appeased by our repentance, the mercy of the Lord will raise us up again, more glorious for the abasement into which he has plunged us. Who could, I say, withhold his tears in so great a disaster, not only according to the principles of our divine religion, which teaches us to weep with the afflicted, but further, from simple motives of humanity, when considering the greatness of the peril, the ferocity of the barbarians, thirsting for the blood of Christians, their endeavours to profane holy things, and to annihilate the name of the true God, in a land in which he was born; pictures which the imagination of the reader will represent to him better than we can paint them. No; the tongue cannot express, the senses cannot comprehend what our affliction has been, what that of the Christian people must be, at learning that this land is now suffering as it suffered under its ancient inhabitants; this land illustrated by so many prophets, from which issued the lights of the world; and, what is still greater and more ineffable, where was incarnate God the creator of all things; where, by an infinite wisdom, and an incomprehensible mercy, he consented to subject himself to the infirmities of the flesh, to suffer hunger, thirst, the punishment of the cross, and by his death and glorious resurrection, effected our salvation. We ought not then to attribute our disasters to the injustice of the judge who chastises, but rather to the iniquity of the people who have sinned; since we see in Scripture that, when the Jews returned to the Lord, he put their enemies to flight, and that one of his angels was sufficient to annihilate the formidable army of Sennacherib. But this land has devoured its inhabitants; it has not been able to enjoy a long tranquillity, and the transgressors of our divine law have not preserved it long; all thus giving this example and this instruction to such as sigh after the heavenly Jerusalem, that it is only by the practice of good works, and amidst numerous temptations, that they can attain it. The people of these countries had beforehand reason to fear that which has now happened to them, when the infidels got possession of a part of the frontier cities. Would to God that they had then had recourse to penitence, and that they had appeased, by a sincere repentance, the God they had offended! for the vengeance of that God is always only delayed. He does not surprise the sinner; he gives him time for repentance, until at length his exhausted mercy gives place to his justice. But we who, amidst the dissolution spread over this country, ought to give our attention, not only to the iniquities of its inhabitants, out to our own, and to those of all Christian people, and who ought, still further, to dread the loss of those of the faithful that still remain in Judæa, and the ravages with which the neighbouring countries are threatened, amidst dissensions which prevail between Christian kings and princes, and between villages and cities; we who see nothing on all sides but scandals and disorders, we ought to weep with the prophet, and repeat with him, "Truth and the knowledge of God are not upon earth; I see nothing reign in their place but falsehood, homicide, adultery, and thirst for blood." It is everywhere urgent to act, to efface our sins by voluntary penance, and, by the help of true piety, to return to the Lord our God, in order that, corrected of our vices, and seeing the malice and ferocity of the enemy, we may do for the support of the cause of the Lord, as much as the infidel does not fear to attempt to do every day against him. Think, my beloved brethren, for what purpose you came into this world, and how you ought to leave it; reflect that you will thus pass through all that concerns you. Employ, then, the time you have to dispose of in good actions, and in performing penance; give that which belongs to you, because you did not make yourself, because you have nothing which is yours alone, and because the faculty of creating a hand-worm is above all the powers of the earth. We will not say, reject us, Lord, but permit us to enter into the celestial granary that you possess; place us amidst those divine fruits, which dread neither the injuries of time nor the attempts of thieves. We will labour to reconquer that land upon which the truth descended from heaven, and where it did not refuse to endure the opprobrium of the cross for our salvation. We will not hold in view either a love of riches or a perishable glory, but your holy will, O my God! you who have taught us to love our brothers as ourselves, and to consecrate to you those riches, the disposal of which, with us, is so often independent of thy will. It is not more astonishing to see this land struck by the hand of God, than it is to see it afterwards delivered by his mercy. The will of the Lord alone can save it; but it is not permitted to ask him why he has acted thus. Perhaps it has been his will to prove us, and to teach us that he who, when the time of repentance is come, embraces it with joy, and sacrifices himself for his brothers, although he may die young, his life comprises a great number of years. Behold with what zeal the Maccabees were inflamed for their holy law, and the deliverance of their brethren, when they precipitated themselves, without hesitation, amidst the greatest perils, sacrificing their wealth and their lives, and exhorting each other, mutually, by such speeches as these: "Let us prepare ourselves, let us show ourselves courageous, because it is better to perish in fight than to behold the evils of our nation, and the profanation of holy things." And they only lived under the law of Moses, whilst you have been enlightened by the incarnation of our Lord Jesus Christ, and by the example of so many martyrs. Show courage, then; do not fear to sacrifice these terrestrial possessions which can last but so short a time, and in exchange for which we are promised eternal ones, above the conception of the senses, and which, in the opinion of the apostle, are worthy of all the sacrifices we can make to obtain them.

We promise, then, to all those who, with a contrite heart and an humble mind, will not fear to undertake this painful voyage, and who will be determined so to do by motives of a sincere faith, and with the view of obtaining the remission of their sins, a plenary indulgence for their faults, and the life everlasting which will follow.

Whether they perish there, or whether they return, let them know that, by the mercy of the all-powerful God, and by the authority of the holy apostles Peter and Paul, and by our own, they are liberated from all other penance that may have been imposed upon them, provided always that they may have made an entire confession of their sins.

The property of the Crusaders and their families will remain under the special protection of the archbishops, bishops, and other prelates of the Church of God.

No examination shall be made as to the validity of the rights of possession of a Crusader, with regard to any property whatever, until his return or his decease be certain; and till that time his property shall be protected and respected.

He cannot be compelled to pay interest, if he owe any to anybody.

The Crusaders are not to march clothed in sumptuous habits, with dogs, birds, or other such objects, which only display luxury and ostentation; but they are to have what is necessary, are to be clothed simply, and are rather to resemble men who are performing a penance, than such as are in search of a vain glory.

Given at Ferrara, the 4th of the calends of November.

[Then follows the ordinance for a general fast, to appease the anger of God, in order that he may enable them to recover Jerusalem.]

The anger of the Supreme Judge being never so effectively appeased as when we seek to subdue our carnal desires, —

Consequently, as we make no doubt that the misfortunes which have recently fallen upon Jerusalem and the Holy Land from the invasion of the Saracens, have been produced by the crimes of the inhabitants and those of the Christian people; we, with the unanimous advice of our brethren, and the approbation of a great number of bishops, order that, from this day, for five years, the fast of Lent shall be observed every Friday, during the whole day.

We further order, that in all places where divine service is celebrated, it shall be at nine o'clock, and that from the Advent of the Lord to his Nativity.

Every one, without distinction, abstaining from eating flesh on the Friday and Saturday of each week, we and our brethren further interdict the use of it on Tuesdays among ourselves, unless personal infirmities, a festival, or some other good cause excuse us; hoping by this means that the Lord will be appeased, and will leave us his benediction.

Such are our regulations on this subject, and whoever shall infringe them shall be considered as a transgressor of the fast of Lent.

Given at Ferrara, the 4th of the calends of November.

— — — —

No. 16.

The Council of Paris, held in 1188, under the Pontificate of Pope Clement III. The Tenths, called Saladin Tenths, were then decreed, to provide for the Expenses of the War against Saladin, King of the Turks.

In the month of March of the year of grace 1188, towards Mid-Lent, a general council, to which were summoned the archbishops, bishops, abbots, and barons of the kingdom, was convoked at Paris by King Philip. An infinite number of soldiers and people there took the cross. It was resolved, with the consent of the clergy and the people, that, considering the urgent wants then experienced (the king having nothing more at heart than the undertaking of the voyage to Jerusalem), a general tenth, from which no one should be exempt, which was named the *Saladin tenth*, [135] should be pre-levied for that year only.

Establishment of the Tenth. — In the name of the holy and indivisible Trinity, greeting. It is ordered by us, Philip, king of France, with the advice of the archbishops, bishops, and barons of our dominions, that the bishops, prelates, and clerks of the churches convoked, and the soldiers who have taken the cross, shall not be troubled for the repayment of the debts they may have before contracted, with Jews or Christians, until two years have revolved, reckoning from the first festival of All Saints which shall follow the decree of our said lord the king: so that at the following All Saints the creditors shall receive a third of that which is due to them, and thus, from year to year, at the same period, until the entire acquittal of the debt. The interests for anterior debts shall run no longer, dating from the day on which the debtor shall have taken the cross. The Crusader who is a legitimate heir, son or son-in-law of a soldier not a Crusader, or of a widow, shall procure for his father or his mother the advantage granted by the present decree, provided he be not in the enjoyment of other revenues than that arising from the labour of his father and mother; but if their son or son-in-law was not at their charge, or even if he did not bear arms and the cross, they shall not enjoy the said advantage; but the debtors who shall have lands and revenues, within the fortnight which follows the approaching festival of John the Baptist, shall point out to his creditors the lands and revenues upon which they shall be able to recover their debts, on the terms above expressed, and according to the form prescribed, by means of the lords in the jurisdiction of whom these lands shall be. The lords shall have no power to oppose this consignment, short of satisfying the creditor themselves. Those who shall not have lands or revenues enough to form such a consignment, shall furnish their creditors guarantees and securities for the acquittal of their debts at the term fixed; if within the fortnight after the festival of St. John the Baptist, they have not satisfied their creditors by a consignment of lands, or by guarantees and securities, if they have no property, as it has been ordered, they shall not enjoy the privilege granted to others. If a clerk or a crusade soldier be the debtor of a clerk or of a crusade soldier, he shall not be troubled before the next All Saints, provided he can furnish him with a good guarantee for payment at that time.

If one of the Crusaders, eight days before the Purification of the Virgin, or later, consign, in favour of his creditor, some money, some work, or some bill, the creditor cannot be forced on that account to consider him liberated. The bargain by which a man has bought of another Crusader the annual produce of an estate is good and valid. If a soldier or a clerk has engaged or consigned his lands or his revenue for some years to another Crusader, or to a clerk or a soldier not crossed, the debtor, for that year, shall collect the produce of the lands or the revenues; but the creditor, after the expiration of the years during which he has enjoyed the consignment or the guarantee, shall continue to enjoy it a year longer, to compensate for the loss of the first year; so that, however, the creditor shall have for that first year half of the revenue for the cultivation, if he has cultivated the vines and the lands which were consigned to him as security. All bargains which shall have been made eight days before the Purification of the Virgin, or which shall be made after, shall be authentic. It will be necessary for all the debts coming within the favour of the present decree, that the debtor shall give a guarantee as good, or even better than that which he had given before. If the parties are not agreed upon the goodness of the guarantee, it shall be referred to the lord of the creditor; if he do not answer to this demand, the affair shall be taken before the suzerain. If the lords or princes under whose direction the creditors or the debtors may be, refuse to give their hand to the execution of that which is ordered by the present decree, on account of the privileges given to the debtor, or of the consignments to be made, and if, warned by the metropolitan or the bishop, they have not done it within forty days, they will be liable to excommunication; but if the lord or the suzerain make it his duty to show, in presence of the metropolitan or the bishop, that he has not failed in this formality towards the creditor, or even the debtor, and that he is ready to execute what is ordered, the metropolitan or the bishop cannot excommunicate him. No Crusader, whether clerk, soldier, or other, shall be held responsible but for debts already demanded legally at the time at which they shall have taken the cross; he shall not be passible to others before his return from the Holy Land. They who are not Crusaders shall pay, at least this year, the tenth of all their property and revenues, except the monks of the order of Citeaux, of the Chartreux, of Fontevraud, and the lazar-houses, with regard to the property which belongs to them. Nobody shall meddle with the property of the communes, unless it be the lord of whom they hold. For the rest, every one shall retain the rights he had before in the commune. The grand justiciary of an estate shall always levy the tenths of it. Let it be observed, that they who are subject to pay the tenth, shall pay it upon all their goods and revenues, without beforehand subtracting their debts. It is not till after they have paid the tenth that they may pay their creditors from the remainder of their property; all laymen, as well soldiers as those that are subject to the *taille* (poll-tax, or something like land-tax), upon taking the oath, under pain of anathema, and clerks under pain of excommunication, shall pay the tenth. The soldier who is not crossed shall pay to his lord who is crossed, and of whom he holds, the tenth of his own property and of the fief which he holds of him. If he holds no fief of him, he will pay him the tenth of his own property, and will pay the tenth to those of whom he holds directly. If he holds of no lord, he will pay the tenth of his own property to him upon whose fief he lives. If a man possessing an estate in proper, finds upon his estate tenths belonging to another than to him to whom he owes them, and if the proprietor can prove that they legitimately belong to him, the former cannot retain these tenths. The crossed soldier, a legitimate heir or son-in-law of a non-crossed soldier, or of a widow, will receive the tenth of his father or mother. Nobody shall lay hands on the property of archbishops, bishops, chapters, or churches that depend upon them, but the archbishops, bishops, chapters, or churches themselves. If the bishops collect the tenths, they shall remit them to those who are appointed to receive them. The Crusader subject to the *taille*, or to the tenth, and who shall refuse to pay them, shall be arrested, and placed at the disposal of him to whom he is indebted. He who has arrested him cannot be excommunicated for doing so. He who shall pay his tenth with readiness, according to the law and without constraint, shall be recompensed by God.

— — — —

No. 17.

Note upon the Greek Fire, taken from the Manuscript Life of Saladin, by Renaudot.

It is certain that the artificial fire called *Greek fire, sea fire,* or *liquid fire,* the composition of which is found in the Greek and Latin historians, was very different from that which the Orientals began at this time to make use of, and the effect of which was the more surprising, from the cause of it being entirely unknown; for whereas the first was prepared of wax, pitch, sulphur, and other combustible materials, there was nothing in this but naphtha or petrol, of which there were springs near Bagdad, like those of which the ancients speak, near Ecbatana and on the frontiers of Media. All naturalists agree that this bituminous matter takes fire very easily, and that it is impossible to extinguish it with anything but sand, vinegar, and urine. An experiment was made with it before Alexander, by lighting a great quantity of it by trains, which burnt for a long time without being able to be extinguished; a buffoon, even, having been rubbed with it, the fire injured him so seriously that there was great difficulty in saving his life. And yet, notwithstanding the ancients were acquainted with it, it is not known that they frequently employed it in war, nor that it entered into the composition of the true Greek fire, invented, according to common opinion, by Callinichus, under Constantine Pogonatus, but which is, notwithstanding, more ancient by many centuries. Thus it is very probable that the Orientals, not having made any use of it before this siege, Ebn-el-Mejas employed it successfully as a new invention; and that the Christians, on account of the resemblance, called it the Greek fire, from the idea they conceived that it might be the same as that with which the whole Levant was acquainted. This fire having been in use for the defence of besieged places, was called *oleum incendiarium, oleum medicum*; and it was employed in the time of Valentinian, under whom Vegetius, a military author, who gives the composition of it, wrote his work. Æneas, an ancient author quoted by Polybius, also speaks of it in his *Treatise upon the Defence of Cities,* and Callinichus added nothing new to it, except the machines, or copper pipes, by means of which they employed it for the first time at sea, and burnt the Arabian fleet near Cyzicus. The Greeks continued afterwards to use these machines, with which they armed their fire-ships, and never communicated the knowledge of it to any other nation; any more than did the Mahometans their naphtha fire, when they had once learned the practice. Thus the names became confounded by the ignorance of the two nations; the Greeks calling, with much reason, the artificial fire of the Mussulmans, *Media fire*, and the Latins comprising both under the name of *Greek fire*; as the Orientals afterwards called gunpowder *naphtha*, from the relation they found between it and that fire which it made them abandon.

— — — —

No. 18.

Memoir upon the Forest of Saron, or the Enchanted Forest of Tasso.

Most of the places in Palestine, in which battles were fought between the Franks and the Saracens, were, towards the end of the eighteenth century, the theatre of many conflicts between the French and the Mussulmans. The French, in 1799, put the Syrians to flight in the neighbourhood of Arsur, on the same spot where Richard gained a great victory over Saladin. We feel pleasure in presenting to our readers the very interesting Memoir of M. Paultre, who made the campaign in Syria, and who identified the forest of Saron, or the enchanted forest of Tasso.

"The 24 Ventose, an 7 (14th of March, 1799), our army, leaving Jaffa to march upon St. Jean d'Acre, after an hour and a half's progress, arrived on the edge of a torrent, which flowed from Lidda, and fell into the sea at a short distance on our left; the crossing of this torrent presented many difficulties to our artillery.

"Before us was a plain of about a league in width, but which, on our left, extended to the sea, where it was inclosed by *dunes*, or small sand-hills, covered with verdure; whilst on our right, it extended for two or three leagues, and was lost in the declivities of the mountains of Gofna and Naplouse, called by the Hebrews, Mount Garizim. The torrent we had just passed was the ancient boundary between the tribes of Dan and Benjamin with that of Ephraim, on the territory of which we were about to march.

"The plain appeared to be closed before us by a wooded ascent, extending from the principal chain which ran along the plains of Palestine, on our left, quite to the seashore; our route was through these woods, and it would have been dangerous to approach them without having reconnoitred them; the more so from our knowing the Syrian army to be at a small distance from us, and it might be expected they had thrown some parties into them, to oppose our passage, and take the advantage which difficult and covered places might offer them. This forest, placed upon a very elevated hill, presented to us a picturesque aspect, which pleasingly recalled the sites of our beautiful wooded countries of France.

"The French general availed himself of the moment which the passage of the torrent retarded the march of the army, to have the different issues of this forest reconnoitred by our vanguard, and to assure himself that the roads were practicable. At nine o'clock in the morning, the general who commanded the cavalry informed him that the route was free, that there was no party of the enemy in the woods, and that the army might advance with safety. According to this advice, the march was resumed, and after proceeding for an hour over a level plain, we began to enter the wood, and ascend a hill, where the road became very difficult for our pieces and our carriages. The route we followed appeared to be very little frequented, although our guides assured us it was the high road to Jaffa, St. Jean d'Acre, and Damascus. Sands, rocks, bushes, ravines, and steep hills, rendered our march very painful; it might have been said that routes had never been traced in these cantons; and I cannot better compare that which we followed than to the cross-roads of our least-frequented forests in France. Branches of trees, whole trunks, fallen from age or accident, with enormous rocks, at every step barred the way, and our sappers had infinite trouble to clear a passage for our carriages and loaded camels. If the enemy had known how to take advantage of the circumstance, and had augmented our difficulties by some redoubts or barricades of trees, it would have been impossible for us to have forced the passage; some parties of infantry, or only some armed peasants, would have been able to do us much injury, and entirely have stopped the march of our army, in places already nearly impassable by their nature. But happily, we had to do with enemies who had no suspicion of even the first elements of military tactics; for, whilst our columns traversed with so much difficulty these woody and rocky mountains, where it would have been so easy to stop us, and fight us with advantage, they awaited us peaceably, four leagues further on, in a clear plain, where our artillery and our manœuvres gave us every advantage over them; as they had good reason to know on the morrow. After a painful march of two leagues, across the forest, the army halted on issuing from the wood, and took up a position on the northern side of the hill, near the village of Meski, where our headquarters were established. A torrent flowed at a small distance in front of our position; and our light troops, who had already passed it, informed us that they could perceive, in a vast plain which extended from the side of St. Jean d'Acre, parties of Syrian and Mameluke cavalry, which indicated the neighbourhood of the enemy's army. Dispositions were then taken to keep us in readiness, in case they should march to attack us; but the evening and the night passed without a blow being struck; and, on the morrow, after having crossed the torrent without opposition, we presented ourselves before them in battle-array in the plain of Quoquoun, at the foot of the mountains of Naplouse, and, after a slight affair, we drove them back to the plain of Esdrelon, whence they effected their retreat upon St. Jean d'Acre.

"Description of the Forest of Saron.—The woods we had just crossed are known in the country under the name of the Forest of Saron; they extend over a vast hill, which is one of the western counterforts of the chain which separates the valley of the Jordan from the plains of Palestine, and which is itself a prolongation of Mount Libanus. This hill, designated by the Hebrews, Mount Saron, is detached from the principal chain below the city of Naplouse, and extends to the sea, where it terminates by low rocks and hills, between Jaffa and Arsouf, the ancient Apollonius; it may be of eight or nine leagues in length, from Mount Garizim, where it quits the principal chain, to the seashore; its mean width is between two and three leagues, and its height is progressive, from Naplouse to the shore of the Mediterranean, where it terminates in rocks and hills of a moderate height. It is bordered on the north by the torrent of Arsouf (Naher-el-Hadder), which has its source below Naplouse, in Mount Garizim; passes near the ruins of ancient Antipatris, and falls into the sea near Arsouf, after a course of seven or eight leagues. To the south, it is parallel with the torrent of Lidda, the ancient Disopolis, which rises in Mount Acrabatene, off Jericho, near Gofna and Gazer, passes Lidda, and falls into the sea at about a league north of Jaffa, after a course of from eight to ten leagues. These two torrents flow parallel with each other, and make almost the same turns, being directed by the declivity of the same hill. The mean distance between their beds is from five to six leagues, which was the width of the land of the ancient tribe of Ephraim, upon the centre of which extended Mount Saron, whose base, two or three leagues wide, terminates at these torrents, by two little lateral plains, of a league in width, or thereabouts.

"The forest covers the side of the hill, from the principal chain to within three-quarters of a league of the seashore; which gives it a length of from seven to ten leagues, and from two to three in width. The chain of Mounts Acrabatene and Garizim appeared to me barren, or covered only with brushwood. The declivities of Mount Saron are more steep and broken on the north than on the south side; its base is a limestone rock, which, in many places of the forest, rises above the surface in great blocks, heaped one upon another. In general, I cannot better compare the sites of this part of Palestine, than to those of the environs of Fontainebleau. The forest of Saron is composed solely of oaks, of the species designated by the ancients, *Quercus cerrus*; its leaves are more smooth and less indented than those of our common oaks. The capsule of the acorns is of very large dimensions; I have seen many of from ten to twelve lines in diameter, at their opening, and which had contained acorns of that size; the scales or shells which cover this capsule were not rounded and placed one upon another, as with that of the oaks of Burgundy, but were terminated in points, and bent outwards in a volute form, or like little hooked points, which has obtained for this oak the name of *Quercus cunita*; the leaves were covered with those tubercles, known in commerce as gall-nuts. These oaks did not appear to me to be susceptible of gaining any considerable size; most of them, although announcing great age, might be embraced by a single man, and had, at most, a square of from seven to eight inches. The trunk was knotty and not very straight, and in few cases was more than from twenty-five to thirty feet high; their top was rather orbicular than pyramidal, like that of our apple and chestnut-trees of Europe. Their bark was, however, more smooth and less furrowed than that of our oaks of the same age. In general, the growth of these trees was nearly like that in the gravelly woods of the dry and elevated coasts of Lower Burgundy, and I believe that the same cause, want of depth of vegetable earth and moisture, may produce this resemblance, although under different climates. And yet I suspect the wood to be very hard, and of good quality; but being knotty, twisted, and of small size, it can be of very little use for building purposes: thus, Solomon, to build his temple, was obliged to get his timber from Libanus, whilst the forest of Saron was at the very gates of Jerusalem. Our first Crusaders, at the time of the siege of the holy city, being obliged to bring thither the wood for the construction of their machines and towers of attack, complained that this forest could only furnish them with pieces of small dimension, which rendered their building labours long and difficult. Perhaps, since that period, there has been no occasion for having recourse to this forest, which now is only used by the inhabitants of the neighbourhood, who cut, on its outskirts, the wood they stand in need of. The government takes no notice of a property which can be turned to no public profit; considering the difficulty of transporting squared timber, in a country where carriages are not used, and where everything is carried upon the backs of camels; besides, so little wood is used for firing in hot climates, that this forest cannot have much value for that purpose even.

"I have now to prove that this forest of Saron was that in which our first Crusaders, at the siege of Jerusalem in 1099, went to cut their timber for the construction of the machines and towers they employed in the attack of the city.

"According to William of Tyre, it was a Syrian who pointed it out to the duke of Normandy and the count of Flanders. This historian places it at a distance of seven or eight miles from Jerusalem, and remarks that the trees of this forest being of small growth, and not capable of furnishing the strong timber of which they stood in need, the difficulty of procuring any other in a country in which woods were very rare, obliged them to form these machines of pieces fastened together, which required much time and labour.

"Casu affuit quidam fidelis indigena natione Syrus, qui in valles quasdam secretiores, sex aut septem ab urbe distantes milliaribus quosdam de principibus direxit, ubi arbores, etsi non ad conceptum opus aptas penitùs, tamen ad aliquem modum bonas invenerunt plures."

William of Tyre is mistaken in the distances, when stating this forest to be six or seven miles from Jerusalem, whilst it is really ten or eleven leagues from it. He places it likewise in a deep valley, which could only be correct if considered with reference to the mountains of Gosna and Naplouse, from which the Crusaders might have descended to cut the wood of which they stood in need.

"Raoul of Caën, equally a contemporary historian, is more exact in the placing of this forest, and proves to us in an irrefutable manner, that it was that of Saron in which the Crusaders went to cut the timbers for the siege; for he places it at the foot of the mountains of Naplouse, exactly where it now exists.

"Lucus erat in montibus, et montes ad Hyerusalem remoti ei, quà modò Neapolis, olim Sebasta, ante Sychar dictus est, propiores, adhuc ignota nostratibus via, nunc celebris et fermè peregrinatium unica." — *Rad. Cad.* cap. 121.

"In fact, to come from St. Jean d'Acre to Jerusalem, it is necessary to pass through this forest; and I do not know how the Crusaders could pass it without observing it, in their march from Antioch to the holy city. Apparently having followed the shores of the sea from Cæsarea to Jaffa, and the high hills that were on their left, prevented their seeing it.

"Le Perè Maimbourg does better; knowing that Palestine is a country in which woods have at all times been rare, in his History of the Crusades,' he doubts the existence of this forest, which is, to the best of my belief, the only one in these cantons.

"Tasso, whose poetical and rich imagination delighted in creating so many wonderful things, was not stopped by such trifling considerations, and in his *Jerusalem Delivered*, the forest of Saron has supplied him with one of the finest episodes of his poem.

"I must here hazard some ideas upon the origin of the name of the forest, of the city, and of the country of Saron. M. D'Anville, in his map of Palestine, gives to the part of the territory of the tribe of Ephraim, comprised between the torrent of Lidda and that of Apollonias, the name of *Saronas*, which he writes as the name of the country; and it is precisely on this spot that the forest of Saron exists, of which, perhaps, M. D'Anville had no kind of knowledge. He likewise places between these two torrents above Lidda, a city called Thamnath Sara, in a country which he denominates *Tamnitica*, which now forms part of the forest where Mount Saron again unites with the principal chain.

"In the map of the Holy Land, by M. Robert, after the manuscripts of the Sieurs Sanson, there is a city of Sarona, situated between Lidda and Antipatris, towards the centre of the present forest. He makes this city a royal city of the Hebrews. He places, as M. D'Anville does, the city of Thamnath Sara; and at a short distance to the north, a city of Ozensara.

"The resemblance of these different names leads me to think they may be all formed from the primitive *Sar*, which, in many languages, signifies oaks, woods, forests as Diodorus points out, in book v., when saying that the Gauls gave the name of *Saronides* to certain philosophers of their country, because they dwelt in forests of oaks, and taught under the shade of those trees. We have preserved this *sar* in the word *sarman*, the wood of the vine; in *serpe* (or *sarpe*, low Breton), an instrument to cut wood; *surbacane*, a perforated stick, to throw small arrows or other projectiles; *sarse*, a wooden cask; *esserter*, or *essarter*, to pull up bushes in a place about to be cultivated.

"I leave it to pens more versed than mine in the science of etymology, to follow this subject in a more learned and certain manner.

———

No. 19.

Ralph Dicet.

Ralph Dicet was of London, and lived, as it is said, in the reign of John; he was a man remarkable for his piety and learning.

He says: "In 1185, the king of England (Henry II.) convoked the conventual abbots, the counts and barons, near the Fountain of the Clerks, [136] at London.

"After having heard the patriarch, and the master of the Hospitallers, the king entreated all who were present to send to Jerusalem all the assistance in their power. They then deliberated whether it was proper for the king to go in person to Palestine, or whether he ought to remain in England, to govern it, as he had engaged to do, before the assembled church. The king promised to furnish succours, in men and money, to repress all violences and iniquities of every kind, and that equity and mercy should preside over all judgments. It appeared most prudent for the king to govern his kingdom with suitable moderation, and to defend it from the irruptions of the barbarians.

"In the same year, the kings of France and England had an interview at Gisors, where they received the cross from the hands of the archbishop of Tyre. It was agreed that all the French Crusaders should wear a red cross, those of England a white cross, and those of the counts of Flanders a green one. [137]

Ralph says that when the cross was taken in England, a general tenth upon all property was levied, for the assistance of Jerusalem. This levy was made with so much violence as to terrify both the clergy and the people. Under the title of alms, it was enforced with a spirit of exaction and rapacity.

After this observation, the historian places the letters patent of Philip, king of France, and Richard, king of England, which order that the Crusaders should set out from both countries in the octave of Easter, under pain of excommunication and interdiction; and forbid any one to do injury to the Crusaders during their absence. These letters are dated 30th December.

Ralph Dicet's work terminates in the year 1199. It is excellent for dates, and for many passages of it.

— — — —

No. 20.

Ralph of Coggershall.

Ralph of Coggershall, an Englishman by birth, flourished about the year 1220, in the reign of Henry III., son of John. He was of the order of Citeaux. His merit and his learning raised him to the dignity of abbot of the monastery of Coggershall, in the county of Essex. He is the author of many works.

D. Martenne, when publishing Ralph's "Chronicon Anglicanum," is astonished, and apparently with reason, that the English, who are so jealous of the glory of their country, have shown such neglect for the works of this author, whom their scholars value so highly.

Ralph, like the other chroniclers, is dry and brief, and it is not before the invasion of Palestine by Saladin that he abandons the style of the chronicler to assume that of the historian.

After having spoken of the arrival of the kings of France and England in Sicily, of that which Richard did in the isle of Cyprus, of the victory which this prince gained over the Saracen vessels before landing at Acre, of the siege and reduction of that place, of the divisions which broke out between Philip Augustus and Richard, of the taking of several maritime cities by Richard, and of the death of the marquis of Montferrat, Ralph of Coggershall relates that the duke of Burgundy, left in Palestine by Philip Augustus, who had returned home, came to join Richard, in order to fight together against the enemies of Christ; and that it was resolved to go and besiege Jerusalem. He describes the victory which Richard gained over a rich caravan which was on its way to that city. He says, that while this prince was in his camp, before the castle of Ernald, and the duke of Burgundy, with his troops, was in the fortress of Betenoble, a spy came to warn the king that in the night he had heard some men and camels come down from the mountains, and that he had followed them. He added, that he had discovered they were sent by Saladin to the duke of Burgundy, and that the camels, to the number of five, were loaded with gold, silver, and silken vestments. The spy had orders from the king to take with him some of the king's guards, and lie in ambush for the messengers of Saladin on their return. All which he did; he surprised them, took them, and brought them to the king. Richard drew from one of them by torture the secret intrusted to them. He acknowledged that the sultan had sent them to the duke. On the following day Richard sent for the duke, the patriarch, and the prior of Bethlehem. He had a private conference with them, and swore, before them, on the Gospel, that he was ready to go with his army and besiege Jerusalem, or Babylonia, or Berytus, without the possession of which places the king could not be crowned. Richard, after having taken this oath, desired the duke to take his. The duke refused, because the Templars and the French had assured him he should incur the anger of Philip, if Richard, by their means, triumphed in Jerusalem. Richard flew into a great rage, treated the duke as a traitor, and reproached him with receiving presents from Saladin. The duke denied all he was accused of. Then Richard sent for the messengers of Saladin. When they had been introduced, and had revealed their secret, the king ordered his guards to shoot them to death with arrows in presence of the whole army; which was done, without the troops of Richard or of the duke knowing the cause of this severity, or whence these messengers came, or what they had done. The duke of Burgundy, much ashamed, immediately retired with his troops, and took the road to Acre. Richard, upon hearing of this retreat, instantly sent messengers to the guards of the city, forbidding them to allow any Frenchman to enter. The duke encamped without the walls. The king struck his camp on the following day; and, following the duke, he also pitched his tents on the outside of the city.

Ralph then gives long details of the battle of Jaffa, which took place soon after. As this battle is one of those in which the valour and skill of Richard were displayed with the greatest advantage, and as the historians we have followed in our account of the third crusade, have only presented us with inexact details of this event, we think it but justice to the lion-hearted king to give an extract from that which Ralph says of it.

Richard had been reposing with his army three days before Ptolemaïs, when he was informed that Saladin was besieging Jaffa with all his troops; and that the city would soon be taken, and the garrison slaughtered, if he did not afford the besieged prompt assistance. Richard, afflicted with this news, endeavoured to bring back the duke of Burgundy to sentiments of concord; but this prince rejected all his advances, and set out with his troops that same night for Tyre. Shortly after arriving there, he finished his life miserably in the delirium of a fever; which Ralph considers as a just chastisement from heaven Richard embarks with a part of his army, and trusts himself to the seas; but the vessels were driven towards the isle of Cyprus, by contrary winds and the fury of the waves, so that they who remained on land believed that the king had retreated secretly. This likewise accounts for some authors having said that Richard went to the isle of Cyprus. The king, and those who accompanied him, after having struggled against the winds and waves for three days, at length succeeded, by rowing obliquely, in anchoring with three vessels in the port of Jaffa.

Saladin, by repeated assaults, had already rendered himself master of the city, and had put to death all the infirm and the wounded. The garrison had retired into the castle, and were already thinking of surrendering by capitulation, when the patriarch, who went freely from one army to the other, told them that Saladin's soldiers had resolved to kill them all, to avenge their relations and friends, whom Richard had put to death without pity on several occasions; and that they would not escape death, if even Saladin should grant them permission to retire. In spite of this information, the garrison hesitated, and saw no hope of avoiding the fate which awaited them, when the vessels of the king appeared in the port. This sight restored their courage. On his part, Richard, perceiving that the fortress of the city was not taken, jumped on shore fully armed, followed by his troops, and like a furious lion, rushes amidst the hosts of enemies that cover the shore. He advances audaciously, through the arrows which pour upon him from all sides, cutting down all in his way. The Turks, unable to stand against such an attack, and believing that Richard had brought a more numerous army with him, precipitately abandoned the siege, and not without experiencing a great loss. They were so terrified, that nothing could stop them before they had got safely within the walls of Rœmula. The king, after this encounter, went boldly and pitched his tents under the walls of the city, in a plain near to Saint Abacue, for the Crusaders could not remain in the city on account of the odour arising from the dead killed on both sides, which had been placed, by mistake, by the side of a number of carcasses of pigs.

When it was announced to Saladin, on the following day, that Richard had arrived with only eighty soldiers, and the four hundred cross-bowmen who formed his guard, he broke into a great rage with his army, for having fled before so small a number. He immediately ordered his cavalry to return to Jaffa, and to bring him, the next day, the king alive and a captive.

That night Richard reposed tranquilly in his camp, suspecting nothing; when, at daybreak, the infidels surrounded his camp so completely, that there was no passage by which he could take refuge in the city. Three thousand Saracens entered Jaffa; and the Christians, awakened by noise and cries, were struck with terror at finding themselves enveloped on all sides.

At the sight of such a sudden danger, Richard quickly assumes his armour, mounts on horseback, and banishing all fear, appears, on the contrary, more bold in proportion with the number of his enemies. He animates his men to the fight; he tells them they ought not to fear death when they have to defend their religion, and avenge the insults offered to Christ; that it would be more glorious for them to fall for the law of Christ, and in falling, courageously to strike down his enemies, than to give themselves basely up to them, or to seek safety in a flight which was become impossible. Whilst addressing them thus, Richard ranged his companions in a close battalion, so that, during the combat, the enemy might be able to find no open space through which to break them. He then caused to be planted, at the foot of every one, tent-poles, which served them for a rampart. Whilst they were thus employed, as well as the time permitted, and that, on their side, the infidels, armed and waited, talking among themselves, one of the chamberlains of the king rushed from the city, and arrived at the camp, crying out with a lamentable voice, as it has been reported to us by Hugh de Nevil, who was in this battle, "Alas! my lord, we shall all perish; we have no resource left. A numberless multitude of pagans have got possession of the city, and we have before us troops as uncountable, who threaten us with death." The king, in great anger, commanded him to be silent; and swore he would strike off his head if he dared to speak such words before any one of the soldiers. Richard immediately harangued his troop afresh; he exhorted them not to be terrified by the numbers of the pagans; he told them he would go into the city to ascertain what was passing; and, taking with him six determined warriors and the royal standard, he intrepidly enters Jaffa, opens himself a road with sword and lance, precipitates himself upon the enemies, who are assembled in the public places, attacks them, cuts them down, kills them. The warriors who accompany him overturn all they meet, and slaughter them without mercy. The irruption of the king was so sudden and so violent, that most who fell were ignorant what power it was that destroyed them. The enemies fled before the king, who pursued them as flocks fly before a lion inflamed by hunger.

Richard having, by his incomparable valour, cut down or put to flight the infidels who were in the city, made some of the soldiers of the garrison, who had retired into the castle, come and take charge of the gates and walls of the place.

After this incredible victory, the king returned with his six warriors to the army. Nevertheless, he was much afflicted at having so few horses; for there were but six and a mule in all the camp. To animate his soldiers still further, Richard related to them what the Lord had done in the city, by means of his arm, and how so small a number had triumphed over such a host of enemies: "For this reason," exclaimed he, "let us invoke the aid of the all-powerful God, in order that he may to-day crush our enemies. Be sure to resist the first shock, and sustain courageously the violence of the first blows. Beware of breaking; for if separated, you will be torn to pieces like sheep, without strength and without defence. If, on the contrary, you can sustain the first charge without breaking, you will have nothing to fear from the courage of your enemies. You will triumph, with the help of God, over the enemies of Christ. But if I see any one of you show the least fear, or leave a passage for the enemy, or turn aside, I swear, by the all-powerful God, I will myself strike off his head."

When the king had thus exhorted and animated his men to the fight, all raised their lances, and, by their prayers, invoked the assistance of God; but whilst many among them, no doubt, were reflecting that they had nothing but a cruel death before them, the sound of trumpets and the noise of clarions announced the approach of the infidels, who came down upon the Christians like a torrent, with their lances directed towards them, and uttering loud and frightful cries. The Turks expected that the Christians would give way at the first charge; that they would disperse over the plain; that their ranks would be broken; and that they would allow themselves to be cut to pieces almost without resistance. But the Christian battalion remained firm and motionless, without yielding a foot to either the terror or the violence of the assault. The Turks wondered at this unheard of audacity in so small a number, and reining up their horses, retired backwards some distance, yet not so far but that they might touch each other with their lances on both sides. Not an arrow was discharged, not a javelin was thrown; they only threatened each other with gesture, voice, and countenance. The Turks remained thus for half an hour, and then returned to their first position, murmuring and talking to themselves. They drew back from the Christians nearly half a stadium. Upon seeing this, the king broke into loud laughter, crying, "Brave soldiers of Christ! did not I tell you so? Did not I tell you they would not dare to measure themselves with you, unless we attacked them first? They have shown us all their courage, and everything that they thought could inspire us with fear and terror. They thought to frighten us by their numbers, and that we should not dare to resist their first charge. They expected us to submit, like women, to their blows, and fly here and there over the plain. Cursed be he now who would seek to avoid their charge, or who would fear to measure himself with them. Sustain their assaults with courage, as you have just done, until, with the help of God, we triumph over them."

Richard had scarcely ceased to speak, when the infidels advanced afresh, uttering their cries, and sounding their trumpets; they, however, halted at a short distance from the Christians. The latter remaining motionless as before, and showing, if possible, greater intrepidity, the infidels returned a second time to their position, without venturing to strike a blow. They repeated this five or six times, from the first hour of the day to the ninth. Richard, who began to be tired of such long inactivity, and whose courage increased proportionately with the intrepidity of those around him, ordered his troop, when the infidels came down again, to launch some arrows and darts at them, and let them feel the points of their lances, so as to provoke them to fight. He commanded his cross-bowmen to march before the soldiers, and discharge their arrows, bolts, and javelins at the enemy, which was done; and when the Turks, according to their custom, advanced uttering hideous cries, and appeared ready to overwhelm the Christians, the latter attacked them with their lances, their swords, and all sorts of weapons, overthrowing them and killing them. The carnage soon produced cries of agony and disorder in the ranks of the enemy. Some were run through with lances, others were cast headlong from their horses; these were wounded in the head, those were pierced by arrows; and a vast number were slain by darts and javelins. The intrepid Richard, whose resplendent arms glittered like fire, and who had till that moment neither given nor received a wound, now all at once dashed amidst the infidel ranks, with his sword in one hand, and his lance in the other, [138] striking sparks from the helmets and armour of all he encountered, right and left. He rushed among the thickest of the enemy's battalions, without seeking to avoid their blows, and without ceasing to deal mortal ones. At one time he was surrounded by a hundred Saracens, who attacked him alone. He falls upon them; he strikes off the head of one at a blow; he divides the shoulders from the body of another; he cuts off the hand of this one, and the arm of that one; others he overthrows, and renders incapable of defence. The rest disperse, and seek to avoid his blows. Richard inspires such terror that no one dares to wait for him, no one dares encounter him. The soldiers of Richard follow their king as they would have followed their standard; they penetrate the enemy, slaughtering without compunction, all who either resist or fall in their way. The infidels fall with lamentable cries; striking the earth with head and feet, and their lives gush out with their blood. Although they attacked the Christians with vigour, and hurled a shower of darts, it pleased God, however, that not one of their blows should be mortal, and that in this fight not a single Christian should perish, with the exception of one soldier, who, separating himself from his comrades, met with the death he wished to avoid by flight. The soldiers to whom Richard had confided the guarding of Jaffa, admiring the invincible courage of the king and his companions, issued in a body from the city, and fell with vigour upon the Turks. The latter, pursued without any intermission by Richard and his little army, took to flight, after losing a great number of their men, and concealed themselves in holes and caves. [139]

Ralph, of Coggershall, after describing this astonishing victory, says that Richard being attacked by the plague, determined to return into Europe. He gives an account, in a few words, of the treaty made with Saladin. He says that that which confirmed the king of England in the resolution of leaving Asia, was the news he received of his brother John's attempts to usurp his authority in his kingdom. The battle of Jaffa was fought in the dog-days, and it was in the autumn that Richard set sail for Europe. The account which the author gives of the manner in which the king was made prisoner in Germany, is sufficiently curious to be repeated here. Ralph is the only one of the chroniclers we have analyzed who furnishes minute details on this subject.

King Richard, says he, with some of his people, was annoyed during six weeks, by a tempestuous sea. When he arrived within three leagues of Marseilles, and learnt that the Count de St. Gilles, and some other nobles, through whose states he must pass, had agreed to place ambushes for him, he resolved to return to England through Germany. He went back, and landed at the isle of Corfu. He found there two pirate vessels, which had had the audacity to attack his, and which his pilot recognised. Richard, on account of the courage and hardihood they had shown, made a bargain with the pirates, and agreed to go on board their vessels. He only took with him a small number of his people. These were Baldwin de Betune; Master Philip, the king's clerk; Anselm, his chaplain, who himself related to us all he saw and heard; and some knights of the Temple. They landed on the coast of Sclavonia, at a city named Gazara. They immediately sent a messenger to the neighbouring castle, to request of the lord, who was master of the province, and nephew to the marquis of Montferrat, liberty to pass through his states. The king, on his return, had purchased three rubies of a Pisan, for which he gave nine hundred byzants. He had had one of these rubies set in a gold ring; and he charged the messenger to offer this ring to the lord of the castle. The latter inquired the names of those who demanded the passage. The messenger replied that they were pilgrims returning from Jerusalem, and he named Baldwin de Betune, adding that it was a merchant called Hugh, who sent him the ring. The lord of the castle, after having for a long time examined the present, replied to the messenger, "His name is not Hugh, but Richard, king of England. I have sworn," added he, "that I will make prisoners of all pilgrims who come into this country, and that I will not receive any present from them; but on account of the value of this, and of the dignity of him who sends it, and who has honoured me thus without knowing me, I return you the ring, and I grant free liberty of passage." The messenger went and reported this answer to the king. The pilgrims, very little satisfied with the message, left the city secretly in the night, mounted upon horses they had purchased, and made the best of their way across the country. But the lord sent a spy after them, to follow their steps and arrest the king. When Richard entered a city in which dwelt the brother of the lord, the latter called to him a trustworthy person, named Roger d'Argenten, a Norman by birth, who had been with him twenty years, and to whom he had given his niece in marriage; and ordered him to go to all the houses in which pilgrims lodged, and endeavour to discover, by language, or by some other sign, if the king were not among them. He promised him half the city if he could arrest the prince. Roger, after a long search, discovered the king, who for a considerable time dissembled, and was only induced to reveal himself by the prayers and tears of Roger. The latter immediately advised Richard to steal away, and gave him the best horse he could procure. He then went to his master, and told him that the news of the arrival of Richard was false, and that it was only Baldwin de Betune and his companions, who were returning from pilgrimage. But the master flew into a great rage, and ordered them all to be arrested. The king had left the city secretly with William de l'Etang, and a servant who understood the German language. He travelled three days and three nights without taking any food. At last, pressed by hunger, he turned from his road, to enter a city called Ginana, in Austria, on the Danube. To complete his ill fortune, the duke of Austria was then at Ginana. The king's servant, on going to the market, displayed several byzants, and created suspicions by his discourse; he was arrested and interrogated. He answered that he served a rich merchant, whom he expected in three days. He was then released; and he went instantly to the king, relating to him what had happened, and advising him to depart without delay. But the king, who was fatigued, determined to rest for a few days. The servant, after going to the market to buy provisions, had one day the imprudence to carry with him the king's gloves, stuck in his girdle. These gloves were very remarkable, and the servant was again arrested. Being taken before a magistrate of the city, he was put to the torture, and threatened with having his tongue cut out if he did not at once reveal the truth. The servant yielding to the agony of the *question*, made the confession demanded of him. Information was instantly sent to the duke; the house in which the king lodged was surrounded, and he was summoned to surrender. The king declared he would only surrender to the duke himself. The latter arrived, and the king, making a few steps to meet him, gave up his sword to him. [140] The duke, highly elated, led away the king, whom he treated honourably. He afterwards placed guards about him, who never left him, night or day, but kept watch, with drawn swords in their hands.

After this recital, Ralph makes many sad reflections upon the captivity of Richard, which he can only explain as a secret judgment of God, so astonishing and deplorable does it appear to him, that a king who had escaped so many dangers in Syria, should become the prisoner of a Christian prince, without having an opportunity to defend himself or give battle. He follows the king through his captivity, and describes his deliverance and return to his dominions. He gives an account of what happened to this prince when he had regained his kingdom, and pursues his history to the time of his death, which was in 1229. Ralph has drawn such a portrait of Richard as cannot fail to interest our readers, on account of the prominent part which that king has played in the history of the crusades.

"We had reason to hope," says he, "that Richard, considering the liberality of his excellent mind and his great skill in the art of war, would be the model of Norman kings. In the early days of his reign he was affable to everybody; being well disposed in religious affairs, and inclined to listen to just demands; he immediately filled up the vacant bishoprics and abbeys. He promised to render justice to all. He restored to many, for sums of money, their charters, privileges, and liberties, or else renewed them. The money he thus obtained served as means for his voyage to Jerusalem. He quitted his kingdom almost immediately afterwards, and commenced his expedition with much devotion, great preparation, and infinite expense. God protected him throughout, and caused him to escape all the dangers of this war; and, by his help, the king wrested from the hands of the infidels a great portion of the Holy Land. God still evidently watched over him during his return and his captivity, and preserved him from the hands of new and numerous enemies. But when Richard was restored to his subjects, he forgot the victorious hand that had preserved him: in the maturity of age he took no pains to correct the vices which had disfigured his youth. He displayed so much harshness and obstinacy, that he tarnished by excessive severity all the virtues that had graced the commencement of his reign. He always turned a threatening eye upon those who talked to him of state affairs; he made reproaches or censures with a terrible air, and showed a furious countenance to those who did not satisfy his demands for money, or perform the promises they had made to pay him some. In private he was affable and winning, and even condescended to play or to joke. He was so greedy of money that he wished to empty every purse. He pressed the English to such a degree, in order to discharge the amount of his ransom, that he spared no order and no condition. Nevertheless, Hubert, archbishop of Canterbury and justiciary of the kingdom, mitigated, as much as he could, the effects of the cruel edicts of the king."

Ralph, in another part of his works, after having praised the new king of England for having restored to the ecclesiastical benefices their revenues and their titularies, adds, that Richard took great delight in the divine service, and particularly in the solemnities of religion. He says that his chapel was richly ornamented; that he accompanied, with his sonorous voice, and encouraged by presents, the singers of the church; but that from the *secrète* of the mass to the *post-communion*, he prayed in silence, and with an earnestness which nothing could disturb. He afterwards names two abbeys which he founded or repaired, both of the order of Citeaux; one was that of Bon-Port, in Normandy, in the diocese of Rouën; the other, that of the Pine, in the diocese of Poictiers.

———

No. 21.

The continuator of the history of William of Tyre relates nothing which is not found in the text, except a little trick which Saladin attempted to play off upon Richard, at the time of the battle of Jaffa, and which we think worthy of being presented to our readers. We quote the chronicle:—

"Saladin asked where the king of England was. They answered him, Sire, see him yonder on the ground, on foot, with his men.' How,' said Saladin, is the king on foot among his men; is he not ashamed?' Then Saladin sent him a horse, and charged the messenger to say, that such a one as he should not be on foot among his men in such danger. The sergeant performed the commands of his lord. He came to the king and presented to him the horse sent by Saladin. The king thanked him for it, and ordered one of his own sergeants to mount it and show its paces before him. After the sergeant had spurred the horse into a gallop, and wished to return towards his master, he found he could not; for the horse, in spite of all he could do, carried him away to the Saracen host. Saladin was much ashamed of this."

This chronicle, when speaking of the deliverance of Richard from his captivity, does not hesitate to say that it was by the advice of Philip Augustus, that such an enormous ransom was required, and that the king of France had a good share of it.

Another chronicler, Gauthier Vinisauf, says that Richard gave eight noble Turkish prisoners in exchange for William de Protelles (others name him Porcelot), who had saved his master, when taken by surprise, by throwing himself in the way of the Saracens, exclaiming, "I am King Richard."

––––

No. 22.

Extract from an anonymous Chronicle contained in the MSS. of the Sorbonne, No. 454, of the Thirteenth Century. [141]

Then the king Richard turned back, and directed his course as straight and as well as he was able towards Germany, where he landed, and, with a small train, wandered about till he came to Austria (Osterriche), where he was watched by spies, and known. When he fancied he was discovered, he took the dress of a servant, and set to work in the kitchen to turn the capons; but the spy knew him, and went and informed the duke; and when the duke heard it, he sent so many knights and people that they were much the stronger, and the king was taken and sent away to a fortress, and his companions to another; and the king was sent from castle to castle, so that no one knew where he was, nor did the soldiers who guarded him know who he was.

How Richard the King was taken out of Prison by Blondel the Minstrel.—We have told you how King Richard was put in prison by the duke of Austria, and that no one knew where he was except the duke and those he trusted. It happened that the king had for a long time entertained a minstrel, born near Artois, whose name was Blondel. This person declared to himself that he would seek his lord over the whole earth till he had found him; and set out, and wandered about from day to day, by land and water, until he had sought for a year and a half without hearing anything of the king. And it so happened that he entered into Austria, and chance led him straight to the castle where the king was confined. And the *Aubergiste*, near the castle was a widow woman, and he asked her to whom that castle belonged, which was so fine, so strong, and well placed. The hostess replied that "it belonged to the duke of Austria." "Pretty hostess," said Blondel, "is there any prisoner confined in it?" "Certes," said she, "there is one, who has been confined nearly four years, but we do not know who he is; they guard him very carefully, and we have no doubt he is a gentleman—somebody of high quality." When Blondel heard this he was infinitely delighted, and his heart whispered him that he had at length found him he sought; but he was careful not to allow the hostess to know this. That night he slept soundly, for his mind was at rest; and when the cock announced the day, he arose and went to the church to pray God to assist him. He then came to the castle, and addressed himself to the castellan, telling him he was a minstrel, and played upon the lute, and that he would willingly remain with him if it were agreeable to him. The castellan was a young and handsome knight, and said he would gladly retain him. Then Blondel was delighted, and went to fetch his lute and his wallet; and he exerted himself so that he greatly pleased the castellan, and became a favourite with his household. Here he remained all the winter without being able to make out who the prisoner was. At length, near the festival of Easter, as he was one day walking in the garden which surrounded the tower, examining it in all directions, in the hope of seeing the prisoner, whilst his thoughts were thus engaged, the king perceived Blondel, and, wishing to make himself known to him, called to his mind a song which they had made together, and which no one knew but the king and Blondel. So he began to sing the first verse of it in a loud and clear voice, for he sang very well. And when Blondel heard it, he became certain it was his lord; and his heart had never experienced such joy as that day. And he went from the orchard to the chamber in which he slept, and fetched his lute; then he began to play, and in his playing expressed his pleasure at having found his lord. Thus Blondel remained till Pentecost, and performed his part so well that nobody suspected him. Then Blondel went to the castellan, and said to him: "Sir, if agreeable to you, I would willingly return to my own country, for it is a long time since I left it." "Blondel, good brother," said the castellan, "you will not do so if you will take my advice; but remain where you are, and I will advance your fortunes." "Certes, sir," said Blondel, "I cannot remain on any account." When the castellan found that he could not detain him, he bade him farewell, and gave him a good new horse. Having left the castellan, Blondel travelled so quickly that he soon arrived in England, and informed the barons and the friends of the king where and how he had found him. When they heard this news they were much delighted, for the king was the bravest knight that ever wore spur. They then determined among themselves that they would send into Austria, to the duke, to procure the deliverance of the king; and selected two of the most valiant and prudent knights for the purpose. They travelled so quickly that they soon reached the duke of Austria, whom they found in his castle. They saluted him on the part of the barons of England, and said: "Sire, they pray and beseech you to take ransom for their lord; they will give you as much as you may require." The duke replied that he would consider of it. And when he had taken advice upon the matter, he said: "If you wish to recover your lord, you must bring two hundred thousand marks sterling; if not, say no more about it, for it will be time and trouble thrown away." Having received the answer, they bade farewell to the duke, and said they would report it to the barons. They then returned to England, and told the barons what the duke had said; and the barons replied that he should never be detained for that. Then they got together the ransom, and sent it to the duke, and the duke delivered the king to them; but not before he had given him good security that he would never molest him.

— — — —

No. 23.

Extract from a Journey made into the country of Wales by Baldwin, Archbishop of Canterbury.

We have spoken, in the seventh book, of the preaching of Archbishop Baldwin, and of the account written by Gerald the Welshman (Giraldus Cambrensis), known also under the name of *Barri*. We think we shall gratify our readers by giving an extract from this relation, which will furnish some idea of the manners of the inhabitants of Wales in the twelfth century. The preachers went first to Hereford and Radnor. In this latter city a bishop of the country and a monk of the order of Cluni took the cross; at the same time was enrolled Rhys, son of Gruffydh, prince of the southern part of Wales. Their example was followed by Eineon, son of Eineon Clyd, prince of Ekenia, and by several other inhabitants. Giraldus relates what had happened to the lord of Radnor, in the reign of Henry I. This nobleman entered a church, where, without respect to the sanctity of the place, he passed the night with his horses and hounds. Rising early, according to the custom of hunters, he found that he was struck blind, and was told that all his hounds were dead. He was conducted back to his castle by the hand, and when he had for a long time led a sad and an unhappy life, he determined to go to Jerusalem, in order that the light of the faith might not be extinguished within him. When arrived in Palestine, he proceeded to fight with the Saracens, and mounting a fiery horse, he rushed amidst the enemies' ranks, and expired with glory.

In the province of Warthrenion, near Radnor, an adventure no less miraculous was related among the people. Einon, son-in-law of Rhys, lord of the country, was one day hunting in the forests. One of his people struck a hind with an arrow. This hind, contrary to custom, had horns of twelve years, and as large as those of the male. This animal was considered as a prodigy of nature; but the hunter who had killed it instantly lost his right eye, was struck with paralysis, and remained during the rest of his life in a languishing state.

The people of this province held in reverence a stick which had belonged to St. Cyricus; this stick was crooked at both ends, in the shape of a cross, and was ornamented with gold and silver. It possessed the special virtue of curing the evil and humours of the neck. Those who were attacked by this sort of complaint, touched the stick, after having paid a denier. "It happened in our time," says Giraldus, "that a man suffering from the evil only placed a single obole before the stick, and the evil was only half cured; upon this the sick man offered a second obole, and was quite cured. Another man obtained his cure by promising a denier, but as he did not perform his promise, his evil returned, and did not entirely disappear until he had offered three deniers."

Near Eleiven, in the church of Glascum, was a bell, which was said to have been that of St. David's. A woman, to liberate her husband, who was shut up in a neighbouring castle, carried thither the bell, which she had secretly taken from St. David's church; but the castellans would not deliver the husband, and retained the bell: the castle was consumed during the night by a miraculous fire, which spared nothing but the wall against which the bell was suspended. An almost similar miracle happened at the little village of Luel. The church, which had been set fire to, was entirely consumed, with all it contained, with the exception of the box which contained the *host*.

In the province of Elevein two great lakes burst their banks, one of which was constructed by nature, and the other by the hand of man. The natural dyke changed its place, and the lake appeared two thousand paces off, in a valley, where it preserved its fish. Giraldus, when relating this singular circumstance, adds, "that in Normandy, some time before the death of Henry II. all the fish in a lake were beheld fighting during a whole night, and that crowds were drawn together to witness this strange spectacle. The next morning, not a single fish was left alive."

In the country of Haga and Brecknock, in a lake across which the river Wye passes, before Glastonbury, the water all at once appeared of a green colour. Old men said this phenomenon took place at the time when the country was desolated by Noël, son of Meredith. It happened in the same country, that a little boy, endeavouring to take a nest of doves, in the church of St. David, his hand remained fastened to a stone, which was considered as a miracle wrought by the saint, who wished to preserve the birds of his church. This boy, followed by his parents and friends, came and threw himself at the foot of the altar, and passed three nights fasting and praying: the stone was detached from his hand, and he was delivered. Giraldus says that he saw this boy, then become an old man, in the course of his journey, and that he related this prodigy to him. The stone was preserved in the church of St. David, and the impression of the five fingers of the boy was still visible.

A miracle not less incredible happened near St. Edmondsbury. A poor woman, with the appearance of devotion, approached the box or *tronc* of a holy personage, and instead of placing an offering in it, found means to steal from it every day some portion of the alms of the faithful. She kissed the tronc in such a manner, that a piece of money stuck to her tongue, which she conveyed to her mouth without being observed. One day, whilst kissing the tronc in her customary manner, her lips became fixed to it; she spit out the money which she had in her mouth, but could not release her lips from the box, during a whole day. A great number of Christians, and even Jews, came to behold this miracle, and were struck with surprise and admiration.

Archbishop Baldwin and his train preached the crusade in the fields where they found the labourers and shepherds. They gave the cross to a great number of men, who joined them in a state of perfect nudity; their wives having concealed their clothes to prevent their enrolling themselves in the crusade.

Whilst crossing the territory of Brecknock, Giraldus heard that in the church of Heveden, the concubine of the rector of the church imprudently sat down on the wooden coffin of St. Orsana, sister of King Ofred. This coffin was more elevated than the altar. When the concubine wished to rise up, she could not release her thighs from the wood, to which they were firmly fixed. The people crowded in, she was overwhelmed with blows, her clothes were torn off her back, and she was only relieved by the help of the Divinity, who, at length, was moved to pity by her tears and prayers.

The psalm-book of Quindreda, sister of St. Kenelmus, likewise operated great prodigies. On the eve of the festival of St. Kenelmus, at Winehelcumbe, a crowd of women came from all the neighbouring places to be present at the festivities given by the monks. The *subcellarius fornicationem incurrit* with one of those in the corridors of the cloister. On the following day, in the procession, he carried the book of psalms of which we have spoken; but when he wished to lay it down, the book remained attached to his hands. He then remembered the sin he had committed the night before; he confessed, performed penance, and, seconded by the prayers of his brethren, at length succeeded in breaking the chains the Divinity had imposed upon him. This book of psalms possessed admirable and frequently tried virtues. When the body of Kenelmus was being carried to the cemetery, and the people, on the way, cried out, "He is a martyr!" Quindreda, who was suspected of having killed her brother, answered, "It is as true that he has been assassinated as it is true that my eyes, drawn from my head, are fastened to this psalter." At these words the two eyes of Quindreda fell from their sockets upon the open book, and left the stains of blood upon the leaves.

They likewise exhibited, in the same country, a collar or crown, which they said had belonged to St. Canaucus. A thief having endeavoured to steal it, was deprived of sight, and spent his life in darkness.

Giraldus related many other prodigies no less extraordinary. We repeat some of them in his own words. A soldier named Gilbert Hagernill, was delivered, *per fenestram ejectionis*, of a foal, in the presence of a great number of witnesses. He had been ill three years before the event. A mare produced an animal of extraordinary swiftness, which in its fore quarters resembled a horse, and in its hind quarters a stag.

Near the rivers Avon and Neth Giraldus was told of an adventure which had happened to a curate named Elidore. This curate, when twelve years of age, had fled from the paternal roof. After having remained two days in a cavern, he perceived two little men, who came towards him, and said: "Will you come with us? We will take you to a land of delights." The youth followed the pigmies along a subterraneous and dark road, and discovered a beautiful country which was intersected by woods, meadows, and rivers, but which was not lighted by the sun. Young Elidore was conducted before the king of this dark country, who, after admiring him for a long time, gave him to the prince, his son. The subjects of this prince were of very small stature; they had light curly hair, which flowed over their shoulders. They had little horses, as big as our hounds. They ate neither meat nor fish, and lived, for the most part, upon milk. They never swore or took oaths, and detested falsehood. When any of them went upon the earth, they could not at all comprehend the inconstancy, perfidy, and ambition of the men whom the sun enlightened. They appeared to have no exterior worship, no religious observances, but confined themselves entirely to the love of truth.

Young Elidore sometimes reascended to the earth, and came to see his mother, to whom he related his discoveries and adventures. His mother advised him to bring with him a little of the gold which he described as being so plentiful in that wonderful country. He wished to obey her, and stole a golden ball, with which the king's son was accustomed to play. As he entered the paternal dwelling, his foot remained fixed to the sill of the door; the golden ball he had brought, rolled to the feet of his mother, but was immediately picked up by two pigmies, who loaded Elidore with jeers and raillery. The latter, quite ashamed of his fault, wishing to return to the country of the Gnomes, in vain endeavoured to find the road; and although he continued his search for more than a year, he never succeeded. He finished by seeking consolation in study, and became a priest. He had learnt, says Giraldus, the language of the pigmies, and retained several words of it: this language very much resembled Greek.

This story, which is very like one of the *Thousand and One Nights*, may have furnished Swift with the idea of *Gulliver*; it is given at great length by Giraldus. The curate, Elidore, adds our traveller, related these marvellous adventures in his old age, and could not repeat them without shedding tears.

In the country of Haverford and Ross, an innumerable multitude of people followed Archbishop Baldwin, and took the cross. The orators of the holy war preached in Latin and in French, and although the people did not understand a word they spoke, they were moved to tears. An old woman, who, during three years, had been blind, sent her son to Archbishop Baldwin, in order to obtain a morsel of the robe of that holy pontiff. The young man not having been able to penetrate the crowd which surrounded the archbishop, brought back to his mother a clod of earth upon which the archbishop had trodden, and left his footmark; the blind woman pressed this clod to her mouth, then applied it to her eyes, and recovered her sight.

The preachers of the crusade appeared in the isle of Mona, or Anglesea. In this isle, Roderick, the youngest of the sons of Awen, took the cross with a great number of his subjects. The inhabitants of this isle pointed out, with great respect, a stone which bore the shape of a man's thigh, and which, by a miraculous virtue, when it was displaced, returned of itself, to the spot it had at first occupied. Count Hugh, of Chester, caused it to be fastened with strong chains to the bottom of the sea; but on the next day, it was again found in the place from which it had been taken.

The archbishop finished his tour by visiting the environs of Deva, or Chester; these countries were not less rich in marvels than the others. Many of the princes and nobles of this country took the cross.

When crossing the river Conway, Giraldus informs us that at the source of that river the enchanter Merlin lived; he gives, on this subject (chap. viii.), a curious notice upon the two Merlins; the one was of Scotland and the other of Wales; the latter was named Ambrose, and was born of a demon, in the city of Caermardyn, which owes its name to him.

— — — —

No. 24.

Letter to M. Michaud upon the Assassins, by Am. Jourdain.

In the course of your labours, you must often, Monsieur, have met with the names of these sectaries, known by the appellation of *Assassins*, whose religious principle consisted in blind obedience to that Old Man of the Mountains, who reigned only by murder, and the most horrible crimes. More than once perhaps you will have attributed to the love of the marvellous which prevails in ages of ignorance, barbarism, and credulity, the accounts of Western authors, contemporaries of the crusades, respecting their perseverance, and their imperturbable audacity in the pursuit and execution of crime. Nevertheless, we must confess, to the disgrace of our species, these accounts are even below the truth, and are confirmed by the unanimous concurrence of Arabian and Persian writers.

I will not describe these sectaries to you according to William of Tyre, James of Vitry, and an infinite number of historians with whom you are well acquainted; I should, if I did so, teach you nothing you did not know before. But I will devote this letter to presenting you with a short sketch of the origin, the dogmas, and history of the Assassins, even of their present state; for some remains of them still exist in the mountains of Syria. I shall be highly gratified if I can add any interest to your work, or give you at least a proof of the pleasure I receive in being serviceable to you.

Before entering on the matter, it will not be useless to recall to your mind the origin of the two great religious sects which divide the Mussulmans— the *Sunnites* and the *Chütes*.

Mahomet dying without naming his successor, there arose two factions among the people, one of which wished to elevate to the caliphat, Ali, the son-in-law of this false prophet, and the other the pious Abou-Bekr. The courageous firmness of Omar cut the difficulties short, and the party of Abou-Bekr triumphed. Omar governed after him, and had Othman for his successor. It was not till the death of this weak prince, that Ali obtained possession of the throne, always regarded by his partisans as his heritage.

Nevertheless, scarcely had his reign begun, than factions arose on all sides, whose aim it was to deprive him of the sceptre. Ali had contributed to this state of things, by disdaining the arts of policy, and by offending by refusals and even by disgraces, some of the officers of Mahomet, whose credit was great. One of these factious persons, Moaviah, an ambitious and powerful rival, aided by the cunning of Ibn-el-Ass, the famous conqueror of Egypt, sustained by Ayesha, the widow of Mahomet, who could not pardon the husband of Fatima, for having suspected her conjugal fidelity, and profiting skilfully by the faults of Ali, succeeded at length in wresting an authority from him whose legitimacy could not be contested; at the same time terminated by murder the course of a life which was about, probably, to end in humiliation and troubles of all kinds. His two sons experienced a fate not in any way more fortunate; they perished, victims of the ambition of the Ommiades, a house of which Moaviah was the first prince.

From that time there existed in the Mussulman empire two parties, whose opposition had religion for its basis, and which exist even at the present day: [142] these are the Sunnites and the Chütes. The first recognised the legitimacy of the succession in the persons of Abou-Bekr, Omar, and Othman, and placed Ali in the same rank with these three caliphs. The second, on the contrary, treat the first vicars of Mahomet as usurpers, and maintain that Ali was his only and veritable successor.

The numbers of the partisans of Ali became very great, particularly in Persia; but these partisans were not long before they themselves were divided into several parties, united in their veneration for Ali and his posterity, but divided with regard to the prerogatives they attached to this noble origin, and to the branch which possessed the rights of the *Imamat*, that is to say, the spiritual and temporal power. Of all the sects to which this difference of opinions gave birth, the most powerful was that of the Ismaëlians. It was thus called because it pretended that the dignity of Imaun had been transmitted by an uninterrupted line of the descendants of Ali, to a prince named Ismaël, and that after his death the Imamat had reposed upon persons unknown to men, up to the moment at which the triumph of the house of Ali was to be effected; to this sect belonged the Carmates and the Fatimite caliphs, who wrested Egypt and Syria from the Abasside caliphs of Bagdad, after having laid the foundation of their power in Africa, and formed a great empire, to the period when Saladin overturned their throne to erect one for a descendant of Abbas. But as the Fatimites acknowledged no other legitimate authority but their own, they employed a great number of missionaries in spreading their dogmas, and gaining proselytes in secret.

Such is, Monsieur, the sketch I have deemed it necessary to make, before proceeding with the founder of the sect which is the object of my letter.

This founder was named Hassan, son of Sabbah. He was born in the environs of Thous, a city of Korassan, celebrated for having given birth to several great men. His father lived in the practices of a mortified life and of an austere doctrine, but he followed in secret the sect of the Rafedhites, or the partisans of Ali. To divert, however, all suspicion from his opinions, he intrusted the education of his son to a famous doctor, Movaffeceddin, of Nichapour, who was a virtuous Sunnite. He pretended to an Arabian origin, and gave himself out as descended from the family of Sabbah-Homairi; but this was a fable to which no one gave faith, and it was very well known that his ancestors inhabited some villages in the dependence of Thous.

Hassan speaks thus of his first years of conversion to the sect of the Ismaëlians:—"From the age of seven years I laboured to acquire knowledge and talents. I made, as my fathers had done, profession of that sect of Chütes who recognise the succession of the twelve Imauns.

I had occasion to become acquainted with a *refik*, named Amireh-Zanab, and a most intimate friendship grew up between us. I believed that the dogmas and opinions of the Ismaëlians were only those of philosophers, and I imagined that the sovereign of Egypt (that is to say, the Fatimite caliph) was a sectary of this philosophy. This persuasion engaged me in warm discussions with Amireh; whenever he wished to defend his own doctrines, we had disputes and controversies respecting the dogmas of them. It was in vain for him to attack the doctrines of my sect, I did not yield at all to his arguments, and yet he insensibly made an impression on my mind. Whilst things were in this state we separated, and I was afflicted with a long illness. I then said inwardly to myself: "The doctrine of the Ismaëlians is conformable with truth, and it is only obstinacy that prevents me from adhering to it. If then, as God forbid! the fatal moment is come for me, I shall die without having embraced the truth." I was, however, restored to health, and soon after made acquaintance with another Ismaëlian, named Abou-Nedjm-Sanadj. I questioned him upon the true system of Ismaëlian belief: he explained it to me clearly, and I very soon penetrated all the depths of it. I afterwards met with an Ismaëlian Dai, named Moumen, to whom the cheik Abdelmelik-ben-Attach, dai of Irac, had given permission to exercise the functions of missionary. I informed him of the wish I had to make my profession of faith to him, and he acceded to my request. At the time that the cheik Abdelmelek came to Rey, I accompanied him, and my conduct having pleased him, he confided to me the ministry of a dai. You must go into Egypt,' said he, in order to render your homage to the Imaun Mostanser, and may that be a blessing to you!' Mostanser-billah, a descendant of Ali, then occupied the caliphat of Egypt and the *Imamat*. When, therefore, the cheik left Rey for Ispahan, I set out for Egypt."

Hassan was received in Egypt with great distinction, for the fame of his merit had preceded him thither, and the Imaun Mostanser admitted him to the most familiar intimacy. This high degree of favour ruined him. The courtiers, jealous of his credit, laboured to procure his disgrace, and a difference having arisen between him and the celebrated Bedr-Al-djemali, generalissimo of the caliph's troops, Hassan succumbed. His enemies seized him and threw him, with some Franks, into a vessel about to sail to Africa. Scarcely was he on the sea when a horrible tempest arose and placed the ship in great danger; all the passengers were overcome by terror, expecting nothing but death; Hassan alone preserved his self-possession and tranquillity. When interrogated upon this extraordinary conduct, "Our lord," answered he, "has promised me that no harm should happen to us;" and, in effect, at the end of a short time, the sea resumed its calm. The cry of miracle soon arose, and Hassan made so many disciples of the companions of his voyage. Another time, the vessel was driven into the port of a Christian city, the governor of which allowed our pious doctor to reimbark, after having treated him with hospitality. At length, the vessel being cast upon the coast of Syria, Hassan abandoned it, and directed his course towards Persia, by land. He passed through Aleppo and Bagdad, and went from thence to Konsistan, Ispahan, Yezd, and Carmania, preaching his doctrine everywhere. From Carmania he returned to Ispahan, where he sojourned more than four months, at the end of which he set out for Konsistan. He remained here three months, and then went to Damegan, where he dwelt for three years, making a great number of proselytes. Hassan, after various other wanderings, took possession of Altamont, a strong castle, situated in the Roudbard, a country near Casbin. Mirkhond, a Persian historian, relates, that he proposed to Mehdi, a descendant of Ali, who possessed this place, to purchase as much land of him as could be comprised within the skin of an ox, for the sum of 3,000 dinars. Mehdi having consented to this bargain, Hassan took the skin of an ox, of which he made thongs, and tying these together, passed the line all round the castle. It was by means of this trick that he made himself master of Altamont, which afterwards became the central point of the power of the Ismaëlians.

This power, by the ability and activity of Hassan, made a rapid progress; it was already established throughout the province of Roudbar, in which his sectaries built a number of strong castles; nobody was talked of in Persia but Hassan, who threatened to bring the whole of that great country under his domination. Melik-chah, alarmed at what he heard, ordered one of his generals to destroy Hassan and his partisans, and to raze his fortresses; but in vain; and death overtook Melik-chah before his troops had obtained the least advantage.

The troubles which followed his death, and the division which arose among the children of this prince, on the subject of the succession to the throne, left the field free for Hassan to augment the number of his proselytes. The best-fortified castles of the north-west of Persia fell into his hands. At length, the sultan Sindjar, having made himself master of this kingdom, set seriously about the destruction of the Ismaëlians. Hassan, by artifice, got rid of this dangerous enemy. He seduced one of the servants of the prince; who, whilst he slept, placed a sharp stiletto near his head. When the sultan, on awaking, saw this poniard, he was seized with great fear; but as he was ignorant of the hand that placed it there, he preserved silence upon the circumstance. At the end of some days he received the following letter from the head of the Ismaëlians:—"If good intentions were not entertained towards the sultan, the poniard which he found near his head would have been plunged into his heart." Sindjar was so terrified, that he consented to make peace with the Ismaëlians upon three conditions: the first was, that they should add no new constructions to their castles; the second, that they should purchase neither arms nor machines of war; and the third, that he should make no new proselytes. He even granted Hassan, by the title of pension, a portion of the revenues of the country of Coumes.

From that time Hassan lived peaceably in the castle of Altamont, in the greatest seclusion, practising the exercises of austere piety, and employing himself in the composition of dogmatic treatises upon his doctrine. It is said that he only ascended to the terrace of his palace, at Altamont, twice during thirty years. He required of his sectaries the most rigid exactitude in the observances of religion. Even paternal tenderness could not lead him to deviate from this severity. Hosséin, his son, having killed the daï of Couhestan, he punished him with death; another son, for having drunk wine, met with the same fate. A man having played upon the flute, in the castle of Altamont, he commanded him to be turned out of the place, and resisted all the prayers that were made to him to obtain his pardon. Some authors pretend, that by sacrificing his sons thus, he wished to prove to the Ismaëlians that he had no intention of fixing the sovereign power in his own family; I doubt whether such a reason can justify Hassan in his barbarity. And yet it would not be the first time that policy has sacrificed the feelings of the heart to state interests.

The ability of this man in the management of affairs equalled his fanaticism. History has preserved several proofs of this, of which I shall only quote the following. Hassan had studied under the imaun Movassek-eddin, in company with Nizam-el-Moulk, one of the greatest statesmen Islamism ever produced; and community of labours established the strictest friendship between them. They entered into a mutual promise that the first of the two that should obtain honours should share them with the other, and that fortune should not affect their attachment. Hassan, after having for a long time led a miserable life, went to Nichapour, where he found Nizam-el-Moulk minister of the great Melik-chah; this was about the year 1073 of the Christian era. Nizam-el-Moulk, faithful to his promise, received Hassan with great kindness, and procured him a post at the court. Endowed with an expansive mind, rare cunning, and great talents for administration, this aspirant was not long in insinuating himself into the good graces of the Sultan, and acquiring his confidence. One day, Melik-chah having conceived some doubt of the probity of his first minister, asked him in how short a time he could draw out a clear statement of the receipts and expenses of the provinces. We should observe, that at that period the dominions of this prince extended from Antioch, in Syria, to Kachkar, in Turkistan. Nizam-el-Moulk said it would require two years; Hassan offered to perform the labour in forty days, provided the Sultan would place at his disposal all the writers of the court; and his offer being accepted, he realized his promise. He was preparing to present the result of his researches to the prince, when Nizam-el-Moulk, who saw his ruin approach, found means to get the statements into his hands, and to mutilate them. When Hassan appeared before the Sultan, the prince put several questions to him relative to the situation and finances of the empire. Hassan had recourse to his papers, and found them incomplete; he hesitated, stammered, and could not answer. Nizam-el-Moulk skilfully took advantage of his tergiversations to degrade Hassan in the mind of Melik-chah. "Wise and prudent men," said he, "required two years to perform the work commanded by your majesty; an ignorant man, who has pretended to terminate it in forty days, is unable to give satisfactory answers to the questions put to him." The prince, in his anger, was desirous of punishing Hassan; but, as he was a creature of his court, he allowed the affair to drop, and satisfied himself with despising him. This anecdote, which does little honour to the character of Nizam-el-Moulk, and shows no delicacy on the part of Hassan, towards the man to whom he owed his fortune, proves at least that the latter possessed great aptitude for business.

Such was the man whom the Ismaëlians, or rather the Assassins of the Crusaders, recognised as their chief, and to whom they gave the name of *Séidouna,*—Our Lord. But before we proceed, it is necessary to enter into some details upon the principles of this sect, upon the denominations that it bore, and upon its organization.

You have seen, sir, the origin of the denomination of Ismaëlian, given to the branch of the partisans of Ali to which Hassan belonged. This name is not, however, the only one under which these heretics were known by orthodox Mussulmans. They were likewise called *Bathenians, Nezzarians, Molaheds,* and *Hachichens;* but the two last epithets alone applied to the proselytes of Hassan.

The title of Bathenian designated the principles established by the Ismaëlians. One of the characters of their religion was to explain, in an allegorical manner, all the precepts of the Mussulman law; and this allegory was carried so far by some of their doctors, that it tended to nothing less than the destruction of all public worship; and to the elevation of a purely philosophical doctrine, and a very licentious morality, upon the ruins of all revelation and all divine authority. This is why they were called *Bathenis,* or *Bathenians;* which is to say, *partisans of interior worship.*

Molahed, the plural of the Arabian word *Molhed,* signifies *impious;* the partisans of Hassan did not receive this epithet till towards the year 1164 of

Christ, and under the reign of one of his successors, named Hassan, the son of Mohammed. This prince, from his youth, gave himself up to the study of the dogmatic books of the sect; and as his father, to whom he succeeded, was unacquainted with science, he appeared in the eyes of the people a very profound scholar, and an extraordinary man. This good opinion, with respect to his person, increased daily, and the Ismaëlians became more blindly willing to execute his orders. Hassan, rendered bold by this success, put forth some extravagant opinions, and gave himself out to be the Imaun of the age. His father was still living; and, in his ignorance, scrupulously followed the doctrines of his sect. The pretensions of his son disgusted him, and he put to death two hundred and fifty of those who favoured them. As long as Mohammed lived, Hassan suppressed his real intentions; but he resumed them the moment the death of his father put him in possession of the throne. He permitted everything that religion prohibited, abolished the exterior practices of the Mussulman faith, allowed his subjects to drink wine, and dispensed with all the obligations which the law of Mahomet imposes on its sectaries; he declared that the knowledge of the allegorical sense of the precepts dispenses with the observance of the literal sense, and at length caused himself to be proclaimed son of Nezzar, son of the caliph Mostanser, and the caliph of God on the surface of the earth. [143] This heretical conduct procured for the Ismaëlians the denomination of *Molahed*, impious.

The surname of Nezzarians is derived from that Nezzar, of whom I have spoken, and was given to those Ismaëlians who adhered to the party of that prince, the eldest son of Mostanser, caliph of Egypt. The sectarians of Hassan were of the party of Nezzar.

I now come to the epithet of *Assassins*. The origin of this word had been the object of numerous researches, which still remained without any satisfactory result, when an illustrious scholar proved, in an evident manner, supporting all he advanced upon various Arabian texts, that it was a corruption of the word *hachichen*; and that it was given to the Ismaëlians, because they made use of an intoxicating liquor called *hachich*. This hachich is a preparation of the leaves of hemp, or some other part of that vegetable, which they employ in different manners; as a liquor, under the form of confections; or as pastilles, sweetened with saccharine substances; and even as fumigations. "The intoxication produced by the *hachich*," says M. Silvestre de Sacy, "throws the person who takes it into an ecstasy similar to that which the Orientals experience in the use of opium; and according to the testimony of a great many travellers, we may be satisfied that men in this state of delirium imagine that they enjoy the ordinary objects of their wishes, and taste of a felicity, the acquisition of which costs them little, but the use of which, too often repeated, changes the animal organization, and leads to marasma and death. Some of them, in this state of transient insanity, losing the consciousness of their weakness, commit actions of a brutal nature, capable of disturbing public order. It cannot be forgotten that, during the sojourn of the French army in Egypt, the general-in-chief was obliged strictly to prohibit the sale and use of these pernicious substances, the indulgence in which has become a necessity for the inhabitants of Egypt, particularly the lower classes of the people. Those who give themselves up to this custom, are still called *Hachichin, Hachachin*; and these two expressions plainly show why the Ismaëlians have been called by the Latin historians of the crusades, sometimes *Assissini*, and sometimes *Assassini*.

With a small acquaintance with the Arabic tongue, and an observation upon the alterations certain words of that language have experienced in being transferred to the works of Latin and Greek authors, it is impossible to raise any objection to the correctness of the etymology advanced by M. Silvestre de Sacy. We may, however, believe that all Ismaëlians did not employ the hachich; that their chief alone was acquainted with this preparation, and that he only administered it to those whom he destined to exercise the infamous trade of *fedai*, or *assassins*; for there prevailed among the partisans of this sect a remarkable hierarchy: the *dai, the refik*, and the *fedaï*, formed three perfectly distinct classes.

The chief of the sect dwelt, as I have said, in the castle of Altamont, placed amidst mountains. It was the situation of this abode which gave him the title of *Cheik Aldjebal,—Lord of the Mountain*; but as *cheik* signifies equally *lord* and *old man*, our historians of the crusades took it in the latter sense, and called the prince of the Assassins the *Old Man of the Mountain*.

The *daïs* formed the first class of the sect; it was reserved to them to propagate the doctrine. [144] They exercised the functions of missionaries, spreading themselves throughout the provinces, preaching the dogmas of their worship, and receiving the profession of faith of such as were converted. There were, still further, degrees among these. They called *dai aldoat,—dai of dais*, him who had several missionaries under his orders, and whose jurisdiction comprised several provinces. The Ismaëlians had *dais aldoat* in Syria, Irac, Dilem, Korassan, &c.

Under the name *refik*, it appears, the body of the sectaries was comprised.

The *fedaïs* were the blind ministers of the Old Man of the Mountain; it was in their hands he placed the knife under which were to fall, without pity, all who opposed the establishment of his doctrine, or combated it by dangerous arguments; princes, generals, doctors,—nobody was safe from their blows; and they showed in the execution of the crime, a perseverance equalled only by their fanaticism.

The word *fedaï*, in its proper signification, means a *devoted man*, and the application of it was very just, since this class of the Ismaëlians had for the orders of their prince a devotedness without example. It is true this blind obedience was purchased by stratagem; for I have not the least doubt that we must apply to the fedaïs that which Marco Paolo relates of the young people brought up by the Old Man of the Mountains. "This traveller, whose veracity is generally acknowledged," says M. de Sacy, "informs us that this prince caused young people to be brought up, chosen from amongst the most robust of the inhabitants of the places over which he ruled, to make of them the executioners of his barbarous decrees. All their education had for object to convince them that by blindly obeying the orders of their chief, they would secure themselves, after their death, the enjoyment of all the pleasures which delight the senses. [145] To attain this aim, this prince caused delicious gardens to be made round his palace. There, in pavilions, decorated with all that Asiatic luxury can imagine that is rich and brilliant, dwelt young beauties, consecrated solely to the pleasures of those for whom these enchanting places were destined. It was to this spot the Ismaëlian princes caused to be transported, from time to time, the young men of whom they meant to make the blind instruments of their will. After having caused them to swallow a draught which plunged them into a profound sleep, and deprived them for some time of the use of all their faculties, they had them conveyed to these pavilions, worthy of the gardens of Armida. Upon awaking, everything which struck their ears or their eyes threw them into a ravishment of delight, which left reason no empire in their minds. Uncertain if they had already entered upon the enjoyment of the felicity of which a picture had so often been held up to their imagination, they abandoned themselves with transport to all the various seductions by which they were surrounded. After they had passed some days in these gardens, the same means as had been employed to bring them there, without their knowledge, were again had recourse to to remove them from them. Advantage was carefully taken of the first moments of an awakening, which for them had put an end to the charm of so much enjoyment, to cause them to describe to their young companions the wonders of which they had been witnesses, and to convince them that the happiness of which they had during several fast-flitting days partaken, was but the prelude or foretaste of what they could secure an eternal possession of by their submission to the orders of their prince."

This draught, endowed with such wonderful powers, was nothing but the *hachich*, with the virtues of which the chief of the sect was acquainted, and the use of which was not spread till some centuries after.

This, sir, is what Oriental historians furnish us with respecting the origin, dogmas, and political organization of the sect of the Assassins. As to its history, the extent of its dominions, and its power, these are points, for the development of which a much greater space would be requisite than that to which I am obliged to limit myself. Nevertheless, I will devote a few lines to these articles, for the gratification of your curiosity.

Mirkhoud has left us, in his work entitled *Bouzat Alsafa*, a history of the Ismaëlians of Persia. This piece is the more valuable and authentic, from having been extracted word for word, from a history written by the celebrated vizier Atha-el-Mulk, who was sent by Holagon, after the ruin of the Ismaëlians, into the castle of Altamont, and had an opportunity of consulting their original historical memoirs. Mirkhoud, or rather Atha-el-Mulk, informs us, then, that the Persian dynasty of the Ismaëlians furnished eight princes, including Hassan-ben-Sabbah, and that it subsisted during a space of 166 years, to the time at which Holagon, at the instigation of several princes who detested the Ismaëlians on account of their excesses, conquered Persia, destroyed the castles of the sect, and sent Rokn-eddin-Karchar, the last sovereign of Altamont, to the other side of the Oxus. This great event took place in 1256.

But this principal branch, or rather this *stock* of the Ismaëlians, is not that of which such frequent mention is made in our crusades; Hassan Sabbah, after having laid the foundation of his power in Persia, sent missionaries, of both the first and second order, into all parts of the Mussulman world; and these missionaries were particularly active in Syria. A certain very celebrated Seljoukide emir, who governed Aleppo, seconded their designs wonderfully. Redoun (that was the name of this prince) formed a friendship with the Ismaëlians, embraced their principles even, and granted them open protection. From that period, that is to say 501 of the Hegyra, dates the origin of the great power they exercised in Syria, which subsisted nearly two hundred years; but these Ismaëlians were subject to the sovereign of Altamont, and were directed by *daïs*: it is even remarkable that most of the *fedaïs*, employed in committing murder in Syria, were Persians by nation, and had doubtless been educated for that execrable profession in the delicious gardens of Altamont, and by the virtue of the *chich*.

Europe has taken too little interest in the history of the Ismaëlians, as obtained from Oriental writers, to be certain of the extent of country occupied by these sectaries. The geography of Persia, likewise, is enveloped in too much obscurity to allow us to assign an exact position to the various castles they inhabited. But what I can affirm is, that the province of Roudbar, in which was placed the seat of their empire, is, according to the *Ferhenk Choouri,*—the Persian dictionary, explained in Turkish, a large district, comprising many villages, and situated between Casbin and Guilan, in the neighbourhood of Theheran, the present capital of Persia.

William of Tyre informs us that the Ismaëlians possessed ten fortresses in Syria, and reckons them at sixty thousand souls. Their principal establishment was at Massiat, an important, well-fortified place, situated to the west of Hamah, at the distance of a day's march. They obtained possession of it in 505 of the Hegyra, after having assassinated the emir who governed it; and have kept it even up to our times. In addition to Massiat, they held seven fortresses in the parallel of Hamah, from Hemes to the Mediterranean, and in the neighbourhood of Tripoli. They began to appear in Syria towards the end of the fifth century of the Hegyra. Their power increased rapidly under the Seljoukide Redevan, who embraced their doctrine. During the whole course of his reign, they had a house in Aleppo, in which they exercised their worship. They were so much dreaded, that they carried off women and children out of the open streets in mid-day, without any one daring to oppose their violences. They publicly plundered people of a sect opposed to their own; gave asylum to the greatest criminals, and gathered from impunity fresh audacity for the commission of new crimes. These barbarians carried their insolence so far as to seize, by force of arms, cities and strong castles; it was thus they entered Apamea, from which place Tancred drove them.

Whatever may have been the extent of the dominions possessed by the Ismaëlians, either in Persia or Syria, it cannot be compared with their power, established by fanaticism, and maintained by the fear they inspired. Spread throughout the whole of the Mussulman world, from the extremities of Asia Minor to the depths of Turkistan, they were everywhere dreaded. In presenting you with a few instances of their fanaticism and audacity, if I do not afford you a precise idea of their power, I shall at least make you acquainted with the nature of it, and with what it may be presumed to have been. Let us begin with devotedness and fanaticism.

History informs us that Henry, count of Champagne, having made a journey into Lesser Armenia, paid a visit, on his return, to the king of the Assassins, and was received with the most distinguished honours. The prince led him to all parts of his abode, and having conducted him up a very lofty tower, upon every step of which stood men clothed in white: "I do not suppose," said he to his guest, "that you have any subjects as obedient as mine?" At the same time he made a sign with his hand, when two of these men precipitated themselves from the top of the tower, and expired instantly. The head of the Ismaëlians added: "If you desire it, at the least signal on my part, those whom you see will precipitate themselves in the same manner." When taking leave of Henry, he made him rich presents, and said: "If you have any enemy who aims at your crown, address yourself to me, and my servants shall soon relieve you from your anxiety, by poniarding him."

Melik-chah, alarmed at the progress of Hassan-ben-Sabbah, sent one of his officers to him to require him to desist from his views, and to surrender his castles. Hassan ordered one of his servants into his presence, and commanded him to kill himself, which the servant instantly did. He then told another to throw himself from the summit of a high tower, and his orders were equally promptly obeyed. "Report to your master," then said he to the ambassador, "what you have seen, and tell him that I have sixty thousand men at my command, whose devotedness and obedience are like that which you have seen."

In 1120, some Bathenians having assassinated Boursiki, prince of Mossoul, they were cut to pieces on the spot. The mother of one of these Ismaëlians having learnt the death of the emir and the fate of the assassins, gave herself up to transports of joy; but her satisfaction was changed into as lively a grief when she learnt that her son, by some fortunate chance, had escaped the destiny of his companions. Thus fanaticism produced the same effect upon this woman as was produced by national honour and patriotism in the case of the Spartan mother, whom history has immortalized as sinking under her grief when she heard that her son had escaped from the massacre of Thermopylæ. What becomes of the charm and power of virtue, if blind fanaticism, the disgrace of our nature, can rival her in the noblest actions she inspires?

The Ismaëlians were the more dangerous and redoubtable, from their practice of insinuating themselves into the courts of most princes, and their skill in adopting such disguises as circumstances required. They assumed the Syrian dress, in order to get rid of that Ahmed Bal, of whom I have just spoken; they entered the service of Tadjelmouth Bouri, prince of Damascus, in the quality of grooms of Korassan, and attacked him with impunity. The murderers of Bouriski took the dress of dervises, to avert all suspicion. The Ismaëlians deputed to poniard the marquis of Montferrat, embraced Christianity, wore religious habits, affected the most austere piety, gained the friendship and esteem of the clergy, acquired the good-will of their victim, and, after having killed him, endured the tortures in which they perished with admirable resignation. The imaun Fakr-eddin, a very celebrated Persian doctor, having been accused of practising the Ismaëlian doctrines in secret, in order to clear himself from the calumny, ascended the pulpit, and pronounced maledictions against the sect. This news reaching Altamont, Mohammed, who then reigned, charged a fedaï with the execution of his vengeance. This man repaired to the dwelling of the imaun, and told him that he was a jurisconsult, that he was desirous of being instructed by so able a master, and with his caresses and flattery, played his part so well, that he was admitted into the family of the doctor; he passed seven months with him without obtaining an opportunity to execute his purpose. At length, finding himself one day alone with the imaun, he shut the doors of the house, drew his poniard, rushed upon the doctor, struck him to the ground, and seated himself upon his chest. "I will rip you up," said he, "from the navel to the breast." "What for?" replied the imaun. Then the fedaï reproached him with having cursed the Ismaëlians from the pulpit. The imaun swore several times never to speak ill of that sect in future; upon which the fedaï released him, saying: "I have no orders to kill you, otherwise I should not delay the execution of those orders, or hesitate in performing them; know, then, that Mohammed salutes you, and desires that you would do him the honour of visiting him at his castle. You will become an all-powerful governor, for we shall obey you blindly." And he added, "We take no account of the discourse of common people; their insults have no effect upon us. But you, you ought never to permit your tongue to utter anything against us, or to censure our conduct; because your words sink into the people's hearts as the strokes of the engraver penetrate the stone." The imaun said: "It is impossible for me to go to the castle, but I will, henceforward, never pronounce a word that may be displeasing to the sovereign of Altamont." After this conversation, the fedaï took from his girdle three hundred and sixty pieces of gold, and said to the imaun: "Here is your salary for one year, and it has been ordered by the *sublime divan*, that you should receive every year a similar sum from the reis Modhaffer. I have in my chamber two Yeman robes; when I am gone your servants must take them, for our master has sent them to you." The fedaï instantly disappeared. The imaun took the pieces of gold and the robes, and during five years received the appointed salary.

This miraculous devotedness, this confidence in an after-life, the felicity of which was beyond description, produced the audacity and perseverance in the execution of the orders of the prince, and the imperturbable courage which led the Ismaëlians to endure death, without allowing the most severe tortures to draw a confession from them. Caliphs and emirs fell beneath their blows, in mosques, in streets, within the walls of palaces, amidst crowds of people and courts of nobles. If they were taken with the fatal knife in their hands, they thanked heaven for bringing them nearer to the goal of their desires, and hailed death as leading them the first step towards felicity. Moudoud and Ac Sancar Albourski, princes of Mossoul, were assassinated as they were coming out of the great mosque of the city, although surrounded by their officers and domestics. Ahmed Bal, governor of some castles of the Azerbaidjan, had several times declared himself an enemy to the Lord of the Mountain; he was struck dead in the midst of the hall of audience of the sultan Mohammed at Bagdad. The great Saladin refused to embrace or protect the Ismaëlian doctrine, and announced his intention of destroying it. Whilst he was carrying on the siege of Akka, or Ptolemaïs, a fedaï threw himself upon him, and dealt him a blow of a poniard upon his head. Saladin seized him by the arm, but the murderer never ceased striking till he was killed. A second and a third fedaï continued the attack, but without obtaining better success. Nevertheless, says the historian, Saladin retired to his tent in great fear.

I have told you, sir, that the irruption of Holagon into Persia, and the expeditions of Biban into Syria, ruined the Ismaëlian power. But, whilst destroying their castles, these two great warriors were not able to completely exterminate the sect. When Tamerlane penetrated into Mezinderan, he found a great number of Ismaëlians. Mention is often made of these sectaries in the history of the conquest of Yemen by the Turks. We know that they are at present scattered through many parts of Persia, and that the government tolerates them. They even pretend that they have preserved their imaun to this moment; that he is descended from Ismaël himself, the son of Djafar Elasdie, and is named Chah Kalil. He dwells in the city of Khekh, near to Kom. This imaun is almost venerated as a god, among his proselytes, who attribute to him the gift of miracles, and often decorate him with the title of caliph. The Ismaëlians are found as far as the banks of the Ganges and the Indus, whence they piously come every year to receive the blessings of their lord in return for the magnificent offerings they bring him. There likewise still exist many families of them in the mountains of Libanus, upon whom M. Rousseau, consul-general of France to Aleppo, has given us some valuable information.

The Ismaëlians of Syria are divided into two classes, —the *Soueidanis* and the *Khedhrewis*. The latter, who form the most numerous part of the sect, have for chief the emir Ali Zoghbi, successor of the emir Mustapha Edris. Their principal place of abode is at Messias, which M. de Sacy thinks ought to be called Mesiat. This ancient fortress is situated at twelve leagues west of Hamah, upon an isolated rock. At three leagues west of Messias, the Ismaëlians possess another fortress, named Kadmous, of not less consequence than the other.

The second class, which comprises the *Soueidanis*, is much less numerous than the preceding one, and is concentrated in the village of Feudara, of the district of Messias. Its poverty has drawn upon it the contempt of the Khedhrewis; its present chief is named *Cheikh Soleiman*.

The sect of the Ismaëlians at the present moment only consists of some wretched families scattered here and there, whom the persecutions of the Turks are daily annihilating. The following is the sinister event which has plunged them into these circumstances. We will leave M. Rousseau to speak:—"The *Reslans*, one of the most distinguished families of the sect of the Nosaïris, possessed from time immemorial the fortress and territory of Messias, when the Ismaëlians, having become sufficiently powerful to encroach upon their domains, suddenly attacked them, and drove them from the country, in which they established themselves. This manifest usurpation increased the inveterate hatred which all the neighbouring peoples entertained for them. The Nosaïris, after having uselessly attempted, by several means, to regain their possessions, at length had recourse to stratagem. They sent some of their people to Messias, who, under borrowed names, and without creating any suspicion of their designs, entered the service of the Chich emir, *Mustafa Edris*, who then commanded in the fortress.

"Abou Ali Hammour and Ali Bacha, chief of the conspirators, had not long to wait for the opportunity they wished for. One day when the emir remained alone in his dwelling, they assailed him, and slew him with several dagger-wounds. This unexpected murder was the signal for great misfortunes for the Ismaëlians. Measures were so well concerted among their enemies, that at a given signal, a numerous band of Nosaïris, posted in the avenues of Messias, were to precipitate themselves upon it on a sudden, and massacre all the inhabitants who attempted to defend themselves. This project was completely carried out. The Ismaëlians, attacked sharply, terrified, and, for the most part, killed in the open streets, offered but weak resistance to their enemies, to whom they were compelled to swear submission and obedience for the future. The booty made on this day was valued at more than a million piastres, reckoning the plunder of the villages and the country. This event took place in the year 1809."

These Ismaëlians have a book which contains the dogmas of their present belief, the practices of their worship, &c. Its author was a certain Cheikh Ibrahim, who seems to have been one of the visionaries of the sect; it was made public after the pillage of Messias. It is an assemblage of absurd reveries and incoherent, ridiculous, insignificant principles, in which the primitive doctrine of these sectaries is joined to a crowd of dogmas which are foreign to it, and which time, communication with other sects, and ignorance, have introduced into their belief. Nevertheless, the study of them ought not to be entirely neglected, as they serve to prove to what a degree the human mind may deceive itself.

To avoid fatiguing your patience, I will pass over that which relates to mystic theology, and the different incarnations of the Imaun or Messiah, who was manifested in the persons of Adam, Noah, Abraham, Moses, Jesus, and Ali, fourth caliph, according to orthodox Mahometans. I will likewise be silent upon the mysteries of the alphabetical letters, which are divided into the luminous and the obscure, the substantial and the corporeal; were at first twenty-two in number, were augmented by six, at the time of the revelation of the Koran; are connected with the houses of the moon, with the signs of the zodiac, with the planets, and the elements; designate sometimes a prophet, sometimes a holy personage; in short, are susceptible of an infinity of allegorical applications; but I will give in its entirety the description of Paradise.

"I have reserved an abode more permanent, and filled with eternal delights for those who follow my law, and fear the effects of my justice. This abode is paradise, to which entrance may be obtained by eight different gates, which lead to the same number of inclosures; there are in each inclosure or division, 70,000 meadows of saffron, and 70,000 abodes of mother-of-pearl and coral; in each dwelling-place or abode, there are 70,000 palaces and 70,000 galleries of topaz; in each gallery there are 70,000 golden saloons; in each saloon, 70,000 silver tables; upon each table, 70,000 exquisite dishes, &c. &c. Each of these 70,000 palaces contains 70,000 springs, or streams of milk and honey with as many purple pavilions, occupied by beautiful young women. Still further, each saloon is surmounted by 70,000 domes of amber, and upon each dome are set forth 70,000 wonders from the hand of Omnipotence. The inhabitants of these enchanted places are immortal and are unacquainted with infirmities, tears, laughter, prayers, or fasting."

I ought to tell you, with regard to this passage, that in the true doctrine of the Ismaëlians, paradise is the true religion, and the epoch of its manifestation, and that this description, or any other like it, must be considered as an allegory.

To this quotation I cannot refrain from adding two others: one upon the duties of man, the other upon the metaphysical ideas of this sect.

"Oh! son of Adam, the empire of the universe belongs to me; all that you possess comes from me; but learn that the aliments which nourish you, will not preserve you from death, nor the clothes which cover you from the infirmities of the flesh; you will advance or go back, as you employ your tongue in falsehood or in truth. Thy being is composed of three parts: the first is mine, the second is thine; and the third belongs to us in common. That which is mine, is thy soul; that which is thine, is thy actions; and that which we share between us, is the prayers which thou addressest to me. Thou oughtest to implore me in thy wants; my delight is to listen to the prayers of the good. Oh! son of Adam, honour me, and thou wilt know me; fear me, and thou wilt see me; adore me, and thou wilt draw near to me. Oh! son of Adam, if kings are cast into flames for their tyranny, magistrates for their treachery, doctors for their jealousies, artisans for their frauds, the great for their pride, the low for their hypocrisy, the poor for their falsehoods, — where will they be found who can aspire to enter into paradise?

There are three sorts of existence: the first, usual and relative, exposed to the influence of the stars, subject to alterations, and susceptible of being and not being at the same time; that is matter: the second, intellectual, which has been preceded by non-existence, but which becomes permanent from the moment it begins; that is the soul, upon which the celestial bodies cannot act: the third, necessary, absolute, and eternal, superior by its nature to the two others, that is the Supreme Being, by whom everything has been produced, who has always subsisted, and will subsist for ever.

"The Being whose existence is eternal, the first principle, is unlimited, One, and without companions.

"Man exists then doubly, — by his soul and by his body; his spiritual existence survives his bodily existence, which, sooner of later, is dissolved.

"The soul is a simple substance, homogeneous and immaterial, an indestructible breath of the Divinity. The body is a compound of material parts heterogeneous and destructible, which only exists as long as its parts remain united together. The soul is not essentially inherent to the body; the latter is not the subject of it; we only know that it is present in it, as we are aware of the splendour of the sun upon the surface of any object whatever.

"The soul is immortal.

Souls were created before bodies: they resided, whilst waiting for them, in the intellectual world, the abode of true essences.

"After their union with the body, they constantly endeavour to preserve the reminiscence of their productive cause; and if, in their new state, they do not forget this first essence, they return to their former dwelling; otherwise they continue wandering and unhappy in the *material* world, there to perpetually experience the vicissitudes and pains of the present life.

"In order not to deteriorate, or lose its rights to proximity with its author, the soul must be constantly filled with the idea of that first cause which is disposed to attract it, unceasingly, towards it. It is its true state of perfection, that in which it maintains itself by becoming insensible to all terrestrial affections.

"In addition to his immaterial and reasonable soul, man has still another, which is the natural soul; this is born and dies with the body; it is a certain inexplicable, but active and actual force, which is common to him and animals devoid of reason, and which elevates him above these; it is the immortal breath which the Divinity has communicated to him, to the exclusion of the other beings of the universe." [146] —Receive, monsieur, I beg, &c. &c.

— — — —

No. 25.

Treaty made under the Walls of Constantinople.

This is certainly one of the most extraordinary documents we have ever seen. A handful of warriors, in a strange and foreign country, without any certainty of reinforcements, are before the second city of the world, well peopled, completely fortified, and prepared for defence; and yet they, before giving an assault, coolly draw up a treaty, by which the city and its empire are divided amongst them; and what completes the wonder is, that they succeeded, and, for a while, obtained what they contemplated.

"We, Henry Dandolo, by the grace of God doge of Venice, Dalmatia, and Croatia, and the very illustrious lords, Boniface, marquis of Montferrat; Baldwin, count of Flanders and Hainault; Louis, count of Blois and Clermont; and Henry, count of St. Pol; each on his own part, in order to maintain among us union and concord, and to avoid every subject of offence, with the co-operation of Him who is our peace, who made everything, and for whose glory we have thought fit to establish the following order, after having reciprocally engaged ourselves with the bonds of an oath. In the first place, we all agree (after having invoked the name of Jesus Christ) to cause the city to be attacked; and if, by the aid of divine power, we succeed in entering it, we will remain and serve under the command of those who shall be established leaders of the army, and follow them as it shall be ordered. All the wealth that shall be found in the city, shall by every one be deposited in a common place, which shall be chosen for this purpose, we reserving always, as well as for our Venetians, three parts of this wealth, which are to be remitted to us as an indemnity for that which the Emperor Alexius was bound to pay to us, as well as to you. On your side, you will retain a fourth part, until we have all obtained equal satisfaction; and if there should be anything left, we will share it equally between us and you, so that all may be satisfied. And if the said wealth should not prove sufficient to discharge that which is due to us, this wealth, from whatever source it may arise, shall be shared in the same manner between you and us, as it has been thereupon agreed, except the provisions and forage, which shall be set aside and divided equally among your people and ours, in order that all may subsist in a suitable manner; and all that may be found besides shall be shared with the other booty, according as it has been agreed thereupon. We and our Venetians are to enjoy, throughout the empire, in a free and absolute manner, and without any kind of contradiction, all the prerogatives and possessions which we have been accustomed to enjoy, as well in spiritual as in temporal matters; as well as all privileges and usages, written or not written. There shall also be chosen six members on our part, and six on yours, who, after having taken an oath, shall choose in the army and raise to the empire, him whom they shall believe to be most fit to exercise it, and to command in this land for the advantage and glory of God, of the holy Romish church, and of the empire. If they agree among themselves, we will recognise as emperor him whom they shall have elected with one common voice. But if it should happen that six shall be on one side and six on the other, it shall be left to chance, and him upon whom the lot shall fall we will acknowledge as emperor. If there should be a majority on one side, we will acknowledge as emperor him in favour of whom this majority shall be declared. If the council should be divided into more than two parts, we will acknowledge for emperor him whom the most numerous party shall have elected. The person who may be chosen emperor, shall have the quarter of all that shall be conquered from the empire, the palace of Blachernæ, and the Lion's Mouth. The three other quarters shall be shared equally among you and us. As to the clerical members who shall be of the side on which the emperor shall not have been chosen, they shall have the privilege of composing the clergy of the Church of St. Sophia, and to elect a patriarch for the glory of God, of the holy Roman church, and the empire. But as regards the clerical members on one side and the other, they shall compose the clergy of the churches which shall fall to their share. As to the wealth of the churches, care will be taken to distribute to the ecclesiastics as much as will be sufficient to provide honourably for them, and to the churches as much as will be requisite to maintain them properly. Whatever may remain of this wealth shall be divided and shared as above directed. We will, in addition, make oath, on both sides, that, dating from the last day of the present month of March, we will remain during the space of an entire year in the service of the emperor, in order to contribute to and strengthen his power, for the glory of God, the holy Romish church, and the empire; and that all those who shall have previously sojourned in the empire, shall swear fidelity to the emperor, according to the good and praiseworthy custom. Thus then, all those who now dwell in the empire, as has been mentioned, shall swear they will hold as good and authentic the regulations and treaties which have been made. It is also proper to observe that, as well on your side as on ours, there shall be chosen twelve members, at most, as it may be convenient, who, after having taken the oath, shall be charged with the duty of distributing the fiefs and honours among individuals, and of regulating the rights of service to which these same individuals shall be subjected as regards the emperor and the empire, according to what these members shall think suitable; that the fief which shall be assigned to any one shall be possessed freely and without any obstacle, by his posterity, as well masculine as feminine, and that the possessor shall have entire power to execute whatever to him may seem good, saving his obedience to the laws and the duty he shall owe to the service of the emperor and the empire. There shall be likewise done for the emperor all the service necessary, independently of that to which the possessors of fiefs and privileges shall be bound, according to the order that shall be assigned to them. It is further enacted, that no inhabitant of a nation which shall be at war with us or our successors, or the Venetians, shall be admitted into the empire until that war shall be entirely terminated. Moreover, each party is held to labour sincerely to obtain from our holy father the pope, that if any one shall attempt to contravene the present constitution, he shall be struck by excommunication. On his side, the emperor is bound to swear that he will hold the acts and gifts which shall be made, irrevocable, conformably with all which has hereupon been named. That if the present treaty should require any addition or suppression, it will be within our power and liberty to make it, assisted by our six counsellors, conjointly with the said lord marquis, assisted equally by his six counsellors. On the other side, the above-named lord doge cannot take the oath to the emperor for any service, for any fief or privilege that may be granted to him; but he or they whom he shall delegate in that which concerns him, shall take the oath to do, towards the emperor and towards the empire, all services required, conformably with all which has been thereupon mentioned.

Given, in the year of grace 1204, the 7th day of the month of March.

No. 26.

In the year 1195, Walter Hemingford, an English chronicler, says that the Old Man of the Mountain sent to all the princes of Europe a letter, in which he exculpates the illustrious king Richard from the death of the marquis of Montferrat. Although this letter may be a little apocryphal, we publish it, to show our readers how the Old Man of the Mountain was then spoken of.

"The Old Man of the Mountain to the princes and all the people of the Christian religion, salutation. As we do not wish ill to him who is innocent and merits it not, we will not allow that the innocence of another should be compromised by any act that we have done. We will never suffer, with the permission of God, that they who have offended us shall rejoice long in the injuries inflicted on our simplicity. We signify then to you all, and we take as witness him by whom we hope to be saved, that it was not by any machinations of the king of England that the marquis was killed. He was justly killed, by our will and by our order, by our satellites, because he had offended us, and had neglected, in spite of our warnings, to make us reparation: for it is our custom first to warn those who have offended us in anything, either us or our friends, in order that they may give us satisfaction; and it is our custom, if they despise our warning, to avenge ourselves by the hands of our ministers, who obey us with the greater devotion from being convinced they shall be gloriously recompensed by God, if they fall whilst executing our orders. We have learnt likewise that it is said of the same king that he had engaged us, as less incorruptible than others, to send some one of our people to lay an ambush for the king of Franco. This is false, and the effect of a vain suspicion. God is our witness, that he never proposed anything of the kind to us, and that our honesty would not permit us to allow anything evil to be attempted against a person who had not merited it. Fare ye well."

— — — —

No. 27.

Fragment from Nicetas Choniates, concerning the Statues
of Constantinople destroyed by the Crusaders. [147]

The Latins manifested that love of gold which characterizes their nation, by thinking of a new species of plunder, till that time unknown to all the former spoilers of this city of cities. After opening the coffins of the emperors which are in the Heroüm, erected near the magnificent church of the disciples of Jesus Christ, they pillaged them all during the night; and, in violation of the laws of equity, they took away all the ornaments in gold, pearls, and precious transparent stones, which had so long remained untouched in that sacred place.

Having found, likewise, the body of the emperor Justinian, still perfect and undecomposed, after the lapse of so many years, this spectacle struck them with admiration; but they paid no more respect, on that account, to the ornaments with which the body had been buried.

It may be affirmed that the Occidentals spared neither the living nor the dead, and beginning with God and his servants, they made all, indifferently, sensible to the effects of their impiety. A short time after, they bore away from the great church that veil which was valued at many thousand silver minæ, and which was ornamented with thick golden embroidery. But as even all these riches could not satisfy the boundless cupidity of these barbarians, they cast their eyes upon the bronze statues, and consigned them to the flames. The Juno of bronze, which stood in the Square of Constantine, was taken to pieces and sent to the melting-house, to be transformed into *staters*; [148] so large was this statue that the head was as much as four pairs of oxen could draw to the palace.

After the Juno, they took down from its base a group of Paris and Venus; the shepherd offering the goddess the golden apple of discord.

Whoever beheld without admiration that square obelisk of bronze, the height of which was almost equal to that of the loftiest columns? Upon it were sculptured all the birds which, in spring, make the air resound with their melodious concerts, the labours of husbandmen, musical instruments, bleating sheep, and bounding lambs. The sea there spread forth its waves, with vast numbers of fish, part of which were taken alive, and the rest, bursting through the nets, were plunging back into their watery home. Naked cupids, sporting by twos and threes, pelting each other with apples, and indulging in the wildest gambols. At the top of this square obelisk, which terminated in a pyramidal form, was placed a female figure, which turned with the least breath of wind; whence she was called *Anemodoulos* (that is to say, the slave of the winds). This work, of admirable beauty, was likewise melted, as was a colossal statue, which stood in the Place of Taurus, and represented a man on horseback in heroic costume. This figure, whose base was a trapezium, was said by some to be Joshua, because his hand was extended towards the declining sun, and that he seemed to be commanding it to stay its course. But most persons thought it was intended for Bellerophon, the hero born and brought up in the Peloponnesus, mounted upon Pegasus; for the horse had no bridle, and it is thus Pegasus is represented, striking, at will, the plain with his hoof, and, whether flying or running, disdaining to submit to his rider. There was an ancient tradition, which was preserved to our times, and known to everybody, that under the left forefoot of this horse was concealed the figure of a man, representing, according to some, a Venetian, and according to others, some other enemy from the West, bearing a Roman name, or else it was a Bulgarian. Efforts had often been made to render this foot so firm and so solid that it might not be possible to discover what was said to be hidden beneath it. When this horse and his rider were taken to pieces to be melted, the figure was really found concealed under the foot of the horse; it was clothed in a mantle, much in appearance like one of wool; but the Latins, troubling themselves very little about the predictions concerning it, cast it also into the fire. Many other statues and admirable works, standing in the Hippodrome, shared the same fate, and were destroyed by these barbarians, who, incapable of admiration for the beautiful, converted all these masterpieces into coin, and annihilated monuments which had cost so much, for the sake of such an inconsiderable amount of money. They broke to pieces a Hercules, reclining upon an osier-basket (or mattress), covered by a lion's skin, the head of which had, even in the bronze, so terrible an aspect, that it appeared about to roar, and spread terror among the idle multitude who stopped to look at it. The hero was seated, without quiver, bow, or club; his right arm and leg were stretched out to their full length, whilst his left leg was bent; placing his left elbow on his knee, he raised his fore-arm, and with an air of sadness, reposed his head upon the palm of his hand. He appeared to deplore his destiny, and to be thinking over with indignation the troubles to which Eurystheus constrained him, from jealousy, and not from necessity. His chest and shoulders were broad, his hair curly, his thighs large, his arms muscular, and his height was such as Lysimachus might, upon conjecture, have assigned to the true Hercules. This bronze Hercules was his first and last work: it was so large that the cord which went round his thumb was long enough for a common man's girdle, and that with which his leg was measured was equal in length to the height of a man. They did not, however, fail to annihilate such a Hercules; these men who had separated courage from the virtues allied to it, who attributed it to themselves particularly, and professed to esteem it above everything! They took away the ass with his pack-saddle, walking and braying, with the ass-driver following him, which Cæsar Augustus had caused to be placed at Actium or Nicopolis, in Greece, to perpetuate the remembrance of his having gone out one night to observe the army of Antony, and having met with this man, of whom he asked who he was, and whither he was going, the man answered his name was Nico, and that of his ass Nicander, and that he was going to Cæsar's army. Neither could they keep their hands from the hyena, and the wolf which suckled Remus and Romulus;—they melted this precious monument of the Roman nation for the sake of some paltry pieces of copper coin. They destroyed, in the same manner, the man contending with a lion; an hippopotamus of the Nile, the body of which ended in a tail covered with scales; the elephant shaking his trunk; the sphynxes, whose upper parts were those of women of rare beauty, but who, below, resembled fearful and horrid animals; these sphynxes were the more admirable from appearing to be able to walk, and at the same time to fly, and to dispute the palm of swiftness with the largest birds. A horse without a bridle, pricking up his ears and neighing; a tamed bull, walking with slow, heavy steps; and Scylla, that ancient monster, a woman to the waist, with her long neck, her large breasts, and an air full of cruelty; her inferior parts divided, to form those animals which attacked the vessels of Ulysses, and devoured several of his companions.

There was, likewise, in the Hippodrome, a bronze eagle, a wonderful monument of the magic art of Apollonius of Tyana. Being at Byzantium, he was implored to put an end to the trouble the inhabitants endured from the bites of serpents. Having recourse to his criminal arts, in which he had been instructed by demons and men initiated in their wicked mysteries, he placed upon a column an eagle which could not be looked upon without pleasure, and which drew passers-by to stop and contemplate it, as the songs of the Syrens fascinated those who listened to them. His wings were extended as if he were about to fly; but the folds of a serpent, which he held in his talons, impeded his efforts. The reptile stretched out its head as if to reach the wings of the bird; but its efforts were in vain; for, pierced by the claws of the eagle, its ardour relaxed, so that it appeared rather to be about to sleep or die than to fasten on the wings of the eagle. Thus the serpent was breathing its last sigh, and its venom was exhaling with it; whilst the eagle, with a haughty glance, and actually appearing to utter cries of victory, endeavoured to raise the serpent, and bear it away into the heavens with him; all which was expressed by the eagle's superb look, and the death of the serpent. It might almost be said, in seeing the serpent thus forced to slacken its flexible folds, and forego its venomous bites, that it drove away, by its example, other serpents from Byzantium, and exhorted them to conceal themselves in their holes. And this was not all that rendered the figure of this eagle admirable; for it indicated, very correctly to the eye of an instructed spectator, the twelve hours of the day, by twelve lines traced upon its wings, when the rays of the sun were not veiled by clouds.

What shall I say of the Helen, with arms whiter than snow, with small delicate feet, and a bosom of alabaster? Of Helen, who brought all Greece together against Troy, who occasioned the ruin of that city, who from the Trojan shores, passed to those of the Nile, and thence at length returned to Lacedæmon? Was she able to subdue these inexorable men, and soften these hearts of iron? She had not the power; she, whose beauty charmed every spectator, whose robing was magnificent, who, although of bronze, was full of delicious languor, and who, even to her tunic, her veil, her diadem, and her elegantly arranged hair, appeared to respire the very spirit of voluptuousness. Her tunic was of a fabric more delicate than the tissues of Arachne; her veil was of the most admirable workmanship; the diadem which encircled her brow, glittered with the brilliancy of gold and precious stones; and her floating tresses, agitated by the wind, were gathered together behind, and descended to her legs. Her lips, slightly separated, like the cup of a rose, appeared ready to breathe soft and pleasant words, whilst her inexpressibly sweet smile seemed, in a manner, to meet the spectator, and fill him with delicious emotion. But language cannot describe or transmit to posterity the charm of her look, the arch so exquisitely marked of her eyebrows, or the graces which adorned her person. But thou, Helen, daughter of Tyndarus, lovely with natural beauty, work of the Loves, object of the cares of Venus, the most admirable gift of nature, the prize of victory proposed to Greeks and Trojans, where is the Nepenthe, that remedy against sadness, which the wife of Thoas remitted to thee? Where are those philters which none can resist? Why didst thou not employ them as formerly? But I see how it was. Thy inevitable destiny was to become the prey of the flames, thou, whose image alone had power to kindle the flames of love in the hearts of all who beheld thee. Perhaps I may say, that these descendants of Æneas condemned thee to the fire, to avenge in thy own person Ilium, consumed by the fires which thy loves had created. But the fury of gold which possessed the Latins, and led them to annihilate in every spot the most beautiful masterpieces of art, is beyond my power of imagining or describing. But I may venture to say this; they separate themselves from their wives, and yield them to the embraces of others for a few oboles; they are incessantly occupied in plunder, or in games of chance; they put on armour, and fight with each other, with a senseless and furious ardour, and not with a prudent, regulated valour; expose all they possess as the prize for victory, without excepting the young brides who have given them the pleasures of paternity, or even their own lives, a treasure so dear and valuable to all other men, and for the preservation of which there is nothing they will not undertake. — Barbarians even, without letters, know and repeat these verses upon thee, Helen: — "It is just that both Greeks and Trojans should undergo long misfortunes for the woman whose beauty equals that of immortal goddesses."

There stood upon a column another woman of singular beauty, apparently in the period of brilliant youth, whose hair descended in tresses on each side of her face, and was fastened behind; she occupied a situation but slightly elevated, so that she could be touched by the hand. In the right hand, although the arm had no support, this statue bore a horseman, whose horse she held by one foot, and that apparently as easily as a cup of wine is carried. This horseman, of a manly, noble bearing, clothed in his cuirass, and with booted legs, seemed actually to breathe war. The horse's ears were raised as if he heard the sound of the trumpet, his head elevated, his look fiery, and the ardour painted in his eyes denoted his impatience for the course; his feet, prancing in the air, seemed springing forward with a warlike bound.

After this statue, next to the eastern boundary of the Quadriges, called of the yellow faction, were placed statues of charioteers, examples and models of the art of skilfully driving a chariot. They appeared almost, by the disposition of their hands, to warn charioteers, not to loosen the reins on approaching the boundary; but to hold the horses with a tight hand whilst turning, and to make a sharp and continual use of the whip, so as to keep as close to the boundary as possible, and leave the unskilful rival charioteer, to make too wide a sweep, and lose the advantage, even with the best horses.

I will only add one particularity, for I have not undertaken to describe everything. That which excited remarkable pleasure and admiration, was a stone basis, upon which was placed an animal in bronze, which might have been taken for an ox, but that its tail was too small; like the oxen of Egypt, it had not long dewlaps, and its hoofs were not cloven. It crushed within its jaws, almost to the point of stifling it, another animal, whose body was bristling with scales, so pointed, that although of bronze, they would wound those who ventured to touch them: this animal was supposed to be a basilisk, and the creature it had seized, an aspick; but by others one was said to be an ox from the banks of the Nile, and the other a crocodile. For my part, I will not undertake to reconcile these opinions; I will content myself with saying that they were engaged in a most astonishing contest, and inflicted serious wounds upon each other; for sometimes the more strong, sometimes the mere weak, they were at the same time conquerors and conquered. The animal, which many supposed to be a basilisk, was all swollen from head to feet, and the poison circulating throughout its body, and flowing through all its members, gave it a colour greener than that of frogs,—a colour of death. It was upon its knees, with languishing eyes, and appeared to have lost all strength and vigour. It might have been believed even, that it had long been dead, had not its hind legs, at least, still stood firmly under it. The other animal which it held in its jaws, still waved its tail a little, and opened its long mouth under the pressure of the teeth which held and stifled it. It appeared to use its utmost efforts to escape from the teeth and jaws which held it so tenaciously, but could not succeed; for its body was fast between the jaws, and transpierced by the teeth of its enemy from the shoulders and the fore-feet to the part next to the tail. It was thus they died, the one by the other; the combat was mutual, the vengeance reciprocal, the victory equal, and the death common. [149] For my part, I believe I may remark on this subject, that it is not only in effigy, or among fierce and strong animals, that beings wicked and fatal to man thus inflict a mutual death upon each other; but that we often see nations, which bring war to the Romans, destroy each other; which is an effect of the power of Christ, who disperses nations that are friends to war, who holds blood in horror, and shows the just marching against the aspick and the basilisk, and trampling under foot the lion and the dragon.

— — — —

No. 28.

Letter to M. Michaud upon the Crusade of Children of 1212, by M. Am. Jourdain.

The expedition beyond the seas, undertaken about 1212, and composed entirely of children, if not one of the most striking events of the crusades, certainly appears to me to be not one of the least extraordinary. That institutions dictated by the spirit of religion, and destined either to propagate our religion, or to elevate its splendour, have not always found in their object a preservative against the corruption attached to human beings, is a truth established by numberless examples; but that fanaticism or the genius of evil, should be sufficiently powerful to extinguish in childhood the natural sentiment of its weakness, and draw it away from its natural supports, to inspire it with this train of ideas, this perseverance in resolutions, this accordance required by every enterprise formed by a numerous concourse of individuals, is what we can scarcely believe, although the memory of the fact is preserved by several historians. Whoever is acquainted with the taste of the middle ages for the marvellous, and has only read the incomplete account of the modern historians of the crusades, is at first tempted to range this expedition among fabulous adventures; and to procure it any credit, it is necessary to produce evidences worthy of our confidence.

In my first incredulity, I employed myself in collecting these evidences; I offer them to you in this letter, monsieur, in order to furnish, if possible, one trait more for the varied picture of the errors of the human mind.

We must distinguish various circumstances in this strange event; its date, the means which prepared it, the places that witnessed it, and its issue. Although criticism has not sufficient data to determine each of these points with precision, nevertheless the chronicles of the middle ages furnish us with documents sufficiently extensive to satisfy a prudent curiosity.

With regard to the date, contemporary historians all place this crusade under the year 1212, [150] or 1213 at the latest. [151] It is only by an error very easy to be reconciled, that others advance it twelve years, [152] or put it back ten. [153]

As to the places that witnessed the birth and growth of such an enterprise, it appears that the Crusaders belonged to two nations, and formed two troops, which followed different routes: one, leaving Germany, traversed Saxony and the Alps, and arrived on the shores of the Adriatic Sea; [154] France furnished the others, who, after collecting in the environs of Paris, crossed Burgundy, and arrived at Marseilles, the place of embarkation. [155]

Prestiges, fanaticism, the announcement of prodigies, were all employed to rouse the youth of these countries, and put them in motion. It was reported, according to Vincent de Beauvais that the Old Man of the Mountain, who was accustomed to educate *arsacides* from the tenderest age, detained two clerks captives, and would only grant them their liberty upon condition that they brought him back some young boys from France. The opinion then was, that these children, deceived by false visions, and seduced by the promises of these two clerks, marked themselves with the sign of the cross.

The promoter of the crusade in Germany was a certain Nicolas, a German by nation. [156] "This multitude of children," says Bezarre, "were persuaded, by the help of a false revelation, that the drought would be so great that year, that the abysses of the sea would be dry; and they went to Genoa, with the intention of passing over to Jerusalem, across the arid bed of the Mediterranean."

The composition of these troops corresponded with the means employed to seduce them. There were children of all ages and conditions, and of both sexes; some of them were not more than twelve years old; they set out from villages and towns, without leaders, without guides, without provisions, and with empty purses. It was in vain their parents or friends thought to dissuade them by showing them the folly of such an expedition: the captivity to which they condemned them redoubled their ardour; breaking through doors, or opening themselves passages through walls, they succeeded in escaping, and went to rejoin their respective bands. If they were questioned upon the object of their voyage, they answered that they were going to visit the holy places. Although a pilgrimage commenced under such auspices, and stained with all sorts of excesses, must have been an object of scandal rather than of edification, there were people senseless enough to see in it an act of the all-powerful God; men and women quitted their houses and their lands to join these vagabond troops, believing they pursued the way of salvation: others furnished them with money and food, thinking they aided souls inspired by God, and guided by sentiments of divine piety. The pope, when informed of their proceedings, exclaimed, with a groan: "These children reproach us with being buried in sleep, whilst they are flying to the defence of the Holy Land." [157] If some few of the clergy, endowed with a little foresight, openly blamed this expedition, their censures were at once attributed to motives of avarice and incredulity; and, in order to avoid public contempt, [158] wisdom and prudence were condemned to silence.

The event, however, proved that all which man undertakes without employing the balance of reason and earnest reflection, does not come to a fortunate issue; "for soon," says Bishop Sicard, "this multitude entirely disappeared:—*quasi evanuit universa.*"

But we must carefully distinguish between the fate of the German and that of the French Crusaders, although a part of the latter directed their course towards Italy.

It required nothing beyond wearing the cross to be admitted into the crusade; if the watchful care of princes and prelates in expeditions directed by ecclesiastical and secular power could not succeed in excluding from them men of bad morals, what sort of people must have been mixed with a host got together without the least care, and under the eye of no superior intelligence, the greater part of whom fled, like the prodigal son, from the paternal dwelling, in order to give themselves up, without restraint, to their vicious inclinations? The account of Godfrey the Monk, therefore, does not at all astonish us when he says that thieves insinuated themselves among the German pilgrims, and disappeared after having plundered them of their baggage and the gifts the faithful had bestowed upon them. One of these thieves being recognised at Cologne, ended his days on the rack. To this first misfortune a crowd of evils quickly succeeded, the necessary result of the want of foresight of the Crusaders. The fatigue of a long journey, heat, disease, and want, swept away a great number of them. Of those who arrived in Italy, some, dispersing themselves over the country, and plundered by the inhabitants, were reduced to servitude; others, to the amount of seven thousand, presented themselves before Genoa. At first the senate gave them permission to remain six or seven days in the city; but reflecting afterwards upon the folly of the expedition, fearing that such a multitude would produce famine, and, above all, apprehending that Frederick, who was then in a state of rebellion against the Holy See and at war with Genoa, might take advantage of the circumstance to excite a tumult, they ordered the Crusaders to depart from the city. Nevertheless, it was a received opinion in the time of Bizarre, that the republic granted the rights of citizenship to several of the young Germans of this formidable body, who were distinguished by birth; they acquired afterwards so much consideration, that they were admitted into the order of patricians; "and it is from them," adds the same historian, "that several of the great families of the present day derive their origin; among whom may be remarked that of the Vivaldi." The others, finding their error, turned back towards their own country again; and these Crusaders, who had been seen advancing in numerous troops, and singing animating songs, returned singly, robbed of everything, walking barefooted, undergoing the pangs of hunger, and subjected to the scoffs and derision of the population of the cities and countries they passed through: it is not to be wondered at, that in such circumstances many young girls lost the chastity which had been their ornament in their homes.

The Crusaders from France experienced a nearly similar fate: a very slender portion of them returned: the rest either perished in the waves or became an object of speculation for two Marseilles merchants. Hugh Ferrers and William Porcus, so were they named, carried on a trade with the Saracens, of which the asle of young boys formed a considerable branch. No opportunity for an advantageous speculation could be more favourable; they offered to transport to the East all the pilgrims who arrived at Marseilles, without any kind of charge for the voyage; assigning piety as the motive for this act of generosity. This proposition was joyfully accepted; and seven vessels, laden with these pilgrims, set sail for the coast of Syria. At the end of two days, when the ships were off the isle of St. Peter, near the rock of the Recluse, a violent tempest arose, and the sea swallowed up two of them, with all the passengers on board. The other five arrived at Bugia and Alexandria, and the young Crusaders were all sold to the Saracens or to slave-merchants. [159] The caliph bought forty of them, all of whom were in orders, and caused them to be brought up with great care in a place set apart for the purpose: twelve of the others perished as martyrs, being unwilling to renounce their religion. None of the clerks purchased by the caliph, according to the account of one of them who afterwards obtained his liberty, embraced the worship of Mahomet: all faithful to the religion of their fathers, practised it constantly in tears and slavery. Hugh and William having at a later period formed the project of assassinating Frederick, were discovered, and perished in an ignominious manner, with three Saracens, their accomplices, receiving, in this miserable end, the wages due to their treachery.

Pope Gregory IX. afterwards caused a church to be built in the island of St. Peter, in honour of those who were shipwrecked, and instituted twelve canonships to provide for the duties of it. In the time of Alberic the spot was still pointed out where the bodies cast up by the waves were buried.

As for the Crusaders who survived so many calamities, and remained in Europe, with the exception of some old and infirm persons, the pope would not release them from their vows; they were obliged either to perform the pilgrimage at a maturer age, or to redeem it by alms.

Such was the issue of this crusade, so justly designated by two chronicles, *expeditio nugatoria, expeditio derisoria*. [160]

Two facts strike us as extraordinary in this account: the condition attached by the Old Man of the Mountain to the liberty of the clerk of whom Vincent of Beauvais speaks, and the trade in children carried on by the merchants of Marseilles.

Upon the first point we can offer nothing but the opinion received among the nations of the West. It was generally believed in the thirteenth century, that the Old Man of the Mountain kept up a connection with Christian

Europe; several princes were even accused of having had recourse to the daggers of his assassins to get rid of their enemies. Frederick received ambassadors from him in Sicily. [161] Roger Bacon complains bitterly of the fascinations secretly employed by the Saracens to seduce the young servants of Christ; [162] the name of *Assassins* had already passed into the vulgar tongue in the thirteenth century, and was the object of general terror. In spite, then, of the opinion of some critics, a more extended examination than comes within the scope of this letter is necessary, before we reject the account of Vincent of Bauvais.

As to the trade in young boys, that is not at all a new fact; many traces of it are to be found much anterior to this period. The Greeks and Venetians practised it openly enough. Pope Zacharias repurchased, in 748, many Christian slaves, who had been taken away from Rome by Venetian merchants; the people of Verdun, as witnessed by Lilprand, were about to sell to the Arabs of Spain some young boys they had mutilated, and who were to serve as guards to the women of seraglios. [163] Besides, the fate of the young Crusaders who embarked at Marseilles, and found degradation and slavery instead of the sacred soil promised to their blind zeal, is attested by two contemporary writers, worthy of perfect confidence: these are the illustrious Thomas de Champré [164] and Roger Bacon. [165] I do not then perceive any reasonable doubt that can be raised against this fact, but I find in it a fresh example of human cupidity, which sacrifices, in order to satisfy its cravings, that which nature and religion hold most sacred.—Receive, Monsieur, &c. &c.

— — — —

No. 29.

A Letter from Pope Innocent III. [166]

Now that motives more pressing than ever call Christians to the assistance of the Holy Land, and that we have reason to expect, from the present aid, more fortunate results than have been hitherto obtained, we again raise our voice, and make you to hear our cries in the name of Him who, when dying, cried with a loud voice from the cross, and who carried obedience towards God, his father, so far as to die upon the cross, crying in order to drag us from the torments of an eternal death; who cried also by himself, and said: "If any one desires to come with me, let him entirely renounce himself, let him take up his cross, and follow me." This is as if he said in a more manifest manner, Let him who desires to follow me to the crown, follow me also to the fight, which is now proposed to all to serve as a trial. There is no doubt that the Omnipotent God was able, if it had been his will, to prevent this land falling into the hands of the enemies; he is able even now, if it were his will, to wrest it from them easily; since nothing can resist his will. But as iniquity was carried almost to its height, and as the zeal of charity was chilled in most, to arouse his faithful servants from the sleep of death, and to recall to them the desire of life, he offers this conflict to them, in order to prove their faith, like gold in the crucible; offering to them in this, an opportunity, nay more, an assured pledge of obtaining salvation. For this, they who shall have fought valiantly for him, shall obtain of him a crown of happiness; but they who, in such a pressing necessity, shall have drawn back from the service they owed to the glory of the Lord, will deserve to hear, at the great day of judgment, their just condemnation pronounced. What happy effects will this holy enterprise produce! How many, turning towards penitence, will range themselves under the standard of the cross, and will merit, by their efforts, a crown of glory, who perhaps would have perished in their iniquity, after having passed a life entirely consecrated to carnal voluptuousness and to the frivolities of this world. This is an old artifice of Jesus Christ, which he has deigned to repeat in our days for the salvation of his faithful servants. In fact, if any earthly monarch were driven by his enemies from his states, would not, when he should have recovered them, such of his vassals be condemned as infidels, and destined to all the punishments which the greatly guilty deserve, as had not exposed for his sake, not only their lives but their persons? In the same manner the King of Kings, our Lord Jesus Christ, who has given you a body and a soul, and all the other blessings you enjoy, will condemn you as guilty of black ingratitude, and of the crime of infidelity, if you fail to march to his succour at a time when he is in a manner driven from the kingdom he has acquired by his blood. Let whoever then shall refuse, in this pressing necessity, to hasten to the help of his Redeemer, know that he will exhibit a criminal hardness, and that he will be grievously guilty. If any one should be unjustly deprived of a portion, however small, of the heritage of his fathers, soon, according to the usages of the world, he would labour with all his strength to have this injustice repaired, and to repel this violence; and would spare neither his person nor his property, until he had succeeded in regaining all that he had lost. What excuse, then, can he bring who shall have declined some trifling labours to punish offences committed against his Redeemer, and avenge the outrages he has received; and who, by sparing his person and his goods, prevents the recovery of the places which witnessed the passion and the resurrection of our Lord, in which God, our king, deigned, some centuries ago, to operate, upon the earth, the salvation of men? How, also, according to the divine precept, can he love his neighbour as himself (as it is written), who knows that his brethren, Christians in belief and in name, are groaning in the prisons of the perfidious Saracens, and are suffering all the horrors of the hardest captivity, and shall refuse to labour in an effective manner for their deliverance, transgressing by this, this precept of the natural law, which God has made known in his Gospel: "Do unto other men that which you wish they should do unto you." Are you ignorant, that among these people, many thousands of Christians groan in slavery and in chains, and are constantly subject to the most cruel tortures? All the provinces now in the power of the Saracens were inhabited by Christian nations till after the time of St. Gregory; but towards that period, there arose a child of perdition, a false prophet, named Mahomet, who, by the attractions of the joys of this world, and by the bait of carnal voluptuousness, found means to seduce a great number and turn them aside from the path of truth. Although his perfidy may have triumphed up to the present day, we place, nevertheless, our confidence in the Lord, who has hitherto so well inspired us, and we hope that we shall soon see the end of this beast, of which, according to the Apocalypse of St. John, "the number is included in six hundred and sixty-six." He will soon end by the operation of the Holy Ghost, who will revive, with the fire of charity, the chilled hearts of the faithful; and of these years, nearly six hundred have already passed away. In addition to the other grave and considerable insults that the perfidious Saracens have inflicted on our Redeemer on account of our sins, lately, upon Mount Tabor, where he revealed to his disciples the image of future glory, these same perfidious Saracens have erected a fortress for the confusion of the Christian name. They hope, by means of this fortress, easily to obtain possession of the city of Acre, which is near to it, and afterwards invade, without the least obstacle, the rest of the Holy Land, almost entirely destitute of strength and means of defence. For this, then, my dear children in Christ, change into sentiments of peace and love your brotherly dissensions and discords, and let every one of you hasten to range himself under the standard of the cross, without hesitating to expose his person and his wealth for Him who offered up his soul for you, and shed his blood for you. March with security, upon this holy expedition, certain that if you are truly repentant, this short and transient labour will be for you a certain means of obtaining life eternal. For us, depositaries of the Divine mercy, and to whom has been transmitted the authority of the blessed St. Peter and St. Paul, according to the power which, although we were unworthy of it, God has given us to bind and unbind, we grant, to all who shall undertake in person and at their own expense this meritorious labour, the absolute pardon of their sins, after they shall heartily have repented of them, and shall have confessed them by word of mouth, and we give them the certain hope, by this means, of obtaining more easily life everlasting. As for those who, without assisting in person in the expedition, shall contribute to it by sending, according to their rank and their means, men fit for the purpose, in the same manner to those who shall go in person, although at the expense of others, we grant to all pardon for their sins. We grant the same pardon, in proportion with the extent of their sacrifices and the fervour of their devotion, to those who shall deprive themselves of a part of their worldly goods to provide for the expenses of the enterprise. We equally take under the protection of Saint Peter and of ourselves, the persons and the property of the faithful, from the moment they shall receive the sign of the cross; we place them under that of the archbishops and bishops, and all the prelates of the Church; and we declare that no infringement shall be made upon the possessions of the absent, until certain intelligence be obtained of their death or of their return. If any one shall make an attempt to do so, he shall be cited before the prelates of the Church, and shall be subjected to ecclesiastical censure. If it should happen, moreover, that any one of those who are disposed to set out for the Holy Land, should be obliged, by oath to pay any usurious amounts, we enjoin the prelates of the Church, to employ the same means to force their creditors to liberate them from their oath, and to desist from their usurious demands; and if it should happen that any one of these creditors should undertake to force his debtor to the payment of the usuries, let him incur the same censure, and be forced to make restitution. As for the Jews, we order that they be forced, by the secular power, to make remission of all usury to them who are going to the Holy Land; and, until they have made that remission, they shall be deprived, by means of excommunication, of all kinds of commerce with Christians. But in order that the succour furnished to the Holy Land should become less burdensome and more easy, from being levied upon a greater number, we beg all the faithful in general, and every one individually, in the name of the Father, the Son, and the Holy Ghost, the only true, the only Eternal God, demanding in the name of Jesus Christ and for Jesus Christ, of all archbishops, bishops, abbots, and priors; of all chapters of churches, whether cathedral or conventual; of all clerks, as well as of all cities, towns, and villages, to furnish each, according to their faculties, the required number of warriors, with everything necessary for their support for three years. If, for this purpose, each individual contribution should appear insufficient, several should be joined together; for we entertain no doubt that enough persons will present themselves, if the means be not wanting. We particularly request kings, princes, counts, barons, and other wealthy men who do not assist in the expedition in person, to contribute their part according to their means. As to maritime cities, we require of them the assistance of vessels. And for fear that we should appear to impose heavy and serious burdens upon others, which we are unwilling to put our hand to ourselves, we declare in our conscience, and before God, that all which we require of others we will eagerly do ourselves. We have thought it our duty to state, with respect to the clerks who shall form part of the expedition, that, all contestation ceasing, they may, to that effect, pledge the revenues of their benefices for three years. But as the succour which the Holy Land requires may meet with many obstacles and delays, if, before conferring the cross upon every one, it were necessary to stop to examine if he were capable of performing personally all the obligations imposed by such a vow, we consent that, regulars excepted, all who desire it shall take the cross; and that, if reasons of a pressing necessity, or of an evident utility require it, their vow may be, in virtue of an apostolic mandatory letter, changed, redeemed, or deferred; and, for the same reason, we revoke the pardons and indulgences granted by us, up to this day, to those who offered to march against the Moors in Spain, or against the heretics of Provence; particularly as they were granted to them for a time which is now entirely passed away, and for reasons which, in a great degree, have ceased to exist. For, with the grace of God, these affairs have so progressed, that they no longer require active measures; and if, by chance, they should again require them, we should take care quickly to turn our attention towards them. We grant, however, that the Provençals and Spaniards should still enjoy these indulgences. Moreover, as corsairs and pirates greatly impede the measures taken for the succour of the Holy Land, by seizing and plundering those who are going thither, we excommunicate them, as well as their principal accomplices and abettors; forbidding under pain of anathema, any person, wittingly, to treat with them for any sale or any purchase, and enjoining the governors of cities and places which they inhabit, to reclaim them from this trade of iniquity, and put an end to their brigandages. Besides, as not being willing to trouble the wicked is nothing else but encouraging them; and as this is not foreign to the manœuvres of a secret society which neglects to oppose these manifest crimes, we cannot refrain from employing ecclesiastical severity against the persons and the property of those who shall be in this condition; because they would become no less dangerous to the Christian name than the Saracens themselves. Moreover, we renew the sentence of excommunication, passed in the Council of the Lateran, against those who supply the Saracens with armour and weapons, or serve as pilots to the corsairs of those nations; we declare also that they shall be deprived of all they possess, and shall remain in slavery, if they chance to fall into it. We order that this sentence be published in all maritime cities, every Sunday and festival. But as we have much more to look for from divine clemency than from human power, we must, in such a conjuncture, contend less with corporeal arms than with spiritual arms; therefore we order and decree, that once in every month there shall be made, separately, a general procession of men, and in the same manner separately, as much as possible, one of women, during which, with minds filled with the spirit of humility, all will ask, with fervent prayers, that it may please the divine mercy to remove from us opprobrium and confusion, by delivering from the hands of pagans, that land upon which all the mysteries of our redemption were effected, and by restoring it, for the glory of the Omnipotent, to the Christian people. Care must always be taken, in these processions, to make a fervent exhortation to the people, and to repeat to them the name of the sign of our salvation. To prayer must be added fasting and charity, in order that they may be like wings to prayer, and carry it more easily and more promptly to the pious ears of the Eternal, who will listen to us with kindness in his own good time. Every day, likewise, at the solemn mass, after the kiss of peace, at the moment in which the salutary host, offered for the sins of the world, is upon the point of being consumed, all present, men as well as women, shall prostrate themselves humbly to the earth, and the clerks shall sing with a loud voice, the psalm, *Deus venerunt gentes in hæreditatem tuam*; to which they shall add: *Exurgat Deus et dissipentur inimici ejus; et fugiant à facie ejus qui oderunt eum*. Then the officiating priest shall sing with a loud voice upon the altar, the prayer, *Deus qui admirabile, &c*. In churches in which the general procession shall assemble, care shall be taken to place a *tronc*, which shall be fastened with three keys, one of which shall remain in the hands of an honest priest, another in those of a devout layman, and the third in those of a monk, that they may be faithfully taken care of. It is in these troncs that clerks, laymen, men, and women shall deposit the alms destined for the aid of the Holy Land, according to the dispositions of those to whom these cares shall have been confided. As to the departure and the voyage, which should be made with modesty and order, we will, as yet, state nothing regarding them until the army of the Lord shall have taken the cross. But as all the circumstances are now prepared for, we will make all the arrangements which may appear necessary, aided by the counsels of wise and prudent men. To this effect, we have chosen our beloved son De Sales, the late abbots of Novo Castro, C. dean of Spire, and the guardian of the Augustines, all men of probity and known fidelity, who, after having associated themselves with other worthy and honest men, shall regulate and dispose, in our name, all that they shall deem necessary for the success of this enterprise, causing their orders to be faithfully and carefully executed by men fit for the business and specially appointed to it. This, therefore, is why we pray you all, we supplicate and conjure you, in the name of the Lord, command you by this present apostolic letters, and enjoin you by the authority of the Holy Ghost, to take care to prove, on every occasion, to these legates of Jesus Christ, by your eagerness to furnish them with all things necessary, that they will find, by you and in you, the means of attaining the so much desired end.

— — — —

No. 30.

Poetry of the Troubadours for the Crusades.

See how great is the folly of him who remains here! Does not Jesus command his apostles to follow him, and that he who should follow him should leave his friends and his wealthy abode? The time is come to obey this order: he who dies beyond the seas is more happy than if he lived; and he who lives on this side of them is more unfortunate than if he died. What is a cowardly, shameful life worth? Ah! he who dies generously triumphs over death itself, and lives again in felicity.

Let him cease to boast of being brave, the knight who does not arm to succour both the cross and the sacred tomb! Yes, with rich equipments, with valour, with courtesy, and with all that is fair and irreproachable, we cannot obtain glory and happiness in paradise. What more could counts and kings require, if, by honourable deeds, they could redeem themselves from hell and from fire eternal, in which so many wretches would live tormented for ever?

Whoever is forced by old age or sickness to remain at home, let him give his money to those who are willing to take arms: it is a good deed to send another in your place; particularly when you are not kept back by cowardice. Ah! at the day of judgment, what will they answer who have remained at home? God will appear, and will say: "False men! men full of cowardice! for your sakes I died, for your sakes I was scourged." Then, the just man himself, will he be without fear?—(Pons de Capducil: *Er nos sia.*)

I would that the king of France and the king of England were at peace! Certes, God would greatly honour him of the two who should consent the first, and would never forget his merits. Yes, that king would be crowned in heaven. Ah! why are the king of Apulia and the emperor not friends and brothers, until the holy tomb be recovered? Are they ignorant that the pardon they grant here, they themselves shall obtain at the day of the great judgment?—(Pons de Capducil: *En honor.*)

What mourning! what despair! what tears! when God shall say, "Go, wretches, go into hell, where you shall be tormented for ever in tortures, in agonies. This is your punishment for not having believed that I underwent a cruel passion: I died for you, and you have forgotten it." But they who, in the crusade, shall meet with death, will be able to say, "And we, Lord, we died for thee."—(Folquet de Romans: *Quan lo dous.*)

To-day will the brave, the gallant, and the courageous show themselves; it will be their audacity and their bravery that will distinguish them: this is the moment to display skill and valour. God calls, he himself calls, he chooses true knights, he who knows them, and he rejects the base who are wanting in courage and faith: it is the valiant alone whom his mercy will distinguish.—(Pierre d'Auvergne: *Lo Senhor*.)

The time is come, the day is arrived, in which it will be put to the test who are the men worthy of serving the Eternal: he calls, but he only calls upon the gallant and the brave. They shall be ever his, who, knowing faithfully how to suffer, devote themselves, and fight, shall be full of frankness, generosity, courtesy, and loyalty. Let the cowardly and the avaricious remain where they are; God only wants the good: he is willing that they should save themselves by their own high deeds. What a worthy and glorious salvation!

If ever William Malespine appeared brave among us, he has now furnished God himself with the proof of it; he took the cross the first, he took the cross voluntarily, to deliver the holy sepulchre and the sacred heritage. What shame! how wrong it is of the kings and the emperor that they do not deign to conclude treaties and truces with one another, in order to be able to succour the kingdom of the law, the holy light, and the tomb and the cross which the Turks have so long retained. The repetition alone of this disaster overwhelms us with profound sadness—(Aimerie de Peguilhan: *Evas pana*.)

It will soon be known what gallant men entertain the noble ambition of meriting the glory of this world and the glory of God. Yes, they may obtain the one and the other, they who devote themselves to the pious pilgrimage to deliver the holy tomb. Great God, what grief! the Turks have assailed and profaned it! Let us be sensible, even to the depths of our hearts, of this mortal disgrace; let us clothe ourselves with the sign of the Crusaders, let us pass over the seas; we have a safe and courageous guide, the sovereign pontiff Innocent himself.

Yes, every one is invited thither, every one is required; let every one march forward and cross himself in the name of that God who was crucified between two thieves, when he was so unjustly condemned by the Jews. If we still set a value on loyalty and bravery, we must fear the opprobrium of leaving Christ thus disinherited; but we love, we wish for that which is evil, and despise that which would be good and useful. But what! life, in our countries, is for us, nothing but a continual danger; and death, in the Holy Land, is for us eternal happiness.

Ah! ought we to hesitate to suffer death in the service of God, of that God who deigned to suffer for our deliverance! Yes, they shall be saved with St. Andrew, they who shall march towards Mount Tabor: let no one feel dread in the passage of this fleshly death. That which is to be feared is spiritual death, which delivers us up to the place where there shall be weeping and gnashing of teeth, as St. Matthew shows and assures us.

Signor, saciez-tu or ne s'en ira
En cele terre u diex fu mors et vis,
Et ki la crois d'outre mer ne prendra
A paines mais ira en Paradis:
Ki a en soi pitié et ramembrance
Au haut Seignor, doit guerre sa vengeance,
Et delivrer sa terre et son pays....
Or s'en iront cil vaillant bacheler
Ki aiment Dieu et l'oneur de cest mont
Ki sagement voilent à Dieu aler,
Et li morveux, li cendreus demourront:
Avugle sunt, de ce ne dont je mie,
Ki au secours ne font Dieu en sa vie
Et por si poc pert la gloire del mont.
Diex se laissa per nos en crois pener;
Et nous dira au jour où tuit venront:
"Vos, ki ma crois m'aidâtes à porfer,
Vos en irez là où li angele sont;
Là me verrez, et ma Mère Marie;
Et vos, par qui je n'oi onques aie,
Descendez tuit en enfer le parfont." [167]

—Thibault, king of Navarre. He took the cross in 1236; he set out from Marseilles in the month of August, 1238 or 1239.

— — — —

No. 31.

Upon the Funeral Ceremonies of the Prussians.

When a man, particularly a noble, died, he was placed upon a seat in the midst of his family and his friends, who said to him, "Hilloa! hadst thou not a comfortable house and a handsome wife, why didst thou die? Hadst thou not large flocks, horses of speed, and dogs of sure scent? What has driven thee from the world?" They then spread out the riches of the dead man, asking him the same questions; and as he made them no answer, those who were present charged him with messages to their deceased friends and relations. [168] They made the defunct funeral presents: for the men, this was a sword, to defend them against their enemies; for the women, it was a needle and thread, with which they might mend their clothes during their long voyage. The poor were buried, the rich were consumed upon a funeral pile. [169] The relations accompanied the convoy on horseback, sword in hand, uttering cries to drive away evil spirits. When arrived at the place of the ceremony, the cortège went three times round the pile, repeating these words: "Hilloa! why hast thou quitted life?" With the dead they burnt household goods, horses, dogs, falcons, everything which had ministered to the wants or pleasures of the deceased upon earth; sometimes even the wives, and the slaves who were attached to him, were cast into the lighted pile. Panegyrists, whom they called *talissons* [170] and *ligastons*, pronounced the eulogy of the dead; and whilst the flames ascended towards the heavens, they fancied they beheld him in the clouds, mounted upon a white horse, clad in brilliant armour, holding three stars in the right hand, a falcon on the left hand, and advancing towards another world in all the splendour of power and glory.

No. 32.

Letter from the Count of Artois upon the taking of Damietta.

To his very excellent and very dear mother, Blanche, by the grace of God, illustrious queen of France, Robert, Count d'Artois, her devoted son, salutation, filial piety, and a will always obedient to hers. As you take much interest in our prosperity, in that of ours and of the Christian people, when you shall learn them with certainty, your excellence will no doubt rejoice to know that the lord, our brother and king, the queen and her sister, and ourselves also, are enjoying, thanks to God, perfect health. We ardently desire that you may be in the enjoyment of the like. Our dear brother, the Count of Anjou, is still afflicted with his quartan fever, but it is less violent than it was. The lord, our brother, with the barons and pilgrims who passed the winter in the isle of Cyprus, assembled on board their vessels, at the port of Limisso, on the evening of the Ascension, in order to proceed against the enemies of the Christian faith. After much labour, and much opposition on the part of the winds, they arrived, under the guardianship of God, on the Friday after Trinity, and towards mid-day, upon the coast, where, having cast anchor, they assembled in the king's vessel, to deliberate upon what was to be done. As they saw before them Damietta, and the port guarded by a great multitude of barbarians, on horseback as well as on foot, and the mouth of the river covered with a great number of armed vessels, it was resolved that on the following day, all should land with our lord the king.

On the morrow, the Christian army, leaving the large vessels, descended into the galleys and small boats. Full of confidence in the mercy of God, and in the succour of the holy cross, which the legate carried near the king, they directed their course towards the shore and against the enemy, who launched a great number of arrows against them. Nevertheless, as the small boats, on account of the too great depth of the sea, could not gain the shore, the Christian army, leaving their boats to the care of Providence, threw themselves into the sea, and gained land, although loaded with their armour. Although a multitude of Turks defended the shores against the Christians, nevertheless, thanks to our Lord Jesus Christ, the latter made themselves masters of it without loss, and killed a great number of the horse and foot soldiers, and some, as we hear, of great name. The Saracens retreated into the city, which was well fortified by the river, its walls and strong towers; but the All-Powerful Lord gave it up, on the next day, which was the octave of the Trinity, to the Christian army; the Saracens flying away, after having abandoned it. This was done by the favour of God alone. Know that these same Saracens have left the city full of provisions of all kinds, and of machines of war. The Christian army, after having fully supplied itself, left half for the provisioning of the city. The king, our lord, has sojourned there with his army, and, during his sojourn, has caused to be brought from the vessels all he requires. We have thought it best to remain here till the retreat of the waters of the Nile, which will, as we hear, inundate the country, and would cause great losses in the Christian army.

The countess of Anjou was confined in the isle of Cyprus, of a fine well-made boy, whom she has left at nurse there. Given at the camp of *Jamas*, in the year of our Lord 1249, in the month of June, and on the eve of St. John the Baptist.

———

No. 33.

Letter of St. Louis upon his Captivity and Deliverance.

Louis, by the grace of God, king of the French, to his beloved and faithful prelates, barons, warriors, citizens, burgesses, and all the other inhabitants of his kingdom, to whom these present letters may come, salutation!

For the honour and glory of the name of God, desiring, with all our soul, to pursue the enterprise of the crusade, we have thought proper to inform you all that after the taking of Damietta, which our Lord Jesus Christ, by his ineffable mercy, as by miracle, gave up to the power of the Christians, as you have no doubt learnt, by the advice of our council, we set out from that city the 20th day of the month of November last. Our armies of land and sea were united; we marched against that of the Saracens, which was gathered together, and encamped in a place vulgarly called Mansourah. During our march, we sustained the attack of the enemy, who constantly experienced considerable loss. Upon one day among others, many men belonging to the Egyptian army, who came to attack ours, were killed. We learnt by the way that the Sultan of Cairo had just terminated his unhappy life; that before dying he sent for his son, who was in the eastern provinces, and made all the officers of his army take the oath of fidelity to this prince; and that he had left the command of all his troops to one of his emirs, named Fakr-eddin. Upon our arrival at the spot I have named, we found the news true. It was on the Thursday before the festival of Christmas that we arrived there; but we were not able to approach the Saracens, on account of a stream of water, which was between the two armies, called the river Thanis, a stream which separates itself at this spot from the great river of the Nile. We placed our camp between these two rivers, and it extended from the greater to the lesser one. We had there some engagements with the Saracens, who had many of their men killed by the swords of ours, but a great number of them were drowned in the waters. As the Thanis was not fordable, on account of the deepness of its waters, and the height of its banks, we began to throw a causeway across it, in order to open a passage for the Christian army; we worked at it for many days with great labour, dangers, and expense. The Saracens opposed all the efforts of our toil: they built machines to act against our machines; and they broke to pieces with stones, and burned with their Greek fire the towers and timbers which we placed upon the causeway. We had almost lost all hope of passing over by means of the causeway, when a Saracen fugitive informed us of a ford by which the Christian army might cross the river. Having called together our barons, and the principal leaders of the army, on the Monday before Ash-Wednesday, it was resolved that on the following day, that is to say, the day of Carême penant (three days before Lent), we should repair early in the morning to the place pointed out for crossing the river, leaving a small part of the army to guard the camp. The next day, having ranged our troops in order of battle, we proceeded to the ford, and crossed the river, not without incurring great dangers; for the ford was deeper and more difficult than it had been represented to us. Our horses were obliged to swim, and it was not easy to get out of the river, on account of the elevation of the banks, which were besides very muddy. When we had crossed the river, we arrived at the place where the Saracens had raised machines in face of our causeway. Our vanguard, attacking the enemy, killed a vast many people, and spared neither sex nor age. Among the number, the Saracens lost a general and several emirs. Our troops having afterwards dispersed themselves over the country, some of our soldiers passed through the camp of the enemy, and arrived at the village named Mansourah, killing all they met with; but the Saracens perceiving the imprudence of our men, resumed their courage, and fell upon them, surrounding them on all sides, and overwhelming them with numbers. A great carnage ensued of our barons and warriors, ecclesiastics as well as others, whom we have with reason deplored, and whose loss we still continue to deplore. There we lost also our brave and illustrious brother, the count d'Artois, worthy of eternal remembrance. It is with bitterness of heart we recall the memory of that painful loss, although we ought to rejoice at it; for we believe and hope that having received the crown of martyrdom, he is gone into the heavenly country, and that he there enjoys the reward accorded to holy martyrs. On that day the Saracens pouring down upon us from all parts, and piercing our troops with showers of arrows, we withstood their fierce assaults till the ninth hour, although we were entirely without the assistance of our cross-bowmen. [171] In the end, after having a great number of our warriors and horses killed and wounded, with the help of our Lord, we preserved our position, and having rallied, we went that same day and pitched our tents close to the machines of the Saracens. We remained there with a small number of our people, and made a bridge of boats, that those who were on the other side of the river might come to us. The next day many of them crossed, and encamped near us. Then the machines of the Saracens being destroyed, our soldiers were able to go and come freely, and safely, from one army to the other, over the bridge of boats. On the following Friday, the children of perdition having collected their forces from all parts, with the intention of exterminating the Christian army, came to attack our lines, with much audacity, and with infinite numbers. The shock was so terrible on both sides, that it is said never was such a one beheld on these shores. With the help of God, we stood our ground on all sides; we repulsed the enemy, and made a great number of them fall beneath our blows. At the end of a few days, the son of the late Sultan, returning from the eastern provinces, arrived at Mansourah. The Egyptians received him as their master, and with transports of joy. His arrival redoubled their courage; but from that moment, we know not by what judgment of God, everything on our side went contrary to our desires. A contagious disease broke out in our army, and carried off men and animals, in such a manner that there were very few who had not to regret companions or attend upon the sick. The Christian army was, in a very short time, much diminished. There was such a scarcity of food, that many died of want and hunger; for the boats of Damietta could not bring to the army the provisions embarked upon the river, because the vessels of pirates and of the enemy cut off the passage. They even captured many of our boats, and afterwards took, successively, two caravans, which were bringing us provisions, and killed a great number of sailors and others who formed part of it. The extreme scarcity of food and forage spread desolation and terror throughout the army, and with the losses we had experienced, forced us to quit our position, and to return to Damietta, if it were the will of God; but *as the ways of man are not within himself, but in Him who directs his steps, and disposes all things according to his will*, whilst we were on the road, that is to say, the 5th of the month of April, the Saracens, having got together all their forces, attacked the Christian army, and by the permission of God, and on account of our sins, we fell into the power of the enemy. We and our dear brothers, the counts of Anjou and Poictiers, and the others who were returning with us by land, were all taken prisoners. The greater part of those who were returning by the river were, in the same manner, either taken prisoners or killed. The vessels on which they were aboard were mostly burnt with the sick who were in them. Some days after our captivity, the sultan proposed a truce to us; he demanded earnestly, but without threats, that Damietta and all that it contained should be given up to him without delay; and that he should be indemnified for all the losses and all the expenses he had incurred up to that day, from the moment the Christians entered Damietta. After many conferences, we concluded a truce with him for ten years, on the following conditions:—

The sultan will deliver from prison, and allow to go whither we will, ourselves and all that have been made prisoners since our arrival in Egypt, and all other Christians, of whatever country they may be, who have been made prisoners since the sultan Kamel, grandfather of the present sultan, made a truce with the emperor; the Christians retaining in peace all the lands they possessed in the kingdom of Jerusalem, at the time of our arrival. On our part, we consent to give up Damietta, with eight hundred thousand Saracen byzants, for the liberty of the prisoners, and for the losses and expenses of which we have just spoken (we have already paid four hundred), and to deliver all Saracen prisoners which the Christians have made since we have been in Egypt, as well as those who had been made captives in the kingdom of Jerusalem, since the truce concluded between the aforesaid sultan and the aforesaid emperor. All our household goods, and those of all others who were at Damietta, shall be, after our departure, placed under the care of the sultan, and be transported into the country of the Christians when an opportunity shall offer itself. All the Christian sick, and those who shall remain at Damietta to sell what they possess there, shall be in equal safety, and shall depart either by land or by sea, when they shall please, without obstacle or molestation.—The sultan was bound to give safe conduct to the countries of the Christians to those who should wish to depart by land.

This truce, concluded with the sultan, had just been sworn to on both sides, and the sultan had already set forward on his march to go with his army to Damietta, and fulfil the conditions which had been stipulated, when, by a judgment of God, some Saracen warriors, doubtless with the connivance of the greater part of the army, rushed upon the sultan at the moment he was rising from table, and wounded him severely. The sultan, in spite of this, came out of his tent, hoping to be able to escape by flight; but he was killed by sword-cuts, in presence of almost all the emirs, and of a multitude of other Saracens. After this many Saracens, in the first moments of their fury, came with arms in their hands to our tent, as if they wished, and as many among us feared, to slay both us and the other Christians; but divine clemency having calmed their fury, they pressed us to execute the conditions of the truce. Their words and their requests were, however, mingled with terrible threats: at last, by the will of God, who is the father of mercies, the consoler of the afflicted, and who listens to the lamentations of his servants, we confirmed by a new oath the truce which we had made with the sultan. We received from all, and from each one in particular of them, a similar oath, sworn according to their law, to observe the conditions of the truce. The time was fixed for the giving up of the prisoners and the city of Damietta. It had not been without difficulty that we agreed with the sultan for the giving up of that place; it was not without difficulty again that we agreed afresh with the emirs. As we could have no hopes of holding it, after what we were told by those who came back from Damietta, and who knew the true state of things; by the advice of the barons of France, and of many others, we judged it would be better for Christendom, that we and the other prisoners should be delivered by means of a truce, than to retain that city with the remains of the Christians that were in it, ourselves and the others remaining prisoners, exposed to all the dangers of such a captivity. For this reason, on the day fixed, the emirs received the city of Damietta, after which they set us at liberty, ourselves, our brothers, the counts of Flanders, Brittany, and Soissons, and many other barons and warriors of the kingdoms of France, Jerusalem, and Cyprus. We had then a firm hope that they would render up and deliver all the other Christians, and that, according to the tenor of the treaty, they would keep their oaths.

This done, we quitted Egypt; after having left the persons charged to receive the prisoners from the hands of the Saracens, and to take care of the things we could not bring away, for want of vessels to convey them in. Upon our arrival here, we sent vessels and commissaries into Egypt, to bring away the prisoners; for the deliverance of these prisoners is the object of all our solicitude; and the other things which we had left behind, such as the machines, arms, tents, a certain number of horses, and several other articles; but the emirs detained our commissaries a long time at Cairo, to whom they have, at length, only delivered four hundred prisoners out of twelve thousand that there are in Egypt. Some of these were only liberated upon the payment of money. As to the other things, the emirs would restore nothing; but what is most odious, after the truce concluded and sworn to, according to the account of our commissaries and captives worthy of credit, who have returned from that country, they have chosen from among their prisoners some young men, whom they have forced, the sword held over their heads, to abjure the Catholic faith, and embrace the law of Mahomet, which many have had the weakness to do; but others, like courageous athletes, rooted in their faith, and constantly persisting in their firm resolution, have not been moved by either the threats or the blows of the enemies, and have received the crown of martyrdom. Their blood, we do not doubt, cries to the Lord for the Christian people; they will be, in the heavenly court, our advocates before the Sovereign Judge; and they will be more useful to us in that country than if we had been able to keep them upon earth. The Mussulmans likewise slaughtered many Christians who were left sick in Damietta. Although we should have observed the conditions of the treaty that we have made with them, and were always ready to observe them, we had no certainty of seeing the Christian prisoners delivered, or of having that restored which belonged to us. When the truce was concluded, and our deliverance had taken place, we had a firm confidence that the country beyond the sea, occupied by the Christians, would remain in a state of peace until the expiration of the truce; and we had both the desire and the intention to return to France. We were already making preparations for our passage; but when we clearly perceived, by that which we have just related, that the emirs were openly violating the truce, and, in contempt of their oath, did not fear to make a sport of us and Christendom, we assembled the barons of France, the prelates, the knights of the Temple, of the Hospital, of the Teutonic order, and the barons of the kingdom of Jerusalem, and we consulted with them upon what was best to be done. The greater number were of opinion that if we were to return at this moment, and abandon this country, which we were upon the point of losing, it would be exposing it entirely to the attacks of the Saracens, particularly in the state of misery and weakness to which it was reduced, and we might consider the deliverance of the Christian prisoners now in the power of the enemy, as lost and hopeless. If, on the contrary, we remained, we had hopes that time would bring about something favourable, such as the deliverance of the captives, the preservation of the castles, and the fortresses of the kingdom of Jerusalem, and other advantages for Christendom; particularly as discord had sprung up between the sultan of Aleppo and those who governed at Cairo. The sultan has already, after gathering together his armies, got possession of Damascus, and some castles belonging to the sovereign of Cairo. It is said he is about to come into Egypt, to avenge the death of the sultan, whom the emirs killed, and to make himself master, if he can, of all the country. In consequence of these considerations and compassionating the miseries and degradation of the Holy Land, we who came to succour it, pitying the captivity and the sorrows of our prisoners, although many dissuade us from remaining longer beyond the seas, we have preferred putting off our passage, and continuing still some time in Syria, to abandoning entirely the cause of Christ, and leaving our prisoners exposed to so many and such great dangers. But we have determined upon sending back into France our dear brothers, the counts of Poictiers and Anjou, for the consolation of our dear lady and mother, and of the whole kingdom. As all those who bear the name of Christian ought to be filled with zeal for the enterprise we have formed, and you in particular, who are descended from the blood of those whom the Lord chose as a privileged people, for the conquest of the Holy Land, which you ought to look upon as your property, we invite you all to serve Him who served you upon the cross, shedding his blood for your salvation; for this criminal nation, in addition to the blasphemies they vomited in the presence of Christian people against the Creator, beat the cross with rods, spat upon it, and trampled it under-foot, in hatred of the Christian faith.

Courage, then, soldiers of Christ! arm, and be ready to avenge these outrages and these affronts. Take example of your ancestors, who distinguished themselves among all nations by their devotion, by the sincerity of their faith, and filled the universe with the fame of their noble actions. We have gone before you in the service of God. Come and join us. Although you arrive late, you will receive from the Lord the recompense which the father of the family, in the Gospel, accorded without distinction to the labourers who came to labour in the vineyard at the end of the day, as to the labourers who came at the beginning of it. They who shall come, or who shall send succour whilst we are here, will obtain, in addition to the indulgences promised to Crusaders, the favour of God and of man. Make, then, your preparations, and let them whom the virtue of the Most High shall inspire to either come themselves or send assistance, be ready by the month of April or of May next. As for such as cannot be prepared for the first passage, let them at least be in a situation to make that which will take place about the festival of St. John. The nature of the enterprise requires promptness, and every delay must produce fatal consequences. For you, prelates and others, faithful servants of Christ, help our cause with the Most High by the fervour of your prayers; order it so that this be done in all places under your direction, so that they may obtain for us from divine clemency the blessings of which our sins render us unworthy.

Done at Acre, the year of our Lord 1250, in the month of August

— — — —

No. 34.

A List of the Great Officers or Knights who followed St. Louis to Tunis, according to Agreements entered into between them and the King, in the year 1269, as set forth in the Manuscript from which this List is taken; which Manuscript was inherited by M. Malet de Graville, formerly Admiral, and was printed at the end of the Preface to the History of St. Louis, *by Joinville, edition of the Louvre.*

Monseigneur de Valery is to go himself, and thirty knights, and the king is to give him eight thousand livres Tournois, and he is to have food for his horses of the king during the passage; but they shall not be fed at court (*n'auront pas bouche à court*), and shall remain a year, he and his people, which year shall commence as soon as they shall have arrived on dry land; and if it should so happen that by agreement or by the accidents of the sea they should sojourn in some island with the king, by which they should remain with the sea behind them, the year shall commence with their sojourn, and the knights must be paid half of their dues when the year begins, and the other half when the first half shall have passed away; and if it be required to know what shall be allowed to each banneret, it is to be two horses; and to each knight not a banneret, one horse; and the horses to carry the groom who shall take care of them; so that grooms have six horses each in charge. [172] The constable shall go likewise, he and fifteen knights, upon the same condition as the sieur de Valery, but he shall only receive four thousand livres Tournois of the king.

Monseigneur Florent de Varannes, the admiral, shall go also upon the same conditions, himself and twelve knights, and shall receive of the king three thousand two hundred livres Tournois.

Monsieur Raoul d'Estrées, the marshal, shall go also on the same conditions, himself and six knights, and shall receive sixteen hundred livres Tournois.

Monseigneur Launcelot de St. Marc, marshal, shall go on the same conditions, himself and five knights, and shall have fourteen hundred livres Tournois.

Monsieur Pierre de Moleines shall go, himself and five knights, on the same conditions, except that he and his companions shall eat at court, and shall receive of the king fourteen hundred livres Tournois, and four hundred livres as a gift.

Monsieur Collart de Moleines, his brother, shall go on the same conditions, and in the same manner as Monsieur Pierre, his brother.

Monsieur Gilles de la Tournerelle shall go, himself and four knights, on the same conditions, and shall eat at court.

Monsieur Malry de Roie shall go, himself and eight knights, on these same conditions, and shall eat at court, and shall have two thousand livres, and two hundred livres separately for himself.

Monsieur Gerard de Mortroise shall go, himself and ten knights, to receive three thousand livres Tournois.

Monsieur Raoul de Neele, himself and fifteen knights, to receive four thousand livres Tournois, and shall eat at their own expense (*à son hostel*).

Monseigneur Almaury de Meulane, himself and fifteen knights, four thousand livres Tournois, and shall eat at their own expense.

Monsieur Ausoat d'Offemont, himself and ten knights, twenty-six hundred livres Tournois, and shall eat at the expense of the king (*en l'hostel du roy*).

Raoul de Flamant, six knights; Baldwin de Longueval, four knights; Louis de Beangen, ten knights; Jean de Ville, four knights; Malry de Tournelle, four knights; William de Courtenay, ten knights; William de Patay, himself and his brother, with many others, all receiving pay in proportion to the number of their knights, and all eating at the king's expense (*en l'hostel du roy*).

The archbishop of Rheims to receive 1,111 m. l.

The bishop of Lengres to receive 1,111 m. l., with a vessel for his thirty-two knights.

Monsieur Robert de Bois-Gencelin, quite alone, one hundred and sixty livres, to eat at the king's expense. Pierre de Sanz, Etienne Gauche, Macy Delene, all the same, that is, quite alone, one hundred and sixty livres, or, as the text is, eight twenty livres each, and eat at the king's expense.

Monsieur Gilles de Mailley, himself and ten knights, three thousand livres, and passage and return for his horses; eat at court.

Monsieur Ytien de Morignac, himself and five knights, twelve hundred livres, and passage and return for his horses; eat at court.

The Fourrier de Vernail, for himself and four knights, twelve hundred livres, and eat at the king's expense.

Monsieur Guillaume de Fresne, ten knights, twenty-six hundred livres, and eat at the king's expense. The count de Guynes, exactly the same.

The count de St. Pol, himself and thirty knights, for passage and return of horses, for eating and for all other things, twelve thousand livres, and two thousand private gift.

Monsieur Lambert des Limons, himself and ten knights in the pay of the king, that is to say, to each, ten sols Tournois per diem, and shall not eat at court,—amounts to eighteen hundred and twenty-five livres.

Monsieur Gerard de Campandu, himself and fifteen knights in the king's pay, shall not eat at court, as with M. Lambert, two thousand seven hundred and thirty-seven livres ten sols Tournois.

Monsieur Raymond Alan, himself and five knights, at the king's pay, amounts to nine hundred and twelve livres ten sols Tournois.

Monsieur Jehan de Debeines, himself and ten knights, three thousand livres, and passage and return for six horses, shall eat at court.

The mareschal de Champagne shall go, with ten knights, and shall receive nothing of the king.

Monsieur Gaillard Darle, himself and five, in the king's pay, nine hundred and twelve livres ten sols.

Monsieur Guillame de Flandres, himself and twenty knights, six thousand livres, and passage and return for his horses, and shall eat at court.

Monsieur Aubert de Longueval, himself and five knights, eleven hundred livres, passage and return for horses, and eat at court.

— — — —

No. 35.

Instructions of St. Louis, addressed, on his
Death-bed, to Philip-le-Hardi. [173]

Dear Son,—As it is the most earnest desire of my heart that thou shouldst be well informed on all subjects, I think thou mayest derive much instruction from this writing; often having heard thee say that thou retainest better that which proceeds from me than from any other person.

Dear Son, my first instruction to thee is, that thou shouldst love God with all thy heart and with all thy power, for without that all that thou doest is nothing worth: thou shouldst avoid all things that thou thinkest may displease him, and which are within thy power, and particularly thou shouldst have so strong a resolution that thou wouldst not commit a mortal sin for anything that could happen to thee, and that thou wouldst suffer all thy members to be hacked off, and thy life taken away by the most cruel martyrdom, rather than knowingly commit a mortal sin.

If our Lord should afflict thee with any persecution, malady, or other thing, thou shouldst suffer cheerfully, and thank him for it and be pleased; for thou must think that he hath done it for thy good, and thou must further think that thou hast merited it, and more still if it be his will; because thou hast but too little served him, or too little loved him, and because thou hast done many things against his will.

If our Lord shall please to send thee any prosperity, health of body, or other thing, thou shouldst thank him humbly, and shouldst take great care not debase thyself by pride, or any other offence; for it is a great sin to wage war against the Lord with his own gifts.

Dear Son, I advise thee to confess frequently, and always to choose a confessor of holy life and sufficient knowledge, by whom thou mayest be instructed upon the things thou shouldst shun and upon the things thou shouldst do; and bear thyself in such a manner that thy confessors and friends may dare boldly to instruct and reprove thee.

Dear Son, I advise thee to hear willingly the service of the Holy Church, and when thou art in the chapel, beware of daring to utter vain words. Repeat thy orisons with earnest attention, either by mouth or by thought, and be particularly observant when the body of our Lord shall be present at the mass.

Dear Son, have a compassionate heart for the poor, and for those whom thou thinkest are enduring sufferings of either heart or body, and according to thy power comfort them willingly with consolation or with alms. If thou art sick at heart, tell it to thy confessor, or any other person whom thou thinkest to be loyal and can keep thy secret: *in order that thou mayest be ever at peace, never do anything that thou canst not tell of.*

Dear Son, entertain willingly the company of good men, whether religious or secular, but eschew the company of the wicked; hold willingly good conversation (parlements) with the good, and willingly hear our Lord spoken of in sermons; and in private seek earnestly for pardon. Love good in others, and hate evil, and never suffer words to be spoken in thy presence that may lead people to sin, never hear willingly others spoken ill of, or any words that may disparage our Lord, or our Lady, or the saints. Never suffer any such speech without reproving it; and if it should proceed from a clerk, or so great a person that thou canst not punish him, cause it to be told to him who can inflict justice for it.

Dear Son, take care that thou beest so good in everything, that it may appear thou art grateful for the blessings and honours that God has heaped upon thee, so that if it please our Lord that thou shouldst come to the honour of governing the kingdom, thou mayest be worthy to receive the holy unction with which the kings of France are consecrated.

Dear Son, if thou shouldst attain the kingdom, take care to possess the qualities which belong to kings; that is to say, be so just as never to swerve from justice, whatever may happen to thee. *If a quarrel should arise between a poor man and a rich man, take the part of the poor man against the rich man, until thou shalt ascertain the truth, and when thou shalt know it, do justice. If it should* so happen that thou shouldst have a dispute with another person, maintain the cause of the stranger before thy council: do not appear to be too forward in thy quarrel, until thou shalt be certain of the truth; for those of thy council might fear to speak against thee, which thou oughtest not to desire.

Dear Son, if thou learnest that thou art possessed of anything wrongfully, either in thy own time or in that of thy ancestors, immediately restore it, however great the matter may be, in land, money, or other property. If the affair be obscure, so that thou canst not arrive at the truth, make such peace, according to the advice of worthy men, that thy soul or that of thy ancestors may be entirely freed from it: and if ever thou hearest that thy ancestors have made any restitution, take great pains to learn whether nothing still remains to be restored; and if thou findest there is, make restitution instantly, for the good of thy soul and that of thy ancestors. Be diligent to protect in thy territories all kinds of people, particularly persons belonging to the holy Church; defend them from injury both in their persons and their property, and I hereupon remind thee of a saying of King Philip, one of my ancestors, as one of his council has told me he heard him speak it. The king was one day with his privy council, and some of his counsellors said that the clerks did him great wrong, and they wondered that he suffered it. He replied: "I believe that they do me great wrong; but when I think of the honours our Lord has conferred on me, I by far prefer suffering my loss or injury, to doing anything which might create a misunderstanding between me and the holy Church." I repeat this to thee, that thou mayest not lightly believe those who speak against persons connected with the holy Church. In such a way honour and protect them, that they may be able to perform the service of our Lord in peace. I teach thee this, in order that thou mayest principally love religious people, and mayest succour them in their wants; and those by whom thou shalt think our Lord is best honoured and served, such love better than others.

Dear Son, I desire that thou shouldst love and honour thy mother, and that thou shouldst willingly receive and observe her good instructions, and be inclined to place faith in her good counsels; love thy brothers, and always watch over their good and their advancement; be to them in the place of a father, to lead them to all that which is good; but take care, that for the love of any one, thou dost not fall off from acting rightly, or do anything that ought not to be done.

Dear Son, I advise thee, that all the benefices of the holy Church which thou shalt have to bestow shall be given to persons judged worthy by the great council of *prud'hommes*; and it appears better to me that thou shouldst give to them who have nothing, and will employ thy gifts well, if thou searchest for them diligently.

Dear Son, I advise thee to avoid, as much as it shall be possible, to enter into war with any Christian; and, if any one do thee wrong, try by every means to learn if there be no way of maintaining thy right without going to war, observing that this is to avoid the sins that are committed in war. And if it should happen that it be proper for thee to make it, or that any one of thy men fail in his duty, or commit wrong against any church, or any poor person whatever, and will not make amends, for which, or for any reasonable cause, it be proper for thee to make war, carefully *give orders that the poor people, who have committed neither crime nor offence, be protected, let no injury fall upon them either by fire or other means*; for it will be much better for thee to contend with the evil-doer, and take his castles by storm or siege: but be sure to be well advised before thou movest in any war; be sure that the cause be perfectly just, that thou hast summoned the evil-doer, and hast waited as long as thy duty will permit.

Dear Son, I advise thee, that when wars shall arise in thy dominions among thy men, that thou shouldst take all possible pains to appease them; for that is a thing which is pleasing to our Lord; and Messire Saint Martin has given a very great example of it, for he went to restore concord among the clerks who were in the archbishop's palace, although at the time he knew from our Lord that he must die; and it appeared to him that by doing so he ended his life worthily.

Dear Son, be sure that thou hast good judges and provosts in thy dominions, and frequently examine whether they are doing justice, and whether they are doing wrong to nobody, and are acting as they ought; in the same manner be sure that they who live in thy court (*ton hostel*), commit no injustice; for however thou mayest hate doing ill to others, thou oughtest still more to hate the ill which should come from those who receive the power from thee, and shouldst take great heed that this never should happen.

Dear Son, I advise thee to be always devoted to the Church of Rome, and to our holy father the pope, and to pay him the respect and honour due to thy spiritual father.

Dear Son, confer power freely upon well-intentioned people who know how to employ it properly, and take great pains to remove all sins from thy territories,—that is to say, profane swearing and everything that may be said or done in contempt of God, our Lady, or the saints; carnal sins, gaming with dice, tavern-drinking and other vices. Suppress, in thy dominions, wisely and prudently, all rebels and traitors against thy power; drive them and all ill-disposed persons from the land, until it be quite purged of them. When, by the sage counsel of worthy people, thou shalt hear of any good thing to be done, forward it by every means in thy power, giving proofs that thou acknowledgest the blessings our Lord has bestowed upon thee, and that thou art willing to return him thanks for them.

Dear Son, I advise thee to take great care that the money thou shalt spend shall be properly expended, and, moreover, that it be justly levied: this is a thing of which I should wish thee to be particularly heedful; that is to say, avoid extravagant expenses and unjust extortion, let thy money be justly received and well employed; and this may our Lord teach thee, with everything that may be profitable and suitable to thee!

Dear Son, I pray thee, if it shall please our Lord that I should quit this life before thee, that thou wilt help me with masses and prayers, and that thou wilt send to the congregations of the kingdom of France, to make them put up prayers for my soul, and that thou wilt desire that our Lord may give me part in all the good deeds thou shalt perform.

Dear Son, I give thee every blessing that a father can and ought to give to a son, and I pray our Lord Jesus Christ, that by his great mercy, and by the prayers and the merits of his blessed mother the Virgin Mary, and of the angels and archangels, and of all the male and female saints, that he will keep and defend thee from committing anything that may be against his will, and that he will give thee grace to perform his will, and that he may be served and honoured by thee: and may he grant to thee and to me, by his unbounded generosity, that after this mortal life, we may come to him for life everlasting, there where we may see him, may love him, and may praise him without end. Amen.

To him be all glory, honour, and praise, who is one God with the Father and the Holy Ghost, without beginning and without end. Amen.

— — — —

No. 36.

Edward I., King of England.

As our author has said but little to show English readers what part this, one of their greatest kings, played in the holy wars, we offer an extract from the chronicler Walter Hemingford, canon of Gisseburne, of whom Michaud speaks highly.

Edward, son of Henry III., took part in the crusade of Louis IX. He set out, about the feast of St. Michael, to Aigues-Mortes, where he embarked, and at the end of ten days, landed at Carthage, and was received with much joy by the Christian princes who were then there; that is to say, Philip of France, who had just succeeded Louis IX., his father; Charles king of Sicily, and the king of Navarre. Walter relates that Edward was disgusted with the treaty made between the Christian kings and the king of Tunis, and would take no part in it. The English prince went to Acre with a thousand picked men, and reposed for a month, in order to refresh his troops, and become acquainted with the country. At the end of the month, many Christians joined him, and leaving Acre, at the head of seven thousand men, he marched to a distance of twenty leagues from that city, took Nazareth, and killed a great number of Saracens. The army then returned towards Acre, but were followed by the enemy, who hoped to surprise them in some valley, or confined place. The Christians, upon becoming aware of their intentions, faced about, killed many, and put the others to flight.

Towards the feast of St. John, Edward, learning that the Saracens were within fifteen miles of Acre, marched out, fell upon them, at break of day, killed about a thousand of them, and put the rest to flight. The name of Edward was soon spread among the enemies of Christ, and beginning to dread him, they devised means to get rid of him. The great emir of Jaffa, feigning a wish to be converted to the Christian faith, sent to him several times a slave, bearing letters, but charged secretly with the commission of assassinating the king, which the slave executed. But fortunately Edward escaped the consequences by the assistance of skilful leeches. As soon as he was cured, he concluded a truce for ten years, and returned to Europe with his Crusaders.

— — — —

No. 37.

The Openings of the Troncs.

M. Michaud has given a very long account of the openings of the troncs, of which we only think it necessary to offer our readers a small portion, to show them the nature of the thing. The continued repetition of the names of French towns, &c., with the amount of money found in the troncs, can be interesting to nobody.

On Low Sunday, the 19th day of April, in the year 1517, between the hours of eight and nine after mid-day, was raised and carried away the tronc of the metropolitan church of St. Stephen of Thoulouse, closed and fastened with three keys, and sealed with two seals, and placed in the archiepiscopal house of the said Thoulouse, by the said commissary, treasurer, or receiver and comptroller, in the presence of Messire Jehan de Verramino, canon and chancellor of the said church; Thomas le Franc, rector of the said church;

Domengo Vaussenet, burgess, and several others; and on the next day, in the presence of as above, the said commissary, receiver, and comptroller opened the said tronc, where they took and found for the confessionals the sum of six hundred and fifty-one livres, six sols, six deniers in full, for one thousand one hundred and fifteen confessions, which have been distributed; for this

6c. 51 liv. 6s. 4d. (sic)

Of other money found in the said tronc on the day and year aforesaid, arising from the pardons and jubilee of the crusade, the sum of four hundred and ninety-nine livres, fifteen sols, four deniers Tournois

ci. 499 liv. 15s. 4d.

From another opening of the trone of Thoulouse, at the feast of the following Christmas, in the said year 1517, the sum of twenty-seven livres, three sols, nine denier Tournois.

27 liv. 3s. 9d.

From another opening of the said trone of Thoulouse, made the first day of May, 1518, which is the second of the year 1518, in which there was found, as well for money for the jubilee as for confessionals, the sum of two hundred and five livres, ten sols, six deniers Tournois; for this

205 liv. 10s. 6d.

From another opening made the 7th day of June, of the said year, there was found, as well for jubilee as for confessionals, the sum of one hundred and twenty-seven livres, two sols Tournois; for this

127 liv. 2s.

From an opening of the tronc of Castannet, in the diocese of Thoulouse, there was found, as well for confessionals as for the jubilee, the sum of fourteen livres, one sol, five deniers Tournois; for this

14 liv. 1s. 5d.

&c. &c. &c.

From the opening of the various troncs in the diocese of Thoulouse, within and without the city, in the years 1517 and 1518, many being opened several times, they collected an amount which stands thus at the end: Summa Totalis *receptæ presentis computi*

3,700 liv. 18s. 6d.

The expenditure of this money is detailed equally minutely; of which we will offer a few examples.

EXPENDITURE

OF THIS PRESENT ACCOUNT,

AND, IN THE FIRST PLACE,

Moneys paid to People who are to account for them.

To Master Jehan Grossier, notary and secretary of the king our lord, and by him commissioned to keep the account, and receive the moneys for the crusade granted by our holy father the pope to the king our lord, in his kingdom and other lands and lordships owing allegiance to him, the sum of fifteen hundred and thirty-two livres, seventeen sols, four deniers Tournois, which the present receiver owes on account of the said receipt which he has made of the moneys for the said crusade to the said city of Thoulouse, which sum has been paid to the said Grossier, in virtue of the letters missive of our lord the king, given at Amboise, the 25th day of January, there rendered, as by his quittance, signed by his hand, the 26th day of February, in the year 1517, thus so rendered, as appears; and for this

1,532 liv. 17s. 4d.

To the said Master Jehan Grossier, by his written quittance, the 10th day of June, in the year one thousand five hundred and eighteen, the sum of two hundred and forty-eight livres, three sols Tournois, which the said receiver ought, upon receiving the said receipt, pay him, by virtue of the letters missive of the king our lord, given at Amboise, the last day of April, as by said quittance, here rendered, as appears; for this

248 liv. 3s.

To the same Master Jehan Grossier, for another written quittance on the 20th day of May, 1520, the sum of six hundred and twenty-five livres, fourteen sols, five deniers Tournois, which the said receiver ought to pay him, as by his said quittance, here rendered, as appears; for this

625 liv. 14s. 5d.

Other Expenses made by the said Master Jehan Clucher, by the order of Messire Josse de la Garde, Doctor of Theology, Vicar-General of the Very Reverend Father in God, Monseigneur the Archbishop of Thoulouse, Commissary, ordered by the King our Lord, on the matter of the Crusade, and according to the Letters Missive and Instructions signed by the hand of the King, transcribed and rendered at the commencement of this Account.

For the expenses of the commissaries, receiver, comptroller, and notary, for having been, with seven horses, setting out on the 22nd day of April, in the year 1517, through the diocese of the archbishopric of

Thoulouse, to collect the troncs and boxes, in which they were engaged for the space of thirteen days, the sum of twenty livres, nine sols, five deniers Tournois, which has been paid by the present receiver by order of the said commissary, as appears by the papers signed and certified by his hand, and by Monsieur Raymond Raffin, canon in the metropolitan church of Thoulouse, comptroller, deputed by our lord the king to assist in collecting the money for the said crusade, [174] containing the expense of this account rendered, and containing likewise a certification of the payment of all the said expense, instead of quittance (receipt); for this the sum of

20 liv. 9s. 5d.

To Pierre Langiere, the sum of sixteen sols Tournois, for having pasted up four hundred articles, and for having placed and fixed about two hundred of them at the doors and cross-ways of the said Thoulouse, for the feast of Easter; for this

16s.

To Messire Pierre Ferrestiere, Anthoine Chassantre, and Durant Veissiere, priests, for having carried the said articles, at the said time, to Montastruc, Versveil, and Carmaing, the sum of sixty sols Tournois; this

60s.

To Georges Ruveres, for having made two tin cases to put over the tronc, the sum of ten sols Tournois; this

10s.

To Thomas Noel, for having made the tronc for the said crusade, at Thoulouse, the sum of sixty-three sols, four deniers Tournois; this

63s. 4d.

To Jehan Dernent, for having bound about with iron the coffer of the said tronc, and made the padlock for the same, the sum of eleven livres, T.; this

11 liv.

To Master Stephen Fabry and Jehan Galmart, for having carried the said articles into several places, and for writing-paper and packthread to tie up the packets, the sum of four livres, two sols, nine deniers Tournois; this

4 liv. 2s. 9d.

To William Perolle, for having carried some confessionals to Cluriac, the sum of twelve sols Tournois; this

12s.

To Lion de Veausclera, for four padlocks for the said tronc, the sum of forty sols Tournois; this

40s.

To the bell-ringers of St. Stephen of Thoulouse, for what may be due to them for having rung the Pardon, at the late festival of Easter, the sum of sixty sols Tournois; this

60s.

To la Roussignolle, for twelve cloth bags to put the money into, the sum of eight sols, six deniers Tournois; this

8s. 6d.

To Master Jehan Galmar, for having been to fix the troncs in various places, and having furnished nails for the padlocks, the sum of twenty-seven sols, six deniers

27s. 6d.

To Bertrand Beix, for having served, or waited at, the tronc of St. Stephen of Thoulouse, for the space of fifteen days, the sum of seventeen sols, six deniers Tournois

17s. 6d.

For the dinner [175] which was made for those who were present to see the money counted from the tronc of the said St. Stephen of Thoulouse, and for the cook, the sum of seventy-two sols Tournois

72s.

To the preachers of Thoulouse, for having preached the said pardons, the sum of eighteen livres Tournois; this

18 liv.

To Master Jehan Bourlier, notary, [176] for having attended the placing and removing of the said troncs, in the said diocese of Thoulouse, for the space of fifteen days, at the period of Easter, the sum of fifteen livres Tournois

15 liv.

To Master Jehan Terrein, of Thoulouse, the sum of a hundred sols Tournois, for having superintended the giving out of the letters, and obtaining the names and surnames of those who took them to the church of Thoulouse, at Easter, this

100s.

To the bell-ringers of the said St. Stephen, for ringing the bells and cleaning the church, the sum of forty sols Tournois; this

40s.

To those who sealed the confessionals of the said crusade and jubilee, the sum of six livres Tournois, this

6 liv.

To Messire Jehan Bonissent, secretary of Monseigneur de Thoulouse, for having made eight mandatory letters on parchment, and having signed four hundred articles to be posted upon the doors of churches, the sum of six livres Tournois, this

6 liv.

To Jehan Grant, printer, for having printed a thousand small articles, and a hundred confessionals, on parchment, the sum of one hundred and ten livres Tournois; this

110 liv.

To Jehan Bodret, apothecary, of Thoulouse, for thirty-one pounds of red wax, and also for four quires of paper, the sum of ten livres, seventeen sols, six deniers Tournois; this

1O liv. 17s. 6d.

To Master Guillaume de Villano, notary, for having signed and filled up the confessionals and commissions, and having made the other acts of the said crusade, the sum of ten livres Tournois; this

10 liv.

To the Receiver of the said crusade, for having been to place the troncs and collect the money, for the attendance of thirteen days, the sum of twenty-eight livres Tournois

28 liv.

To Monsieur the Comptroller of the said crusade, for the same cause, the sum of twenty-eight livres Tournois; this

28 liv.

To Monsieur the Commissary of the said crusade, with three horses, for the same cause, the sum of forty livres Tournois; this

40 liv.

To Master Jehan Bourlier, for having made two duplicates of the receipt and expense of the said crusade, the sum of thirty sols Tournois; this

30s.

To Raymond de Vlino, for having made three hundred and fifty coats of arms, at twelve deniers Tournois each, amounting to the sum of seventeen livres, ten sols Tournois; this

17 liv. 10s.

To those who sealed the said confessionals, both on parchment and on paper, and for having folded them, the sum of four livres Tournois

4 liv.

Then follows a list of amounts paid to preachers of the crusade, which is far too long for insertion, but all tending to prove that the task was not performed gratuitously. We have extracted the above articles from the interminable account to show our readers something of the nature of the charges made by various classes for work done early in the sixteenth century, but more particularly to point out, after the money had been extorted from the pious or the charitable, how many hands were dipped into the troncs before their contents were applied to their destined purpose. *The preachers, as appears by the following items and many others of the account, took a fifth part of what was found in the troncs at the time of opening them.*

To the preachers who have preached in the city of Thoulouse, for the fifth part of four hundred and nine livres, sixteen sols, eight deniers Tournois, which have been found in the said tronc, opened at several festivals, has been paid over the sum of eighty-one livres, nineteen sols, four deniers Tournois; this

81 liv. 19s. 4d.

To the preacher of Lisle en Jourdain, for HIS fifth part of one hundred and ninety-eight livres, three sols, seven deniers Tournois; this

39 liv. 3s. 7d.

Nobody seems to have touched the tronc without benefit; thus there are sixty sols to Jehan Turein for taking charge of the tronc, at Easter; and fifteen sols to a child who *cried* at the tronc. The high officials took each one hundred livres per annum whilst the crusade was being preached, and their underlings did nothing without remuneration.

— — — —

No. 38.

Memoir of Leibnitz, addressed to Louis XIV.

After the example of M. Michaud, we do not hesitate to lay before our readers the following paper, although it bears little relation to our history. A document passing between two such men as Leibnitz and Louis XIV., upon a speculative, yet an important question, cannot be without interest; besides which, there is very little doubt that it fell into the hands of Buonaparte before he undertook his expedition to Egypt. It is generally believed that this Memoir of Leibnitz, upon the expedition to Egypt, was preserved, up to the period of the revolution, in the archives of Versailles, and that this historical document disappeared during the political troubles of France. An extract from it was published in an English pamphlet in 1805; and another extract was made in a book entitled *Voyage en Hanovre*, published in 1805. M. Michaud has made more use of the English pamphlet than of the latter publication. M. Mangourit, the author of the Voyage, saw in the library of Hanover a copy of the Memoir addressed to Louis XIV., written by the hand of Leibnitz; it had for title, *De Expeditione Egyptiatica, Epistola ad Regem Franciæ scripta*. M. Mangourit informs us that Marshal Mortier ordered a copy to be made of it, to be sent to Paris, where it was placed in the library of the king. It appears that the Memoir was sent a short time before the famous passage of the Rhine and the war against Holland. M. Mangourit is persuaded that Leibnitz, whom he represents as the instrument of some cabinet, had no other motive in persuading Louis to invade Egypt but to divert him from his threatened attack upon the Batavian republic. M. Michaud says that this opinion appears improbable, and that the author gives no satisfactory proof of it. We think some of our readers, at least, will incline to the opinion of M. Mangourit.

Leibnitz commences his Memoir by declaring that the fame of his majesty's wisdom has induced him to present to him some reflections upon a subject familiar to preceding ages, but recently neglected and forgotten; it concerns an enterprise, "the greatest that can be attempted, and at the same time the most easy of such as are considered great. I venture to add," continues he, "that it is the most holy, the most just (*addere audeo, sanctissimum justissimumque*), and that it is not accompanied by any danger, even should it be attempted in vain. It agrees likewise so well with the kind of preparations already made, that it would appear to have been a long time in contemplation, and would thus increase the admiration of those who justly call the conceptions of your majesty *the miracle of secrecy*. It would do more harm to Holland than could be hoped for from the most brilliant success of an open war, without leaving them the power of opposing any obstacle to it. It would accomplish the object of the present armament, by procuring for France the empire of the seas and of commerce. In short, all hatreds and all jealousies being thus extinguished at a single blow, your majesty would find yourself raised by it, with general assent, to the rank of supreme arbiter of Christendom—the highest possible to be conceived, and it would cover your name with an immortal glory, for having cleared, whether for yourself or your descendants, the route for exploits similar to those of Alexander."

After having made it plain that the present moment was exceedingly favourable, that there was no sovereign more powerful than the king of France, or one more beloved by his subjects; "I am persuaded," says he, "that there is not in the known world any country the conquest of which deserves so much to be attempted, or which would be so likely to give supremacy, as the Egypt which I delight in calling the Holland of the East, as I call France the China of the West."

"The marriage between this prince and this country, that is to say, between the king of France and Egypt, appears to me to interest equally the human race and the Christian religion."

Leibnitz afterwards says, that upon examining the motives which determined Louis IX. to attempt the conquest of Egypt rather than that of Jerusalem, he had become convinced that they merit the greatest attention.

"After the death of the Emperor Frederick Barbarossa, Philip, surnamed Augustus, and Richard, king of England, besieged and took St. Jean d'Acre. There was among the prisoners an Arabian named Caracous, whom history represents as a prophet. This man, hearing Philip frequently speak of the aim the Christian powers proposed to themselves in this war, declared that they could never retain Jerusalem and the Christian sovereignty in Asia, unless the Egyptian monarchy were overthrown; and for that purpose it was of the greatest importance to get possession of Damietta. From this arose a dissension between Philip and Richard, &c. Richard himself, after having failed in Palestine, wished to undertake an expedition against Egypt, but death prevented him.

"The Christian powers at length became aware of their error, and Pope Innocent III. promoted an expedition against Egypt, the issue of which was unfortunate. Then came the expedition of St. Louis, which failed from the imprudence and want of skill in the leaders. Louis exposed his army in the interior of the country, between two branches of the Nile, with his rear and the course of the river in the power of the enemy. Instead of getting possession of the coasts and securing the Nile for his fleet, the only means of establishing his conquest, provisioning his army, and making himself safe from all attacks, he allowed himself to be surrounded; the Saracens intercepted his supplies, and finished by destroying the Christian army.

"Afterwards, the wars between France and England, as well as those which broke out between France and the house of Austria, put an end to all idea of invading Egypt, till the time of Ximenes, who was the author of a league, formed for the conquest of this country, by Ferdinand of Castile, Emanuel of Portugal, and Henry VIII. of England. [177] Three princes," says Leibnitz, "of whom it may, with reason, be said, that each of them laid the foundation of the power and commerce of their respective people; and that it is which France now expects from Louis XIV.

"This project was defeated by the death of Ferdinand, which caused the crown of Spain to pass to the house of Austria."

Leibnitz then gives a sketch of the revolutions of Egypt, from the earliest ages to the time it was subdued by the Turks; to show the importance that has always been attached to the possession of Egypt, and to prove that it has never opposed much resistance to a skilful and powerful conqueror.

"Egypt, now become a province of the Turkish empire, will be, on that account, more easily subdued; not only from the difficulty the Port will have in throwing in succours, and the inclination the inhabitants always have for revolt, but still more from its being no longer the seat of an empire."

After this preamble, Leibnitz, developing his plan, argues that the conquest of Egypt is the most certain road to supremacy in Europe; or, in other terms, that it will strengthen the best interests of France,—that, considering the magnitude of the object, the enterprise is very easy;—that there is no risk;—that it is in accordance with sound policy;—that it should not be delayed;—in short, that it is great, just, and pious.

"This supremacy, which it is so important for France to obtain, consists in the possession of as much power as can be reasonably hoped for; for it cannot look to a universal monarchy, but only the general direction or arbitration of affairs. Universal monarchy is an absurdity; the history of Europe proves it. By making war upon Christian states, weak aggrandisements can alone be obtained, and a small accession of territory acquired. Such means are not suitable for a most Christian king, or a great monarch:—marriages, elections, and successions produce more.

"War should alone be directed against barbarous nations; and among these, it is incontestable that by a single fortunate blow (and the French are particularly formed to strike such), empires may be in an instant overthrown and founded. In such wars are found the elements of high power, and of an exalted glory.

"It is certain that the power of France must increase with the peace of Europe, and that it must be weakened by ill-timed wars. Let it then be employed against the barbarians, and for the restoration of Egypt. In America, the Spaniards, the English, and the Dutch would render every enterprise impossible; but, directed towards Turkey, no one would dare to oppose it; Egypt being once invaded, the war that we should then make would be rendered sacred by universal approbation; and instead of the deserted countries of Palestine, only celebrated by its ruins, we should have, as the rewards of our efforts, *that eye of countries, that mother of grain, that seat of commerce. (Non, deserta illa, ruinis tantùm nobilis Palæstina, sed oculus regionum, mater frugum, sedes commerciorum acquiretur.)*

"Of all the regions of the earth, Egypt ought to be considered, after China, as the first. It possesses so many advantages, that the imagination can add nothing to them. It is the principal isthmus of the globe, the seas of which it divides in such a manner, as to create the necessity for passing round Africa. It is at the same time the barrier and the passage between Africa and Asia. It is the point of communication, and the general entrepôt of the commerce, on one side, of India, and on the other, of Europe. It is in some sort the eye of the adjacent countries, rich by the fertility of its soil, and by its great population, amidst the deserts which surround it. It unites the wonders of nature and of art, which, after so many ages, ever appear to furnish subjects for fresh admiration."

After having supported his opinions by numerous quotations upon the resources Egypt possesses, Leibnitz continues thus:—

"Suppose Egypt should be occupied by an army of the most Christian king, we shall see how much this event must contribute to political supremacy. (*Pars melior Franciæ cedet; hæc maris Mediterranei domina, imperium Orientalis resuscitabit.*)

"It is evident that the Turkish empire might be overthrown by the attacks of the Germans and the Poles, if the germs of rebellion, which are there now forming, were developed generally; and there is no doubt that Muscovy and Persia would take advantage of that circumstance. Then, the most valuable portion of that monarchy would fall to France; which, becoming thus mistress of the Mediterranean, would reëstablish the Eastern empire. From Egypt it would extend its empire over the ocean, and would take, without difficulty, possession of the Red Sea, and the isles near Madagascar. It would not be long in gaining the Sea of Ethiopia, the Persian Gulf, and the isle of Ormuz, which commands it.

"The conquest of Egypt would likewise be followed by great and important changes in Europe. The king of France could then, by incontestable right, and with the consent of the pope, assume the title of emperor of the East; he could add to his title of eldest son, that of patron (*advocatus*) of the Church, and by the great advantages procured to the Holy See, hold the pontiffs much more in his power than if they resided at Avignon. Italy and Germany would be definitively delivered from the fear of the Turks, and

Spain from that of the Moors. The commerce of the world would be shared between France and the house of Austria; at length, the reconciliation between the most powerful families would be cemented to the satisfaction of both, France having for its share the East, and Spain the West. [178] And if they should wish to be united by the indissoluble tie of their common interest, they would gain the object which the wisest of ministers have endeavoured to attain in the conferences of the Pyrenees; they would become the arbitrators between other powers; they would prepare the happiness of the human race, and they would create an everlasting reverence for the memory of the great king, to whom so many miracles were due.

"With Egypt, the Dutch might easily be deprived of the commerce of India, upon which great part of their power depends, and they would by that be more directly and necessarily injured than by the most brilliant success in an open war. The Christian religion would again flourish in Asia; the world would obey the same laws, and the whole human race would be united by the same ties; so *that, with the exception of the philosopher's stone, I know nothing that can be imagined of more importance than the conquest of Egypt."*

When discussing the facility of the execution, Leibnitz considers siders— "The forces to be employed—the means of transporting the troops—the climate of the country—its fortifications and military strength—the manner of making war there—the interior troubles of Egypt—the dispositions of the neighbouring nations—and the allies and auxiliaries, as well of the aggressors as of the invaded country."

With respect to the forces of France, Leibnitz refers to Louis, who must be better acquainted with their numbers than he; he however believes that there is in fact already more strength than would be required.

Francis, duke of Urbino, demanded 50,000 men to overturn the Ottoman empire. For the conquest of Egypt, thirty thousand picked men would be sufficient. Emanuel the Wise, king of Portugal, flattered himself that he could succeed with a much smaller number. "There is no doubt," adds Leibnitz, "that our numbers would prodigiously increase in a short time, by the accession of Arabs and Numidians, whilst the Turkish forces in that province must be very inconsiderable.

"But suppose," continues Leibnitz, "we were compelled to embark 50,000 men; that is a force which France would easily provide. For, although I am persuaded that 20,000 would amply suffice to occupy and guard the coast of Egypt, it would be prudent to draw advantage from the forces now assembled, and to effect by one stroke, by one vigorous operation, the conquest of the whole of Egypt." Leibnitz further advises that the troops should be encouraged by speeches, indulgences, rewards, honours, &c. &c.; thinks it of much less importance to employ a great number of troops than it is to select them well.

"Some persons are averse to the transporting of large armies by sea; but wiser persons are of a contrary opinion, and think that the trifling inconveniences of this mode of transport are more than compensated by very great advantages. The first inconveniences to which they are subject on board, are neither dangerous nor of long duration; they may be considered even as evacuations favourable to health. Scorbutic affections appear only in long voyages, and acute diseases are occasioned by intemperance, which discipline may prevent, or by a change of climate, which cannot be experienced in the Mediterranean. No mutiny need be apprehended, because the soldiers are in some sort in the power of the sailors."

The memorial of Leibnitz here presents an historical summary of the armies embarked at different periods, from the Punic wars to the last conquests made in Asia and America, by the Spaniards, the Portuguese, the English, &c.; and whilst recommending that the vessels should not be too heavily laden as regards troops, he remarks that the navigation of the Mediterranean has, for a long time, become familiar to French sailors, and that there could be no danger, if proper attention were paid to seasons. French and Venetian vessels constantly visit Candia, and from that island to Egypt the passage is not difficult. Let us add, that the isle of Malta is a secure station for the fleet, that isle being united to France by an infinite number of ties, since the major part of the knights and the grand master of the order are French.

"After the port of Alexandria shall have been taken by a coup-de-main (which cannot fail of succeeding), the coasts of Syria, as well as the isles of Cyprus and Candia, will necessarily fall, provided that the Turks are not able to undertake anything by sea to oppose it."

The memorial of Leibnitz then rejects all fear of the insalubrity of the climate of Egypt; he expatiates upon the healthy qualities of the waters of the Nile, gives dietic rules, recommends abstinence from wine, and points out the variations in the weather in the different months of the year.

Then he speaks of the saltpetre which Egypt produces in such abundance, and continues: "The means of the natural defences of Egypt are the deserts and seas that surround it, and the Nile; its artificial means are its castles and its cities. The sea and the Nile, far from injuring, facilitate the employment of naval forces, and the deserts will interrupt communications with the other parts of the Ottoman empire, and will prevent the Turks from throwing imposing succours into the Egyptian territory. The strong places are either upon the Red Sea or upon the Mediterranean." Here Leibnitz describes Alexandria, Rosetta, and Damietta, with the Bozag, pointing out the weakness of these places. "The coast of the Red Sea is still more neglected, and would fall quickly into the power of a Portuguese fleet, acting in concert with a French force from Madagascar;" for Leibnitz supposes that the Portuguese would be more disposed to second the views of the French than to oppose them.

The memorial describes very minutely the Arabian Gulf and the Strait of Bab-el-Mandel; he affirms that all places on the coast want fortifications; he speaks particularly of Suez, Cossier, Souakem, and at length of Cairo, which would not offer, any more than the rest, a strong resistance.

"Could the resistance of Cairo," says Leibnitz, "alone prevent France from raising itself above all glory past or present? It would be disgraceful for so powerful a nation, when engaged in such a mighty enterprise, to entertain a moment's doubt of final success in presence of this last obstacle. For France would not be fighting then for either Dunkirk or Gravelines, or for Maëstricht; but for the dominion of the seas, for the empire of the East, for the overthrow of the Port, and for universal supremacy;—all results from the conquest of Egypt."

Then follow some geographical details upon the coast of Syria, and the ports and cities of that country; that is to say, El-Aresch, Byblos, Tripoli, Alexandretta, Aleppo, and Damascus.

"Alexandretta commands the defiles of Cilicia. By the possession of this place, an army marching from Asia Minor upon Palestine could be forced to make a long and painful circuit, across a country half desert, and across portions of Cilicia, Armenia, and Mesopotamia.

"Aleppo and Damascus are the only cities capable of resisting for a moment our ulterior operations after the reduction of Cairo. Although they are distant from the sea, they must be secured, since then we shall command all the country on this side of Mount Amanus.

"The Turks may, it is true, if they are warned, place reinforcements in Egypt, and even fortify Alexandria and render Egypt nearly inaccessible. It will therefore be essential to preserve the most profound secrecy upon the project, and accelerate the departure of the armament for its destination. When the expedition shall be once made, it will be no longer in the power of the Turks to place an obstacle in the way of its success, since the departure of so formidable a fleet will give alarm for the seat of government itself. Under this point of view it will be even useful to spread a report that it is in fact destined against Constantinople, in order that the Port should unite and concentrate, for the protection of the capital, its divided forces, and thus render the distant provinces the weaker. The French army being thus suddenly thrown into Egypt, it would require six months for the Turks to assemble an equal force, or even a much longer time, if Turkey were at the same time engaged in a Polish or Hungarian war. Moreover, as soon as the expedition should have succeeded, Persia, which cannot declare itself upon our promises alone, will not fail to rise likewise. And if the expedition took place in that season of the year which, according to the opinion of experienced persons, would appear the most suitable, it would be absolutely impossible for the Turks to arrive in any useful time, if even they had 100,000 disposable forces; because Egypt would be then inundated with the waters of the Nile, in which our fleet would dominate; and because the Turkish army could not set out on its march before the following winter, &c.

"Suppose now that Egypt should be in our power, and, which is not at all improbable, the Turks should find themselves at peace with all their neighbours, that there should be no trouble among themselves, and that they should be in a condition to advance with 100,000 effective men; suppose, on the other side, that we were only able to oppose this force with 30,000 men, since we must leave 20,000 behind, to maintain our position in Egypt, and reduce the places not yet subdued: I affirm that these 30,000 men would be sufficient to repulse the Turks: let us add, that if measures be well taken, there is no doubt that considerable reinforcements might arrive from Europe, and that the Christian subjects of the Port, as well as the natives, would flock eagerly to range themselves under our Banners. But suppose our force did not exceed 30,000 men, this troop would be perfectly in a state to resist the Turks by two different manœuvres, whether by waiting for them in the plains of Egypt, between Suez and Cairo; or whether in marching forward to meet them in Arabia Petræa, between Gaza and the mountains, or in Syria between Alexandretta and Mount Amanus, called now the mount of Scanderoun, or El Lucan.

"There are in Arabia Petræa three narrow defiles, through which the caravans pass on their way from Egypt into Asia. One of these defiles is on the right, when we are coming from Egypt, and leads to the eastern shores of the Red Sea; another passage is on the left, on the shores of the Mediterranean,—it leads into Palestine and Syria; the third, situated between the two preceding ones, comes out at Mount Horeb, and at the monastery of St. Catherine. The two first passages lead into Arabia, where no army could penetrate without great difficulty. There only remains then the third route, which goes from Egypt into Palestine, across Idumea. But this passage is so narrowed on one side by the Mediterranean Sea, and on the other by the foot of the mountains of Arabia Petræa, that the sultan of

Egypt would easily have expelled the army of Selim from his country, if he had taken care to secure the passage between Syria and Cilicia: it was by neglecting this precaution that Darius very much facilitated the conquest of Asia by Alexander. If the sultan of the Mamelukes, abandoning Palestine, had taken up a position in the narrow strait near Gaza, or near Sihor (called in Scripture the river of Egypt), which is a species of hollow ravine, running from the mountains to the sea, and if he had there awaited his enemy, it is certain that in that position, 30,000 men would have been able to resist hundreds of thousands.

"Suppose the Turks were able to force not only the passage of Alexandretta, but likewise that of Gaza, they yet could not recover Egypt; for, in this case, our army would keep in its rear the Nile and a very fertile country, whilst the enemy would have nothing in their rear but the deserts of Arabia. And if, in this position, we were to avoid a pitched battle, which would be easy from the nature of the country, the Turkish army would necessarily waste away, and would be forced, by want of provisions, to retire into Syria, and leave us in the tranquil enjoyment of our conquests."

Leibnitz brings several historical facts to the support of his opinion; he proves that the Turks are much less formidable, less warlike, less numerous than they formerly were; he enters into details upon the seraglio, the revenues, and the military and maritime establishments of the Ottoman empire.

The author assigns reasons for hoping that, after the first news of the success of Louis XIV., there would ensue partial revolts, and then a general insurrection of the pachas, the civil functionaries, the soldiers, the Christians, and finally of the whole people. "I venture to affirm," says he, "that all the subjects of the Ottoman empire are unhappy, discontented, anxious for change, and that at this moment they are only restrained by the disheartening remembrance of their former attempts to throw off the yoke.

"A French author, very well acquainted with the affairs of Turkey, and who is surprised that an empire so constituted subsists so long, forms the conjecture that God, who does everything for the best, had raised and sustained this powerful nation for the good of his Church, and to punish Christians for their sins and vices;' but I," continues Leibnitz,—"I am convinced that the time approaches in which the Omnipotent will visit his people, in which the fury of barbarians will be at an end, in which a far happier epoch will open on the Christian world. Much might be said with regard to prophecies; upon periods in human affairs; upon the inevitable catastrophes of empires; even upon the traditions of the Turks themselves, which make them look for their destruction from a country between two seas. This prediction has been commonly applied to Constantinople, and sometimes to the Morea; but no one has hitherto thought of Egypt.

"Let us, however, without presuming to penetrate the secrets of destiny, draw our conclusions from the ordinary course of affairs. It is notorious that the Sultan has entirely lost, in the opinion of his subjects, his character of inviolability, and this circumstance must necessarily facilitate his defeat."

All that follows this is but a picture of the disorder which reigns in the political organization of the Turkish empire. Therefore, Leibnitz thinks that the conquest of Egypt would shake the Port to its foundation. He adds: *"Audaciter dico, flagrabit Turcia seditionibus, si volumus;* and if the Port were at the same time engaged in a war with Poland or Hungary, *jam ruina ipsa,"* says he, *"et totius corporis paralysis universalis indubitata est."*

―――

No. 39.

Capitulations between France and the Ottoman Port.

Francis I. was the first of our kings who made treaties with the Port. He obtained in 1535, from Soliman the Canonist, the first capitulations in favour of commerce and of the Catholic religion, in the states of the Grand Seignor; in 1604, Henry IV. obtained from the Sultan Ahmid I. the renewal of them with some additions; in 1675 they were renewed and augmented under the reign of the Sultan Mehemed IV., at the demand of Louis XIV.; in 1740, Louis XV. obtained from the Sultan Mahmoud the renewal of the ancient treaties, with considerable additions.

France has had since that period other negotiations with the Port; but these negotiations have not produced any treaty, the dispositions of which are either new or important. The documents necessary for the history of the relations of France with the Ottoman empire have always been carefully preserved in the chancery of the French embassy at Constantinople. It is there we must search for exact notices to add to that which we have been able to advance upon this question.

We will give, from these capitulations, as much as particularly concerns the subject of our history, or which may throw a light upon the Ottoman policy.

"The Emperor Sultan Mahmoud, son of Sultan Moustapha, ever victorious. [179]

"Here is that which ordains this glorious and imperial signature, conqueror of the world, this noble and sublime mark, whose efficacy proceeds from divine aid.

"I, who by the excellence of the favours of the Most High, and by the eminence of the miracles filled with blessings from the chief of the prophets (to whom be the most ample salutations, as well as to his family and his companions), am the Sultan of glorious sultans, the emperor of puissant emperors, the distributor of crowns to the Cosroes, who are seated on thrones, the shadow of God upon earth, the servant of the two illustrious cities of Mecca and Medina, august and holy places, to which Mussulmans address their vows; the protector and master of the holy Jerusalem; the sovereign of the three great cities of Constantinople, Adrianople, and Broussa, as well as of Damascus, the odour of Paradise; of Tripoli, of Syria, of Egypt, the wonder of ages, and renowned for its delights; of all Arabia; of Africa, of Cairovan, of Aleppo, of Irak, Arab, and Adgen; of Bassora, of Lahra, of Dilem, and particularly of Bagdad, capital of the caliphs; of Rakka, of Mossoul, of Chehregour, of Diarbeker, of Zulkadric, of Ergerum the Delightful; of Sebarta, of Adana, of Caramenia, of Kars, of Ichidder, of Van, of the isles of the Morea, of Candia, of Cyprus, Chio, and Rhodes; of Barbary, of Ethiopia; of the places of war, Algiers, Tripoli, and Tunis; of the isles and the coasts of the White Sea and of the Black Sea; of the countries of Natolia, and the kingdom of Romelia; of all Kurdestan, of Greece, of Turkomania, of Tartary, of Circassia, of Cabarta, and of Georgia; of the noble tribes of the Tartars, and of all the hordes which depend upon them; of Caffa, and other surrounding places; of all Bosnia and its dependencies; of the fortress of Belgrade, a place of war; of Servia, as well as of the fortresses and castles existing in it; of the countries of Albania, of all Wallachia, of Moldavia, and of the forts and holds which are in these cantons; possessor besides of a number of cities and fortresses, of which it is superfluous to repeat or boast the names. I, who am emperor, asylum of justice and king of kings, the centre of victory, Sultan, son of the Sultan, Emperor Mahmoud the conqueror, son of Sultan Mustafa, son of Sultan Muhammed: I, who by my power, the origin of facility, am adorned with the title of emperor of the two lands, and as a crowning grandeur to my caliphate, am illustrated by the title of emperor of the two seas.

"The glory of the great princes of the faith of Jesus, the elect of the great and the magnificent of the religion of the Messiah, the arbitrator and mediator in the affairs of Christian nations, clothed with true marks of dignity and honour, filled with grandeur, with glory and majesty, the emperor of France, and of other vast kingdoms which depend upon it, our very magnificent, very honoured, sincere, and ancient friend, Louis XV., to whom God grant all success and felicity, having sent to our august court, which is the seat of the caliphate, a letter containing evidences of the most perfect sincerity, and of the most particular affection, candour, and uprightness, and the same letter being destined for our Sublime Port of felicity, which, by the infinite goodness of the incontestably majestic Supreme Being, is the abode of sultans the most magnificent, of emperors the most respectable; the model of Christian nobles, skilful, prudent, esteemed, and honoured minister, Louis Sauveur, marquis de Villeneuve, your present counsellor of state, and your ambassador to our Port of felicity (may the end of which be crowned with good fortune), having demanded permission to present and remit the said letter, which has been granted to him by our imperial consent, conformably with the ancient usages of our court; and consequently the said ambassador having been admitted to the foot of our imperial throne, surrounded with the light of glory, he has there delivered the said letter, and has been the representative of your majesty, in participating our imperial grace and favour; the translation of its friendly tenor was afterwards presented and reported, according to the ancient customs of the Ottomans, at the foot of our sublime throne, by the channel of the very honoured Elhadjy Mehemed Pacha, our first minister, the absolute interpreter of our ordinances, the ornament of the world, the support of the good order of nations, the orderer of the grades of our empire, the instrument of the glory of our crown, the channel for the favours of royal majesty, the very virtuous Grand Vizier, my venerable and fortunate minister and lieutenant-general, of whose power and prosperity may God perpetuate the triumph!

"And as the expressions of this friendly letter make known the desire and eagerness of your majesty to preserve, as heretofore, all the honours and ancient friendship, hitherto maintained from time immemorial between our glorious ancestors (may the light of God be upon them), and the very magnificent emperors of France; and as in the said letter there is question, in consideration of the sincere friendship and the particular attachment that France has always evinced towards our imperial house, again to renew, during the happy period of our glorious reign, and to strengthen and enlighten, by the addition of some articles, the imperial capitulations, already renewed in the year of the Hegyra 1084, under the reign of the late Sultan Mehemed, our august grandfather, noble and generous during his life, and happy in his death; which capitulations had for object, *that the ambassadors, consuls, interpreters, merchants, and other subjects of France, should be protected and maintained in all peace and tranquillity,* [180] and it has at length arrived at our imperial knowledge that these points have been conferred upon by the said ambassador and the minister of the Sublime Port: the foundations of the friendship which, from time immemorial, has subsisted with firmness between the court of France and our Sublime Port, and the convincing proofs which your majesty has given of it, particularly during our glorious reign, giving reason to hope that the ties of such a friendship can only be drawn closer, and become stronger from day to day; these motives have inspired us with sentiments conformable with your desires; and wishing to procure activity in commerce, and security to goers and comers, which are the fruits such a friendship ought to produce; we not only confirm by these presents in their full extent, the ancient and renewed capitulations, as well as the articles concerted at the above date, but to procure more ease for our merchants and greater vigour in commerce, we have granted them exemption from the right of *Mezeterie*, which they have paid at all times, as well as several other points concerning commerce, and the safety of comers and goers, which have been discussed, treated of, and regulated, in good and due form, in the divers conferences which have been held upon the subject, between the said ambassador, furnished with sufficient power, and the persons deputed on the part of our Sublime Port. After the entire conclusion of all, my supreme and absolute Grand Vizier, having rendered an account of it to our imperial Stirrup, and it being our will to show specially on this occasion the value and esteem that we entertain for the ancient and constant friendship of the emperor of France, who has just given us fresh and particular marks of the sincerity of his heart, we have granted our sign imperial for the execution of the articles newly concluded, and consequently of the ancient and renewed capitulations; having been transcribed and reported exactly, word for word from the commencement, and followed by the articles newly regulated and granted; these present imperial capitulations have been placed and consigned, in the above-said order, in the hands of the aforesaid ambassador."

Articles 32, 33, 34, 35, and 36 of the capitulations contain what follows:—"As inimical nations, who have no positive ambassadors at my Port of felicity, formerly went and came in our states, under the banner of the emperor of France, whether for commerce, whether for pilgrimage, according to the imperial permission they had had for it under the reigns of our ancestors of glorious memory, as likewise it was granted by the ancient capitulations accorded to the French: and as afterwards, for certain reasons, the entrance to our states was positively prohibited to these same nations, and they were even withdrawn from the said capitulations; nevertheless, the emperor of France having evinced by the letter he has sent to our Port of felicity, that he should wish that the inimical nations, to whom trading in our states has been forbidden, might have liberty to come and go to Jerusalem, in the same manner as they were accustomed to go and come, without being in any way interrupted; and that if consequently it were permitted them to come and traffic in our states, it should be under the banner of France, as formerly, the demand of the emperor of France has been complied with, in consideration of the ancient friendship, which from the times of my glorious ancestors has subsisted, from father to son, between your majesty and the Sublime Port, and we have issued an imperial edict, of which the following is the tenor:—That the Christian and inimical nations which are at peace with the emperor of France, and who shall desire to visit Jerusalem, may go thither and return, within the boundaries of their state, in the customary manner, and in full liberty and security, without any person causing them trouble or impediment; and if it should afterwards prove convenient to grant to the said nations the liberty of trading in our states, they will then go and come under the banner of the emperor of France as formerly, without being allowed to go and come under any other banner.

"The ancient imperial capitulations, which have been in the hands of the French since the reigns of my magnificent ancestors to the present day, and which have just been reported in detail above, having been now renewed with an addition of some new articles, conformably with the imperial order, issued in virtue of my khatt-cherif; the first of these articles declares, that the bishops dependent upon France, and the other ecclesiastics who profess the French religion, of whatever nation or race they may be, as long as they shall keep within the limits of their state, shall not be troubled in the exercise of their functions in those parts of our empire where they have been long settled.

"The French ecclesiastics who, according to ancient custom, are established within and without the city of Jerusalem, in the church of the Holy Sepulchre called Kamama, shall not be disturbed in the places of visitation which they inhabit, and which are in their hands, which shall remain still in their hands as formerly, without being disturbed in that respect, or by the imposition of tributes; and should any dispute arise, which cannot be decided on the spot, it shall be sent to my Sublime Port.

"The French, or those who depend upon them, of whatever nation or quality they may be, who desire to go to Jerusalem, shall not be molested either in going or returning.

"The two religious orders which are at Galata, that is to say, the Jesuits and the Capuchins, having two churches there, which have been in their hands *ab antiquo*, they shall remain in their hands, and they shall retain the possession and the advantages of them: and as one of these churches has been burnt, it shall be rebuilt as justice requires, and it shall remain, as formerly, in the hands of the Capuchins, without molestation or disturbance. There shall be no uneasiness entertained with regard to the churches the French have at Smyrna, Seyda, Alexandria, and other *Echelles*; and no money shall be required of them under any pretence.

"The French shall not be disturbed, when, within the bounds of their own quarter, they read the Gospel in their hospital of Galata."

Several of these dispositions not having been strictly executed, the Port renewed them in 1740; this is the renewal, as it is expressed in article 82.

"When the places, of which the ecclesiastics dependent upon France have possession at Jerusalem, as has been mentioned in the articles solemnly granted and now renewed, shall be in want of repair, to prevent the ruin to which they would be exposed by the course of time, it shall be permitted to grant, at the request of the ambassador of France, residing at my Port of felicity, orders for their being repaired in a way conformable to justice; and the cadis, commandants, and other officers, shall not be allowed to throw any impediment in the way of the things granted by order; and as it has happened that our officers, under pretext of having made secret repairs in the said places, made many visits in the course of the year, and extorted money from the ecclesiastics, we command that, on the part of the cadis, commandants, and other officers who may be there, there shall be only one visit made in the year to the church of the place that is called the Sepulchre of Jesus; and the same in the other churches and places of visitation. The bishop and ecclesiastics dependent upon the emperor of France, who are in my empire, shall be protected as long as they confine themselves to the limits of their own state, and nobody shall prevent them from performing their rites according to their own customs, in the churches which are in their hands, as well as in the other places in which they dwell: and when our tributary subjects and the French shall go and come among one another, for the purpose of buying, selling, or other affairs, they shall not be molested, against the same laws, on account of this intercourse; and as it is decreed in the preceding stipulated articles that they shall be allowed to read the Scriptures in the hospital of Galata, and this has, nevertheless, not been done, we order, that in whatever place that hospital may for the future be, in a juridical form, they may be allowed to read the Scripture there, as is their duty, without any inquietude upon the subject."

The capitulations or treaties with the Port are too extensive to allow us to give them entirely here. The articles, which amount to eighty-five, regulate the rights of persons and the commercial privileges of which the Port has granted the enjoyment to all the French established or travelling in the countries of its domination; they regulate also the diplomatic relations between the two powers, and the prerogatives of the ambassadors of the king of France.

———

Note by M. Raynouard upon the Work by M. Hammer, entitled Mysterium Baphometi Revelatum, &c.

Since the proscription of the knights of the Temple and the abolition of the order, five hundred years had passed away, when accusations, evidences, and judgments, were again submitted to the revision of history;—the renown of the order and the memory of the knights are again reëstablished in the opinion of impartial persons.

A new adversary of the Templars presented himself, and setting aside the accusations which contemporary persecutors had imagined, invented other crimes. In spite of the interval of time, he boasted of being able to produce material proofs: "There is no need of words," says M. Hammer, "when stones serve as witnesses."

What are these monuments with which the persons who prepared and achieved the ruin of the Templars were unacquainted, or which they neglected? How did they escape the industrious perquisitions of the envy, hatred, and sagacity of the inquisitors? Why did not the divers apostates, who, from ambition or fear, gave evidence against the order, point out monuments which then would have been more numerous and more striking, and whose existence might have justified their shameful desertion? And when the churches and houses of the Templars were occupied by successors who had so much interest in procuring pardon for the rigour of the spoliation, how was it that none of these successors discovered these material proofs, which, according to M. Hammer, proclaim to the present day the apostasy of the Templars?

The work of this scholar is entitled, Le Mystère du Baphomet révélé; or, the Brothers of the Military Order of the Temple convicted, by their own Memorials, of sharing the Apostasy, Idolatry, and Impiety of the Gnostics, and even of the Ophianites.

The following contains the exposition, the analysis, and the recapitulation of M. Hammer.

"We read, in the procedure undertaken against the order of the Temple, that the knights worshipped an idol of Bafomet form—in figuram Bafometi. [181] The decomposition of this word furnishes bafo and meti. Bafo, in Greek, signifies dyeing, or dipping, and, by extension, baptism; meti, signifies spirit. The Bafomet of the Templars was then the baptism of the spirit—the Gnostic baptism, which was not performed by the waters of redemption, but which was a spiritual lustration by fire. Bafomet signifies, then, the illumination of the spirit.

"As the Gnostics had furnished the Templars with Bafometic ideas and images, the word *meti* (*metis*) became venerated among the Templars: "I shall, therefore," adds M. Hammer, "furnish proofs of this decisive circumstance.

"The Gnostics were accused of infamous vices. The *metis* was represented under symbolical forms, principally under that of serpents, and of a truncated cross in the shape of *Tau—T*.

"The Gnostics," continues M. Hammer, "did not always employ the word *meti* in their monuments; they likewise made use of the word *gnosis*, which is synonymous, and is found among the Templars."

Developing his system of accusation, M. Hammer constantly maintains that it is proved by the proceedings instituted against the Templars, that they adored Bafometic figures; he produces medals which bear these pretended Bafometic figures, and particularly some medals upon which may be read, *meti*, with a truncated cross, [182] and others which represent a temple, with the legend, *Sanctissima Quinosis*, that is to say, *Gnosis*. He indicates likewise Gnostic vases and chalices; and attributing them to the Templars, advances, that the romance of the *Saint Graal*, or holy cup, is a symbolic romance, which at the same time conceals and proves the apostasy of the knights; and believes that he recognises in churches which formerly belonged to the Templars, or which he pretends to have belonged to them, Bafometic figures, and Gnostic and ophitic symbols.

M. Hammer expends much erudition in describing the various and numerous systems which preceded and produced the sect of the Gnostics; at length he comes to the Bafometic figures; he produces twenty-four of them, which appear to him to bear the characters of the *Bafomet*; they are covered with astrological signs; many are encircled by a serpent, and hold this cross by a handle, which was called *key of the Nile* by the Egyptians, and which has been considered the symbol of fecundity; they bear inscriptions, some in Latin, some in Greek, which denote nothing but proper names; and others in Arabic would be unintelligible, if we had not the means of comparing them with those upon the vases. The principal vase bears an Arabic inscription, which refers to the worship of a divinity named *Mété*; it has the title of *Teala*—all-powerful, and of *Nasch*—producer. M. Hammer pretends that the *Mété* was the same as the *Sophia* and *Achamet* of the various sects of Gnostics.

But no relation presents itself, either near or remote, with the Templars.

It was M. Nicolaï who, in a German work, entitled, *An Essay upon the Secret of the Templars*, first employed this word *Bafomet*, and who attached to it the idea of the image of the supreme God, in the state of quietude attributed to him by the Manichean Gnostics; it was this learned man who first supposed that the Templars had a secret doctrine and initiations of several grades; and he pretends that the Saracens had communicated this doctrine to them.

In order to destroy all these systems, it is sufficient to prove that it is impossible to prove that the word *Bafometi*, which is reported in the proceedings against the Templars, signified anything but *Mahomet*.

M. le Baron Sylvestre de Sacy had already condemned this explanation of M. Hammer; and if the latter persisted in not recognising in *Bafomet* the name of *Mahomet*, it would be easy to prove to him that authors of the middle ages often wrote Bafomet for Mahomet;—authorities are not wanting.

If the word even of the Bafometic or Gnostic sect does not exist, if it never has existed, the entire system is without a basis.

But even if it could be proved that a Bafometic sect had existed, if we were in possession of certain details upon its opinions and mysteries, how could M. Hammer prove that the Templars belonged to this sect?

M. Hammer has collected and caused to be engraved as many as a hundred medals and other monuments which he attributes to the Templars, because he fancies he finds upon them the *Mete* and the *Tau* of the Gnostics.

The medals he produces are not even proofs of the existence of a sect of Gnostics; and even if this existence could be demonstrated, these medals and these monuments being entirely foreign to the Templars, why should they be applied to them? [183]

To give an idea of the manner in which M. Hammer tries to prove, by the medals, that the Templars were Gnostics, I will cite only these upon which this savant fancies he reads the word *Quinosis* or *Gnosis*.

In the coin 80, we see, according to M. Hammer, the temple of Jerusalem with four towers; the inscription is: S. S. SIMOONJU[prostrate d]A; but reading it the reverse way, and beginning, not by the final A, but by the prostrate d, which M. Hammer has taken for a Q, whilst other savants, who have quoted this medal, have thought it a D, he reads SSTA QUINOMIS, although there is no T in the inscription; and considering the M as a sigma reversed, M. Hammer has found Quinosis; then Qui into G, and only making a single O of the two, he obtains Gnosis; which, according to his account, reveals and proves the secret of the Gnostic Templars.

M. Hammer not only reads it backwards, but he begins by the penultimate letter, and leaves the A, after which is a which separates the beginning of the inscription from its end. He adds a T, and supposes a Greek letter mixed with the Latin inscription; and yet, after all these changes, he cannot produce the word Gnosis.

And what prevented him from seeing in this inscription what it really is, SS. SIMON JUDA?

In the medal 99 we read in the same manner, S. Simon Vel Juda; in the 93rd, S. Simon Juda, &c. Nothing was more common in the middle ages than coins which, on one side bear the name of a saint, and on the other side the name of a city or prince.

Two of the coins upon which, instead of St. Simon and St. Jude, M. Hammer records Saint Gnostic, bear also the name of *Otto*, or *Otto* Marchio. This circumstance is embarrassing for M. Hammer; he explains it by saying that this Marquis Otho was a Gnostic, a protector of the Templars, and initiated into their secret doctrines.

Seelander only reads St. Simon and St. Jude upon these coins; he believes that this Otho might be Otho II., marquis of Brandenburg, who lived about the year 1200. If the opinion of Seelander will not induce M. Hammer to adopt this simple, natural, and evident explanation, he may find in Otto Sperlingius the explanation of a similar coin, with the inscription of St. Simon and St. Jude. The heads of the two saints are close together, under the same crown. A. Mellen thought that this coin was struck at Goslar, and Sperlengius adopts his opinion.

But even if it were allowed that these coins belonged to a sect of Gnostics, I should continue to assert that M. Hammer does not at all prove that the Templars made use of them. The reasoning of this savant is reduced almost to this:—"These monuments are Gnostic, therefore they relate to the Templars;" and to this:—"These monuments relate to the Templars, therefore they are Gnostic."

But let me be permitted to say once more, if the Templars had had amongst them such Gnostic signs, how was it that these signs were not made known and denounced when the question was to destroy the order? How is it that they are never found anywhere but in Germany?

I should obtain the same result if I were to examine in this manner in detail all that relates to the cups and chalices in which M. Hammer believes he sees Gnostic emblems; not only is there nothing upon them concerning the Templars, but M. Hammer has only collected them in places and upon monuments quite foreign to the order of the Templars.

As to the Gnostic sculptures which M. Hammer persists in seeing in some churches, is it not well known that we find in the churches of the middle ages sculptures and monuments which it is very difficult to explain, either on account of the moral and religious ideas which the artists of the time expressed under very unsuitable images; or on account of the pious allegories, the tradition of which is not come down to us?

The relievos of the capitals of the church of St. Germaine des Prés have embarrassed antiquaries, and if M. Hammer had found such in a church of the Templars, he would not have failed to magnify by them his act of accusation.

He cites seven churches in Germany, in which he pretends to recognise Gnostic emblems: but he offers no proof that these churches belonged to the Templars; and, even if the Order had built them, is it to be conceived, that if there existed a secret doctrine among them, the leaders would have exposed the symbols of it in public in their churches? And how is it that they selected seven German churches to receive these irreligious signs, whilst they did nothing of the same kind in the three thousand churches they possessed in Christendom?

M. Hammer is not more fortunate when he seeks in romances, which speak of the Saint Graal, the emblematic history, or the symbol of the order of the Temple.

These romances present nothing contrary to religion; the knights, who are the personages, promise fidelity to God and the ladies; they arm and fight for religion and beauty. Can we then be astounded that at the period when these romances were composed, the search for the St. Graal, or holy cup, was considered an exploit worthy of chivalry?

M. Hammer fancies he finds something very favourable to him in the following passage:—"As the St. Graal came to Tramelet on the day of Pentecost,"—he remarks that the festival of St. Graal was not celebrated on Christmas-day, but at Pentecost; "if by this cup," says he, "had been meant, as some people suppose, the Lord's cup, the festival would have been celebrated either on Christmas-day or Holy Thursday, and not on the day of Pentecost, which the Gnostics regarded as very holy, as the day of the Holy Ghost, which was for the Gnostics Sophia, and for the Templars Mete."

The reply to this is very easy:—1st. King Artus held his plenary court on the great festivals of the year; it is not, then, surprising that the St. Graal should arrive at Pentecost. 2nd. The author of the romance could not choose the day of Christmas-day, which festival was not appointed in the time of King Artus. 3rd. It is even probable that the romance in question was composed before the institution of that festival by Urban IV., in 1264.

M. Hammer has been sensible that it was strange to form, after a lapse of five centuries, an accusation against the Templars quite different from that which served as a pretext for the contemporary oppressors. Therefore he advances that the pope, by the sentence which was pronounced against the Templars, was willing to conceal the knowledge of their true crimes; but he maintains, that when the archives of Rome shall come to light, as everything does sooner or later, we shall there find the proof of the crimes he now denounces.

How is it possible to be believed, that if the knights had been guilty of the crimes M. Hammer attributes to them, the pope and kings would have preferred the absurd system of accusation which they employed, to a system such as that which M. Hammer puts forth?

But, besides, it is very certain that ALL the pieces which the archives of Rome contained are now known: they are ALL marked with their numbers in the notice of the unpublished pieces which have assisted in the composition of *Les Monuments Historiques relatifs à la Condemnation des Chavaliers du Temple, etc.* M. Hammer has nothing, therefore, to hope from the archives of the Vatican.

This distinguished savant will some day acknowledge that he ought not to have yielded to the desire of putting forth a new system of denunciation against the order and the knights of the Temple. Their terrible and celebrated catastrophe imposes the obligation of being very circumspect and very severe in the choice of the means by which we may allow ourselves to endeavour to deprive them of the just pity which posterity has not refused to their fate.

INDEX

A

Abaga, khan of the Tartars, sends ambassadors to Rome

Abassides persecute the Christians, Decline of their empire

Aboubeker, his interview with Richard I. of England

Abou-bekr, founder of one of the Mohammedan sects

Accien, sovereign of Antioch

Achard de Montmerle

Adel, the son of Saladin

Adhémar de Monteil, bishop of Puy, engages in the first crusade

His enthusiastic bravery

Adonis, the river

Adrianople, besieged by the Latins

Battle of

Siege raised

Æneas Sylvius, bishop of Sienna, preaches a crusade against the Turks et seq

Elected pope, under the title of Pius II.

See *Pius II.*

Afdhal, son of Saladin, and commander of the Mussulman forces of Egypt

His extensive empire

Civil contests of et seq

Oath taken by the emirs of

Rebellion against

Africa invaded by the Christian forces et seq

and take it by storm

Godfrey de Bouillon elected king

Great victory over the Egyptian forces on the plain of Ascalon

Many of the leaders return to Europe

Fresh bodies of Crusaders leave Europe for the East

Their leaders

Take the city of Ancyra, *ib.*

Defeated with great slaughter by the Turks

Reflections on their heroism and exploits et seq

Kingdom founded by their victories et seq

Death of their great leader, Godfrey de Bouillon, king of Jerusalem

His brother Baldwin elected as his successor, on whose family the sovereignty devolves et seq

Hostilities carried on against the infidels of Palestine and Egypt, with alternate success and defeat et seq

Their conquests and high state of prosperity under Baldwin du Bourg

Their military orders of knighthood

Their calamitous defeat at Edessa by the armies of Zengui and Noureddin

Their consternation and despair

— — The Second Crusade, a.d. 1142-1148. — The Christian colonies of the East being threatened by the Mussulmans, call upon the princes of Europe to assist them,

All Christendom aroused by St. Bernard to the impending dangers of the Holy Land et seq

Louis VII., king of France, and Pope Eugenius III., determine on a second crusade

The multitudes assembled for the occasion

The cities of Metz and Ratisbon the general rendezvous

Measures for raising money to defray the expenses

The crusaders depart from Europe, headed by Louis VII. and the Emperor Conrad

Arrive at Constantinople

Death of Louis IX.

The Crusaders conclude a ten years' truce with the king of Tunis

Their fleet is nearly destroyed by a tempest

The ancient spirit of the Crusaders suspended

Prince Edward of England arrives in Palestine, *ib.*;

but soon returns

Causes of the failure of this crusade et seq

Gregory X. convokes the council of Lyons, and endeavours, but in vain, to revive a new crusade

Severe losses and sanguinary contests of the Christians of Palestine with the Saracens, et seq

The slaughter of, at the capture of Ptolemaïs et seq

Abandoned by their leaders

Capture and destruction of all the Christian cities along the coast of Syria

Indifference of the Western world to the melancholy fate of the Christian inhabitants

— — Attempted Crusades against the Turks, a.d. 1291-1396.—Pope Nicholas IV. directs his attention to the preaching of another crusade,

The hopes of the West revived by the successes of the Tartars against the Mussulmans et seq

Proclaimed by Clement V. at the council of Vienna

Philip, king of France, Edward III. of England, and other illustrious personages, prepare for a formidable crusade, which is checked by the death of Pope John XXI.

Persecutions of the Christians of the East in consequence of these attempts

Benedict XI. endeavours to stir up a crusade

Assembly of sovereigns and nobles at Avignon

They capture and burn Alexandria

Invade the coast of Barbary

Miraculous interpositions related

Treaty with the sultan of Egypt

A crusade against the Turks determined on

Its illustrious leaders

Their fatal contests with Bajazet

Pope Eugenius exhorts to a fresh crusade

and large armies are collected

The Christians enter into a treaty with Amurath, which they violate

and undertaking another crusade are defeated and annihilated

The Crusaders full of bravery but deficient in qualities

European crusades terminate with the capture of Constantinople, and the destruction of the Greek empire by the Ottoman forces, in 1453

— — Defensive Crusades against the Turks, a.d. 1453-1481,

Meeting of Philip of Burgundy, John Capistran, Æneas Sylvius, Frederick III. of Germany, Pope Nicholas V., Calixtus III., and others, to endeavour to stir up a crusade against the Turks

The crusade preached in France, England, Germany, Spain, and Portugal

General assembly at Mantua, convoked by Pius II.

His holiness endeavours to arouse the Christian states against the victorious career of the Turks et seq

Accompanies the crusade, and dies at Ancona

Paul II. and Sextus V. preach the crusade

Partial successes of the Crusaders, and the discord attending them

The Christians lose all their previous conquests, except Cyprus and Rhodes

Charles VIII. of Naples engages in a pretended crusade against the Turks

Pope Alexander VI. endeavours in vain to stir up the crusade

The crusading spirit becomes enfeebled

Exertions of Leo X. for its revival et seq

Great preparations for

Curious historical documents respecting

Clement VII. renounces all further hopes

Career of the Turks checked by their signal defeat in the Gulf of Lepanto

His zealous endeavours to resist the advance of the Turks et seq

Engages in the crusade

and dies at Ancona

Plague in Egypt

Plaisance, papal council at

Poictiers, count of, his capture and release

Poitevins, their severe conflicts with the Saracens

Pons, abbot of Vézelai, preaches in favour of the second crusade

— — de Balasu, death and character of

Popedom, contests for the, ;

Popelicains, religious principles of the

Popes, increase of their power during the progress of Christianity

Their political pretensions and quarrels,

Their domination during the age of the crusades et seq

See *Rome*

Portugal submits to Alphonso

The sultan of Egypt's expedition against

Pourcelet, Wm., his heroic self-sacrifice

Prester John, notices of

Printing, instrumental in preserving the literary treasures of the East

Prodigies, miraculous, seen at Antioch

Provençalex, origin of the name

Provisions, scarcity and dearness of and

Prudhommes, maritime code drawn up by the

Prussia, paganism of, in the thirteenth century

Manners and customs of the inhabitants

Their religious belief, and festivals

Subdued and converted by the Holy See

Reflections on the papal crusade against

Funeral ceremonies of (App.)

Ptolemaïs, the Crusaders march through the country of

SUPPLEMENTARY CHAPTER

M. Michaud has told the story of the crusades with such fulness and accuracy that, so far as these religious pilgrimages in arms are concerned, nothing need be added. The movement of the West upon the East is traced and described in minute detail, with every accessory of personal incident and achievement, and the work has been done so thoroughly that probably no later historian will feel drawn to the same field. It may be profitable, however, to supplement this trustworthy and spirited narrative by a rapid survey of the wide and fruitful changes which the crusades directly and indirectly introduced into the social and political life of Europe. It is one of the gains of time that its lapse discloses those larger relations of great events which are hidden from the observation of an earlier age; and while the earlier historian has the advantage of being near the historical movement which he describes, and of collecting at first hand the fullest information of its origin, direction, and personality, the later writer is far more fully equipped for the work of setting the movement in right relation to its social and political environment. Thucydides must remain preëminently the historian of the Peloponnesian War; but Grote and Curtius, largely deriving their facts from him, are able to discuss the decisive struggle between Athens and Sparta with wider grasp of the elements of Greek character and politics which brought about the conflict, and to trace its influence in later Greek history. This chapter will add no newly discovered facts concerning the crusades; but, taking advantage of later studies in this important field, it will indicate some of the results of these expeditions as they have disclosed themselves in the subsequent political development of Europe.

The Council of Clermont in 1095 found the feudal system fully developed in Western Europe. The Holy Roman Empire which, in the person of Charlemagne, had given brief promise of a restoration of authority to government, and of cohesion to society, had become a mere shadow among the warring, aggressive factions of feudalism. The tremendous energy of Charles was potent enough to drive back the boundaries of barbarism, and make for a little time a comparatively clear field for efforts toward an organized and stable society; but the task of subduing the social and political anarchy about him was too great even for a ruler of his genius. The time was not ripe, and when the laboriously gathered lines of power fell from the strong hand, there was no successor to grasp them. Anarchy became well-nigh universal. The royal authority was everywhere, with here and there a passing exception, a vague and indefinite thing, hemmed in and jealously watched by barons, more powerful than the king in everything but name. Society was broken up into small communities, with apparently no common direction of movement or impulse of progress. Every castle was a centre of power, which might be hostile to every other authority about it. There were no common ties binding races into the larger fellowship of kindred aims and aspirations. Men of the same blood were arrayed in more deadly hostility to each other than were men of alien races.

No large enterprises were possible, because the community of sentiment and the harmony of action which made them possible, were alike absent. The principle of individualism—the greatest contribution of the northern races to the political development of Europe—had reached its fullest growth, and everywhere asserted itself in the most aggressive forms. Western Europe had gone so far in this direction that no further progress in the arts, industries, and institutions of civilization was possible without the introduction of a new element into the problem. What was needed was the cohesive influence of some common purpose, which should give a new unity by disclosing to men the larger possibilities of organized social and political life. Organization is the necessary condition of progress, and so long as Europe remained without the conception of government with well-defined powers, regularity of administration, and ability to suppress opposition and impress its authority, in all sections of its territory, with a firm and steady hand, no forward movement was possible.

This spell of political and social impotence was broken by the crusades. Peter the Hermit was a voice crying in the wilderness, the forerunner of a historical movement which was to be the salvation of Europe. Returning from Syria with a heart hot with indignation at the insults and persecutions which beset the pilgrim to the Holy Sepulchre, his call to arms had all the authority which a genuine religious conviction could give it, and all the persuasive eloquence of a call for which men had been longing and waiting in silence and despair. No one will deny the strength of the religious sentiment which, in answer to that message, speedily marshalled the hosts of the first crusade; but the restless life of oppressed and burdened races found in the new enterprise an outlet through which it poured itself like a rising tide. For the first time in its history Western Europe had a common purpose and united in a common undertaking. In the farthest hamlet the overshadowing power of the feudal lord became for the time being tributary to the authority of the Church, summoning Europe to fight its battles and protect its sacred places. Europe awoke to the fact, unsuspected before, that it was larger than its warring feudatories, that the possibilities of its life were far more varied and rich than men had dreamed under the iron pressure of the feudal system, and thus the needed element of association and coöperation asserted itself.

Like all great social and political changes, the transition from feudal communities to national organization was unconscious and undiscovered. In the minds of the crusaders and of the communities whose faith they represented and whose impulse they carried into action, no clearly defined ideal of national life answered the call of Peter. That ideal grew slowly, but its roots were planted in this movement. Spaniards, Germans, Italians, Englishmen, and Frenchmen found themselves acting in harmony for a common purpose. They bore different banners, they marched under different leaders, they took different roads; but a common impulse sent them forth and a common goal drew them on. Their community of sentiment was often marred by mutual jealousies, and their unity of action impaired by mutual antagonisms; but the substantial harmony which underlay these disorders and which secured the positive results of the earlier crusades, gave Europe a conception of life which it had thoroughly learned before the last crusaders returned from their fruitless quest.

That which drew together various nationalities and races, disclosing to them the religious and social aims and tastes which they possessed in common, brought about a similar result through the widely separated ranks of society. European society had no homogeneity when the first crusade was preached. It was divided into ranks sharply discriminated from each other, bound together by the pressure of external force, rather than by the cohesive power of organic structure. There was no mutuality of interest or feeling. King, baron, burgher, and peasant were so widely apart by virtue of the education of their circumstances that they could not understand each other. That common language of experience and aspiration, which to-day finds a response among men of all social ranks, would have been incomprehensible in the age of the first crusade. Baron and peasant had indeed acted together in feudal warfare; but only as the lower was forced to serve the higher, the weaker to do the work of the stronger. No common impulse had ever before stirred the common humanity of all classes; no call had ever before summoned them as individuals to a service in which each stood in a spiritual equality with every other. Men had moved in classes before, but they moved as classes and not as men.

The Church had seen its early dream of an imperial power with which it could keep itself in friendly and influential alliance fade like a mist before the iron individualism of feudalism, and had been compelled to begin almost anew its conquest over the governing powers of Europe. The work which a few skilful ecclesiastics could have done at the courts of kings in a few capital cities was relegated for centuries to an army of priests attached to baronial households, and conducting the sacred offices of their religion in the chapels of castles over the vast territory of Western Europe. The Church and feudalism were in radical antagonism; they represented ideas which could not, in the extremes in which each held them, be harmonized in practical life. The Church had yielded to feudalism, as in an earlier age she had yielded to the barbarian conquest of Southern Europe, because surrender, in form at least, was inevitable. But, in the latter case, as in the former, the struggle was renewed at once upon a new plan of action. The orderly campaign by massing of forces at a few strategic points was abandoned for incessant watchfulness and a perpetual skirmish along an immensely extended frontier. Every barony became a scene of action, every castle a stronghold to be won by the most skilful devices of the spiritual warfare. The Church was the only representative of the idea of universal authority and order, but as yet no occasion had arisen by which it might profit to make that conception an active principle in society. It was in deadly antagonism to the system which broke society up into small, hostile communities; but the time had not come when it could bring to bear a force powerful enough to destroy its antagonist, or to set at work an influence which would inevitably result in the disintegration of the feudal order.

The preaching of the first crusade was an opportunity which the Church was quick to recognise and to follow up with that persistent and consummate ability which characterized all its earlier and much of its later history. It was possible now to call not only separate feudatories but all Europe to arms. Feudalism would keep men divided into fixed classes, and society broken up into permanent groups; the Church, on the other hand, would prevent the oppression of one class by another by binding all in a universal allegiance to herself, and would impress upon society the unity of a common service and a common faith.

The crusades sprang out of a feeling which was as strong in the heart of the peasant as in that of the noble. A great cause and a universal sentiment gave the Church the opportunity for which it sought. A solemn council made the preaching of Peter the Hermit the voice of the Church herself. Feudal distinctions were forgotten in the enthusiasm of a service which transcended in its sanctions and its aims all earthly duties, and in which earthly differences were for the moment laid aside. The power of the feudal nobility, hitherto the dominant authority in Western Europe, became, for the time being, secondary to that of the Church. Men were summoned no longer to the service of their lords, but to the service of their Church. The change was radical. It was the introduction of a principle which is still struggling to assert itself in practical legislation and political action. Its development has been slow, but it has revolutionized society, and what its ultimate outcome is to be no man can predict. King, baron, burgher, and peasant found themselves side by side in the same cause, one class serving another, not by virtue of a feudal but of a spiritual authority; comrades in arms in an enterprise which addressed what was common and eternal in them all rather than what was distinctive and conventional. Not suddenly, but by the slow processes of growth which belong to great moral changes, men forgot their abasement and slavery under feudalism in the dawning light of a liberty conferred by a superior and a spiritual power. A conception of a higher authority than that lodged in the hands of the feudal lord took root in the mind of Europe and became fruitful of vast change. In Syria the leaders of the crusades were not able to keep their followers in subjection when they attempted to follow their personal ambitions. The commanding purpose which drew them thither overmastered all private designs and made insubordination a virtue. An influence more powerful than feudalism entered into European life with the crusades, and was perhaps the most far-reaching and potential effect which they produced upon the world.

The crusades found Europe stationary and without the power of progress. Society had crystallized into forms so rigid and fixed that strong pressure from without was essential to any movement toward liberation. Not only were communities circumscribed and reduced in numbers, and individuals held in their places by a power against which it was hopeless to strive; but the whole population was bound to the soil by a system of servitude the most exacting and the most pervasive known in history. Contiguous communities spoke dialects differing so widely as to make communication between men of the same race almost as difficult as between men of widely separated nationalities.

There was almost no interchange of knowledge, no commerce of ideas. Where men were born they spent their lives, and were buried with no sense of any larger relationships in life than those of the locality which formed their little sphere of action. Feudalism, in disintegrating society and reducing the individual to an unimportant factor in a vast system, had paralyzed the power of development, which comes only through interchange and combination of energy. The Chinese Empire of a century ago was hardly more securely walled in from external influence and condemned to absolute stagnation than were the countries over which feudalism had spread its iron network. Into this close, dense atmosphere the crusades sent a vigorous current of new thought. The hopeless and weary routine to which great populations were condemned explains much of that enthusiasm with which multitudes rushed into a dangerous and laborious service. Men were stifled in an air which they and their fathers before them had breathed without any possibility of change. In the crusade epoch the religious impulse was strong, but the impulse toward freedom was doubtless the sentiment next in importance.

Between 1095 A.D. and 1291 A.D., there was an immense change. The first crusade found men of all nationalities eager to follow its leaders, the preachers of the last crusade appealed to deaf ears. Europe was indifferent to the cause which for two centuries had found orators as eloquent as Bernard of Clairvaux and leaders as pure as Godfrey, as daring as Richard, as devoted as St. Louis, and yet religious zeal was not dead, nor had the sanctions of religion lost their sacredness. The secret of the change in European sentiment lay in the enlargement and liberation of European life which the crusades had secured. There was a comparatively free interchange between the different sections. The incessant movements of the crusading hosts, the intermingling of so many different races had broken down many barriers and set many unifying influences at work. The German knew the Frenchman, and the Frenchman the Englishman, and this mutual knowledge was fruitful in quickened and stimulated life everywhere. Men began to better their condition by a change of location. Emigration, which in the earlier centuries of the Christian era had changed the face of Europe and then had been checked by feudalism, began once more in ways so small and insignificant as to remain long unnoticed, but of immense importance in the light of subsequent history.

The modification and disintegration of the feudal system is unquestionably the greatest contribution of the crusades to the development of humanity. This result was brought about, as has been shown, by the liberation of thought and life throughout Western Europe; but there were other and important elements which entered into the solution of the problem of European progress.

The expeditions to the East were, for that age, enormously expensive. Very many of the great feudal lords who fitted out expeditions were not able, out of their ordinary resources, to meet the necessary outlay. Money was raised by all kinds of expedients. Cities took advantage of the needs of their feudal lords to purchase their freedom, great estates that for centuries had increased by continued accumulation and conquest were encumbered or sold. There was an interchange of landed property altogether unprecedented in European history. Many great fiefs disappeared entirely during the two centuries which saw the gathering of the successive expeditions for the East. By purchase and by escheat and confiscation, which the disorder of the times made possible, the royal authority made immense inroads into the territory of feudalism, and when the last hopeless struggle in Syria was over, the principle of centralization, represented everywhere by the royal power, had gained vastly upon the extreme individualism of feudalism.

The advance of the Church in influence and authority was, however, the most immediate and marked result of the crusades. Religious ideas, Guizot declares, had experienced no change, but power had changed hands no less than property. The Church, quick to profit by every opportunity which the troubled age and the vicissitudes of war afforded, had pushed steadily forward, occupying every defenceless position and fortifying every exposed point. The authority which Urban had exercised at the Council of Clermont, in calling all men to arms as subjects of the Church, was asserted upon every occasion with that steadiness and universality of policy which is one of the secrets of papal power. A new principle of allegiance was substituted for feudal subordination. Differences between great barons were settled by the voice of the Church, and in the councils of kings the pope spoke by his personal representatives. Legates from Rome became familiar figures in every capital, and the persistence with which they made themselves heard in all public matters rapidly and continually enlarged the popular conception of the scope and weight of the authority of Rome.

In the East results of equal moment were brought about by the campaigns of the crusaders. Communication was reopened between the East and the West. The rude hand of war threw open the doors, which were never again to remain permanently closed.

The fierce struggles of the contending parties did not blind them to the fact that each had much to learn from the other. Oriental magnificence and culture had charms even for the warriors whose mailed hands were sworn to destroy the civilization under which they were developed. The positive and immediate gain to Western knowledge was doubtless less than was formerly believed, but the ulterior gain is incalculable. If the West is not indebted to the East for the art of printing and the compass, it is indebted for a substantial enrichment of thought, for a great enlargement of mental horizon. The interchange of thought which was set in motion by the crusades is still to work out its richest results; and in contemporaneous history there is no more impressive feature than the confluence of these two ancient civilizations.

FOOTNOTES:

[1] We find copious details upon these disputes, and their origin, in Sanuti, which we have thought it best to abridge.

[2] We have adopted the version of M. Deguignes as the most probable. (See *History of the Huns*.)

[3] One of the principal difficulties that an historian of this epoch experiences, is, to preserve the connection in his narrative, from having to speak at the same time of the West and of the East, of the Christians, the Mamelukes, and the Tartars. Here a new people start up upon the stage, there an old empire falls to decay: all the events are hurried and confounded together, and the march of history is embarrassed among so many ruins. We endeavour to be as clear as possible.

[4] Many chronicles say that Oulagon shut the caliph up in the midst of all his treasures, and left him to die of hunger: this circumstance is not at all probable, and has not been acknowledged by M. Deguignes.

[5] Most historians have taken their accounts of this war of the Moguls from an esteemed work, entitled *Fragmentum de Statu Saracœnorum*; it, however, contains many errors, and ought to be rectified in several places by the study of the Oriental historians. Some valuable information respecting this war of the Tartars may also be found in the Armenian Hayton, and in Sanuti; but these authors must be read with precaution and suspicion.

[6] Bela IV., king of Hungary, wrote to the pope, that if he were not speedily succoured he should form an alliance with the Tartars. The pope reproved him warmly. Alexander IV. wrote to all Christian princes, prelates, and communities, to consult upon the means of resisting the barbarians, as well in the East as in the West. In Raynaldi—the year 1262, Nos. 29 and 30— his letter may be seen, in which he enters into many details upon the levy of soldiers, and upon subsidies. This letter has been preserved by Matthew Paris, who speaks of the councils held on this subject; some facts relative to the invasion of the Tartars may likewise be found in William of Nangis and Matthew of Westminster, as well as in the *Collection of Councils*.

[7] This singular fact is related by the Arabian historian Aboulfeda, and repeated by M. Deguignes, vol. iv. p. 133.

[8] This circular is reported by Raynaldi, Nos. 68 and 69. The motives alleged by the pope, in his letter, astonish the wise Fleuri, who observes upon the spirit of contradiction which we have mentioned.

[9] These expeditions of Bibars are related with all their details in the chronicles of Ibn-Ferat and in Makrizi. Although we have much abridged our account, we fear we shall be accused of tediousness. We have yielded to our inclination of filling up the deficiencies which exist in all the chronicles of the West in their accounts of this period. The life of Bibars has likewise been of great service to us.

[10] The Arabian chronicles describe this event in a very obscure and equivocal manner; they scarcely mention the massacre of the prisoners, and say but little of the capitulation; they accuse the Franks of having taken Mussulman prisoners away with them, which is not very probable.

[11] We are afraid M. Michaud carries the partialities of Biography into the pages of History: in the former, such are sometimes excusable; in the latter, never. Our readers who look back to the taking of Jerusalem or Ptolemaïs, will at once see how weak is the claim of the Christians to a superiority over their adversaries in mercy. As to the religious portion of the account, history teems with wholesale conversions of conquered armies and nations. See Charlemagne and our own Alfred, for instance. We thought that the idea of Mahometanism being *a religion of the sword* was exploded. Gibbon positively denies it to be so, and asserts that no precept or passage of the Koran inculcates it.—Trans.

[12] Sanuti is almost the only Christian writer that affords information on the taking of Sefed.

[13] "I cannot tell the amount," says Joinville, "of what the king laid out for the fortification of Jaffa, it was so great. He closed the canal between the two seas, he built twenty-four towers, and cleansed the ditches without and within. There were three gates, of which the legate built one, and likewise part of the walls. And in order to show you what the king must have expended, I will tell you what the legate said when I asked him how much that gate and the wall had cost him. I had reckoned that the first cost him five hundred livres, and the latter three hundred livres; but he told me, as God might help him, that the gate and the wall had cost him thirty thousand livres."

[14] This little incident is quite dramatic, and, in good hands, would not look badly on canvass. Would it not assist art, if historians, when forcibly struck by the scenes they describe, would suggest to painters, who so frequently prove they are at a loss for subjects by their injudicious choice, events, persons, and passions fit for the pencil?—Trans.

[15] This letter of Bibars, which was written by his secretary, the author of the life we have of this sultan, does not only speak of the taking and the destruction of Antioch, but of the ravages committed by the Mamelukes in the territory of Tripoli. This letter is of great length, but we find in it more declamatory sentences and Oriental figures than facts for the pen of the historian.

[16] Sirvente is a kind of poem peculiar to the troubadours.

[17] This *sirvente*, which is attributed to a knight of the Temple, has been translated by the Abbé Millot, who appears to have altered the sense of it. It is printed in the fourth volume, p. 131, of the *Choix des Poésies des Troubadours*, by M. Raynouard, perpetual secretary to the French Academy. We make use of a literal translation that M. Raynouard has kindly communicated to us.

[18] These details, as well as the most of those that precede them, concerning the Mussulmans, are taken from the valuable chronicle of Ibn-Ferat.

[19] "He was of opinion," says William de Nangis, "that the kingdom of France had undergone great disgrace in the first pilgrimage." Le père Maimbourg expresses himself thus upon the king's determination:—"St. Louis, great saint as he was, could not help thinking that much shame lay upon him for having succeeded so ill in Egypt."

[20] *Hist. de St. Louis*, by Filleau de la Chaise.

[21] See the letters of Clement, in Duchesne, epist. 269.

[22] Joinville, when present at the mass in the chapel, heard two knights conferring; one said, that if the king took the cross, it would be one of the most fatal days ever seen in France; for if we take the cross, we shall ruin the king; and again, if we take the cross, we shall lose God's grace, because we do not take the cross for the sake of him.

[23] When our readers look back to the means employed in former crusades to extort money from all classes, as well as from the clergy, we think they will partake of our surprise at this assertion. The clergy had been, in most cases, the recipients of the taxes upon the laity, and according to our author himself, had not always proved trustworthy collectors.—Trans.

[24] All these details upon the tenths are of great importance for the history of the crusades: for this negotiation the following authorities may be consulted: Raynaldi, No. 59; the *Spicilège*, vol. xiii. p. 221; the *Supplement* to Raynaldi, book lxix. No. 42; Fleury's *Ecclesiastical History*, and the *Acts* of Rymer.

[25] As historians, we should hesitate to assert this, and should advise our readers to adopt it with much caution, and many limitations.—Trans.

[26] This dissertation, which has been sent to us by the author, bears for title, *An Historical Dissertation upon the Part the Spaniards took in the Wars beyond the Seas, and upon the Influence of these Expeditions, from the Eleventh to the Fifteenth Century*, by Don Fernandez de Crevarette. This work, in which a learned criticism and a sound erudition prevail, contains many valuable documents; we shall often have occasion to quote it.

[27] Migeray thus describes the murder of Conradin:—"As Charles had determined to go into Africa with the king, St. Louis, not knowing what to do with Conradin and Frederick, whom it was dangerous to keep, and still more to release, in a kingdom filled with faction and revolt, he ordered them to be brought to trial before the syndics of the cities of the kingdom."

[28] For the preparations for the voyage of Louis IX., William of Nangis, Geoffrey de Beaulieu, the *Gestes* of St. Louis, the continuator of Matthew Paris, and Joinville, may be consulted.

[29] "It is true that before the king Louis took the cross, he had had several messages from the king of Tunis, and at divers times, and many had been sent to him; these messages gave Louis to understand that the king of Tunis was willing to become a Christian, and that he would the more willingly change his faith if an opportunity should occur in which his own honour and the welfare of his people would be secured. The good Christian king believed that if he and his renowned hosts should come to Tunis suddenly, scarcely could the king of Tunis refuse or excuse such a reasonable opportunity for receiving holy baptism," &c.—*Annals of the Reign of St. Louis*, by William of Nangis.

[30] Some classical authorities name it Tunetum; others, Tunes.—Trans.

[31] Louis makes use of the expression: "Je vous dis le *ban*," &c. which word cannot be used in this sense in English, but is very effective in French, and was employed in many legal proclamations connected with royal or seignorial rights,—as, for instance: *ban* is a proclamation by which all who held lands of the crown of France were summoned to serve the king in his wars.—Trans.

[32] William of Nangis says on this subject:—"This was great treachery on the part of the Saracens, and great simplicity on the part of the Christians."

[33] Geoffrey de Beaulieu has given an account of these instructions in Latin. They are in old French in Joinville and in the *Annals of the Reign of St. Louis*. These three authors give them with remarkable differences.

Moreau, in the twentieth volume of his *Discours sur l'Histoire de France*, gives another new version, which he declares to have been copied from one of the registers of the Chamber of Accounts, in which, probably, Philip le Hardi was desirous this monument should be preserved. It is this version we have principally followed in the extract we have here given.

[34] Details upon the death of St. Louis may be found in Geoffrey de Beaulieu, William of Chartres, William of Nangis, and in a letter from the bishop of Tunis, reported by Martenne; Joinville relates a few circumstances of it; but it is very much to be regretted that the good seneschal was not present at the last moments of St. Louis; how touching would his relation have been! and how much better would it have been than that which is given to us by eyewitnesses, who have written with such unfeeling dryness and conciseness!

[35] This letter, which has been translated into Latin, may be found in the collection of Martenne. We will give an extract from it in our Appendix.

[36] We read in the life of Bibars and in the chronicle of Ibn-Ferat, that the sultan of Cairo was much dissatisfied with the conduct of the king of Tunis. The peace which the latter made, left the Crusaders at liberty to carry their arms into Egypt. Bibars would have wished the Christian army to have been detained on the coast of Africa. He threatened to dethrone his ally, and told the ambassadors of the king of Tunis, that such a prince as he was not worthy to reign over Mussulmans.

[37] For the events that followed the death of St. Louis, see Duchesne, and *le Spicilège*, vol. i.

[38] We hope our readers, while they peruse the latter part of this otherwise good paragraph, will not forget that we are only translators.— Trans.

[39] Among the numerous panegyrics of Louis IX. there are few that have stood the test of time. Voltaire has drawn a fine portrait of the good king. M. Dampmartin, in his work upon the kings of France, has spoken of this great prince with ability and truth.

[40] Words of the *Bull of Canonization*.

[41] The Arabian chroniclers have preserved several of these treaties: we find in the extracts from Oriental manuscripts, a treaty between the sultan of Cairo and the little city of Tortosa. When reading the titles and the dependencies of the masters and the inhabitants of Tortosa, we may fancy we read the lease of a bailiwick or a farm, made before a notary.

[42] In Ibn-Ferat we may read the letter which the sultan of Cairo wrote on the subject of the princess of Berouth, who had left her little principality without the consent of the sultan. (See the extracts from Arabic manuscripts.)

[43] This account is much longer in Ibn-Ferat; whilst endeavouring to preserve the tone and the Oriental colouring of it, we have felt it necessary to abridge it. The chronicle of Ibn-Ferat, which is a collection of many other chronicles, contains several different versions; this appears to us the most probable, and, at the same time, the one best calculated to show what were the resources of the nations of Asia against the excesses of despotism.

[44] Many historians think that Charles's preparations were intended to be directed against Constantinople. Without contradicting this opinion, we may believe that the king of Sicily thought likewise of the kingdom of Jerusalem. Charles was always very secret in his political projects; and very frequently the dissimulation of princes causes as much embarrassment to historians as it could have done ill to the countries exposed to its attempts.

[45] The text of this treaty may be read in the life of Kelaoun.

[46] M. de Sacy has translated a treaty concluded between the sultan of Egypt and the kings of Sicily and Arragon. The following is one of the clauses of this treaty:—"If the case should happen that the pope of Rome, the kings of the Franks, of the Greeks, of the Tartars, or others, should ask the king of Arragon or his brothers, or should cause to be asked in the states of their dominions, auxiliary troops or any succour, whether of cavalry, infantry, money, vessels, clothing, or arms, the said princes would give no consent to it, either openly or in secret; they would grant them no succour, and would consent to nothing of the kind. If the king of Arragon should learn that one of the above-named kings should have any intention of carrying war into the states of the sultan, or to cause him any prejudice, he will send and advise the sultan of it, and will inform him on what side his enemies propose to attack him, and that with the shortest delay possible, before they shall be put in motion, and he will conceal nothing concerning it from him." This treaty is very long, and provides against all difficulties. We may here make a general remark, which is, that most of the treaties made between the Orientals and the Christians surpass, in some sort, the sagacity of modern diplomacy; so much mistrust gave foresight to the negotiators and the contracting powers.

[47] We can find no document on this subject in the chronicles of the West; our guide has been Ibn-Ferat.

[48] All these curious details upon Ptolemaïs, its morals, and the mode of living of its inhabitants, are furnished by Herman Cornarius (Ekard's Collection). A more extensive extract will be found in our analysis of the German authors.

[49] We find this fact in two Austrian chronicles, which have for title, one, *Chronicon Anonymi Leobensis*; the other, *Thomæ Ebendorfeiri de Haselbach Chronicon*. The first says that the legate called together the people of Ptolemaïs, that he launched against them the anathemas of the Church, and then embarked to return to Rome. This last circumstance appears to us improbable, and we have, therefore, passed it over in silence.

[50] This circumstance is related in the life of the sultan Kelaoun. (See the extracts from Arabian manuscripts in our Appendix.)

[51] For the siege of Ptolemaïs we have consulted Sanuti, Herman, and a manuscript relation. This relation, written in the French of the time, appears to have been drawn from a letter from John de Vile, marshal of the hospital of St. John, who wrote to his brother, William de Vile, prior of St. Gilles, in Provence. Either John de Vile was at Ptolemaïs, or he wrote from the evidence of some Hospitallers who had escaped the swords of the Mussulmans, and had retired to the isle of Cyprus. This manuscript chronicle, which we often use, is divided into twenty-two chapters It is in the King's Library, No. 1290.

[52] This fact is related in the chronicle we have before quoted.

[53] A manuscript account of the siege and taking of Acre by the Saracens.

[54] This extraordinary fact is related in a discourse addressed to Pope Nicholas IV. by Brother Arsene, a Greek priest, who had been on a pilgrimage to Jerusalem in the time of the siege of Ptolemaïs. This account is found in Muratori; we have translated it entirely, as will be seen in our Appendix.

[55] This fact is likewise attested by the chronicle of Herman Cornarius, which we have already quoted.

[56] A German chronicle of Thomas Ebendorft relates the miraculous stories that were circulated among the Saracens. According to this chronicle, when a Christian expired, another issued from his mouth, *ex ore*. There were two souls in every body; *in uno corpore duo fuerunt hominis*.

[57] The Arabian chronicles speak of the sieur de Télema or Barthélemi, who never ceased to provoke the fury of the Saracens. The Western chronicles

say nothing of him; one of them merely says that a Frank, banished from Ptolemaïs on account of murder, took refuge with the sultan of Egypt, and pointed out to him the means of taking the city.

[58] Wadin, the author of a chronicle entitled *Annales Minorum*, tom. ii. p. 585, quotes a circumstance which St. Antonine relates in the third part of his *Somme Historique*. After having said that the greater part of the French Cordeliers were killed by the Saracens, he adds these words: "But not one of the virgins of St. Claire escaped." The abbess of this order, who possessed a masculine spirit, having learnt that the enemy had entered the city, called all her sisters together by the sound of the bell, and by the force of her words persuaded them to hold the promise they had made to Jesus Christ, their spouse, to preserve their chastity: "My dear daughters, my excellent sisters," said she, "we must, in this certain danger of life and modesty, show ourselves above our sex. The enemies are near to us; not so much to our bodies as to our souls; these barbarians, who, after having satisfied their brutal lusts upon all they meet, slay them with their swords. In this crisis we cannot hope to escape their fury by flight, but we can by a resolution, painful it is true, but sure. Most men are seduced by the beauty of women; let us deprive ourselves of this attraction, let us seek a preservative for our modesty in that which serves as a cause for its violation. Let us destroy our beauty to preserve our virginity pure. I will set you the example; let those who desire to meet their heavenly spouse imitate their mistress." At these words she cut her nose off with a razor; the others did the same, and boldly disfigured themselves, to present themselves more beautiful before Jesus Christ. By these means they preserved their purity, for the Saracens, on beholding their bleeding faces, conceived a disgust for them, and killed them all, without sparing one.

[59] Quand il fut revenu au milieu de la cité, son dextrier fut molt las, et lui-même aussi; le dextrier resista en contre les espérons, et s'arresta dans la rue comme qui n'en peut plus. Les Sarrasins, à coups de flèches, ruèrent à terre frère Guillaume; ainsi ce loyal champion de Jesus-Christ rendit l'âme à son Créateur.

[60] Among the marvellous accounts to which the destruction of the Christian colonies in Syria gave birth, history has preserved the following:—"In the year 1291, the house of the holy Virgin at Nazareth, in which she conceived the Son of God, was transported by angels to the top of a little mountain in Dalmatia, on the shore of the Adriatic Sea: three years afterwards it was transported to another shore of the same sea, in a wood

which belonged to a widow named Loretto. There have been since built upon this spot a small city and a magnificent church, which still preserve the name of this widow."

[61] We are not able to add anything to the learned researches of M. Raynouard upon the condemnation of the Templars. We refer our readers to his work, and to our Appendix.

[62] This article of the will of Charles-le-Bel is related by Ducange. It has been remarked that it is dated the 24th of October, 1324, and that Charles died in 1327: we may suppose that the date is incorrect, or that Charles-le-Bel did not perform his vow.

[63] We have before us a will made at this period, in which a gentleman of the name of Castellen, already illustrious in the times of the crusades, gives a sum for the expenses of the holy war. We regret we are not able to publish the text of this document, which has been communicated to us by the family of the testator.

[64] A memoir on the part which the Spaniards took in the crusades, read at the Academy of Madrid, describes the labours, the adventures, and wanderings of Raymond Lulli. The *Histoire Ecclesiastique* of Fleury may likewise be consulted.

[65] We have taken these particulars of Raymond Lulli from the Spanish dissertations upon the crusades, which we have already quoted in the preceding book.

[66] See what Sanuti himself relates in his book, from which we shall take many extracts.

[67] It appears almost incomprehensible that our author should, in these reflections, omit that which must strike every one else as the principal cause of the change he affects to lament. In the days of Peter the Hermit, a crusade was a golden day-dream, in which ambition and cupidity indulged as strongly as piety or superstition. But experience had not only proved it to be "a baseless fabric," but a cruel and a bitter scourge to all who had embarked in one. The first Crusaders were visionary—later ones must have been mad.—Trans.

[68] Et venoist à tous seigneurs moult grande plaisance, et spécialement à ceux qui vouloient le temps dispenser en armes, et qui adonc ne le tuvoient mie bien raisonnablement employer ailleurs.—*Froissart*.

[69] The eternal production of the Holy Ghost, which proceeds from the Father and the Son.—Trans.

[70] Our readers will observe by this, that the crescent, which has generally, but falsely, been taken as the standard of all Saracens, belongs to the Ottomans: it has never been mentioned in this history before.—Trans.

[71] The character of Constantine was worthy of being celebrated by the epic muse. One of our most distinguished statesmen has undertaken this glorious task.—See the poem of *The Last Constantine*, by M. de Vaublanc. [We wonder our author is not here struck by the very palpable reflection, that empires, kingdoms, and other institutions, which have richly merited their fall, frequently expire under the immediate rule of men who have not been instrumental in bringing about their ruin—they are but the last step of a headlong declivity,—if they are of adamant they must yield. The history of his own country and of ours might have supplied him with hints for such a reflection.—Trans.]

[72] For the siege of Constantinople, the very detailed account of Gibbon, and the rapid but complete picture of M. Salabury, in his *History of the Turkish Empire*, may be consulted.

[73] Olivier de la Marche, after giving a description of the festival and of the divers spectacles offered to the eyes of the guests, adds: "Such were the dainty mundane dishes of this festival, of which I will leave others to speak, to give an account of a pitiable portion of it, which appears to me of more consequence than the others," &c.

[74] Olivier de la Marche says, that the duke of Burgundy had already undertaken, three years before, to make a crusade against the Turks, in an assembly held at Mons.

[75] Some modern historians who have spoken of these vows of the knights, have exaggerated the fantasticalness of them. I find, among others, in one of these historians, this sentence: "In short, what gives the best idea of the devotion of these new Crusaders is, that one vowed that if, *up to the moment of his departure, he could not obtain the favours of his mistress, he would marry the first demoiselle he should meet with having twenty thousand crowns.*" We have found nothing like this in either Montstrelet or Olivier de la Marche, who are the only authors of the times who speak of this festival.

[76] We smile when reading this strange scene of safe and ignorant boasting; but if a Grand Turk ever indulges in mirth, we should think it would have excited the laughter of Mahomet, if he chanced to hear of it.—Trans.

[77] He should have reminded him of glorious old Henry Dandolo.—Trans.

[78] Nothing can be more unaccountable than such reflections! What did these wretched outcasts know or care about the dangers of Europe? What they sought was relief from the destitution they suffered; and if the Turks had been in Europe, they would have enlisted with them.—Trans.

[79] Jacques Cœur was condemned to death, and his property was confiscated. Charles VII. contented himself with banishing Jacques Cœur; but his property was not restored for a long time. Sixty of the clerks of Jacques Cœur subscribed together, and made up a sum of 60,000 crowns, with which he retired to the isle of Cyprus and reëstablished his trade. He founded an hospital for pilgrims there, and a Carmelite convent, in which he was buried. Jacques Cœur built many houses at Marseilles, Montpellier, and Bourges: among others, the beautiful house which is now the municipality. It was Louis XI. who reinstated the memory of Jacques Cœur. The inscription which is here mentioned must have been also in the hospital for pilgrims at Cyprus.

[80] The saying of the Abbé de Vertot was but an expression of politeness addressed to somebody who offered him documents, not in the interests of truth, but in the interest of some families, who wished that their names should be mentioned. In fact, if the documents they offered him concerned the truth, they had nothing to do but to publish them; now, we see nothing that has been published upon the siege of Rhodes that proves that the Abbé de Vertot was mistaken, or forgot anything of importance. It has not even been attempted to attack the authenticity of the facts he relates by any criticism that has survived to our times. There only remains the famous expression, *my siege is completed*, without any one having sought to explain in what sense and upon what subject this expression was made.

[81] Mahomet II. took Constantinople in 1453, and died in 1481.—Trans.

[82] The reflections this passage gives birth to might fill pages; but almost the most striking is, to observe how the operations of men's minds and industry, in their progress, obliterate that which is gone before, and then again, after a season, which season has done its work in spreading civilization and intelligence, return to old courses. Though science is bringing us back to the old route to India, what wonders the discovery of Vasco de Gama has effected for the progress of the Great Scheme!—Trans.

[83] To what extent this sort of profanation is carried, even by so-called civilized nations, may be seen by the story (we hope not a true one)

of Sir Sidney Smith and a party of English sailors, after the siege of Acre, singing "God save the king," in full chorus, in the great mosque of Omar, at Jerusalem.—Trans.

[84] This is the passage of the ordinance that relates to the banners that were to be carried in procession:—"There shall be made, at the same time, a handsome banner, upon which shall be painted our holy father the pope, in his full pontificals, accompanied by several cardinals and other prelates, being in pontificals, and mitred with white mitres; the pope shall be on the dexter, the king on the sinister, armed completely in white except his armour of state, which shall be borne by his squire, accompanied by several princes and other lords, all armed; on the other side of the said banner, histories and other pictures, full of Turks and other Infidels."

[85] All these documents are unpublished, and very voluminous; we will give some extracts from them in our Appendix.

[86] Some writers have pretended, against the opinion of Bossuet and David Hume, that Luther was not drawn into his opposition by a motive of jealousy, and by a sentiment of self-love. In spite of their objections, the fact is demonstrated. The learned Mosheim, in his history, has not thought proper to justify Luther on this head; which is besides of very little importance.

[87] The fruit became ripe in the age of Leo, and therefore he generally has the merit of the cultivation. Nicholas V. promoted the growth of intelligence and the arts quite as earnestly as Leo, and with more prudence and less pretension. But this is a common error: no age was ever more forgetful that all knowledge is progressive, than the present; we enjoy much, and claim all the merit of it; but very unjustly.—Trans.

[88] This question, we think, will admit of another decision. M. Michaud confounds the aristocracy with the middle class. When a class becomes raised, by any means, to an hereditary superiority, not purchased by individual merit of any other kind, manners are too frequently set at defiance, and morals become corrupt. What he says of the middle class is quite correct. The whole history of the world cannot furnish such an instance of stability and prosperity, as is now offered in England by the influence of an intelligent, prudent, moral middle class.—Trans.

[89] Will not much of this apply to all religions, all times, and all countries? Success hallows everything—it makes rebellion, revolution; assassination, patriotism; crimes, virtues. The Jesuits are said to be the warmest religionists in the world. Could Mussulman priests have expressed more delight in the advent and success of the strongest despotism that Europe ever witnessed, than they have done recently?—Trans.

[90] I look for you six months hence on the shores of the Hellespont.

[91] The last capitulations are of the reign of Louis XV.

[92] This resignation is expressed in a very singular manner in an extract from the manuscript of the library of Berne,—"Upon the cause why the Saracens possess the Holy Land."

Brother Vincent, in a sermon which he made, and which had for its text, "Ecce ascendimus Hierosoleman," gives three reasons for it:—"The first," said he, "is to excuse the Christians; the second is for the confusion of the Saracens; and the third is for the conversion of the Jews. As to the first reason, we ought all to know that there is no Christian, however holy, who does not sin, and has not sinned, except Jesus and his mother, the glorious Virgin Mary; and God is not willing that Christians should sin in the land in which Jesus Christ, his son, suffered the passion for the sins of men; and would account it a great offence. But He is not thus offended by the Saracens; for they are dogs. It would displease the king if his children or his knights should make water in his chamber; but when a dog makes water there, he takes no account of it."

See *Catalogus Codicum MSS. Bibliothecæ Bernensis*, &c. tom. i. p. 79.

[93] This account of the crusades at first appeared in the *Mercury*, and was afterwards printed in a little volume. It is now merged in Voltaire's *Histoire Générale*.

[94] Two memorials obtained prizes; one was by M. Hercen, the other by M. Choisseul d'Aullecourt. Both are remarkable for erudition and spirit of criticism; they marked out the way we have followed, and we take pleasure in acknowledging all we owe them.

[95] When a person moderately read in French history remembers the selfish, sensual, *wicked* characters here so unduly eulogized, he may forgive himself for the smile with which he must read the "impotent conclusion."— Trans.

[96] Say, rather—rendered so infamous by his cruelties.—Trans.

[97] The chronicle of Tours tells us, with the greatest simplicity, that Charlemagne was called the *Great* on account of his *great good luck*; thus historians confounded, as the vulgar do, glory with fortune.

[98] These must be exceedingly remote times, indeed; such as we have no account of. The oldest poems, the oldest histories, describe no such state; the savage tribes of the forest and the desert have something of a pride of

ancestry, and are known as the sons of their fathers, as well as Achilles was known as Pelides, or Gaul as the son of Morni.—Trans.

[99] It does not become us, as translators, to enter into controversy with our original, otherwise, much might be said in reply to this truly *conservative* paragraph. But, as readers of history, we think we may be permitted to observe, that *the advantages* pointed out in the first lines of it do not appear in the history of Venice. She was never so great or so prosperous as when purely mercantile. When territory was acquired, and nobility arose, corruption and decay soon followed.—Trans.

[100] And yet we cannot think that the custom of the Scotch *lairds*, who assume the name of their estates, can be traced to this source, although they do it in the same way. It seems probable that the French *de*, generally admitted as a proof of gentility, at least, was adopted upon such an occasion; but even this *de* is subject to doubt, as implying the lord *of* the estate, country, or city, or the man who raised himself into note *from* the country or city.—Trans.

[101] How was it, then, that William of Normandy, on his conquest of England, two centuries before, created so many of his knights, earls and barons, giving them titles of the places and estates he at the same time bestowed? Philip-le-Hardi, no doubt, gave the newly-created nobles means to support their honours and nobility was connected with property, as it had been.—Trans.

[102] In this suggestive passage we are sorry to find the prejudices of our original inducing him to give a false colouring to his picture. Monarchs granted no immunities to the people out of love for either liberty or the people, but to gain their assistance against their enemies, the great vassals or barons—thence the consequences; the principle was carried so far, that the monarch was elevated into the despot; and then another change ensued; when his power was so complete that his old enemies looked upon him as the source of all honours and riches, they united with him; both joined in their endeavours to oppress and plunder the people; and then came the last phase.—Trans.

[103] And yet he lived under Richelieu, in the nominal reign of Louis XIII., and in the reign of Louis XIV.!—Trans.

[104] Most political economists call man's labour *property*; M. Michaud has shown that the bulk of the people, under the feudal system, paid society *labour*, *life*, and *liberty*; and yet he calls these *nothing*!—Trans.

[105] I do not recollect this prediction; but I perfectly remember Montesquieu foretells that *France will perish by the sword.*—Trans.

[106] What can this mean? Taxation is as old as governments of any kind.—Trans.

[107] Servez Dieu, et il vous aidera: soyez doux et courtois à tout gentil-homme en otant de vous tout orgueil; ne soyez flatteur ne rapporteur; car telles manières de gens ne viennent pas à gran le perfection. Soyez loyal en faits et en dits; tenez votre parole; soyez secourables à pauvres et orphelins, et Dieu vous le guerdonnera.

[108] Le Père Hélyot, in his *Histoire des Ordres Monastiques*, vol. i. p. 263, expresses himself thus, when speaking of the order of St. Lazarus:—"What is very remarkable is, that they could only elect as grand-master, a leprous knight of the hospital of Jerusalem, which lasted up to the time of Innocent IV., that is to say, about the year 1253, when, having been obliged to abandon Syria, they addressed the pontiff, and represented to him, that always having had, from their foundation, a leprous knight for grand-master, they found themselves in the impossibility of electing one, because the infidels had killed all the leprous knights of their hospital at Jerusalem. For this reason, they prayed the pontiff to allow them to elect, for the future, as grand-master, a knight who had not been attacked by leprosy, and who might be in good health; and the pope referred them to the bishop of Trascate, that he might accord them this permission, after having examined if that could be done according to the will of God. This is reported by Pope Pius IV., in his bull of the year 1565, so extended and so favourable to the order of St. Lazarus, by which he renews all the privileges and all the gifts that his predecessors had granted to it, and gives it fresh ones. Here is what he says of the election these knights ought to make of a leprous grand-master:—Et Innocentius IV., per eum accepto, quod licet de antiquâ approbatâ et hactenùs pacificè observatâ consuetudine obtentum esset, ut miles leprosus domûs Sancti-Lazari Hierosolymitani in ejus magistrum assumeretur; verùm quia ferè omnes milites leprosi dictæ domûs ab inimicis fidei miserabiliter interfecti fuerant, et hujusmodi consuetudo nequiebat commodè observari: idcircò tunc episcopo Tusculano per quasdam commiserat, ut, si sibi secundùm Deum visum foret expedire fratribus ipsis licentiam, aliquem militem sanum et fratribus prædictæ domûs Sancti-Lazari in ejus magistrum (non obstante consuetudine hujusmodi de cætero eligendi) auctoritate apostolicâ concederet.

[109] For serfs this might be a blessing, but for free labour it was complained of as an evil. La Fontaine's Cobbler, when describing his state to the Financier, says:—

"Chaque jour amène son pain,
Tantôt plus, tantôt moins: le mal est que toujours
(Et sans cela nos gains seraient assez honnêtes),
Le mal est que dans l'an s'entremêlent des jours
Qu'il faut chômer; on nous ruine en fêtes;
L'une fait tort à l'autre; et monsieur le curé
De quelque nouveau saint charge toujours son prône."

Every day brings its bread; sometimes more, sometimes less: the worst is that always (and without that our gains would be very tolerable), the evil is, that in the year so many days creep in in which we must be idle—we are ruined in festivals; one treads upon the heels of another; and master curate is always introducing some new saint into his sermon.—Trans.

[110] We are constantly withheld, by the respect due from translators to originals, from making remarks in opposition to our author, when he lays down the historian's pen to get into the philosopher's chair. In the course of this chapter, our readers must have observed much reflection that is not deep, and some passages that are contradictory of others; but all has one great merit—*it is extremely suggestive.*—Trans.

[111] How could the clergy be said to pay for these wars? What became of the vast sums raised by the sale of indulgences of all kinds? The clergy had the collecting of the offerings of the faithful, which we have seen was sometimes *profitable.* Besides, the barons and knights paid for their own and their vassals' equipments as long as they had a coin left; then the king or leader, as Louis IX. did, sometimes helped them.—Trans.

[112] This is one of innumerable instances in the course of the work, in which the reader must regret that M. Michaud was not aware he was writing for the world; his views, and, I am sorry to say, his biasses, are exclusively French.—Trans.

[113] Surely he should have added to these, the human passions and mundane interests of these ignorant, independent tyrants.—Trans.

[114] Is not there always some such dominant principle in society? Is not *money* now as powerful as brute force or skill in arms were in the middle ages?—Trans.

[115] Nothing has been better said upon the influence of the clergy and religion, in the middle ages, than that which we read in a work entitled *Des Intérêts et des Opinions*, by M. Fievée:—"At a time in which the Church imposed public penitences, whilst the tribunals only ordered judgments by arms, we cannot see how the high police could not have fallen into the hands of the ecclesiastics; and it was because they alone exercised it, that, in the civil wars, fortunate princes confided to the monks the guarding of princes, from whom the fate of battle or treachery took the rights they possessed to share the kingdom. It was necessary that the void left by the laws should be filled up, or the state would perish; and the priests alone enjoyed a moral authority sufficiently great to supply the weakness of legislation;—exalted passions, more powerful virtues, great crimes, great remorse; a proud independence, salutary fears; an excess of force, and no regulations; courage in everything and everywhere: such was, at this period, the state of society;—it is easy to perceive that religion alone contended with barbarism." We regret not to be able to quote more than a fragment of a work filled with ingenious perceptions and profound views, upon the march of civilization in the middle ages.

[116] The author of *A Memoir to serve as a New History of Louis XII.* carries the first appearance of judicial reform in France to the reign of that monarch. He has prosecuted on this subject learned researches, and his work has given us much information upon the spirit and the march of our legislation in the middle ages. Although we do not always agree as to the consequences of the principles he develops, particularly as to their application to that which is passing at present, we take pleasure in rendering justice to the rare sagacity with which he has cleared up questions which have been scarcely perceived by our best historians.

[117] La Fontaine.

[118] And yet Marseilles had been a flourishing port for ages. In the early crusades it did not belong to the French monarchy.—Trans.

[119] "A skilful man, appointed to view and make a report of a thing," in this case; but it has several other meanings; as a man of worth, probity, or even valour.—Trans.

[120] Hotspur says to his lady—

> "Swear me, Kate, like a lady, as thou art,
> A good mouth-filling oath!"

The queen's anathema upon Joinville, is, in the original, something of this character.—Trans.

[121] M. de Choiseul d'Aillecourt gives in his *Mémoire* a very extended nomenclature of the inventions brought from the East into Europe by the Crusaders.

[122] And has not this been the case with all rich and prosperous nations? What invariably follows this high state of opulence, of the fine arts, and their attendant sensuality, is a question for every great nation that is so circumstanced to ask itself.—Trans.

[123] We are not positive whether the small-pox was known in Europe previously to the Crusaders. Its introduction amongst us is frequently attributed to them; and we observe, in reading the history of Mahomet and his successors, many persons were marked with the scars left by this disease. We wonder Michaud does not mention it.—Trans.

[124] The Moors of Spain may be adduced as an example against this opinion. It is true that the Moors of Granada cultivated the arts and sciences for a long time, and with much success; but what became of them when they returned to the coast of Africa?

[125] Lord Bolingbroke said: "After all, it is Nicholas V. to whom Europe is obliged for its present state of learning" (Spence).—Trans.

[126] The best answer to this is, that the too widely extended Mussulman power was as much split into sections by discord and ambition as Europe was. At the time of the first crusade there was no dread of invasion from the East; and the invasion of the Christians produced unanimity in defence of Mahomedanism.—Trans.

[127] It is somewhat remarkable, that in this very interesting summary, Michaud makes no mention of the exact sciences. We are generally supposed to be indebted to the Arabians for great improvement, if not for entire knowledge of mathematics; and although that knowledge may have come to us through Spain, we cannot think mention of the circumstance would have been out of its place here.—Trans.

[128] Although we cannot pretend to be perfectly acquainted with all the saints of these ages, we think this may be the same Paulinus who had been bishop of Nola, and who, if not the first inventor of bells, was the first who applied them to sacred purposes.—Trans.

[129] M. Michaud says, we must consider this Itinerary as the first account of the voyage to the Holy Land that we are in possession of.

Bordeaux, at the time of the pilgrims' departure, was one of the principal cities of the Gauls. It is situated at the mouth of the Garonne, in the Bay of Biscay, and is strongly associated with English history, as having been for a long time the residence of the Black Prince, and the birth-place of the unfortunate Richard II.—Trans.

[130] Our readers will judge, by two or three humorous traits in this description, that our monk of Malmesbury had no objection to a joke. The national characteristics here mentioned are curious, as proving how long our northern friends have been jeered at for their *scratching propensities*, and that the love of drinking was peculiar to the Dane before it was reprobated by Hamlet:—

> "This heavy-headed revel, east and west,
> Makes us traduced, and taxed of other nations:
> They clepe us drunkards, and with swinish phrase
> Soil our addition,"

[131] This was St. Hugh, consecrated in the year 1081, by Pope Gregory VII., the same who, a short time after, received St. Bruno and his companions, and gave them the solitude of the Chartreuse, to found a new order there. The church of Tours was then governed by Rodolph II.

[132] Saladin here speaks of the battle of Tiberias.

[133] The count of Tripoli.

[134] To understand this phrase, we must remember that the author of the letter compares the fortifications of Jerusalem to a *necklace*.

[135] This is a most extraordinary circumstance and proclaims to us not only the fame of Saladin, the monarch of such a distant country, but likewise the fear in which he was held in Europe. Notwithstanding his greater proximity, we did not call our income-tax the *Buonaparte tax*, as we might have done.—Trans.

[136] Here is a little bit for the antiquaries of *Clerkenwell*, which is, no doubt, meant by this.—Trans.

[137] This is a valuable hint for poets, painters, and novelists.—Trans.

[138] This may appear improbable; but there is no doubt Richard was a perfect horseman; and we very well remember Mr. Goldham, of the London and Westminster volunteer light-horse, performing the broad sword exercise with a sword in each hand, and his horse at speed, before George III., in Hyde Park.—Trans.

[139] Although our chronicler does not tell us so, we may presume that when one of Richard's troop cut down a Turkish horseman, he did not leave his saddle long empty, and that such accessions enabled the Christians to make an effective pursuit.—Trans.

[140] If any limner had the skill to paint Richard's countenance at parting with such a friend as his "good sword," this would make a fine picture. The feelings, which must have nearly suffocated his lion heart, would furnish matter for a poem.—Trans.

[141] We give a translation of this extract because it is very curious; but we have no faith in it with respect to the date; it appears to us to be much more modern, and some parts of the language inconsistent with others.— Trans.

[142] But, as in most such cases, religion was rather the cloak than the basis of ambition. The Mussulman empire, after the three first caliphs, became too large and too complicated to be governed by a simple Arab; and the miraculous conquests of the sect naturally made the generals who achieved them ambitious of governing what they conquered. The religious feud was but an excuse.—Trans.

[143] This doctrine prevailed among the Ismaëlians of Persia during nearly fifty years; but Djelah-ed Din, grandson of Hassan, reëstablished the worship in its purity.

[144] Dai, an Arabian participle, signifies properly him who calls,— *advocans*; and by extension it designates a person who preaches to men, and invites them to embrace some doctrine. The title of *dai* was common in the first century of Islamism. Every sect had its own.

[145] A passage of the historian Mirkhoud supports this account; he informs us that Hassan, after getting possession of the castle of Altamont, caused a canal to be dug, and brought water from a great distance to the foot of his castle. Fruit-trees were planted round it, and he encouraged the inhabitants to sow the land. It was thus that the air of this place, which had been unwholesome, became pure and salubrious.

[146] M. Jourdain, who addressed this interesting letter to me, has published a work entitled *La Perse, ou le Tableau de l'Histoire du Gouvernement, de la Littérature, de cet Empire, des Mœurs et Coutumes des Habitants*. This work, in five vols. in 18mo., contains many new notions and curious details, and does honour to the talent as well as to the erudition of the Orientalist.

[147] The original of this fragment is in the *Bibl. Græc.* of Fabricius, vol. vi, p. 405, and in the first volume of the *Imperium Orientiale* of Bandière. It is not in the editions of Nicetas.

[148] Coins worth two shillings and fourpence each.

[149] This is an extraordinary description of what must have been a surprising work of art; but we cannot reconcile the idea we entertain of a basilisk with that of the animal mentioned—we thought a basilisk was a kind of serpent.—Trans.

[150] Vincent Bellev. *Specul. Hist.* book xxx. chap. 5; Albert Stad. *Chron.* fol. 202; Godefr. Monach. *Annal. ap. Frch. Collect. Alberici*, p. 489; Sicard. *Chron. ap. Murat.* vol. vii. p. 623.

[151] Thomas de Cantipr. *De Apibus.*

[152] *Chron. Argent, ap. Urtii, Collect.* vol. i. p. 1.

[153] Jacob de Vorrag. *Chron. Januense, ap. Murat.* vol. ix. p. 46. What proves the error of this date is, that Bizarre (*Hist. Genuens.*), who has copied this chronicle, places the event under the year 1212. I do not know by what authority John Massey places it in his chronicle in 1210.

[154] See the *Chron. Anon.* of Strasburg, Godfrey the Monk, James of Varagine, and Bishop Sicard.

[155] Alberic enters into copious details; and though this historian generally sins on the side of extravagant credulity, his evidence cannot, in this case, be doubted.

[156] Jacques de Vorrag.

[157] Albert de Stadt.

[158] *Anonymous Chronicle* of Strasburg.

[159] This account is furnished by Alberic, and is confirmed by Thomas of Champré and Roger Bacon.

[160] *Chron. Augus.; Chron. Argent.*

[161] Godfrey the Monk.

[162] *Opus Majus*, p. 254, ed. in fol.

[163] See Marin, *Storia Civile e Politica del Commercia de' Veneziani*, vol. i. p. 206; Do Guignes, *Mémoires sur le Commerce des Francs dans le Levant*, &c.; vol. xxxvii. of *Les Mémoires de l'Acad. des Inscr.*

[164] Videmus anno incarn. Di. 1213, infinitam puerorum multitudinem spiritu deceptionis arreptos, cum signaculo crucis iter Hierosolymitanum agressos fuisse, periisseque diversis in locis; et maximam ex eis multitudinem per malefices quosdam Sarracenis in mari venditos extitisse. — *Lib. de Apibus.*

[165] Forsan vidistis aut audivistis pro certo quod pueri de regno Franciæ semel occurrebant in infinitâ multitudine post quemdem malignum hominem, ita quod nec à patribus, nec à matribus, nec ab amicis poterant detineri, et positi sunt in navibus et Sarracenis venditi, et non sunt adhuc 64 annis. — *Opus Majus*, p. 254.

[166] We promised to give in the Appendix some letters and the Bull of this pope relative to the crusade of 1197; but as the contents of these pieces are all alike, with the exception of some trifling expressions, we shall confine ourselves to this one.

[167] Lord, know that he who shall not go to that land where God was both living and dead, and who shall not take the cross beyond the seas, shall have no chance of going into Paradise: he who has pity and remembrance of the Lord, ought from war and vengeance to deliver his land and his country.... Now, every valiant bachelor will go who loves God and honours the holy mountain; they who act wisely will go to God, the base and the vile will stay behind: they are blind, as I think, who in their lives offer no assistance to God, and lose the glory of the mount for such a trifle. God suffered for us on the cross; and will say to us on the day to which all will come: — "You who helped me to bear my cross, you shall go where angels dwell, and shall there see both me and my mother Mary; and you from whom I have received nothing, descend all into the depths of hell!"

[168] Mrs. Hemans' beautiful poem, *Messages to the Dead*, is upon this subject; and in a note, quoted from Mr. Brunton's *Discipline*, she says that the custom was not uncommon in the Highlands. — Trans.

[169] In the regulations which were made for the Prussian converts, the popes particularly condemned the funeral customs of these people. "The neophytes," say these regulations, "promise not to burn their dead, and not to bury with them men, or horses, arms, clothes, or valuable things. They will no longer have those impostors called *ligastons*, who resemble pagan priests, and who, at funerals, praise the dead for robberies, impieties, and other sins," &c. These regulations enable us to become acquainted with many of the ancient customs of the Prussians.

[170] This is a most remarkable resemblance to the word signifying bard in Welsh, and to the name of the Welsh bard, *par excellence*. — Trans.

[171] The reader may remember they were left in the camp with the duke at Burgundy.

[172] This passage is very obscure.

[173] These instructions were inscribed in a register of the Chamber of Accounts. To facilitate the reading of them to the public, some impressions have been modernized.

[174] That is, the papers or accounts. We have given it exactly as it stands, that our readers may the more plainly perceive the nature of these documents.—Trans.

[175] By which we may perceive that *dining* at parish meetings is not a custom confined to modern times.

[176] By which we learn that the charge of a notary was one livre per diem.

[177] This must be Henry VII. from the dates, the contemporary princes, and the character given of the monarch.—Trans.

[178] How amusing, and, at the same time, wonderfully instructive it is, to read these schemes of philosophers and statemen a hundred and fifty years after they have occupied their thoughts by day and their visions by night!—Trans.

[179] Words intertwined with the letters of the cipher of the Grand Seignor.

[180] This passage being the basis of all the privileges of the French in Turkey, it often serves as a motive in the requests of ambassadors, and as a foundation for the firmans of the Grand Seignor.

[181] Much more is wanting to show that the informations received against the Templars furnished either moral or legal proof of the existence of the Bafometic figures. The act of accusation says not one word of it. There is no mention of it in the great procedure instituted at Paris, or in the numerous depositions of the witnesses whom the inquisitor and the commissaries of the pope questioned. Of the six witnesses heard at Carcassonne, who declared that an idol was presented to them, only two designated it in Figuram Bafometi. One, Gaucerand de Montpesat, when brought to Paris, retracted all preceding confession; there only then remained one single witness, of whose ulterior conduct and end nothing is known. It is proved, that of the other four persons interrogated at Carcassonne, Jean Cassauhas and Peter de Mossi retracted their first deposition, and Jean Cassauhas was burnt in that city.

[182] The pretended truncated cross, which M. Hammer believed he recognised upon the medals, which otherwise have nothing to do with the Templars, is nothing but the effect of the superposition of a hand upon the upper part of an ordinary cross; this hand, which holds the cross by the top, is found upon many medals and coins which M. Hammer himself would not dare to attribute to the Templars.

[183] Raimundus de Agiles says of the Mahometans: In ecclesiis autem magnis Bafumarias faciebant ... habebant monticulum ubi duæ erant Bafumariæ. The troubadours employ Baformaria for mosque, and Bafomet for Mahomet.